16th Conference of the European Chapter of the Association for Computational Linguistics (EACL 2021)

System Demonstrations

Held online due to COVID-19

Kiev, Ukraine
21 – 23 April 2021

ISBN: 978-1-7138-2916-4

Printed from e-media with permission by:

Curran Associates, Inc.
57 Morehouse Lane
Red Hook, NY 12571

CURRAN ASSOCIATES INC.
proceedings
.com

Some format issues inherent in the e-media version may also appear in this print version.

Association for Computational Linguistics
209 N. Eighth Street
Stroudsburg, Pennsylvania 18360

Phone: 1-570-476-8006
Fax: 1-570-476-0860

acl@aclweb.org

Additional copies of this publication are available from:

Curran Associates, Inc.
57 Morehouse Lane
Red Hook, NY 12571 USA
Phone: 845-758-0400
Fax: 845-758-2633
Email: curran@proceedings.com
Web: www.proceedings.com

EACL 2021

The 16th Conference of the European Chapter of the Association for Computational Linguistics

Proceedings of the System Demonstrations

April 19 - 23, 2021

Introduction

Welcome to the proceedings of the EACL System Demonstration Sessions. This volume contains the papers of the system demonstrations presented at the 16th conference of the European Chapter of the Association for Computational Linguistics (EACL) on April 19th - April 23rd, 2021.

The EACL 2021 demonstrations track welcomed submissions ranging from early research prototypes to mature production-ready systems. We received 56 submissions this year, of which 39 were selected for inclusion in the program after having been reviewed by two members of the program committee. This year, the EACL demo track received a very large amount of high-quality research papers. We therefore decided to feature an inclusive programme where all excellent publications were chosen to be presented at the meeting. Following current practice, we further asked the programme committee to pay special attention to issues related to ethics. We would like to warmly thank the members of the program committee for their timely help in reviewing the submissions.

Lastly, we thank the many authors that submitted their work to the demonstrations track. Because this year the EACL conference is completely virtual, the demonstration paper talks are therefore pre-recorded and authors are invited to present their work with posters during the two live demo sessions through gather.town.

Dimitra Gkatzia and Djamé Seddah
EACL 2021 Demonstration Track Chairs

Organizing Committee

- **System Demonstration Chairs:**
  Dimitra Gkatzia, Djamé Seddah

- **Program Committee:**
  Omri Abend, Nikolaos Aletras, Shlomo Argamon, Rachel Bawden, Timothée Bernard, Marie Candito, Xavier Carreras, Alberto Cetoli, Jhih-Jie Chen, Manuel R. Ciosici, Miruna-Adriana Clinciu, Raphael Cohen, Michael Desmond, Sourav Dutta, Catherine Finegan-Dollak, Dimitra Gkatzia, Johannes Heinecke, Daniel Hershcovich, David M. Howcroft, Ganesh Jawahar, Giannis Karamanolakis, Rabeeh Karimi Mahabadi, Andrew Kirby, Arne Köhn, Philippe Laban, Dong-Ho Lee, Manling Li, Xuezhe Ma, Prodromos Malakasiotis, Yuval Marton, Ivan Vladimir Meza Ruiz, Khalil Mrini, Pedro Javier Ortiz Suárez, Xutan Peng, Benoît Sagot, Sashank Santhanam, Sebastin Santy, Thomas Scialom, Djamé Seddah, Somayajulu Sripada, Carl Strathearn, Simon Wells, Guillaume Wisniewski, Runxin Xu, Hamada Zahera, Yi Zhang

Table of Contents

Conference Program

Using and comparing Rhetorical Structure Theory parsers with rst-workbench
Arne Neumann

SF-QA: Simple and Fair Evaluation Library for Open-domain Question Answering
Xiaopeng Lu, Kyusong Lee and Tiancheng Zhao

Finite-state script normalization and processing utilities: The Nisaba Brahmic library
Cibu Johny, Lawrence Wolf-Sonkin, Alexander Gutkin and Brian Roark

CovRelex: A COVID-19 Retrieval System with Relation Extraction
Vu Tran, Van-Hien Tran, Phuong Nguyen, Chau Nguyen, Ken Satoh, Yuji Matsumoto and Minh Nguyen

MATILDA - Multi-AnnoTator multi-language InteractiveLight-weight Dialogue Annotator
Davide Cucurnia, Nikolai Rozanov, Irene Sucameli, Augusto Ciuffoletti and Maria Simi

AnswerQuest: A System for Generating Question-Answer Items from Multi-Paragraph Documents
Melissa Roemmele, Deep Sidhpura, Steve DeNeefe and Ling Tsou

T-NER: An All-Round Python Library for Transformer-based Named Entity Recognition
Asahi Ushio and Jose Camacho-Collados

Forum 4.0: An Open-Source User Comment Analysis Framework
Marlo Haering, Jakob Smedegaard Andersen, Chris Biemann, Wiebke Loosen, Benjamin Milde, Tim Pietz, Christian Stöcker, Gregor Wiedemann, Olaf Zukunft and Walid Maalej

SLTEV: Comprehensive Evaluation of Spoken Language Translation
Ebrahim Ansari, Ondřej Bojar, Barry Haddow and Mohammad Mahmoudi

Trankit: A Light-Weight Transformer-based Toolkit for Multilingual Natural Language Processing
Minh Van Nguyen, Viet Dac Lai, Amir Pouran Ben Veyseh and Thien Huu Nguyen

DebIE: A Platform for Implicit and Explicit Debiasing of Word Embedding Spaces
Niklas Friedrich, Anne Lauscher, Simone Paolo Ponzetto and Goran Glavaš

A Dashboard for Mitigating the COVID-19 Misinfodemic
Zhengyuan Zhu, Kevin Meng, Josue Caraballo, Israa Jaradat, Xiao Shi, Zeyu Zhang, Farahnaz Akrami, Haojin Liao, Fatma Arslan, Damian Jimenez, Mohammed Samiul Saeef, Paras Pathak and Chengkai Li

No Day Set (continued)

T2NER: Transformers based Transfer Learning Framework for Named Entity Recognition
Saadullah Amin and Guenter Neumann

European Language Grid: A Joint Platform for the European Language Technology Community
Georg Rehm, Stelios Piperidis, Kalina Bontcheva, Jan Hajic, Victoria Arranz, Andrejs Vasiljevs, Gerhard Backfried, Jose Manuel Gomez-Perez, Ulrich Germann, Rémi Calizzano, Nils Feldhus, Stefanie Hegele, Florian Kintzel, Katrin Marheinecke, Julian Moreno-Schneider, Dimitris Galanis, Penny Labropoulou, Miltos Deligiannis, Katerina Gkirtzou, Athanasia Kolovou, Dimitris Gkoumas, Leon Voukoutis, Ian Roberts, Jana Hamrlova, Dusan Varis, Lukas Kacena, Khalid Choukri, Valérie Mapelli, Mickaël Rigault, Julija Melnika, Miro Janosik, Katja Prinz, Andres Garcia-Silva, Cristian Berrio, Ondrej Klejch and Steve Renals

A New Surprise Measure for Extracting Interesting Relationships between Persons
Hidetaka Kamigaito, Jingun Kwon, Young-In Song and Manabu Okumura

Paladin: an annotation tool based on active and proactive learning
Minh-Quoc Nghiem, Paul Baylis and Sophia Ananiadou

Story Centaur: Large Language Model Few Shot Learning as a Creative Writing Tool
Ben Swanson, Kory Mathewson, Ben Pietrzak, Sherol Chen and Monica Dinalescu

FrameForm: An Open-source Annotation Interface for FrameNet
Büşra Marşan and Olcay Taner Yıldız

OCTIS: Comparing and Optimizing Topic models is Simple!
Silvia Terragni, Elisabetta Fersini, Bruno Giovanni Galuzzi, Pietro Tropeano and ANTONIO CANDELIERI

ELITR Multilingual Live Subtitling: Demo and Strategy
Ondřej Bojar, Dominik Macháček, Sangeet Sagar, Otakar Smrž, Jonáš Kratochvíl, Peter Polák, Ebrahim Ansari, Mohammad Mahmoudi, Rishu Kumar, Dario Franceschini, Chiara Canton, Ivan Simonini, Thai-Son Nguyen, Felix Schneider, Sebastian Stüker, Alex Waibel, Barry Haddow, Rico Sennrich and Philip Williams

Breaking Writer's Block: Low-cost Fine-tuning of Natural Language Generation Models
Alexandre Duval, Thomas Lamson, Gaël de Léséleuc de Kérouara and Matthias Gallé

OPUS-CAT: Desktop NMT with CAT integration and local fine-tuning
Tommi Nieminen

Domain Expert Platform for Goal-Oriented Dialog Collection
Didzis Goško, Arturs Znotins, Inguna Skadina, Normunds Gruzitis and Gunta Nešpore-Bērzkalne

Which is Better for Deep Learning: Python or MATLAB? Answering Comparative Questions in Natural Language
Viktoriia Chekalina, Alexander Bondarenko, Chris Biemann, Meriem Beloucif, Varvara Logacheva and Alexander Panchenko

No Day Set (continued)

PunKtuator: A Multilingual Punctuation Restoration System for Spoken and Written Text
Varnith Chordia

Conversational Agent for Daily Living Assessment Coaching Demo
Raymond Finzel, Aditya Gaydhani, Sheena Dufresne, Maria Gini and Serguei Pakhomov

HULK: An Energy Efficiency Benchmark Platform for Responsible Natural Language Processing
Xiyou Zhou, Zhiyu Chen, Xiaoyong Jin and William Yang Wang

Using and comparing Rhetorical Structure Theory parsers with rst-workbench

Arne Neumann
Independent researcher
rst-workbench@arne.cl

Abstract

I present rst-workbench, a software package that simplifies the installation and usage of numerous end-to-end Rhetorical Structure Theory (RST) parsers.[1] The tool offers a web-based interface that allows users to enter text and let multiple RST parsers generate analyses concurrently. The resulting RST trees can be compared visually, manually post-edited (in the browser) and stored for later usage.

1 Introduction

Rhetorical Structure Theory (RST) provides a formalism for hierarchical text organization that can be applied to a wide range of natural language processing tasks, ranging from text generation (Marcu, 1997; Konstas and Lapata, 2013) to the assessment of conversational patterns of Alzheimer's patients (Abdalla et al., 2018; Paulino et al., 2018).

Most research on RST parsing is focused on parser engineering, i.e. the evaluation of parsers against a "gold standard" hand-annotated dataset. Although RST corpora exist for a variety of other languages (e.g. German, Dutch and Spanish), end-to-end discourse parsers are usually only trained and evaluated on English data, with the notable exception of Braud et al. (2017a,b,c).

There are a number of RST parsers that were developed for other languages, but either are they not publicly available (e.g. Reitter (2003) for German and English as well as Pardo and Nunes (2008) for Portuguese) or they do not produce complete RST analyses, e.g. Sumita et al. (1992) for Japanese (no intra-sentence relations) and da Cunha et al. (2012) for Spanish (no inter-sentence relations).

Compared to other NLP tasks like syntax parsing, the amount of available training data is limited, with corpora being in the range from dozens to a few hundred hand-annotated texts. There is also little work evaluating RST parsers beyond the Parseval-based procedure proposed by Marcu (2000).[2]

For example, machine learning models are usually not compared with respect to their ability to detect rare rhetorical relations. Zhang and Liu (2016) found that rhetorical relations in RST-DT at different levels—i.e. between clauses within sentences, between sentences within paragraphs and between paragraphs—all follow the same Zipf's law–related distribution. Individual relations show different patterns, e.g. *Attribution* is more common in intra-sentential relations than on higher levels.

In addition, no systematic review exists of the impact of the preprocessing steps—sentence splitting, syntax parsing and segmentation into Elementary Discourse Units (EDUs)—on the quality of the resulting RST parses. There is some work in this direction, though.

For example, Surdeanu et al. (2015) implemented two RST parsers that only differ in the syntax parser used—the constituent-based RST parser produced slightly better results, but the dependency-based equivalent was 2.5 times faster. Braud et al. (2017c) evaluated the influence of syntactic information (using either constituency parses, dependency parses or only POS tags) on discourse segmentation. Rutherford et al. (2017) reviewed the impact of different neural network architectures on implicit discourse relation detection.

While Huber and Carenini (2020) showed that RST parser performance can be improved by train-

[1] The rst-workbench and all related Docker configuration files, images and REST API wrappers around the RST parsers are available from `https://github.com/arne-cl/rst-workbench`. An online demo is provided at `https://rst-workbench.arne.cl/`.

[2] In a replication study, Morey et al. (2017) found that most recently reported increases in RST parser performance (9 parsers published between 2013 to 2017) are caused by implementation differences of Marcu's evaluation procedure.

Proceedings of the 16th Conference of the European Chapter of the Association for Computational Linguistics: System Demonstrations, pages 1–6
April 19 - 23, 2021. ©2021 Association for Computational Linguistics

ing them on large RST treebanks automatically generated using distant supervision, I hypothesize that RST parsers can profit even more from larger human-annotated training corpora.

In turn, the annotation of RST corpora can likely be sped up by leveraging RST parsers. In the same vein that translators can produce high-quality translations by post-editing machine-translated texts more quickly than by manual translation alone (Gaspari et al., 2014; Koponen, 2016), I assume that linguists can produce RST analyses faster with machine support (i.e. by selecting the best automatic analysis from a number of RST parsers and then post-editing it) than by relying on hand-annotation alone.

If the goal is to make annotators use RST parsers productively, the parsers need to be adapted to meet their needs. While the primary focus of RST parser development is improving upon state-of-the-art benchmark results, this work focuses on usability and compatibility, i.e. the parsers need to be easy to install and run while supporting the same format(s) that common RST annotation and visualization tools use.

To achieve this, I implemented rst-workbench, which:

- acts as a web-based front-end to six different RST parsers,
- provides an easy way to install the parsers on all modern desktop operating systems using Docker containers,
- facilitates their integration into NLP pipelines by wrapping them in REST APIs,
- enables the RST analyses produced by the parsers to be visualized by and edited in the rstWeb annotation tool (Zeldes, 2016) by amending it with a REST API and by providing converters from the parsers' output formats to rstWeb's input format.

The remainder of this paper is organized as follows. Section 2 gives a brief overview of related work, while Section 3 describes the architecture and usage of the system. Section 4 summarizes the main conclusions and outlines areas of future work.

2 Related work

To the best of my knowledge, rst-workbench is the first tool that offers a graphical user interface for and integrates several RST parsers. Besides rstWeb (Zeldes, 2016), which is integrated in this software, there are two other annotation tools specifically made for rhetorical structures: RSTTool (O'Donnell, 2000) and TreeAnnotator (Helfrich et al., 2018). For visualizing RST trees and querying RST corpora, there is ANNIS3 (Krause and Zeldes, 2014).

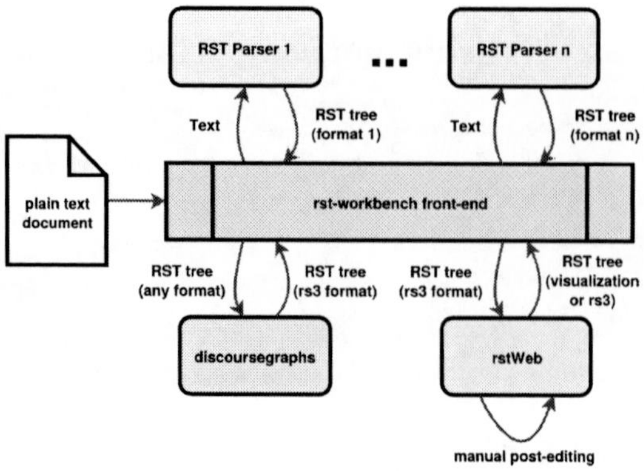

Figure 1: Components and workflow of the rst-workbench.

While I implemented very minimal REST APIs around the individual RST parsers in Python, CLAM (van Gompel and Reynaert, 2014) could be used to create REST API wrappers around command-line NLP tools by writing a configuration file. For simple cases, it is slightly more complicated to setup than my approach (cf. Section 3.2), but it comes with many additional features (e.g. user authentication, batch processing and a generic web interface for each API) and can be extended with additional format converters and visualization components.

3 Software architecture and usage

The rst-workbench provides a simple way to install multiple RST parsers on a computer, run them as well as visually compare and edit their analyses in a web browser. Its architecture and usage is summarized in Figure 1. Screenshots of the workflow are provided in Figures 2 and 3.

At the core, the rst-workbench consists of six existing open-source RST parsers—HILDA (Hernault et al., 2010), Feng and Hirst (2014), DPLP (Ji and Eisenstein, 2014), Heilman and Sagae (2015), CODRA (Joty et al., 2015) and StageDP (Wang et al., 2017, 2018)—packaged as Docker containers to make them easily installable without any user intervention (cf. Section 3.1).

Users do not have to learn the different

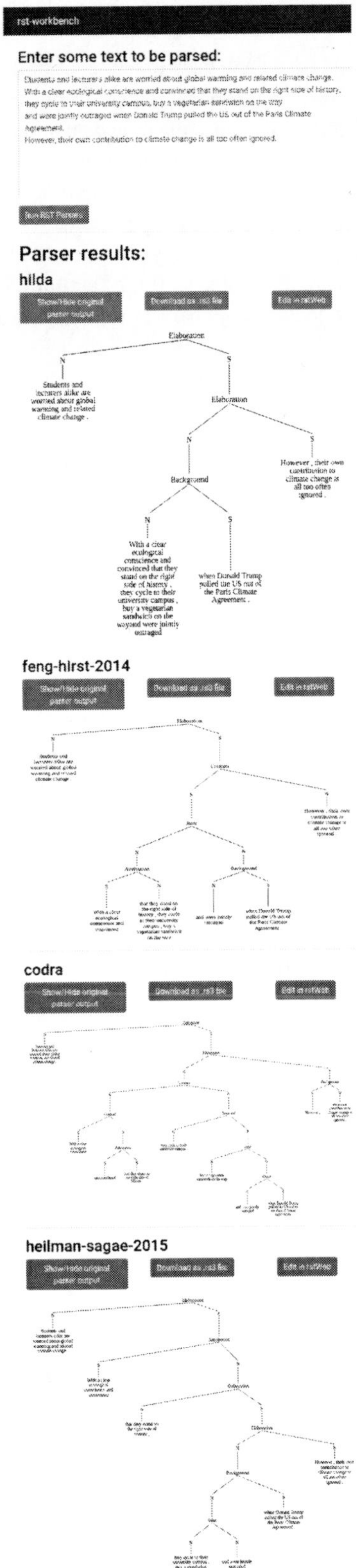

Figure 2: Screenshot of rst-workbench showing the result of parsing the beginning of a newspaper article with various RST parsers.

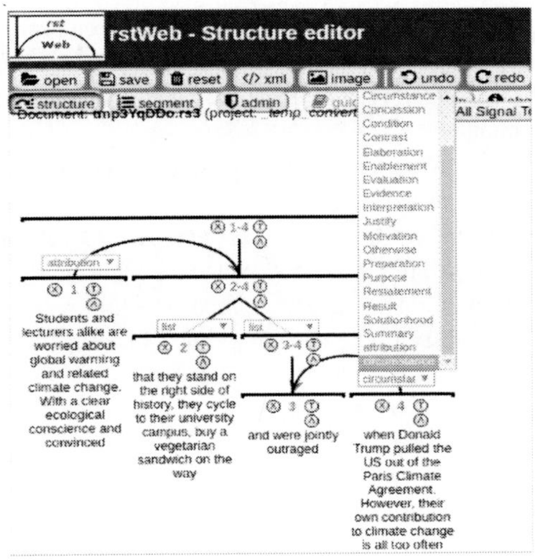

Figure 3: Post-editing a parse result in rstWeb (here: changing the relation that holds between two EDUs).

command-line interfaces of the parsers, but can simply interact with them via a web browser. To make this possible, I added a REST API to each of the parsers, which the browser can talk to (cf. Section 3.2).

In the browser, annotators can enter text or upload a plain text document. After clicking the "Run Parsers" button, all RST parsers are started concurrently to analyze the given text. The results appear asynchronously in the browser, i.e. the user sees the result of the fastest parser immediately when it is available and does not have to wait for the remaining parsers to finish processing. Users can now select the parse tree that most resembles their linguistic intuition, and click "Edit in rstWeb" to load the analysis into the rstWeb annotation tool. Here, all aspects of the RST tree can be modified, e.g. rhetorical relations between EDUs and/or larger subtrees can be replaced (Figure 3). Afterwards, the result can be saved locally for further inspection or corpus creation.

The technical setup needed to integrate all these stand-alone tools into one software package with a unified interface is described in the following subsections.

3.1 Docker

Docker is a tool that allows programmers to bundle a piece of software with all its dependencies into a *container*, which a user can reproducibly install on any computer with Linux, Mac OSX or Windows without having to know any details about the software. The step-by-step installation process of a software package is described in a so-called *Dockerfile*, which is both readable by machines and humans.

Installing an RST parser from a Dockerfile will save the user the effort of finding its dependencies, installation parameters and training settings. This will not, however, reduce the run time of the installation and training process, as that will happen on the user's local machine. This process can be drastically sped up by using a Docker *image*, which is a compressed file that contains the results of running a Dockerfile. I provide Docker images for all but one of the RST parsers available in the rst-workbench.[3] If Docker is already running on the target system, the installation of an RST parser boils down to a one-line command.[4]

At this point, the parsers can be used without tedious installation procedures, but are still only available as individual command-line tools with different parameters and output formats. To improve their *usability*, I make them available as web services with a common interface (cf. Section 3.2). To improve their *comparability*, I offer a simple way to convert their output to a common format and generate visualizations of the resulting RST trees (Section 3.3).

3.2 Web application and REST APIs

With rst-workbench, I aim to make RST parsers more accessible to a wider audience, by providing a common (graphical) interface for them. I chose to implement this in form of a web application, which talks to the individual RST parsers via REST (Fielding, 2000), a simple text-based protocol commonly used by programs running on different computers to communicate with each other via the Internet. I implemented REST interfaces for each of the parsers using the Python hug library[5]. They receive requests containing the text to be analyzed, run the actual (command-line) RST parsers in the background on the given input, capture their outputs and send them back to the requesting program.

Using REST allows the user to run the parsers on different machines than the web application (in case one computer does not have enough RAM or processing power to run all RST parsers at the same time) and even to use the parsers as web services without the front-end, e.g. to integrate them into custom NLP pipelines. It also simplifies the process of adding more parsers to the rst-workbench, as it only needs to know where the parsers run and which output format they use.

3.3 discoursegraphs and rstWeb

The interoperability of RST tools is hindered by the lack of a standard format for encoding RST analyses. While corpora are either using the LISP-like `dis` or the XML-based `rs3` format, RST parsers are using a plethora of custom formats. rst-workbench is able to convert many of them into rs3—the format supported by RST annotation tools like RSTTool (O'Donnell, 2000) and rstWeb (Zeldes, 2016)— by utilizing a REST service I implemented on top of the discoursegraphs converter library (Neumann, 2015, 2016), which supports all RST file formats of the given parsers.

Using the rs3 format and integrating rstWeb into the rst-workbench allows it to leverage rstWeb's capabilities to visualize and (post)-edit RST trees.[6]

4 Conclusions

In this paper, I presented a software package that simplifies the installation, usage and visual comparison of RST parsers. I showed how it can help linguists to produce manual RST analyses with less effort.

I plan to integrate the rst-workbench directly into rstWeb to facilitate corpus annotation projects. In rstWeb, an "administrator" can create an annotation project, upload documents to be annotated and assign them to annotators. With an integrated rst-workbench, the administrator could precompute and store the automatic RST analyses once for all annotators, which would reduce wait time for the annotators and allow them to work without switching browser tabs and tools.

In the current setup, analyzing a text with all parsers may take up to two minutes. Most of this

[3]All Docker images for the rst-workbench are available at `https://hub.docker.com/u/nlpbox`. I can't provide an image for the HILDA RST parser (Hernault et al., 2010), as its license does not allow its source code to be freely distributed. Nevertheless, if you have access to the HILDA source code, you can simply build an image using the Dockerfile provided at `https://github.com/NLPbox/hilda-docker`.

[4]For example `docker run nlpbox/heilman-sagae-2015` for the (Heilman and Sagae, 2015) parser.

[5]`http://www.hug.rest/`

[6]To achieve this, I added a REST interface to rstWeb. For lack of time, it is not yet part of the official rstWeb source code, but is available here: `https://github.com/arne-cl/rstWeb/tree/add-rest-api`

time is spent on loading the models of the underlying syntax parsers. This can be drastically reduced by "outsourcing" the syntax parsers into their own web services, as I have already done for DPLP.[7]

References

Mohamed Abdalla, Frank Rudzicz, and Graeme Hirst. 2018. Rhetorical structure and Alzheimers disease. *Aphasiology*, 32(1).

Chloé Braud, Maximin Coavoux, and Anders Søgaard. 2017a. Cross-lingual RST Discourse Parsing. In *Proceedings of the 15th Conference of the European Chapter of the Association for Computational Linguistics: Volume 1, Long Papers*, pages 292–304, Valencia, Spain. Association for Computational Linguistics.

Chloé Braud, Ophélie Lacroix, and Anders Søgaard. 2017b. Cross-lingual and cross-domain discourse segmentation of entire documents. In *Proceedings of the 55th Annual Meeting of the Association for Computational Linguistics (Volume 2: Short Papers)*, pages 237–243, Vancouver, Canada. Association for Computational Linguistics.

Chloé Braud, Ophélie Lacroix, and Anders Søgaard. 2017c. Does syntax help discourse segmentation? Not so much. In *Proceedings of the 2017 Conference on Empirical Methods in Natural Language Processing*, pages 2432–2442, Copenhagen, Denmark. Association for Computational Linguistics.

Iria da Cunha, Eric SanJuan, Juan-Manuel Torres-Moreno, M. Teresa Cabré, and Gerardo Sierra. 2012. A Symbolic Approach for Automatic Detection of Nuclearity and Rhetorical Relations among Intra-sentence Discourse Segments in Spanish. In *Proceedings of the 13th International Conference in Computational Linguistics and Intelligent Text Processing (CICLing 2012)*.

Vanessa Wei Feng and Graeme Hirst. 2014. A Linear-Time Bottom-Up Discourse Parser with Constraints and Post-Editing. In *Proceedings of the 52nd Annual Meeting of the Association for Computational Linguistics (Volume 1: Long Papers)*, pages 511–521, Baltimore, Maryland. Association for Computational Linguistics.

Roy Thomas Fielding. 2000. *Architectural Styles and the Design of Network-based Software Architectures*. Ph.D. thesis, University of California, Irvine.

Federico Gaspari, Antonio Toral, Sudip Kumar Naskar, Declan Groves, and Andy Way. 2014. Perception vs Reality: Measuring Machine Translation Post-Editing Productivity. In *Proc. Third Workshop on Post-Editing Technology and Practice*.

[7]See the Dockerfile in `https://github.com/NLPbox/dplp-docker`.

Maarten van Gompel and Martin Reynaert. 2014. CLAM: Quickly deploy NLP command-line tools on the web. In *Proceedings of COLING 2014, the 25th International Conference on Computational Linguistics: System Demonstrations*, pages 71–75, Dublin, Ireland. Dublin City University and Association for Computational Linguistics.

Michael Heilman and Kenji Sagae. 2015. Fast Rhetorical Structure Theory Discourse Parsing. *arXiv preprint arXiv:1505.02425*.

Philipp Helfrich, Elias Rieb, Giuseppe Abrami, Andy Lücking, and Alexander Mehler. 2018. TreeAnnotator: Versatile Visual Annotation of Hierarchical Text Relations. In *Proceedings of the Eleventh International Conference on Language Resources and Evaluation (LREC-2018)*, Miyazaki, Japan. European Languages Resources Association (ELRA).

Hugo Hernault, Helmut Prendinger, David A. duVerle, and Mitsuru Ishizuka. 2010. HILDA: A Discourse Parser Using Support Vector Machine Classification. *Dialogue & Discourse*, 1(3).

Patrick Huber and Giuseppe Carenini. 2020. MEGA RST Discourse Treebanks with Structure and Nuclearity from Scalable Distant Sentiment Supervision. In *Proceedings of the 2020 Conference on Empirical Methods in Natural Language Processing (EMNLP)*, pages 7442–7457, Online. Association for Computational Linguistics.

Yangfeng Ji and Jacob Eisenstein. 2014. Representation Learning for Text-level Discourse Parsing. In *Proceedings of the 52nd Annual Meeting of the Association for Computational Linguistics (Volume 1: Long Papers)*, pages 13–24, Baltimore, Maryland. Association for Computational Linguistics.

Shafiq Joty, Giuseppe Carenini, and Raymond T. Ng. 2015. CODRA: A Novel Discriminative Framework for Rhetorical Analysis. *Computational Linguistics*, 41(3):385–435.

Ioannis Konstas and Mirella Lapata. 2013. Inducing Document Plans for Concept-to-Text Generation. In *Proceedings of the 2013 Conference on Empirical Methods in Natural Language Processing*, pages 1503–1514, Seattle, Washington, USA. Association for Computational Linguistics.

Maarit Koponen. 2016. Is machine translation post-editing worth the effort? A survey of research into post-editing and effort. *The Journal of Specialised Translation*, 25:131–148.

Thomas Krause and Amir Zeldes. 2014. ANNIS3: A new architecture for generic corpus query and visualization. *Literary and Linguistic Computing*.

Daniel Marcu. 1997. *The Rhetorical Parsing, Summarization, and Generation of Natural Language Text*. Ph.D. thesis, Department of Computer Science. University of Toronto.

Daniel Marcu. 2000. The rhetorical parsing of unrestricted texts: a surface-based approach. *Computational Linguistics*, 26(3):395–448.

Mathieu Morey, Philippe Muller, and Nicholas Asher. 2017. How much progress have we made on RST discourse parsing? A replication study of recent results on the RST-DT. In *Proceedings of the 2017 Conference on Empirical Methods in Natural Language Processing*, pages 1319–1324, Copenhagen, Denmark. Association for Computational Linguistics.

Arne Neumann. 2015. discoursegraphs: A graph-based merging tool and converter for multilayer annotated corpora. In *Proceedings of the 20th Nordic Conference of Computational Linguistics (NODALIDA 2015)*, pages 309–312, Vilnius, Lithuania. Linköping University Electronic Press, Sweden.

Arne Neumann. 2016. Merging and validating heterogenous, multi-layered corpora with discoursegraphs. *Journal for Language Technology and Computational Linguistics*, 31(1):101–115.

Michael O'Donnell. 2000. RSTTool 2.4 - A markup Tool for Rhetorical Structure Theory. In *INLG'2000 Proceedings of the First International Conference on Natural Language Generation*, pages 253–256, Mitzpe Ramon, Israel. Association for Computational Linguistics.

Thiago Alexandre Salgueiro Pardo and Maria das Graças Volpe Nunes. 2008. On the Development and Evaluation of a Brazilian Portuguese Discourse Parser. *RITA*, 15(2):43–64.

Anayeli Paulino, Gerardo Sierra, Laura Hernández-Domínguez, Iria da Cunha, and Gemma Bel-Enguix. 2018. Rhetorical relations in the speech of Alzheimers patients and healthy elderly subjects: An approach from the RST. *Computación y Sistemas*, 22(3).

David Reitter. 2003. Simple Signals for Complex Rhetorics: On Rhetorical Analysis with Rich-Feature Support Vector Models. *LDV Forum*, 18(1).

Attapol Rutherford, Vera Demberg, and Nianwen Xue. 2017. A Systematic Study of Neural Discourse Models for Implicit Discourse Relation. In *Proceedings of the 15th Conference of the European Chapter of the Association for Computational Linguistics: Volume 1, Long Papers*, pages 281–291, Valencia, Spain. Association for Computational Linguistics.

K. Sumita, K. Ono, T. Chino, T. Ukita, and S. Amano. 1992. A Discourse Structure Analyzer for Japanese Text. In *Proceedings International Conference on Fifth Generation Computer Systems*, pages 1133–1140.

Mihai Surdeanu, Tom Hicks, and Marco Antonio Valenzuela-Escárcega. 2015. Two Practical Rhetorical Structure Theory Parsers. In *Proceedings of the 2015 Conference of the North American Chapter of the Association for Computational Linguistics: Demonstrations*, pages 1–5, Denver, Colorado. Association for Computational Linguistics.

Yizhong Wang, Sujian Li, and Houfeng Wang. 2017. A Two-Stage Parsing Method for Text-Level Discourse Analysis. In *Proceedings of the 55th Annual Meeting of the Association for Computational Linguistics (Volume 2: Short Papers)*, pages 184–188, Vancouver, Canada. Association for Computational Linguistics.

Yizhong Wang, Sujian Li, and Jingfeng Yang. 2018. Toward Fast and Accurate Neural Discourse Segmentation. In *Proceedings of the 2018 Conference on Empirical Methods in Natural Language Processing*, pages 962–967, Brussels, Belgium. Association for Computational Linguistics.

Amir Zeldes. 2016. rstWeb - A Browser-based Annotation Interface for Rhetorical Structure Theory and Discourse Relations. In *Proceedings of the 2016 Conference of the North American Chapter of the Association for Computational Linguistics: Demonstrations*, pages 1–5, San Diego, California. Association for Computational Linguistics.

Hongxin Zhang and Haitao Liu. 2016. Quantitative Aspects of RST Rhetorical Relations across Individual Levels. *Glottometrics*, 33:8–24.

SF-QA: Simple and Fair Evaluation Library for Open-domain Question Answering

Xiaopeng Lu[2]*, **Kyusong Lee**[1] **and Tiancheng Zhao**[1]
SOCO Inc.
[1]{kyusongl,tianchez}@soco.ai
Language Technologies Institute, Carnegie Mellon University
[2]xiaopen2@andrew.cmu.edu

Abstract

Although open-domain question answering (QA) draws great attention in recent years, it requires large amounts of resources for building the full system and it is often difficult to reproduce previous results due to complex configurations. In this paper, we introduce SF-QA: simple and fair evaluation framework for open-domain QA. SF-QA framework modularizes the pipeline open-domain QA system, which makes the task itself easily accessible and reproducible to research groups without enough computing resources. The proposed evaluation framework is publicly available and anyone can contribute to the code and evaluations.

1 Introduction

Open-domain Question Answering (QA) is the task of answering open-ended questions by utilizing knowledge from a large body of unstructured texts, such as Wikipedia, world-wide-web and etc. This task is challenging because researchers have to face issues in both scalability and accuracy. In the last few years, rapid progress has been made and the performance of open-domain QA systems has been improved significantly (Chen et al., 2017; Qi et al., 2019; Yang et al., 2019). Several different approaches were proposed, including two-stage ranker-reader systems (Chen et al., 2017), end-to-end models (Seo et al., 2019) and retrieval-free models (Raffel et al., 2019). Despite people's increasing interest in open-domain QA research, there are still two main limitations in current open-domain QA research communities that makes research in this area not easily accessible:

The first issue is the high cost of ranking large knowledge sources. Most of the prior research used Wikipedia dumps as the knowledge source. For example, the English Wikipedia has more than 7 million articles and 100 million sentences. For many researchers, indexing data of this size with a classic search engine (e.g., Apache Lucene (McCandless et al., 2010)) is feasible but becomes impractical when indexing with a neural ranker that requires weeks to index with GPU acceleration and consumes very large memory space for vector search. Therefore, research that innovates in ranking mostly originates from the industry.

The second issue is about reproducibility. Open-domain QA datasets are collected at different time, making it depends on different versions of Wikipedia as the correct knowledge source. For example, SQuAD (Rajpurkar et al., 2016) uses the 2016 Wikipedia dump, and Natural Question (Kwiatkowski et al., 2019) uses 2018 Wikipedia dump. Our experiments found that a system's performance can vary greatly when using the wrong version of Wikipedia. Moreover, indexing the entire Wikipedia with neural methods is expensive, so it is hard for researchers to utilize others' new rankers in their future research. Lastly, the performance of an open-domain QA system depends on many hyperparameters, e.g. the number of passages passed to the reader, fusion strategy, etc., which is another confounding factor to reproduce a system's results.

Thus, this work proposes SF-QA (Simple and Fair Question-Answering), a Python library to solve the above challenges for two-stage QA systems. The key idea of SF-QA is to provide pre-indexed large knowledge sources as public APIs or cached ranking results; a hub of reader models; and a configuration file that can be used to precisely reproduce an open-domain QA system for a task. The pre-indexed knowledge sources enable researchers to build on top of the previously proposed rankers without worrying about the tedious work needed to index the entire Wikipedia. Then the executable configuration file provides a complete

* This work was done during an internship at SOCO

Proceedings of the 16th Conference of the European Chapter of the Association for Computational Linguistics: System Demonstrations, pages 7–13
April 19 - 23, 2021.

snapshot that captures all of the hyperparameters in order to reproduce a result.

Experiments are conducted to validate the effectiveness of SF-QA. We show that one can easily reproduce previous state-of-the-art open-domain QA results on four QA datasets, namely Open SQuAD, Open Natural Questions, Open CMRC, and Open DRCD. More datasets will be included in the future. Also, we illustrate several use cases of SF-QA, such as efficient reader comparison, reproducible research, open-source community, and knowledge-empowered applications.

SF-QA is also completely open-sourced [1] and encourages the research community to contribute their rankers or readers into the repository, so that their methods can be used by the rest of the community.

In short, the contributions of this paper include:

1. The proposed open-source SF-QA project that provides a complete pipeline for simplifying open-domain QA research.
2. A hub of pre-indexed Wikipedia at different years with different ranking algorithms as public APIs or cached results.
3. Experiments and tutorials that explain use cases and scenarios of SF-QA and validate its effectiveness.

2 Related Work

Existing deep learning open-domain QA approaches can be broadly divided into three categories.

2.1 Two-stage Approach

Recent open-domain QA systems mostly use a two-stage ranker-reader approach. Dr.QA (Chen et al., 2017) uses a modified TF-IDF bag-of-words method as the first-stage retriever. Selected documents are then fed into an RNN-based document reader to extract the final answer span. Wang et al. (2018) leverage reinforcement learning to update both ranker and reader components and shows improvement over Dr.QA in open-domain QA task. Lee et al. (2018) focuses on the ranker improvement and uses a learned reranker to boost first stage answer recall.

Some other works focus on second-stage reader improvement. Yang et al. (2019) adopts a BERT-based reader model (Devlin et al., 2018) instead of the previous RNN-based model and that significantly improved the end-to-end performance. To deal with span extraction in a multi-document setting, Wang et al. (2019) uses the global normalization approach (Clark and Gardner, 2017) to make the span scores comparable among candidate documents, which improved the performance by a large amount.

The graph-based ranker-reader approach has also been explored recently. Asai et al. (2019) proposes a graph-based retriever to retrieve supporting documents recursively based on entity link evidence, and then uses a BERT-based reader model to complete open-domain QA task.

2.2 End-to-End Approach

Open-domain QA using the end-to-end approach was not feasible for a long time, because this needs humongous memory to index the corpus and do the vector search. With the emergence of a large pre-trained language model (PLM), researchers revisit this idea and make the end-to-end open-domain QA feasible. Lee et al. (2019) proposed Open-retrieval QA (ORQA) model, which updates the ranker and reader model in an end-to-end fashion by pre-training the model with an Inverse Cloze Task (ICT). Seo et al. (2019) experiments with considering open-domain QA task as a one-stage problem, and indexing corpus at phrase level directly. This approach shows promising inference speed with compromise in worse performance.

2.3 Retrieval-free Approach

Pre-trained language models have got rapid development in recent years. Querying a language model directly to get phrase-level answers becomes a possibility. The T5 model (11B version) (Raffel et al., 2019) can reach comparative scores on several open-domain QA datasets, compared with two-stage approaches with far less number of parameters ($\sim$330M). However, as reported in Guu et al. (2020), decreasing the number of parameters hurts the model performance drastically. This leaves large room for future research on how to make retrieval-free open-domain QA feasible in the real-world setting.

3 The Proposed Method

3.1 Background

A typical ranker-reader-based open-domain QA system operates as follows: first, a large text

[1] `https://github.com/soco-ai/SF-QA.git`

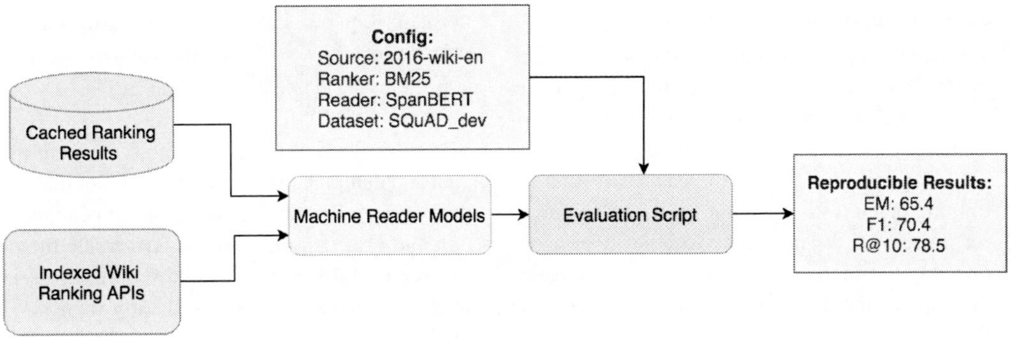

Figure 1: Overall pipeline for open-domain QA

knowledge-base is indexed by a ranker, e.g. a full-text search engine. Given a query, the ranker can return a list of relevant passages that may contain the correct answer. How to choose the size of a passage is still an open research question and many choices are available, e.g. paragraph, fixed-size chunks, and sentences. Note that it is not necessary that the ranker needs to return the final passages in one-shot: advanced ranker can iteratively refine the passage list to support multi-hop reasoning (Yang et al., 2018; Asai et al., 2019).

Then given the returned passages, a machine reader model will process all passages jointly and extract potential phrase-level answers from them. A fusion strategy is needed to combine candidate answers and scores from each passage and to create a final list of N-best phrase-level answers by reading these passages. The reason to combine ranker with the reader is to solve the scalability challenge since the state-of-the-art readers are prohibitively slow to process very large corpus in real-time (Chen et al., 2017; Devlin et al., 2018).

3.2 The Proposed Library Overview

SF-QA is a library that is designed to make it easy to evaluate and reproduce open-domain systems that use ranker-reader architecture. SF-QA decreases the cost of indexing, hosting, and querying large unstructured text knowledge base, e.g. Wikipedia, and also provides a complete configuration snapshot that can be used to replicate a QA system's performance. It is also a place for open-domain QA researchers to share their work, no matter it is innovating in better information retrieval or it is in stronger machine reading comprehension.

There are four main components in SF-QA: *ranker service*, *reader hub*, *evaluation*, and *pipeline configuration*.

3.3 Ranker Service

The goal of the ranker service is to reduce the cost and time to index and query large knowledge source for open-domain QA research using a variety of ranking technologies. Up to date, we have included the BM25 (Robertson et al., 2009) and SPARTA (Zhao et al., 2020) ranking methods with several configurations detailed below. More methods will be included and we also welcome community contributions.

Currently, SF-QA supports four ways of document splitting for indexing:

1. Sentence: sentence-level indexing
2. Paragraph: paragraph-level indexing
3. Chunk: fixed word size indexing
4. Context: context-level indexing, where the full sentence is always kept, with a maximum number of tokens

Also, Wikipedia dumps at different times are indexed separately so that users can choose to use the same dump as benchmark datasets used. The following versions are included:

1. English Wikipedia: 2016/2018/2020
2. Chinese Wikipedia: 2017/2018/2020

The returned passage is in the following JSON format: $\{\langle question\_id \rangle$: [*"score": 42.86,"answer": "Super Bowl V, the fifth edition of the Super Bowl..."*, ...]}, which contains all question ids as key, and top-k retrieved documents and scores as value.

There are two methods to use the ranking results: *cached ranking results* and *ranking API*.

3.3.1 Cached Ranking Results

The fastest way to use ranking service for experiments is via cached ranking results. SF-QA provides top-K ranked passages in JSON format for training, validation and test (if publicly available) set. One can directly use the cached results for training or for testing, saving time, and resources for processing the raw data. Another use case is one may use more computationally expensive re-ranking methods to re-rank the top-K passages and then feed them into the reader component.

3.3.2 Ranking APIs

The cached results are very useful for researchers who work on existing datasets and who do not need to have a live system. However, only cached results do not work for new datasets or live QA system that needs to handle user queries. Therefore, SF-QA also provides public API as a service to solve this need. The API is available as a RESTful API and can be reached via HTTPs. Detailed connection documentation can be found on the GitHub.

3.4 Reader Hub

Reader hub allows SF-QA's user to specify which reader model to use to extract phrase-level answers. One can either uses their own models by implementing an abstract function or directly load any reader models that are compatible with the Hugging Face Transformer library (Wolf et al., 2019). SF-QA also includes its own reader model that is optimized for open-domain QA. For example, it offers a BERT reader that is globally normalized (Wang et al., 2019), which provides more reliable answer scores to compare multiple candidates' answers from different passages.

Moreover, the reader hub allows the user to define the fusion mechanism that combines the ranking results with reading results. The current implementation supports a linear combination with two free variables, namely the type of score and the weight on reader score. Concretely, the final answer score is computed as follows:

$$y = (1 - \alpha)y_{reader} + \alpha y_{rank} \quad (1)$$

where α is a coefficient between 0 and 1. y_{reader} is the reader score, which can either be logits or probability after the softmax layer. y_{ranker} is the ranker score, which depends on the ranking method. One may also specify different normalization strategies to normalize the score from ranker or reader. Normalization strategies include z-normalization, floor normalization etc. Lastly, one may easily add their own strategy by overriding the fusion function.

3.5 Evaluation

SF-QA evaluation is designed to offer a multilingual and comprehensive evaluation script that computes the performance of an open-domain QA system and also outputs useful intermediate metrics that are useful for analysis and visualization. For language support, SF-QA evaluation supports English and Chinese. For metrics, it has the most common EM (exact match) and F1 score for the final performance. It also provides other relevant metrics. The following is a list of metrics that are in the output:

- Exact match (EM)
- F-1 Score
- Ranking recall at K
- Oracle ranker score
- Mean reciprocal rank (MRR)

3.6 Pipeline Configurations

The pipeline configuration file is in YAML format, which defines all the hyperparameter for an open-domain QA system to do a forward inference. One can set the configuration for data, ranker ID, and reader ID, fusion strategy and etc. Therefore, the easiest way to share an open-domain QA system for results replication is via providing the right YAML configuration. The following is an example.

```yaml
# config.yaml
data:
    lang: en
    name: squad
    split: dev-v1.1
ranker:
    use_cached: False
    model:
        name: sparta
        es_index_name: en-wiki-2016
reader:
    model_id: squad-context-spanbert
param:
    n_gpu: 2
    score_weight: 0.8
    top_k: 10
```

4 Use Cases

SF-QA is designed to be modular and ready to use, with the hope that it can connect people from researchers interested in Question Answering (QA), Information Retrieval (IR), and developers from industries. In this section, we illustrate several use cases of SF-QA.

4.1 Efficient Reader Comparison

In open-domain QA, the first stage ranker consumes humongous resources in both time, memory, and storage. For researchers without enough computing power, it is not feasible to start open-domain QA research, even if they only want to improve the system on the reader stage. SF-QA provides solutions for researchers with this need. In SF-QA, existing publicly available open-domain QA datasets are already indexed with multiple rankers used in previous open-domain QA research work, currently including BM25 (Robertson et al., 2009), and SPARTA (Zhao et al., 2020), both with different granularity options. Researchers can call the RESTful API to get the cached ranking results directly if they want to focus on existing open-domain QA datasets, for example, Open SQuAD, Open CMRC, etc. Alternatively, they can call the backend live ranker to get the top retrieved results regarding the input query. We design SF-QA to be completely modular: the researcher is able to pick up a cached ranker and plug in their own reader model to evaluate the open-domain QA results.

4.2 Reproducible Research

Reproducibility is another problem that existed in current open-domain QA research. Since the first-stage retriever model needs researchers to collect large-scale data by themselves, it is hard to keep all the settings the same to make fair comparisons. In SF-QA, we collected data following the earliest works' setting (Chen et al., 2017; Yang et al., 2019; Kwiatkowski et al., 2019). Therefore, researchers can check SF-QA to get data specifications for existing models. Moreover, parameter settings for different models are recorded and saved in another separate configuration file, as shown in the section3.6. Therefore, any existing models in the current SF-QA project can be directly reproduced, which would greatly facilitate researchers in establishing benchmark scores and doing fair comparisons.

4.3 Knowledge-empowered Applications

SF-QA framework also considers the needs from an industry perspective. To show the potential of open-domain QA and to encourage more people to join the development of this task, we also provide a RESTful API (with a ready-to-use open-domain QA model in the backend) for users to ask questions and get the phrase-level answers directly as output. We also provide a tutorial to demonstrate that SF-QA can be seamlessly incorporated into RASA (Bocklisch et al., 2017), a popular open-source chatbot building platform, with only a few lines of code. We hope that this effort can attract people from different backgrounds to open-domain QA research.

5 Experiment Results

	Reported		Reproduced	
	EM	F1	EM	F1
Bertserini (Yang et al., 2019)	38.6	46.1	41.2	48.6
+DS (Xie et al., 2020)	51.2	59.4	51.6	59.2
Multipassage (Wang et al., 2019)	53.0	60.9	53.2	60.7
SpartaQA (Zhao et al., 2020)	59.3	66.5	59.3	66.5

Table 1: Comparison between reported performance and reproduced performance on Open SQuAD.

5.1 Reproducing Prior Art

Results in Table 1 shows the performance comparison between several reported open-domain QA systems and our reproduced results. The first experiment conducted is to reproduce some prior results using SF-QA. We choose Bertserini (Yang et al., 2019), Bertserini with distant supervision (Xie et al., 2020), Multi-passage Bert (Wang et al., 2019), and SPARTA (Zhao et al., 2020) as three benchmark systems to reproduce.

To reproduce Bertserini (Yang et al., 2019), we follow the implementation described in the original paper and first index the 2016 English Wikipedia in paragraph level to get 29.5M documents in total. A BERT-base-cased model is trained with global normalization, following descriptions in the paper. We observe a slight improvement in the open-domain QA result, which may due to the usage of a newer version of the BM25 retriever. The same

	Indexing	Uploading	Retrieval	Reader	Total
Traditional Approach	16.2 h	5.2 h	6.1 h	4.4 h	21.9 h
SF-QA	-	-	-	4.4 h	4.4h

Table 2: Time elapsed to evaluate open-domain QA using Open SQuAD development set

open-domain QA setting	wiki 2016*			wiki 2018			wiki 2020		
	EM	F1	R@1	EM	F1	R@1	EM	F1	R@1
BM25 + SpanBERT	**49.2**	**56.7**	**41.9**	45.8	53.8	39.4	41.5	49.5	35.4
Sparta + SpanBERT	**59.3**	**66.5**	**50.8**	46.5	54.4	39.3	46.4	53.9	42.2

Table 3: Open SQuAD performance using Wikipedia dumps from different years. * represents the dump which SQuAD originally used for annotation.

phenomenon has also been reported in (Xie et al., 2020).

For Bertserini with distant supervision (Xie et al., 2020), we follow the two-stage distant supervision strategy proposed by the original author, where the model was first fine-tuned using the original SQuAD dataset, and then fine-tuned on the distantly supervised data retrieved from the full Wikipedia. The score we get matches the score reported by the original author.

To reproduce Multi-passage BERT (Wang et al., 2019), we first index the Wikipedia corpus using chunk size equals to 100, with a stride of 50 words. A BERT reranker is then trained to rerank the retrieved top 100 documents and the top 30 documents are passed to the reader. In the reader training stage, we train the model using BERT-large-cased model, also with global normalization to make the span score comparable. Our reproduced score matches the score reported in the original paper.

For SpartaQA, we follow the original author's implementation on SPARTA retriever, and index the Wikipedia in the context level with a size of 150. During the reader stage, a SpanBERT (Joshi et al., 2020) model is used to train the model with distantly supervised data retrieved from Wikipedia with global normalization strategy. The score matches the reported score.

5.2 Time saved by SF-QA

This experiment shows results for elapsed time to evaluate open domain question answering with and without the SFQA evaluation framework (Table 2). Traditionally, we need to build the complete pipeline in order to evaluate the open-domain QA as following steps: (1) **Indexing**: converting full Wikipedia into sparse or dense representations; (2) **Uploading:** inserting the text and representations to Elasticsearch (or similar database); 3) **Retriever**: retrieval n-best candidates from Elasticsearch; 4) **Reader:** span prediction using machine reading comprehension. We use GeForce RTX 2080 Ti GPU to index the entire Wikipedia dump of the total 89,544,689 sentences. The total amount of elapsed time for open-domain QA is 29 hours without using SF-QA for one experimental setting. In comparison to this, using cached retrieved results provided from SF-QA saves repetitive work in heavy indexing, and it only takes $\sim$ 4 hours to get the final scores.

5.3 Model Accuracy v.s. Corpus release year

We conduct the last experiment to test the robustness of the state-of-the-art system against temporal shifting. Results are reported in Table 3. We observe that model accuracy is largely affected by the version of the Wikipedia dump, showing that it is essential to track the version of the input data and make sure that all open-domain QA researches are reproducible starting from the data input level.

6 Conclusion

In conclusion, this paper presents SF-QA, a novel evaluation framework to make open-domain QA research simple and fair. This framework fixes the gap among researchers from different fields, and make the open-domain QA more accessible. We show the robustness of this framework by successfully reproducing several existing models in open-domain QA research. We hope that SF-QA can make the open-domain QA research more accessible and make the evaluation easier. We expect to further improve our framework by including more models in both ranker and reader side, and encourage community contributions to the project as well.

References

Akari Asai, Kazuma Hashimoto, Hannaneh Hajishirzi, Richard Socher, and Caiming Xiong. 2019. Learning to retrieve reasoning paths over wikipedia graph for question answering. *arXiv preprint arXiv:1911.10470*.

Tom Bocklisch, Joey Faulkner, Nick Pawlowski, and Alan Nichol. 2017. Rasa: Open source language understanding and dialogue management. *arXiv preprint arXiv:1712.05181*.

Danqi Chen, Adam Fisch, Jason Weston, and Antoine Bordes. 2017. Reading Wikipedia to answer open-domain questions. In *Association for Computational Linguistics (ACL)*.

Christopher Clark and Matt Gardner. 2017. Simple and effective multi-paragraph reading comprehension. *arXiv preprint arXiv:1710.10723*.

Jacob Devlin, Ming-Wei Chang, Kenton Lee, and Kristina Toutanova. 2018. Bert: Pre-training of deep bidirectional transformers for language understanding. *arXiv preprint arXiv:1810.04805*.

Kelvin Guu, Kenton Lee, Zora Tung, Panupong Pasupat, and Ming-Wei Chang. 2020. Realm: Retrieval-augmented language model pre-training. *arXiv preprint arXiv:2002.08909*.

Mandar Joshi, Danqi Chen, Yinhan Liu, Daniel S Weld, Luke Zettlemoyer, and Omer Levy. 2020. Spanbert: Improving pre-training by representing and predicting spans. *Transactions of the Association for Computational Linguistics*, 8:64–77.

Tom Kwiatkowski, Jennimaria Palomaki, Olivia Redfield, Michael Collins, Ankur Parikh, Chris Alberti, Danielle Epstein, Illia Polosukhin, Jacob Devlin, Kenton Lee, et al. 2019. Natural questions: a benchmark for question answering research. *Transactions of the Association for Computational Linguistics*, 7:453–466.

Jinhyuk Lee, Seongjun Yun, Hyunjae Kim, Miyoung Ko, and Jaewoo Kang. 2018. Ranking paragraphs for improving answer recall in open-domain question answering. *arXiv preprint arXiv:1810.00494*.

Kenton Lee, Ming-Wei Chang, and Kristina Toutanova. 2019. Latent retrieval for weakly supervised open domain question answering. *arXiv preprint arXiv:1906.00300*.

Michael McCandless, Erik Hatcher, Otis Gospodnetić, and O Gospodnetić. 2010. *Lucene in action*, volume 2. Manning Greenwich.

Peng Qi, Xiaowen Lin, Leo Mehr, Zijian Wang, and Christopher D Manning. 2019. Answering complex open-domain questions through iterative query generation. *arXiv preprint arXiv:1910.07000*.

Colin Raffel, Noam Shazeer, Adam Roberts, Katherine Lee, Sharan Narang, Michael Matena, Yanqi Zhou, Wei Li, and Peter J Liu. 2019. Exploring the limits of transfer learning with a unified text-to-text transformer. *arXiv preprint arXiv:1910.10683*.

Pranav Rajpurkar, Jian Zhang, Konstantin Lopyrev, and Percy Liang. 2016. Squad: 100,000+ questions for machine comprehension of text. *arXiv preprint arXiv:1606.05250*.

Stephen Robertson, Hugo Zaragoza, et al. 2009. The probabilistic relevance framework: Bm25 and beyond. *Foundations and Trends® in Information Retrieval*, 3(4):333–389.

Minjoon Seo, Jinhyuk Lee, Tom Kwiatkowski, Ankur Parikh, Ali Farhadi, and Hannaneh Hajishirzi. 2019. Real-time open-domain question answering with dense-sparse phrase index. In *Proceedings of the 57th Annual Meeting of the Association for Computational Linguistics*, pages 4430–4441.

Shuohang Wang, Mo Yu, Xiaoxiao Guo, Zhiguo Wang, Tim Klinger, Wei Zhang, Shiyu Chang, Gerry Tesauro, Bowen Zhou, and Jing Jiang. 2018. R 3: Reinforced ranker-reader for open-domain question answering. In *Thirty-Second AAAI Conference on Artificial Intelligence*.

Zhiguo Wang, Patrick Ng, Xiaofei Ma, Ramesh Nallapati, and Bing Xiang. 2019. Multi-passage bert: A globally normalized bert model for open-domain question answering. *arXiv preprint arXiv:1908.08167*.

Thomas Wolf, Lysandre Debut, Victor Sanh, Julien Chaumond, Clement Delangue, Anthony Moi, Pierric Cistac, Tim Rault, Rémi Louf, Morgan Funtowicz, et al. 2019. Huggingface's transformers: State-of-the-art natural language processing. *ArXiv*, pages arXiv–1910.

Yuqing Xie, Wei Yang, Luchen Tan, Kun Xiong, Nicholas Jing Yuan, Baoxing Huai, Ming Li, and Jimmy Lin. 2020. Distant supervision for multi-stage fine-tuning in retrieval-based question answering. In *Proceedings of The Web Conference 2020*, pages 2934–2940.

Wei Yang, Yuqing Xie, Aileen Lin, Xingyu Li, Luchen Tan, Kun Xiong, Ming Li, and Jimmy Lin. 2019. End-to-end open-domain question answering with bertserini. *arXiv preprint arXiv:1902.01718*.

Zhilin Yang, Peng Qi, Saizheng Zhang, Yoshua Bengio, William W Cohen, Ruslan Salakhutdinov, and Christopher D Manning. 2018. Hotpotqa: A dataset for diverse, explainable multi-hop question answering. *arXiv preprint arXiv:1809.09600*.

Tiancheng Zhao, Xiaopeng Lu, and Kyusong Lee. 2020. Sparta: Efficient open-domain question answering via sparse transformer matching retrieval. *arXiv preprint arXiv:2009.13013*.

Finite-state script normalization and processing utilities: The Nisaba Brahmic library

Cibu Johny[†] **Lawrence Wolf-Sonkin**[‡] **Alexander Gutkin**[†] **Brian Roark**[‡]
Google Research
[†]United Kingdom and [‡]United States
{cibu,wolfsonkin,agutkin,roark}@google.com

Abstract

This paper presents an open-source library for efficient low-level processing of ten major South Asian Brahmic scripts. The library provides a flexible and extensible framework for supporting crucial operations on Brahmic scripts, such as NFC, visual normalization, reversible transliteration, and validity checks, implemented in Python within a finite-state transducer formalism. We survey some common Brahmic script issues that may adversely affect the performance of downstream NLP tasks, and provide the rationale for finite-state design and system implementation details.

1 Introduction

The Unicode Standard separates the representation of text from its specific graphical rendering: text is encoded as a sequence of characters, which, at presentation time are then collectively rendered into the appropriate sequence of glyphs for display. This can occasionally result in many-to-one mappings, where several distinctly-encoded strings can result in identical display. For example, Latin script letters with diacritics such as "é" can generally be encoded as either: (a) a pair of the base letter (e.g., "e" which is `U+0065` from Unicode's Basic Latin block, corresponding to ASCII) and a diacritic (in this case `U+0301` from the Combining Diacritical Marks block); or (b) a single character that represents the grapheme directly (`U+00E9` from the Latin-1 Supplement Unicode block). Both encodings yield visually identical text, hence text is often normalized to a conventionalized normal form, such as the well-known Normalization Form C (NFC), so that visually identical words are mapped to a conventionalized representative of their equivalence class for downstream processing. Critically, NFC normalization falls far short of a complete handling of such many-to-one phenomena in Unicode.

In addition to such normalization issues, some scripts also have well-formedness constraints, i.e., not all strings of Unicode characters from a single script correspond to a valid (i.e., legible) grapheme sequence in the script. Such constraints do not apply in the basic Latin alphabet, where any permutation of letters can be rendered as a valid string (e.g., for use as an acronym). The Brahmic family of scripts, however, including the Devanagari script used to write Hindi, Marathi and many other South Asian languages, do have such constraints. These scripts are alphasyllabaries, meaning that they are structured around orthographic syllables (akṣara) as the basic unit.[1] One or more Unicode characters combine when rendering one of thousands of legible akṣara, but many combinations do not correspond to any akṣara. Given a token in these scripts, one may want to (a) normalize it to a canonical form; and (b) check whether it is a well-formed sequence of akṣara.

Brahmic scripts are heavily used across South Asia and have official status in India, Bangladesh, Nepal, Sri Lanka and beyond (Cardona and Jain, 2007; Steever, 2019). Despite evident progress in localization standards (Unicode Consortium, 2019) and improvements in associated technologies such as input methods (Hinkle et al., 2013) and character recognition (Pal et al., 2012), Brahmic script processing still poses important challenges due to the inherent differences between these writing systems and those which historically have been more dominant in information technology (Sinha, 2009; Bhattacharyya et al., 2019).

In this paper, we present Nisaba, an open-source software library,[2] which provides processing utilities for ten major Brahmic scripts of South Asia: Bengali, Devanagari, Gujarati, Gurmukhi, Kannada, Malayalam, Oriya (Odia), Sinhala, Tamil,

[1]See §3 for details on the scripts.
[2]`https://github.com/google-research/nisaba/`

Proceedings of the 16th Conference of the European Chapter of the Association for Computational Linguistics: System Demonstrations, pages 14–23
April 19 - 23, 2021.

and Telugu. In addition to string normalization and well-formedness processing, the library also includes utilities for the deterministic and reversible romanization of these scripts, i.e., transliteration from each script to and from the Latin script (Wellisch, 1978). While the resulting romanizations are standardized in a way that may or may not correspond to how native speakers tend to romanize the text in informal communication (see, e.g., Roark et al., 2020), such a default romanization can permit easy inspection of an approximate version of the linguistic strings for those who read the Latin script but not the specific Brahmic script being examined.

As a whole, the library provides important utilities for language processing applications of South Asian languages using Brahmic scripts. The design is based on the observation that, while there are considerable superficial differences between these scripts, they follow the same encoding model in Unicode, and maintain a very similar character repertoire having evolved from the same source — the Brāhmī script (Salomon, 1996; Fedorova, 2012). This observation lends itself to the script-agnostic design (outlined in §4) that, unlike other approaches reviewed in §2, is based on the weighted finite state transducer (WFST) formalism (Mohri, 2004). The details of our system are provided in §5.

2 Related Work

The computational processing of Brahmic scripts is not a new topic, with the first applications dating back to the early formal syntactic work by Datta (1984). With an increased focus on the South Asian languages within the NLP community, facilitated by advances in machine learning and the increased availability of relevant corpora, multiple script processing solutions have emerged. Some of these toolkits, such as statistical machine translation-based Brahmi-Net (Kunchukuttan et al., 2015), are model-based, while others, such as URoman (Hermjakob et al., 2018), IndicNLP (Kunchukuttan, 2020), and Aksharmukha (Rajan, 2020), employ rules. The main focus of these libraries is script conversion and romanization. In this capacity they were successfully employed in diverse downstream multilingual NLP tasks such as neural machine translation (Zhang et al., 2020; Amrhein and Sennrich, 2020), morphological analysis (Hauer et al., 2019; Murikinati et al., 2020), named entity recognition (Huang et al., 2019) and part-of-speech tagging (Cardenas et al., 2019).

Similar to the software mentioned above, our library does provide romanization, but unlike some of the packages, such as URoman, we guarantee reversibility from Latin back to the native script. Similar to others we do not focus on faithful invertible transliteration of named entities which typically requires model-based approaches (Sequiera et al., 2014). Unlike the IndicNLP package, our software does not provide morphological analysis, but instead offers significantly richer script normalization capabilities than other packages. These capabilities are functionally separated into normalization to Normalization Form C (NFC) and visual normalization. Additionally, our library provides extensive script-specific well-formedness grammars. Finally, in contrast to these other approaches, grammars in our library are maintained separately from the code for compilation and application, allowing for maintenance of existing scripts and languages plus extension to new ones without having to modify any code. This is particularly important given that Unicode standards do change over time and there remain many languages left to cover.

To the best of our knowledge this is the first publicly available general finite-state grammar approach for low-level processing of multiple Brahmic scripts since the early formal syntactic work by Datta (1984) and is the first such library designed based on an observation by Sproat (2003) that the fundamental organizing principles of the Brahmic scripts can be algebraically formalized. In particular, all the core components of our library (inverse romanization, normalization and well-formedness) are compactly and efficiently represented as finite state transducers. Such formalization lends itself particularly well to run-time or offline integration with any finite state processing pipeline, such as decoder components of input methods (Ouyang et al., 2017; Hellsten et al., 2017), text normalization for automatic speech recognition and text-to-speech synthesis (Zhang et al., 2019), among other natural language and speech applications.

3 Brahmic Scripts: An Overview

The scripts of interest have evolved from the ancient Brāhmī writing system that was recorded

Name	Id	IV	DV	C	CO
Bengali	BENG	16	13	43	5
Devanagari	DEVA	19	17	45	4
Gujarati	GUJR	16	15	39	5
Gurmukhi	GURU	12	9	39	8
Kannada	KNDA	17	15	39	3
Malayalam	MLYM	16	16	38	10
Oriya	ORYA	14	13	38	5
Sinhala	SINH	18	17	41	2
Tamil	TAML	12	11	27	1
Telugu	TELU	16	15	38	5

Table 1: Sizes of core graphemic classes: Independent vowels (IV), dependent vowel diacritics (DV), consonants (C), coda symbols (CO).

from the 3rd century BCE and fell out of use by the 5th century CE (Salomon, 1996; Strauch, 2012; Fedorova, 2012). The main unit of linear graphemic representation in Brahmic scripts is known by its traditional Sanskrit-derived name *akṣara*. As Bright (1999) notes, it is often translated as "syllable" although it does not bear direct correspondence to a syllable of speech, but rather to an orthographic syllable. The structure, or "grammar" of an akṣara is based on the following common principles: an akṣara often consists of a consonant symbol C, by default bearing an unmarked *inherent* vowel or attached diacritic (*dependent*) vowel sign v (C^v); but it may also be an *independent* vowel symbol V, or a consonant symbol with its inherent vowel "muted" by a special *virama* diacritic $\emptyset$ ($C^\emptyset$). In any of these preceding scenarios, the base consonant C can be replaced by a consonant cluster where all but the last consonant lose their inherent vowel. When the individual component consonants of the cluster combine to form a composite form, precluding the use of an overt *virama* diacritic, this is known as a "consonant conjunct" (e.g., $C_i^\emptyset C_j^\emptyset C_k$ vs $[C_iC_jC_k]^3$) (Fedorova, 2013; Bright, 1999; Coulmas, 1999; Share and Daniels, 2016).

The elements of the akṣara grammar described above can be grouped into several natural classes. The sizes of the core classes are shown in Table 1 for each writing system and its corresponding ISO 15924 identifier in uppercase format (ISO, 2004). The major classes are the independent vowels (e.g., the Devanagari diphthong औ), the dependent vowel diacritics (e.g., the Gujarati ી), and the consonants (e.g., the Gurmukhi ਝ). Another important class consists of the coda consonant sym-

[3]Here, surrounding the consonants in square brackets will serve to indicate that the enclosed consonants form a conjunct together.

Visual	Legacy sequence	NFC normalized
ऩ	NA NUKTA (U+0928 ·U+093C)	NNNA (U+0929)
क़	QA (U+0958)	KA NUKTA (U+0915 U+093C)

Table 2: NFC examples for Devanagari.

bols, like *anusvara*, *chandrabindu*, and *visarga*, which modify the akṣara as a whole (and follow and vowel signs in the memory representation). Finally, there is a class of special characters, such as the religious symbol *Om* ॐ, that behave like independent akṣara.[4]

Unicode Normalization Unicode defines several *normalization forms* which are used for checking whether the two Unicode strings are equivalent to each other (Unicode Consortium, 2019). In our library we support Normalization Form C (NFC) which is well suited for comparing visually identical strings. This normalization generally converts strings to the equivalent form that uses composite characters. Table 2 shows two examples of legacy sequences corresponding canonically equivalent forms for Devanagari.

Visual Normalization As was mentioned above, an akṣara may be represented by multiple Unicode character sequences and the goal of NFC normalization is to convert them to their unique canonical form. However, there are many Unicode character sequences that fall outside the scope of NFC algorithm. We provide visual normalization that, in addition to providing the NFC functionality, also supports transforming such legacy sequences. Some of the rules are provided as "Do Not Use" tables by the Unicode Consortium (2019) that recommends transformations from legacy sequences to their corresponding canonical form, such as Devanagari { अ (U+0905), ॅ (U+0945) } → ॲ (U+0972). We also included transformations for visually identical sequences (under many implementations) which are commonly found on the Web, such as Devanagari { ऐ (U+0910), े (U+0947) } → ऐ (U+0910).[5]

Well-formedness Check A well-formedness acceptor verifies whether the given text is readable in a particular script or not. It would be hard for the native reader to visually parse the text if the script rules are not followed. For example, the reader

[4]These classes are documented in `https://github.com/google-research/nisaba/blob/main/nisaba/brahmic/mappings.md`.

[5]Here the combining vowel sign `U+0947` does not affect the compound glyph's visual appearance hence is removed.

Script ID	Visual	Character(s)	Translit.
BENG	ৎ	KHANDA TA	⟨tʼ⟩
DEVA	इ	Non-word initial VOWEL I	⟨.i⟩
GUJR	ૐ	Religious sign OM	⟨ōm̐⟩
GURU	ੱ	ADDAK	⟨˙⟩
MLYM	ൻ	CHILLU N	⟨nʼ⟩
SINH	ඥ	JNYA	⟨ňj⟩
TAML	ஃப	VISARGA, PA	⟨f⟩

Table 3: Examples for additions to ISO 15919.

does not expect two vowels signs on a single consonant and such a thing may not even be possible to reasonably draw. Furthermore, unlike the Latin script, acronyms are not written using arbitrary letter sequences, they are formed only as a sequence of akṣara. Our approach verifies whether the text is a sequence of well-formed akṣara using the grammar described above.

Reversible ISO Transliteration ISO 15919 represents a unified 8-bit Latin transliteration scheme for major South Asian Brahmic scripts (ISO, 2001). Since it has not been updated with the characters that were introduced to the Unicode standard after 2001, we have added additional mappings, with some examples shown in Table 3. These additions are crucial because they allow us to reverse the romanizations to get the original Brahmic strings back reliably. This property allows various data processing pipelines to use the romanized text as an internal representation and convert it back to the original native script at the output stage.

Language-specific Logic Several South Asian languages often share the same script with some, often minor, language-specific differences. Our library supports language-specific customizations that can be combined with language-agnostic script logic. For example, the modern Bengali–Assamese script (Beng) is shared by both Bengali and Assamese languages, among others (Brandt and Sohoni, 2018). For both of these languages our library provides customizations,[6] such as the transformations required for visual normalization of Assamese that transform Bengali letter *ra* into its Assamese equivalent when it participates in a consonant conjunct (which generally occurs when following or preceding *virama*, e.g., { র (U+09B0), ◌্ (U+09CD) } → { ৰ (U+09F0), ◌্ (U+09CD) }).

[6] https://github.com/google-research/nisaba/tree/main/nisaba/brahmic/data/lang

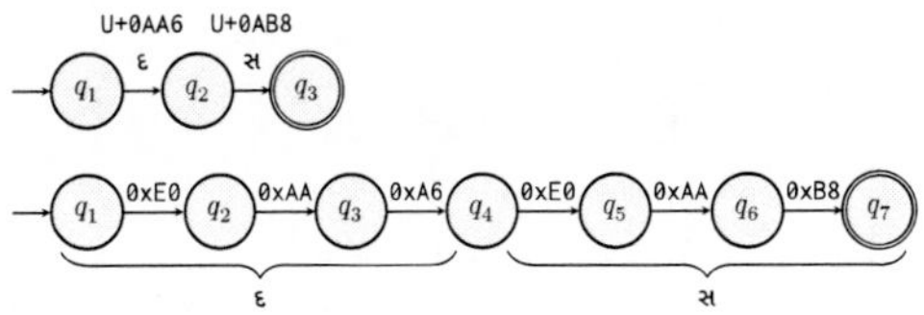

Figure 1: String acceptors for Gujarati word દસ (⟨dasa⟩, "ten") over an alphabet of Unicode code points (top) and bytes (bottom).

Require: FSAs: *consonant*, *vowel*, *vowel_sign*, *coda*, *standalone*, *virama*, *dead_consonant*, *accept*.

function $\mathcal{W}$(*consonant*, *vowel*, *vowel_sign*, *coda*, *standalone*, *virama*, *dead_consonant*, *accept*)
    $cluster \leftarrow (consonant + virama)^* + consonant$
    $codable \leftarrow (vowel \cup (cluster + vowel\_sign^?) \cup accept) \cup coda^?$
    $akshara \leftarrow codable \cup (cluster + virama + dead\_consonant^?)$
    $T \leftarrow akshara \cup standalone$
    return T^+ ▷ Kleene plus

Figure 2: Simplified construction of the well-formed automaton $\mathcal{W}$.

4 The Finite-State Approach

The Brahmic script manipulation operations described above have a natural intepretation grounded in formal language theory. We treat the text corpus in a given script as a set of strings over some finite alphabet Σ that defines a set of admissable script symbols. The set of zero or more strings is known as *language* which, in its simplest (regular) form, can be succintly described (or *recognized*) by a finite state automaton (FSA) or acceptor (Yu, 1997). Two simple FSAs that represent the Gujarati word દસ are shown in Figure 1, where the top automaton represents the word over an alphabet of Unicode code points for Gujarati, while the bottom one represents the same string over the corresponding byte symbols in UTF-8 encoding (Unicode Consortium, 2019). Our library supports both representations.

The akṣara grammar outlined in the previous section can be expressed via elementary formal operations on the FSAs that describe grammar constituents. Such set-theoretic operations include union ($\cup$), concatenation ($+$) and closure, where closure is defined as an arbitrary natural number of concatenations of a language L over Σ with itself, either accepting an empty input $\{\epsilon\}$ or not, denoted L^* (Kleene star) and L^+ (Kleene plus), respectively (Kuich and Salomaa, 1986). These operations represent non-trivial automata which are compiled offline resulting in compact and efficient representations. A simplified process for constructing the automaton $\mathcal{W}$ to perform the well-

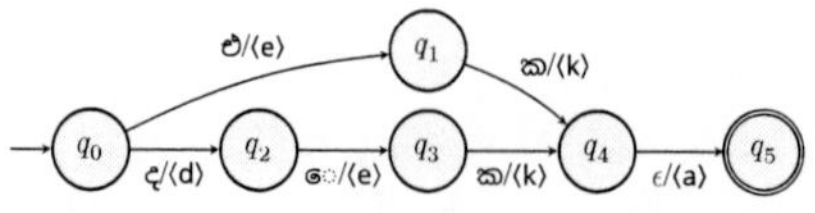

Figure 3: Romanization of Sinhala words එක ("one") and දෙක ("two") into ⟨eka⟩ and ⟨deka⟩, respectively.

```
Require: FSTs: consonant, vowel, vowel_sign, coda, standalone, virama.

1: function 𝒯(consonant, vowel, vowel_sign, coda, standalone, virama)
2:     del_virama ← virama × Ø                          ▷ Delete virama
3:     ins_schwa ← Ø × {⟨a⟩}                             ▷ Insert inherent vowel
4:     deweight ← (ϵ, ϵ, w ↓)                            ▷ De-prioritize the path
5:     T ← (
6:         (consonant + vowel_sign) ∪     ▷ (ස,⟨sa⟩) + (ු,⟨u⟩) → (සු,⟨su⟩)
7:         (consonant + del_virama + deweight) ∪
8:         (consonant + ins_schwa + deweight) ∪
9:         (vowel + deweight) ∪ coda ∪ standalone ∪
10:        ...)                                          ▷ Further logic
11:    return T*                                         ▷ Kleene star
```

Figure 4: Simplified construction of the transliteration transducer $\mathcal{T}$.

formed check from the previous section is shown in Figure 2. In this simplified example, the paths through the automaton that define a legal consonant cluster (line 2 of the algorithm) are represented by a sub-automaton that recognizes the language that consists of strings formed from the consonant and virama symbols only, where each consonant, apart from the last one, must be followed by the virama that removes an inherent vowel.

The rest of the operations on the Brahmic scripts, namely the normalization and transliteration, involve modifications of the Brahmic script inputs. Such operations are naturally expressed by finite state transducers (FSTs), which are a generalization of the FSA concept used to encode string-string *relations* (or transductions), by modifying the automata arcs to have pairs of labels from input and output alphabets, instead of single labels. A trivial romanization in our representation of the two Sinhala words එක (⟨eka⟩, "one") and දෙක (⟨deka⟩, "two") is shown in Figure 3. Note the "vocalization" of the final consonant by insertion of a schwa via an input ϵ-transition. Also note that the path accepting the second word is longer. The word දෙක consists of three akṣara and requires modification of the inherent vowel by the dependent vowel in order to produce ⟨de⟩.

The basic operations on the FSAs outlined above also extend to the FST case and allow for similarly succinct final compiled representations (Mohri, 2000), such as the simplified construction of the ISO romanization transducer $\mathcal{T}$ for converting from Brahmic scripts to Latin alphabet, shown in Figure 4. An important extension of FSAs and FSTs are the weighted finite state automata (WFSAs) and transducers (WFSTs) (Mohri, 2004, 2009) that equip each arc in the automaton or transducer with a weight, thus allowing optimization and search algorithms to compute the costs of distinct paths, which can be used to determine their relative importance. We use weights in some of our grammars to indicate the relative priority of a particular akṣara modification. For example, in Figure 4, the paths corresponding to consonants followed by dependent vowels (line 6) have priority over the akṣara-initial independent vowels (line 9).

The two remaining operations on akṣara, namely NFC and visual normalization, are represented in our library using the context-dependent rewrite rules from the formal approach popularized by Chomsky and Halle (1968). The normalization rules are represented as a sequence $\{\phi \rightarrow \psi / \lambda \_\_ \rho\}$, where the source ϕ is rewritten as ψ if its left and right contexts are λ and ρ. For an earlier example from §3, a single NFC normalization rule rewrites the Devanagari string $\phi =$ "न" (*na*, `U+0928`) + "़" (*nukta* sign, `U+093C`) into its canonical composition $\psi =$ "ऩ" (*nnna*, `U+0929`). Kaplan and Kay (1994) proposed an algorithm for compiling such sequences into an FST. This approach was further improved and extended to WFSTs by Mohri and Sproat (1996), whose algorithm we use to compile sequences of NFC and visual normalization rules into transducers denoted $\mathcal{N}$ and $\mathcal{V}$.

Finally, the transducers representing language-specific customizations of a particular script operation are compiled by composing the generic language-agnostic transducer, such as the Devanagari visual normalizer, with the transducer representing transformations that capture language-specific use of the script, e.g., Devanagari for Nepali.

5 System Details and Demo

The core of the Nisaba Brahmic script manipulation library resides under the `brahmic` directory of the distribution. In this section we provide details for how to build and use the library and also explore its application to visual normalization of Wikipedia-based text in 9 of these scripts.

Prerequisites We use Bazel (Google, 2020) as a primary build environment. For compiling the

Op.	Symb.	Prop.	BENG	DEVA	GUJR	GURU	KNDA	MLYM	ORYA	SINH	TAML	TELU
			Script									
$\mathcal{T}$	Unicode	N_s	127	130	113	93	119	122	105	122	75	112
		N_a	475	546	476	418	487	522	452	513	326	485
	Byte	N_s	248	235	195	171	210	201	178	192	126	181
		N_a	384	399	334	288	350	345	305	339	229	318
$\mathcal{N}$	Unicode	N_s	9	17	1	8	21	8	9	17	11	4
		N_a	158	248	75	78	349	261	160	352	228	163
	Byte	N_s	31	55	1	28	70	27	31	55	37	14
		N_a	1,812	1,841	255	1,047	2,884	2,322	1,813	2,611	3,098	1,543
$\mathcal{V}$	Unicode	N_s	103	51,710	98	119	1764	287	60	182	209	57
		N_a	2,423	121,157	2,234	2,322	6,136	3,021	1,732	2,129	1,280	2,249
	Byte	N_s	369	165,168	356	425	5,611	965	232	624	703	225
		N_a	18,896	266,441	18,684	20,733	30,422	18,598	16,146	15,363	11,830	18,717
$\mathcal{W}$	Unicode	N_s	11	7	7	7	10	10	7	7	4	6
		N_a	427	446	388	341	465	485	380	361	158	335
	Byte	N_s	38	23	21	23	33	33	22	22	11	19
		N_a	297	321	284	257	309	297	279	195	130	239

Table 4: Properties of script FSTs arranged by operation and symbol types (Unicode code points and UTF-8 bytes), where $\mathcal{T}$ denotes the ISO transliteration operation, $\mathcal{N}$ is the NFC normalization, $\mathcal{V}$ denotes visual normalization, and $\mathcal{W}$ is the well-formed check. The numbers of states and arcs are denoted by N_s and N_a, respectively.

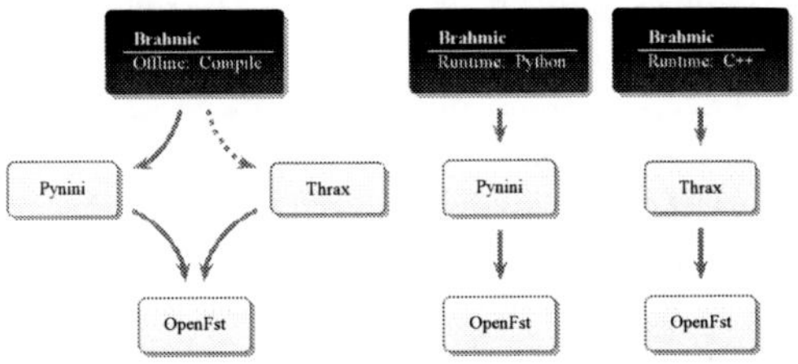

Figure 5: Software dependency diagrams for the three modes of operation: compile stage (left), Python run-time (center) and C++ run-time (right).

automata and transducers we employ Pynini[7], a Python library for constructing finite-state grammars and for performing operations on WFSTs (Gorman, 2016; Gorman and Sproat, in press). In addition, the library depends on Thrax[8], an older relative of Pynini, that provides a custom grammar manipulation language for WFSTs (Tai et al., 2011; Roark et al., 2012). Although Thrax has been mostly superseded by Pynini, we still rely on some of its utilities for unit testing and its C++ run-time components. At their core, both Pynini and Thrax depend on the OpenFst library[9] for the implementation of most WFST algorithms (Allauzen et al., 2007; Riley et al., 2009). The overall dependency diagram is shown on the left-hand side of Figure 5 (the minimal dependency on Thrax is indicated by a dotted arrow). At build time, Bazel pulls in these dependencies remotely from their respective repositories.

[7]`http://pynini.opengrm.org/`
[8]`http://thrax.opengrm.org`
[9]`http://www.openfst.org`

Compiling the Transducers Figure 6 presents the sequence of steps to compile the transducers, including downloading the repository (line 2), compiling the library and its artifacts (line 5) and running the unit tests (line 7). The artifacts are compiled by Bazel using Pynini and consist of the finite state archive (FAR) files that contain collections of WFSTs (Roark et al., 2012). For each of the four Brahmic script operations we generate two FAR files: one for WFSTs over the byte alphabet, and another over the Unicode code point alphabet.[10] Each FAR file contains ten script-specific transducers whose names correspond to the upper-case ISO 15924 script codes. Since the transliteration operation is bidirectional, the name of each script-specific transliteration transducer has the prefix `FROM_` for the native-to-Latin direction, and `TO_` for the inverse. The numbers of states (N_s) and arcs (N_a) of the resulting transliteration ($\mathcal{T}$), NFC ($\mathcal{N}$), visual normalization ($\mathcal{V}$) transducers and well-formedness acceptors ($\mathcal{W}$) for each script and alphabet type are shown in Table 4.

Offline and Online Usage Once the transducers are compiled, they can be applied offline to the input files using the `rewrite-tester` tool provided by Thrax, as shown in lines 8–13 of the example in Figure 6, where the visual normalization transducer $\mathcal{V}$ for Kannada that resides in the `visual_norm.far` archive is applied to words in input file `words.txt`.

We provide lightweight run-time interfaces for

[10]The Unicode code point FARs rather misleadingly have the suffix `utf8` in their name for historical reasons.

```
# Download Nisaba repository.
git clone https://github.com/google-research/nisaba.git
cd nisaba
# Compile the transducers and tests.
bazel build -c opt //nisaba/brahmic/...
# Run the unit tests.
bazel test -c opt //nisaba/brahmic/...
# Compile Thrax rewrite helper tool.
bazel build -c opt @org_opengrm_thrax//:rewrite-tester
# Run visual normalization for Kannada.
bazel-bin/external/org_opengrm_thrax/rewrite-tester \
    --far=bazel-bin/nisaba/brahmic/visual_norm.far \
    --rules=KNDA < words.txt
```

Figure 6: Compiling the transducers.

```
import unittest
from nisaba import brahmic

class BrahmicTest(unittest.TestCase):
  def testBasicOperations(self):
    # Check romanization.
    iso_to_deva = brahmic.IsoTo('Deva')
    self.assertEqual('क्लब',
       iso_to_deva.ApplyOnText('⟨k·laba⟩'))
    # Check valid inputs.
    wellformed_mlym = brahmic.WellFormed('Mlym')
    self.assertTrue(wellformed_mlym.AcceptText('ന്യൂഠം'))
    # Visual normalizer.
    visual_norm_deva = brahmic.VisualNorm('Deva')
    self.assertEqual('औ', visual_norm_deva.ApplyOnText('अौ'))
```

Figure 7: Run-time Python interface example.

both Python and C++, their dependencies shown in the center and the right-hand side of Figure 5, respectively. The Python interface is provided via several wrappers around the `pynini.Fst` abstraction, with a simple example shown in Figure 7. In addition to performing simple operations on individual strings, more WFST-specific operations, such as transducer composition, are provided by Pynini. The C++ interface is provided by the `Grammar` helper class, shown in Figure 8, that includes the necessary methods for initializing the WFSTs and performing rewrites (for transducers) and acceptance tests (for acceptors). In addition, many more operations on WFSTs are available through the OpenFst library, if required.

Prevalence of Normalization To demonstrate the prevalence of text requiring normalization in

```
#include <string>

// Generic wrapper around FST archive with Brahmic transducers.
class Grammar {
  public:
  // Constructs given the FAR path, its name and the name of WFST.
  Grammar(const std::string& far_path, const std::string& far_name,
          const std::string& fst_name);
  // Initializes the transducer.
  bool Load();
  // Rewrites <input> into <output>.
  bool Rewrite(const std::string& input, std::string *output) const;
  // Checks whether the grammar accepts <input>.
  bool Accept(const std::string& input) const;
};
```

Figure 8: Run-time C++ interface.

Language	Script	% Changed Types	Tokens
Bengali	BENG	0.53	0.06
Gujarati	GUJR	0.46	0.09
Hindi	DEVA	1.41	0.18
Kannada	KNDA	4.19	1.66
Malayalam	MLYM	6.33	4.19
Marathi	DEVA	1.51	0.40
Punjabi	GURU	1.67	0.33
Sinhala	SINH	3.55	0.71
Tamil	TAML	0.59	0.17
Telugu	TELU	1.97	0.63

Table 5: Percentage of types and tokens changed by visual normalization from native script Wikipedia training partitions of the Dakshina dataset.

these scripts, we normalized publicly available corpora and measured how frequently words in the samples were modified. The Dakshina dataset (Roark et al., 2020) includes (among other things) collections of monolingual Wikipedia sentences in 12 South Asian languages, 10 of which use Brahmic scripts. We applied visual normalization to the training partitions of the collections in these 10 languages, and Table 5 presents the percentage of both types and tokens that were changed by the normalization.[11] Malayalam is the language with the highest percentage of both types and tokens changed by visual normalization, largely due to frequent conversion to chillu letters from alternative encodings. For example, the relatively frequent word തന്റെ ("yours") is normalized to the encoding with the chillu letter ൻ instead of ന.

6 Conclusion and Future Work

We presented finite-state automata-based utilities for processing the major Brahmic scripts. The finite state transducer formalism provides an efficient and scalable framework for expressing Brahmic script operations and is suitable for many NLP applications, such as those reported in Kumar et al. (2020) and Kakwani et al. (2020), which may benefit from the reduction in "noise" present in unnormalized text. In the future, we will continue to improve the support for existing scripts and extend our work to other Brahmic scripts.

[11]Tokenization was simply based on whitespace, with no other processing such as punctuation separation, so the total number of distinct types is accordingly relatively high. The texts from that dataset were already NFC normalized.

Acknowledgments

The authors would like to thank Işın Demirşahin for valuable discussion on this project.

References

Cyril Allauzen, Michael Riley, Johan Schalkwyk, Wojciech Skut, and Mehryar Mohri. 2007. OpenFst: A general and efficient weighted finite-state transducer library. In *International Conference on Implementation and Application of Automata*, pages 11–23. Springer.

Chantal Amrhein and Rico Sennrich. 2020. On Romanization for model transfer between scripts in neural machine translation. In *Findings of the Association for Computational Linguistics: EMNLP 2020*, pages 2461–2469, Online. Association for Computational Linguistics.

Pushpak Bhattacharyya, Hema Murthy, Surangika Ranathunga, and Ranjiva Munasinghe. 2019. Indic language computing. *Communications of the ACM*, 62(11):70–75.

Carmen Brandt and Pushkar Sohoni. 2018. Script and identity – the politics of writing in South Asia: an introduction. *South Asian History and Culture*, 9(1):1–15.

William Bright. 1999. A matter of typology: Alphasyllabaries and abugidas. *Written Language & Literacy*, 2(1):45–55.

Ronald Cardenas, Ying Lin, Heng Ji, and Jonathan May. 2019. A grounded unsupervised universal part-of-speech tagger for low-resource languages. In *Proceedings of the 2019 Conference of the North American Chapter of the Association for Computational Linguistics: Human Language Technologies, Volume 1 (Long and Short Papers)*, pages 2428–2439, Minneapolis, Minnesota. Association for Computational Linguistics.

George Cardona and Danesh Jain. 2007. *The Indo-Aryan Languages*. Routledge Language Family Series. Routledge, New York.

Noam Chomsky and Morris Halle. 1968. *The Sound Pattern of English*. Harper & Row, New York.

Florian Coulmas. 1999. *The Blackwell Encyclopedia of Writing Systems*. John Wiley & Sons, Oxford.

A. K. Datta. 1984. A generalized formal approach for description and analysis of major Indian scripts. *IETE Journal of Research*, 30(6):155–161.

Liudmila L Fedorova. 2012. The development of structural characteristics of Brahmi script in derivative writing systems. *Written Language & Literacy*, 15(1):1–25.

Liudmila L. Fedorova. 2013. The development of graphic representation in abugida writing: The akshara's grammar. *Lingua Posnaniensis*, 55(2):49–66.

Google. 2020. Bazel. `http://bazel.build`. [Online], Accessed: 2020-12-10.

Kyle Gorman. 2016. Pynini: A Python library for weighted finite-state grammar compilation. In *Proceedings of the SIGFSM Workshop on Statistical NLP and Weighted Automata*, pages 75–80, Berlin, Germany. Association for Computational Linguistics.

Kyle Gorman and Richard Sproat. in press. *Finite-State Text Processing*. Human Language Technologies. Morgan & Claypool, Williston, VT.

Bradley Hauer, Amir Ahmad Habibi, Yixing Luan, Rashed Rubby Riyadh, and Grzegorz Kondrak. 2019. Cognate projection for low-resource inflection generation. In *Proceedings of the 16th Workshop on Computational Research in Phonetics, Phonology, and Morphology*, pages 6–11, Florence, Italy. Association for Computational Linguistics.

Lars Hellsten, Brian Roark, Prasoon Goyal, Cyril Allauzen, Françoise Beaufays, Tom Ouyang, Michael Riley, and David Rybach. 2017. Transliterated mobile keyboard input via weighted finite-state transducers. In *Proceedings of the 13th International Conference on Finite State Methods and Natural Language Processing (FSMNLP 2017)*, pages 10–19, Umeå, Sweden. Association for Computational Linguistics.

Ulf Hermjakob, Jonathan May, and Kevin Knight. 2018. Out-of-the-box universal Romanization tool uroman. In *Proceedings of ACL 2018, System Demonstrations*, pages 13–18, Melbourne, Australia. Association for Computational Linguistics.

Lauren Hinkle, Albert Brouillette, Sujay Jayakar, Leigh Gathings, Miguel Lezcano, and Jugal Kalita. 2013. Design and evaluation of soft keyboards for Brahmic scripts. *ACM Transactions on Asian Language Information Processing (TALIP)*, 12(2):1–37.

Xiaolei Huang, Jonathan May, and Nanyun Peng. 2019. What matters for neural cross-lingual named entity recognition: An empirical analysis. In *Proceedings of the 2019 Conference on Empirical Methods in Natural Language Processing and the 9th International Joint Conference on Natural Language Processing (EMNLP-IJCNLP)*, pages 6395–6401, Hong Kong, China. Association for Computational Linguistics.

ISO. 2001. ISO 15919: Transliteration of Devanagari and related Indic scripts into Latin characters. `https://www.iso.org/standard/28333.html`. International Organization for Standardization.

ISO. 2004. ISO 15924: Codes for the representation of names of scripts. `https://www.iso.org/obp/ui/#iso:std:iso:15924:ed-1:v1:en`. International Organization for Standardization.

Divyanshu Kakwani, Anoop Kunchukuttan, Satish Golla, Gokul N. C., Avik Bhattacharyya, Mitesh M. Khapra, and Pratyush Kumar. 2020. iNLPSuite: Monolingual corpora, evaluation benchmarks and pre-trained multilingual language models for Indian languages. In *Proc. of the 2020 Conference on Empirical Methods in Natural Language Processing: Findings, EMNLP 2020*, pages 4948–4961, Online Event. Association for Computational Linguistics.

Ronald M. Kaplan and Martin Kay. 1994. Regular models of phonological rule systems. *Computational Linguistics*, 20(3):331–378.

Werner Kuich and Arto Salomaa. 1986. *Semirings, Automata, Languages*, volume 5 of *Monographs in Theoretical Computer Science*. Springer, Berlin.

Saurav Kumar, Saunack Kumar, Diptesh Kanojia, and Pushpak Bhattacharyya. 2020. "A passage to India": Pre-trained word embeddings for Indian languages. In *Proc. of the 1st Joint Workshop on Spoken Language Technologies for Under-resourced languages (SLTU) and Collaboration and Computing for Under-Resourced Languages (CCURL)*, pages 352–357, Marseille, France. European Language Resources association.

Anoop Kunchukuttan. 2020. The IndicNLP Library. https://github.com/anoopkunchukuttan/indic_nlp_library.

Anoop Kunchukuttan, Ratish Puduppully, and Pushpak Bhattacharyya. 2015. Brahmi-net: A transliteration and script conversion system for languages of the Indian subcontinent. In *Proceedings of the 2015 Conference of the North American Chapter of the Association for Computational Linguistics: Demonstrations*, pages 81–85, Denver, Colorado. Association for Computational Linguistics.

Mehryar Mohri. 2000. Minimization algorithms for sequential transducers. *Theoretical Computer Science*, 234(1-2):177–201.

Mehryar Mohri. 2004. Weighted finite-state transducer algorithms. An overview. In Carlos Martín-Vide, Victor Mitrana, and Gheorghe Păun, editors, *Formal Languages and Applications*, pages 551–563. Springer, Berlin; Heidelberg.

Mehryar Mohri. 2009. Weighted automata algorithms. In Manfred Droste, Werner Kuich, and Heiko Vogler, editors, *Handbook of Weighted Automata*, Monographs in Theoretical Computer Science, pages 213–254. Springer.

Mehryar Mohri and Richard Sproat. 1996. An efficient compiler for weighted rewrite rules. In *34th Annual Meeting of the Association for Computational Linguistics*, pages 231–238, Santa Cruz, California, USA. Association for Computational Linguistics.

Nikitha Murikinati, Antonios Anastasopoulos, and Graham Neubig. 2020. Transliteration for cross-lingual morphological inflection. In *Proceedings of the 17th SIGMORPHON Workshop on Computational Research in Phonetics, Phonology, and Morphology*, pages 189–197, Online. Association for Computational Linguistics.

Tom Ouyang, David Rybach, Françoise Beaufays, and Michael Riley. 2017. Mobile keyboard input decoding with finite-state transducers.

Umapada Pal, Ramachandran Jayadevan, and Nabin Sharma. 2012. Handwriting recognition in Indian regional scripts: A survey of offline techniques. *ACM Transactions on Asian Language Information Processing (TALIP)*, 11(1):1–35.

Vinodh Rajan. 2020. Aksharamukha. https://github.com/virtualvinodh/aksharamukha.

Michael Riley, Cyril Allauzen, and Martin Jansche. 2009. OpenFst: An open-source, weighted finite-state transducer library and its applications to speech and language. In *Proceedings of Human Language Technologies: The 2009 Annual Conference of the North American Chapter of the Association for Computational Linguistics, Companion Volume: Tutorial Abstracts*, pages 9–10, Boulder, Colorado. Association for Computational Linguistics.

Brian Roark, Richard Sproat, Cyril Allauzen, Michael Riley, Jeffrey Sorensen, and Terry Tai. 2012. The OpenGrm open-source finite-state grammar software libraries. In *Proceedings of the ACL 2012 System Demonstrations*, pages 61–66, Jeju Island, Korea. Association for Computational Linguistics.

Brian Roark, Lawrence Wolf-Sonkin, Christo Kirov, Sabrina J. Mielke, Cibu Johny, Isin Demirsahin, and Keith Hall. 2020. Processing South Asian languages written in the Latin script: the Dakshina dataset. In *Proc. of 12th Language Resources and Evaluation Conference (LREC)*, pages 2413–2423, Marseille, France.

Richard G. Salomon. 1996. Brahmi and Kharoshthi. In Peter T. Daniels and William Bright, editors, *The World's Writing Systems*, pages 373–383. Oxford University Press, New York, NY.

Royal Denzil Sequiera, Shashank S. Rao, and B. R. Shambavi. 2014. Word-level language identification and back transliteration of romanized text. In *Proceedings of the Forum for Information Retrieval Evaluation*, pages 70–73, Bangalore, India.

David L. Share and Peter T. Daniels. 2016. Aksharas, alphasyllabaries, abugidas, alphabets and orthographic depth: Reflections on Rimzhim, Katz and Fowler (2014). *Writing systems research*, 8(1):17–31.

R. Mahesh K. Sinha. 2009. A journey from Indian scripts processing to Indian language processing. *IEEE Annals of the History of Computing*, 31(1):8–31.

Richard Sproat. 2003. A formal computational analysis of Indic scripts. In *In International Symposium on Indic Scripts: Past and Future*, Tokyo, Japan.

Sanford B. Steever. 2019. *The Dravidian Languages*, 2nd edition. Routledge Language Family Series. Routledge, New York.

Ingo Strauch. 2012. The character of the Indian Kharoṣṭhī script and the "Sanskrit Revolution": A writing system between identity and assimilation. In Alexander J. de Voogt and Joachim Friedrich Quack, editors, *The Idea of Writing: Writing Across Borders*, pages 131–168. Brill, Leiden; Boston.

Terry Tai, Wojciech Skut, and Richard Sproat. 2011. Thrax: An open source grammar compiler built on OpenFst. In *Proc. of IEEE Automatic Speech Recognition and Understanding Workshop (ASRU)*, volume 12, Hawaii, USA.

Unicode Consortium. 2019. The Unicode Standard. Online: `http://www.unicode.org/versions/Unicode12.1.0/`. Version 12.1.0, Mountain View, CA.

Hans H. Wellisch. 1978. *The Conversion of Scripts: Its Nature, History, and Utilization*. Information sciences series. John Wiley & Sons, New York.

Sheng Yu. 1997. Regular languages. In Grzegorz Rozenberg and Arto Salomaa, editors, *Handbook of Formal Languages*, volume 1: Word, Language, Grammar, pages 41–110. Springer, Berlin.

Hao Zhang, Richard Sproat, Axel H Ng, Felix Stahlberg, Xiaochang Peng, Kyle Gorman, and Brian Roark. 2019. Neural models of text normalization for speech applications. *Computational Linguistics*, 45(2):293–337.

Yuhao Zhang, Ziyang Wang, Runzhe Cao, Binghao Wei, Weiqiao Shan, Shuhan Zhou, Abudurexiti Reheman, Tao Zhou, Xin Zeng, Laohu Wang, Yongyu Mu, Jingnan Zhang, Xiaoqian Liu, Xuanjun Zhou, Yinqiao Li, Bei Li, Tong Xiao, and Jingbo Zhu. 2020. The NiuTrans machine translation systems for WMT20. In *Proceedings of the Fifth Conference on Machine Translation*, pages 338–345, Online. Association for Computational Linguistics.

CovRelex: A COVID-19 Retrieval System with Relation Extraction

Vu Tran[1] **Van-Hien Tran**[2] **Phuong Minh Nguyen**[1] **Chau Minh Nguyen**[1]
Ken Satoh[3] **Yuji Matsumoto**[4] **Minh Le Nguyen**[1]

[1]Japan Advanced Institute of Science and Technology
{vu.tran,phuongnm,chau.nguyen,nguyenml}@jaist.ac.jp
[2]Nara Institute of Science and Technology, Japan
tran.van_hien.ts1@is.naist.jp
[3]National Institute of Informatics, Japan
ksatoh@nii.ac.jp
[4]RIKEN Center for Advanced Intelligence Project (AIP), Japan
yuji.matsumoto@riken.jp

Abstract

This paper presents CovRelex, a scientific paper retrieval system targeting entities and relations via relation extraction on COVID-19 scientific papers. This work aims at building a system supporting users efficiently in acquiring knowledge across a huge number of COVID-19 scientific papers published rapidly. Our system can be accessed via https://www.jaist.ac.jp/is/labs/nguyen-lab/systems/covrelex/.

Keywords: COVID-19, biomedical domain, scientific paper analysis, relation extraction, entity recognition, document retrieval.

1 Introduction

This work aims at facilitating knowledge acquisition from a huge number of COVID-19 scientific papers. Due to the COVID-19 outbreak, researchers have been focusing on studying the virus and publishing a huge number of papers rapidly. According to the estimation of Silva et al. (2020), 23,634 unique documents were published in just 6 months between January 1st and June 30th, 2020. In the records of the COVID-19 Open Research Dataset (CORD-19) Challenge[1], the number of collected papers about COVID-19, SARS-Cov-2 and related coronaviruses is more than 400K by January 9th, 2021. The rapid speed of new publication and the huge number of related papers challenges specialists to seek knowledge by connecting findings across papers efficiently and timely.

When focusing on knowledge acquisition of biomedical entities, several questions can be asked regarding the entities and their relations:

- Which papers mention entity E_1?
- Which papers mention the relation R between entity E_1 and entity E_2?
- Which papers mention the relation R_1 between entity E_1 and entity E_2, and the relation R_2 between entity E_2 and entity E_3?
- What relations R_x exist between entity E_1 and entity E_2 and in which papers?
- What entity E_x has relation R with entity E_1 and in which papers?

Such questions can be answered by our system.

2 Related Work

FACTA+ (Tsuruoka et al., 2011, 2008) was presented as a text search engine that helps users discover and visualize indirect associations between biomedical concepts from MEDLINE abstracts. Liu et al. (2015) introduced an online text-mining system (PolySearch2) for identifying relationships between biomedical entities over 43 million articles covering MEDLINE abstracts, PubMed Central full-text articles, Wikipedia full-text articles, US Patent abstracts, open access textbooks from NCBI and MedlinePlus articles. More recently, LitVar (Allot et al., 2018), a semantic search engine, utilized advanced text mining techniques to compute and extract relationships between genome

[1]https://www.kaggle.com/allen-institute-for-ai/CORD-19-research-challenge

Proceedings of the 16th Conference of the European Chapter of the Association for Computational Linguistics: System Demonstrations, pages 24–31
April 19 - 23, 2021. ©2021 Association for Computational Linguistics

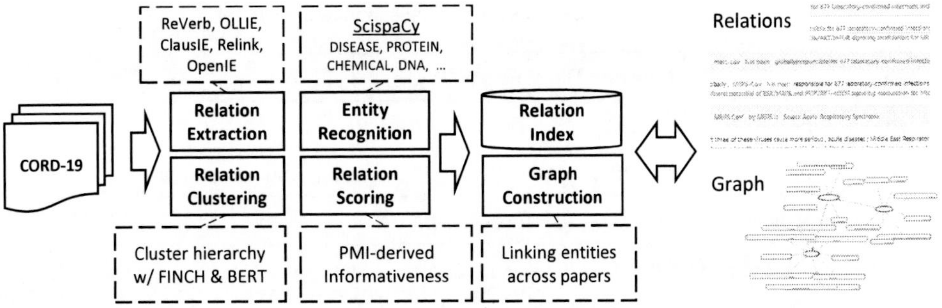

Figure 1: System Overview.

arg_1	rel	arg_2
[MERS-CoV]$_{GGP}$	include	[fever]$_{DISEASE}$, [chills/rigors]$_{DISEASE}$, [headache]$_{DISEASE}$, non-productive [cough]$_{DISEASE}$
[MERS-CoV]$_{GGP}$	is responsible for causing	lower [respiratory infections]$_{DISEASE}$ with [fever]$_{DISEASE}$ and [cough]$_{DISEASE}$

Figure 2: An example of relations extracted from COVID-19 papers.

variants and other associated entities such as diseases and chemicals/drugs. Wei et al. (2019) presented a web service PubTator Central (PTC) that provides automated bioconcept annotations in full text biomedical articles, in which bioconcepts are extracted from state-of-the-art text mining systems.

Due to the COVID-19 outbreak, it is essential to grasp valuable knowledge from a huge number of COVID-19-related papers for dealing with the pandemic effectively. Sohrab et al. (2020) introduced the BENNERD system that detects named entities in biomedical text and links them to the unified medical language system (UMLS) to facilitate the COVID-19 research. Hope et al. (2020) created a dataset annotated for mechanism relations and trained an information extraction model on this data. Then, they used the model to extract a Knowledge Base (KB) of mechanism and effect relations from papers relating to COVID-19. Zhang et al. (2020) built Covidex, a search infrastructure that provides information access to the COVID-19 Open Research Dataset such as answering questions. Esteva et al. (2020) also presented Co-Search, a retriever-ranker semantic search engine designed to handle complex queries over the COVID-19 literature. Wang et al. (2020) created the EvidenceMiner web-based system. Given a query as a natural language statement, EvidenceMiner automatically retrieves sentence-level textual evidence from the CORD-19 corpus.

Clearly, previous works made a great effort to acquire useful knowledge from the COVID-19 literature, such as recognizing biomedical entities (Sohrab et al., 2020), extracting mechanism relations between entities (Hope et al., 2020), or retrieving relevant text segments based on the user query (Zhang et al., 2020; Wang et al., 2020). However, there is still a lack of a system that has the ability to automatically detect both entities with various types and their diverse relations through papers, especially when COVID-19 papers are published rapidly. This motivates us to build the CovRelex system, which aims to exploit such information.

3 Method

3.1 Overview

The core of our system is built from extracting an enormous number of relations from COVID-19 related scientific papers (in CORD-19 corpus) by several open domain relation extraction methods. The extracted relations are represented not only by their original form from the extraction methods but also by the contained biomedical entities. Furthermore, the relations are clustered and scored for their informativeness over the corpus (Fig. 1).

A **relation** is a triplet in the form (arg_1, rel, arg_2), where arg_1, and arg_2 are noun phrases which may contain biomedical entities, and rel is an expression describing the directed relation from arg_1 to arg_2 (shown in Fig. 2).

Table 1: SciSpacy models used in our system.

Name	Training Data	Entity Types
en_ner_craft_md	CRAFT	GGP, SO, TAXON, CHEBI, GO, CL
en_ner_jnlpba_md	JNLPBA	DNA, CELL_TYPE, CELL_LINE, RNA, PROTEIN
en_ner_bc5cdr_md	BC5CDR	DISEASE, CHEMICAL
en_ner_bionlp13cg_md	BIONLP13CG	AMINO_ACID, ANATOMICAL_SYSTEM, CANCER, CELL, CELLULAR_COMPONENT, DEVELOPING_ANATOMICAL_STRUCTURE, GENE_OR_GENE_PRODUCT, IMMATERIAL_ANATOMICAL_ENTITY, MULTI-TISSUE_STRUCTURE, ORGAN, ORGANISM, ORGANISM_SUBDIVISION, ORGANISM_SUBSTANCE, PATHOLOGICAL_FORMATION, SIMPLE_CHEMICAL, TISSUE

3.2 Relation Extraction

With the objective of extracting as many relations as possible, we employ several relation extraction methods. Each method has their own characteristics, thus, may extract different kinds of relations. By combining several methods, we can obtain higher extraction coverage. The methods are briefly described as follows.

- ReVerb (Fader et al., 2011) tackles the problems of incoherent and uninformative extractions by introducing constraints on binary, verb-based relation phrases.
- OLLIE (Mausam et al., 2012) addresses the problems that Open IE systems such as ReVerb only extract relations that are mediated by verbs. Not only by verbs, OLIEE extracts relations mediated also by nouns, adjectives, and more.
- ClausIE (Del Corro and Gemulla, 2013) is a clause-based approach to open information extraction. It separates the detection of clauses and clause types from the actual generation of propositions.
- Relink (Tran and Nguyen, 2020) is a method partly inherited from ReVerb, extracts relations from the connected phrases, not for identifying clause type like ClauseIE.
- OpenIE (Angeli et al., 2015) extracts relations by breaking a long sentence into short, coherent clauses, and then finds the maximally simple relations.

The extracted relations are also tagged with biomedical entities recognized by using entity recognition models presented in the next subsection.

3.3 Entity Recognition

We use biomedical entity recognition models specialized for predicting entity type and provided by SciSpacy (Neumann et al., 2019) (Table 1). Each of the models is trained on a different annotated corpus, thus, covers a different set of biomedical entities. By using multiple entity systems, we can obtain various specialized entity information: chemicals and diseases with BCD5CDR (Li et al., 2016), cell types, chemicals, proteins, and genes with CRAFT (Bada et al., 2012), cell lines, cell types, DNAs, RNAs, and proteins with JNLPBA (Collier and Kim, 2004), and cancer genetics with BioNLP13CG (Pyysalo et al., 2015).

3.4 Relation Clustering

We build a cluster hierarchy on a subset of the extracted relations (this subset contains all relations in which both arg_1 and arg_2 are biomedical entities), so users can quickly find their interested relation expressions or they can choose some clusters which may contain their interested relation expressions.

We utilize FINCH (Sarfraz et al., 2019), hierarchical clustering method, and BERT (Devlin et al., 2019) for this task. First, BERT-Base model is used to encode each relation as a simple sentence " arg_1 rel arg_2" into a 768-dimensional vector. Then, FINCH is used to build the cluster hierarchy. For each cluster, representative expressions of the cluster are selected from its $rels$ from top informative relations scored by the formula presented in the next subsection. The result cluster hierarchy is illustrated in Fig. 3.

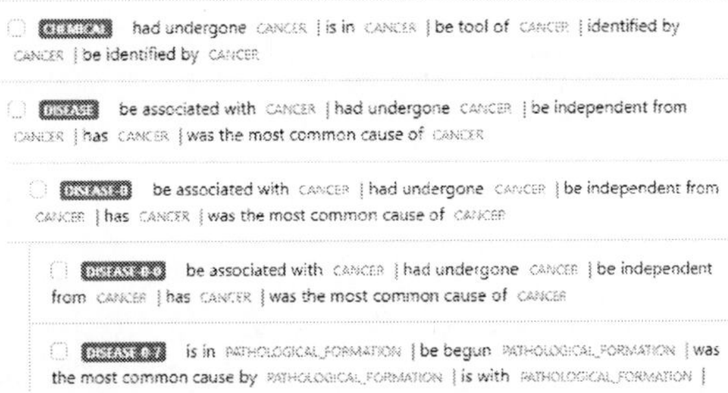

Figure 3: Illustration of cluster hierarchy. "DISEASE-0-7": the type of an entity contained in the arg_1 is DISEASE, the id of the level 0 (root) cluster is 0, the id of the level 1 cluster is 7. An expression has the form of ENTITY TYPE (in arg_1, omitted) relation/verb phrase ENTITY TYPE (in arg_2). Expressions are separated by |.

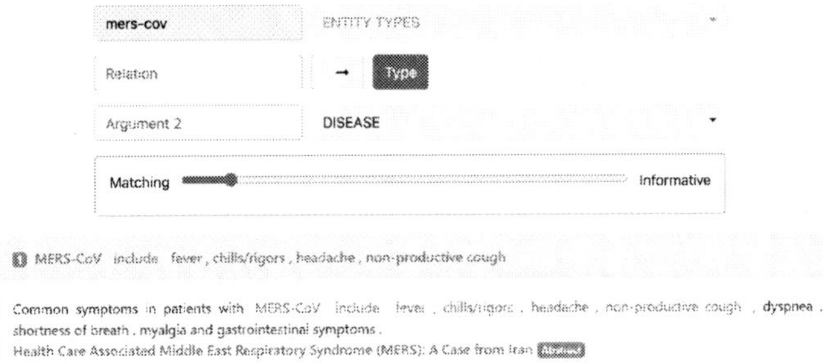

Figure 4: An example of **Single-Relation Query** for (mers-cov, any-relation, DISEASE).

3.5 Relation Scoring

Relations are scored for informativeness based from Pointwise Mutual Information (PMI) (Church and Hanks, 1990), the association ratio for measuring word association norms, based on the information-theoretic concept of mutual information. The informativeness of a relation (arg_1, rel, arg_2) can be regarded as PMI (Eq. 1) of two points: arg-pair $args = (arg_1, arg_2)$ and its relation expression rel through occurrence $p(.)$.

$$\text{PMI}(args, rel) = \log_2 \frac{p(args, rel)}{p(args)\, p(rel)} \quad (1)$$

It is difficult to apply Eq. 1, which computes the occurrence by exact matching, for our system because of the variation and noise in the contents of the extracted relations. To mitigate the difficulty of using exact match, we propose to use cosine similarity with Tf-idf vectorization (Sparck Jones, 1988). While exact match counting of occurrence indicates the presence of an instance ($args$ or rel) in the relation set, our use of cosine similarity indicates the presence of the *contents* of the instance in the relation set, thus can adapt to the variation and noise in the contents of the relations.

With our approach, the relation's informativeness InfoScore$(args, rel)$ is computed following Eq. 2.

$$\text{InfoScore}(args, rel) = \log_2 \frac{S(args, rel)}{S(args)S(rel)} \quad (2)$$

$$S(args, rel) = \sum_{(args', rel')} \cos(v(args, rel), v(args', rel'))$$

$$S(args) = \sum_{args'} \cos(v(args), v(args'))$$

$$S(rel) = \sum_{rel'} \cos(v(rel), v(rel'))$$

where $(args', rel')$ are all relations other than $(args, rel)$, $args'$ are arg-pairs in all relations other than $(args, rel)$, rel' are expressions in all relations other than $(args, rel)$, and $v(t_1, t_2, ...t_n)$ is the vectorization function which concatenates the input texts $t_1, t_2, ..., t_n$ and converts the concatenated text into a single Tf-idf vector.

3.6 Retrieval System

The retrieval system provides two kinds of queries: **Single-Relation Query** and **Graph Query**. While **Single-Relation Query** provides simple way to

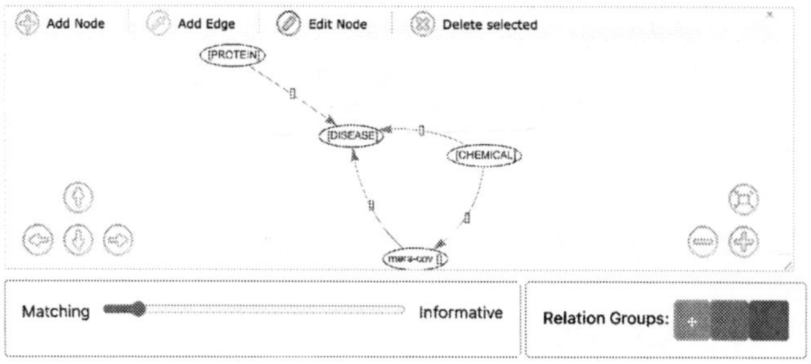

Figure 5: Graph Query: searching for a paper containing relations matching the query graph.

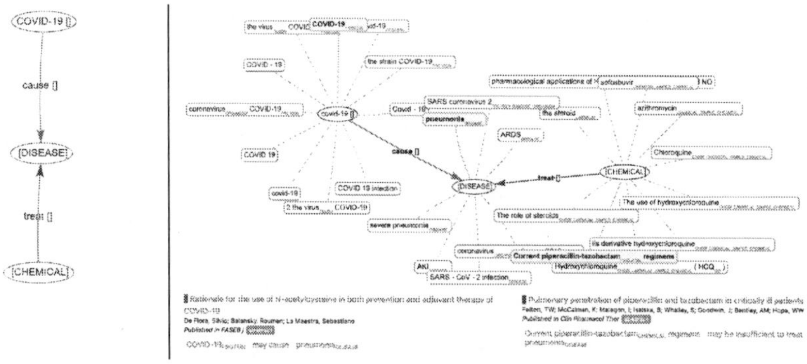

Figure 6: Example of **Multi-Paper Graph Query**. Left-hand side graph is the query. The right-hand side graph is the summary of the results showing candidate entities. The highlighted nodes of the summary graph show entities related to each other and mentioned in the two papers at the bottom.

search for specific relations, **Graph Query** provides a sophisticated way to search for papers containing entities connected in a complex relation graph.

3.6.1 Single-Relation Query

A query consists of partial information of a relation which can contains keywords about arg_1, arg_2, and rel, types of entities possibly included in the arg_1 or arg_2, or clusters which the relation belongs to. The retrieved results are relevant relations with their corresponding papers. An example of **Single-Relation Query** is illustrated in Fig. 4. The query relation is (mers-cov, any-relation, DISEASE). The results are best matched relations, for instance, (MERS-CoV, include, "fever, chills/rigors, headache, non-productive cough").

The candidate relations are retrieved based on the keyword matching score by BM25 (Schütze et al., 2008) and InfoScore (Eq. 2), then filtered by the entity types and the clusters. Keyword matching score and InfoScore can be weighed for the need of searching candidates that have high lexical matching with the query or candidates that are highly informative.

3.6.2 Graph Query

This extends **Single-Relation Query** by enabling more sophisticated paper search covering a complex graph describing relations among entities. An example of **Graph Query** is illustrated in Fig. 5 with a query consists of 4 relations: (mers-cov, cause, DISEASE), (CHEMICAL, any-relation, mers-cov), (CHEMICAl, any-relation, DISEASE), and (PROTEIN, any-relation, DISEASE). The result graph is built from linking entities and relations obtained from each paper, which matches the query graph. The entity linking is done through lexical matching and type matching. This approach faces the challenges from entities with synonyms and performance of entity recognition.

One special feature of **Graph Query** is **Multi-Paper Graph Query** which supports searching relations across multiple papers. The important use case is that interested relations are not described in one single paper, i.e., one entity is mentioned in different papers and thus engaged in different relations. For example, if users want to *"find some*

Table 2: Evaluation results on relation extraction. **Correct I**, **II**, and **I&II**: evaluated as correct relations (can be entailed from the corresponding sentences) by the first, the second, and both the evaluators, respectively. **Overall**: evaluation on the unique relations per sentence from all methods. **Kappa**: Cohen's kappa coefficient.

Method	Total	Correct I	Correct II	Correct I&II	Kappa
ReVerb	255	183 (72%)	224 (88%)	181 (71%)	0.47
OLLIE	398	304 (76%)	303 (76%)	275 (69%)	0.60
ClausIE	1,061	880 (83%)	760 (72%)	720 (68%)	0.47
Relink	302	210 (70%)	193 (64%)	173 (57%)	0.58
OpenIE	1,609	1,042 (65%)	901 (56%)	700 (44%)	0.30
Overall	3,477	2,479 (71%)	2,242 (64%)	1,913 (55%)	0.41

Table 3: Statistics of extracted relations.

Method	Non-uniq. /corpus	Uniq. /corpus	Uniq. /abstract
ReVerb	2.3M	1.7M	8
OLLIE	4.7M	3.6M	16
ClausIE	9.0M	6.9M	31
Relink	5.5M	4.1M	19
OpenIE	24.4M	18.6M	84
Overall	45.9M	33.3M	150

Table 4: Statistics of recognized entities.

Model	/corpus	/abstract
en_ner_craft_md	1.8M	6
en_ner_jnlpba_md	3.1M	11
en_ner_bc5cdr_md	1.8M	6
en_ner_bionlp13cg_md	1.4M	5
Total	6.4M	22

CHEMICAL that can treat some DISEASE caused by COVID-19", they will look for two relations: (COVID-19, cause, DISEASE), and (CHEMICAL, treat, DISEASE). In that case, the two relations may be retrieved from two different papers. Therefore, aggregating information scattering over multiple papers is necessary for building a more comprehensive understanding. It is done through relation grouping allowing users to segment the query graph into several segments each belonging to different papers. With the above example, users can define a query graph (the left-hand side of Fig. 6) and our system could find that "pneunomia" is a DISEASE caused by COVID-19 and is treated with "Current [piperacillin-tazobactam]$_{\text{CHEMICAL}}$ regimens" (the right-hand side of Fig. 6) from two separate papers, and more.

4 Results

4.1 Corpus

We performed relation extraction and entity recognition from the CORD19 corpus provided in the COVID-19 Open Research Dataset Challenge updated by January 3rd, 2021. The corpus contains ≈400K entries to COVID-19 related papers. Relation extraction and entity recognition were performed on the abstracts of the papers.

4.2 Relation Extraction

As shown in Table 3, we extracted 40.5 million relations including 29.8 million unique relations. Among the relation extraction methods, OpenIE outputs the largest number. The other three relation extraction methods tend to output long and composite relations while OpenIE tends to break down and output shorter and simpler relations. However, OpenIE also outputs small variations of similar relations.

For assessing the quality of relation extraction, we conduct an evaluation on a small data sample consisting of 100 papers selected from the corpus. The evaluation was conducted by two human evaluators with the criteria to answer *whether the relation can be entailed from the sentence*.

The results (Table 2) show that the evaluation is a difficult task. The evaluation agreement between the two evaluators is 0.41 in term of Cohen's kappa coefficient (McHugh, 2012). It's considered fair agreement (Fleiss et al., 2003). Among the relation extraction methods, OLLIE yields the best kappa coefficient of 0.60 (good agreement), OpenIE yields the worst coefficient of 0.30 (poor agreement), and the others yield the coefficients of 0.47 to 0.58 (fair to good agreement). One of the possible reasons is the complexity of biomedical texts: sentences with 31 tokens in average and up to 167 tokens in the evaluated sample, and common use of conjunctions and nested clauses.

4.3 Entity Recognition

As shown in Table 4, a total of 6.4M entities were recognized from the corpus with the four entity recognition models. For each abstract of a COVID-19 related paper, an average of 22 entities were recognized. Among the four models, **en_ner_jnlpba_md** outputs the largest number of entities, about 1.7 to 2.2 times more than the other models, where this model's specialized entity types are cell lines, cell types, DNAs, RNAs, and proteins.

5 Conclusion

We have presented our COVID-19 scientific paper retrieval system which focuses on analysing entities and their relations. The system is empowered with several relation extraction and entity recognition methods. The system supports users in acquiring knowledge efficiently across a huge number of COVID-19 scientific papers published rapidly. There, however, exist extremely challenging problems to tackle for making the system more practical: dealing with the newly created and unknown data, solving the performance gap when utilizing present methods, and do these in the nick of time of fighting with pandemics.

Acknowledgment

This work was supported by JST CREST Grant Number JPMJCR1513, Japan.

References

Alexis Allot, Yifan Peng, Chih-Hsuan Wei, Kyubum Lee, Lon Phan, and Zhiyong Lu. 2018. LitVar: a semantic search engine for linking genomic variant data in PubMed and PMC. *Nucleic Acids Research*, 46(W1):W530–W536.

Gabor Angeli, Melvin Jose Johnson Premkumar, and Christopher D. Manning. 2015. Leveraging linguistic structure for open domain information extraction. In *Proceedings of the 53rd Annual Meeting of the Association for Computational Linguistics and the 7th International Joint Conference on Natural Language Processing (Volume 1: Long Papers)*, pages 344–354, Beijing, China. Association for Computational Linguistics.

Michael Bada, Miriam Eckert, Donald Evans, Kristin Garcia, Krista Shipley, Dmitry Sitnikov, William A Baumgartner, K Bretonnel Cohen, Karin Verspoor, Judith A Blake, and Lawrence E Hunter. 2012. Concept annotation in the CRAFT corpus. *BMC Bioinformatics*, 13(1).

Kenneth Ward Church and Patrick Hanks. 1990. Word association norms, mutual information, and lexicography. *Computational Linguistics*, 16(1):22–29.

Nigel Collier and Jin-Dong Kim. 2004. Introduction to the bio-entity recognition task at JNLPBA. In *Proceedings of the International Joint Workshop on Natural Language Processing in Biomedicine and its Applications (NLPBA/BioNLP)*, pages 73–78, Geneva, Switzerland. COLING.

Luciano Del Corro and Rainer Gemulla. 2013. Clausie: clause-based open information extraction. In *Proceedings of the 22nd international conference on World Wide Web*, pages 355–366.

Jacob Devlin, Ming-Wei Chang, Kenton Lee, and Kristina Toutanova. 2019. BERT: Pre-training of deep bidirectional transformers for language understanding. In *Proceedings of the 2019 Conference of the North American Chapter of the Association for Computational Linguistics: Human Language Technologies, Volume 1 (Long and Short Papers)*, pages 4171–4186, Minneapolis, Minnesota. Association for Computational Linguistics.

Andre Esteva, Anuprit Kale, Romain Paulus, Kazuma Hashimoto, Wenpeng Yin, Dragomir Radev, and Richard Socher. 2020. Co-search: Covid-19 information retrieval with semantic search, question answering, and abstractive summarization.

Anthony Fader, Stephen Soderland, and Oren Etzioni. 2011. Identifying relations for open information extraction. In *Proceedings of the 2011 Conference on Empirical Methods in Natural Language Processing*, pages 1535–1545, Edinburgh, Scotland, UK. Association for Computational Linguistics.

Joseph L. Fleiss, Bruce Levin, and Myunghee Cho Paik. 2003. *Statistical Methods for Rates and Proportions*. John Wiley & Sons, Inc.

Tom Hope, Aida Amini, David Wadden, Madeleine van Zuylen, E. Horvitz, Roy Schwartz, and Hannaneh Hajishirzi. 2020. Extracting a Knowledge Base of Mechanisms from COVID-19 Papers .

Jiao Li, Yueping Sun, Robin J. Johnson, Daniela Sciaky, Chih-Hsuan Wei, Robert Leaman, Allan Peter Davis, Carolyn J. Mattingly, Thomas C. Wiegers, and Zhiyong Lu. 2016. BioCreative v CDR task corpus: a resource for chemical disease relation extraction. *Database*, 2016:baw068.

Yifeng Liu, Yongjie Liang, and David Wishart. 2015. PolySearch2: a significantly improved text-mining system for discovering associations between human diseases, genes, drugs, metabolites, toxins and more. *Nucleic Acids Research*, 43(W1):W535–W542.

Mausam, Michael Schmitz, Stephen Soderland, Robert Bart, and Oren Etzioni. 2012. Open language learning for information extraction. In *Proceedings of the 2012 Joint Conference on Empirical Methods in Natural Language Processing and Computational Natural Language Learning*, pages 523–534, Jeju Island, Korea. Association for Computational Linguistics.

Marry L. McHugh. 2012. Interrater reliability: the kappa statistic. *Biochemia Medica*, pages 276–282.

Mark Neumann, Daniel King, Iz Beltagy, and Waleed Ammar. 2019. ScispaCy: Fast and robust models for biomedical natural language processing. In *Proceedings of the 18th BioNLP Workshop and Shared Task*, pages 319–327, Florence, Italy. Association for Computational Linguistics.

Sampo Pyysalo, Tomoko Ohta, Rafal Rak, Andrew Rowley, Hong-Woo Chun, Sung-Jae Jung, Sung-Pil Choi, Jun'ichi Tsujii, and Sophia Ananiadou. 2015. Overview of the cancer genetics and pathway curation tasks of bionlp shared task 2013. *BMC bioinformatics*, 16(S10):S2.

Saquib Sarfraz, Vivek Sharma, and Rainer Stiefelhagen. 2019. Efficient parameter-free clustering using first neighbor relations. In *Proceedings of the IEEE/CVF Conference on Computer Vision and Pattern Recognition (CVPR)*.

Hinrich Schütze, Christopher D Manning, and Prabhakar Raghavan. 2008. *Introduction to information retrieval*, volume 39. Cambridge University Press Cambridge.

Jaime A Teixeira da Silva, Panagiotis Tsigaris, and Mohammadamin Erfanmanesh. 2020. Publishing volumes in major databases related to covid-19. *Scientometrics*, pages 1–12.

Mohammad Golam Sohrab, Khoa Duong, Makoto Miwa, Goran Topić, Ikeda Masami, and Hiroya Takamura. 2020. Bennerd: A neural named entity linking system for covid-19. In *Proceedings of the 2020 Conference on Empirical Methods in Natural Language Processing: System Demonstrations*, pages 182–188, Online. Association for Computational Linguistics.

Karen Sparck Jones. 1988. A statistical interpretation of term specificity and its application in retrieval. In *Document retrieval systems*, pages 132–142. Taylor Graham Publishing.

Xuan-Chien Tran and Le-Minh Nguyen. 2020. ReLink: Open information extraction by linking phrases and its applications. In *Distributed Computing and Internet Technology*, pages 44–62. Springer International Publishing.

Yoshimasa Tsuruoka, Makoto Miwa, Kaisei Hamamoto, Jun'ichi Tsujii, and Sophia Ananiadou. 2011. Discovering and visualizing indirect associations between biomedical concepts. *Bioinformatics*, 27(13):i111–i119.

Yoshimasa Tsuruoka, Jun'ichi Tsujii, and Sophia Ananiadou. 2008. FACTA: a text search engine for finding associated biomedical concepts. *Bioinformatics*, 24(21):2559–2560.

Xuan Wang, Weili Liu, Aabhas Chauhan, Yingjun Guan, and Jiawei Han. 2020. Automatic textual evidence mining in covid-19 literature. *arXiv preprint arXiv:2004.12563*.

Chih-Hsuan Wei, Alexis Allot, Robert Leaman, and Zhiyong Lu. 2019. PubTator central: automated concept annotation for biomedical full text articles. *Nucleic Acids Research*, 47(W1):W587–W593.

Edwin Zhang, Nikhil Gupta, Raphael Tang, Xiao Han, Ronak Pradeep, Kuang Lu, Yue Zhang, Rodrigo Nogueira, Kyunghyun Cho, Hui Fang, and Jimmy Lin. 2020. Covidex: Neural ranking models and keyword search infrastructure for the COVID-19 open research dataset. In *Proceedings of the First Workshop on Scholarly Document Processing*, pages 31–41, Online. Association for Computational Linguistics.

MATILDA: Multi-AnnoTator multi-language Interactive Light-weight Dialogue Annotator

Davide Cucurnia[◇] **Nikolai Rozanov**[♠] **Irene Sucameli**[◇]
Augusto Ciuffoletti[◇] **Maria Simi**[◇]

[◇]Department of Computer Science, University of Pisa, Pisa, Italy
[♠]Wluper Ltd., London, United Kingdom
[◇]{d.cucurnia2@studenti., irene@phd., augusto.ciuffoletti@, maria.simi@}unipi.it
[♠]{nikolai}@wluper.com

Abstract

Dialogue Systems are becoming ubiquitous in various forms and shapes, from virtual assistants (like Siri, Alexa and various chat-bots) to customer support systems embedded within websites. Recent publications and advancements with natural language modelling have opened up NLP (and its more advanced applications like conversational AI) to a wider audience. Unfortunately, the lack of labelled data within this field remains a significant barrier and so we have developed MATILDA (the first multi-annotator, multi-language dialogue annotation tool) as an initial contribution to help the community overcome this barrier. MATILDA is a tool for creating high-quality corpora via a user-friendly interface so as to facilitate the annotation of dialogues, resolve inter-annotator disagreement and manage multiple users at scale. We have evaluated the tool on ease of use, annotation speed and inter-annotation resolution for both experts and novices and can confidently conclude that MATILDA offers a novel, streamlined, end-to-end solution to dialogue annotation and is intuitive enough to use, even for a non-technical audience. The tool is completely open-sourced at https://github.com/wluper/matilda and is easily adaptable to any language. We are also providing a complementary tutorial video[1].

1 Introduction

As a community, we have observed great advances in the last decade that include word-embeddings (Mikolov et al., 2013), seq-to-seq models for a variety of tasks (Sutskever et al., 2014) and pre-trained, transformer-based language models (Devlin et al., 2019). Relying on these seminal works, a plethora of downstream tasks (e.g. NMT, Q&A, dialogues, summarisation, etc.) have seen notable improvements and some have even been "solved". Many of the advancements made in computational modelling and power owe a lot of their success to the careful curation and annotation of huge datasets, which are thus equally pivotal to recent advancements and progress in general. In particular, datasets such as (Budzianowski et al., 2018) and (Byrne et al., 2019) have allowed data-hungry neural-models to advance the field of task-oriented dialogues.

In the field of annotation tools and data generation, recent advances such as (Collins et al., 2019) show similar promise by open-sourcing technology and developing it with modern usability-related principles in mind. Following in the spirit of such similar research, we present MATILDA (a full dialogue annotation tool specifically focused on the inclusivity for all languages and facilitating multiple annotators). We evaluate it on a variety of usability aspects, both with experienced and untrained users, and conclude that both our dialogue annotation and creation tools are easy-to-use. Furthermore, MATILDA offers more features than any comparable tool in the research community; comfortably supporting multiple annotators as well as multiple languages during the annotation process. Therefore, we have open-sourced it and provided precompiled docker images for easy setup.

MATILDA's main contributions are: 1) a native annotation tool that is quick-to-adapt[2] for multi-language support; 2) a user-friendly interface to simply and intuitively manage multiple users as well as easily distribute datasets to crowd-workers for annotation; 3) task-oriented multi-speaker annotation capabilities (in the style of MultiWoz and Taskmaster); 4) inter-annotator resolution; and 5) integrated recommendations to assist annotators.

[1]https://vimeo.com/500125248

[2]As an example the full adaptation of the annotation tool from English to German took roughly 30 minutes.

Proceedings of the 16th Conference of the European Chapter of the Association for Computational Linguistics: System Demonstrations, pages 32–39
April 19 - 23, 2021.

2 Related Work

Table 1 compares MATILDA with other recent annotation tools.

TWIST (Pluss, 2012) is a dialogue annotation tool which consists of two stages: turn segmentation and content feature annotation. Turn segmentation allows users to create new turn segments from raw text. After this, users can annotate sections of text in a segment by highlighting them and selecting from a predefined feature list. However, this tool doesn't allow users to specify custom annotations or labels and doesn't support classification or slot-value annotation. This is not compatible with modern dialogue datasets which require such annotations (Budzianowski et al., 2018). INCEpTION (Klie et al., 2018) is a semantic annotation platform for interactive tasks that require semantic resources like entity linking. It provides machine learning models to suggest annotations and allows users to collect and model knowledge directly in the tool. GATE (Cunningham, 2002) is an open source tool that provides predefined solutions for many text processing tasks. It is powerful because it allows annotators to enhance the provided annotation tools with their own Java code, making it easily extensible and provides a great number of predefined features. However, GATE is a large and complicated tool with a significant setup cost - its instruction manual alone is over 600 pages long[3]. Despite their large feature sets, INCEpTION and GATE are not designed for annotating dialogue and cannot display data as turns, an important feature for dialogue datasets. BRAT (Stenetorp et al., 2012) and Doccano[4] are web-based annotation tools for tasks such as text classification and sequence labelling. They have intuitive and user-friendly interfaces which aim to make the creation of certain types of dataset such as classification or sequence labelling datasets as fast as possible. BRAT also supports annotation suggestions by integrating ML models. However, like INCEpTION[5] and GATE[6], they are not designed for annotating dialogues and do not support the generation of formatted conversational data from a raw text file such as might be outputted by a transcription service. LIDA (Collins et al., 2019) provides an easy-to-setup annotation tool for modern task-oriented dialogues and also supports the integration of recommendations. However, LIDA is not accessible for multiple users and is only intended for the English language. MATILDA addresses these shortcomings and adds features such as: annotation styles compatible with modern dialogue datasets, inter-annotation resolution, customisable recommendations and user administration. DialogueView's (Heeman et al., 2002) main use-cases are focused on segmenting recorded conversations, annotating audio files and discourse segmentation. Granular labelling of the dialogue, recommenders, inter-annotator agreement, and slot-value labelling are not possible.

3 System Overview

We introduce an annotator service that extends previous successful experiences, like LIDA, by introducing features that address large-scale, task-oriented dialogue annotation projects. In particular, we allow for distributed multi-annotators, multi-language support, interannotator resolution and custom recommenders to assist the annotation process. Furthermore, our modern and modularised implementation simplifies extension to additional languages, use-cases and annotation styles. A typical use-case follows this workflow:

Creation of a Dataset We envision two main ways to create a corpus: either interactively or by uploading existing data. We adopt data representations that allow backward compatibility with other tools based on text files with a simple syntax, and a JSON format that is easy to operate.

User Administration Once a corpus consisting of several collections is created, administrators can then proceed to assign those collections to one or more different annotators. The assigned partition will then be shown to the designated annotators in their "Collection" view, ready to be annotated. According to the typical use case, we need two roles for the users, which we call *Annotators* and *Administrators*. We want our system to include user management with a simple interface for creation, editing and removal.

Annotation and Supervision Each annotator has access only to the subsets of dialogues assigned to them to add/modify annotations and monitor

[3] https://gate.ac.uk/sale/tao/tao.pdf

[4] https://github.com/chakki-works/doccano

[5] A plugin allows calculation of scores not resolution: https://dkpro.github.io/dkpro-statistics/dkpro-agreement-poster.pdf

[6] Again inter-annotator score calculation capabilities are available as separate plug-in https://gate.ac.uk/releases/gate-5.1-beta1-build3397-ALL/doc/tao/splitch10.html - however support for resolutions is not apparent

Annotation Tool	Dialogue-specific Annotation	Multi-language Support	Crowd Multi-annotator Support	Recommenders	Inter-Annotator Disagreement Resolution	Language
MATILDA	YES	YES	YES	YES	YES	PYTHON
LIDA (Collins et al., 2019)	YES	NO	NO	YES	YES	PYTHON
INCEpTion (Klie et al., 2018)	NO	NO	NO	YES	YES/NO[3]	JAVA
GATE (Cunningham, 2002)	NO	NO	NO	NO	YES/NO [4]	JAVA
TWIST (Pluss, 2012)	YES	NO	NO	NO	NO	-
BRAT (Stenetorp et al., 2012)	NO	NO	NO	YES	NO	PYTHON
DOCCANO[3]	NO	NO	NO	NO	NO	PYTHON
DialogueView (Heeman et al., 2002)	YES	NO	NO	NO	NO	TcK/TK

Table 1: Annotator Tool Comparison Table
Dialogue-specific Annotation: Support to annotate datasets such as MultiWoz or Taskmaster. Multi-language Support: The ability to localise the annotation tool for different languages. Crowd Multi-annotator Support: The possibility to manage users and easily deploy to many annotators in different locations. Recommenders: ML models to suggest annotations. Inter-Annotator Disagreement Resolution: whether the system has an interface to resolve disagreements between different annotators. Language: what programming language the system uses

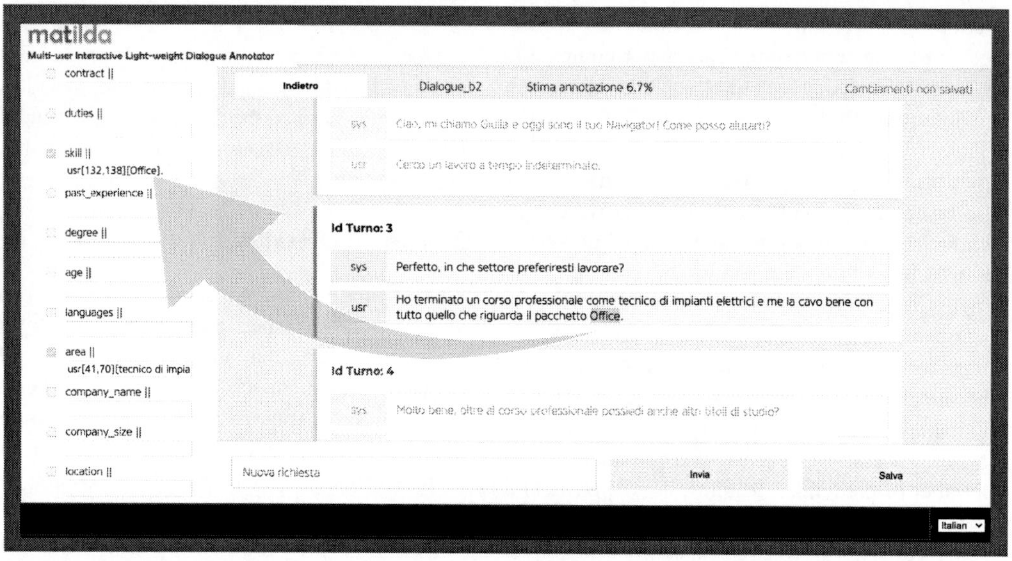

Figure 1: Dialogue annotation interface: filling slots by selection of text fragments.

work progress. Figure 1 shows a screenshot of the annotation interface and highlights the slot-filling functionality. Administrators inspect annotators' work and resolve conflicts in the *interannotation* interface. When annotators provide diverging annotations, a designated supervisor provides a *gold standard* either opting for one of them or introducing an alternative one. Besides, the system computes interannotator agreement metrics, such as Cohen's Kappa. Gold standard annotations provided by supervisors are recorded separately and do not overwrite the original ones.

The Interannotator is designed to confront two or more annotated dialogue collections and resolve annotation conflicts between them. MATILDA automatically retrieves all annotated versions of one corpus partition present in the database; administrators are also allowed to upload a file to add to the confrontation. This can be seen in Figure 2

3.1 System architecture

MATILDA is designed as a Web Service: a browser hosts the user interface while the server supports data and control. Our use case envisions all components running on user premises, but it is straightforward to distribute them on distinct hosts.

On the server side, MATILDA is a bundle of two components: a web server and a database server.

Each of them is encapsulated in a Docker, so that complex configurations are carried out by the designer and invisible to the non-technical end-user. In fact, MATILDA operation depends only on Docker support, which is available for major operating systems. In order to have MATILDA operational, the end-user installs the Docker support and launches a Docker script that downloads and deploys on the user's PC the server-side Dockers. MATILDA is then reachable from the browser

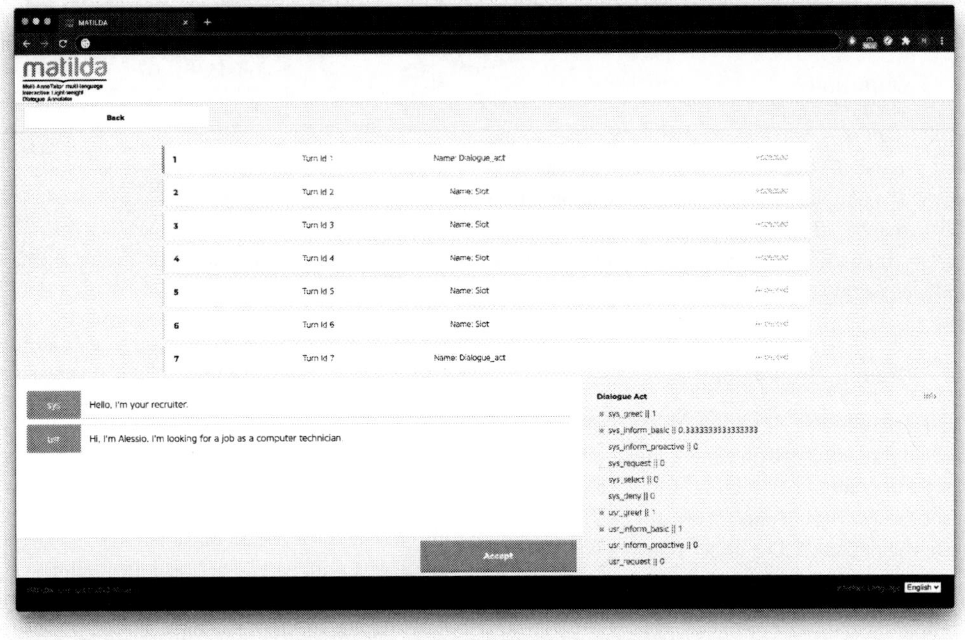

Figure 2: Inter-annotation Resolution Interface.

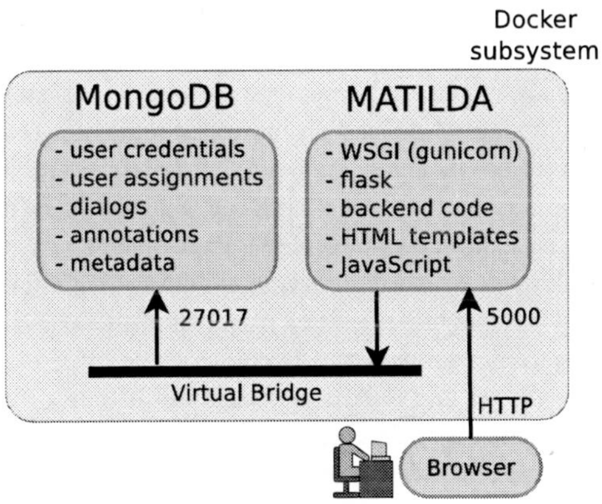

Figure 3: architecture

at the URL `http://localhost/index.html`. The tech-inclined user has the option to configure some features, like the use of an external database or the access through a network interface. The installation script and the operation manual are distributed on GitHub `https://github.com/wluper/matilda`, while the Dockers are available from `https://hub.docker.com`.

As seen in Figure 3, the MATILDA engine is written in Python using the *Flask* framework, while the client-side JavaScript uses the *Vue* framework.

The MongoDB database provides NoSQL access to the dialogs, the annotations and their metadata. This technology meets the required flexibility, allowing heterogeneous types of documents and an agile structure. The native support of JSON documents matches with the format used for the internal representation of the dialogs. Finally, the availability of both an open-source server and a public service is useful when implementing either a service on-premises, according to the reference use-case, or, in a more advanced use-case, to implement a cloud database for sharing dialogs.

The most stringent requirement on host hardware is that the processor must belong to the 64-bit family; this is inherited from Docker. To analyse the footprint of MATILDA components, we installed it on a system based on the Intel Celeron J3355, a 2-core microprocessor dated 2016, created for entry level desktop systems and with a 2GB RAM. During a significant processing peak, induced with an upload, the footprint did not exceed a few percent of hardware capacity.

The developer can find the engine source code in the GitHub repository mentioned above; this allows them to customize or to add new features to MATILDA and to produce a new Docker. Locale-dependent information is recorded in an independent JSON document, and so introducing a different localization of the interface is non-intrusive (?).

4 Evaluation

MATILDA was evaluated on two experiments: the first evaluated MATILDA's admin-related capabilities while and the second evaluated its annotation performance. Both experiments were conducted across three different languages (English, Italian and German) to assess MATILDA's cross-language adaptability.

4.1 Quantitative Evaluation

4.1.1 Administration and Supervision

The administration experiment involved a total of six participants, each representing different supervisory roles: i) an expert supervisor (**ES**) who is familiar with MATILDA or has relevant background knowledge in NLP and dialogue annotation and ii) an untrained supervisor (**US**) who has never used MATILDA before and has little to no experience with dialogue annotation in general. The initial *admin task* consisted of adding two new users (A1 and A2) into MATILDA and assigning them as annotators, then creating a new dialogue collection and defining its features (e.g. collection's title, its description, etc.) and assigning the new collection to all the annotators. The second *inter-annotator task* consisted of resolving inter-annotator conflicts which may occur at the end of the annotation work, which involved the supervisor comparing conflicts on MATILDA for each annotator disagreement and selecting one, thus creating a final, gold dataset.

During the two phases of the experiment, we record the time needed for ES and US to complete the tasks. Table 2 describes and compares the time taken on the admin task for the two supervisors across the three languages considered. It also shows the time taken to resolve inter-annotator disagreements as well as the total number of disagreements resolved.

The quantitative evaluations show that both trained and untrained supervisors were able to successfully complete the predefined tasks, with the untrained supervisors performing only marginally worse, despite having never used an annotation tool before. The untrained supervisors were provided with a 15 minute guided training prior to the inter-annotation task as they were unfamiliar with the task (having no prior NLP knowledge or experience).

Time(min:sec) per admin task			
	English	**Italian**	**German**
ES	03:45	03:05	02:20
US	02:52	02:55	03:30
Time(min:sec) per inter-annotator task			
ES	22:05	09:31	17:30
US	26:30*	25:02	15:13*
Conflicts	38	40	25
Total Labels	130	130	130

Table 2: Comparison of the time taken by different supervisors to carry out admin and inter-annotators resolution tasks. *Needed additional training before being able to perform the task

The evaluation revealed a strong dependency on the execution of admin tasks with the supervisor's familiarity with MATILDA and annotation systems in general. However, the results also indicate that users who are unfamiliar with annotation tools are still able to easily use MATILDA and complete administration and inter-annotation tasks.

4.1.2 Annotation

The second evaluation focuses on quantitatively analysing the tool's annotation interface. An expert annotator (**EA**) and an untrained annotator (**UA**) were both asked to annotate five dialogues and the time taken to complete the task was recorded (the results are shown in Table 3). Each dialogue, across all languages tested, had an average of eight turns (wherein a turn consisted of one user utterance and system response) and twenty-four possible class labels per turn (10 dialogue acts and 14 slots). This complexity is comparable with those of public dialogue datasets, like Multiwoz or Taskmaster-1 (Budzianowski et al., 2018; Byrne et al., 2019).

Time(min:sec) per annotation task			
	English	**Italian**	**German**
EA	34:27	16:35	27:55
UA	37:30	49:48	45:00

Table 3: Time taken to annotate a set of 5 dialogues by different native-speaker annotators

The results of this experiment show that even untrained annotators were able to use MATILDA to successfully complete the annotation task. In fact, a substantial increase in the users' annotation speed can be observed within just a few annotations, demonstrating a fast learning curve for MATILDA.

For expert annotators, the average annotation time was 26:17 minutes for five dialogues (giving an average of approximately 5:16 minutes per dialogue). For untrained annotators, this increases to approximately 8:50 minutes per dialogue. Therefore, annotating a data-set of 10,000 dialogues (with two annotations per dialogue) can be calculated as requiring 1,756 hours or 100x 8-hour working days for two expert annotators to complete on MATILDA. However, this time can be massively reduced using untrained crowd-workers, wherein approximately 52 untrained workers could complete the annotation of such a dataset within a week. Thus highlighting the importance of such tools and software as MATILDA, that can manage, collate and resolve annotation conflicts across the crowd-workers.

4.2 Qualitative Evaluation & User Feedback

4.2.1 Questionnaire

In addition to the quantitative evaluations, a qualitative analysis was conducted in the form of a questionnaire about MATILDA's usability, provided to each annotator and supervisor as an an anonymous feedback form. Each supervisor was asked to evaluate the following features with a *Low-Medium-High* score:

- Q1: ease of completing the admin task;
- Q2: ease of resolving inter-annotator conflicts;
- Q3: quality of the feedback provided by the tool.
- Q4: overall usability of MATILDA admin interface.

Supervisors evaluation			
	Low	**Medium**	**High**
Q1	0.0%	16.7%	83.3%
Q2	16.7%	50.0%	33.3%
Q3	33.3%	50.0%	16.7%
Q4	0.0%	33.3%	66.7%

Table 4: Evaluation of MATILDA usability

Similarly, we ask annotators to evaluate:

- Q1: ease of annotation;
- Q2: ease of understanding how to work on a dialogue collection and how to sent it to supervisors at the end of the annotation;
- Q3: quality of the feedback provided by the tool.
- Q4: overall usability of MATILDA annotator interface.

Annotators evaluation			
Q1	0.0%	66.7%	33.3%
Q2	0.0%	33.3%	66.7%
Q3	66.6%	16.7%	16.7%
Q4	0.0%	33.3%	66.7%

Table 5: Evaluation of MATILDA usability

Tables 4 and 5 show the percentages of responses to each question for supervisors and annotators respectively. Question 4 (Q4) about overall usability shows 66.7% Good usability, 33.3% Medium usability and nobody answered with Low usability (including the untrained annotators) which confirm the quantitative results regarding MATILDA's low-friction usability. Questions about the individual aspects of the tasks (Q1 and Q2) also confirm the overall usability of the tool, receiving mostly Good or Medium scores. The main point for improvement, according to the responses, was the level of feedback the tool provides to the user (i.e. prompts that show whether a user action was successful at a task, like the successful creation of a user, etc)

4.2.2 Feedback

We have also provided the study participants the venue to express their feedback in an unstructured way, by prompting them, "Please provide feedback in a couple of sentences on the usability of the annotation and supervision aspects of the app and the improvements you would suggest".

The feedback can be summarised in three categories:

1. Feedback and Information Prompts by the tool
2. Improving slot-filling for the annotation tool
3. Improving the layout of the inter-annotator resolution

The first feedback was also apparent from the feedback forms provided in the previous section. We have accepted this feedback to improve our tool and the to-be-published version is planned to include these improvements.

The second feedback point was very important and the future version of the tool will work on improving the slot-filling annotation format.

The final feedback was more of an aesthetic feedback about the location and visibility of certain aspects of the interannotator resolution screen.

5 Conclusion and future work

We have presented MATILDA the first, to the best of our knowledge, multi-annotator, multi-language dialogue annotation tool that allows the user to annotate, distribute annotation work among crowdworkers or colleagues and to resolve annotation conflicts. We evaluate the tool based on the ease and rapidity of use and show that even untrained novices can quickly learn to use it.

Thanks to the open-source nature of the original LIDA project, we hope the community will pick-up on this work both in terms of using it to create strongly needed corpora for different languages as well as extending it to allow even more use-cases and more advanced annotation styles.

To this end we have conducted qualitative feedback sessions with study participants and provided a potential avenue of concrete improvements. We hope that this work will be a meaningful stepping stone for our community to create more useful resources in many languages.

6 Acknowledgements

In this work we would like to acknowledge the great input from EACL Reviewers that helped us push the paper to a new level.

We particularly would like to thank the thoughtful input of our colleagues in the University of Pisa, especially Clara Casandra and Carla Congiu.

We would also like to thank members of the Wluper team that acted as Testers, Annotators and Paper Reviewers. In particular, special thanks go to Mohammed Terry-Jack, Lamia El Afani, Andrew Burnie, Ed Collins and Maurice von Sturm. Furthermore, additional thanks goes to the authors and developers of the previous version of this annotation tool - LIDA - Ed Collins and Bingbing Zhang.

Furthermore, the work of Nikolai Rozanov was done under the Research Lab of Wluper Ltd. (UK/ 10195181) and part of the contribution of this lab was supported by the *Innovate UK Smart Grants: October 2019*.

References

Paweł Budzianowski, Tsung-Hsien Wen, Bo-Hsiang Tseng, Iñigo Casanueva, Stefan Ultes, Osman Ramadan, and Milica Gašić. 2018. Multiwoz-a large-scale multi-domain wizard-of-oz dataset for task-oriented dialogue modelling. *arXiv preprint arXiv:1810.00278*.

Bill Byrne, Karthik Krishnamoorthi, Chinnadhurai Sankar, Arvind Neelakantan, Daniel Duckworth, Semih Yavuz, Ben Goodrich, Amit Dubey, Kyu-Young Kim, and Andy Cedilnik. 2019. Taskmaster-1: Toward a realistic and diverse dialog dataset.

Edward Collins, Nikolai Rozanov, and Bingbing Zhang. 2019. LIDA: lightweight interactive dialogue annotator. In *Proceedings of the 2019 Conference on Empirical Methods in Natural Language Processing and the 9th International Joint Conference on Natural Language Processing, EMNLP-IJCNLP 2019, Hong Kong, China, November 3-7, 2019 - System Demonstrations*, pages 121–126. Association for Computational Linguistics.

Hamish Cunningham. 2002. Gate, a general architecture for text engineering. *Computers and the Humanities*, 36(2):223–254.

Jacob Devlin, Ming-Wei Chang, Kenton Lee, and Kristina Toutanova. 2019. BERT: Pre-training of deep bidirectional transformers for language understanding. In *Proceedings of the 2019 Conference of the North American Chapter of the Association for Computational Linguistics: Human Language Technologies, Volume 1 (Long and Short Papers)*, pages 4171–4186, Minneapolis, Minnesota. Association for Computational Linguistics.

Peter A. Heeman, Fan Yang, and Susan E. Strayer. 2002. DialogueView - an annotation tool for dialogue. In *Proceedings of the Third SIGdial Workshop on Discourse and Dialogue*, pages 50–59, Philadelphia, Pennsylvania, USA. Association for Computational Linguistics.

Jan-Christoph Klie, Michael Bugert, Beto Boullosa, Richard Eckart de Castilho, and Iryna Gurevych. 2018. The inception platform: Machine-assisted and knowledge-oriented interactive annotation. In *Proceedings of the 27th International Conference on Computational Linguistics: System Demonstrations*, pages 5–9.

Tomas Mikolov, Ilya Sutskever, Kai Chen, Greg S Corrado, and Jeff Dean. 2013. Distributed representations of words and phrases and their compositionality. In C. J. C. Burges, L. Bottou, M. Welling, Z. Ghahramani, and K. Q. Weinberger, editors, *Advances in Neural Information Processing Systems 26*, pages 3111–3119. Curran Associates, Inc.

Brian Pluss. 2012. Twist dialogue annotation tool. `http://mcs.open.ac.uk/nlg/non-cooperation/resources/user-guide.pdf`.

Pontus Stenetorp, Sampo Pyysalo, Goran Topić, Tomoko Ohta, Sophia Ananiadou, and Jun'ichi Tsujii. 2012. Brat: a web-based tool for nlp-assisted text annotation. In *Proceedings of the Demonstrations at the 13th Conference of the European Chapter of the Association for Computational Linguistics*, pages 102–107. Association for Computational Linguistics.

Ilya Sutskever, Oriol Vinyals, and Quoc V Le. 2014. Sequence to sequence learning with neural networks. In Z. Ghahramani, M. Welling, C. Cortes, N. D. Lawrence, and K. Q. Weinberger, editors, *Advances in Neural Information Processing Systems 27*, pages 3104–3112. Curran Associates, Inc.

AnswerQuest: A System for Generating Question-Answer Items from Multi-Paragraph Documents

Melissa Roemmele[†] **Deep Sidhpura**[◇] **Steve DeNeefe**[†] **Ling Tsou**[†]
SDL Research, Los Angeles, CA, USA
[†]{mroemmele, sdeneefe, ltsou}@sdl.com
[◇]deepsidhpura777@gmail.com

Abstract

One strategy for facilitating reading comprehension is to present information in a question-and-answer format. We demo a system that integrates the tasks of question answering (QA) and question generation (QG) in order to produce Q&A items that convey the content of multi-paragraph documents. We report some experiments for QA and QG that yield improvements on both tasks, and assess how they interact to produce a list of Q&A items for a text. The demo is accessible at qna.sdl.com.

1 Introduction

Automated reading comprehension is one of the current frontiers in AI and NLP research, evidenced by the frequently changing state-of-the-art among competing approaches on standard benchmark tasks (e.g. Wang et al., 2018). These systems aim to reach the standard of human performance, but they also have the potential to further enhance human reading comprehension. For instance, many demonstrations of reading comprehension involve eliciting answers to questions about a text. Meanwhile, educational research and conventional writing advice indicate that structuring information in a question-and-answer format can aid comprehension (Knight, 2010; Raphael, 1982). Accordingly, systems that present content in this format by automatically generating and answering relevant questions may help users better understand the content.

The two NLP tasks essential to this objective, question answering (QA) and question generation (QG), have received a lot of attention in recent years. Recent work has started to explore the intersection of QA and QG for the purpose of enhancing performance on one or both tasks (Sachan and Xing, 2018; Song et al., 2018; Tang et al., 2018; Yuan et al., 2017). Among application interfaces that demo these tasks, most have focused on either one or the other (Kaisser, 2008; Kumar et al., 2019). Krishna and Iyyer (2019) presented a system that integrated these tasks to simulate a pedagogical approach to human reading comprehension. In our work, we demo an end-to-end system that applies QA and QG to multi-paragraph documents for the purpose of user content understanding. The system generates a catalog of Q&A items that convey a document's content. This paper first presents some focused contributions to the individual tasks of QA and QG. In particular, we examine the challenging task of QA applied to multi-paragraph documents and show the impact of incorporating a pre-trained text encoding model into an existing approach. Additionally, we report a new set of results for QA that assesses generalizability between datasets that are typically evaluated separately. For QG, we demonstrate the benefit of data augmentation by seeding a model with automatically generated questions, which produces more fluent and answerable questions beyond a model that observes only the original human-authored data. In combining the two tasks into a single pipeline, we show that the information given by the generated Q&A items is relevant to the information humans target when formulating questions about a text.

The demo is implemented as a web application in which users can automatically generate Q&A pairs for any text they provide. The web application is available at qna.sdl.com, and our code is at github.com/roemmele/answerquest.

2 Question Answering

2.1 Model Overview

Our demo implements extractive QA, where answers to questions are extracted directly from some given reference text. State-of-the-art systems have utilized a classification objective to predict indices

[◇]Current affiliation: eBay Inc., San Jose, CA, USA

Proceedings of the 16th Conference of the European Chapter of the Association for Computational Linguistics: System Demonstrations, pages 40–52
April 19 - 23, 2021. ©2021 Association for Computational Linguistics

of answer spans in the text. This approach has achieved success when the reference text is limited to a single paragraph (Devlin et al., 2019). However, QA for multi-paragraph documents has proven to be more difficult. Our system addresses this challenging document-level QA task by adapting an existing method to additionally leverage a pre-trained text encoding model.

Existing work on document-level QA has proposed a pipelined approach that first applies a retrieval module to select the most relevant paragraphs from the document, and then a reader module for extracting answers from the retrieved paragraphs (Chen et al., 2017; Yang et al., 2019). During training, each of the retrieved paragraphs and the corresponding questions are observed independently. To predict answers, the model scores candidate answer spans within each of the paragraphs, ultimately predicting the one with the highest score across all paragraphs. One problem is that the candidate answer scores across paragraphs might not be comparable, since each paragraph-question pair is treated as an independent training instance. To address this issue, Clark and Gardner (2018) suggested a shared-normalization approach (which we refer to here as BIDAF SHARED-NORM) where paragraph-question pairs are still processed independently, but answer probability scores are globally normalized across the document. In their work, they selected the top-k most relevant paragraphs for a given question using a TF-IDF heuristic. They then encoded the question and these paragraphs into a neural architecture consisting of GRU layers and a Bi-Directional Attention Flow (BiDAF) mechanism (Seo et al., 2017). On top of this model is a linear layer that predicts the start and end token indices of the answer within a paragraph, using an adapted softmax function with normalization across all top-k paragraphs for the question.

Another document-level QA system, RE^{3}QA (Hu et al., 2019), incorporated the text encoding model BERT (Devlin et al., 2019). BERT has been successfully used for numerous reading comprehension tasks. In contrast to BIDAF SHARED-NORM, RE^{3}QA combined paragraph retrieval and answer prediction into a single end-to-end training process, applying BERT to both steps. Because it obtained favorable results relative to the BIDAF SHARED-NORM approach, we were curious to assess the isolated impact of BERT specifically on the answer prediction component of the pipeline. Therefore we adapted Clark and Gardner's shared-normalization approach by replacing their GRU BiDAF encoder with the BERT-BASE-UNCASED encoder. Wang et al. (2019) used a similar approach for open-domain QA, where answers are mined from the entirety of Wikipedia. We instead evaluate QA with reference to a single document, for which the impact of BERT on the shared-normalization approach has not yet been documented.

We refer to our model here as BERT SHARED-NORM. To rank paragraph relevance to a question, we rely on TF-IDF similarity. During training, we retrieved the top k=4 paragraphs. The BERT SHARED-NORM model consists of the BERT-BASE-UNCASED pre-trained model, which encodes the paragraph and question in the same manner as Devlin et al.'s paragraph-level QA model. The rest of our model is the same as BIDAF SHARED-NORM: the softmax output layer predicts the start and end answer tokens and the same shared-normalization objective function is applied during training. The model can predict that a question is 'unanswerable' by observing an index of 0 for the end token. During inference, the highest-scoring answer span across paragraphs is predicted as the answer. See Appendix A.1 for more details.

2.2 Dataset

Our QA experiments utilized the SQUAD (Rajpurkar et al., 2016) and NEWSQA (Trischler et al., 2017) datasets. SQUAD is derived from Wikipedia articles, while NEWSQA consists of CNN news articles. Both datasets were developed through crowdsourcing tasks where participants authored questions and identified their answers, resulting in text-question-answer items where each answer is a span within the text. There are two versions of SQUAD. SQUAD-1.1 contains 87,599 train and 10,570 test items. SQUAD-2.0 contains an additional 42,720 train and 1,303 test items (a total of 130,319 and 11,873, respectively), distinguished from SQUAD-1.1 by including questions that do not have answers in the text. NEWSQA contains 107,674 and 5,988 train and test items, respectively. As with SQUAD-2.0, some of these questions are unanswerable.[1]

[1]The SQUAD test items we use are actually the items from their 'dev' (development) set: rajpurkar.github.io/SQuAD-explorer. Their official test set is withheld. The other published systems we compare against also report evaluations on this dev set, so for simplicity we refer to it here as the test set. Similarly, we use the dev NEWSQA items as our held-out test set: github.com/Maluuba/newsqa.

SQuAD questions pertain to a single paragraph. Paragraphs are grouped by document and can be concatenated for document-level QA. There are on average 43 paragraphs per document. Paragraph boundaries are not explicit in the NewsQA texts, so we treated each text as a multi-paragraph document by splitting it into chunks of 300 tokens, resulting in 2.55 average paragraphs per document.

2.3 Evaluation

2.3.1 Comparison with other Systems

We first evaluated our BERT Shared-Norm model on SQuAD-1.1 for comparison with the BiDAF Shared-Norm and RE^{3}QA results reported for this dataset. We used the official SQuAD evaluation scripts provided by the website. For direct comparison with BiDAF Shared-Norm, we replicated their setting of k=15 for paragraph retrieval. Table 1 shows the results in terms of the exact match (EM) and F1 accuracy of answers. We improve upon the result for BiDAF Shared-Norm, demonstrating the beneficial impact of incorporating BERT into this approach. The BERT-based RE^{3}QA still outperforms our model, suggesting that its other components outside the BERT encoding for answer prediction additionally contribute to its success.

Model	EM	F1
BiDAF Shared-Norm	64.08	72.37
RE^{3}QA	77.90	84.81
BERT Shared-Norm	72.85	80.58

Table 1: QA results on SQuAD-1.1

2.3.2 Generalizability across Datasets

Our demo accepts any arbitrary text supplied by a user, and we ultimately aim to produce informative Q&A items for varying content domains. State-of-the-art QA systems have matched human-level performance on individual datasets like SQuAD, but it is unclear how much this performance generalizes across different datasets. As a narrow assessment of this issue, we examined the generalizability between SQuAD and NewsQA by alternatively training and evaluating BERT Shared-Norm on different combinations of these datasets.

Table 2 shows the results of this experiment. We trained three different BERT Shared-Norm models on separate datasets: SQuAD-2.0, NewsQA, and SQuAD-2.0 + NewsQA combined (which we term MegaQA). We then evaluated each of these models on the SQuAD-2.0 and NewsQA test sets. Note that the experiments in Section 2.3.1 were evaluated on SQuAD-1.1 for comparison with the other approaches. Here, we only evaluate on SQuAD-2.0, which involves additionally predicting when a question does not have an answer span in the document. For these evaluations, consistent with training, we retrieved the top k=4 paragraphs from each document for answer prediction.

Train Data	Test Data			
	SQuAD-2.0		NewsQA	
	EM	F1	EM	F1
SQuAD-2.0	71.37	74.65	40.88	48.67
NewsQA	45.85	49.88	52.68	61.26
MegaQA	70.29	73.55	53.85	62.46

Table 2: Generalizability of BERT Shared-Norm across datasets

The results reveal a generalizability problem, where the model trained on SQuAD-2.0 fails to perform as well on NewsQA and vice-versa, presumably due to their domain difference (Wikipedia vs. Newswire). However, combining the datasets with the MegaQA model generalizes well to both. Related to this, Talmor and Berant (2019) found combining multiple datasets from different domains to be advantageous for BERT-based reading comprehension models. Based on these results, the BERT Shared-Norm MegaQA model is currently integrated into our demo.

3 Question Generation

3.1 Model Overview

We follow the same paradigm of much recent work on QG, which has applied encoder-decoder (i.e. sequence-to-sequence) models to text-question pairs (Du et al., 2017; Duan et al., 2017; Scialom et al., 2019; Song et al., 2018; Zhao et al., 2018). Similar to Scialom et al., we utilize the Transformer architecture for the encoder and decoder layers of the model, and enhance the decoder with a copy mechanism. The encoder input is a single sentence and the decoder output is a question, where the input sentence contains the answer to the question. Following the standard procedure for sequence-to-sequence model training, we used the cross-entropy of the output question tokens as the loss function. When generating questions, we use a beam size of 5. See Appendix A.2 for further details.

3.2 Dataset

We trained and evaluated the model on SQUAD and NEWSQA concatenated, the same datasets used for the QA experiments. Our QG model aims to produce questions whose answers are contained in their corresponding input texts, so we only included SQUAD-1.1 items and answerable NEWSQA items (this excluded 32,764 NEWSQA items from the train and test sets). For each paragraph-question-answer item, we sentence-segmented the paragraph, isolated the sentence with the answer span, and inserted special tokens into the sentence (<ANSWER> and </ANSWER>) designating the start and end of the span. These answer-annotated sentences were the model inputs and the aligned questions were the target outputs. We applied Byte-Pair-Encoding (BPE) tokenization (Sennrich et al., 2016) to the inputs and targets (see Appendix A.2). We used the same train-test dataset splits as the QA experiments, allocating a small subset of training items to a validation set for hyperparameter tuning. Overall the train, validation, and test sets consisted of 160,876, 3,281, and 14,910 sentence-question pairs, respectively.

3.3 Data Augmentation Experiments

We examined three different versions of the model described in 3.1, differentiated by their training inputs. The purpose of this experiment was to assess using the output of a rule-based QG system as a means of augmenting the training data. We specifically evaluated the three configurations below:

STANDARD: In this model, no data augmentation was applied. We trained the model directly on the SQUAD/NEWSQA items described in 3.2.

RULEMIMIC: This model observed only the automatically generated augmentation data, without the original data. The source of the augmentation data was the QG system by Heilman and Smith (2010)[2]. This system applies linguistic rule-based transformations (i.e. clause simplification, verb decomposition, subject-auxiliary inversion, and wh-movement) to convert a sentence into a question answered by the sentence, then scores the fluency of the question using a statistical model. Du et al. (2017) found favorable results for a neural sequence-to-sequence approach relative to this rule-based system, but we were curious about its use as a strategy for augmenting our training data. We anticipated that a neural model could learn to 'mimic' the system's generic transformation rules by observing its inputs and outputs. Thus, we applied the system to the raw paragraphs in the SQUAD/NEWSQA training set, which resulted in 1,531,233 questions, each aligned with a sentence. We then followed the same steps described in 3.2 to tokenize the sentence and mark the answer span. The training set for this model consisted only of these automatically generated questions (1,500,610 train items with 30,623 used for validation), with no human-authored questions.

AUGMENTED: This model observed both the original data seen by the STANDARD model and the augmentation data seen by the RULEMIMIC model, via a two-stage fine-tuning process. After training the RULEMIMIC model, we used its parameters to initialize another model, then fine-tuned this new model on the STANDARD model dataset. The hypothesis behind this approach is that it can simulate linguistic rules underlying question formulation, while also capturing the more abstractive features of human questions that are harder to derive using deterministic syntactic and lexical transformations.

3.4 Evaluation

Many QG systems are evaluated using BLEU or similar metrics that reward overall token overlap between generated and human-authored questions. However, Nema and Khapra (2018) argue that these metrics are ill-suited for QG. In particular, comparatively fluent questions with the same answer could have few tokens in common. Moreover, certain tokens within a question have far more impact than others on its perceived quality. They encourage alternative metrics that focus instead on the 'answerability' of questions. Guided by this, we conducted both automated and human ratings-based evaluations in order to assess the answerability of our QG output. Because our demo performs extractive QA, our evaluations focus on whether questions are answerable relative to the input text from which the question is generated.

3.4.1 Automated Evaluation

Some work has utilized automated QA as a scoring metric for QG systems, based on the rationale that a QA system's ability to predict correct answers to generated questions indicate how well the ques-

[2]Code at cs.cmu.edu/~ark/mheilman/questions

tions are formulated to elicit these answers (Duan et al., 2017; Zhang and Bansal, 2019). Following this idea, we generated questions for sentence inputs in the SQuAD/NewsQA test set. As with the training inputs, these inputs were derived by annotating the answer span of the corresponding human-authored question for the paragraph, and isolating the sentence containing that span. We then provided each generated question and corresponding paragraph to the BERT Shared-Norm MegaQA model described in Section 2. The results for each QG model in terms of answer F1 accuracy are shown in Table 3, compared alongside the result for human-authored questions.

As shown, the questions generated by the RuleMimic model are much better at eliciting the designated answers than the Standard model questions, indicating that observing the rule-generated questions alone is impactful. Additionally, the Augmented model generates more answerable questions than the RuleMimic model, showing the usefulness of combining rule-generated questions with human-authored questions as a data augmentation strategy.

Model	F1
Standard	0.354
RuleMimic	0.503
Augmented	0.551
Human	0.718

Table 3: Accuracy of QA system on QG output

3.4.2 Human Evaluation

Model	Rating	Answer Present
Standard	2.813	0.225
RuleMimic	2.934	0.381
Augmented	3.140	0.399
Human	3.776	0.793

Table 4: Human assessment of QG output

We also elicited human judgments for a subset of the same generated questions. Participants were recruited from an internal team of linguists as well as Amazon Mechanical Turk (AMT). We selected questions corresponding to 175 inputs. Table 5 in the appendix shows examples of these items. Participants read the input sentence in its paragraph context, then observed all four questions associated with the input (one generated by each of the three models plus the corresponding human-authored question). The presentation order of the questions for a given paragraph was randomized. Participants rated the fluency and answerability of questions on a scale of 1-4 based on the following statements:

1: *Question is completely ungrammatical. It's impossible to know what this question is asking.*

2: *Question is mostly grammatical, but it doesn't fully make sense. It's not clear what this question is asking.*

3: *Question is strangely worded, vague, or contains errors. However, I can make a guess about what the question is asking.*

4: *Question is clearly worded. I understand what this question is asking.*

If the participant indicated that the question was answerable by rating it a 3 or 4, they were then asked if the answer to the question was contained in the paragraph. If they indicated 'yes', they were asked to verify this by selecting all text spans in the paragraph that qualified as correct answers to the question. Based on this, we scored a question as having an 'answer present' if it was marked as being answerable and if at least one of the participant-selected answer spans was the same one the question was conditioned upon when generated (signifying that the question actually elicited the answer the model observed in the input). 41 participants assessed a total of 1,560 paragraph-question items, with each item being rated by at least two participants (see Appendix A.3 for inter-rater reliability statistics). We averaged the scores for the same questions across participants. Table 4 shows the mean ratings and answer presence for each set of generated questions including the Human questions. In terms of ratings, the results follow the same pattern as the automated evaluation: the RuleMimic questions are rated higher than the Standard questions, and the Augmented questions are rated higher than the RuleMimic questions. All sets of generated questions are rated much lower than the Human questions. The models are ordered the same in terms of answer presence, though the difference between the RuleMimic and Augmented models is slight. Overall these results again show the benefit of augmenting the training data with automatically generated questions. Accordingly, our demo currently runs the Augmented model.

4 Generating Q&A Pairs

We combined our best-performing QG and QA models into a system that takes a text as input and returns a list of Q&A pairs. Our web demo illustrates this system (see Appendix A.4 for details).

For our evaluations in Section 3, the QG models observed annotated answer spans upon which the generated questions were conditioned. However, these annotations are obviously not available by default for any arbitrary text. Consequently, after splitting the text into sentences, we automatically identify syntactic chunks and named entities as candidate answers to questions (see Appendix A.5 for details). For each candidate answer in a sentence, we produce an input consisting of that sentence annotated with that span. We also include sentences with no answer annotations as inputs, since they are not formally required by the model. We provide all inputs for a given sentence to the AUGMENTED QG model to get a list of questions that can be passed to the QA component. Note that even though some of the questions are already associated with annotated answers, we still apply QA as an additional means of verifying their answerability, and defer to the QA-predicted answer. To prepare the QA inputs, for each sentence-question item, we extend the sentence to include the sentences immediately preceding and following it, so each question becomes aligned with a 3-sentence passage. This enables the QA system to possibly retrieve additional context beyond the sentence that it may deem as part of the answer span. We provide these passage-question pairs to the BERT SHARED-NORM MEGAQA model, then retain output items for which answers are found. We reduce the redundancy of items by filtering those with duplicate questions or answers, as well as items where the question and answer concatenated share 60% or more of the same tokens. In these cases, we only retain the item with the highest QG probability.

4.1 Human Evaluation

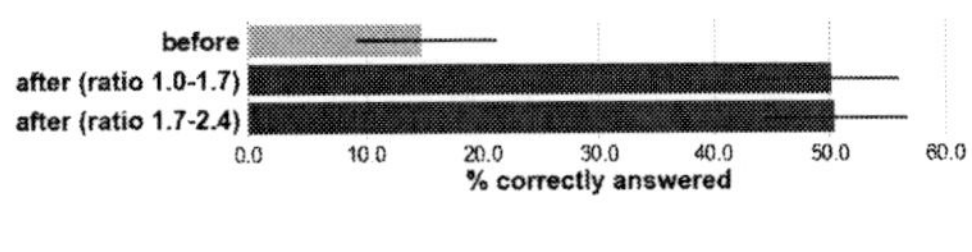

Figure 1: Human accuracy on target questions before and after observing generated Q&A pairs

We used our system to generate Q&A pairs for ten texts from the SQUAD test set. Appendix Table 6 shows an example of a generated Q&A list for one text. We conducted an evaluation of the informativeness of these pairs with 38 AMT participants. In the first stage of the evaluation, participants were shown only the title of one text (e.g. "Tesla") and the human-authored SQUAD questions (no answers) corresponding to the text. Without referencing any material, they were asked to answer these target questions or respond with "X" for questions they couldn't answer. Because no generated Q&A pairs were shown to participants during this stage, the accuracy of their answers indicated their prior mental knowledge of the information in the text. In the second stage, the generated Q&A pairs for the same text were revealed to them and they answered the same target questions again. Participants never observed the original text itself. The logic of this design is that the more questions people could correctly answer in the second stage relative to the first, the more informative the generated Q&A list could be deemed. The ratio of generated Q&A pairs to target questions per text varied from 1 to 2.4 (e.g. ratio = 2 for a text with 30 generated pairs and 15 target questions). Figure 1 shows the percentage of target questions participants answered correctly before and after observing the Q&A list, grouped by ratio. The overall difference in these conditions (14.74% vs. 50.26%) shows that the generated items were partially informative for answering the target questions, signifying that the system does highlight some of the same content people ask questions about. However, accuracy did not markedly improve as participants saw more items (50.18% for the lower ratio vs. 50.38% for the higher ratio), suggesting that the information coverage of the items could be improved. See Appendix A.6 for more details about this evaluation.

5 Conclusion and Future Work

In this paper, we present a system that automatically produces Q&A pairs for multi-paragraph documents. We report some novel experiments for QA and QG that motivate techniques for improving these tasks. We show that combining these components can produce informative Q&A items. Our future work will focus on more advanced modeling of information structure in documents. For example, the ideal design of Q&A items varies by domain (e.g. news stories vs. financial reports vs. opinion editorials), and items should target the content readers find most substantial in each domain.

References

Danqi Chen, Adam Fisch, Jason Weston, and Antoine Bordes. 2017. Reading Wikipedia to answer open-domain questions. In *Proceedings of the 55th Annual Meeting of the Association for Computational Linguistics (Volume 1: Long Papers)*, pages 1870–1879, Vancouver, Canada. Association for Computational Linguistics.

Christopher Clark and Matt Gardner. 2018. Simple and effective multi-paragraph reading comprehension. In *Proceedings of the 56th Annual Meeting of the Association for Computational Linguistics (Volume 1: Long Papers)*, pages 845–855, Melbourne, Australia. Association for Computational Linguistics.

Jacob Devlin, Ming-Wei Chang, Kenton Lee, and Kristina Toutanova. 2019. BERT: Pre-training of deep bidirectional transformers for language understanding. In *Proceedings of the 2019 Conference of the North American Chapter of the Association for Computational Linguistics: Human Language Technologies, Volume 1 (Long and Short Papers)*, pages 4171–4186, Minneapolis, Minnesota. Association for Computational Linguistics.

Xinya Du, Junru Shao, and Claire Cardie. 2017. Learning to ask: Neural question generation for reading comprehension. In *Proceedings of the 55th Annual Meeting of the Association for Computational Linguistics (Volume 1: Long Papers)*, pages 1342–1352, Vancouver, Canada. Association for Computational Linguistics.

Nan Duan, Duyu Tang, Peng Chen, and Ming Zhou. 2017. Question generation for question answering. In *Proceedings of the 2017 Conference on Empirical Methods in Natural Language Processing*, pages 866–874, Copenhagen, Denmark. Association for Computational Linguistics.

Michael Heilman and Noah A. Smith. 2010. Good question! statistical ranking for question generation. In *Human Language Technologies: The 2010 Annual Conference of the North American Chapter of the Association for Computational Linguistics*, pages 609–617, Los Angeles, California. Association for Computational Linguistics.

Minghao Hu, Yuxing Peng, Zhen Huang, and Dongsheng Li. 2019. Retrieve, read, rerank: Towards end-to-end multi-document reading comprehension. In *Proceedings of the 57th Annual Meeting of the Association for Computational Linguistics*, pages 2285–2295, Florence, Italy. Association for Computational Linguistics.

Michael Kaisser. 2008. The QuALiM question answering demo: Supplementing answers with paragraphs drawn from Wikipedia. In *Proceedings of the ACL-08: HLT Demo Session*, pages 32–35, Columbus, Ohio. Association for Computational Linguistics.

Guillaume Klein, Yoon Kim, Yuntian Deng, Jean Senellart, and Alexander M. Rush. 2017. OpenNMT: Open-source toolkit for neural machine translation. In *Proc. ACL*.

Chris Knight. 2010. Question & answer article template.

Kalpesh Krishna and Mohit Iyyer. 2019. Generating question-answer hierarchies. In *Association for Computational Linguistics*.

Vishwajeet Kumar, Sivaanandh Muneeswaran, Ganesh Ramakrishnan, and Yuan-Fang Li. 2019. Paraqg: A system for generating questions and answers from paragraphs. In *Proceedings of the 2019 Conference on Empirical Methods in Natural Language Processing and the 9th International Joint Conference on Natural Language Processing (EMNLP-IJCNLP): System Demonstrations*, pages 175–180.

Preksha Nema and Mitesh M Khapra. 2018. Towards a better metric for evaluating question generation systems. In *Proceedings of the 2018 Conference on Empirical Methods in Natural Language Processing*, pages 3950–3959.

Pranav Rajpurkar, Jian Zhang, Konstantin Lopyrev, and Percy Liang. 2016. SQuAD: 100,000+ questions for machine comprehension of text. In *Proceedings of the 2016 Conference on Empirical Methods in Natural Language Processing*, pages 2383–2392, Austin, Texas. Association for Computational Linguistics.

Taffy E Raphael. 1982. Improving question-answering performance through instruction. *Reading education report; no. 32.*

Stephen Robertson, Hugo Zaragoza, et al. 2009. The probabilistic relevance framework: Bm25 and beyond. *Foundations and Trends® in Information Retrieval*, 3(4):333–389.

Mrinmaya Sachan and Eric Xing. 2018. Self-training for jointly learning to ask and answer questions. In *Proceedings of the 2018 Conference of the North American Chapter of the Association for Computational Linguistics: Human Language Technologies, Volume 1 (Long Papers)*, pages 629–640, New Orleans, Louisiana. Association for Computational Linguistics.

Thomas Scialom, Benjamin Piwowarski, and Jacopo Staiano. 2019. Self-attention architectures for answer-agnostic neural question generation. In *Proceedings of the 57th Annual Meeting of the Association for Computational Linguistics*, pages 6027–6032.

Rico Sennrich, Barry Haddow, and Alexandra Birch. 2016. Neural machine translation of rare words with subword units. In *Proceedings of the 54th Annual Meeting of the Association for Computational Linguistics (Volume 1: Long Papers)*, pages 1715–1725.

Min Joon Seo, Aniruddha Kembhavi, Ali Farhadi, and Hannaneh Hajishirzi. 2017. Bidirectional attention flow for machine comprehension. In *5th International Conference on Learning Representations, ICLR 2017, Toulon, France, April 24-26, 2017, Conference Track Proceedings*.

Linfeng Song, Zhiguo Wang, Wael Hamza, Yue Zhang, and Daniel Gildea. 2018. Leveraging context information for natural question generation. In *Proceedings of the 2018 Conference of the North American Chapter of the Association for Computational Linguistics: Human Language Technologies, Volume 2 (Short Papers)*, pages 569–574, New Orleans, Louisiana. Association for Computational Linguistics.

Alon Talmor and Jonathan Berant. 2019. MultiQA: An empirical investigation of generalization and transfer in reading comprehension. In *Proceedings of the 57th Annual Meeting of the Association for Computational Linguistics*, pages 4911–4921, Florence, Italy. Association for Computational Linguistics.

Duyu Tang, Nan Duan, Zhao Yan, Zhirui Zhang, Yibo Sun, Shujie Liu, Yuanhua Lv, and Ming Zhou. 2018. Learning to collaborate for question answering and asking. In *Proceedings of the 2018 Conference of the North American Chapter of the Association for Computational Linguistics: Human Language Technologies, Volume 1 (Long Papers)*, pages 1564–1574, New Orleans, Louisiana. Association for Computational Linguistics.

Adam Trischler, Tong Wang, Xingdi Yuan, Justin Harris, Alessandro Sordoni, Philip Bachman, and Kaheer Suleman. 2017. NewsQA: A machine comprehension dataset. In *Proceedings of the 2nd Workshop on Representation Learning for NLP*, pages 191–200, Vancouver, Canada. Association for Computational Linguistics.

Alex Wang, Amanpreet Singh, Julian Michael, Felix Hill, Omer Levy, and Samuel Bowman. 2018. GLUE: A multi-task benchmark and analysis platform for natural language understanding. In *Proceedings of the 2018 EMNLP Workshop BlackboxNLP: Analyzing and Interpreting Neural Networks for NLP*, pages 353–355, Brussels, Belgium. Association for Computational Linguistics.

Zhiguo Wang, Patrick Ng, Xiaofei Ma, Ramesh Nallapati, and Bing Xiang. 2019. Multi-passage bert: A globally normalized bert model for open-domain question answering. In *Proceedings of the 2019 Conference on Empirical Methods in Natural Language Processing and the 9th International Joint Conference on Natural Language Processing (EMNLP-IJCNLP)*, pages 5881–5885.

Wei Yang, Yuqing Xie, Aileen Lin, Xingyu Li, Luchen Tan, Kun Xiong, Ming Li, and Jimmy Lin. 2019. End-to-end open-domain question answering with BERTserini. In *Proceedings of the 2019 Conference of the North American Chapter of the Association for Computational Linguistics (Demonstrations)*, pages 72–77, Minneapolis, Minnesota. Association for Computational Linguistics.

Xingdi Yuan, Tong Wang, Caglar Gulcehre, Alessandro Sordoni, Philip Bachman, Saizheng Zhang, Sandeep Subramanian, and Adam Trischler. 2017. Machine comprehension by text-to-text neural question generation. In *Proceedings of the 2nd Workshop on Representation Learning for NLP*, pages 15–25, Vancouver, Canada. Association for Computational Linguistics.

Shiyue Zhang and Mohit Bansal. 2019. Addressing semantic drift in question generation for semi-supervised question answering. In *Proceedings of the 2019 Conference on Empirical Methods in Natural Language Processing and the 9th International Joint Conference on Natural Language Processing (EMNLP-IJCNLP)*, pages 2495–2509.

Yao Zhao, Xiaochuan Ni, Yuanyuan Ding, and Qifa Ke. 2018. Paragraph-level neural question generation with maxout pointer and gated self-attention networks. In *Proceedings of the 2018 Conference on Empirical Methods in Natural Language Processing*, pages 3901–3910, Brussels, Belgium. Association for Computational Linguistics.

A Appendices

A.1 QA Model Details

The TF-IDF method for ranking paragraph relevance to the question specifically uses the BM-25 ranker[3] (Robertson et al., 2009). We implemented the QA model in PyTorch using the HuggingFace Transformers library[4]. As described in Section 2.1, we use the pre-trained BERT-BASE-UNCASED model, which has 12 layers, 768 nodes per layer, 12 heads per layer, and 110M parameters overall. The maximum sequence length for BERT-BASE-UNCASED is 384 tokens (including both paragraph and question tokens combined), so we truncated paragraphs when this total was exceeded. The output layer consists of a 384 x 2 matrix whose dimensions correspond to token indices for the start and end of the answer span. We trained the model in parallel across 4 Nvidia Tesla V100 GPUs with a paragraph-question batch size of 48 with gradient accumulation at step 1 (12 paragraph-question pairs per GPU, which was the maximum size a single V100 GPU could accommodate). Following Devlin et al.'s BERT-based fine-tuning procedure for paragraph-level QA, the model was trained for 3 epochs and a learning rate of 3e-5 using Adam optimization.

A.2 QG Model Details

We used OpenNMT-py[5] (Klein et al., 2017) for implementation of the QG model. For BPE tokenization, we use the OpenAI GPT-2 tokenizer implemented by the HuggingFace transformers library cited above. The vocabulary included all tokens observed in the training data. The Transformer encoder and decoder each consist of 4 layers with 2048 nodes and 8 heads each. We include position encodings on the token embeddings and a copy attention layer in the decoder. We used a training batch size of 4096 tokens, normalizing gradients over tokens and computing gradients based on 4 batches. We trained for a maximum of 100,000 steps and validated every 200 steps, with early stopping after one round of no improvement in validation loss. We applied the other hyperparameter settings recommended for training transformer sequence-to-sequence models on the OpenNMT-py website[6]. This included Adam optimization with $\beta_1 = 0.998$, gradient re-normalization for norms exceeding 0, Glorot uniform parameter initialization, 0.1 dropout probability, noam decay, 8000 warmup steps for decay, learning rate = 2, and label smoothing $\epsilon = 0$.

A.3 QG Evaluation Details

The sentence inputs for the evaluated questions were randomly sampled after filtering for those inside paragraphs longer than 500 characters, to ensure participants could efficiently complete the evaluation. AMT workers were paid $7 for their participation in this evaluation, with the expected time commitment of about 35 minutes.

The Cohen's kappa inter-rater agreement on the fluency/answerability ratings of 1-4 was 0.422, indicating moderate agreement. The kappa for answer presence in the paragraph was 0.465, also indicating moderate agreement.

A.4 System Implementation Details

The system UI is implemented using React JS with Bootstrap CSS for styling. Figure 2 shows a screenshot of the interface. The QA and QG functionalities run as web services implemented using Flask.

As an additional feature of the UI, users have the option to obtain answers to their own custom questions. They supply the question via a text box. The QA system receives the entire document text as input along with the question. We enforce paragraph boundaries by splitting the document into non-overlapping paragraphs of 300 tokens, and then apply the BERT SHARED-NORM MEGAQA model with top k=4 for paragraph retrieval[7]. If the model predicts the answer is not in the text, the user sees a message indicating this.

A.5 Candidate Answers for QG

We use the spaCy[8] library to extract all named entities and noun chunks. Additionally, we extract all dependency parse subtrees whose head is labeled as one of the following: clausal complement (xcomp), attribute (attr), prepositional modified (prep), object (obj), indirect object (iobj), flat multiword expression (flat), fixed multiword expression (fixed), clausal subject (csubj), clausal

[3] pypi.org/project/rank-bm25

[4] huggingface.co/transformers

[5] github.com/OpenNMT/OpenNMT-py

[6] opennmt.net/OpenNMT-py/FAQ.html#how-do-i-use-the-transformer-model

[7] Section 2.3.1 reported the result for k=15, but k=4 performs only slightly lower (71.21 EM and 78.89 F1 vs. 72.85 and 80.58, respectively) with significantly higher efficiency.

[8] spacy.io

complement (ccomp), adjectival clause (acl), and conjunct (conj). All extracted chunks are annotated as answer spans.

A.6 Q&A List Evaluation

We truncated each of the ten SQuAD documents to its first three paragraphs. There were on average 334.5 tokens per truncated document. For each document we selected all SQuAD questions corresponding to the first three paragraphs as the list of target questions participants were prompted to answer. There were on average 16.2 target questions per truncated document. We provided the truncated document to the system to generate a list of Q&A items. As described in Section 4.1, the ratio of generated Q&A items per target questions varied from 1 to 2.4 with an average of 1.66, resulting in an overall average of 26.3 generated items per document.

Each of the 38 AMT participants answered the target questions for a single document, so approximately four participants answered each unique list of target questions. They were paid $8 for their participation, with the expected time commitment of around 30 minutes. The instructions emphasized that they should not use any external information to answer the questions other than the reference Q&A list (which was only used when participants answered the questions for the second time). They were told their participation would not be judged based on the number of questions correctly answered. Participants were not informed that the reference Q&A items were automatically generated.

Because all answers were provided as free text and there could be some token variation in correct answers for the same question (e.g. "Parliament of the United Kingdom" vs. "UK Parliament"), we used a fuzzy metric for judging answers as correct. We counted a participant answer as correct if it had at least one token in common with the answer given in the SQuAD dataset. This is a permissive threshold that can yield false positives (e.g. "300 years" vs. "500 years"), but because it was consistently applied across both stages of the evaluation (i.e. before and after observing the Q&A list), we deemed it sufficient for quantifying the relative impact of the generated items in the 'after' condition.

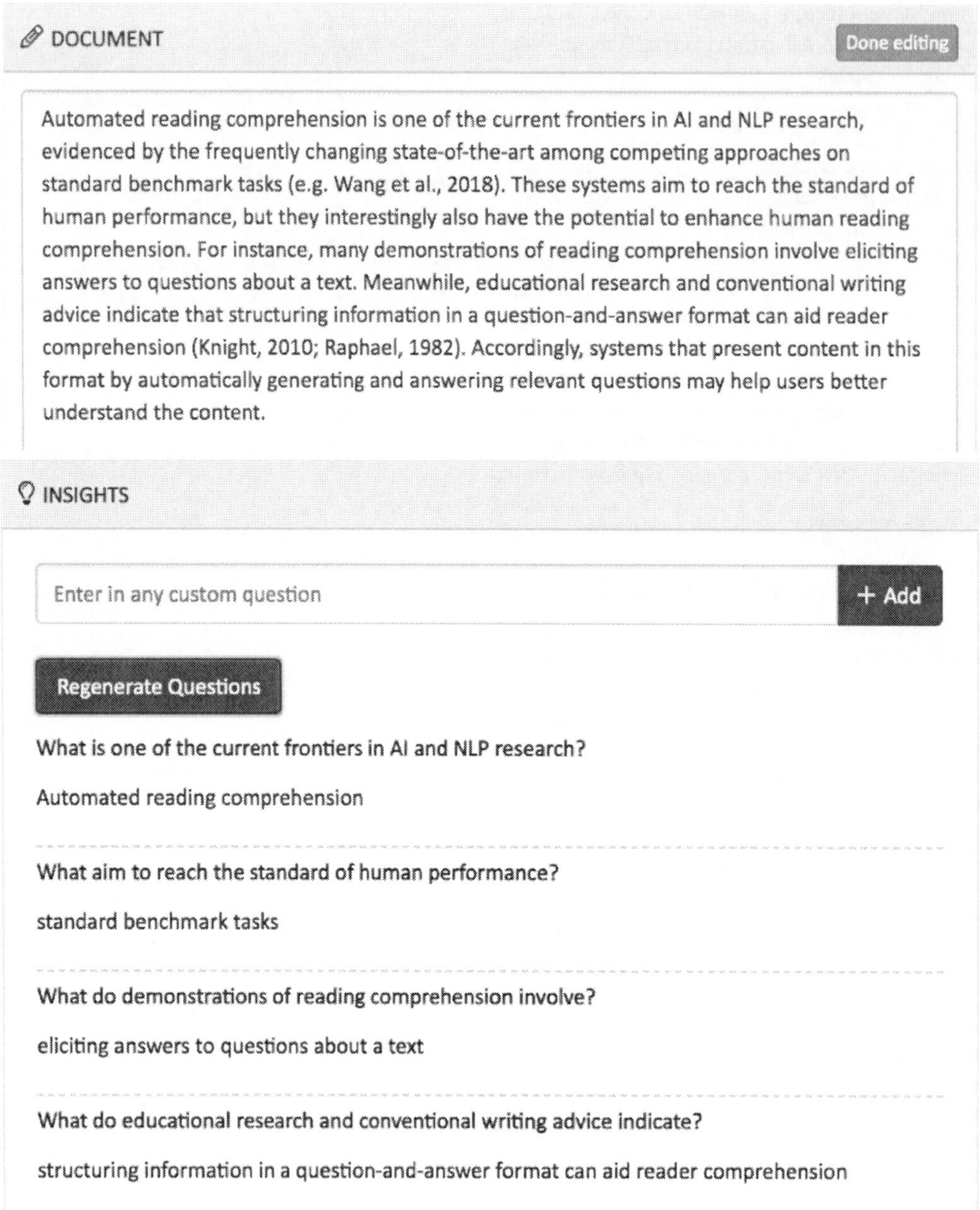

Figure 2: Screenshot of UI with generated Q&A pairs for the displayed document

Input Sentence	Model	Output Question
By far the most famous work of Norman art is the <ANSWER> Bayeux Tapestry </ANSWER>, which is not a tapestry but a work of embroidery.	Standard	What is the name of the work of Norman art?
	RuleMimic	What is not a tapestry but a work of embroidery?
	Augmented	What is the most famous work of Norman art?
	Human	What is Norman art's most well known piece?
Later in life, Tesla made claims concerning a "teleforce" weapon after studying the <ANSWER> Van de Graaff generator </ANSWER>.	Standard	What was the name of the weapon that studying the Teslaforce?
	RuleMimic	What did Tesla make claims concerning a "teleforce" weapon after studying?
	Augmented	What did Tesla study?
	Human	What was he studying that gave him the teleforce weapon idea?
The Super Bowl 50 Host Committee has vowed to be "the most giving Super Bowl ever", and will dedicate <ANSWER> 25 percent </ANSWER> of all money it raises for philanthropic causes in the Bay Area.	Standard	How much of the Super Bowl raises?
	RuleMimic	What will the Super Bowl 50 Host Committee dedicate it raises for philanthropic causes in the Bay Area?
	Augmented	What is the Super Bowl 50 Host Committee?
	Human	How many will the host committee dedicate to local charities?
In 1899, John Jacob Astor IV invested $100,000 for Tesla to further <ANSWER> develop and produce a new lighting system </ANSWER>.	Standard	What did Jacob Astor IV do?
	RuleMimic	What did John Jacob Astor IV invest $100,000 for in 1899?
	Augmented	Why did Jacob Astor IV invest $100,000?
	Human	What did Astor expect the money be used for?
Most influential among these was the definition of Turing machines by Alan Turing in <ANSWER> 1936 </ANSWER>, which turned out to be a very robust and flexible simplification of a computer.	Standard	When was the definition of the definition of Turing?
	RuleMimic	When turned out to be a very robust and flexible simplification of a computer?
	Augmented	When did Alan Turing write machines?
	Human	In what year was the Alan Turing's definitional model of a computing device received?
In addition to the <ANSWER> Vince Lombardi </ANSWER> Trophy that all Super Bowl champions receive, the winner of Super Bowl 50 will also receive a large, 18-karat gold-plated "50".	Standard	What is the name of the Super Bowl?
	RuleMimic	Who will the winner of Super Bowl 50 also receive a large in addition to the Vince Lombardi Trophy that all Super Bowl champions receive?
	Augmented	Who wrote the Super Bowl 50?
	Human	Who is the trophy given to the Super Bowl champion named for?
In 1874, Tesla evaded being drafted into the Austro-Hungarian Army in Smiljan by running away to <ANSWER> Tomingaj </ANSWER>, near Gračac.	Standard	What was the name of Tesla's Army in 1874?
	RuleMimic	Who was near Gračac?
	Augmented	Where did Tesla travel to?
	Human	Where did Tesla run to avoid the army draft?

Table 5: Examples of questions produced by each evaluated QG model for the given input sentences

Q: What is separate from the combustion products? A: working fluid	Q: Where was the water supply for driving waterels? A: factories
Q: What is solar power? A: Non-combustion heat sources	Q: What did the mine provide? A: water supply
Q: What is the ideal thermodynamic cycle used for? A: to analyze this process	Q: Where was it employed? A: draining mine workings
Q: What is heated and transforms into steam? A: water	Q: Where was the storage reservoir? A: above the wheel
Q: Why is mechanical work done? A: When expanded through pistons or turbines	Q: What was passed over the wheel? A: Water
Q: What is then condensed and pumped back into the boiler? A: reduced-pressure steam	Q: When was the first railway journey? A: 21 February 1804
Q: Who invented the first commercially true engine? A: Thomas Newcomen	Q: Where was the train? A: along the tramway from the Pen-y-darren ironworks, near Merthyr Tydfil to Abercynon in south Wales
Q: What could generate power? A: atmospheric engine	Q: What was built by Richard Trevithick? A: The first full-scale working railway steam locomotive
Q: Who proposed the piston pump? A: Papin	Q: The design incorporated a number of what? A: important innovations that included using high-pressure steam which reduced the weight of the engine and increased its efficiency
Q: What happened to Newcomen's engine? A: relatively inefficient	Q: What did England become the leading centre for? A: experimentation and development of steam locomotives
Q: What was the engine used for? A: pumping water	Q: Where was the railways colliery? A: north-east England
Q: What was the vacuum worked by? A: condensing steam under a piston within a cylinder	Q: Who visited the Newcastle area in 1804? A: Trevithick
Q: What was the reason for draining watarelswheels? A: providing a reusable water supply	

Table 6: Generated Q&A list for the first three paragraphs of the SQUAD document titled "Steam engine"

T-NER: An All-Round Python Library for Transformer-based Named Entity Recognition

Asahi Ushio and **Jose Camacho-Collados**
School of Computer Science and Informatics
Cardiff University, United Kingdom
{ushioa,camachocolladosj}@cardiff.ac.uk

Abstract

Language model (LM) pretraining has led to consistent improvements in many NLP downstream tasks, including named entity recognition (NER). In this paper, we present **T-NER**[1] (**T**ransformer-based **N**amed **E**ntity **R**ecognition), a Python library for NER LM finetuning. In addition to its practical utility, T-NER facilitates the study and investigation of the cross-domain and cross-lingual generalization ability of LMs finetuned on NER. Our library also provides a web app where users can get model predictions interactively for arbitrary text, which facilitates qualitative model evaluation for non-expert programmers. We show the potential of the library by compiling nine public NER datasets into a unified format and evaluating the cross-domain and cross-lingual performance across the datasets. The results from our initial experiments show that in-domain performance is generally competitive across datasets. However, cross-domain generalization is challenging even with a large pretrained LM, which has nevertheless capacity to learn domain-specific features if finetuned on a combined dataset. To facilitate future research, we also release all our LM checkpoints via the Hugging Face model hub[2]

1 Introduction

Language model (LM) pretraining has become one of the most common strategies within the natural language processing (NLP) community to solve downstream tasks (Peters et al., 2018; Howard and Ruder, 2018; Radford et al., 2018, 2019; Devlin et al., 2019). LMs trained over large textual data only need to be finetuned on downstream tasks to outperform most of the task-specific designed models. Among the NLP tasks impacted by LM pretraining, named entity recognition (NER) is one of the most prevailing and practical applications. However, the availability of open-source NER libraries for LM training is limited.[3]

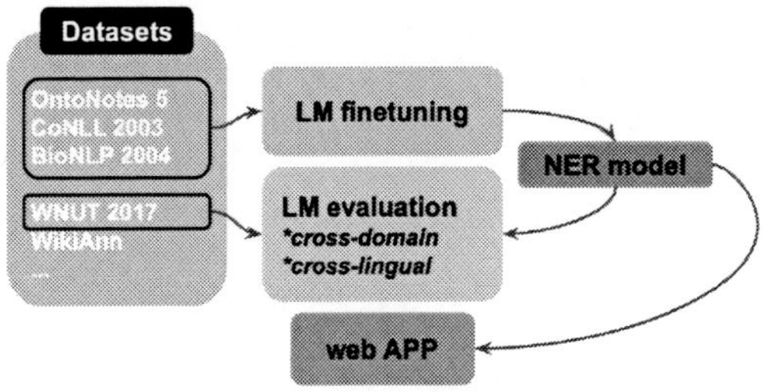

Figure 1: System overview of T-NER.

In this paper, we introduce **T-NER**, an open-source Python library for cross-domain analysis for NER with pretrained Transformer-based LMs. Figure 1 shows a brief overview of our library and its functionalities. The library facilitates NER experimental design including easy-to-use features such as model training and evaluation. Most notably, it enables to organize cross-domain analyses such as training a NER model and testing it on a different domain, with a small configuration. We also report initial experiment results, by which we show that although cross-domain NER is challenging, if it has an access to new domains, LM can successfully learn new domain knowledge. The results give us an insight that LM is capable to learn a variety of domain knowledge, but an ordinary finetuning scheme on single dataset most likely causes overfitting and results in poor domain generalization.

As a system design, T-NER is implemented in

[1] https://github.com/asahi417/tner

[2] https://huggingface.co/models?search=asahi417/tner.

[3] Recently, spaCy (https://spacy.io/) has released a general NLP pipeline with pretrained models including a NER feature. Although it provides a very efficient pipeline for processing text, it is not suitable for LM finetuning or evaluation on arbitrary NER data.

Proceedings of the 16th Conference of the European Chapter of the Association for Computational Linguistics: System Demonstrations, pages 53–62
April 19 - 23, 2021. ©2021 Association for Computational Linguistics

Pytorch (Paszke et al., 2019) on top of the Transformers library (Wolf et al., 2019). Moreover, the interfaces of our training and evaluation modules are highly inspired by Scikit-learn (Pedregosa et al., 2011), enabling an interoperability with recent models as well as integrating them in an intuitive way. In addition to the versatility of our toolkit for NER experimentation, we also include an online demo and robust pre-trained models trained across domains. In the following sections, we provide a brief overview about NER in Section 2, explain the system architecture of T-NER with a few basic usages in Section 3 and describe experiment results on cross-domain transfer with our library in Section 4.

2 Named Entity Recognition

Given an arbitrary text, the task of NER consists of detecting named entities and identifying their type. For example, given a sentence *"Dante was born in Florence."*, a NER model are would identify *"Dante"* as a person and *"Florence"* as a location. Traditionally, NER systems have relied on a classification model on top of hand-engineered feature sets extracted from corpora (Ratinov and Roth, 2009; Collobert et al., 2011), which was improved by carefully designed neural network approaches (Lample et al., 2016; Chiu and Nichols, 2016; Ma and Hovy, 2016). This paradigm shift was mainly due to its efficient access to contextual information and flexibility, as human-crafted feature sets were no longer required. Later, contextual representations produced by pretrained LMs have improved the generalization abilities of neural network architectures in many NLP tasks, including NER (Peters et al., 2018; Devlin et al., 2019).

In particular, LMs *see* millions of plain texts during pretraining, a knowledge that then can be leveraged in downstream NLP applications. This property has been studied in the recently literature by probing their generalization capacity (Hendrycks et al., 2020; Aharoni and Goldberg, 2020; Desai and Durrett, 2020; Gururangan et al., 2020). When it comes to LM generalization studies in NER, the literature is more limited and mainly restricted to in-domain (Agarwal et al., 2021) or multilingual settings (Pfeiffer et al., 2020a; Hu et al., 2020b). Our library facilitates future research in cross-domain and cross-lingual generalization by providing a unified benchmark for several languages and domain as well as a straightforward implementation of NER LM finetuning.

3 T-NER: An Overview

A key design goal was to create a self-contained universal system to train, evaluate, and utilize NER models in an easy way, not only for research purpose but also practical use cases in industry. Moreover, we provide a demo web app (Figure 2) where users can get predictions from a trained model given a sentence interactively. This way, users (even those without programming experience) can conduct qualitative analyses on their own or existing pre-trained models.

In the following we provide details on the technicalities of the package provided, including details on how to train and evaluate any LM-based architecture. Our package, T-NER, allows practitioners in NLP to get started working on NER with a few lines of code while diving into the recent progress in LM finetuning. We employ Python as our core implementation, as is one of the most prevailing languages in the machine learning and NLP communities. Our library enables Python users to access its various kinds of features such as model training, in- and cross-domain model evaluation, and an interface to get predictions from trained models with minimum effort.

3.1 Datasets

For model training and evaluation, we compiled nine public NER datasets from different domains, unifying them into same format: OntoNotes5 (Hovy et al., 2006), CoNLL 2003 (Tjong Kim Sang and De Meulder, 2003), WNUT 2017 (Derczynski et al., 2017), WikiAnn (Pan et al., 2017), FIN (Salinas Alvarado et al., 2015), BioNLP 2004 (Collier and Kim, 2004), BioCreative V CDR[4] (Wei et al., 2015), MIT movie review semantic corpus,[5] and MIT restaurant review.[6] These unified datasets are also made available as part of our T-NER library. Except for WikiAnn that contains 282 languages, all the datasets are in English, and only the MIT corpora are lowercased. As MIT corpora are com-

[4]The original dataset consists of long documents which cannot be fed on LM because of the length, so we split them into sentences to reduce their size.

[5]The movie corpus includes two datasets (*eng* and *trivia10k13*) coming from different data sources. While both have been integrated into our library, we only used the largest *trivia10k13* in our experiments.

[6]The original MIT NER corpora can be downloaded from `https://groups.csail.mit.edu/sls/downloads/`.

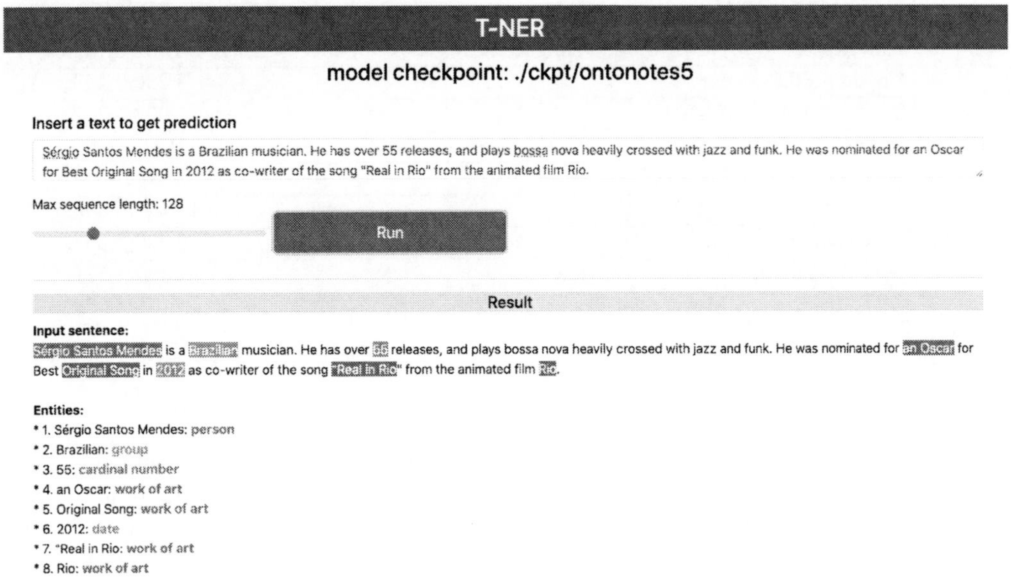

Figure 2: A screenshot from the demo web app. In this example, the NER transformer model is fine-tuned on OntoNotes 5 and a sample sentence is fetched from Wikipedia (`en.wikipedia.org/wiki/Sergio_Mendes`).

monly used for slot filling task in spoken language understanding (Liu and Lane, 2017), the characteristics of the entities and annotation guidelines are quite different from the other datasets, but we included them for completeness and to analyze the differences across datasets.

Table 1 shows statistics of each dataset. In Section 4, we train models on each dataset, and assess the in- and cross-domain accuracy over them.

Dataset format and customization. Users can utilize their own datasets for both model training and evaluation by formatting them into the IOB scheme (Tjong Kim Sang and De Meulder, 2003) which we used to unify all datasets. In the IOB format, all data files contain one word per line with empty lines representing sentence boundaries. At the end of each line there is a tag which states whether the current word is inside a named entity or not. The tag also encodes the type of named entity. Here is an example from CoNLL 2003:

```
EU B-ORG
rejects O
German B-MISC
call O
to O
boycott O
British B-MISC
lamb O
. O
```

3.2 Model Training

We provide modules to facilitate LM finetuning on any given NER dataset. Following Devlin et al. (2019), we add a linear layer on top of the last embedding layer in each token, and train all weights with cross-entropy loss. The model training component relies on the Huggingface transformers library (Wolf et al., 2019), one of the largest Python frameworks for distributing pretrained LM checkpoint files. Our library is therefore fully compatible with the Transformers framework: once new model was deployed on the Transformer hub, one can immediately try those models out with our library as a NER model. To reduce computational complexity, in addition to enabling multi-GPU support, we implement mixture precision during model training by using the apex library[7].

The instance of model training in a given dataset[8] can be used in an intuitive way as displayed below:

```
from tner import TrainTransformersNER
model = TrainTransformersNER(
        dataset="ontonotes5",
        transformer="roberta-base")
model.train()
```

With this sample code, we would finetune

[7] `https://github.com/NVIDIA/apex`

[8] To use custom datasets, the path to a custom dataset folder can simply be included in the dataset argument.

Name	Domain	Entity types	Data size
OntoNotes5	News, Blog, Dialogue	18	59,924/8,582/8,262
CoNLL 2003	News	4	14,041/3,250/3,453
WNUT 2017	SNS	6	1,000/1,008/1,287
WikiAnn	Wikipedia (282 languages)	3	20,000/10,000/10,000
FIN	Finance	4	1,164/-/303
BioNLP 2004	Biochemical	5	18,546/-/3,856
BioCreative V	Biomedical	5	5,228/5,330/5,865
MIT Restaurant	Restaurant review	8	7,660/-/1,521
MIT Movie	Movie review	12	7,816/-/1,953

Table 1: Overview of the NER datasets used in our evaluation and included in T-NER. Data size is the number of sentence in training/validation/test set.

RoBERTa$_{BASE}$ (Liu et al., 2019) on the OntoNotes5 dataset. We also provide an easy extension to train on multiple datasets at the same time:

```
TrainTransformersNER(
    dataset=[
        "ontonotes5", "wnut2017"
        ],
    transformer="roberta-base")
```

Once training is completed, checkpoint files with model weights and other statistics are generated. These are automatically organized for each configuration and can be easily uploaded to the Hugging Face model hub. Ready-to-use code samples can be found in our Google Colab notebook[9], and details for additional options and arguments are included in the github repository. Finally, our library supports Tensorboard[10] to visualize learning curves.

3.3 Model Evaluation

Once a NER model is trained, users may want to test the models in the same dataset or a different one to assess its general performance across domains. To this end, we implemented flexible evaluation modules to facilitate cross-domain evaluation comparison, which is also aided by the unification of datasets into the same format (see Section 3.1) with a unique label reference lookup.

The basic usage of the evaluation module is described below.

```
from tner import TrainTransformersNER
model = TrainTransformersNER(
    "path-to-model-checkpoint"
    )
model.test("ontonotes5")
```

Here, the model would be tested on OntoNotes5 dataset, and it could be evaluated on any other test set including custom dataset. As with the model training module, we prepared a Google Colab notebook[11] for an example use case, and further details can be found in our github repository.

4 Evaluation

In this section, we assess the reliability of T-NER with experiments in standard NER datasets.

4.1 Experimental Setting

4.1.1 Implementation details

Through the experiments, we use *XLM-R* (Liu et al., 2019), which has shown to be one of the most reliable multi-lingual pretrained LMs for discriminative tasks at the moment. In all experiments we make use of the default configuration and hyperpameters of Huggingface's *XLM-R* implementation. For WikiAnn/ja (Japanese), we convert the original character-level tokenization into proper morphological chunk by MeCab[12].

4.1.2 Evaluation metrics and protocols

As customary in the NER literature, we report *span micro-F1 score* computed by seqeval[13], a Python library to compute metrics for sequence prediction evaluation. We refer to this F1 score as *type-aware* F1 score to distinguish it from the the type-ignored metric used to assess the cross-domain performance, which we explain below.

[9] https://colab.research.google.com/drive/1AlcTbEsp8W1lyflT7SyT0L4C4HG6MXYr?usp=sharing

[10] www.tensorflow.org/tensorboard

[11] https://colab.research.google.com/drive/1jHVGnFN4AU8uS-ozWJIXXe2fV8HUj8NZ?usp=sharing

[12] https://pypi.org/project/mecab-python3/

[13] https://pypi.org/project/seqeval/

In a cross-domain evaluation setting, the *type-aware* F1 score easily fails to represent the cross-domain performance if the granularity of entity types differ across datasets. For instance, the MIT restaurant corpus has entities such as *amenity* and *rating*, while *plot* and *actor* are entities from the MIT movie corpus. Thus, we report *type-ignored* F1 score for cross-domain analysis. In this *type-ignored* evaluation, the entity type from both of predictions and true labels is disregarded, reducing the task into a simpler entity span detection task. This evaluation protocol can be customized by the user at test time.

4.2 Results

We conduct three experiments on the nine datasets described in Table 1: (i) in-domain evaluation (Section 4.2.1), (ii) cross-domain evaluation (Section 4.2.2), and (iii) cross-lingual evaluation (Section 4.2.3). While the first experiment tests our implementation in standard datasets, the second experiment is aimed at investigating the cross-domain performance of transformer-based NER models. Finally, as a direct extension of our evaluation module, we show the zero-shot cross-lingual performance of NER models on the WikiAnn dataset.

4.2.1 In-domain results

The main results are displayed in Table 2, where we report the *type-aware* F1 score from $XLM\text{-}R_{BASE}$ and $XLM\text{-}R_{LARGE}$ models along with current state-of-the-art (SoTA). One can confirm that our framework with $XLM\text{-}R_{LARGE}$ achieves a comparable SoTA score, even surpassing it in the WNUT 2017 dataset. In general, $XLM\text{-}R_{LARGE}$ performs consistently better than $XLM\text{-}R_{BASE}$ but, interestingly, the base model performs better than large on the FIN dataset. This can be attributed to the limited training data in this dataset, which may have caused overfitting in the large model.

Generally, it can be expected to get better accuracy with domain-specific or larger language models that can be integrated into our library. Nonetheless, our goal for these experiments were not to achieve SoTA but rather to provide a competitive and easy-to-use framework. In the remaining experiments we report results for $XLM\text{-}R_{LARGE}$ only, but the results for $XLM\text{-}R_{BASE}$ can be found in the appendix.

Dataset	*BASE*	*LARGE*	**SoTA**
OntoNotes5	89.0	89.1	92.1
CoNLL 2003	90.8	92.9	94.3
WNUT 2017	52.8	58.5	50.3
FIN	81.3	76.4	82.7
BioNLP 2004	73.4	74.3	77.4
BioCreative V	88.0	88.6	89.9
MIT Restaurant	79.4	79.6	-
MIT Movie	69.9	71.2	-
WikiAnn/en	82.7	84.0	84.8
WikiAnn/ja	83.8	86.5	73.3
WikiAnn/ru	88.6	90.0	91.4
WikiAnn/es	90.9	92.1	-
WikiAnn/ko	87.5	89.6	-
WikiAnn/ar	88.9	90.3	-

Table 2: In-domain *type-aware* F1 score for test set on each dataset with current SoTA. SoTA on each dataset is attained from the result of *BERT-MRC-DSC* (Li et al., 2019) for OntoNotes5, *LUKE* (**?**) for CoNLL 2003, *CrossWeigh* (Wang et al., 2019) for WNUT 2017, (Pfeiffer et al., 2020a) for WikiAnn (en, ja, ru, es, ko, ar), (Salinas Alvarado et al., 2015) for FIN, (Lee et al., 2020) for BioNLP 2004, (Nooralahzadeh et al., 2019) for BioCreative V and (Pfeiffer et al., 2020a) for WikiAnn/en.

4.2.2 Cross-domain results

In this section, we show cross-domain evaluation results on the English datasets[14]: OntoNotes5 (ontonotes), CoNLL 2003 (conll), WNUT 2017 (wnut), WikiAnn/en (wiki), BioNLP 2004 (bionlp), and BioCreative V (bc5cdr), FIN (fin). We also report the accuracy of the same XLM-R model trained over a combined dataset resulting from concatenation of all the above datasets.

In Table 3, we present the *type-ignored* F1 results across datasets. Overall cross-domain scores are not as competitive as in-domain results. This gap reveals the difficulty of transferring NER models into different domains, which may also be attributed to different annotation guidelines or data construction procedures across datasets. Especially, training on the bionlp and bc5cdr datasets lead to a null accuracy when they are evaluated on other datasets, as well as others evaluated on them. Those datasets are very domain specific dataset, as they have entities such as *DNA*, *Protein*, *Chemical*, and *Disease*, which results in a poor adaptation to other domains. On the other hand, there are datasets

[14]We excluded the MIT datasets in this setting since they are all lowercased.

train\test	ontonotes	conll	wnut	wiki	bionlp	bc5cdr	fin	avg
ontonotes	**91.6**	65.4	53.6	47.5	0.0	0.0	18.3	40.8
conll	62.2	**96.0**	69.1	61.7	0.0	0.0	22.7	35.1
wnut	41.8	85.7	**68.3**	54.5	0.0	0.0	20.0	31.7
wiki	32.8	73.3	53.6	**93.4**	0.0	0.0	12.2	29.6
bionlp	0.0	0.0	0.0	0.0	**79.0**	0.0	0.0	8.7
bc5cdr	0.0	0.0	0.0	0.0	0.0	**88.8**	0.0	9.8
fin	48.2	73.2	60.9	58.9	0.0	0.0	**82.0**	38.1
all	90.9	93.8	60.9	91.3	78.3	84.6	75.5	81.7

Table 3: *Type-ignored* F1 score in cross-domain setting over non-lower-cased English datasets. We compute average of accuracy in each test set, named as **avg**. The model trained on all datasets listed here, is shown as **all**.

	test					
train	**en**	**ja**	**ru**	**ko**	**es**	**ar**
en	**84.0**	46.3	73.1	58.1	71.4	53.2
ja	53.0	**86.5**	45.7	57.1	74.5	55.4
ru	60.4	53.3	**90.0**	68.1	76.8	54.9
ko	57.8	62.0	68.6	**89.6**	66.2	57.2
es	70.5	50.6	75.8	61.8	**92.1**	62.1
ar	60.1	55.7	55.7	70.7	79.7	**90.3**

Table 4: Cross-lingual *type-aware* F1 results on various languages for the WikiAnn dataset.

that are more easily transferable, such as wnut and conll. The wnut-trained model achieves 85.7 on the conll dataset and, surprisingly, the conll-trained model actually works better than the wnut-trained model when evaluated on the wnut test set. This could be also attributed to the data size, as wnut only has 1,000 sentences, while conll has 14,041. Nevertheless, the fact that ontonotes has 59,924 sentences but does not perform better than conll on wnut reveals a certain domain similarity between conll and wnut.

Finally, the model trained on the training sets of all datasets achieves a *type-ignored* F1 score close to the in-domain baselines. This indicates that a LM is capable of learning representations of different domains. Moreover, leveraging domain similarity as explained above can lead to better results as, for example, distant datasets such as bionlp and bc5cdr surely cause performance drops. This is an example of the type of experiments that could be facilited by T-NER, which we leave for future work.

4.2.3 Cross-lingual results

Finally, we present some results for zero-shot cross-lingual NER over the WikiAnn dataset, where we include six distinct languages: English (en), Japanese (ja), Russian (ru), Korean (ko), Spanish (es), and Arabic (ar). In Table 4, we show the cross-lingual evaluation results. The diagonal includes the results of the model trained on the training data of the same target language. There are a few interesting findings. First, we observe a high correlation between Russian and Spanish, which are generally considered to be distant languages and do not share the alphabet. Second, Arabic also transfers well to Spanish which, despite the Arabic (lexical) influence on the Spanish language (Stewart et al., 1999), are still languages from distant families.

Clearly, this is a shallow cross-lingual analysis, but it highlights the possibilities of our library for research in cross-lingual NER. Recently, (Hu et al., 2020a) proposed a compilation of multilingual benchmark tasks including the WikiAnn datasets as a part of it, and *XLM-R* proved to be a strong baseline on multilingual NER. This is in line with the results of Conneau et al. (2020), which showed a high capacity of zero-shot cross-lingual transferability. On this respect, Pfeiffer et al. (2020b) proposed a language/task specific adapter module that can further improve cross-lingual adaptation in NER. Given the possibilities and recent advances in cross-lingual language models in recent years, we expect our library to help practitioners to experiment and test these advances in NER.

5 Conclusion

In this paper, we have presented a Python library to get started with Transformer-based NER models. This paper especially focuses on LM finetuning, and empirically shows the difficulty of cross-domain generalization in NER. Our framework is designed to be as simple as possible so that any level of users can start running experiments on

NER on any given dataset. To this end, we have also facilitated the evaluation by unifying some of the most popular NER datasets in the literature, including languages other than English. We believe that our initial experiment results emphasize the importance of NER generalization analysis, for which we hope that our open-source library can help NLP community to convey relevant research in an efficient and accessible way.

Acknowledgements

We would like to thank Dimosthenis Antypas for testing our library and the anonymous reviewers for their useful comments.

References

Oshin Agarwal, Yinfei Yang, Byron C Wallace, and Ani Nenkova. 2021. Entity-switched datasets: An approach to auditing the in-domain robustness of named entity recognition models. *arXiv preprint arXiv:2004.04123*.

Roee Aharoni and Yoav Goldberg. 2020. Unsupervised domain clusters in pretrained language models. In *Proceedings of the 58th Annual Meeting of the Association for Computational Linguistics*, pages 7747–7763, Online. Association for Computational Linguistics.

Jason P.C. Chiu and Eric Nichols. 2016. Named entity recognition with bidirectional LSTM-CNNs. *Transactions of the Association for Computational Linguistics*, 4:357–370.

Nigel Collier and Jin-Dong Kim. 2004. Introduction to the bio-entity recognition task at JNLPBA. In *Proceedings of the International Joint Workshop on Natural Language Processing in Biomedicine and its Applications (NLPBA/BioNLP)*, pages 73–78, Geneva, Switzerland. COLING.

Ronan Collobert, Jason Weston, Léon Bottou, Michael Karlen, Koray Kavukcuoglu, and Pavel Kuksa. 2011. Natural language processing (almost) from scratch. *Journal of machine learning research*, 12(ARTICLE):2493–2537.

Alexis Conneau, Shijie Wu, Haoran Li, Luke Zettlemoyer, and Veselin Stoyanov. 2020. Emerging cross-lingual structure in pretrained language models. In *Proceedings of the 58th Annual Meeting of the Association for Computational Linguistics*, pages 6022–6034, Online. Association for Computational Linguistics.

Leon Derczynski, Eric Nichols, Marieke van Erp, and Nut Limsopatham. 2017. Results of the WNUT2017 shared task on novel and emerging entity recognition. In *Proceedings of the 3rd Workshop on Noisy User-generated Text*, pages 140–147, Copenhagen, Denmark. Association for Computational Linguistics.

Shrey Desai and Greg Durrett. 2020. Calibration of pre-trained transformers. *arXiv preprint arXiv:2003.07892*.

Jacob Devlin, Ming-Wei Chang, Kenton Lee, and Kristina Toutanova. 2019. BERT: Pre-training of deep bidirectional transformers for language understanding. In *Proceedings of the 2019 Conference of the North American Chapter of the Association for Computational Linguistics: Human Language Technologies, Volume 1 (Long and Short Papers)*, pages 4171–4186, Minneapolis, Minnesota. Association for Computational Linguistics.

Suchin Gururangan, Ana Marasović, Swabha Swayamdipta, Kyle Lo, Iz Beltagy, Doug Downey, and Noah A Smith. 2020. Don't stop pretraining: Adapt language models to domains and tasks. *arXiv preprint arXiv:2004.10964*.

Dan Hendrycks, Xiaoyuan Liu, Eric Wallace, Adam Dziedzic, Rishabh Krishnan, and Dawn Song. 2020. Pretrained transformers improve out-of-distribution robustness. *arXiv preprint arXiv:2004.06100*.

Eduard Hovy, Mitchell Marcus, Martha Palmer, Lance Ramshaw, and Ralph Weischedel. 2006. OntoNotes: The 90% solution. In *Proceedings of the Human Language Technology Conference of the NAACL, Companion Volume: Short Papers*, pages 57–60, New York City, USA. Association for Computational Linguistics.

Jeremy Howard and Sebastian Ruder. 2018. Universal language model fine-tuning for text classification. In *Proceedings of the 56th Annual Meeting of the Association for Computational Linguistics (Volume 1: Long Papers)*, pages 328–339, Melbourne, Australia. Association for Computational Linguistics.

Junjie Hu, Sebastian Ruder, Aditya Siddhant, Graham Neubig, Orhan Firat, and Melvin Johnson. 2020a. XTREME: A massively multilingual multi-task benchmark for evaluating cross-lingual generalisation. In *International Conference on Machine Learning (ICML)*.

Junjie Hu, Sebastian Ruder, Aditya Siddhant, Graham Neubig, Orhan Firat, and Melvin Johnson. 2020b. Xtreme: A massively multilingual multi-task benchmark for evaluating cross-lingual generalization. *arXiv preprint arXiv:2003.11080*.

Guillaume Lample, Miguel Ballesteros, Sandeep Subramanian, Kazuya Kawakami, and Chris Dyer. 2016. Neural architectures for named entity recognition. In *Proceedings of the 2016 Conference of the North American Chapter of the Association for Computational Linguistics: Human Language Technologies*, pages 260–270, San Diego, California. Association for Computational Linguistics.

Jinhyuk Lee, Wonjin Yoon, Sungdong Kim, Donghyeon Kim, Sunkyu Kim, Chan Ho So, and Jaewoo Kang. 2020. Biobert: a pre-trained biomedical language representation model for biomedical text mining. *Bioinformatics*, 36(4):1234–1240.

Xiaoya Li, Xiaofei Sun, Yuxian Meng, Junjun Liang, Fei Wu, and Jiwei Li. 2019. Dice loss for data-imbalanced nlp tasks. *arXiv preprint arXiv:1911.02855*.

Bing Liu and Ian Lane. 2017. Multi-domain adversarial learning for slot filling in spoken language understanding. *arXiv preprint arXiv:1711.11310*.

Yinhan Liu, Myle Ott, Naman Goyal, Jingfei Du, Mandar Joshi, Danqi Chen, Omer Levy, Mike Lewis, Luke Zettlemoyer, and Veselin Stoyanov. 2019. Roberta: A robustly optimized bert pretraining approach. *arXiv preprint arXiv:1907.11692*.

Xuezhe Ma and Eduard Hovy. 2016. End-to-end sequence labeling via bi-directional LSTM-CNNs-CRF. In *Proceedings of the 54th Annual Meeting of the Association for Computational Linguistics (Volume 1: Long Papers)*, pages 1064–1074, Berlin, Germany. Association for Computational Linguistics.

Farhad Nooralahzadeh, Jan Tore Lønning, and Lilja Øvrelid. 2019. Reinforcement-based denoising of distantly supervised ner with partial annotation. In *Proceedings of the 2nd Workshop on Deep Learning Approaches for Low-Resource NLP (DeepLo 2019)*, pages 225–233.

Xiaoman Pan, Boliang Zhang, Jonathan May, Joel Nothman, Kevin Knight, and Heng Ji. 2017. Cross-lingual name tagging and linking for 282 languages. In *Proceedings of the 55th Annual Meeting of the Association for Computational Linguistics (Volume 1: Long Papers)*, pages 1946–1958, Vancouver, Canada. Association for Computational Linguistics.

Adam Paszke, Sam Gross, Francisco Massa, Adam Lerer, James Bradbury, Gregory Chanan, Trevor Killeen, Zeming Lin, Natalia Gimelshein, Luca Antiga, et al. 2019. Pytorch: An imperative style, high-performance deep learning library. In *Advances in neural information processing systems*, pages 8026–8037.

Fabian Pedregosa, Gaël Varoquaux, Alexandre Gramfort, Vincent Michel, Bertrand Thirion, Olivier Grisel, Mathieu Blondel, Peter Prettenhofer, Ron Weiss, Vincent Dubourg, et al. 2011. Scikit-learn: Machine learning in python. *the Journal of machine Learning research*, 12:2825–2830.

Matthew Peters, Mark Neumann, Mohit Iyyer, Matt Gardner, Christopher Clark, Kenton Lee, and Luke Zettlemoyer. 2018. Deep contextualized word representations. In *Proceedings of the 2018 Conference of the North American Chapter of the Association for Computational Linguistics: Human Language Technologies, Volume 1 (Long Papers)*, pages 2227–2237, New Orleans, Louisiana. Association for Computational Linguistics.

Jonas Pfeiffer, Ivan Vulić, Iryna Gurevych, and Sebastian Ruder. 2020a. Mad-x: An adapter-based framework for multi-task cross-lingual transfer. *arXiv preprint arXiv:2005.00052*.

Jonas Pfeiffer, Ivan Vulić, Iryna Gurevych, and Sebastian Ruder. 2020b. MAD-X: An Adapter-Based Framework for Multi-Task Cross-Lingual Transfer. In *Proceedings of the 2020 Conference on Empirical Methods in Natural Language Processing (EMNLP)*, pages 7654–7673, Online. Association for Computational Linguistics.

Alec Radford, Karthik Narasimhan, Tim Salimans, and Ilya Sutskever. 2018. Improving language understanding by generative pre-training.

Alec Radford, Jeffrey Wu, Rewon Child, David Luan, Dario Amodei, and Ilya Sutskever. 2019. Language models are unsupervised multitask learners.

Lev Ratinov and Dan Roth. 2009. Design challenges and misconceptions in named entity recognition. In *Proceedings of the Thirteenth Conference on Computational Natural Language Learning (CoNLL-2009)*, pages 147–155, Boulder, Colorado. Association for Computational Linguistics.

Julio Cesar Salinas Alvarado, Karin Verspoor, and Timothy Baldwin. 2015. Domain adaption of named entity recognition to support credit risk assessment. In *Proceedings of the Australasian Language Technology Association Workshop 2015*, pages 84–90, Parramatta, Australia.

Miranda Stewart et al. 1999. *The Spanish language today*. Psychology Press.

Erik F. Tjong Kim Sang and Fien De Meulder. 2003. Introduction to the CoNLL-2003 shared task: Language-independent named entity recognition. In *Proceedings of the Seventh Conference on Natural Language Learning at HLT-NAACL 2003*, pages 142–147.

Zihan Wang, Jingbo Shang, Liyuan Liu, Lihao Lu, Jiacheng Liu, and Jiawei Han. 2019. Crossweigh: Training named entity tagger from imperfect annotations. In *Proceedings of the 2019 Conference on Empirical Methods in Natural Language Processing and the 9th International Joint Conference on Natural Language Processing (EMNLP-IJCNLP)*, pages 5157–5166.

Chih-Hsuan Wei, Yifan Peng, Robert Leaman, Allan Peter Davis, Carolyn J Mattingly, Jiao Li, Thomas C Wiegers, and Zhiyong Lu. 2015. Overview of the biocreative v chemical disease relation (cdr) task. In *Proceedings of the fifth BioCreative challenge evaluation workshop*, volume 14.

Thomas Wolf, Lysandre Debut, Victor Sanh, Julien Chaumond, Clement Delangue, Anthony Moi, Pierric Cistac, Tim Rault, Rémi Louf, Morgan Funtowicz, Joe Davison, Sam Shleifer, Patrick von Platen, Clara Ma, Yacine Jernite, Julien Plu, Canwen Xu, Teven Le Scao, Sylvain Gugger, Mariama Drame, Quentin Lhoest, and Alexander M. Rush. 2019. Huggingface's transformers: State-of-the-art natural language processing. *ArXiv*, abs/1910.03771.

A Appendices

In all experiments we make use of the default configuration and hyperpameters of Huggingface's *XLM-R* implementation.

A.1 Cross-lingual Results

In this section, we show cross-lingual analysis on *XLM-R$_{BASE}$*, where the result is shown in Table 5. For these cross-lingual results, we rely on the WikiAnn dataset where zero-shot cross-lingual NER over six distinct languages is conducted: English (en), Japanese (ja), Russian (ru), Korean (ko), Spanish (es), and Arabic (ar).

A.2 Cross-domain Results

In this section, we show a few more results on our cross-domain analysis, which is based on non-lowercased English datasets: OntoNotes5 (ontonotes), CoNLL 2003 (conll), WNUT 2017 (wnut), WikiAnn/en (wiki), BioNLP 2004 (bionlp), and BioCreative V (bc5cdr), and FIN (fin). Table 6 shows the type-aware F1 score of the *XLM-R$_{LARGE}$* and *XLM-R$_{BASE}$* models trained on all the datasets. Furthermore, Table 7 shows additional results for *XLM-R$_{BASE}$* in the type-ignored evaluation.

	test					
train	**en**	**ja**	**ru**	**ko**	**es**	**ar**
en	**82.8**	38.6	65.7	50.4	73.8	44.5
ja	53.8	**83.9**	46.9	60.1	71.3	46.3
ru	51.9	39.9	**88.7**	51.9	66.8	51.0
ko	54.7	51.6	53.3	**87.5**	63.3	52.3
es	65.7	44.0	66.5	54.1	**90.9**	59.4
ar	53.1	49.2	49.4	59.7	73.6	**88.9**

Table 5: Cross-lingual *type-aware* F1 score over WikiAnn dataset with *XLM-R$_{BASE}$*.

Cross-domain results with lowercased datasets. In this section, we show cross-domain results on the English datasets including lowercased corpora such as MIT Restaurant (restaurant) and MIT Movie (movie). Since those datasets are lowercasd, we converted all datasets into lowercase. Tables 8 and Table 9 show the *type-ignored* F1 score across models trained on different English datasets including lowercased corpora with *XLM-R$_{LARGE}$* and *XLM-R$_{BASE}$*, respectively.

	uppercase		lowercase	
Datasets	*BASE*	*LARGE*	*BASE*	*LARGE*
ontonotes	85.8	87.8	81.7	85.6
conll	87.2	90.3	82.8	87.6
wnut	49.6	55.1	43.7	51.3
wiki	79.1	82.7	75.2	80.8
bionlp	72.9	74.1	71.7	74.0
bc5cdr	79.4	85.0	78.0	84.2
fin	72.4	72.4	72.4	73.5
restaurant	-	-	76.8	80.9
movie	-	-	67.8	71.8

Table 6: *Type-aware* F1 score across different test sets of models trained on all **uppercase/lowercase** English datasets with *XLM-R$_{BASE}$* or *XLM-R$_{LARGE}$*.

train\test	ontonotes	conll	wnut	wiki	bionlp	bc5cdr	fin	avg
ontonotes	**91.8**	62.2	51.7	44.7	0.0	0.0	31.8	40.3
conll	60.5	**95.7**	66.6	60.8	0.0	0.0	33.5	45.3
wnut	41.3	81.3	**63.0**	56.3	0.0	0.0	20.5	37.5
wiki	30.2	71.8	45.3	**92.6**	0.0	0.0	11.5	35.9
bionlp	0.0	0.0	0.0	0.0	**78.5**	0.0	0.0	11.2
bc5cdr	0.0	0.0	0.0	0.0	0.0	**87.5**	0.0	12.5
fin	49.0	73.5	62.2	60.7	0.0	0.0	**82.8**	46.9
all	89.7	92.4	55.8	89.3	78.2	80.0	74.8	80.0

Table 7: *Type-ignored* F1 score in cross-domain setting over non-lower-cased English datasets with *XLM-R*$_{BASE}$. We compute average of accuracy in each test set, named as **avg**. The model trained on all datasets listed here, is shown as **all**.

train\test	ontonotes	conll	wnut	wiki	bionlp	bc5cdr	fin	restaurant	movie	avg
ontonotes	89.3	59.9	50.1	44.7	0.0	0.0	15.1	4.5	88.6	39.1
conll	57.7	94.8	67.0	57.9	0.0	0.0	20.5	23.9	0.0	35.7
wnut	39.8	80.3	61.3	52.3	0.0	0.0	19.5	18.8	0.0	30.2
wiki	28.5	69.7	51.2	92.4	0.0	0.0	12.0	3.0	0.0	28.5
bionlp	0.0	0.0	0.0	0.0	79.0	0.0	0.0	0.0	0.0	8.7
bc5cdr	0.0	0.0	0.0	0.0	0.0	88.9	0.0	0.0	0.0	9.8
fin	46	72.0	61.5	54.8	0.0	0.0	83.0	24.5	0.0	37.9
restaurant	4.6	21.7	22.9	22.3	0.0	0.0	5.4	83.4	0.0	17.8
movie	10.9	0.0	0.0	0.0	0.0	0.0	0.0	0.0	73.1	9.3
all	88.5	92.1	58.0	90.0	79.0	84.6	74.5	85.3	74.1	80.7

Table 8: *Type-ignored* F1 score in cross-domain setting over lower-cased English datasets with *XLM-R*$_{LARGE}$. We compute average of accuracy in each test set, named as **avg**. The model trained on all datasets listed here, is shown as **all**.

train\test	ontonotes	conll	wnut	wiki	bionlp	bc5cdr	fin	restaurant	movie	avg
ontonotes	**88.3**	56.7	49.0	41.4	0.0	0.0	11.7	4.2	88.3	37.7
conll	55.1	**93.7**	60.5	56.8	0.0	0.0	20.4	21.9	0.0	34.3
wnut	38.1	73.0	**57.5**	49.1	0.0	0.0	21.1	20.4	0.0	28.8
wiki	26.3	66.5	41.4	**90.9**	0.0	0.0	9.7	7.6	0.0	26.9
bionlp	0.0	0.0	0.0	0.0	**78.7**	0.0	0.0	0.0	0.0	8.7
bc5cdr	0.0	0.0	0.0	0.0	0.0	**88.0**	0.0	0.0	0.0	9.8
fin	41.3	64.4	45.8	57.8	0.0	0.0	**81.5**	22.0	0.0	34.8
restaurant	8.1	19.1	19.6	19.1	0.0	0.0	13.5	**83.6**	0.0	18.1
movie	14.5	0.0	0.0	0.0	0.0	0.0	0.0	0.0	**73.1**	9.7
all	86.1	89.5	49.9	86.2	76.9	78.8	75.4	82.4	72.2	77.5

Table 9: *Type-ignored* F1 score in cross-domain setting over lower-cased English datasets with *XLM-R*$_{BASE}$. We compute average of accuracy in each test set, named as **avg**. The model trained on all datasets listed here, is shown as **all**.

Forum 4.0: An Open-Source User Comment Analysis Framework

Marlo Haering[1] and **Jakob Smedegaard Andersen**[1] and **Chris Biemann**[1]
and **Wiebke Loosen**[2] and **Benjamin Milde**[1] and **Tim Pietz**[1] and **Christian Stoecker**[3]
and **Gregor Wiedemann**[2] and **Olaf Zukunft**[3] and **Walid Maalej**[1]
Universität Hamburg[1], Leibniz Institute for Media Research[2],
Hamburg University of Applied Sciences[3]
{haering,andersen,biemann,milde,5pietz,maalej}
@informatik.uni-hamburg.de
{w.loosen,g.wiedemann}@leibniz-hbi.de
{christian.stoecker,olaf.zukunft}@haw-hamburg.de

Abstract

With the increasing number of user comments in diverse domains, including comments on online journalism and e-commerce websites, the manual content analysis of these comments becomes time-consuming and challenging. However, research showed that user comments contain useful information for different domain experts, which is thus worth finding and utilizing. This paper introduces Forum 4.0, an open-source framework to semi-automatically analyze, aggregate, and visualize user comments based on labels defined by domain experts. We demonstrate the applicability of Forum 4.0 with comments analytics scenarios within the domains of online journalism and app stores. We outline the underlying container architecture, including the web-based user interface, the machine learning component, and the task manager for time-consuming tasks. We finally conduct machine learning experiments with simulated annotations and different sampling strategies on existing datasets from both domains to evaluate Forum 4.0's performance. Forum 4.0 achieves promising classification results (ROC-AUC $\geq$ 0.9 with 100 annotated samples), utilizing transformer-based embeddings with a lightweight logistic regression model. We explain how Forum 4.0's architecture is applicable for millions of user comments in real-time, yet at feasible training and classification costs.

1 Introduction

Comment sections are omnipresent in today's online environments, for example, on news websites, blogs, online shops, or app stores. In these sections, users submit their feedback and opinion, request features and information, or report issues and bugs. Also, in social media such as Twitter or Facebook, users regularly comment on specific topics, events, products, or services. In many domains, including e-commerce and journalism, users discuss with each other, read others' opinions to e.g. assess the quality of the service or the product (Springer et al., 2015; Kümpel and Springer, 2016), and provide feedback to other users and other domain experts like the journalist (Häring et al., 2018), who wrote the article or the developer who created the app (Maalej et al., 2016b).

Even though research has criticized phenomena such as "dark participation" (Frischlich et al., 2019), comments can contain constructive information for different domain experts in different fields (Loosen et al., 2018; Maalej et al., 2016a). For example, in app development, vendors use app reviews in app stores to collect new feature ideas, bug reports, or ideas of additional user scenarios for their app (Stanik et al., 2019). Software vendors consider the reviews to decide which bug or feature request to prioritize in the next development cycle (Martens and Maalej, 2019). In online journalism, media outlets harness user comments to acquire a broader perspective on additional arguments, collect resonance about their articles, or identify and contact experts or persons concerned for follow-up stories (Loosen et al., 2018). However, the quality of the comments varies significantly, and their amount is sometimes overwhelming, which makes manual monitoring and analysis a real challenge (Pagano and Maalej, 2013; Park et al., 2016a).

In this work, we propose Forum 4.0, an open-source user comment analysis framework to semi-automatically analyze a large number of user comments for domain experts from various domains. Forum 4.0 leverages a combination of transfer learning (Howard and Ruder, 2018), human-in-the-loop (Bailey and Chopra, 2018), and active learning (Settles, 2012) strategies to automatically analyze the comments' content. To enable replication and further research, we share Forum 4.0's source code,

Proceedings of the 16th Conference of the European Chapter of the Association for Computational Linguistics: System Demonstrations, pages 63–70
April 19 - 23, 2021.

the scripts, and datasets we used for our research[1] and a video, which showcases Forum 4.0[2].

2 Usage of Forum 4.0

We describe exemplary usage scenarios of Forum 4.0 for journalists and product managers in their respective online journalism and app development domains and introduce Forum 4.0's user interface.

2.1 Online Journalism

The manual effort for comment moderation in online journalism is high (Park et al., 2016b). One the one hand, media outlets filter hate speech (Gao and Huang, 2017), as it might negatively affect their credibility (Naab et al., 2020). On the other hand, user comments can also be useful for different journalistic purposes (Diakopoulos, 2015). For example, journalists can obtain new perspectives and opinions on an article, learn from users' described personal experiences, or identify potential interview partners among the commenting users (Loosen et al., 2018). Journalists can also aggregate user comments to identify and visualize their audience's opinion on current news topics (Wang et al., 2013). Users can also point out errors in reporting, contribute additional or missing sources and information, provide new ideas for further news, or even address the editorial team or authors directly, for example, by criticizing the article's quality (Häring et al., 2018).

Journalists first define a useful user comment label in Forum 4.0. Examples for such labels could be: "criticism towards corona measures," or "pros/cons regarding a legislative proposal". Journalists or forum moderators annotate user comments regarding these labels, gradually increasing the number of training samples. Forum 4.0 trains a machine learning model using the annotated comments and classifies all other user comments. The automatic classification will improve with more annotations until it reaches sufficient precision so that journalists can conduct quantitative and qualitative analyses with the comments.

2.2 App Development

In app stores, product managers utilize user comments for multiple purposes: users report crashes and bugs in app reviews with valuable context information (e.g., device or app version), helping developers identifying and fixing them (Pagano and Maalej, 2013). This is particularly helpful to acquire immediate feedback after a new major release or update (Guzman and Maalej, 2014). Additionally, users suggest desired and useful app feature ideas (Maalej et al., 2016a). Thereby, the product managers get an overview of current app issues, which they can consider for their further development. In the field of mobile learning, the product manager can utilize comments for the automatic evaluation of education apps (Haering et al., 2021).

Similar to the online journalism domain, the product manager can use Forum 4.0 to first create labels for constructive app reviews. In the app development domain, useful labels include "problems since the last app update", "positive/negative feedback on a certain app feature", or "missing or requested features". The domain expert further annotates app reviews, compiling a training set. Forum 4.0 trains a model and classifies the other app reviews for the domain expert to analyze.

2.3 User Interface

Figure 1 shows Forum 4.0's user interface. The domain expert can log in to create a new label or annotate user comments. Below the title bar, the expert can select a data source containing the comments to analyze. In the figure, we selected comments from the Austrian newspaper DER STANDARD[3], which contains the comments of the "One Million Posts Corpus" published by Schabus et al. (2017). Next to the data source selector, the domain expert can create a new label or select relevant existing labels to analyze and annotate the comments.

The pie chart shows the comment distribution among the document categories (news article or app categories). The bar chart shows the number of positive classifications for the selected labels over time with different granularity options. We train one classification model for each label and show the accuracy and the development of the F1-scores with an increasing number of training samples.

The lower part of the Forum 4.0 interface lists the actual user comments for exploration and annotation. With a full-text search, the domain expert can further filter the comment results. The list contains the comment text, the timestamp, and a column for each selected label. Each label column

[1]https://forum40.informatik.uni-hamburg.de/git/

[2]https://forum40.informatik.uni-hamburg.de/demo.mp4

[3]https://www.derstandard.at/

Figure 1: Main user interface of Forum 4.0.

has two sub-columns. The first sub-column with the person symbol shows either existing human annotations when logged out or the own annotations when logged in. A logged-in user can correct the automatic classification or annotate comments as a positive or negative sample for the selected labels. The second sub-column with the robot icon shows binary labels and confidence scores. The domain expert has three sorting options for the classifications: (1) positives first, (2) negatives first, (3) uncertain first (circle with tick mark). Forum 4.0 supports finding positive samples for rare comment labels by suggesting semantically similar user comments. Thereby, Forum 4.0 employs the rapid annotation approach to quickly retrieve additional positive samples for a specific comment label.

3 Architecture

We describe Forum 4.0's container-based architecture and its machine learning pipelines.

3.1 Container-based Architecture

Forum 4.0 is composed of containers, interacting with each other via a restful API. Figure 2 outlines a UML deployment diagram.

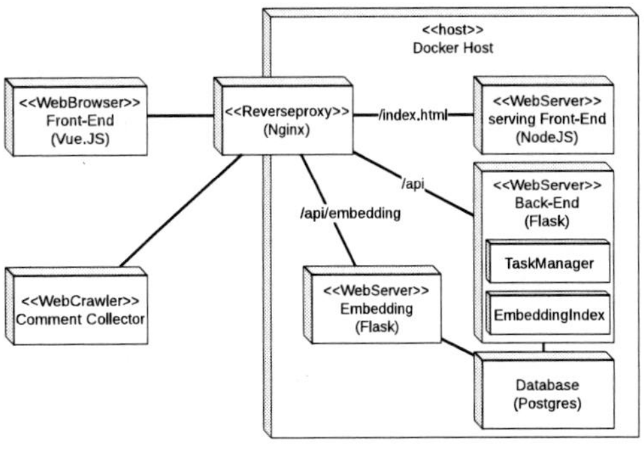

Figure 2: Forum 4.0's container architecture.

The *Comment Collector* aggregates user comments from various sources, including media sites, app stores, and social media. Forum 4.0 currently contains the "One Million Posts Corpus" and imports comments from the Google Play store and the German news site SPIEGEL Online[4].

The client accessing Forum 4.0's web page requests the *Reverse Proxy*, which forwards the requests depending on the URL path to the responsible container. The first request loads the single page application (Flanagan and Like, 2006) from the *Front-End* web server, which further communicates via a restful API with the Back-End container.

The containers on the Docker host are only accessible from the outside through the reverse proxy for security. The *Back-End* provides the restful API. It invokes all machine learning, NLP, and embedding tasks via a task manager in isolated processes as they are time-consuming and would exceed the HTTP request time out. It further calculates the comment embedding index and queries the database. The *Embedding Container* calculates the embeddings for newly imported user comments. This container can also run on a dedicated host to calculate the embeddings with GPU support.

After login, the *Back-End* issues a JSON web token (Jánoky et al., 2018) for the *Front-End*. All sensitive API endpoints of the *Back-End* are protected and require a valid JSON web token in the request's body. Protected actions include the comment and document import, the creation of new labels, and posting annotations.

3.2 Machine Learning Pipelines

Two essential parts of the architecture are the Model Training Pipeline (Figure 3a) and the Comment Import Pipeline (Figure 3b).

The Model Training Pipeline applies supervised machine learning, and active learning strategies (Settles, 2012) to improve the comment classification continuously. To define a label and train a model for the automatic classification, the domain expert must first log in and create a new label. Domain experts can select the new label from the menu and start annotating samples. The domain expert is the human in the loop (Bailey and Chopra, 2018), who annotates and enlarges the training set to improve the automatic classification iteratively.

Annotators can sort the user comments according to the uncertainty score to keep the annotation process most rewarding (Andersen et al., 2020). Forum 4.0 uses the label probability as the uncertainty value. Uncertain instances are those whose classification is the least confident, i.e. $P(c|d) \approx 0.5$ for comment d belonging to class c.

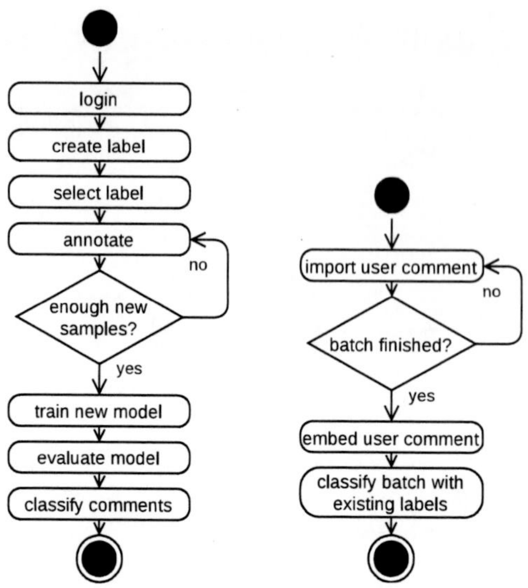

(a) The Model Training Pipeline. (b) The Comment Import Pipeline.

Figure 3: Machine Learning Pipelines

Forum 4.0 provides rapid annotation techniques to support and accelerate the collection of training samples. Forum 4.0 lists semantically similar comments to an existing comment based on the similarity of the comment embeddings. In case the annotator found a positive training example, chances are higher that semantically similar user comments are also positive user comments, which the annotator can quickly check.

We can adjust the number of required new training samples, which trigger the training of a new model. After each annotation, Forum 4.0 checks whether enough new training samples are available to invoke (re-)training of the model. The task manager executes each model training as a dedicated process, logs its training, and records the evaluation results. Forum 4.0 evaluates each model using tenfold cross-validation (Stone, 1974) to determine the classification performance. The newly trained model classifies all other user comments, which are not part of the training set, and Forum 4.0 persists its classification scores for that label.

The Data Import Pipeline enables the import and processing of new user comments. After importing a new user comment batch, the task manager triggers the embedding process, which calculates the embeddings for the imported user comments.

[4] `https://spiegel.de/`

Forum 4.0 employs transfer learning (Howard and Ruder, 2018) by using the embeddings of well-established pre-trained language models, for example, BERT embeddings (Devlin et al., 2019), as machine learning features for the classification model. Subsequently, all existing models classify the new user comment batch.

4 Machine Learning Experiments

To preliminary evaluate the applicability of Forum 4.0 and the performance of its machine learning models, we conducted experiments with comments from news sites and app stores. For the online journalism domain, we used the One Million Post (OMP) corpus (Schabus et al., 2017). It consists of ~1M German user comments submitted to the Austrian newspaper DER STANDARD, partly annotated by forum moderators. For the app store domain, we used an existing annotated app review dataset (ARD) (Stanik et al., 2019).

We used 9,336 annotated German comments (1,625 positives and 7,711 negatives) regarding OMP's "personal story" label. These user comments share the users' personal stories regarding the respective topic, including experiences and anecdotes. We used 6,406 annotated English app reviews (1,437 positives and 4,969 negatives) regarding the ARD's "bug report" label. In bug reports, users describe problems with the app that should be fixed, such as a crash, an erroneous behavior, or a performance issue.

We simulated the human annotator, who gradually annotates a batch of user comments, triggering a new training and evaluation cycle. We trained the classifier on the training set and evaluated the model on the remaining comments. We started our first training with ten samples and triggered new training for every ten new annotations.

Forum 4.0 allows random sampling and uncertainty sampling for new annotations, which we compared in our experiments. With random sampling, we randomly chose and added ten new samples to our training set. With uncertainty sampling, we added the user comments for which the classifier's output is closest to 0.5. We stopped adding more user comments to the training set as soon as the balanced accuracy score converged.

We evaluated the classification model on the remaining user comments after each training, using the *balanced accuracy*, *F1-score*, and the Receiver Operating Characteristics (*ROC-AUC*) metrics.

For the comment embeddings, we used two different multi-lingual pre-trained language models to embed the comments: (1) BERT (Devlin et al., 2019) is based on a transformer architecture, which learns contextual relations between sub-(word) units in a text. We used an average token embedding of the four last layers of the BERT model as the comment embeddings. (2) Sentence-BERT (S-BERT) (Reimers and Gurevych, 2019) is based on a modification of the BERT network and infers semantically meaningful sentence embeddings. We used a lightweight logistic regression model as a classifier due to performance requirements for quick updates of machine labels during human-in-the-loop coding. To assess the feasibility of our architecture, we further timed the model's training and evaluation. To mitigate the noise of our results, we performed 50 rounds for each experiment. The line plots show the average results of all rounds and the standard deviation.

5 Experiments Results

Figure 4 shows the balanced accuracy, ROC-AUC, and F1-scores for all our classification experiments. Overall, all classification metrics improve with increasing training data. Additionally, the uncertainty sampling strategy outperforms random sampling, and the S-BERT embeddings outperform the BERT embeddings given the same sampling strategy. All evaluation metrics significantly improve within the first 100 training samples and converge afterward.

On the OMP dataset, we achieved a balanced accuracy of 0.86 with 100 training samples using uncertainty sampling and S-BERT embeddings. With 500 training samples, we reached 0.91. Within the first 100 training samples, S-BERT embeddings outperformed the BERT embeddings. We achieved a similar F1-score as Schabus et al. (2017) with ~50 training samples (0.70) and outperformed their model using 500 training samples with an F1-score of 0.82. On the app review dataset, we achieved a balanced accuracy of 0.92, a ROC-AUC of 0.96, and an F1-score of 0.85 using 500 training samples.

Figure 5 shows the time measurements for training the logistic regression model. In all cases, the training size has a linear increase. Overall, the training time with the S-BERT embeddings (0.1s for 500 samples) takes a shorter time than training with the BERT embeddings (0.4s for 500 samples) on both datasets. We also measured the classification time on the remaining test set, which takes less

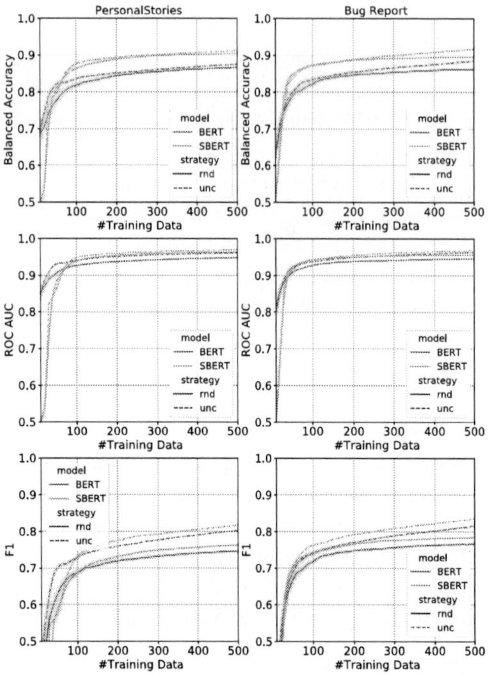

Figure 4: Balanced accuracy (top), ROC-AUC (center), and F1-scores (bottom) for all classification experiments on the OMP (left column) and the ARD (right column).

than ∼3ms on the OMP (∼8,000 test samples) and the ARD (∼6,000 test samples) dataset.

6 Related Work

Previous work in the app development domain automatically analyzed comments on apps including, app reviews (Guzman and Maalej, 2014; Dhinakaran et al., 2018; Harman et al., 2012) and tweets (Guzman et al., 2016; Williams and Mahmoud, 2017), to understand and summarize users' needs and support development decisions (Stanik and Maalej, 2019). A typical analysis goal is to reduce the noisy user feedback and classify the remaining ones into bug reports, feature requests, and experience reports (Maalej et al., 2016a).

Similarly, in online journalism, previous work aimed to reduce noise and hate speech (Gao and Huang, 2017), identify high-quality contributions (Park et al., 2016a; Diakopoulos, 2015; Wang and Diakopoulos, 2021), summarize the audiences' sentiment (Wang et al., 2013), or identify comments, which address journalistic aspects (Häring et al., 2018). Park et al. (2018) and Fast et al. (2016) developed a prototype, which supports the analysis of documents and comments regarding a custom concept based on seed terms.

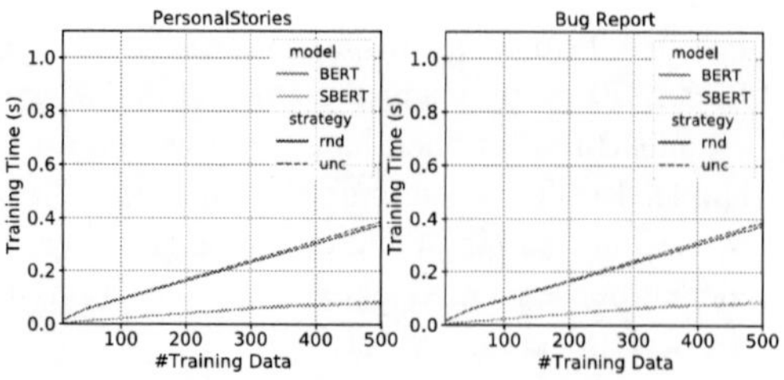

Figure 5: Training time of the logistic regression model.

Forum 4.0 builds upon this previous work and features a domain-independent comment analysis framework for domain experts. Domain experts can create or reuse useful labels, annotate user comments regarding these labels, and train machine-learning models, which automatically classify the comments for further utilization.

7 Conclusion

We presented Forum 4.0, an open-source framework to semi-automatically analyze user comments in various domains including, online journalism and app store. Domain experts can flexibly define or reuse comment analysis dimensions as classification labels in our framework. Forum 4.0's architecture leverages state-of-the-art semantic text embeddings with a lightweight logistic regression model to address the labeling flexibility and the scalability requirements for an application to millions of user comments. Forum 4.0 starts a new model training after the domain expert annotated additional comments for the concerned label. Forum 4.0 evaluates each new model and classifies the remaining user comments for further analysis.

We achieved promising results with our machine learning experiments in both domains with different semantic embedding and sampling strategies already after n $\geq$ 100 annotations with a low training time ($t = 0.1s$). Our evaluation suggests that Forum 4.0 can also be applied at a larger scale with millions of user comments.

Acknowledgments

This work is partly funded by the Hamburg's *ahoi.digital* program in the Forum 4.0 project.

References

Jakob Smedegaard Andersen, Tom Schöner, and Walid Maalej. 2020. Word-Level Uncertainty Estimation for Black-Box Text Classifiers using RNNs. In *Proceedings of the 28th International Conference on Computational Linguistics*, pages 5541–5546, Barcelona, Spain (Online). International Committee on Computational Linguistics.

Katherine Bailey and Sunny Chopra. 2018. Few-shot text classification with pre-trained word embeddings and a human in the loop. *arXiv preprint arXiv:1804.02063*.

Jacob Devlin, Ming-Wei Chang, Kenton Lee, and Kristina Toutanova. 2019. BERT: Pre-training of deep bidirectional transformers for language understanding. In *Proceedings of the 2019 Conference of the North American Chapter of the Association for Computational Linguistics: Human Language Technologies, Volume 1 (Long and Short Papers)*, pages 4171–4186, Minneapolis, MN, USA. Association for Computational Linguistics.

Venkatesh T. Dhinakaran, Raseshwari Pulle, Nirav Ajmeri, and Pradeep K. Murukannaiah. 2018. App Review Analysis Via Active Learning: Reducing Supervision Effort without Compromising Classification Accuracy. In *2018 IEEE 26th International Requirements Engineering Conference (RE)*, pages 170–181, Banff, AB. IEEE.

Nicholas Diakopoulos. 2015. Picking the NYT picks: Editorial criteria and automation in the curation of online news comments. *#ISOJ*, page 147.

Ethan Fast, Binbin Chen, and Michael S. Bernstein. 2016. Empath: Understanding topic signals in large-scale text. In *Proceedings of the 2016 CHI Conference on Human Factors in Computing Systems*, pages 4647–4657, San Jose, CA, USA. ACM.

David Flanagan and Will Sell Like. 2006. Javascript: The definitive guide, 5th.

Lena Frischlich, Svenja Boberg, and Thorsten Quandt. 2019. Comment Sections as Targets of Dark Participation? Journalists' Evaluation and Moderation of Deviant User Comments. *Journalism Studies*, 20(14):2014–2033.

Lei Gao and Ruihong Huang. 2017. Detecting online hate speech using context aware models. In *Proceedings of the International Conference Recent Advances in Natural Language Processing, RANLP 2017*, pages 260–266, Varna, Bulgaria. INCOMA Ltd.

Emitza Guzman, Rana Alkadhi, and Norbert Seyff. 2016. A Needle in a Haystack: What Do Twitter Users Say about Software? In *2016 IEEE 24th International Requirements Engineering Conference (RE)*, pages 96–105, Beijing, China.

Emitza Guzman and Walid Maalej. 2014. How Do Users Like This Feature? A Fine Grained Sentiment Analysis of App Reviews. In *2014 IEEE 22nd Int. Requirements Engineering Conf. (RE)*, pages 153–162, Karlskrona, Sweden.

Marlo Haering, Muneera Bano, Didar Zowghi, Matthew Kearney, and Walid Maalej. 2021. Automating the evaluation of education apps with app store data. *IEEE Transactions on Learning Technologies (TLT)*, pages 1–12.

Marlo Häring, Wiebke Loosen, and Walid Maalej. 2018. Who is Addressed in This Comment?: Automatically Classifying Meta-Comments in News Comments. *Proc. ACM Hum.-Comput. Interact.*, 2(CSCW):67:1–67:20.

Mark Harman, Yue Jia, and Yuanyuan Zhang. 2012. App Store Mining and Analysis: MSR for App Stores. In *Proceedings of the 9th IEEE Working Conference on Mining Software Repositories*, MSR '12, pages 108–111, Piscataway, NJ, USA. IEEE, IEEE Press.

Jeremy Howard and Sebastian Ruder. 2018. Universal Language Model Fine-tuning for Text Classification. In *Proceedings of the 56th Annual Meeting of the Association for Computational Linguistics (Volume 1: Long Papers)*, pages 328–339, Melbourne, Australia. Association for Computational Linguistics.

László Viktor Jánoky, János Levendovszky, and Péter Ekler. 2018. An analysis on the revoking mechanisms for JSON Web Tokens. *International Journal of Distributed Sensor Networks*, 14(9):155014771880153.

Anna Sophie Kümpel and Nina Springer. 2016. Qualität kommentieren. Die Wirkung von Nutzerkommentaren auf die Wahrnehmung journalistischer Qualität. *Studies in Communication — Media*, 5(3):353–366.

Wiebke Loosen, Marlo Häring, Zijad Kurtanović, Lisa Merten, Julius Reimer, Lies van Roessel, and Walid Maalej. 2018. Making sense of user comments: Identifying journalists' requirements for a comment analysis framework. *SCM Studies in Communication and Media*, 6(4):333–364.

Walid Maalej, Zijad Kurtanović, Hadeer Nabil, and Christoph Stanik. 2016a. On the automatic classification of app reviews. *Requirements Engineering*, 21(3):311–331.

Walid Maalej, Maleknaz Nayebi, Timo Johann, and Guenther Ruhe. 2016b. Toward data-driven requirements engineering. *IEEE Software*, 33(1):48–54.

Daniel Martens and Walid Maalej. 2019. Release early, release often, and watch your users' emotions: Lessons from emotional patterns. *IEEE Software*, 36(5):32–37.

Teresa K. Naab, Dominique Heinbach, Marc Ziegele, and Marie-Theres Grasberger. 2020. Comments and Credibility: How Critical User Comments Decrease Perceived News Article Credibility. *Journalism Studies*, 21(6):783–801.

Dennis Pagano and Walid Maalej. 2013. User feedback in the appstore: An empirical study. In *2013 21st IEEE International Requirements Engineering Conference (RE)*, pages 125–134, Rio de Janeiro, Brasil.

Deokgun Park, Seungyeon Kim, Jurim Lee, Jaegul Choo, Nicholas Diakopoulos, and Niklas Elmqvist. 2018. ConceptVector: Text visual analytics via interactive lexicon building using word embedding. *IEEE transactions on visualization and computer graphics*, 24(1):361–370.

Deokgun Park, Simranjit Sachar, Nicholas Diakopoulos, and Niklas Elmqvist. 2016a. Supporting comment moderators in identifying high quality online news comments. In *Proceedings of the 2016 CHI Conference on Human Factors in Computing Systems*, CHI '16, page 1114–1125, New York, NY, USA. Association for Computing Machinery.

Deokgun Park, Simranjit Sachar, Nicholas Diakopoulos, and Niklas Elmqvist. 2016b. Supporting comment moderators in identifying high quality online news comments. In *Proceedings of the 2016 CHI Conference on Human Factors in Computing Systems*, pages 1114–1125, San Jose, CA, USA. ACM.

Nils Reimers and Iryna Gurevych. 2019. Sentence-BERT: Sentence embeddings using Siamese BERT-networks. In *Proceedings of the 2019 Conference on Empirical Methods in Natural Language Processing and the 9th International Joint Conference on Natural Language Processing (EMNLP-IJCNLP)*, pages 3982–3992, Hong Kong, China. Association for Computational Linguistics.

Dietmar Schabus, Marcin Skowron, and Martin Trapp. 2017. One million posts: A data set of German online discussions. In *Proceedings of the 40th International ACM SIGIR Conference on Research and Development in Information Retrieval*, pages 1241–1244, Miyazaki, Japan. ACM Press.

Burr Settles. 2012. *Active Learning*. Morgan & Claypool Publishers.

Nina Springer, Ines Engelmann, and Christian Pfaffinger. 2015. User comments: Motives and inhibitors to write and read. *Information, Communication & Society*, 18(7):798–815.

Christoph Stanik, Marlo Haering, and Walid Maalej. 2019. Classifying multilingual user feedback using traditional machine learning and deep learning. In *IEEE 27th International Requirements Engineering Conference Workshops*, pages 220–226, Jeju Island, South Korea.

Christoph Stanik and Walid Maalej. 2019. Requirements intelligence with OpenReq analytics. In *2019 IEEE 27th International Requirements Engineering Conference (RE)*, pages 482–483, Jeju Island, South Korea.

Mervyn Stone. 1974. Cross-Validatory Choice and Assessment of Statistical Predictions. *Journal of the Royal Statistical Society: Series B (Methodological)*, 36(2):111–133.

Changbo Wang, Zhao Xiao, Yuhua Liu, Yanru Xu, Aoying Zhou, and Kang Zhang. 2013. SentiView: Sentiment Analysis and Visualization for Internet Popular Topics. *IEEE Transactions on Human-Machine Systems*, 43(6):620–630.

Yixue Wang and Nicholas Diakopoulos. 2021. The Role of New York Times Picks in Comment Quality and Engagement. In *Hawaii International Conference on System Sciences*, page to appear, Hawaii.

Grant Williams and Anas Mahmoud. 2017. Mining Twitter feeds for software user requirements. In *2017 IEEE 25th International Requirements Engineering Conference (RE)*, pages 1–10, Lisbon, Portugal.

SLTEV: Comprehensive Evaluation of Spoken Language Translation

Ebrahim Ansari
Charles University MFF ÚFAL
and IASBS

Ondřej Bojar
Charles University
MFF ÚFAL

Barry Haddow
University of Edinburgh

Mohammad Mahmoudi
IASBS

surname@ufal.mff.cuni.cz except bhaddow@ed.ac.uk

Abstract

Automatic evaluation of Machine Translation (MT) quality has been investigated over several decades. Spoken Language Translation (SLT), especially when simultaneous, needs to consider additional criteria and does not have a standard evaluation procedure and a widely used toolkit. To fill the gap, we introduce SLTEV, an open-source tool for assessing SLT in a comprehensive way. SLTEV reports the quality, latency, and stability of an SLT candidate output based on the time-stamped transcript and reference translation into a target language. For quality, we rely on sacreBLEU which provides MT evaluation measures such as chrF or BLEU. For latency, we propose two new scoring techniques. For stability, we extend the previously defined measures with a normalized Flicker in our work. We also propose a new averaging of older measures.

A preliminary version of SLTEV was used in the IWSLT 2020 SHARED TASK. Moreover, a growing collection of test datasets directly accessible by SLTEV are provided for system evaluation comparable across papers.

1 Introduction

Spoken Language Translation (SLT), i.e. translation of human speech across languages, is an application at least as important as Machine Translation (MT). Many approaches have been examined so far, ranging from translation of transcript chunks (Fügen et al., 2008; Bangalore et al., 2012) to fully end-to-end, speech-to-speech neural systems, (Jia et al., 2019). In recent years, simultaneous translation systems aim at behavior similar to human interpreters, digesting and producing an infinite sequence of words. Some systems (Grissom II et al., 2014; Gu et al., 2017; Arivazhagan et al., 2019b; Press and Smith, 2018; Xiong et al., 2019; Ma et al., 2019; Zheng et al., 2019) do not consider any revision of their outputs and can be evaluated in two main criteria: quality and latency, allowing users to trade a bigger delay (including waiting for more input text) for a more accurate translation. Simultaneous translation systems aimed at automatic subtitling (Niehues et al., 2016; Müller et al., 2016; Niehues et al., 2018; Arivazhagan et al., 2019a) may revise their outputs, demanding a new evaluation measure: the stability, i.e. the amount of revision. Trading these qualities for one another is again possible: It is obvious that if a system creates the translations with a longer Delay or revises them more (higher Flicker), the quality of the final translation (i.e., the output text) can be better. Given the existence of three evaluation criteria and a multitude of possible definitions for each of them, the need for some robust and standard metrics to evaluate SLT is inevitable.

Recently, the MT community tackled a similar problem (i.e., the inconsistency in the reporting of BLEU scores) by introducing a tool named sacreBLEU (Post, 2018) with a canonical implementation of the widely user metric. In this work, we propose SLTEV,[1] an open-source tool to calculate the quality of SLT systems based on three different criteria: translation quality, latency, and stability, in a standardized way. Furthermore, we complement SLTEV with a growing collection of freely-available test sets for Automatic Speech Recognition (ASR), MT and SLT for a number of languages, so that these technologies can be evaluated in comparable settings, similarly to what the WMT news test sets (Barrault et al., 2020) offer in MT.

2 Related Work

SLTEV is designed to be versatile enough to score automatic SLT as well as transcribed human interpretation. Shimizu et al. (2014) are probably the first to score human interpretation with automatic

[1] https://github.com/ELITR/SLTev

Proceedings of the 16th Conference of the European Chapter of the Association for Computational Linguistics: System Demonstrations, pages 71–79
April 19 - 23, 2021. ©2021 Association for Computational Linguistics

P	0	50	Good	P	60	0	50	Gut
P	0	65	Good mor	P	80	0	65	Guten Morgen!
P	0	119	Good morning how	P	130	0	119	Guten wie morgen
P	0	195	Good morning. How are you?	P	201	0	195	Guten Morgen! Wie geht es dir?
C	0	102	Good morning.	C	201	0	102	Guten Morgen!
P	102	218	How are you? I	P	220	102	218	Wie geht es dir? Ich
C	102	195	How are you?	C	220	102	195	Wie geht es dir?
P	195	239	I am	P	245	195	239	Ich bin
...	...	...	...	...	...	...	...	...
(a) Time-stamped transcript				(b) SLT candidate output				

Figure 1: Example of SLTEV file formats. All timestamps in centiseconds.

measures but they segment the output manually and assess only the quality using BLEU (Papineni et al., 2002), WER (Matusov et al., 2005), TER (Snover et al., 2006), and RIBES (Isozaki et al., 2010).

Most SLT evaluations require sentence segmentation of the candidate to match the reference one. Using *mwerSegmenter* (Matusov et al., 2005), they re-segment the candidate automatically, minimizing WER against the reference. We complement this approach with time-based segmentation.

Niehues et al. (2016) introduced the retranslation approach to simultaneous SLT, and define latency based on the time between a word expected and actually displayed, considering only the final version of the word, not early revisions. They did not provide any evaluation of stability. However, in follow-up work (Niehues et al., 2018) they assess the level of SLT stability (i.e., the number of corrections) by measuring the overlap between consecutive updates. As soon as a word is changed, all the following words are counted as updated, suggesting than any word change forces the user to reread all the rest.

Gu et al. (2017) consider two versions of delay when assessing their reinforcement learning based simultaneous SLT model: Average Proportion (of waiting compared to producing words) and Consecutive Wait (the silence duration so far), and prescribe a target value for each of them to steer the learning, also balancing it with quality estimated by smoothed BLEU (Lin and Och, 2004). Since their model does not allow corrections, they do not require a measure of stability.

The delay measures of (Gu et al., 2017) were criticised by Ma et al. (2019) when they introduced their wait-k model. They defined a measure Average Lag (AL), which measures how far, in words, the translation is behind an ideal wait-k model. Since wait-k does not allow corrections, they do not need a stability measure. AL was improved by Cherry and Foster (2019), with Differentiable Average Lag (DAL), which not only is differentiable, but fixes some undesirable behaviour of AL around sentence boundaries. However DAL, like AL, is defined in terms of word count and on segmented text (although it could be extended to fix these shortcomings).

Arivazhagan et al. (2019a) extended the retranslation model of Niehues et al. (2016), and so needed a measure of stability. For evaluation, they check the output of ASR and the output of the MT system as recorded over time in their simple logging system. They assess the quality, latency, and stability (i.e., Flicker). The quality is estimated using BLEU after *mwerSegmenter* re-segmentation. For the assessment of latency (translation lag) and stability (the number of erased tokens in temporary translations per final target token, "Normalized Erasure" in the paper), they do not use any segmentation at all and instead calculate the scores for ten-minute long audio chunks.

The closest to our work is *SIMULEVAL* (Ma et al., 2020), a client-server toolkit measuring the latency of SLT including any network effects between the evaluated system (client) and the mock user (SIMULEVAL server). SIMULEVAL offers a nice visualization interface but the required client-server approach may be unsuitable for research prototypes solving SLT only partially. Most importantly, updates of output (Flicker) are not supported and no test set for reproducible scoring is provided.

3 Input Formats

SLTEV can evaluate separate ASR and MT systems as well as cascaded and end-to-end SLT systems. We focus on SLT here. Three input files are used for SLT evaluation: a time-stamped golden transcript in the source language (Section 3.1), a reference translation (or translations in multi-reference format; Section 3.2) and candidate output (Section 3.3) in the target language. The intermediate ASR output can be provided as the fourth input file to calculate the accuracy of the ASR system if it was part of the cascade (Section 3.3).

3.1 File Format of Time-Stamped Transcript

Time-stamped transcript files (golden transcript and ASR output, both in the source language) are line-oriented text files. The lines contain gradually growing "partial" (P) segments, until the segment is "completed" (C);[2] see Figure 1 (a). All lines are equipped with timestamps measured in centiseconds from the start of the sound file: the *start time* and *end time* of the given segment.

Partial segments add one or more words at once, sub-word updates are possible but SLTEV is not ready for them. We expect that a well-aligned transcript file (such as the golden reference) should have the exact same number of completed (C) segments as the reference translation file.

3.2 File Format of the Reference Translation

Each line of the reference translation file shows the translation of the corresponding complete (C) line in the time-stamped transcript file. The number of lines in the reference translation thus equals the number of C lines in the time-stamped transcript.

3.3 File Format of ASR, MT or SLT Output

An ideal SLT system will report all the details as in Figure 1 (b): partial (P) vs. complete (C) flag, the *display time* when the segment was produced and the *start time* and *end time* indicating the time span supposedly containing the given message. Partial segments allow the user to provide finer timing information and to provide revisions of outputs,[3] trading lower Delay for higher Flicker.

For the output of ASR, the segment is in the source language. For the output of MT as the second step or the output of end-to-end SLT, the segment is in the target language but the start and end timestamps should reflect the span in the *original* sound, i.e., when the source was uttered.

Again, "P"artial candidates allow for revising the output so far, and the "C"omplete candidates are required. The concatenation of all the (C) segments corresponds to the whole document but their number and segmentation may differ from the reference one. If the ASR, MT or SLT outputs lack some of the timestamp information, zeros should be used for format consistency. SLTEV then calculates limited results based on the provided information.

[2] We use the term "segment" for generality but typically, completed segments correspond to sentences. Usually, a sentence ends with a punctuation mark.

[3] Revisions do not occur in golden transcripts but we want the same format to suit both golden and candidate outputs.

4 Proposed Metrics

In this section, all evaluation metrics and strategies introduced in our evaluation framework are described. Our evaluations are based on three criteria: latency, stability, and the quality of MT outputs.

4.1 Delay to Assess Latency

In our point of view, *latency* should reflect the delay with which the recipient receives the message from the sender. Words are reasonable smallest units that the message can be broken into but there is not a 1-to-1 correspondence between source and target words. Ideally, we would know the alignment between the source words and the words in the candidate translation, and we would have exact timing information for both.

Defining latency as the sum of how long we had to wait for a target word given the time of the corresponding source word[4] would render the values dependent on the language pair in question. When translating, e.g., from English into German, all verbs in subordinate clauses would increase the value of latency because they simply have to appear at the end of the German clause, so the recipient receives them much later than their English source verb was uttered. We thus focus on the extra delay beyond what the language pair implies.

We propose two approaches to delay calculation. Both measure the difference between the time that a target word was displayed and an estimate of when it should have been displayed but differ in estimating the expected display time:[5] The first one is proportional while the second one uses automatic word alignment between the source and reference translations to account for word order differences across languages, see Sections 4.2.1 and 4.2.2 below.

Both approaches produce a two-dimensional matrix $T(i, j)$ storing the expected time of the jth word of the reference sentence i.

[4] In this calculation, we only include reference words which also appear in the SLT output, because they are the only ones that contribute meaningfully to the delay. A reference word which never appears in the SLT output has an infinite delay, and a word appearing in the output but not in the reference is, well, unexpected, so no delay makes sense. We acknowledge that this design decision brings the risk of gaming Delay by producing words different from the reference; this would however lead to a clear loss in Quality.

[5] If the reference translation was also time-stamped at the word level, this estimate would be easier to make but we do not assume that. We are however experimenting with reference *interpretation*, where a human interpreter produces translation in time. This exploration is left for future.

Given T, our Delay is calculated by summing differences between the expected word emission time in T and the reported emission time in the segments of the SLT candidate output. If the SLT system predicts the word earlier than its expected time, its delay is set to zero, not negative.

4.2 Segmentation Strategies

Note that delay calculation operates on the individual *segments* of the transcript. We use two segmentation strategies to re-segment the candidate to match the reference as described below. In both cases, only completed (C) segments are re-segmented, but partial (P) segments are used to estimate timings of individual words.

Time-Based Segmentation: Using the *starting time* and *ending time* of each segment in the reference transcript, the corresponding words in the SLT output are selected (i.e., words with their time between the *starting* and *ending time*). To compensate for minor timing errors, we expand this span by one word in each direction in the SLT output. All the words from the starting to the ending one are taken as the candidate segment, see Figure 3.

Word-Based Segmentation: We use the 1-1 correspondence between segments in the golden source transcript and reference translation. We apply *mwerSegmenter* to re-segment candidate translation (the concatenation of "C" segments) to match exactly the segmentation of the reference translation and then work with source–candidate segment pairs. Again, minor *mwerSegmenter* errors are compensated by expanding candidate segments by one word at each end, see Figure 4.

4.2.1 Proportional Delay Calculation

We need to attribute an "expected" time to each word in the reference and then compare it with the time the word was displayed in SLT output.

For proportional delay calculation, we first estimate the timing of each source word based on partial (P) segments[6] in the golden transcript and then attribute these times to words in the reference translation, proportionally along the sequence of words.[7] This is an oversimplification because word alignment is not monotonic and also because the reference translation was created in written form with access to the full source, so even the first word of the reference may well be influenced by some late source words.

Formally, we are populating table $T(i,j)$ with expected times of jth word in the ith segment of the reference translation. First we estimate the times of *source* words in the ith complete segment of the golden transcript based on *starting* and *ending time* of the (partial) source segment where the source word first appeared. For example, when three new words are added in a partial segment ending at t_2 compared to the previous partial segment which ended at t_1, we need to divide the time interval (t_1, t_2) among these three words. We estimate that the first word appeared at $t_1 + (t_2 - t_1)/3$, the second one at $t_1 + 2 * (t_2 - t_1)/3$ and the last one at t_2.

This source word timing is transferred to the target word timing proportionally. With l_i being the length in words of source segment i and m_i the corresponding reference length, we denote $P = j * l_i/m_i$ as a shortcut for the fractional index of the *source* word which corresponds to the j word in the reference segment i. We then define:

$$T(i,j) = t_{\lfloor P \rfloor} + \left((t_{\lceil P \rceil} - t_{\lfloor P \rfloor}) * (P - \lfloor P \rfloor) \right) \quad (1)$$

t_x is the expected time of the xth word of the *source* sentence i and $\lfloor \cdot \rfloor$, $\lceil \cdot \rceil$ round to the nearest integer.

To see how the proportional delay calculation works in practice, consider the example in Figure 2. We first need to estimate the times for each source word. Since the first source partial segment consists of 3 words, we estimate the times of "We","would" and "like" by dividing the 760–827 interval into three equal parts, whereas the other source words are assigned to the end timestamps of their time intervals, since they appear in individual increments. The estimated source times are therefore:

We	would	like	to	introduce	our	company
782	805	827	846	919	961	1062

In order to perform the proportional delay calculation, we note that the source-reference length ratio is 7/6, so that the value P in Equation 1 is equal to $7j/6$ for the jth reference word. Substituting into Equation 1 gives the following expected times for the reference words:

Wir	würden	gern	unser	Unternehmen	vorstellen
786	812	836	895	954	1062

Comparing the expected times with the actual times in Figure 2b, we can see that the total delay

[6] Partial segments provide more accurate word-level timing but we can and do resort to equidistant division of the complete segment time span if golden transcript lacks partial segments.

[7] Word lengths could be used as an additional refinement.

P	760	827	We would like
P	760	847	We would like to
P	760	919	We would like to introduce
P	760	961	We would like to introduce our
C	760	1062	We would like to introduce our company.

(a) Time-stamped golden source transcript

P	800	720	760	Wir
P	870	720	860	Wir möchten
P	910	720	905	Wir möchten vorstellen
C	1200	720	1110	Wir möchten unser Unternehmen vorstellen.

(b) SLT output

Wir würden gern unser Unternehmen vorstellen

(c) Reference

Figure 2: Example for proportional delay calculation.

is given by:

$$(800-786)+(1200-895)+(1200-954)+0 = 565$$

In this sum, "würden" and "gern" are not included at all because they do not appear in the hypothesis. "unser" and "Unternehmen" both appeared at the same time 1200 and "vorstellen" has zero delay, since it arrives at 910, *before* its expected time.

4.2.2 Delay Calculation using Alignments

The SLT system should not be expected to produce any word earlier than the reference produced it, e.g. due to grammatical constraints of the target language. (If it does, we do not penalize it. Giving a bonus for such an earlier appearance is yet to be considered.)

We use the word alignment between source words (which are time-stamped in the golden transcript) and reference words to attribute timing information to reference words, see "Table T" in the middle of Figures 3 and 4.

We set the expected time of each reference word as the maximum of the timestamp of the last source word aligned to this reference word (the reference translator "had to wait" for the respective source piece of information) and the expected time of the preceding reference word (the translator "had to postpone" any words he or she already knew until the missing one became available to respect target language grammatical order). With this definition, any SLT system is allowed to "wait" for the source or "postpone" its output without penalization same as the reference translator did. E.g. the word "vorstellen" (introduce) is expected at 1062 in the proportional delay calculation (upper Tables T). Based on alignment only, it would be expected at 919 (struck out in the figures), because that is the time when the aligned "introduce" appeared but we max it out to 1062 because the preceding "Unternehmen" (company) was available only at 1062.

For "unser", SLTEV selects the expected time as the maximum between 895 (its expectation time under proportional delay) and 961 (the time that its aligned source word "our" appeared) . In other words, SLTEV gives more time to the SLT system to display the "unser" because its aligned word is output a bit later than the proportional expectation of "unser". Under the alignment-based delay, we do not expect that the word will be output earlier than its alignment indicates.

Technically, we rely on automatic word alignments by MGIZA (Gao and Vogel, 2008) which is a multi-threaded version of GIZA++ (Och and Ney, 2003), aligning the completed segments of the golden source transcript and the reference translation. The effect of alignment errors on the reliability of the evaluation is yet to be explored.

4.2.3 Multi-Reference Delay Calculation

With multiple references, we create a separate table T for each and calculate the delay of each segment individually, taking the minimum across all references. The final delay is the sum of these minima. We use this strategy for both delay calculation methods and both segmentation strategies introduced above.

4.3 Flicker to Assess Stability

For systems that revise their outputs, (in)stability of the output is important because it could distract the user. Following Niehues et al. (2018), "flicker" commonly reflects the number of words after the first difference between two consecutive output updates. We report two variants of Flicker:

Average revision count per segment:

The revision count RC for each completed ("C") segment k is calculated as: $RC_k = \sum_{i=2}^{n_k} (|s_{i-1}| - |\text{LCP}(s_{i-1}, s_i)|)$, where s_i is the ith partial segment preceding the current complete segment k and n_k is the number of partial segments between complete segments $k-1$ and k. LCP gets the longest common prefix. If segment k has no

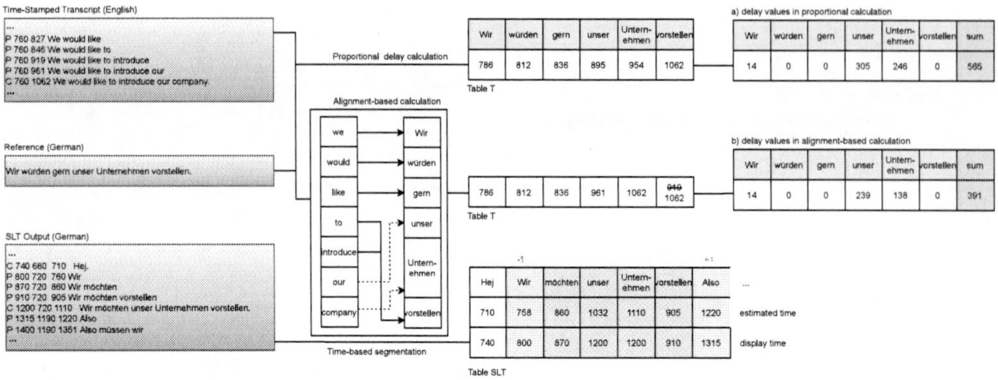

Figure 3: Time-based segmentation for proportional (a) and alignment-based (b) delay calculation. Using time-stamped transcript and reference translation, Table T is pre-computed. Then using timings in SLT output, word-level timestamps are estimated ("Table SLT"). The a) and b) value of delay is the sum of differences between expected word times in Table T and display times in Table SLT.

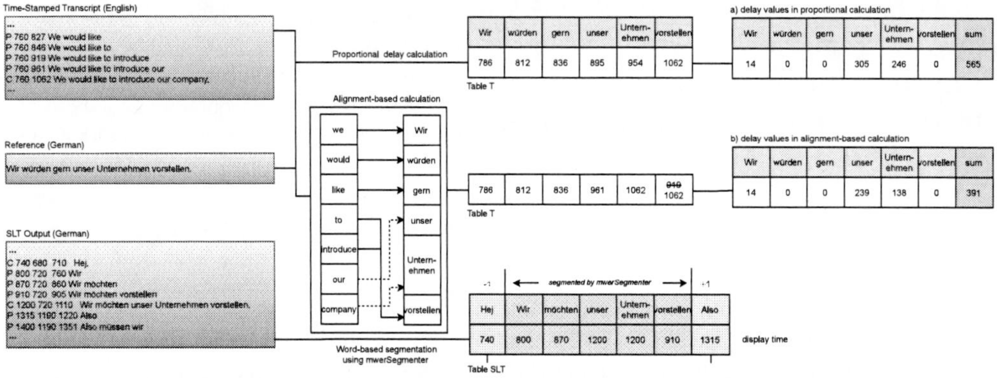

Figure 4: Word-based segmentation (*mwerSegmenter*) for proportional (a) and alignment-based (b) delay calculation. The main difference from Figure 3 is in finding the span of words that form the candidate segment, i.e. contribute to "Table SLT". Table SLT now needs to contain only display time of words.

preceding partial segments, RC_k is zero. Average revision count is calculated as: $\frac{1}{K}\sum_{k=1}^{K} RC_k$, where K is the total number of complete segments.

A disadvantage of this strategy is that if the system makes a little change (1-2 chars) at the start of the sentence, it gets heavily penalised.

Normalized revision count:

Similar to Arivazhagan et al. (2019a), normalized revision is the total revision count ($\sum_{k=1}^{K} RC_k$) divided by the output length (sum of lengths of completed segments).

4.4 sacreBLEU to Assess Quality

Early versions of SLTEV used NLTK (Bird et al., 2009) implementation of BLEU but it behaved badly on empty segments and used a less common tokenization scheme. We fully switched to sacreBLEU, calculating three variants of the score: (1) disregarding segmentation, we concatenate all completed segments and evaluate them against the concatenated reference as if it was a single segment, (2) force the candidate to reference segmentation using *mwerSegmenter* and calculate standard BLEU, (3) time-span quality. The third option divides the whole document into chunks of a fixed duration (e.g. 30 seconds) and treats all words in that span as a single segment. These single-segment BLEUs are reported, providing an estimate of translation quality over time, and also averaged for a summary.

If multiple references are available, we pass them to sacreBLEU which follows standard multi-reference BLEU and chrF calculations. In word-based segmentation, we use the first reference as the basis for *mwerSegmenter* re-segmentation.

5 A Growing Test Set

To allow for continued and comparable evaluation of SLT by the research community, we create and keep extending a publicly available dataset which contains source audio, time-stamped golden transcripts and reference translations for different types of inputs called `elitr-testset`.[8] The dataset currently focuses on European languages, as needed by the ELITR project (Bojar et al., 2020, 2021), but it is designed to be easily extensible in both languages and domains. With the help of commit IDs, full reproducibility of evaluations is ensured, even as the dataset will be growing.

In simple words, the `elitr-testset` is an assorted collection of documents, with inputs and expected outputs for ASR, MT and/or SLT systems. We expect our users to pick a relevant subset of these documents depending on their application needs and evaluate on this subset. For comparability, we standardize some of these selections by introducing the concept of "indices".

Each index is simply a file list of documents and it is also versioned in the `elitr-testset`. For example, we provide indices of documents which are good for purposes like: (1) SLT of English into Czech/German in the auditing domain, (2) English ASR in the computational linguistics domain, and (3) Czech/German ASR, regardless of the domain.

Another feature of `elitr-testset` is a collection of automatic checks that verify formal integrity of the documents (e.g. character encoding, line ends, number of lines) before every commit.

All datasets included in `elitr-testset` are free for public use but some indices include confidential files.

SLTEV can be used as a stand-alone tool to evaluate ASR, MT or SLT using source, candidate and reference files you provide, or it can be used very conveniently with `elitr-testset`. Running `SLTev -g index-name` will provide you with input files that your system should process and a second run of SLTEV will report your system's scores for the given index.

5.1 Practical Check

A preliminary version of SLTEV evaluated the submitted systems participating in the "Non-Native Speech Translation" shared task of IWSLT 2020 (Ansari et al., 2020). We ran simplified configurations of SLTEV (i.e., without calculating Delay and Flicker) for systems that did not provide enough information in their output.

Five teams from three institutions took part in the IWSLT 2020 SHARED TASK which was designed for English-Czech and English-German language pairs. The main test sets used in the shared task (and now included in `elitr-testset`) were:

Antrecorp: 37 files each of which is an up to 90-second mock business presentation given by high school students in very noisy conditions. None of the speakers is a native speaker of English and their English contains many lexical, grammatical and pronunciation errors as well as disfluencies due to the spontaneous nature of the speech.

KhanAcademy: six files each of which is an educational video. The speaker is not a native speaker of English but his accent is generally rather good.

SAO: six files illustrating interpretation needs of the Supreme Audit Office of the Czech Republic. The speakers' nationality affects their accent. The Dutch file is a recording of a remote conference call with further distorted sound quality.

6 Conclusion

In this paper, we introduced SLTEV, a framework for comprehensive and fine-grained evaluation of the output of simultaneous SLT systems, i.e., systems for live speech translation, and their components (ASR, MT). In contrast to text translation systems, simultaneous SLT systems cannot be judged just based on translation quality. For example, if the system waits for the whole sentence to be analyzed and processed, the translation quality will likely be better but the high latency may not be acceptable to the end user. SLTEV evaluates quality, latency, and stability (the number of corrections the system makes). In order to tackle the problem of the output segmentation, we proposed a new time-based segmentation method, in addition to the classical re-segmentation strategy of *mwerSegmenter*.

We complement the release of SLTEV with `elitr-testset`, a publicly available dataset of source speech and reference translations, so that truly comparable evaluations are available for the research community. SLTEV directly accesses this growing collection for easy and comparable scoring of your systems in various domains. We used a preliminary version of SLTEV to evaluate systems in one of the IWSLT 2020 shared tasks.

[8] `https://github.com/ELITR/elitr-testset/`

Acknowledgments

This work has received funding from the European Union's Horizon 2020 Research and Innovation Programme under Grant Agreement No 825460 (ELITR) and the grant 19-26934X (NEUREM3) of the Czech Science Foundation.

The authors are grateful to Rishu Kumar, Dominik Macháček, Sangeet Sagar, Matúš Žilinec, and other members of the ELITR project for their valuable technical support on SLTEV and their help in improving it.

References

Ebrahim Ansari, Amittai Axelrod, Nguyen Bach, Ondřej Bojar, Roldano Cattoni, Fahim Dalvi, Nadir Durrani, Marcello Federico, Christian Federmann, Jiatao Gu, Fei Huang, Kevin Knight, Xutai Ma, Ajay Nagesh, Matteo Negri, Jan Niehues, Juan Pino, Elizabeth Salesky, Xing Shi, Sebastian Stüker, Marco Turchi, Alexander Waibel, and Changhan Wang. 2020. FINDINGS OF THE IWSLT 2020 EVALUATION CAMPAIGN. In *Proceedings of the 17th International Conference on Spoken Language Translation*, pages 1–34, Online. Association for Computational Linguistics.

Naveen Arivazhagan, Colin Cherry, Te I, Wolfgang Macherey, Pallavi Baljekar, and George Foster. 2019a. Re-translation strategies for long form, simultaneous, spoken language translation.

Naveen Arivazhagan, Colin Cherry, Wolfgang Macherey, Chung-Cheng Chiu, Semih Yavuz, Ruoming Pang, Wei Li, and Colin Raffel. 2019b. Monotonic infinite lookback attention for simultaneous machine translation. In *Proceedings of the 57th Annual Meeting of the Association for Computational Linguistics*, pages 1313–1323, Florence, Italy. Association for Computational Linguistics.

Srinivas Bangalore, Vivek Kumar Rangarajan Sridhar, Prakash Kolan, Ladan Golipour, and Aura Jimenez. 2012. Real-time incremental speech-to-speech translation of dialogs. In *Proceedings of the 2012 Conference of the North American Chapter of the Association for Computational Linguistics: Human Language Technologies*, pages 437–445, Montréal, Canada. Association for Computational Linguistics.

Loïc Barrault, Magdalena Biesialska, Ondřej Bojar, Marta R. Costa-jussà, Christian Federmann, Yvette Graham, Roman Grundkiewicz, Barry Haddow, Matthias Huck, Eric Joanis, Tom Kocmi, Philipp Koehn, Chi-kiu Lo, Nikola Ljubešić, Christof Monz, Makoto Morishita, Masaaki Nagata, Toshiaki Nakazawa, Santanu Pal, Matt Post, and Marcos Zampieri. 2020. Findings of the 2020 conference on machine translation (wmt20). In *Proceedings of the Fifth Conference on Machine Translation*, pages 1–55, Online. Association for Computational Linguistics.

Steven Bird, Ewan Klein, and Edward Loper. 2009. *Natural Language Processing with Python*, 1st edition. O'Reilly Media, Inc.

Ondřej Bojar, Dominik Macháček, Sangeet Sagar, Otakar Smrž, Jonáš Kratochvíl, Ebrahim Ansari, Dario Franceschini, Chiara Canton, Ivan Simonini, Thai-Son Nguyen, Felix Schneider, Sebastian Stücker, Alex Waibel, Barry Haddow, Rico Sennrich, and Philip Williams. 2020. ELITR: European live translator. In *Proceedings of the 22nd Annual Conference of the European Association for Machine Translation*, pages 463–464, Lisboa, Portugal. European Association for Machine Translation.

Ondřej Bojar, Dominik Macháček, Sangeet Sagar, Otakar Smrž, Jonáš Kratochvíl, Peter Polák, Ebrahim Ansari, Mohammad Mahmoudi, Rishu Kumar, Dario Franceschini, Chiara Canton, Ivan Simonini, Thai-Son Nguyen, Felix Schneider, Sebastian Stüker, Alex Waibel, Barry Haddow, Rico Sennrich, and Philip Williams. 2021. ELITR Multilingual Live Subtitling: Demo and Strategy. In *Proceedings of the System Demonstrations of the 16th Conference of the European Chapter of the Association for Computational Linguistics*, Kyiv, Ukraine. Association for Computational Linguistics.

Colin Cherry and George Foster. 2019. Thinking slow about latency evaluation for simultaneous machine translation.

Christian Fügen, Alex Waibel, and Muntsin Kolss. 2008. Simultaneous translation of lectures and speeches. *Springer Netherlands, Machine Translation, MTSN 2008, Springer, Netherland*, 21(4).

Qin Gao and Stephan Vogel. 2008. Parallel implementations of word alignment tool. *Association for Computational Linguistic*, 8(1):49—-57.

Alvin Grissom II, He He, Jordan Boyd-Graber, John Morgan, and Hal Daumé III. 2014. Don't until the final verb wait: Reinforcement learning for simultaneous machine translation. In *Proceedings of the 2014 Conference on Empirical Methods in Natural Language Processing (EMNLP)*, pages 1342–1352, Doha, Qatar. Association for Computational Linguistics.

Jiatao Gu, Graham Neubig, Kyunghyun Cho, and Victor O.K. Li. 2017. Learning to translate in real-time with neural machine translation. In *Proceedings of the 15th Conference of the European Chapter of the Association for Computational Linguistics: Volume 1, Long Papers*, pages 1053–1062, Valencia, Spain. Association for Computational Linguistics.

Hideki Isozaki, Tsutomu Hirao, Kevin Duh, Katsuhito Sudoh, and Hajime Tsukada. 2010. Automatic evaluation of translation quality for distant language pairs. In *Proceedings of the 2010 Conference on Empirical Methods in Natural Language Processing*, pages 944–952, Cambridge, MA. Association for Computational Linguistics.

Ye Jia, Ron J. Weiss, Fadi Biadsy, Wolfgang Macherey, Melvin Johnson, Zhifeng Chen, and Yonghui Wu. 2019. Direct speech-to-speech translation with a sequence-to-sequence model.

Chin-Yew Lin and Franz Josef Och. 2004. Automatic evaluation of machine translation quality using longest common subsequence and skip-bigram statistics. In *Proceedings of the 42nd Annual Meeting of the Association for Computational Linguistics (ACL-04)*, pages 605–612, Barcelona, Spain.

Mingbo Ma, Liang Huang, Hao Xiong, Renjie Zheng, Kaibo Liu, Baigong Zheng, Chuanqiang Zhang, Zhongjun He, Hairong Liu, Xing Li, Hua Wu, and Haifeng Wang. 2019. STACL: Simultaneous translation with implicit anticipation and controllable latency using prefix-to-prefix framework. In *Proceedings of the 57th Annual Meeting of the Association for Computational Linguistics*, pages 3025–3036, Florence, Italy. Association for Computational Linguistics.

Xutai Ma, Mohammad Javad Dousti, Changhan Wang, Jiatao Gu, and Juan Pino. 2020. SIMULEVAL: An evaluation toolkit for simultaneous translation. In *Proceedings of the 2020 Conference on Empirical Methods in Natural Language Processing: System Demonstrations*, pages 144–150, Online. Association for Computational Linguistics.

Evgeny Matusov, Gregor Leusch, Oliver Bender, and Hermann Ney. 2005. Evaluating machine translation output with automatic sentence segmentation. In *International Workshop on Spoken Language Translation*, pages 148–154, Pittsburgh, PA, USA.

Markus Müller, Thai Son Nguyen, Jan Niehues, Eunah Cho, Bastian Krüger, Thanh-Le Ha, Kevin Kilgour, Matthias Sperber, Mohammed Mediani, Sebastian Stüker, and Alex Waibel. 2016. Lecture translator - speech translation framework for simultaneous lecture translation. In *Proceedings of the 2016 Conference of the North American Chapter of the Association for Computational Linguistics: Demonstrations*, pages 82–86, San Diego, California. Association for Computational Linguistics.

J. Niehues, T. S. Nguyen, E. Cho, T.-L. Ha, K. Kilgour, M. Müller, M. Sperber, S. Stüker, and A. Waibel. 2016. Dynamic transcription for low-latency speech translation. In *17th Annual Conference of the International Speech Communication Association, INTERSPEECH 2016; Hyatt Regency San FranciscoSan Francisco; United States; 8 September 2016 through 16 September 2016*, volume 08-12-September-2016 of *Proceedings of the Annual Conference of the International Speech Communication Association. Ed. : N. Morgan*, pages 2513–2517. International Speech and Communication Association, Baixas.

Jan Niehues, Ngoc-Quan Pham, Thanh-Le Ha, Matthias Sperber, and Alex Waibel. 2018. Low-latency neural speech translation. In *Interspeech 2018*, Hyderabad, India.

Franz Josef Och and Hermann Ney. 2003. A systematic comparison of various statistical alignment models. *Computational Linguistics*, 29(1):19–51.

Kishore Papineni, Salim Roukos, Todd Ward, and Wei-Jing Zhu. 2002. Bleu: a method for automatic evaluation of machine translation. In *Proceedings of the 40th Annual Meeting of the Association for Computational Linguistics*, pages 311–318, Philadelphia, Pennsylvania, USA. Association for Computational Linguistics.

Matt Post. 2018. A call for clarity in reporting BLEU scores. In *Proceedings of the Third Conference on Machine Translation: Research Papers*, pages 186–191, Belgium, Brussels. Association for Computational Linguistics.

Ofir Press and Noah A. Smith. 2018. You may not need attention.

Hiroaki Shimizu, Graham Neubig, Sakriani Sakti, Tomoki Toda, and Satoshi Nakamura. 2014. Collection of a simultaneous translation corpus for comparative analysis. In *Proceedings of the Ninth International Conference on Language Resources and Evaluation (LREC'14)*, pages 670–673, Reykjavik, Iceland. European Language Resources Association (ELRA).

Matthew Snover, Bonnie Dorr, Richard Schwartz, Linnea Micciulla, and John Makhoul. 2006. A study of translation edit rate with targeted human annotation. In *In Proceedings of Association for Machine Translation in the Americas*, pages 223–231.

Hao Xiong, Ruiqing Zhang, Chuanqiang Zhang, Zhongjun Hea, Hua Wu, and Haifeng Wang. 2019. Dutongchuan: Context-aware translation model for simultaneous interpreting.

Baigong Zheng, Renjie Zheng, Mingbo Ma, and Liang Huang. 2019. Simpler and faster learning of adaptive policies for simultaneous translation. In *Proceedings of the 2019 Conference on Empirical Methods in Natural Language Processing and the 9th International Joint Conference on Natural Language Processing (EMNLP-IJCNLP)*, pages 1349–1354, Hong Kong, China. Association for Computational Linguistics.

Trankit: A Light-Weight Transformer-based Toolkit for Multilingual Natural Language Processing

Minh Van Nguyen, Viet Lai, Amir Pouran Ben Veyseh, Thien Huu Nguyen
Department of Computer and Information Science
University of Oregon, Eugene, Oregon, USA
{minhnv,vietl,apouranb,thien}@cs.uoregon.edu

Abstract

We introduce **Trankit**, a light-weight **Tran**sformer-based Tool**kit** for multilingual Natural Language Processing (NLP). It provides a trainable pipeline for fundamental NLP tasks over 100 languages, and 90 pretrained pipelines for 56 languages. Built on a state-of-the-art pretrained language model, Trankit significantly outperforms prior multilingual NLP pipelines over sentence segmentation, part-of-speech tagging, morphological feature tagging, and dependency parsing while maintaining competitive performance for tokenization, multi-word token expansion, and lemmatization over 90 Universal Dependencies treebanks. Despite the use of a large pretrained transformer, our toolkit is still efficient in memory usage and speed. This is achieved by our novel plug-and-play mechanism with Adapters where a multilingual pretrained transformer is shared across pipelines for different languages. Our toolkit along with pretrained models and code are publicly available at: `https://github.com/nlp-uoregon/trankit`. A demo website for our toolkit is also available at: `http://nlp.uoregon.edu/trankit`. Finally, we create a demo video for Trankit at: `https://youtu.be/q0KGP3zGjGc`.

1 Introduction

Many efforts have been devoted to developing multilingual NLP systems to overcome language barriers (Aharoni et al., 2019; Liu et al., 2019a; Taghizadeh and Faili, 2020; Zhu, 2020; Kanayama and Iwamoto, 2020; Nguyen and Nguyen, 2021). A large portion of existing multilingual systems has focused on downstream NLP tasks that critically depend on upstream linguistic features, ranging from basic information such as token and sentence boundaries for raw text to more sophisticated structures such as part-of-speech tags, morphological features, and dependency trees of sentences (called fundamental NLP tasks). As such, building effective multilingual systems/pipelines for fundamental upstream NLP tasks to produce such information has the potentials to transform multilingual downstream systems.

There have been several NLP toolkits that concerns multilingualism for fundamental NLP tasks, featuring spaCy[1], UDify (Kondratyuk and Straka, 2019), Flair (Akbik et al., 2019), CoreNLP (Manning et al., 2014), UDPipe (Straka, 2018), and Stanza (Qi et al., 2020). However, these toolkits have their own limitations. spaCy is designed to focus on speed, thus it needs to sacrifice the performance. UDify and Flair cannot process raw text as they depend on external tokenizers. CoreNLP supports raw text, but it does not offer state-of-the-art performance. UDPipe and Stanza are the recent toolkits that leverage word embeddings, i.e., word2vec (Mikolov et al., 2013) and fastText (Bojanowski et al., 2017), to deliver current state-of-the-art performance for many languages. However, Stanza and UDPipe's pipelines for different languages are trained separately and do not share any component, especially the embedding layers that account for most of the model size. This makes their memory usage grow aggressively as pipelines for more languages are simultaneously needed and loaded into the memory (e.g., for language learning apps). Most importantly, none of such toolkits have explored contextualized embeddings from pretrained transformer-based language models that have the potentials to significantly improve the performance of the NLP tasks, as demonstrated in many prior works (Devlin et al., 2019; Liu et al., 2019b; Conneau et al., 2020).

In this paper, we introduce **Trankit**, a multilingual Transformer-based NLP Toolkit that over-

[1] `https://spacy.io/`

Proceedings of the 16th Conference of the European Chapter of the Association for Computational Linguistics: System Demonstrations, pages 80–90
April 19 - 23, 2021. ©2021 Association for Computational Linguistics

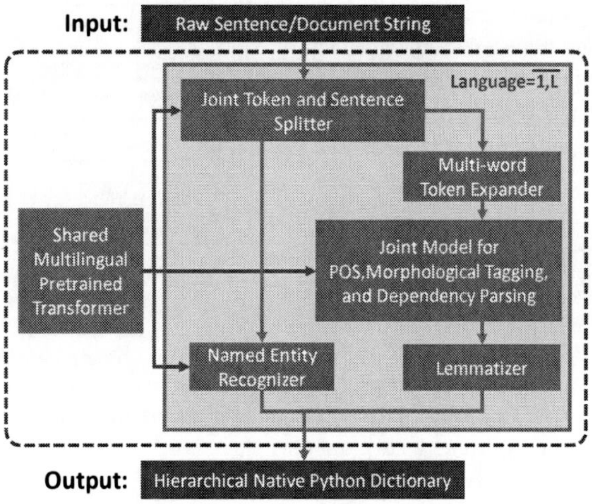

Figure 1: Overall architecture of Trankit. A single multilingual pretrained transformer is shared across three components (pointed by the red arrows) of the pipeline for different languages.

comes such limitations. Our toolkit can process raw text for fundamental NLP tasks, supporting 56 languages with 90 pre-trained pipelines on 90 treebanks of the Universal Dependency v2.5 (Zeman et al., 2019). By utilizing the state-of-the-art multilingual pretrained transformer *XLM-Roberta* (Conneau et al., 2020), Trankit advances state-of-the-art performance for sentence segmentation, part-of-speech (POS) tagging, morphological feature tagging, and dependency parsing while achieving competitive or better performance for tokenization, multi-word token expansion, and lemmatization over the 90 treebanks. It also obtains competitive or better performance for named entity recognition (NER) on 11 public datasets.

Unlike previous work, *our token and sentence splitter is wordpiece-based* instead of character-based to better exploit contextual information, which are beneficial in many languages. Considering the following sentence:

> *"John Donovan from Argghhh! has put out a excellent slide show on what was actually found and fought for in Fallujah."*

As such, Trankit correctly recognizes this as a single sentence while character-based sentence splitters of Stanza and UDPipe are easily fooled by the exclamation mark *"!"*, treating it as two separate sentences. To our knowledge, this is the first work to successfully build a wordpiece-based token and sentence splitter that works well for 56 languages.

Figure 1 presents the overall architecture of Trankit pipeline that features three novel transformer-based components for: (i) the joint token and sentence splitter, (ii) the joint model for POS tagging, morphological tagging, dependency parsing, and (iii) the named entity recognizer. One potential concern for our use of a large pretrained transformer model (i.e., *XML-Roberta*) in Trankit involves GPU memory where different transformer-based components in the pipeline for one or multiple languages must be simultaneously loaded into the memory to serve multilingual tasks. This could extensively consume the memory if different versions of the large pre-trained transformer (finetuned for each component) are employed in the pipeline. As such, we introduce a novel plug-and-play mechanism with Adapters to address this memory issue. Adapters are small networks injected inside all layers of the pretrained transformer model that have shown their effectiveness as a lightweight alternative for the traditional finetuning of pretrained transformers (Houlsby et al., 2019; Peters et al., 2019; Pfeiffer et al., 2020a,b). In Trankit, a set of adapters (for transfomer layers) and task-specific weights (for final predictions) are created for each transformer-based component for each language while only one single large multilingual pretrained transformer is shared across components and languages. Adapters allow us to learn language-specific features for tasks. During training, the shared pretrained transformer is fixed while only the adapters and task-specific weights are updated. At inference time, depending on the language of the input text and the current active component, the corresponding trained adapter and task-specific weights are activated and plugged into the pipeline to process the input. This mechanism not only solves the memory problem but also substantially reduces the training time.

2 Related Work

There have been works using pre-trained transformers to build models for character-based word segmentation for Chinese (Yang, 2019; Tian et al., 2020; Che et al., 2020); POS tagging for Dutch, English, Chinese, and Vietnamese (de Vries et al., 2019; Tenney et al., 2019; Tian et al., 2020; Che et al., 2020; Nguyen and Nguyen, 2020); morphological feature tagging for Estonian and Persian (Kittask et al., 2020; Mohseni and Tebbifakhr, 2019); and dependency parsing for English and Chinese (Tenney et al., 2019; Che et al., 2020). However, all of these works are only developed for some specific language, thus potentially unable to support and scale to the multilingual setting.

Some works have designed multilingual transformer-based systems via multilingual training on the combined data of different languages (Tsai et al., 2019; Kondratyuk and Straka, 2019; Üstün et al., 2020). However, multilingual training is suboptimal (see Section 5). Also, these systems still rely on external resources to perform tokenization and sentence segmentation, thus unable to consume raw text. To our knowedge, this is the first work to successfully build a multilingual transformer-based NLP toolkit where different transformer-based models for many languages can be simultaneously loaded into GPU memory and process raw text inputs of different languages.

3 Design and Architecture

Adapters. Adapters play a critical role in making Trankit memory- and time-efficient for training and inference. Figure 2 shows the architecture and the location of an adapter inside a layer of transformer. We use the adapter architecture proposed by (Pfeiffer et al., 2020a,b), which consists of two projection layers Up and Down (feed-forward networks), and a residual connection.

$$c_i = \text{AddNorm}(r_i), h_i = \text{Up}(\text{ReLU}(\text{Down}(c_i))) + r_i \quad (1)$$

where r_i is the input vector from the transformer layer for the adapter and h_i is the output vector for the transformer layer i. During training, all the weights of the pretrained transformer (i.e., gray

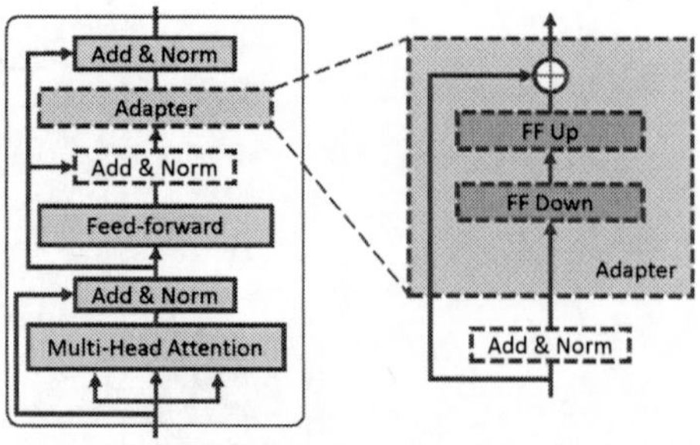

Figure 2: **Left**: location of an adapter (green box) inside a layer of the pretrained transformer. Gray boxes represent the original components of a transformer layer. **Right**: the network architecture of an adapter.

boxes) are fixed and only the adapter weights of two projection layers and the task-specific weights outside the transformer (for final predictions) are updated. As demonstrated in Figure 1, Trankit involves six components described as follows.

Multilingual Encoder with Adapters. This is our core component that is shared across different transformer-based components for different languages of the system. Given an input raw text s, we first split it into substrings by spaces. Afterward, Sentence Piece, a multilingual subword tokenizer (Kudo and Richardson, 2018; Kudo, 2018), is used to further split each substring into wordpieces. By concatenating wordpiece sequences for substrings, we obtain an overall sequence of wordpieces $\mathbf{w} = [w_1, w_2, \ldots, w_K]$ for s. In the next step, $\mathbf{w}$ is fed into the pretrained transformer, which is already integrated with adapters, to obtain the wordpiece representations:

$$x_{1:K}^{l,m} = \text{Transformer}(w_{1:K}; \theta_{AD}^{l,m}) \quad (2)$$

Here, $\theta_{AD}^{l,m}$ represents the adapter weights for language l and component m of the system. As such, we have specific adapters in all transformer layers for each component m and language l. Note that if K is larger than the maximum input length of the pretrained transformer (i.e., 512), we further divide $\mathbf{w}$ into consecutive chunks; each has the length less than or equal to the maximum length. The pretrained transformer is then applied over each chunk to obtain a representation vector for each wordpiece in $\mathbf{w}$. Finally, $x_{1:K}^{l,m}$ will be sent to component m to perform the corresponding task.

Joint Token and Sentence Splitter. Given the wordpiece representations $x_{1:K}^{l,m}$ for this component, each vector $x_i^{l,m}$ for $w_i \in \mathbf{w}$ will be consumed by a feed-forward network with softmax in the end to predict if w_i is the end of a single-word token, the end of a multi-word token, or the end of a sentence. The predictions for all wordpieces in $\mathbf{w}$ will then be aggregated to determine token, multi-word token, and sentence boundaries for s.

Multi-word Token Expander. This component is responsible for expanding each detected multi-word token (MWT) into multiple syntactic words[2]. We follow Stanza to deploy a character-based seq2seq model for this component. This decision is made based on our observation that the task is done best at character level, and the character-based model (with character embeddings) is very small.

Joint Model for POS Tagging, Morphological Tagging and Dependency Parsing. In Trankit, given the detected sentences and tokens/words, we use a single model to jointly perform POS tagging, morphological feature tagging and dependency parsing at sentence level. Joint modeling mitigates error propagation, saves the memory, and speedups the system. In particular, given a sentence, the representation for each word is computed as the average of its wordpieces' transformer-based representations in $x_{1:K}^{l,m}$. Let $t_{1:N} = [t_1, t_2, \ldots, t_N]$ be the representations of the words in the sentence. We compute the following vectors using feed-forward networks FFN$_*$:

$$r_{1:N}^{upos} = \text{FFN}_{upos}(t_{1:N}), r_{1:N}^{xpos} = \text{FFN}_{xpos}(t_{1:N})$$
$$r_{1:N}^{ufeats} = \text{FFN}_{ufeats}(t_{1:N}), r_{0:N}^{dep} = [x_{cls}; \text{FFN}_{dep}(t_{1:N})]$$

Vectors for the words in $r_{1:N}^{upos}$, $r_{1:N}^{xpos}$, $r_{1:N}^{ufeats}$ are then passed to a softmax layer to make predictions for UPOS, XPOS, and UFeats tags for each word. For dependency parsing, we use the classification token <s> to represent the root node, and apply Deep Biaffine Attention (Dozat and Manning, 2017) and the Chu-Liu/Edmonds algorithm (Chu, 1965; Edmonds, 1967) to assign a syntactic head and the associated dependency relation to each word in the sentence.

Lemmatizer. This component receives sentences and their predicted UPOS tags to produce the canonical form for each word. We also employ a character-based seq2seq model for this component as in Stanza.

[2]For languages (e.g., English, Chinese) that do not require MWT expansion, tokens and words are the same concepts.

Named Entity Recognizer. Given a sentence, the named entity recognizer determines spans of entity names by assigning a BIOES tag to each token in the sentence. We deploy a standard sequence labeling architecture using transformer-based representations for tokens, involving a feed-forward network followed by a Conditional Random Field.

4 Usage

Detailed documentation for Trankit can be found at: `https://trankit.readthedocs.io`.

Trankit Installation. Trankit is written in Python and available on PyPI: `https://pypi.org/project/trankit/`. Users can install our toolkit via pip using:

```
pip install trankit
```

Initialize a Pipeline. Lines 1-4 in Figure 3 shows how to initialize a pretrained pipeline for English; it is instructed to run on GPU and store downloaded pretrained models to the specified cache directory. Trankit will not download pretrained models if they already exist.

Multilingual Usage. Figure 3 shows how to initialize a multilingual pipeline and process inputs of different languages in Trankit:

```
1  from trankit import Pipeline
2
3  # initialize a multilingual pipeline
4  p = Pipeline(lang='english', gpu=True, cache_dir='./cache')
5  langs = ['arabic', 'chinese', 'dutch']
6  for lang in langs:
7          p.add(lang)
8
9  # tokenize English input
10 p.set_active('english')
11 en = p.tokenize('Rich was here before the scheduled time.')
12
13 # get ner tags for Arabic input
14 p.set_active('arabic')
15 ar = p.ner('[illegible]')
```

Figure 3: Multilingual pipeline initialization.

Basic Functions. Trankit can process inputs which are untokenized (raw) or pretokenized strings, at both sentence and document levels. Figure 4 illustrates a simple code to perform all the supported tasks for an input text. We organize Trankit's outputs into hierarchical native Python dictionaries, which can be easily inspected by users. Figure 5 demonstrates the outputs of the command line 6 in Figure 4.

Training your own Pipelines. Trankit also provides a trainable pipeline for 100 languages via the class `TPipeline`. This ability is inherited from

Treebank	System	Tokens	Sents.	Words	UPOS	XPOS	UFeats	Lemmas	UAS	LAS
Overall (90 treebanks)	**Trankit**	99.23	**91.82**	**99.02**	**95.65**	**94.05**	**93.21**	**94.27**	**87.06**	**83.69**
	Stanza	**99.26**	88.58	98.90	94.21	92.50	91.75	94.15	83.06	78.68
Arabic-PADT	**Trankit**	99.93	**96.59**	**99.22**	**96.31**	**94.08**	**94.28**	**94.65**	**88.39**	**84.68**
	Stanza	**99.98**	80.43	97.88	94.89	91.75	91.86	93.27	83.27	79.33
	UDPipe	99.98	82.09	94.58	90.36	84.00	84.16	88.46	72.67	68.14
Chinese-GSD	**Trankit**	**97.01**	**99.7**	**97.01**	**94.21**	**94.02**	**96.59**	**97.01**	**85.19**	**82.54**
	Stanza	92.83	98.80	92.83	89.12	88.93	92.11	92.83	72.88	69.82
	UDPipe	90.27	99.10	90.27	84.13	84.04	89.05	90.26	61.60	57.81
English-EWT	**Trankit**	98.48	**88.35**	98.48	**95.95**	**95.71**	**96.26**	96.84	**90.14**	**87.96**
	Stanza	**99.01**	81.13	**99.01**	95.40	95.12	96.11	**97.21**	86.22	83.59
	UDPipe	98.90	77.40	98.90	93.26	92.75	94.23	95.45	80.22	77.03
	spaCy	97.44	63.16	97.44	86.99	91.05	-	87.16	55.38	37.03
French-GSD	**Trankit**	**99.7**	**96.63**	**99.66**	**97.85**	-	**97.16**	**97.80**	**94.00**	**92.34**
	Stanza	99.68	94.92	99.48	97.30	-	96.72	97.64	91.38	89.05
	UDPipe	99.68	93.59	98.81	95.85	-	95.55	96.61	87.14	84.26
	spaCy	99.02	89.73	94.81	89.67	-	-	88.55	75.22	66.93
Spanish-Ancora	**Trankit**	99.94	**99.13**	99.93	**99.02**	**98.94**	**98.8**	**99.17**	**94.11**	**92.41**
	Stanza	**99.98**	99.07	**99.98**	98.78	98.67	98.59	99.19	92.21	90.01
	UDPipe	99.97	98.32	99.95	98.32	98.13	98.13	98.48	88.22	85.10
	spaCy	99.95	97.54	99.43	93.43	-	-	80.02	89.35	83.81

Table 1: Systems' performance on test sets of the Universal Dependencies v2.5 treebanks. Performance for Stanza, UDPipe, and spaCy is obtained using their public pretrained models. The overall performance for Trankit and Stanza is computed as the macro-averaged F1 over 90 treebanks. Detailed performance of Trankit for 90 supported treebanks can be found at our documentation page.

```
from trankit import Pipeline

p = Pipeline(lang='english', gpu=True, cache_dir='./cache')

doc = '''Hello! This is Trankit.'''
# perform all tasks on the input
all = p(doc)
```

Figure 4: A function performing all tasks on the input.

the XLM-Roberta encoder which is pretrained on those languages. Figure 6 illustrates how to train a token and sentence splitter with `TPipeline`.

Demo Website. A demo website for Trankit to support 90 pretrained pipelines is hosted at: `http://nlp.uoregon.edu/trankit`. Figure 7 shows its interface.

```
// Output
{
  'text': 'Hello! This is Trankit.', // input string
  'sentences': [ // list of sentences
    {
      'id': 1, 'text': 'Hello!', 'dspan': (0, 6), 'tokens': [...]
    },
    {
      'id': 2, // sentence index
      'text': 'This is Trankit.', 'dspan': (7, 23), // sentence span
      'tokens': [ // list of tokens
        {
          'id': 1, // token index
          'text': 'This', 'upos': 'PRON', 'xpos': 'DT',
          'feats': 'Number=Sing|PronType=Dem',
          'head': 3, 'deprel': 'nsubj', 'lemma': 'this', 'ner': 'O',
          'dspan': (7, 11), // document-level span of the token
          'span': (0, 4)    // sentence-level span of the token
        },
        {'id': 2...},
        {'id': 3...},
        {'id': 4...}
      ]
    }
  ]
}
```

Figure 5: Output from Trankit. Some parts are collapsed to improve visualization.

5 System Evaluation

5.1 Datasets & Hyper-parameters

To achieve a fair comparison, we follow Stanza (Qi et al., 2020) to train and evaluate all the models on the same canonical data splits of 90 Universal Dependencies treebanks v2.5 (UD2.5)[3] (Zeman et al., 2019), and 11 public NER datasets provided in the following corpora: AQMAR (Mohit et al., 2012), CoNLL02 (Tjong Kim Sang, 2002), CoNLL03 (Tjong Kim Sang and De Meulder, 2003), GermEval14 (Benikova et al., 2014), OntoNotes (Weischedel et al., 2013), and WikiNER (Nothman et al., 2012). Hyper-parameters for all models and datasets are selected based on the development data in this work.

5.2 Universal Dependencies performance

Table 1 compares the performance of Trankit and the latest available versions of other popular toolkits, including Stanza (v1.1.1) with current state-of-the-art performance, UDPipe (v1.2), and spaCy (v2.3) on the UD2.5 test sets. The performance for all systems is obtained using the official scorer

[3]We skip 10 treebanks whose languages are not supported by *XLM-Roberta*.

System	Tokens	Sents.	Words	UPOS	XPOS	UFeats	Lemmas	UAS	LAS
Trankit (plug-and-play with adapters)	**99.05**	**95.12**	**98.96**	**95.43**	**89.02**	**92.69**	**93.46**	**86.20**	**82.51**
Multilingual	96.69	88.95	96.35	91.19	84.64	88.10	90.02	72.96	68.66
No-adapters	95.06	89.57	94.08	88.79	82.54	83.76	88.33	66.63	63.11

Table 2: Model performance on 9 different treebanks (macro-averaged F1 score over test sets).

```
from trankit import TPipeline

tp = TPipeline(training_config={
        'task': 'tokenize',
        'save_dir': './saved_model',
        'train_txt_fpath': './train.txt',
        'train_conllu_fpath': './train.conllu',
        'dev_txt_fpath': './dev.txt',
        'dev_conllu_fpath': './dev.conllu'})

trainer.train()
```

Figure 6: Training a token and sentence splitter using the CONLL-U formatted data (Nivre et al., 2020).

of the CoNLL 2018 Shared Task[4]. On five illustrated languages, Trankit achieves competitive performance on tokenization, MWT expansion, and lemmatization. Importantly, Trankit outperforms other toolkits over all remaining tasks (e.g., POS and morphological tagging) in which the improvement boost is substantial and significant for sentence segmentation and dependency parsing. For example, English enjoys a 7.22% improvement for sentence segmentation, a 3.92% and 4.37% improvement for UAS and LAS in dependency parsing. For Arabic, Trankit has a remarkable improvement of 16.16% for sentence segmentation while Chinese observes 12.31% and 12.72% improvement of UAS and LAS for dependency parsing.

Over all 90 treebanks, Trankit outperforms the previous state-of-the-art framework Stanza in most of the tasks, particularly for sentence segmentation (+3.24%), POS tagging (+1.44% for UPOS and +1.55% for XPOS), morphological tagging (+1.46%), and dependency parsing (+4.0% for UAS and +5.01% for LAS) while maintaining the competitive performance on tokenization, multi-word expansion, and lemmatization.

5.3 NER results

Table 3 compares Trankit with Stanza (v1.1.1), Flair (v0.7), and spaCy (v2.3) on the test sets of 11 considered NER datasets. Following Stanza, we report the performance for other toolkits with their pretrained models on the canonical data splits if they are available. Otherwise, their best configurations are used to train the models on the same data splits (inherited from Stanza). Also, for the Dutch datasets, we retrain the models in Flair as those models (for Dutch) have been updated in version v0.7. As can be seen, Trankit obtains competitive or better performance for most of the languages, clearly demonstrating the benefit of using the pretrained transformer for multilingual NER.

Language	Corpus	Trankit	Stanza	Flair	spaCy
Arabic	AQMAR	**74.8**	74.3	74.0	-
Chinese	OntoNotes	**80.0**	79.2	-	69.3
Dutch	CoNLL02	**91.8**	89.2	91.3	73.8
	WikiNER	**94.8**	**94.8**	**94.8**	90.9
English	CoNLL03	92.1	92.1	**92.7**	81.0
	OntoNotes	**89.6**	88.8	89.0	85.4
French	WikiNER	92.3	**92.9**	92.5	88.8
German	CoNLL03	**84.6**	81.9	82.5	63.9
	GermEval14	**86.9**	85.2	85.4	68.4
Russian	WikiNER	92.8	**92.9**	-	-
Spanish	CoNLL02	**88.9**	88.1	87.3	77.5

Table 3: Performance (F1) on NER test sets.

System	GPU		CPU	
	UD	NER	UD	NER
Trankit	4.50×	1.36×	19.8×	31.5×
Stanza	3.22×	1.08×	10.3×	17.7×
UDPipe	-	-	4.30×	-
Flair	-	1.17×	-	51.8×

Table 4: Run time on processing the English EWT treebank and the English Ontonotes NER dataset. Measurements are done on an NVIDIA Titan RTX card.

Model Package	Trankit	Stanza
Multilingual Transformer	1146.9MB	-
Arabic	38.6MB	393.9MB
Chinese	40.6MB	225.2MB
English	47.9MB	383.5MB
French	39.6MB	561.9MB
Spanish	37.3MB	556.1MB
Total size	1350.9MB	2120.6MB

Table 5: Model sizes for five languages.

5.4 Speed and Memory Usage

Table 4 reports the relative processing time for UD and NER of the toolkits compared to spaCy's CPU processing time[5]. For memory usage comparison, we show the model sizes of Trankit and

[4]https://universaldependencies.org/conll18/evaluation.html

[5]spaCy can process 8140 tokens and 5912 tokens per second for UD and NER, respectively.

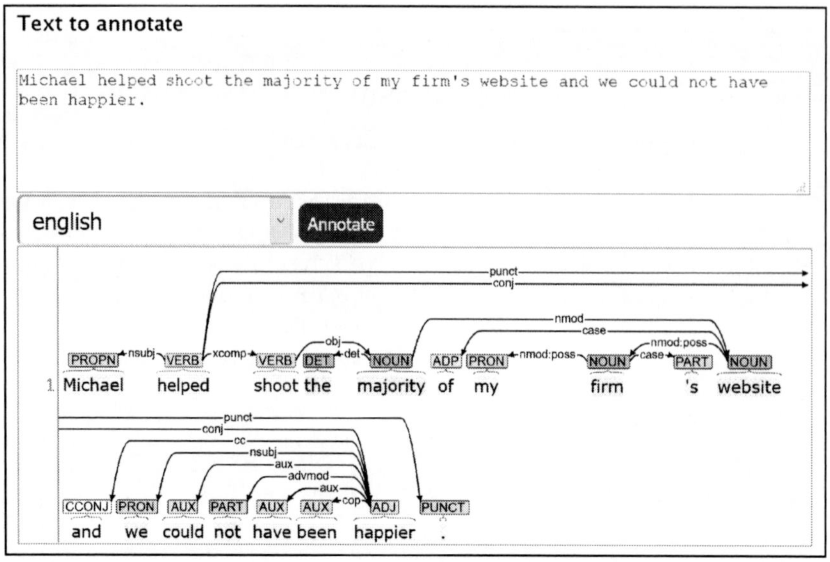

Figure 7: Demo website for Trankit.

Stanza for several languages in Table 5. As can be seen, besides the multilingual transformer, model packages in Trankit only take dozens of megabytes while Stanza consumes hundreds of megabytes for each package. This leads to the Stanza's usage of much more memory when the pipelines for these languages are loaded at the same time. In fact, Trankit only takes 4.9GB to load all the 90 pretrained pipelines for the 56 supported languages.

5.5 Ablation Study

This section compares Trankit with two other possible strategies to build a multilingual system for fundamental NLP tasks. In the first strategy (called "*Multilingual*"), we train a single pipeline where all the components in the pipeline are trained with the combined training data of all the languages. The second strategy (called "*No-adapters*") involves eliminating adapters from *XLM-Roberta* in Trankit. As such, in "*No-adapters*", pipelines are still trained separately for each language; the pretrained transformer is fixed; and only task-specific weights (for predictions) in components are updated during training.

For evaluation, we select 9 treebanks for 3 different groups, i.e., high-resource, medium-resource, and low-resource, depending on the sizes of the treebanks. In particular, the high-resource group includes Czech, Russian, and Arabic; the medium-resource group includes French, English, and Chinese; and the low-resource group involves Belarusian, Telugu, and Lithuanian. Table 2 compares the average performance of Trankit, "*Multilingual*", and "*No-adapters*". As can be seen, "*Multilingual*" and "*No-adapters*" are significantly worse than the proposed adapter-based Trankit. We attribute this to the fact that multilingual training might suffer from unbalanced sizes of treebanks, causing high-resource languages to dominate others and impairing the overall performance. For "*No-adapters*", fixing pretrained transformer might significantly limit the models' capacity for multiple tasks and languages.

6 Conclusion and Future Work

We introduce Trankit, a transformer-based multilingual toolkit that significantly improves the performance for fundamental NLP tasks, including sentence segmentation, part-of-speech, morphological tagging, and dependency parsing over 90 Universal Dependencies v2.5 treebanks of 56 different languages. Our toolkit is fast on GPUs and efficient in memory use, making it usable for general users. In the future, we plan to improve our toolkit by investigating different pretrained transformers such as mBERT and XLM-Roberta$_{large}$. We also plan to provide Named Entity Recognizers for more languages and add modules to perform more NLP tasks.

References

Roee Aharoni, Melvin Johnson, and Orhan Firat. 2019. Massively multilingual neural machine translation. In *Proceedings of the 2019 Conference of the North American Chapter of the Association for Computational Linguistics: Human Language Technologies, Volume 1 (Long and Short Papers)*, pages 3874–3884, Minneapolis, Minnesota. Association for Computational Linguistics.

Alan Akbik, Tanja Bergmann, Duncan Blythe, Kashif Rasul, Stefan Schweter, and Roland Vollgraf. 2019. FLAIR: An easy-to-use framework for state-of-the-art NLP. In *Proceedings of the 2019 Conference of the North American Chapter of the Association for Computational Linguistics (Demonstrations)*, pages 54–59, Minneapolis, Minnesota. Association for Computational Linguistics.

Darina Benikova, Chris Biemann, and Marc Reznicek. 2014. NoSta-d named entity annotation for German: Guidelines and dataset. In *Proceedings of the Ninth International Conference on Language Resources and Evaluation (LREC-2014)*, pages 2524–2531, Reykjavik, Iceland. European Languages Resources Association (ELRA).

Piotr Bojanowski, Edouard Grave, Armand Joulin, and Tomas Mikolov. 2017. Enriching word vectors with subword information. *Transactions of the Association for Computational Linguistics*, 5:135–146.

Wanxiang Che, Yunlong Feng, Libo Qin, and Ting Liu. 2020. N-ltp: A open-source neural chinese language technology platform with pretrained models. *arXiv preprint arXiv:2009.11616*.

Yoeng-Jin Chu. 1965. On the shortest arborescence of a directed graph. *Scientia Sinica*.

Alexis Conneau, Kartikay Khandelwal, Naman Goyal, Vishrav Chaudhary, Guillaume Wenzek, Francisco Guzmán, Edouard Grave, Myle Ott, Luke Zettlemoyer, and Veselin Stoyanov. 2020. Unsupervised cross-lingual representation learning at scale. In *Proceedings of the 58th Annual Meeting of the Association for Computational Linguistics*, pages 8440–8451, Online. Association for Computational Linguistics.

Jacob Devlin, Ming-Wei Chang, Kenton Lee, and Kristina Toutanova. 2019. BERT: Pre-training of deep bidirectional transformers for language understanding. In *Proceedings of the 2019 Conference of the North American Chapter of the Association for Computational Linguistics: Human Language Technologies, Volume 1 (Long and Short Papers)*, pages 4171–4186, Minneapolis, Minnesota. Association for Computational Linguistics.

Timothy Dozat and Christopher D Manning. 2017. Deep biaffine attention for neural dependency parsing. In *Proceedings of the International Conference on Learning Representations*.

Jack Edmonds. 1967. Optimum branchings. *Journal of Research of the national Bureau of Standards B*.

Neil Houlsby, Andrei Giurgiu, Stanislaw Jastrzebski, Bruna Morrone, Quentin De Laroussilhe, Andrea Gesmundo, Mona Attariyan, and Sylvain Gelly. 2019. Parameter-efficient transfer learning for nlp. In *Proceedings of the International Conference on Machine Learning*.

Hiroshi Kanayama and Ran Iwamoto. 2020. How universal are Universal Dependencies? exploiting syntax for multilingual clause-level sentiment detection. In *Proceedings of the 12th Language Resources and Evaluation Conference*, pages 4063–4073, Marseille, France. European Language Resources Association.

Claudia Kittask, Kirill Milintsevich, and Kairit Sirts. 2020. Evaluating multilingual bert for estonian. *Volume*, 328:19–26.

Dan Kondratyuk and Milan Straka. 2019. 75 languages, 1 model: Parsing Universal Dependencies universally. In *Proceedings of the 2019 Conference on Empirical Methods in Natural Language Processing and the 9th International Joint Conference on Natural Language Processing (EMNLP-IJCNLP)*, pages 2779–2795, Hong Kong, China. Association for Computational Linguistics.

Taku Kudo. 2018. Subword regularization: Improving neural network translation models with multiple subword candidates. In *Proceedings of the 56th Annual Meeting of the Association for Computational Linguistics (Volume 1: Long Papers)*, pages 66–75, Melbourne, Australia. Association for Computational Linguistics.

Taku Kudo and John Richardson. 2018. SentencePiece: A simple and language independent subword tokenizer and detokenizer for neural text processing. In *Proceedings of the 2018 Conference on Empirical Methods in Natural Language Processing: System Demonstrations*, pages 66–71, Brussels, Belgium. Association for Computational Linguistics.

Jian Liu, Yubo Chen, Kang Liu, and Jun Zhao. 2019a. Neural cross-lingual event detection with minimal parallel resources. In *Proceedings of the 2019 Conference on Empirical Methods in Natural Language Processing and the 9th International Joint Conference on Natural Language Processing (EMNLP-IJCNLP)*, pages 738–748, Hong Kong, China. Association for Computational Linguistics.

Yinhan Liu, Myle Ott, Naman Goyal, Jingfei Du, Mandar Joshi, Danqi Chen, Omer Levy, Mike Lewis, Luke Zettlemoyer, and Veselin Stoyanov. 2019b. Roberta: A robustly optimized bert pretraining approach. *arXiv preprint arXiv:1907.11692*.

Christopher Manning, Mihai Surdeanu, John Bauer, Jenny Finkel, Steven Bethard, and David McClosky. 2014. The Stanford CoreNLP natural language processing toolkit. In *Proceedings of 52nd Annual*

Meeting of the Association for Computational Linguistics: System Demonstrations, pages 55–60, Baltimore, Maryland. Association for Computational Linguistics.

Tomas Mikolov, Ilya Sutskever, Kai Chen, Greg S Corrado, and Jeff Dean. 2013. Distributed representations of words and phrases and their compositionality. In *Proceedings of the Conference on Neural Information Processing Systems*.

Behrang Mohit, Nathan Schneider, Rishav Bhowmick, Kemal Oflazer, and Noah A. Smith. 2012. Recall-oriented learning of named entities in Arabic Wikipedia. In *Proceedings of the 13th Conference of the European Chapter of the Association for Computational Linguistics*, pages 162–173, Avignon, France. Association for Computational Linguistics.

Mahdi Mohseni and Amirhossein Tebbifakhr. 2019. MorphoBERT: a Persian NER system with BERT and morphological analysis. In *Proceedings of The First International Workshop on NLP Solutions for Under Resourced Languages (NSURL 2019) co-located with ICNLSP 2019 - Short Papers*, pages 23–30, Trento, Italy. Association for Computational Linguistics.

Dat Quoc Nguyen and Anh Tuan Nguyen. 2020. PhoBERT: Pre-trained language models for Vietnamese. In *Findings of the Association for Computational Linguistics: EMNLP 2020*, pages 1037–1042, Online. Association for Computational Linguistics.

Minh Van Nguyen and Thien Huu Nguyen. 2021. Improving cross-lingual transfer for event argument extraction with language-universal sentence structures. In *Proceedings of the Sixth Arabic Natural Language Processing Workshop (WANLP) at EACL 2021*.

Joakim Nivre, Marie-Catherine de Marneffe, Filip Ginter, Jan Hajič, Christopher D. Manning, Sampo Pyysalo, Sebastian Schuster, Francis Tyers, and Daniel Zeman. 2020. Universal Dependencies v2: An evergrowing multilingual treebank collection. In *Proceedings of the 12th Language Resources and Evaluation Conference*, pages 4034–4043, Marseille, France. European Language Resources Association.

Joel Nothman, Nicky Ringland, Will Radford, Tara Murphy, and James R. Curran. 2012. Learning multilingual named entity recognition from Wikipedia. *Artificial Intelligence*, 194:151–175.

Matthew E. Peters, Sebastian Ruder, and Noah A. Smith. 2019. To tune or not to tune? adapting pretrained representations to diverse tasks. In *Proceedings of the 4th Workshop on Representation Learning for NLP (RepL4NLP-2019)*, pages 7–14, Florence, Italy. Association for Computational Linguistics.

Jonas Pfeiffer, Andreas Rücklé, Clifton Poth, Aishwarya Kamath, Ivan Vulić, Sebastian Ruder, Kyunghyun Cho, and Iryna Gurevych. 2020a. AdapterHub: A framework for adapting transformers. In *Proceedings of the 2020 Conference on Empirical Methods in Natural Language Processing: System Demonstrations*, pages 46–54, Online. Association for Computational Linguistics.

Jonas Pfeiffer, Ivan Vulić, Iryna Gurevych, and Sebastian Ruder. 2020b. MAD-X: An Adapter-Based Framework for Multi-Task Cross-Lingual Transfer. In *Proceedings of the 2020 Conference on Empirical Methods in Natural Language Processing (EMNLP)*, pages 7654–7673, Online. Association for Computational Linguistics.

Peng Qi, Yuhao Zhang, Yuhui Zhang, Jason Bolton, and Christopher D. Manning. 2020. Stanza: A python natural language processing toolkit for many human languages. In *Proceedings of the 58th Annual Meeting of the Association for Computational Linguistics: System Demonstrations*, pages 101–108, Online. Association for Computational Linguistics.

Milan Straka. 2018. UDPipe 2.0 prototype at CoNLL 2018 UD shared task. In *Proceedings of the CoNLL 2018 Shared Task: Multilingual Parsing from Raw Text to Universal Dependencies*, pages 197–207, Brussels, Belgium. Association for Computational Linguistics.

Nasrin Taghizadeh and Heshaam Faili. 2020. Cross-lingual adaptation using universal dependencies. *arXiv preprint arXiv:2003.10816*.

Ian Tenney, Dipanjan Das, and Ellie Pavlick. 2019. BERT rediscovers the classical NLP pipeline. In *Proceedings of the 57th Annual Meeting of the Association for Computational Linguistics*, pages 4593–4601, Florence, Italy. Association for Computational Linguistics.

Yuanhe Tian, Yan Song, Xiang Ao, Fei Xia, Xiaojun Quan, Tong Zhang, and Yonggang Wang. 2020. Joint Chinese word segmentation and part-of-speech tagging via two-way attentions of auto-analyzed knowledge. In *Proceedings of the 58th Annual Meeting of the Association for Computational Linguistics*, pages 8286–8296, Online. Association for Computational Linguistics.

Erik F. Tjong Kim Sang. 2002. Introduction to the CoNLL-2002 shared task: Language-independent named entity recognition. In *COLING-02: The 6th Conference on Natural Language Learning 2002 (CoNLL-2002)*.

Erik F. Tjong Kim Sang and Fien De Meulder. 2003. Introduction to the CoNLL-2003 shared task: Language-independent named entity recognition. In *Proceedings of the Seventh Conference on Natural Language Learning at HLT-NAACL 2003*, pages 142–147.

Henry Tsai, Jason Riesa, Melvin Johnson, Naveen Arivazhagan, Xin Li, and Amelia Archer. 2019. Small and practical BERT models for sequence labeling. In *Proceedings of the 2019 Conference on Empirical Methods in Natural Language Processing and the 9th International Joint Conference on Natural Language Processing (EMNLP-IJCNLP)*, pages 3632–3636, Hong Kong, China. Association for Computational Linguistics.

Ahmet Üstün, Arianna Bisazza, Gosse Bouma, and Gertjan van Noord. 2020. UDapter: Language adaptation for truly Universal Dependency parsing. In *Proceedings of the 2020 Conference on Empirical Methods in Natural Language Processing (EMNLP)*, pages 2302–2315, Online. Association for Computational Linguistics.

Wietse de Vries, Andreas van Cranenburgh, Arianna Bisazza, Tommaso Caselli, Gertjan van Noord, and Malvina Nissim. 2019. Bertje: A dutch bert model. *arXiv preprint arXiv:1912.09582*.

Ralph Weischedel, Martha Palmer, Mitchell Marcus, Eduard Hovy, Sameer Pradhan, Lance Ramshaw, Nianwen Xue, Ann Taylor, Jeff Kaufman, Michelle Franchini, et al. 2013. Ontonotes release 5.0. *Linguistic Data Consortium*.

Haiqin Yang. 2019. Bert meets chinese word segmentation. *arXiv preprint arXiv:1909.09292*.

Daniel Zeman, Joakim Nivre, Mitchell Abrams, Noëmi Aepli, Željko Agić, Lars Ahrenberg, Gabrielė Aleksandravičiūtė, Lene Antonsen, Katya Aplonova, Maria Jesus Aranzabe, Gashaw Arutie, Masayuki Asahara, Luma Ateyah, Mohammed Attia, Aitziber Atutxa, Liesbeth Augustinus, Elena Badmaeva, Miguel Ballesteros, Esha Banerjee, Sebastian Bank, Verginica Barbu Mititelu, Victoria Basmov, Colin Batchelor, John Bauer, Sandra Bellato, Kepa Bengoetxea, Yevgeni Berzak, Irshad Ahmad Bhat, Riyaz Ahmad Bhat, Erica Biagetti, Eckhard Bick, Agnė Bielinskienė, Rogier Blokland, Victoria Bobicev, Loïc Boizou, Emanuel Borges Völker, Carl Börstell, Cristina Bosco, Gosse Bouma, Sam Bowman, Adriane Boyd, Kristina Brokaitė, Aljoscha Burchardt, Marie Candito, Bernard Caron, Gauthier Caron, Tatiana Cavalcanti, Gülşen Cebiroğlu Eryiğit, Flavio Massimiliano Cecchini, Giuseppe G. A. Celano, Slavomír Čéplö, Savas Cetin, Fabricio Chalub, Jinho Choi, Yongseok Cho, Jayeol Chun, Alessandra T. Cignarella, Silvie Cinková, Aurélie Collomb, Çağrı Çöltekin, Miriam Connor, Marine Courtin, Elizabeth Davidson, Marie-Catherine de Marneffe, Valeria de Paiva, Elvis de Souza, Arantza Diaz de Ilarraza, Carly Dickerson, Bamba Dione, Peter Dirix, Kaja Dobrovoljc, Timothy Dozat, Kira Droganova, Puneet Dwivedi, Hanne Eckhoff, Marhaba Eli, Ali Elkahky, Binyam Ephrem, Olga Erina, Tomaž Erjavec, Aline Etienne, Wograine Evelyn, Richárd Farkas, Hector Fernandez Alcalde, Jennifer Foster, Cláudia Freitas, Kazunori Fujita, Katarína Gajdošová, Daniel Galbraith, Marcos Garcia, Moa Gärdenfors, Sebastian Garza, Kim Gerdes, Filip Ginter, Iakes Goenaga, Koldo Gojenola, Memduh Gökırmak, Yoav Goldberg, Xavier Gómez Guinovart, Berta González Saavedra, Bernadeta Griciūtė, Matias Grioni, Normunds Grūzītis, Bruno Guillaume, Céline Guillot-Barbance, Nizar Habash, Jan Hajič, Jan Hajič jr., Mika Hämäläinen, Linh Hà Mỹ, Na-Rae Han, Kim Harris, Dag Haug, Johannes Heinecke, Felix Hennig, Barbora Hladká, Jaroslava Hlaváčová, Florinel Hociung, Petter Hohle, Jena Hwang, Takumi Ikeda, Radu Ion, Elena Irimia, Ọlájídé Ishola, Tomáš Jelínek, Anders Johannsen, Fredrik Jørgensen, Markus Juutinen, Hüner Kaşıkara, Andre Kaasen, Nadezhda Kabaeva, Sylvain Kahane, Hiroshi Kanayama, Jenna Kanerva, Boris Katz, Tolga Kayadelen, Jessica Kenney, Václava Kettnerová, Jesse Kirchner, Elena Klementieva, Arne Köhn, Kamil Kopacewicz, Natalia Kotsyba, Jolanta Kovalevskaitė, Simon Krek, Sookyoung Kwak, Veronika Laippala, Lorenzo Lambertino, Lucia Lam, Tatiana Lando, Septina Dian Larasati, Alexei Lavrentiev, John Lee, Phương Lê Hồng, Alessandro Lenci, Saran Lertpradit, Herman Leung, Cheuk Ying Li, Josie Li, Keying Li, KyungTae Lim, Maria Liovina, Yuan Li, Nikola Ljubešić, Olga Loginova, Olga Lyashevskaya, Teresa Lynn, Vivien Macketanz, Aibek Makazhanov, Michael Mandl, Christopher Manning, Ruli Manurung, Cătălina Mărănduc, David Mareček, Katrin Marheinecke, Héctor Martínez Alonso, André Martins, Jan Mašek, Yuji Matsumoto, Ryan McDonald, Sarah McGuinness, Gustavo Mendonça, Niko Miekka, Margarita Misirpashayeva, Anna Missilä, Cătălin Mititelu, Maria Mitrofan, Yusuke Miyao, Simonetta Montemagni, Amir More, Laura Moreno Romero, Keiko Sophie Mori, Tomohiko Morioka, Shinsuke Mori, Shigeki Moro, Bjartur Mortensen, Bohdan Moskalevskyi, Kadri Muischnek, Robert Munro, Yugo Murawaki, Kaili Müürisep, Pinkey Nainwani, Juan Ignacio Navarro Horñiacek, Anna Nedoluzhko, Gunta Nešpore-Bērzkalne, Lương Nguyễn Thị, Huyền Nguyễn Thị Minh, Yoshihiro Nikaido, Vitaly Nikolaev, Rattima Nitisaroj, Hanna Nurmi, Stina Ojala, Atul Kr. Ojha, Adédayọ Olúòkun, Mai Omura, Petya Osenova, Robert Östling, Lilja Øvrelid, Niko Partanen, Elena Pascual, Marco Passarotti, Agnieszka Patejuk, Guilherme Paulino-Passos, Angelika Peljak-Łapińska, Siyao Peng, Cenel-Augusto Perez, Guy Perrier, Daria Petrova, Slav Petrov, Jason Phelan, Jussi Piitulainen, Tommi A Pirinen, Emily Pitler, Barbara Plank, Thierry Poibeau, Larisa Ponomareva, Martin Popel, Lauma Pretkalniņa, Sophie Prévost, Prokopis Prokopidis, Adam Przepiórkowski, Tiina Puolakainen, Sampo Pyysalo, Peng Qi, Andriela Rääbis, Alexandre Rademaker, Loganathan Ramasamy, Taraka Rama, Carlos Ramisch, Vinit Ravishankar, Livy Real, Siva Reddy, Georg Rehm, Ivan Riabov, Michael Rießler, Erika Rimkutė, Larissa Rinaldi, Laura Rituma, Luisa Rocha, Mykhailo Romanenko, Rudolf Rosa, Davide Rovati, Valentin Roșca, Olga Rudina, Jack Rueter, Shoval Sadde, Benoît Sagot,

Shadi Saleh, Alessio Salomoni, Tanja Samardžić, Stephanie Samson, Manuela Sanguinetti, Dage Särg, Baiba Saulīte, Yanin Sawanakunanon, Nathan Schneider, Sebastian Schuster, Djamé Seddah, Wolfgang Seeker, Mojgan Seraji, Mo Shen, Atsuko Shimada, Hiroyuki Shirasu, Muh Shohibussirri, Dmitry Sichinava, Aline Silveira, Natalia Silveira, Maria Simi, Radu Simionescu, Katalin Simkó, Mária Šimková, Kiril Simov, Aaron Smith, Isabela Soares-Bastos, Carolyn Spadine, Antonio Stella, Milan Straka, Jana Strnadová, Alane Suhr, Umut Sulubacak, Shingo Suzuki, Zsolt Szántó, Dima Taji, Yuta Takahashi, Fabio Tamburini, Takaaki Tanaka, Isabelle Tellier, Guillaume Thomas, Liisi Torga, Trond Trosterud, Anna Trukhina, Reut Tsarfaty, Francis Tyers, Sumire Uematsu, Zdeňka Urešová, Larraitz Uria, Hans Uszkoreit, Andrius Utka, Sowmya Vajjala, Daniel van Niekerk, Gertjan van Noord, Viktor Varga, Eric Villemonte de la Clergerie, Veronika Vincze, Lars Wallin, Abigail Walsh, Jing Xian Wang, Jonathan North Washington, Maximilan Wendt, Seyi Williams, Mats Wirén, Christian Wittern, Tsegay Woldemariam, Tak-sum Wong, Alina Wróblewska, Mary Yako, Naoki Yamazaki, Chunxiao Yan, Koichi Yasuoka, Marat M. Yavrumyan, Zhuoran Yu, Zdeněk Žabokrtský, Amir Zeldes, Manying Zhang, and Hanzhi Zhu. 2019. Universal dependencies 2.5. LINDAT/CLARIAH-CZ digital library at the Institute of Formal and Applied Linguistics (ÚFAL), Faculty of Mathematics and Physics, Charles University.

Xingran Zhu. 2020. Cross-lingual word sense disambiguation using mbert embeddings with syntactic dependencies. *arXiv preprint arXiv:2012.05300*.

DEBIE: A Platform for Implicit and Explicit Debiasing of Word Embedding Spaces

Niklas Friedrich, Anne Lauscher, Simone Paolo Ponzetto and Goran Glavaš
Data and Web Science Group
School of Business Informatics and Mathematics
University of Mannheim
nfriedri@mail.uni-mannheim.de
{anne,simone,goran}@informatik.uni-mannheim.de

Abstract

Recent research efforts in NLP have demonstrated that distributional word vector spaces often encode stereotypical human biases, such as racism and sexism. With word representations ubiquitously used in NLP models and pipelines, this raises ethical issues and jeopardizes the fairness of language technologies. While there exists a large body of work on bias measures and debiasing methods, to date, there is no platform that would unify these research efforts and make bias measuring and debiasing of representation spaces widely accessible. In this work, we present DEBIE, the first integrated platform for (1) measuring and (2) mitigating bias in word embeddings. Given an (i) embedding space (users can choose between the predefined spaces or upload their own) and (ii) a bias specification (users can choose between existing bias specifications or create their own), DEBIE can (1) compute several measures of implicit and explicit bias and modify the embedding space by executing two (mutually composable) debiasing models. DEBIE's functionality can be accessed through four different interfaces: (a) a web application, (b) a desktop application, (c) a REST-ful API, and (d) as a command-line application.[1] DEBIE is available at: `debie.informatik.uni-mannheim.de`

1 Introduction

Ethical and fair natural language processing is an essential precondition for widespread societal adoption of language technologies. In recent years, however, distributional language representations built from large corpora have been shown to encode human-like biases, like racism and sexism (Bolukbasi et al., 2016; Zhao et al., 2019; Lauscher et al., 2020a; Nadeem et al., 2020, *inter alia*). At the word level, most embedding spaces, across a range of embedding models and languages (Lauscher and Glavaš, 2019), encode human biases that can be exemplified in biased analogies, such as the famous example of sexism: $\overrightarrow{\text{man}} - \overrightarrow{\text{programmer}} \approx \overrightarrow{\text{woman}} - \overrightarrow{\text{homemaker}}$ (Bolukbasi et al., 2016). While this is not surprising, given the distributional nature of word representation models (Harris, 1954) it is – depending on the sociotechnical context – an undesired artefact of distributional representation learning (Blodgett et al., 2020) which can, in turn, lead to unfair decisions in downstream applications. A number of different measures for quantifying biases in representation spaces have been proposed in recent years (Caliskan et al., 2017; Gonen and Goldberg, 2019; Dev and Phillips, 2019; Garg et al., 2018; Lauscher et al., 2020a) and even more models for removing or attenuating such biases have been developed (Zhao et al., 2019; Bordia and Bowman, 2019; Dinan et al., 2020; Webster et al., 2020; Qian et al., 2019, *inter alia*). What is still missing, however, is the ability to seamlessly apply different bias measures and debiasing models on arbitrary embedding spaces and for custom (i.e., user-specified) bias specifications.

In this work, we address this gap by introducing DEBIE, the first integrated platform offering bias measurement and mitigation for arbitrary static embedding spaces and bias specifications. The DEBIE platform is grounded in the general framework for *implicit* and *explicit* debiasing of word embedding spaces (Lauscher et al., 2020a). Within this framework, an implicit bias consists of measurable discrepancies between two target term sets, which can, for instance, describe a dominant and a minoritized social group (D'Ignazio and Klein, 2020). In contrast, an explicit bias is a bias between such target term sets towards certain attribute terms groups. Our platform allows for both implicit and

[1] Videos demonstrating the usage of the DEBIE application and command-line tool are available at `https://tinyurl.com/y2ymujus`

Proceedings of the 16th Conference of the European Chapter of the Association for Computational Linguistics: System Demonstrations, pages 91–98
April 19 - 23, 2021. ©2021 Association for Computational Linguistics

explicit bias specifications, incorporating a range of different measures for quantifying embedding space bias (Caliskan et al., 2017; Gonen and Goldberg, 2019; Dev and Phillips, 2019) and a pair of mutually composable methods for bias mitigation. DEBIE's functionality for measuring and mitigating biases in distributional word vector spaces is accessible via four different interfaces: as a web application, desktop application, via a RESTful application programming interface (API), and as a command-line tool. We believe that *DebIE* will, by offering to test arbitrary embedding spaces for custom user-defined biases, stimulate a wider exploration of the presence of a broader set of human biases in distributional representation spaces.

2 Related Work

First, we describe related research on bias evaluation and debiasing and then turn our attention to existing bias mitigation platforms.

Bias Measures and Mitigation Methods. There is an extensive body of research on bias detection and bias mitigation in natural language processing. Due to space limitations, here we only provide a brief overview and refer the reader to a recent survey of the field for more information (Blodgett et al., 2020). Bolukbasi et al. (2016) were the first to show stereotypical bias to exist in word embedding models and proposed *hard debiasing*, the first word embedding bias mitigation algorithm. Subsequently, Caliskan et al. (2017) introduced the well-known Word Embedding Association Test (WEAT), inspired by the Implicit Association Test (Nosek et al., 2002), which measures biased associations in human subjects in terms of response times when exposed to sets of stimuli. WEAT, in turn, reflects the strength of associations in terms of semantic similarity between word vectors. McCurdy and Serbetci (2017) study gender bias with WEAT in three other languages (Dutch, German, and Spanish). Extending upon this, Lauscher and Glavaš (2019) translated the WEAT tests to 6 more languages (German, Spanish, Italian, Russian, Croatian, Turkish), allowing for multilingual and cross-lingual analysis of biases captured by the specifications of the original WEAT. They later extended the set of supported languages with Arabic (Lauscher et al., 2020b).

Dev and Phillips (2019) proposed a linear projection model for debiasing along with two bias evaluation measures: the Embedding Coherence Test (ECT) and the Embedding Quality Test (EQT) and propose methods for removing the (explicit) bias based on computing the direction vector of the bias. While their method successfully removes the *explicit* bias, i.e., bias between sets of *target* terms (e.g., male terms like *man*, *father*, and *boy* vs. female terms like *woman*, *mother*, and *girl*) *with respect to* sets of *attribute* terms (e.g., profession terms, such as *scientist* or *artist*), Gonen and Goldberg (2019) show that *implicit* bias between the sets of target terms remains even after (explicit debiasing) and that the terms from one target set are still clearly discernible from the terms of the other set in the embedding space. Based on this finding, Lauscher et al. (2020a) systematized the preceding work and proposed a general framework for bias measurement and debiasing, encompassing a range of existing and newly proposed measures and mitigation methods, which operate either on *explicit* or *implicit* bias specifications. Their framework arguably allows for a more holistic assessment of bias in word vector spaces and ensures interoperability between bias mitigation models and bias specifications. Our DEBIE platform makes this holistic framework for measuring and mitigating biases widely accessible and applicable (1) for arbitrary user-defined bias specification to (2) arbitrary pretrained word embedding spaces.

Bias mitigation platforms. The landscape of the *off-the-shelf* solutions for measuring and mitigating bias for machine learning applications is extremely scarce. To the best of our knowledge, the only such tool is *AI Fairness 360* (Bellamy et al., 2018), an extensible open-source toolkit which offers a set of algorithms for detecting and mitigating unwanted bias in datasets and machine learning models. It addresses bias by integrating fairness algorithms along the machine learning pipeline, i.e., fair pre-processing, fair in-processing, and fair post-processing. In contrast, DEBIE specifically targets biases in distributional word vector spaces (as an ubiquitous component of modern NLP pipelines) by integrating a series of word embedding bias tests and mitigation algorithms not covered by more general tools like AI Fairness 360.

3 DEBIE: System Description

We first explain the two types of bias specifications support by DEBIE (*implicit* and *explicit*), then proceed to describe the concrete bias specifications and debiasing algorithms bundles in the system. Finally, we provide details of DEBIE's architecture and interfaces through which the bias measuring and mitigation functionality can be accessed. All code is publicly available on GitHub.[2]

3.1 Implicit and Explicit Bias Specifications

DEBIE supports measuring of *implicit* or *explicit* biases for a given word embedding space and, respectively, implicit or explicit *debiasing* of the given space. Both implicit bias specifications B_I and explicit bias specifications B_E specify two sets of *target* terms, T_1 and T_2 that capture the dimension of the bias. For example, if measuring a *gender* bias, T_1 would contain male terms (e.g., *man, father*) and T_2 female terms (e.g., *woman, girl, grandma*).[3] While an implicit bias specification is fully specified with the two target lists, $B_I = (T_1, T_2)$, an explicit specification additionally requires two sets of attributes A_1 and A_2, $B_E = (T_1, T_2, A_1, A_2)$, capturing the groups of terms towards which the target groups are expected to exhibit significantly different level of association. For example, for a gender bias, one would expect male terms to be more strongly associated with career terms (e.g., A_1 could contain terms like *programmer*), whereas female terms could be closer to family-related terms (e.g., A_2 could contain terms like *homemaker*). The input for DEBIE consists of an embedding space $\mathbf{X} \in \mathbb{R}^d$ and a bias specification, (implicit or explicit). Explicit debiasing methods (i.e., methods that operate on explicit bias specifications) cannot be executed when the provided bias specification is implicit (B_I).[4]

3.2 Bias Measures

DEBIE provides three measures that capture explicit bias (i.e., apply only if an explicit bias specification is provided), and two tests that measure implicit bias. Because debiasing methods (see §3.3) make perturbations to the embedding space, we additionally couple the bias tests with measures of semantic quality of the distributional space.

[2]https://github.com/umanlp/debie-frontend
https://github.com/umanlp/debie-backend

[3]The bias measures implemented in DEBIE do not require the terms between the target lists to be paired. Accordingly, the two lists also do not need to be of the same length.

[4]Conversely, implicit debiasing methods, i.e., ones that require only T_1 and T_2, can be applied if an explicit specification is provided. In that case, we simply convert B_E to B_I by discarding the provided attribute sets.

Word Embedding Association Test (WEAT). Given an explicit bias test specification $B_E = (T_1, T_2, A_1, A_2)$, WEAT (Caliskan et al., 2017) computes the effect size quantifying the amount of bias as follows:

$$s(T_1, T_2, A_1, A_2) = \sum_{t_1 \in T_1} s(t_1, A_1, A_2) - \sum_{t_2 \in T_2} s(t_2, A_1, A_2),$$

with associative difference of term t given as:

$$s(t, A_1, A_2) = \frac{1}{|A_1|} \sum_{a_1 \in A_1} \cos(\mathbf{t}, \mathbf{a_1}) - \frac{1}{|A_2|} \sum_{a_2 \in A_2} \cos(\mathbf{t}, \mathbf{a_2}),$$

with $\mathbf{t}$ as the word embedding of the target term t and cos as the cosine of the angle between the two vectors. To estimate the significance of the effect size, we follow Caliskan et al. (2017) and compute the non-parametric permutation test in which the $s(T_1, T_2, A_1, A_2)$ is compared to $s(X_1, X_2, A_1, A_2)$, where (X_1, X_2) denotes a random, equally-sized split of terms from $T_1 \cup T_2$.

Embedding Coherence Test (ECT). Given an explicit bias specification with a single attribute set $B_E = (T_1, T_2, A)$ with $A = A_1 \cup A_2$, ECT (Dev and Phillips, 2019) quantifies the presence of the bias as the (lack of) correlation of the distances of the mean vectors of the target term sets T_1 and $T2$ with the attribute terms in A. The lower the correlation, the higher the bias. To this end, we compute the mean vectors $\mathbf{t_1}$ and $\mathbf{t_2}$ as averages of the vector representations of the terms in T_1 and T_2. Next, we compute two vectors containing the cosine similarities of each of the terms in A with $\mathbf{t_1}$, as well as with $\mathbf{t_2}$, respectively. The final score is Spearman's rank correlation coefficient of the obtained vectors of cosine similarity scores.

Bias Analogy Test (BAT). BAT (Lauscher et al., 2020a) assesses the amount of biased analogies that can be retrieved from an embedding space based on the explicit bias specification $B_E = (T_1, T_2, A_1, A_2)$. We first create all possible biased analogies from B_E: $\mathbf{t}_1 - \mathbf{t}_2 \approx \mathbf{a}_1 - \mathbf{a}_2$ for $(t_1, t_2, a_1, a_2) \in T_1 \times T_2 \times A_1 \times A_2$. Next, from each of these analogies, two query vectors are computed: $\mathbf{q}_1 = \mathbf{t}_1 - \mathbf{t}_2 + \mathbf{a}_2$ and $\mathbf{q}_2 = \mathbf{a}_1 - \mathbf{t}_1 + \mathbf{t}_2$ for each 4-tuple (t_1, t_2, a_1, a_2). We then rank all attribute vectors in $\mathbf{X}$ according to the Euclidean distance to the query vector. We report the percentage of cases in which: (1) a_1 is ranked higher than a term $a'_2 \in A_2 \setminus \{a_2\}$ for $\mathbf{q}_1$ and (2) a_2 is ranked higher than a term $a'_1 \in A_1 \setminus \{a_1\}$ for $\mathbf{q}_2$.

Implicit Bias Tests (IBT). As proposed by Gonen and Goldberg (2019), the amount of implicit bias corresponds to the accuracy with which two target term sets can be separated. We report the score of two methods: (1) clustering accuracy with K-Means++ (Arthur and Vassilvitskii, 2007), and (2) classification accuracy based on Support Vector Machines with Gaussian kernel. We carry out the latter via leave-one-out cross-validation (i.e., we train on all words from both target lists, leaving one term for prediction).

Semantic Quality Tests (SQ). The debiasing models (3.3) modify the embedding space. While they reduce the bias, they may reduce the general semantic quality of the embedding space, which could be detrimental for model performance in downstream applications. This is why we couple the bias tests with measures of semantic word similarity on two established word-similarity datasets: SimLex-999 (Hill et al., 2015) or WordSim-353 (Finkelstein et al., 2001). We compute the Spearman correlation between the human similarity scores assigned to word pairs and corresponding cosines computed from the embedding space.

3.3 Debiasing Methods

DEBIE encompasses implementations of two debiasing models from (Lauscher et al., 2020a), for which an implicit bias specification suffices:[5]

General Bias Direction Debiasing (GBDD). As an extension of the linear projection model of Dev and Phillips (2019), GBDD relies on identifying the bias direction in the distributional space. Let (t_1^i, t_2^j) be word pairs with $t_1^i \in T_1$, $t_2^j \in T_2$, respectively. First, we obtain partial bias direction vectors $\mathbf{b_{ij}}$ by computing the difference between the respective vectors for each pair $\boldsymbol{b}_{ij} = \boldsymbol{t}_1^i - \boldsymbol{t}_2^j$. We then stack all partial direction vector, obtaining the bias matrix $\boldsymbol{B}$. The global bias direction vector $\boldsymbol{b}$ then corresponds to the top singular value of $\boldsymbol{B}$, i.e., the first row of matrix $\boldsymbol{V}$, with $\boldsymbol{U\Sigma V}^\top$ as the singular value decomposition of $\boldsymbol{B}$. We then obtain the debiased version of the space $\boldsymbol{X}$ as:

$$\text{GBDD}(\mathbf{X}) = \mathbf{X} - \langle \mathbf{X}, \mathbf{b} \rangle \mathbf{b},$$

with $\langle \boldsymbol{X}, \boldsymbol{b} \rangle$ denoting dot products between rows of $\boldsymbol{X}$ and $\boldsymbol{b}$. As such, the closer the word embedding is to the bias direction, the more it gets corrected.

Bias Alignment Model (BAM). Inspired by previous work on projection-based cross-lingual word embedding spaces (Smith et al., 2017; Glavaš et al., 2019), BAM focuses on *implicit* debiasing by treating the target term sets T_1, and T_2 of an implicit bias specification B_I as "translations" of each other and learning the linear projection of the embedding spaces w.r.t. itself (Lauscher et al., 2020a). First, we build all possible word pairs (t_1^i, t_2^j), $t_1^i \in T_1$, $t_2^j \in T_2$ and stack the respective word vectors of the left and right pairs to obtain matrices $\boldsymbol{X}_{T_1}$ and $\boldsymbol{X}_{T_2}$. We then learn the orthogonal mapping matrix $\boldsymbol{W_X} = \boldsymbol{UV}^\top$, with $\boldsymbol{U\Sigma V}^\top$ as the singular value decomposition of $\boldsymbol{X}_{T_2}\boldsymbol{X}_{T_1}^\top$. In the last step, the original space and its "translation" $\boldsymbol{X} = \boldsymbol{XW_X}$ (which is equally biased), are averaged to obtain the debiased embedding space:

$$\text{BAM}(\boldsymbol{X}) = \frac{1}{2}(\boldsymbol{X} + \boldsymbol{XW_X}).$$

Note that DEBIE can trivially compose the two debiasing models – the resulting space after applying GBDD (BAM) can be the input for BAM (GBDD).

3.4 Integrated Data

DEBIE is designed as a general tool, which allows user to upload their own embedding spaces and define their own bias specifications for testing and/or debiasing. Nonetheless, we include into the platform a set of commonly used bias specifications and word embedding spaces. Concretely, DEBIE includes the whole WEAT test collection (Caliskan et al., 2017), containing the explicit bias specifications summarized in Table 1. DEBIE also comes with three word embedding spaces, pretrained with different models: (1) fastText (Bojanowski et al., 2017),[6] (2) GloVe (Pennington et al., 2014),[7] and (3) CBOW (Mikolov et al., 2013).[8] All three spaces are 300-dimensional and their vocabularies are limited to 200K most frequent words.

3.5 System Architecture

DEBIE's architecture, illustrated in Figure 1, adheres to the principles of modern extensible web application design and consists of four components: (1) the backend, (2) the frontend, which together

[5]Note that any explicit bias specification is trivially reduced to an implicit one by discarding the attribute term sets.

[6]https://dl.fbaipublicfiles.com/fasttext/vectors-wiki/wiki.en.vec

[7]http://nlp.stanford.edu/data/glove.6B.zip

[8]https://drive.google.com/file/d/0B7XkCwpI5KDYNlNUTTlSS21pQmM/edit?usp=sharing

Test	Type	Target Set #1	Target Set #2	Attribute Set #1	Attribute Set #2
1	Universal	Flowers (e.g., *aster, tulip*)	Insects (e.g., *ant, flea*)	Pleasant (e.g., *health, love*)	Unpleasant (e.g., *abuse*)
2	Militant	Instruments (e.g., *cello, guitar*)	Weapons (e.g., *gun, sword*)	Pleasant	Unpleasant
3	Racist	Euro-American names (e.g., *Adam*)	Afro-American names (e.g., *Jamel*)	Pleasant (e.g., *caress*)	Unpleasant (e.g., *abuse*)
4	Racist	Euro-American names (e.g., *Brad*)	Afro-American names (e.g., *Hakim*)	Pleasant	Unpleasant
5	Racist	Euro-American names	Afro-American names	Pleasant (e.g., *joy*)	Unpleasant (e.g., *agony*)
6	Gender	Male names (e.g., *John*)	Female names (e.g., *Lisa*)	Career (e.g. *management*)	Family (e.g., *children*)
7	Gender	Math (e.g., *algebra, geometry*)	Arts (e.g., *poetry, dance*)	Male (e.g., *brother, son*)	Female (e.g., *woman, sister*)
8	Gender	Science (e.g., *experiment*)	Arts	Male	Female
9	Disease	Physical condition (e.g., *virus*)	Mental condition (e.g., *sad*)	Long-term (e.g., *always*)	Short-term (e.g., *occasional*)
10	Age	Older names (e.g., *Gertrude*)	Younger names (e.g., *Michelle*)	Pleasant	Unpleasant

Table 1: WEAT bias test specifications provided by DEBIE.

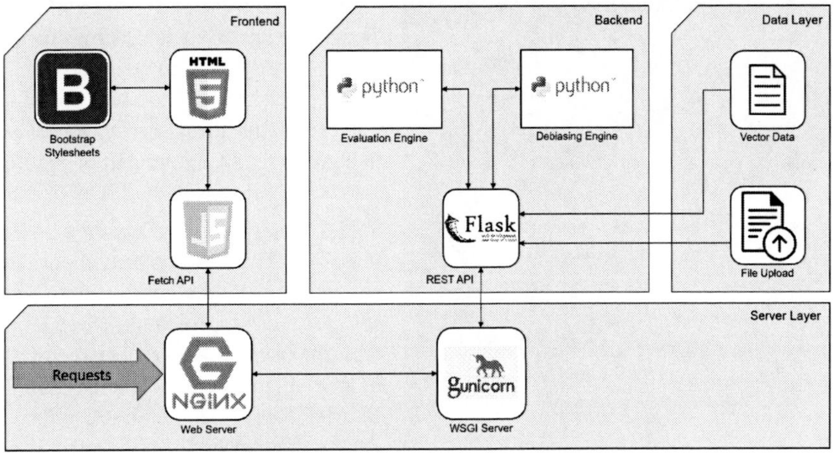

Figure 1: Software Architecture of the DEBIE platform.

represent the core of the application, (3) the data layer, and (4) the server layer facing the web.

Backend. DEBIE's backend consists of two main modules: (1) the bias evaluation engine, which computes the bias test scores (see §3.2), and (2) the debiasing engine, which runs the word embedding debiasing models (see §3.3). The backend interacts with the data layer for retrieving data (bias specifications and vectors from embedding spaces) and its functionality is exposed via a RESTful API, which offers endpoints for programmatically (i) uploading and retrieving data as well as for (ii) running bias evaluation and (iii) debiasing.

There are dedicated controllers and handlers for each of this primary functionalities: vector retrieval, bias evaluation, and debiasing. These are responsible for computing results and delivering content to relevant web pages. The second group of controllers and handlers is responsible for retrieving data out of integrated and external embedding spaces and for parsing and generating JSON data. All bias measures and debiasing methods are implemented as separate modules so that the platform can be extended seamlessly with additional bias measures and debiasing models. A new bias measure or a new debiasing model can be integrated by simply adding the computation scripts (i.e., a function that implements the functionality) and adapting the responsible handler. The backend is purely implemented in Python.

Frontend, Data Layer, and Server Layer. The frontend is written in HTML and plain JavaScript, and relies on the Bootstrap library.[9] The `fetch` functionality is used for sending requests to the RESTful API of the backend. For the visualization of embedding spaces (see bottom part of Figure 2), we rely on the the `chart.js` library.[10]

Embedding spaces are stored as two files: (1) the *.vocab* file is the serialized dictionary that maps words to indices of the embedding matrix; (2) the *.vectors* file is an embedding matrix (serialized 2D `numpy` array) rows of which are the actual word vectors. At the start of the web applicatiob, all bias specifications and intergated embedding spaces are fully loaded into the memory completely.

DEBIE is hosted on a Linux server, running De-

[9]`https://getbootstrap.com/`
[10]`https://www.chartjs.org/`

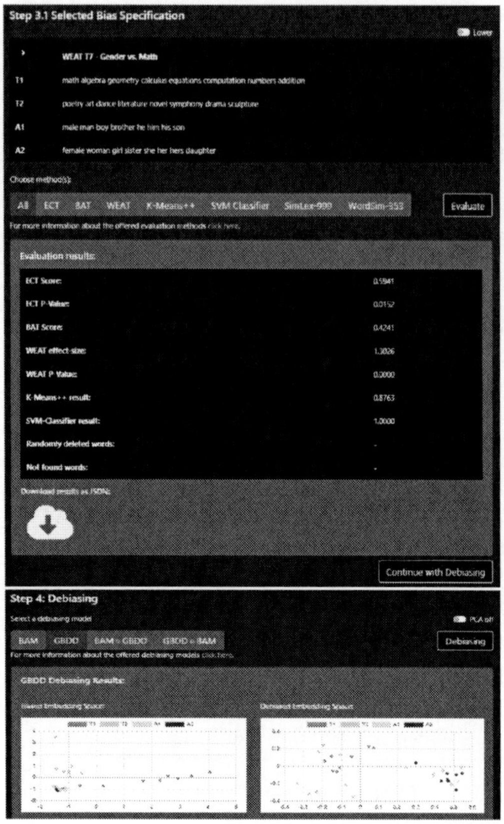

Figure 2: DEBIE'S web UI.

bian 10 as the operating system. The python WSGI-server `gunicorn` is used to serve the RESTful API. We opt for `nginx` as the web server for hosting the frontend and redirecting the API-requests to the internal endpoints of the WSGI-server.

3.6 Accessibility: Interfaces

Users can interact with DEBIE through four different interfaces. The simplest way is by using the provided web interface. For programmatic access, we offer the RESTful-API accessible directly via HTTP requests. As a third option, a desktop version of the tool is available for download: this tools runs completely offline and, depending on the hardware, may perform faster. Finally, we offer a command-line interface intended for shell usage.

Web User Interface. DEBIE is primarily imagined as a web application with a full extendable web user interface (see Figure 2). The web-UI enables users to evaluate and debias with predefined or custom bias specifications. Designed as a *one-page application*, the web UI guides the user via five simple steps through the full process:

Step 1: Selection of the Embedding Space. In the first step, the user has to select with which embedding space to work. The users can select one of three integrated embedding spaces (§3.4) uploaded or their own pretrained vector space.

Step 2: Selection of the Bias Specification. The user next chooses a bias specification: they can select one of the integrated WEAT bias specifications or define a bias specification of their own.

Step 3: Selection and Computation of the Bias Tests. The user next selects bias measures/scores (see §3.2) to be applied on the selected embedding space given the selected bias specification. The bias (and semantic similarity) scores are displayed in a table (see the upper part of Figure 2) and can also be exported as in the JSON format.

Step 4: Selection and Execution of Debiasing Algorithms. The user can next choose to debias the selected embedding space (Step 1) based on the selected bias specification (Step 2). To this effect, the user can choose between GBDD, BAM, or one of their compositions (GBDD∘BAM or BAM∘GBDD). The debiased embeddings space can be downloaded. To visualize the differences between the original (biased) and debiased embedding space, we visualize the 2D PCA-compressions of the terms from the bias specification in both spaces (see bottom part of Figure 2).

Step 5: Computation of Bias Tests on the Debiased space. Finally, the user can evalute the effects of debiasing with the desired set of bias measures. This is like Step 3, only now we subject to testing the debiased instead of the original embedding space.

RESTful API. For programmatic access, we offer a RESTful API. The API can deliver vector representations of words, compute and fetch the bias evaluation scores, as well as debiased word embeddings based on a provided bias specification. The API endpoints are accessible online.[11] API documentation is available in the `swagger` format on the DEBIE website.[12]

Desktop Application. We offer an adapted offline-version of the web application providing the same functionality, runnable on Windows OS. The desktop app has been created with the python module `flaskwebgui`, using the source files of

[11] http://debie.informatik.uni-mannheim.de:8000/REST/

[12] http://debie.informatik.uni-mannheim.de:8000/swagger/

the web application. The desktop application is available both as a windows executable file (`.exe`) and as a python script.

Command-line Interface. Finally, we expose DEBIE's functionality through a command-line interface, intended for shell (e.g., `bash`) usage. We employ the Python framework `click` to parse the command line arguments.

4 Ethical Considerations

Given the high sensitivity of the issue of bias in text representations, we would like the reader to consider the following three aspects.

(i) Our platform allows for measuring and mitigating biases based on bias specifications, which need to be defined by the user. In actual deployment scenarios, those specifications need to be designed with extreme care and the concrete sociotechnical environment in mind. For instance, it would be wrong to assume that by using one of the predefined gender bias specifications provided with this platform, all stereotypical gender associations will be removed from the representation space. In contrast, for each individual application scenario, the user should make sure that the bias specification matches the bias evaluation and debiasing intent.

(ii) Though the user's main role is to choose appropriate bias specifications, we think it is important that the user has enough technical proficiency to understand potential issues of the provided measures and mitigation methods.

(iii) The gender bias specifications from previous work provided with this platform only consider bias between *male* and *female* term sets, i.e., they follow a binary notion of gender. However, it is important to keep in mind that gender is a spectrum. We fully acknowledge the importance of the inclusion of *all gender identities*, e.g., nonbinary, gender fluid, polygender, etc., in language technologies.

5 Conclusion

We have presented DEBIE, an integrated platform for measuring and attenuating implicit and explicit biases in distributional word vector spaces. Via four different interfaces, we enable fast and easy access to a variety of bias measures and debiasing methods, allowing users to experiment with arbitrary embedding spaces and bias specifications. We hope DEBIE facilitates an exploration of a wider set of human biases in language representations.

Acknowledgments

Anne Lauscher and Goran Glavaš are supported by the Eliteprogramm of the Baden-Württemberg Stiftung (AGREE grant). We would like to thank the anonymous reviewers for their helpful comments.

References

David Arthur and Sergei Vassilvitskii. 2007. K-means++: The advantages of careful seeding. In *Proceedings of SODA*, pages 1027–1035.

Rachel Bellamy, Kuntal Dey, Michael Hind, Samuel Hoffman, Stephanie Houde, Kalapriya Kannan, Pranay Lohia, Jacquelyn Martino, Sameep Mehta, Aleksandra Mojsilovic, Seema Nagar, Karthikeyan Natesan Ramamurthy, John Richards, Diptikalyan Saha, Prasanna Sattigeri, Moninder Singh, Ramazon Kush, and Yunfeng Zhang. 2018. Ai fairness 360: An extensible toolkit for detecting, understanding, and mitigating unwanted algorithmic bias.

Su Lin Blodgett, Solon Barocas, Hal Daumé III, and Hanna Wallach. 2020. Language (technology) is power: A critical survey of "bias" in nlp. In *Proceedings of the 58th Meeting of the Association for Computational Linguistics*, pages 5454–5476, Online. Association for Computational Linguistics.

Piotr Bojanowski, Edouard Grave, Armand Joulin, and Tomas Mikolov. 2017. Enriching word vectors with subword information. *Transactions of the ACL*, 5:135–146.

Tolga Bolukbasi, Kai Wei Chang, James Zou, Venkatesh Saligrama, and Adam Kalai. 2016. Man is to computer programmer as woman is to homemaker? Debiasing word embeddings. pages 4356–4364.

Shikha Bordia and Samuel Bowman. 2019. Identifying and reducing gender bias in word-level language models. In *Proceedings of the 2019 Conference of the North American Chapter of the Association for Computational Linguistics: Student Research Workshop*, pages 7–15.

Aylin Caliskan, Joanna J. Bryson, and Arvind Narayanan. 2017. Semantics derived automatically from language corpora necessarily contain human biases. *Science*, 356:183–186.

Sunipa Dev and Jeff Phillips. 2019. Attenuating bias in word vectors. In *Proceedings of Machine Learning Research*, volume 89 of *Proceedings of Machine Learning Research*, pages 879–887. PMLR.

Catherine D'Ignazio and Lauren F Klein. 2020. The power chapter. In *Data Feminism*. The MIT Press.

Emily Dinan, Angela Fan, Adina Williams, Jack Urbanek, Douwe Kiela, and Jason Weston. 2020. Queens are powerful too: Mitigating gender bias in dialogue generation. In *Proceedings of the 2020 Conference on Empirical Methods in Natural Language Processing (EMNLP)*, pages 8173–8188, Online. Association for Computational Linguistics.

Lev Finkelstein, Evgeniy Gabrilovich, Yossi Matias, Ehud Rivlin, Zach Solan, Gadi Wolfman, and Eytan Ruppin. 2001. Placing search in context: The concept revisited. In *Proceedings of the 10th international conference on World Wide Web*, pages 406–414.

Nikhil Garg, Londa Schiebinger, Dan Jurafsky, and James Zou. 2018. Word embeddings quantify 100 years of gender and ethnic stereotypes. *Proceedings of the National Academy of Sciences*, 115(16):3635–3644.

Goran Glavaš, Robert Litschko, Sebastian Ruder, and Ivan Vulić. 2019. How to (properly) evaluate cross-lingual word embeddings: On strong baselines, comparative analyses, and some misconceptions. In *Proceedings of ACL*, pages 710–721.

Hila Gonen and Yoav Goldberg. 2019. Lipstick on a Pig: Debiasing Methods Cover up Systematic Gender Biases in Word Embeddings But do not Remove Them. In *Proceedings of NAACL-HLT*, pages 609–614.

Zellig S. Harris. 1954. Distributional structure. *Word*, 10(23):146–162.

Felix Hill, Roi Reichart, and Anna Korhonen. 2015. Simlex-999: Evaluating semantic models with (genuine) similarity estimation. *Computational Linguistics*, 41(4):665–695.

Anne Lauscher and Goran Glavaš. 2019. Are We Consistently Biased? Multidimensional Analysis of Biases in Distributional Word Vectors. pages 85–91.

Anne Lauscher, Goran Glavaš, Simone Paolo Ponzetto, and Ivan Vulić. 2020a. A general framework for implicit and explicit debiasing of distributional word vector spaces. In *Proceedings of the Thirty-Fourth AAAI Conference on Artificial Intelligence (AAAI)*, pages 8131–8138.

Anne Lauscher, Rafik Takieddin, Simone Paolo Ponzetto, and Goran Glavaš. 2020b. AraWEAT: Multidimensional analysis of biases in Arabic word embeddings. In *Proceedings of the Fifth Arabic Natural Language Processing Workshop*, pages 192–199, Barcelona, Spain (Online). Association for Computational Linguistics.

Katherine McCurdy and Oguz Serbetci. 2017. Grammatical gender associations outweigh topical gender bias in crosslinguistic word embeddings. In *Proceedings of WiNLP*.

Tomas Mikolov, Ilya Sutskever, Kai Chen, Greg S Corrado, and Jeff Dean. 2013. Distributed representations of words and phrases and their compositionality. In *Proceedings of NeurIPS*, pages 3111–3119.

Moin Nadeem, Anna Bethke, and Siva Reddy. 2020. Stereoset: Measuring stereotypical bias in pretrained language models. *arXiv preprint arXiv:2004.09456*.

Brian A. Nosek, Anthony G. Greenwald, and Mahzarin R. Banaji. 2002. Harvesting implicit group attitudes and beliefs from a demonstration web site. *Group Dynamics*, 6:101–115.

Jeffrey Pennington, Richard Socher, and Christopher Manning. 2014. Glove: Global vectors for word representation. In *Proceedings of EMNLP*, pages 1532–1543.

Yusu Qian, Urwa Muaz, Ben Zhang, and Jae Won Hyun. 2019. Reducing gender bias in word-level language models with a gender-equalizing loss function. In *Proceedings of the 57th Annual Meeting of the Association for Computational Linguistics: Student Research Workshop*, pages 223–228.

Samuel L. Smith, David H.P. Turban, Steven Hamblin, and Nils Y. Hammerla. 2017. Offline bilingual word vectors, orthogonal transformations and the inverted softmax. In *Proceedings of ICLR*.

Kellie Webster, Xuezhi Wang, Ian Tenney, Alex Beutel, Emily Pitler, Ellie Pavlick, Jilin Chen, and Slav Petrov. 2020. Measuring and reducing gendered correlations in pre-trained models. *arXiv preprint arXiv:2010.06032*.

Jieyu Zhao, Tianlu Wang, Mark Yatskar, Ryan Cotterell, Vicente Ordonez, and Kai-Wei Chang. 2019. Gender bias in contextualized word embeddings. In *Proceedings of the 2019 Conference of the North American Chapter of the Association for Computational Linguistics: Human Language Technologies, Volume 1 (Long and Short Papers)*, pages 629–634.

A Dashboard for Mitigating the COVID-19 Misinfodemic

Zhengyuan Zhu[1], Kevin Meng[2], Josue Caraballo[1], Israa Jaradat[1],
Xiao Shi[1], Zeyu Zhang[1], Farahnaz Akrami[1], Haojin Liao[1], Fatma Arslan[1],
Damian Jimenez[1], Mohammed Samiul Saeef[1], Paras Pathak[1], and Chengkai Li[1]

[1]The University of Texas at Arlington
[2]Massachusetts Institute of Technology

Abstract

This paper describes the current milestones achieved in our ongoing project that aims to understand the surveillance of, impact of, and effective interventions against the COVID-19 misinfodemic on Twitter. Specifically, it introduces a public dashboard which, in addition to displaying case counts in an interactive map and a navigational panel, also provides some unique features not found in other places. Particularly, the dashboard uses a curated catalog of COVID-19 related facts and debunks of misinformation, and it displays the most prevalent information from the catalog among Twitter users in user-selected U.S. geographic regions. The paper explains how to use BERT-based models to match tweets with the facts and misinformation and to detect their stance towards such information. The paper also discusses the results of preliminary experiments on analyzing the spatio-temporal spread of misinformation.

1 Introduction

Alongside the COVID-19 pandemic, there is a raging global misinfodemic (Mian and Khan, 2020; Roozenbeek et al., 2020) just as deadly. As fear grows, false information related to the pandemic goes viral on social media and threatens to affect an overwhelmed population. Such misinformation misleads the public on how the virus is transmitted, how authorities and people are responding to the pandemic, as well as its symptoms, treatments, and so on. This onslaught exacerbates the vicious impact of the virus, as the misinformation drowns out credible information, interferes with measures to contain the outbreak, depletes resources needed by those at risk, and overloads the health care system. Although health misinformation is not new (Oyeyemi et al., 2014), such a dangerous interplay between a pandemic and a misinfodemic is unprecedented. It calls for studying not only the outbreak but also its related misinformation; the fight on these two fronts must go hand-in-hand.

This demo paper describes the current milestones achieved in our ongoing project that aims to understand the surveillance of, impact of, and effective interventions against the COVID-19 misinfodemic. 1) For *surveillance*, we seek to discover the patterns by which different types of COVID-19 misinformation spread. 2) To understand the *impact* of misinformation, we aim to compare the spreading of the SARS-CoV-2 virus and misinformation and derive their correlations. 3) To understand what types of *interventions* are effective in containing misinformation, we will contrast the spreading of misinformation before and after debunking efforts. 4) To understand whether the outcomes related to 1), 2) and 3) differ by geographical locations and demographic groups, we will study the variability of misinformation and debunking efforts across geographical and demographic groups.

While we continue to pursue these directions, we have built an online dashboard at https://idir.uta.edu/covid-19/ to directly benefit the public. A screencast video of the dashboard is at bit.ly/3c6v5xf. The dashboard provides a map, a navigation panel, and timeline charts for looking up numbers of cases, deaths, and recoveries, similar to a number of COVID-19 tracking dashboards. [1][2][3] However, our dashboard also provides several features not found in other places.

[1]https://www.covid19-trials.com/
[2]https://coronavirus.jhu.edu/map.html
[3]https://www.cdc.gov/covid-data-tracker/index.html

Proceedings of the 16th Conference of the European Chapter of the Association for Computational Linguistics: System Demonstrations, pages 99–105
April 19 - 23, 2021.

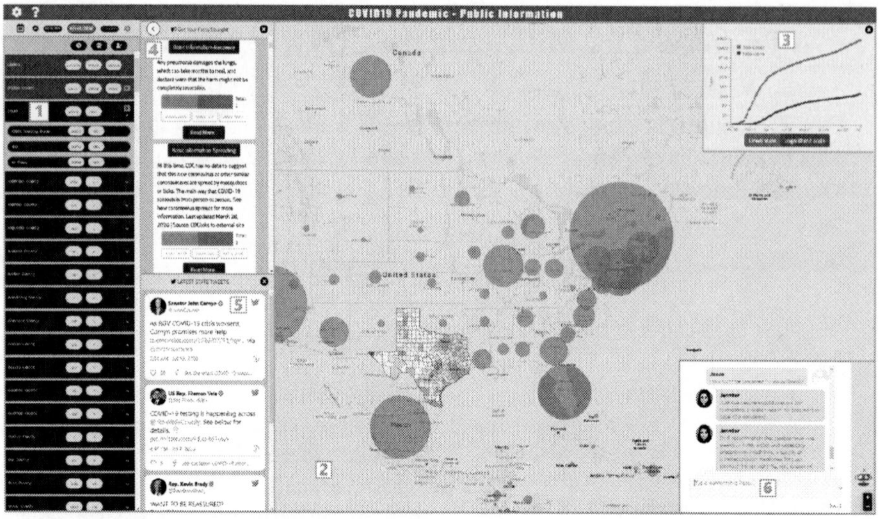

Figure 1: The user interface of the dashboard for mitigating the COVID-19 misinfodemic

1) It displays the most prevalent factual information among Twitter users in any user-selected U.S. geographic region. 2) The "factual information" comes from a catalog that we manually curated. It includes statements from authoritative organizations, verdicts, debunks, and explanations of (potentially false) factual claims from fact-checking websites, and FAQs from credible sources. The catalog's entries are further organized into a taxonomy. For simplicity, we refer to it as the *catalog and taxonomy of COVID-19 facts* or just *facts* in ensuing discussion. 3) The dashboard displays COVID-19 related tweets from local authorities of user-selected geographic regions. 4) It embeds a chatbot built specifically for COVID-19 related questions. 5) It shows case-statistics from several popular sources which sometimes differ.

The codebase of the dashboard's frontend, backend, and data collection tools are open-sourced at https://github.com/idirlab/covid19. All collected data are at https://github.com/idirlab/covid19data. Particularly, the catalog and taxonomy of facts are also available through a SPARQL endpoint at https://cokn.org/deliverables/7-covid19-kg/ and the corresponding RDF dataset can be requested there.

What is particularly worth noting about the underlying implementation of the dashboard is the adaptation of state-of-the-art textual semantic similarity and stance detection models. Tweets are first passed through a *claim-matching* model, which selects the tweets that semantically match the facts in our catalog. Then, the *stance detection* model determines whether the tweets agree with, disagree with, or merely discuss these facts. This enables us to pinpoint pieces of misinformation (i.e., tweets that disagree with known facts) and analyze their spread.

A few studies analyzed and quantified the spread of COVID-19 misinformation on Twitter (Kouzy et al., 2020; Memon and Carley, 2020; Al-Rakhami and Al-Amri, 2020) and other social media platforms (Brennen et al., 2020). However, these studies conducted mostly manual inspection of small datasets, while our system automatically sifts through millions of tweets and matches tweets with our catalog of facts.

2 The Dashboard

Figure 1 shows the dashboard's user interface, with its components highlighted.

Geographic region selection panel (Component 1). A user can select a specific country, a U.S. state, or a U.S. county by using this panel or the interactive map (Component 2). Once a region is selected, the panel shows the counts of confirmed cases, deaths and recovered cases for the region in collapsed or expanded modes. When a region is expanded by the user, counts from all available sources are displayed; on the other hand, if it is collapsed, only counts from the default (which the user can customize) data source are displayed. These sources do not provide identical numbers.

Interactive map (Component 2). On each country and each U.S. state, a red circle is displayed, with an area size proportional to its number of confirmed cases. When a state is selected, the circle is replaced with its counties' polygons in different shades of red, proportional to the counties' confirmed cases.

Timeline chart (Component 3). It plots the counts of the selected region over time and can be viewed in linear or logarithmic scale.

Panel of facts (Component 4). For the selected region, this panel displays facts from our catalog, and the distribution of people discussing, agreeing, or disagreeing with them on Twitter. A large number of people refuting these facts would indicate wide spread of misinformation. To avoid repeating misconceptions, the dashboard displays facts from authoritative sources only.

Government tweets (Component 5). It displays COVID-19 related tweets in the past seven days from officials of the user-selected geographic region. These tweets are from a curated list of 3,744 Twitter handles that belong to governments, officials, and public health authorities at U.S. federal and state levels.

Chatbot (Component 6). This component embeds the *Jennifer Chatbot* built by the New Voices project of the National Academies of Sciences, Engineering and Medicine (Li et al., 2020), which was built specifically for answering COVID-19 related questions. As part of the collaborative team behind this chatbot, we are expanding it using the aforementioned catalog.

3 The Datasets

The dashboard uses the following three datasets.

1) Counts of confirmed cases, deaths, and recoveries. We collected these counts daily from Johns Hopkins University, [4] the New York Times (NYT) [5] and the COVID Tracking Project. [6] These sources provide statistics at various geographic granularities (country, state, county).

2) Tweets. We are using a collection of approximately 250 million COVID-19 related tweets from January 1st, 2020 to May 16th, 2020, obtained from (Banda et al., 2020) (version 10.0). We removed tweets and Twitter handles (and their tweets) that do not have location information, resulting in 34.6 million remaining tweets. We then randomly selected 10.4% of each month's tweets, leading to 3.6 million remaining tweets. We used the OpenStreetMap (Quinion et al., 2020) API to map the locations of Twitter accounts from user-entered free text to U.S. county names. We used the ArcGIS API [7] to map the locations of tweets from longitude/latitude to counties.

3) A catalog and a taxonomy of COVID-19 related facts.

The manually curated catalog currently has 9,512 entries from 21 credible websites, including statements from authoritative organizations (e.g., WHO, CDC), verdicts, debunks, and explanations of factual claims (of which the truthfulness varies) from fact-checking websites (e.g., the IFCN CoronaVirusFacts Alliance Database, [8] PolitiFact), and FAQs both from credible sources (e.g., FDA, NYT) and a dataset curated by (Wei et al., 2020).

We organized the entries in this catalog into a taxonomy of categories, by integrating and consolidating the available categories from a number of source websites, placing entries from other websites into these categories or creating new categories, and organizing the categories into a hierarchical structure based on their inclusion relationship. The taxonomy is as follows, in the format of {level-1 categories [*level-2 categories* (`level-3 categories`)]}: [9]
{Animals, Basic Information [*Causes, Definition, Disease Alongside, Recovery, Spreading, Symptoms, Testing*], Cases, Contribution, Diplomacy, Economics/Finance [*Crisis, Grants/Stimulus, Tax, Unemployment*], Family Preparation, Funeral, Government Control [*Administration* (`Lockdown, Reopen, Staff`), *Law, Medical Support, Military*], Mental Health, Prevention [*Actions to Prevent* (`Hand Hygiene, Isolation, Masks, Social Distancing`), *Medication, Vaccines*], Religion, Schools/Universities, Travel, Treatment [*Medication, Minor Symptom, Severe Symptom*], Violence/Crime}.

We also stored the catalog and the taxonomy

[4] https://github.com/CSSEGISandData/COVID-19

[5] https://github.com/nytimes/covid-19-data

[6] https://covidtracking.com/

[7] https://developers.arcgis.com/python/guide/reverse-geocoding/

[8] https://www.poynter.org/ifcn-covid-19-misinformation/

[9] Not every level-1 or level-2 category has subcategories.

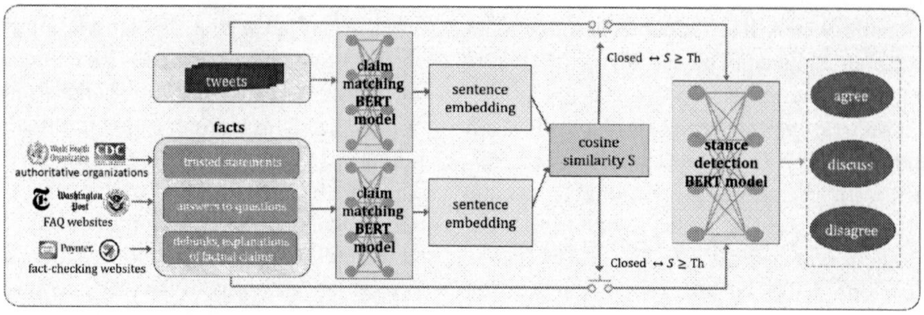

Figure 2: Matching tweets with facts and stance detection

Tweet	Fact	Taxonomy Categories	Similarity	Stance
Coronavirus cannot be passed by dogs or cats but they can test positive.	There has been no evidence that pets such as dogs or cats can spread the coronavirus.	Animals, Spreading	0.817	agree
More people die from the flu in the U.S. in 1 day than have died of the Coronavirus across the world ever.	Right now, it appears that COVID-19, the disease caused by the new coronavirus, causes more cases of severe disease and more deaths than the seasonal flu.	Cases	0.816	disagree

Table 1: Example results of matching tweets with facts and stance detection

as an RDF dataset, in which each entry of the catalog is identified by a unique resource identifier (URI). It is connected to a mediator node that represents the multiary relation associated with the entry. For example, Figure 3 shows a question about COVID-19, its answer and source, and the lowest-level taxonomy nodes that the entry belongs to, all connected to a mediator node. This RDF dataset, with 12 relations and 78,495 triples, is published in four popular RDF formats—N-Triples, Turtle, N3, and RDF/XML. Furthermore, we have set up a SPARQL query endpoint at https://cokn.org/deliverables/7-covid19-kg/ using OpenLink Virtuoso.[10]

4 Matching Tweets with Facts and Stance Detection

Given the catalog of COVID-19 related facts F and the tweets T, we first employ *claim-matching* to locate a set of tweets $\mathbf{t}^f \in T$ that discuss each fact $f \in F$. Next, we apply *stance detection* on pairs $\mathbf{p}^f = \{(t, f) \mid t \in \mathbf{t}^f\}$ to determine whether each t is agreeing with, disagreeing with, or neutrally discussing f. Finally, aggregate results are displayed on Component 4 of the dashboard to summarize the public's view on each fact. Figure 2 depicts the overall claim-matching and stance detection pipeline. For both tasks, we employed Bidirectional Encoder Representations from Transformers (BERT) (Devlin et al., 2019). Table 1 shows some example results of claim matching and stance detection.

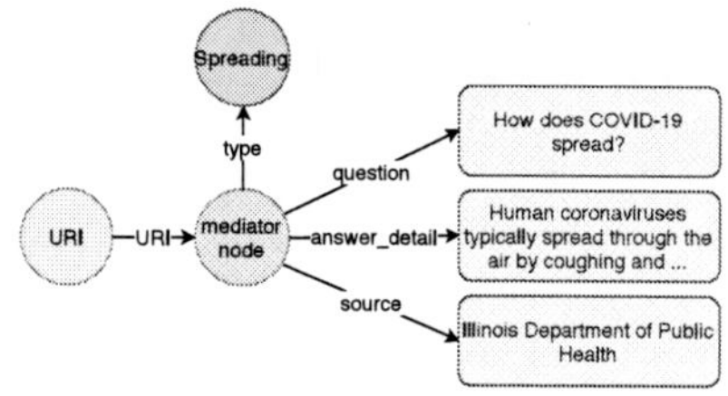

Figure 3: An entry of the catalog stored in RDF

Claim matching.

We generate sentence embeddings $\mathbf{s}^t$ and $\mathbf{s}^f$, for t and f respectively, using the mean-tokens pooling strategy in Sentence-BERT (Reimers and Gurevych, 2019). The relevance between t and f is then calculated as:

$$R^{t,f} = \frac{\mathbf{s}^t \cdot \mathbf{s}^f}{\|\mathbf{s}^t\| \times \|\mathbf{s}^f\|} \tag{1}$$

Given $R^{t,f}$, we model claim-matching as a ranking task on the relevance between facts and tweets. Thus, the output of this stage is $\mathbf{t}^f = \{t \in T \mid R^{t,f} \geq \theta\}$ for each fact $f \in F$, where the threshold θ is 0.8 in our implementation.

[10]https://virtuoso.openlinksw.com/

Stance detection. Given $\mathbf{t}^f$, we detect the stance that each tweet t takes toward fact f. There could be 3 classes of stance: agree (t supports f), discuss (t neutrally discusses f), and disagree (t refutes f). For this task, we obtained a pre-trained $\text{BERT}_{\text{Base}}$ model [11] and trained it on the Fake-News Challenge Stage 1 (FNC-1) dataset. [12] We denote this model Stance-BERT.

We first pre-process $\mathbf{p}^f$ to conform with BERT input conventions by 1) applying $W(\cdot)$, the WordPiece tokenizer (Wu et al., 2016), 2) applying $C(a_1, a_2, \ldots, a_n)$, a function that concatenates arguments in appearance order, and 3) inserting specialized BERT tokens [CLS] and [SEP]. Since BERT has a maximum input length of $M = 512$ and some facts can exceed this limit, we propose a sliding-window approach inspired by (Devlin et al., 2019) to form input $\mathbf{x}^f$:

$$\mathbf{x}^f = \Big\{\{C([\text{CLS}], W(t), [\text{SEP}], W(f)_{[i*S, i*S+L]}, [\text{SEP}]) \mid 0 \le i < \left\lceil \frac{|W(f)|}{S} \right\rceil\} \mid (t, f) \in \mathbf{p}^f\Big\} \quad (2)$$

where S defines the distance between successive windows and $L = M - (|W(t)| + 3)$ is the sequence length available for each fact. If $i * S + L$ is an out-of-bounds index for $W(f)$, the extra space is padded using null tokens.

Each element $\mathbf{w} \in \mathbf{x}^f$ contains a set of windows representing a tweet-fact pair. Each window $w_i \in \mathbf{w}$ is passed into Stance-BERT, which returns probability distributions (each containing 3 entries, 1 for each class) $\hat{\mathbf{y}}^f_{w_i}$ for each window.

Stance aggregation. For each fact f, the stance detection results are accumulated to generate scores S^f_C, where $C \in \{\text{agree}, \text{discuss}, \text{disagree}\}$ that denote the percentage of tweets that agree, discuss, and disagree with f: [13]

$$S^f_C = \frac{\sum_{\mathbf{w} \in \mathbf{x}^f} [\operatorname{argmax} \sigma(\{\hat{\mathbf{y}}^f_{w_i} \mid w_i \in \mathbf{w}\}) = C]}{|\mathbf{x}^f|} \quad (3)$$

where $\sigma(\cdot)$ is a function that averages the model's output scores for each class across all windows of tweet-fact pair. The 3 final stance scores are passed to the dashboard's panel of facts (Component 4) for display.

[11] https://github.com/google-research/bert

[12] http://www.fakenewschallenge.org/

[13] We use the Iverson bracket: $[P] = 1$ if P is true, else 0

5 Evaluation and Results

5.1 Performance of Claim Matching

To evaluate the performance of the claim matching component, we first created a Cartesian product of the 3.6 million tweets with 500 "facts" from the catalog (see Section 3 for description of datasets), followed by randomly selecting 800 tweet-fact pairs from the Cartesian product. To retain a balanced dataset, 400 pairs were drawn from those pairs scored over 0.8 by the claim matching component, and another 400 pairs were drawn from the rest. To obtain the ground-truth labels on these 800 pairs, we used three human annotators. 183 pairs were labeled "matched" (i.e., the tweet and the fact have matching topics) and 617 pairs "unmatched". Table 2 shows the claim matching component's performance on these 800 pairs, measured by precision@k and nDCG@k(normalized Discounted Cumulative Gain at k). Both precision@k and nDCG@k are metrics of ranking widely used in classification problem, the order of top k prediction is considered in nDCG@k but not in precision@k.

Metric	@5	@10	@20	@50	@100
Precision	0.80	0.80	0.70	0.56	0.52
nDCG	0.62	0.72	0.78	0.81	0.83

Table 2: Performance of claim matching on the 800 tweet-fact pairs

5.2 Performance of Stance-BERT

Model	F1 score			
	agree	discuss	disagree	macro
$\text{Stance-BERT}_{\text{window}}$(FNC-1)	0.65	0.45	0.84	0.65
$\text{Stance-BERT}_{\text{trunc}}$(FNC-1)	0.66	0.41	0.82	0.63
(Xu et al., 2018)(FNC-1)	0.55	0.15	0.73	0.48
$\text{Stance-BERT}_{\text{window}}$(COVID-19)	0.75	0.03	0.58	0.45

Table 3: Performance of Stance-BERT on the FNC-1 test dataset and 200 matched tweet-fact pairs

Table 3 shows Stance-BERT's performance on the FNC-1 competition test dataset and our tweet-fact pairs, using F1 scores for all 3 classes as well as macro-F1. On FNC-1, we tested 2 variations of the same model: $\text{Stance-BERT}_{\text{window}}$, which uses the sliding-window approach (Section 4), and $\text{Stance-BERT}_{\text{trunc}}$, a model that truncates/discards all inputs after M tokens but is otherwise identical to $\text{Stance-BERT}_{\text{window}}$. Both variants significantly outperformed the method used in (Xu et al., 2018), one of the recent competitive methods on FNC-1.

Note that FNC-1 also includes a fourth "unrelated" class that we discarded, since we already have a claim-matching component. Because other recent stance detection methods (Mohtarami et al., 2018; Fang et al., 2019) only reported macro-F1 scores calculated using all four classes including "unrelated", we cannot report a direct comparison with their methods. However, we argue that our macro-F1 of 0.65 remains highly competitive. The model of (Xu et al., 2018) achieved a 0.98 F1 score on "unrelated", which suggests that "unrelated" (i.e., separating related and unrelated pairs) is far easier than the other 3 classes (i.e., discerning between different classes of related pairs). Given that Stance-BERT significantly outperformed (Xu et al., 2018) on all other 3 classes, it is plausible that Stance-BERT will remain a top performer under all four classes.

To evaluate Stance-BERT's performance on our tweet-fact pairs, the three human annotators produced ground-truth labels on another set of 481 randomly selected tweet-fact pairs. 200 pairs are labeled as "matched". These 200 pairs are further labeled as "agree"/"discuss"/"disagree", in a distribution of 110/73/17 tweet-fact pairs. Ultimately, we discovered that Stance-BERT performs remarkably well on "agree" and "disagree" classes but falters on "discuss".

5.3 Misinformation Analysis

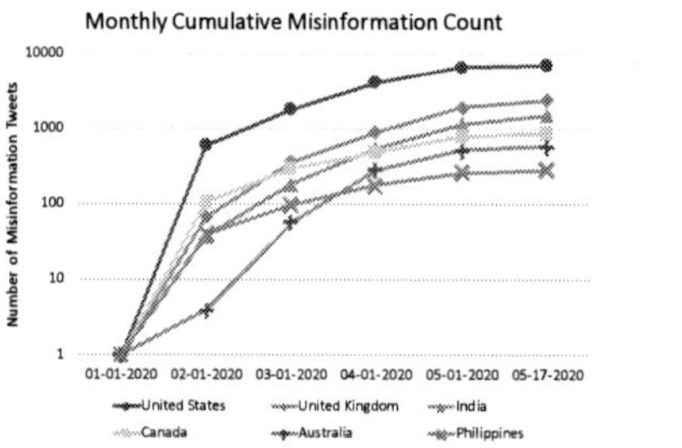

Figure 4: 6 countries with the most misinformation tweets

Figure 4 is the cumulative timeline for the top-6 countries with the most COVID-19 misinformation tweets in the dataset. "Misinformation tweets" refer to tweets that go against known facts as judged by our stance detection model.

We also conducted a study on the correlation between misinformation tweet counts and COVID-19 case counts. We looked at the percentage of cases relative to a country's population size, and the percentage of misinformation tweets relative to the total number of tweets from a country. The Pearson correlation coefficients between them are in Table 4. We find that the number of misinformation tweets most positively correlates with the number of confirmed cases. In contrast, its correlation with the number of recovered cases is weaker.

Country	Confirm	Death	Recover
United States	0.763	0.738	0.712
United Kingdom	0.862	0.833	-
India	0.794	0.798	0.755
Canada	0.706	0.667	0.663
Australia	0.954	0.922	0.887
Philippines	0.720	0.696	0.618

Table 4: Correlation between the percentage of confirmed/deceased/recovered cases and the percentage of misinformation tweets. The number of recovered cases in U.K. after April 13th is missing from the data source.

Finally, we manually categorized the misinformation tweets based on the taxonomy (Section 3). Table 5 lists the five most frequent categories of misinformation tweets. These five categories make up 49.9% of all misinformation tweets, with the other 50.1% being spread out over the other 33 categories.

Category	Count	Percentage
Definition	2503	15.1
Spreading	2118	12.7
Other	1450	8.7
Testing	1301	7.8
Disease Alongside	936	5.6
Total	8308	49.9

Table 5: Most frequent categories of misinformation tweets

6 Conclusion

This paper introduces an information dashboard constructed in the context of our ongoing project regarding the COVID-19 misinfodemic. Going forward, we will focus on developing the dashboard at scale, including more comprehensive tweet collection and catalog discovery and collection. We will also introduce more functions into the dashboard that are aligned with our project goal of studying the surveillance of, impact of, and intervention on COVID-19 misinfodemic.

References

Mabrook S Al-Rakhami and Atif M Al-Amri. 2020. Lies kill, facts save: Detecting covid-19 misinformation in twitter. *IEEE Access*, 8:155961–155970.

Juan M. Banda, Ramya Tekumalla, Guanyu Wang, Jingyuan Yu, Tuo Liu, Yuning Ding, Katya Artemova, Elena Tutubalin, and Gerardo Chowell. 2020. A large-scale COVID-19 twitter chatter dataset for open scientific research - an international collaboration.

J Scott Brennen, Felix M Simon, Philip N Howard, and Rasmus Kleis Nielsen. 2020. Types, sources, and claims of COVID-19 misinformation. *Reuters Institute*.

Jacob Devlin, Ming-Wei Chang, Kenton Lee, and Kristina Toutanova. 2019. BERT: Pre-training of deep bidirectional transformers for language understanding. In *NAACL*, pages 4171–4186.

Wei Fang, Moin Nadeem, Mitra Mohtarami, and James Glass. 2019. Neural multi-task learning for stance prediction. In *EMNLP Workshop on Fact Extraction and Verification*, pages 13–19.

Ramez Kouzy, Joseph Abi Jaoude, Afif Kraitem, Molly B El Alam, Basil Karam, Elio Adib, Jabra Zarka, Cindy Traboulsi, Elie W Akl, and Khalil Baddour. 2020. Coronavirus goes viral: quantifying the COVID-19 misinformation epidemic on twitter. *Cureus*, 12(3).

Yunyao Li, Tyrone Grandison, Patricia Silveyra, Ali Douraghy, Xinyu Guan, Thomas Kieselbach, Chengkai Li, and Haiqi Zhang. 2020. Jennifer for COVID-19: An nlp-powered chatbot built for the people and by the people to combat misinformation. In *ACL Workshop on Natural Language Processing for COVID-19*, pages 1–9.

Shahan Ali Memon and Kathleen M Carley. 2020. Characterizing covid-19 misinformation communities using a novel twitter dataset. *arXiv preprint arXiv:2008.00791*.

Areeb Mian and Shujhat Khan. 2020. Coronavirus: the spread of misinformation. *BMC medicine*, 18(1):1–2.

Mitra Mohtarami, Ramy Baly, James Glass, Preslav Nakov, Lluís Màrquez, and Alessandro Moschitti. 2018. Automatic stance detection using end-to-end memory networks. In *NAACL*, pages 767–776.

Sunday Oluwafemi Oyeyemi, Elia Gabarron, and Rolf Wynn. 2014. Ebola, twitter, and misinformation: a dangerous combination?. *BMJ*, 349:g6178.

Brian Quinion, Sarah Hoffmann, and Marc T. Metten. 2020. Nominatim: A search engine for openstreetmap data.

Nils Reimers and Iryna Gurevych. 2019. Sentence-bert: Sentence embeddings using siamese bert-networks. In *EMNLP-IJCNLP*, pages 3973–3983.

Jon Roozenbeek, Claudia R Schneider, Sarah Dryhurst, John Kerr, Alexandra LJ Freeman, Gabriel Recchia, Anne Marthe Van Der Bles, and Sander Van Der Linden. 2020. Susceptibility to misinformation about covid-19 around the world. *Royal Society open science*, 7(10):201199.

Jerry Wei, Chengyu Huang, Soroush Vosoughi, and Jason Wei. 2020. What are people asking about covid-19? a question classification dataset. *arXiv preprint arXiv:2005.12522*.

Yonghui Wu, Mike Schuster, Zhifeng Chen, Quoc V Le, Mohammad Norouzi, Wolfgang Macherey, Maxim Krikun, Yuan Cao, Qin Gao, Klaus Macherey, et al. 2016. Google's neural machine translation system: Bridging the gap between human and machine translation. *arXiv preprint arXiv:1609.08144*.

Brian Xu, Mitra Mohtarami, and James Glass. 2018. Adversarial domain adaptation for stance detection. In *NeurIPS*.

Gap in pagination due to unavailable paper.

Pages 106-112

ASAD: Arabic Social media Analytics and unDerstanding

Sabit Hassan, Hamdy Mubarak, Ahmed Abdelali, Kareem Darwish
Qatar Computing Research Institute
Hamad bin Khalifa University
Doha, Qatar
{sahassan2,hmubarak,aabdelali,kdarwish}@hbku.edu.qa

Abstract

This system demonstration paper describes the Arabic Social media Analysis and unDerstanding (ASAD) toolkit, which is a suite of seven individual modules that allows users to determine dialects, sentiment, news category, offensiveness, hate speech, adult content, and spam in Arabic tweets[1]. The suite is made available through a web API and a web interface where users can enter text or upload files.

1 Introduction

Since Arabic is spoken across a vast region, the Arabic Twittersphere presents a valuable scope into social and linguistic phenomena, such as the multitude of dialects being used across different regions. The Arabic Social Media and unDerstanding (ASAD) suite [2], which we present herein, offers valuable tools for exploring such phenomena and for the automated processing of Arabic social media texts. Specifically, ASAD offers dialect identification, sentiment analysis, news category detection, offensive language detection, including hate speech and vulgar language, and spam detection. These tools are valuable for many downstream NLP application. For example, dialect identification can help improve author profiling and machine translation (Abdelali et al., 2020). Sentiment analysis can aid in quantifying public opinions (Abu Farha and Magdy, 2019). Detecting news categories can aid in content analysis. Further, offensive language and spam detection can help identify potentially malicious content on social media. Although there has been a growing interest in analyzing Arabic social media, there is a deficiency in publicly available tools or such tools are not integrated into one framework or toolkit. For example, we are not aware of any publicly available systems for offensive language, hate speech, adult content, or spam. Similarly, ADIDA (Obeid et al., 2019) and CAMeL (Obeid et al., 2020) dialect identification systems were not trained with Twitter data. Thus, ASAD fills an important gap in the Arabic social media analysis space. For ease of use, we make ASAD available via an i) online interface where users can enter text or upload files, and ii) web APIs that accept POST requests, making ASAD accessible from any programming language.

During the development of ASAD, we weighed different trade-off between effectiveness and efficiency to achieve competitive results at low computational costs. Thus, ASAD utilizes Support Vector Machine (SVM) classification for six out of the seven modules. As we show later, with the exception of dialect identification, we achieve results that are comparable or slightly lower than deep neural network models (DNN), namely fine-tuned BERT, while being significantly more efficient with no need for GPUs. Due to a larger difference in performance, we deploy a fine-tuned BERT model for dialect identification only. We hope that ASAD will aid researchers, analysts, and system integrators in incorporating Arabic social media analytics and understanding into their models and applications. We also hope that ASAD will motivate researchers to build similar suites for other languages.

2 Related Work

Analysis of Arabic social media has gained much recent interest. Offensive language and hate speech detection have yielded datasets, shared tasks (Mubarak et al., 2020b; Zampieri et al., 2020), and strong systems based on machine learning and contextual embedding models (Hassan et al., 2020a,b). Sentiment analysis is a well addressed problem yielding datasets (Elmadany et al., 2018)

[1] We will add more functionalities in the future.

[2] Demonstration: `https://www.youtube.com/watch?v=Boe_JYWK7cM`

Proceedings of the 16th Conference of the European Chapter of the Association for Computational Linguistics: System Demonstrations, pages 113–118

and systems based on and deep learning techniques (Abu Farha and Magdy, 2019) among others. Fine-tuned BERT models have been used for identifying categories of news posts on social media (Chowdhury et al., 2020). Adult content and spam detection have been relatively less explored with the focus mainly on creating resources (Alshehri et al., 2018; Al Twairesh et al., 2016; Mubarak et al., 2017, 2021, 2020a). Dialect ID has been the focus of the MADAR project (Bouamor et al., 2019) and other works (Abdelali et al., 2020; Abdul-Mageed et al., 2020; Zaidan and Callison-Burch, 2011).

Despite the abundance of literature in the aforementioned topics, there has been very little effort toward making tools available for public use. Most of the tools available in Arabic NLP tasks concentrate on NLP tasks such as segmentation, parsing, lemmatization, and POS tagging (Pasha et al., 2014; Abdelali et al., 2016; Darwish and Mubarak, 2016; Darwish et al., 2014). Along with text processing tools, CAMeL Tools (Obeid et al., 2020) allows sentiment analysis and dialect ID via a Python package. ADIDA (Obeid et al., 2019) is a web interface for dialect ID. The dialect ID systems of CAMeL Tools and ADIDA are based a parallel corpus of 25 Arabic city dialects in the travel domain.

3 Datasets

Dialect ID: We use the QADI dataset containing dialectal tweets from 18 countries (Abdelali et al., 2020). The training set contains 540K tweets automatically tagged for dialect and the test set contains 3.3K manually annotated tweets by native speakers from the 18 countries.

Sentiment Analysis: We use the ArSAS dataset (Elmadany et al., 2018) that contains 21K tweets that are labeled as Positive, Negative, Mixed or Neutral. We merge the Mixed and Neutral classes together (resulting in three classes) and split the data into 80/20 training and test splits.

News Categorization We use an in-house annotated dataset consisting of 30K news items from Aljazeera channel[3]. 80% of the data are used for training and 20% are used for testing. These news are manually annotated for different categories, namely: politics, economy, sports, culture-art, etc.

Offensive Language Detection: We use data of OffensEval 2020 shared task (Zampieri et al., 2020). The data consists of 8K tweets for training and 2K tweets tweets for testing that were manually annotated with whether they are offensive or not.

Hate Speech Detection: There are limited publicly available data for Arabic hate speech detection (Mubarak et al., 2020b). We use a publicly available dataset[4] that consists of tweet IDs annotated for whether they contain hate speech or not. Ignoring tweets that were not available at download time, we end up with 6.9K tweets.[5] We use 80% of the data for training and 20% for testing.

Adult Content Detection: We use the dataset presented in Mubarak et al. (2021). The data contains 50K tweets split into 80% for training and 20% for testing. Around 6K tweets (12% of all tweets) are manually verified to contain adult content. The rest are random tweets that are assumed not contain adult material since the percentage of adult content in tweets is very small.

Spam Detection: We use the dataset presented in Mubarak et al. (2020a). The dataset contains 9.8K tweets from 80 spam accounts (manually verified) that post spam tweets, along with 86K random tweets for training. The test set contains 2.7K tweets from 20 spam accounts (manually verified) that post spam tweets along with 25.6K random tweets. The assumption is that tweets from spam accounts are spam and that the vast majority of random tweets are not spam, because the percentage of spam is very small.

4 Classification Models

Some state-of-the-art (SOTA) techniques use complex models, typically DNN models, to achieve the best results. For ASAD, we want to have models that are small in size and easy to deploy while providing good results. To this end, we compare performances of fine-tuned BERT models and SVMs with character n-gram vectors weighted by term frequency-inverse document frequency (tf-idf) as features. As we show, the SVM models we employ are competitive with SOTA DNN models for majority of the modules of ASAD. The range of n-gram can influence the size of models and their performance. For each component in our suite, we experimented with different ranges of n-gram and calculated model size along with respective performance. Table 1 illustrates this study for offensive

[3] www.aljazeera.net

[4] https://github.com/raghadsh/Arabic-Hate-speech

[5] We plan to merge other datasets in future.

Classifier	Features	Size (classifier + vectorizer)	Acc%	P	R	F1
SVM	W[1-3]	30.7 MB	86.6	78.9	82.6	80.5
SVM	**C[1-3]**	**3.9 MB**	**91.2**	**88.8**	**82.4**	**85.0**
SVM	C[2-4]	14.5 MB	91.6	89.2	83.4	85.8
SVM	C[2-5]	37.5 MB	92.0	89.1	85.1	86.9
SVM	C[2-6]	73.4 MB	91.8	87.6	86.4	87.0
SVM	C[2-7]	120.5 MB	91.8	86.9	88.1	87.4

Table 1: Comparison of size vs performance on offensiveness detection. Ideal setting is bolded.

Module	Classes	Classifier	Features	Acc%	P	R	F1	BERT F1
Dialect ID	18	SVM	C[2-4]	54.5	60.9	54.6	54.1	**60.6**
Sentiment	3	SVM	C[1-3]	75.5	74.6	73.2	73.7	**75.8**
News Category	16	SVM	C[2-4]	84.2	57.3	54.1	54.8	**55.9**
Offensiveness	2	SVM	C[1-3]	91.2	88.8	82.4	85.0	**86.6**
Hate Speech	2	SVM	C[2-4]	79.1	74.4	76.2	**75.2**	75.1
Adult Content	2	SVM	C[1-3]	95.4	91.9	85.79	**88.5**	88.1
Spam	2	SVM	C[1-3]	99.4	99.3	97.3	98.3	**98.9**

Table 2: Performance of different ASAD modules compared to fine-tuned BERT models.

language detection (C and W refer to character and word, [a-b] denotes n-gram ranging from a to b. P, R and F1 stand for macro-averaged precision, recall and F1 respectively). We can see that going from an n-gram range of C[1-3] to C[2-7] increases model size (classifier + vectorizer) from 3.9 MB to 120.5 MB while improving the F1 score by 2.4. Although C[2-7] is a better system, C[1-3] is more suitable for deployment due to its small size. Table 2 lists performance of SVMs version compared to using BERT. When comparing to BERT models, we fine-tuned AraBERT(Antoun et al., 2020), a BERT-based model, pre-trained on Arabic news articles and Arabic Wikipedia. We fine-tune AraBERT by adding a fully-connected dense layer followed by a softmax classifier, minimizing the binary cross-entropy loss function for the training data. We use the PyTorch[6] implementation by HuggingFace[7] as it provides pre-trained weights and vocabulary. Aside from dialect ID, SVM models either beat BERT models or are within 1-2% away. We suspect that the SVM models were competitive because they were trained on Twitter data as opposed to BERT, which is trained on more formal text. For dialect ID, we opt to use the fine-tuned AraBERT model because it outperforms SVMs by a larger margin of 6.5%.

[6]https://pytorch.org/

[7]https://github.com/huggingface/transformers

5 Interface

Design The ASAD web interface is available at: http://asad.qcri.org/

The user can select any of the modules from the tabs and test the performance on random samples and classify them to easily understand the different modules. The user can type a text to be classified. The classification results appear in a table so that earlier results can be referred to. We recognize that users may want to classify many tweets in one go without having to type them one at a time. To allow this, the users can upload a text file. Each line is classified by our system and users can download a file that contains predicted class and class probabilities. To prevent excessive usage, we limit allowed files to have at most 100 lines. We also use Google reCaptcha V2[8] to prevent bots from abusing our file upload system. Figure 1 shows the common layout for all components except for Dialect ID. For Dialect ID, we use a map to visualize results. To this end, we provide a heatmap showing the distribution of probabilities for different dialects. This allows users to easily determine which part of the world the input text is likely to come from. Figure 2 illustrates layout for dialect ID. We also allow users to send feedback to us. This will help us improve ASAD in the future.

[8]https://developers.google.com/recaptcha/

Figure 1: ASAD interface for Offensiveness module (top half) and outputs of other modules (lower half)

Figure 2: ASAD interface for Dialect ID module

Implementation We use Flask[9], a lightweight web application framework for backend development. Input from the user is first transformed into n-gram vectors using tf-idf vectorizer and then are passed to the classifiers (described in Section 4). The classifiers return predicted labels alongside probabilities of different classes. The class probabilities were calculated using Platt calibration (Platt, 1999). We use scikit-learn[10] to train all the SVM classifiers and vectorizers. We use javascript for functionality at frontend and for communication between the frontend and the backend. To display probabilities on a map for the dialect ID module, we use the heatmap layer plugin[11] with leaflet.js[12] and OpenStreetMap[13].

[9] https://palletsprojects.com/p/flask/
[10] https://scikit-learn.org/stable/index.html
[11] https://www.patrick-wied.at/static/heatmapjs/plugin-leaflet-layer.html
[12] https://leafletjs.com/
[13] https://www.openstreetmap.org/#map=8/25.322/51.197

Module	API URL	Body of request
Dialect ID	`https://asad.qcri.org.com/dialect`	KEY : text VALUE : arabic_text
Sentiment	`https://asad.qcri.org/sentiment`	
News Category	`https://asad.qcri.org/news`	
Offensiveness	`https://asad.qcri.org/offensive`	
Hate Speech	`https://asad.qcri.org/hate_speech`	
Adult Content	`https://asad.qcri.org/adult`	
Spam	`https://asad.qcri.org/spam`	

Table 3: API endpoints for ASAD

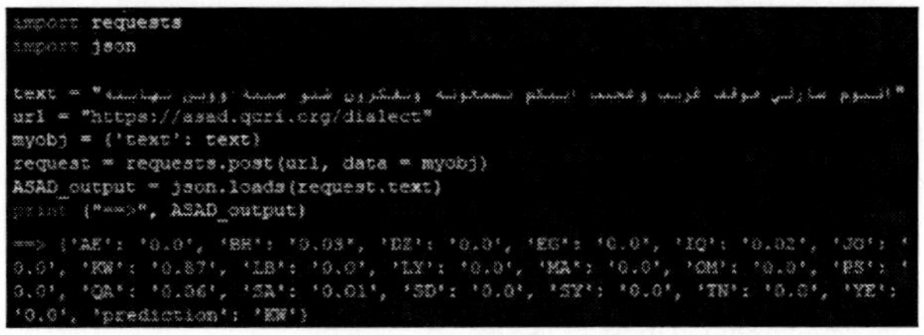

Figure 3: Example usage of ASAD Dialect ID API

Web API To facilitate using ASAD from different programming languages, we provide Web APIs via POST requests. Table 3 lists available API routes and Figure 3 illustrates example usage. Response from ASAD contains predicted class and class probabilities.

6 Conclusion

We presented ASAD, a system that can be used for analysis of tweets in multiple ways. Using one system, users can detect offensive language, hate speech, sentiment, news category, adult content, spam, and also identify dialects. For the ease of usage, our system can be both accessed via Web APIs and an online interface. In the future, we plan to release ASAD through the *pip* Python packaging tool.

References

Ahmed Abdelali, Kareem Darwish, Nadir Durrani, and Hamdy Mubarak. 2016. Farasa: A fast and furious segmenter for Arabic. In *Proceedings of the 2016 Conference of the North American Chapter of the Association for Computational Linguistics: Demonstrations*, pages 11–16, San Diego, California. Association for Computational Linguistics.

Ahmed Abdelali, Hamdy Mubarak, Younes Samih, Sabit Hassan, and Kareem Darwish. 2020. Arabic dialect identification in the wild. *ArXiv*, abs/2005.06557.

Muhammad Abdul-Mageed, Chiyu Zhang, Houda Bouamor, and Nizar Habash. 2020. Nadi 2020: The first nuanced arabic dialect identification shared task. In *Proceedings of the Fifth Arabic Natural Language Processing Workshop*, pages 97–110.

Ibrahim Abu Farha and Walid Magdy. 2019. Mazajak: An online Arabic sentiment analyser. In *Proceedings of the Fourth Arabic Natural Language Processing Workshop*, pages 192–198, Florence, Italy. Association for Computational Linguistics.

Nora Al Twairesh, Mawaheb Al Tuwaijri, Afnan Al Moammar, and Sarah Al Humoud. 2016. Arabic spam detection in twitter. In *The 2nd Workshop on Arabic Corpora and Processing Tools 2016 Theme: Social Media*, page 38.

Ali Alshehri, El Moatez Billah Nagoudi, Hassan Alhuzali, and Muhammad Abdul-Mageed. 2018. Think before your click: Data and models for adult content in arabic twitter.

Wissam Antoun, Fady Baly, and Hazem Hajj. 2020. Arabert: Transformer-based model for arabic language understanding. In *Proceedings of The 4th Workshop on Open-Source Arabic Corpora and Processing Tools*, pages 9–15.

Houda Bouamor, Sabit Hassan, and Nizar Habash. 2019. The MADAR shared task on Arabic fine-grained dialect identification. In *Proceedings of the Fourth Arabic Natural Language Processing Workshop*, pages 199–207, Florence, Italy. Association for Computational Linguistics.

Shammur Absar Chowdhury, Ahmed Abdelali, Kareem Darwish, Jung Soon-Gyo, Joni Salminen, and Bernard J. Jansen. 2020. Improving Arabic text categorization using transformer training diversification.

In *Proceedings of the Fifth Arabic Natural Language Processing Workshop*, pages 226–236, Barcelona, Spain (Online). Association for Computational Linguistics.

Kareem Darwish, Ahmed Abdelali, and Hamdy Mubarak. 2014. Using stem-templates to improve arabic pos and gender/number tagging. In *LREC*, pages 2926–2931. Citeseer.

Kareem Darwish and Hamdy Mubarak. 2016. Farasa: A new fast and accurate arabic word segmenter. In *Proceedings of the Tenth International Conference on Language Resources and Evaluation (LREC'16)*, pages 1070–1074.

AbdelRahim A. Elmadany, Hamdy Mubarak, and Walid Magdy. 2018. An arabic speech-act and sentiment corpus of tweets. In *Proceedings of the Eleventh International Conference on Language Resources and Evaluation (LREC 2018)*. European Language Resources Association (ELRA). The 3rd Workshop on Open-Source Arabic Corpora and Processing Tools, OSACT3 ; Conference date: 08-05-2018.

Sabit Hassan, Younes Samih, Hamdy Mubarak, and Ahmed Abdelali. 2020a. ALT at SemEval-2020 task 12: Arabic and English offensive language identification in social media. In *Proceedings of the Fourteenth Workshop on Semantic Evaluation*, pages 1891–1897, Barcelona (online). International Committee for Computational Linguistics.

Sabit Hassan, Younes Samih, Hamdy Mubarak, Ahmed Abdelali, Ammar Rashed, and Shammur Absar Chowdhury. 2020b. ALT submission for OSACT shared task on offensive language detection. In *Proceedings of the 4th Workshop on Open-Source Arabic Corpora and Processing Tools, with a Shared Task on Offensive Language Detection*, pages 61–65, Marseille, France. European Language Resource Association.

Hamdy Mubarak, Ahmed Abdelali, Sabit Hassan, and Kareem Darwish. 2020a. Spam detection on arabic twitter. In *Social Informatics*, pages 237–251, Cham. Springer International Publishing.

Hamdy Mubarak, Kareem Darwish, and Walid Magdy. 2017. Abusive language detection on arabic social media. In *Proceedings of the First Workshop on Abusive Language Online*, pages 52–56.

Hamdy Mubarak, Kareem Darwish, Walid Magdy, Tamer Elsayed, and Hend Al-Khalifa. 2020b. Overview of osact4 arabic offensive language detection shared task. In *Proceedings of the 4th Workshop on Open-Source Arabic Corpora and Processing Tools, with a Shared Task on Offensive Language Detection*.

Hamdy Mubarak, Sabit Hassan, and Ahmed Abdelali. 2021. Adult content detection on arabic twitter: Analysis and experiments. In *Proceedings of the Sixth Arabic Natural Language Processing Workshop*.

Ossama Obeid, Mohammad Salameh, Houda Bouamor, and Nizar Habash. 2019. ADIDA: Automatic dialect identification for Arabic. In *Proceedings of the 2019 Conference of the North American Chapter of the Association for Computational Linguistics (Demonstrations)*, pages 6–11, Minneapolis, Minnesota. Association for Computational Linguistics.

Ossama Obeid, Nasser Zalmout, Salam Khalifa, Dima Taji, Mai Oudah, Bashar Alhafni, Go Inoue, Fadhl Eryani, Alexander Erdmann, and Nizar Habash. 2020. CAMeL tools: An open source python toolkit for Arabic natural language processing. In *Proceedings of The 12th Language Resources and Evaluation Conference*, pages 7022–7032, Marseille, France. European Language Resources Association.

Arfath Pasha, Mohamed Al-Badrashiny, Mona Diab, Ahmed El Kholy, Ramy Eskander, Nizar Habash, Manoj Pooleery, Owen Rambow, and Ryan Roth. 2014. MADAMIRA: A fast, comprehensive tool for morphological analysis and disambiguation of Arabic. In *Proceedings of the Ninth International Conference on Language Resources and Evaluation (LREC-2014)*, pages 1094–1101, Reykjavik, Iceland. European Languages Resources Association (ELRA).

John C. Platt. 1999. Probabilistic outputs for support vector machines and comparisons to regularized likelihood methods. In *ADVANCES IN LARGE MARGIN CLASSIFIERS*, pages 61–74. MIT Press.

Omar F Zaidan and Chris Callison-Burch. 2011. The Arabic Online Commentary Dataset: an Annotated Dataset of Informal Arabic With High Dialectal Content. In *Proceedings of the Conference of the Association for Computational Linguistics (ACL)*, pages 37–41.

Marcos Zampieri, Preslav Nakov, Sara Rosenthal, Pepa Atanasova, Georgi Karadzhov, Hamdy Mubarak, Leon Derczynski, Zeses Pitenis, and Çağrı Çöltekin. 2020. SemEval-2020 Task 12: Multilingual Offensive Language Identification in Social Media (OffensEval 2020). In *Proceedings of SemEval*.

CoCo-Ex: A Tool for Linking Concepts from Texts to ConceptNet

Maria Becker, Katharina Korfhage, and Anette Frank
Department of Computational Linguistics, Heidelberg University, Germany
(mbecker, korfhage, frank)@cl.uni-heidelberg.de

Abstract

In this paper we present CoCo-Ex, a tool for **Ex**tracting **Co**ncepts from texts and linking them to the **Co**nceptNet knowledge graph. CoCo-Ex extracts meaningful concepts from natural language texts and maps them to conjunct concept nodes in ConceptNet, utilizing the maximum of relational information stored in the ConceptNet knowledge graph. CoCo-Ex takes into account the challenging characteristics of ConceptNet, namely that – unlike conventional knowledge graphs – nodes are represented as non-canonicalized, free-form text. This means that i) concepts are not normalized; ii) they often consist of several different, nested phrase types; and iii) many of them are uninformative, over-specific, or misspelled. A commonly used shortcut to circumvent these problems is to apply string matching. We compare CoCo-Ex to this method and show that CoCo-Ex enables the extraction of meaningful, important rather than overspecific or uninformative concepts, and allows to assess more relational information stored in the knowledge graph. [1]

1 Introduction

ConceptNet (Speer et al., 2017) is a semantic network which contains general commonsense facts about the world, e.g. *Birds can fly* or *Computers are used for sending e-mails* (Liebermann, 2008). It originates from the crowdsourcing project *Open Mind Common Sense* (Speer et al., 2008) that acquired commonsense knowledge from contributions over the web. The current version also includes expert-created resources such as WordNet (Fellbaum, 1998) and JMDict (Breen, 2004), other crowdsourced resources such as Wiktionary, knowledge obtained through games with a purpose such as Verbosity, and automatically extracted knowledge (cf. Speer et al. (2008)). Knowledge facts in ConceptNet are represented as triples, e.g. [*dog*,IsA,*domestic animal*]. The current version, ConceptNet 5, comprises 37 relations, such as UsedFor, IsA, PartOf, or LocatedAt.

ConceptNet has been proven a useful resource of background knowledge for various NLP downstream tasks, and is thus widely used, e.g., for reading comprehension (Mihaylov and Frank, 2018), machine comprehension (Wang et al., 2018; González et al., 2018), dialog modelling (Young et al., 2018), argument classification (Paul et al., 2020), textual entailment (Weissenborn et al., 2018), question answering (Ostermann et al., 2018) or for explaining sentiment (Paul and Frank, 2019).

As opposed to conventional knowledge bases such as NELL (Carlson et al., 2010), Freebase (Bollacker et al., 2008), or YAGO (Nickel et al., 2012), the nodes in ConceptNet are represented as non-canonicalized, free-form text. This means that (I) concept nodes are not normalized: e.g. *bake cake, bake cakes, baking cake*, and *baking cakes* are represented as distinct nodes; likewise *bin bag, binbag, bin bags*, and *bin-bag* are separate nodes in ConceptNet. (II) concept nodes often consist of multi-word expressions, which can be very long and complex. Often they consist of several nested phrase types, e.g., *buying the ingredients of the recipe*, or *a friend was celebrating a birthday*. (III) Since large parts of ConceptNet have been crowdsourced, it contains noise (e.g., typos), uninformative concepts (e.g., *there, it's*), or very specific concepts (e.g., the second concept in the triple: [*compute*,HasProp,*more complex than pencil*]).

These specific properties lead to a larger amount of nodes and a substantially sparser graph compared to conventional knowledge bases. This in turn is challenging for tasks such as knowledge

[1]We provide a demo video (https://www.youtube.com/watch?v=bgqVhE2vR9A&feature=youtu.be) and the code (https://github.com/Heidelberg-NLP/CoCo-Ex) for CoCo-Ex.

Proceedings of the 16th Conference of the European Chapter of the Association for Computational Linguistics: System Demonstrations, pages 119–126
April 19 - 23, 2021. ©2021 Association for Computational Linguistics

base completion (cf. Li et al. (2016); Saito et al. (2018); Bosselut et al. (2019); Malaviya et al. (2020)); the semantic representation of nodes and edges (Speer and Lowry-Duda, 2017); or the learning of new relations (dos Santos et al., 2015; Becker et al., 2019; Trisedya et al., 2019).

Moreover, non-canonicalized nodes become challenging when merging knowledge bases, as in Faralli et al. (2020), who introduce a graph database merging multiple hypernymy graphs extracted from ConceptNet, DBpedia, WebIsAGraph, WordNet, and Wikipedia. They find that only 25% of the edges connect nodes from ConceptNet to other databases, which can be traced back to the fact that ConceptNet nodes are non-canonicalized, as opposed to common knowledge bases.

Finally, free-form concept nodes become problematic when we aim to project a ConceptNet subgraph from natural language texts by mapping phrases from natural language text to nodes in ConceptNet. In recent approaches, simple string matching has been applied to perform such a mapping (e.g. Lin et al. (2019); Wang et al. (2020)). Given the non-normalized nature of the concepts in ConceptNet, this can, however, result in an incomplete and noisy mapping: e.g., if the word "brains" occurs in a text, it can be mapped to the ConceptNet node *brains* (which is connected by 131 edges within ConceptNet), but not to *brain* (which is connected by 1799 edges). Therefore, a lot of relational knowledge stored in ConceptNet gets lost when mapping natural language text to concepts in ConceptNet via string matching. Moreover, since ConceptNet contains many nodes that don't represent meaningful concepts (e.g. *yes, there, it's, the*), simple string matching can lead to the extraction of concepts that will most likely be useless for downstream applications.

Motivated by these observations, we built a Concept Extraction Tool for ConceptNet, **CoCo-Ex**, which we present in this paper. CoCo-Ex is a tool written in Python 3.6 that selects *meaningful* concepts, possibly consisting of multiple tokens from natural language texts; it maps them to a *collection* of concept nodes in ConceptNet, utilizing the maximum of relational information stored in the knowledge graph. It is thus perfectly suited for identifying and extracting concepts from natural language texts and mapping them to ConceptNet, e.g., to project knowledge subgraphs from texts (Paul and Frank, 2019), or for detecting and classifying knowledge relations instantiated within texts (Becker et al., 2019).

We describe our Concept Extraction Tool CoCo-Ex in Section 2. In Section 3 we evaluate the benefits of CoCo-Ex in a practical application scenario, comparing it to simple string matching, by evaluating the retrieved concepts and their connectivity both automatically and manually. We conclude with a summary and results in Section 4.

2 CoCo-Ex: Extracting Concepts from Text and Mapping them to ConceptNet

CoCo-Ex is a pipeline implementation comprising several stages as shown in Figure 1.

In **Step 1**, we extract candidate phrases from a given text, which we preprocess in **Step 2**. In **Step 3**, we map the preprocessed phrases to ConceptNet concepts, which we preprocess in the same manner: We first create a dictionary based on ConceptNet, where we gather all concepts that are conceptually related (that is, referring to a similar or the same entity or event), but represented as distinct nodes. In this dictionary we then look up the preprocessed candidate phrases and get all ConceptNet nodes which contain them. In order to avoid obtaining conceptually unrelated nodes, in **Step 4** we establish a method that allows us to filter out nodes that are not similar enough to the candidate phrase using similarity metrics and vector space representations.

Step 1: Extracting Candidate Phrase Types. We start by extracting candidate phrases from a given text using the Stanford Constituency parser (Mi and Huang, 2015). We extract noun phrases, verb phrases and adjective phrases.[2] We find that some verb phrases are very long and specific and therefore unlikely to find exact matches in ConceptNet (e.g., "be sorted into different wheelie bins"). Yet, ConceptNet concepts often consist of general verb-object phrases, such as *walk the dog; cook dinner; bake a cake.* To accommodate for this, we create, for every verbal phrase we extract from the text, additional versions (i.e., chunks) that exclude subordinated prepositional phrases and/or noun phrases (e.g., for "be sorted into different wheelie bins" we additionally extract "be sorted into" and "be sorted"). Addressing the fact that nodes in ConceptNet are of different lengths and often consist

[2]We extract leaves (= tokens) of all subtrees that have one of the following phrase types or POS-tags: 'NP', 'VP', 'ADJP', 'JJ', 'JJR', 'JJS', 'NN', 'NNS', 'NNP', 'NNPS', 'VB', 'VBG', 'VBD', 'VBN', 'VBP', 'VBZ'.

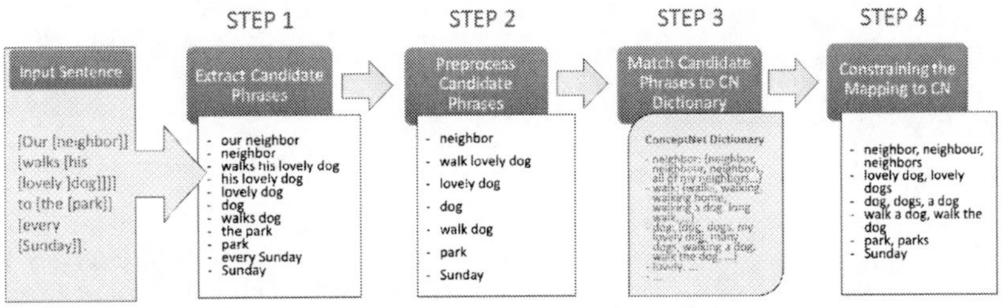

Figure 1: Our pipeline for extracting and mapping phrases from texts to nodes in ConceptNet.

of several nested phrases, we keep all the original complex verbal phrases; the reduced chunks; and the split-off nested, subordinated phrases, which we again split into chunks (here: "different wheelie bins", "wheelie bins", and "bins").

Step 2: Preprocessing Candidate Phrase Types and ConceptNet Nodes. Next, we preprocess the candidate phrases we extracted from the text to prepare the mapping in Step 3. We apply spacy (Honnibal and Montani, 2017) to lemmatize the candidate phrases extracted from the texts, and remove articles, pronouns, adverbs, conjunctions, interjections and punctuation. The very same process we apply in Step 3 to nodes in ConceptNet, which are not normalized, in order to build a dictionary from ConceptNet.

Step 3: Matching Candidate Phrase Types to a Dictionary Based on ConceptNet. We then map the preprocessed phrases to the preprocessed ConceptNet concepts as follows: We create a dictionary based on ConceptNet where we collect all concepts that are conceptually related – in the sense that they involve at least one common content word – but are represented as distinct nodes in ConceptNet. I.e., we aim to subsume, e.g., *dog, dogs, nice dog,* and *my neighbour's dog* under one entry in the dictionary (cf. Figure 2). In our dictionary, keys are lemmatized words contained in concept node phrases (e.g. ⟨dog⟩ for the concept *my dog*), and the corresponding value assigned to a key is a list of all ConcepNet nodes that contain this lemma (e.g. *dog, dogs, my dog, my neigbor's dog*), as determined by the lemmatization of the nodes (see Step 2 for the applied process). Therefore, in our dictionary all ConceptNet nodes that contain the same lemma, the lemma of the key, are clustered together in one entry. Note that we lemmatize the ConcepNet nodes only for the purpose of mapping and clustering, while they remain unchanged (in their original form and inflection) as values in the dictionary. I.e., we compare a key (lemma) to the lemmatized version of the concepts, and include all nodes, or concept phrases in their original, inflected form, that contain this lemma.

An example of how we create an entry in the dictionary is given in Figure 2 and Figure 3: for the key ⟨dog⟩, all conceptually related nodes are retrieved from ConceptNet (Figure 2) by matching the (lemmatized) key and the lemmatized ConceptNet concepts (Figure 3, left side). All the retrieved ConceptNet nodes that contain the key lemma in their lemmatized form are stored as the key's values (middle of Figure 3). In case the lemmatized candidate phrase from the text contains further lemmas, we apply the same procedure for each of these, and construct additional entries, if they have not yet been created and stored.

Using this dictionary we are now able to assess the maximum of relational information stored in the ConceptNet knowledge graph for a given candidate phrase from a text, since it allows us to jointly look up the in- and outgoing edges of all values (nodes) assigned to the same key, e.g., [*dogs*,ISA,*domestic animal*]; [*dog*,HASPROPERTY,*nice*]; ..) (Figure 3, right-hand side). In case a candidate phrase contains multiple lemmas, we collect the union of ConceptNet nodes defined for the respective lemmas (keys) as their values, and apply a filtering step, which we describe below, to select the concept nodes that best correspond to the complex phrase.

Specifically, when looking up extracted candidate phrases that contain *a single lemma* (e.g. ⟨dog⟩), we consider the complete list of nodes stored in the dictionary for that lemma (key) – that is, all concepts containing (inflected versions of) ⟨dog⟩, including also multiword phrases which are linked with other keys. When looking up extracted candidate phrases that contain *more than one lemma* (e.g. "walk the dog"), we obtain sets of ConceptNet nodes (values) that are defined for each (non-stopword) lemma (key) – here: ⟨dog⟩

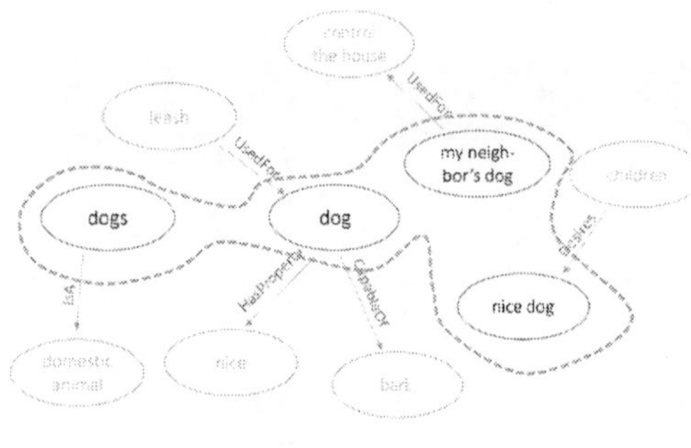

Figure 2: Collecting conceptually related nodes in ConceptNet, here: for the phrase "the dog".

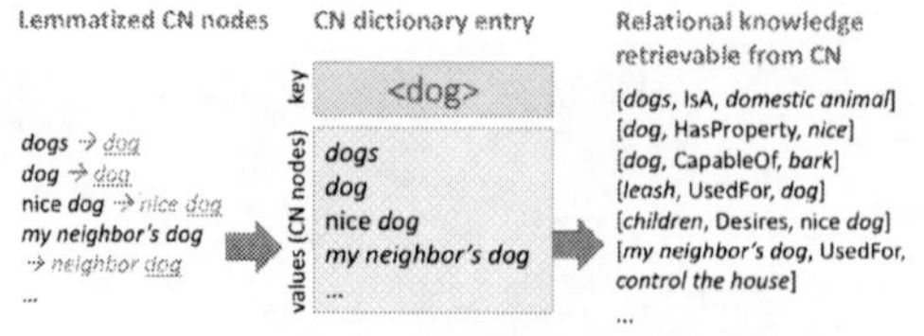

Figure 3: Example of the ConceptNet Dictionary entry for ⟨dog⟩. Left: lemmatized ConceptNet nodes (grey) that contain ⟨dog⟩ (underlined); middle: CN dictionary entry (containing the original CN nodes); right: relational knowledge (in- and outgoing edges for each value (CN node) assigned to the key) which can be retrieved from ConceptNet based on the dictionary entry.

and ⟨walk⟩ – and retrieve all ConceptNet nodes from their respective list of values. From these sets, instead of building their union, we construct their intersection, which yields the set of phrases from all keys' values that contain the maximum of lemmas contained in the candidate phrase.

For our example "walk the dog", we would obtain the two lemmas ⟨walk⟩ and ⟨dog⟩, together with their values:

⟨walk⟩ → *walk, walks, walking, walking home,* ***walking a dog****, long walk,* ***walk the dog****, ...* ; and

⟨dog⟩ → *dog, dogs, nice dog, my neigbor's dog,* ***walking a dog, walk the dog****, ...*;

and extract *walking a dog* and *walk the dog* that are contained as values in both keys.

During the mapping process that collects values (ConceptNet concepts) for the lemmatized keys of candidate phrases, we are also resolving ambiguities. E.g., the forms *fly* or *flies* can be either a noun or a verb. We resolve this ambiguity by comparing the POS tags obtained during preprocessing the extracted candidate phrases to the POS tags that are associated with concepts in ConceptNet.[3] Specifically, we retrieve POS information for the extracted candidate phrases by applying the POS tagger implemented in spacy (Honnibal and Montani, 2017) on the sentence level, while for ConceptNet nodes we assess the POS labels available as metadata. In case we find several concepts with the same surface form but different POS tags in ConceptNet (e.g. *fly/noun* and *fly/verb*), we use the POS annotations from the extracted candidate phrases and from ConceptNet tags to restrict the mapping to matching POS, hence we do not include any concepts with conflicting POS information in the list of values for the phrase's keys.

To summarize, the dictionary we obtain from Step 3 allows us to look up concepts for any preprocessed candidate phrases, and obtain from it all ConceptNet nodes which contain them or inflected versions of them. In case of multiple lemmas contained in a candidate phrase, we retrieve all nodes that contain *all lemmas* included in the given phrase, by computing an intersection over the values associated with all keys (lemmas) evoked by the phrase.[4] Since we lemmatize both the ConceptNet nodes and the extracted candidate phrases as described above, we maximize the number of matches, and hence, the associated ConceptNet relation tuples, while selecting maximally specific nodes. At the same time, since we construct *chunked* phrases from the extracted concepts, we also allow for more constrained matches (limited, e.g., to single lemmata) with equally constrained ConceptNet concepts, preventing over-specific phrases and an ensuing loss of recall. Finally, we apply POS filtering, and hence avoid the retrieval of ConceptNet concepts that do not match the POS category of the concepts mentioned in the candidate phrase, relying on the sentential context of the phrase candidate for disambiguation.

Step 4: Constraining the Mapping to ConceptNet Concepts. While in Step 3 we constrain the selected concept nodes by intersection in case the phrase candidate contains multiple lemmata, we still obtain many ConceptNet nodes when mapping short phrases containing a single content word to ConceptNet, since we retrieve all nodes that include the lemma of the candidate phrase. In practice, this yields a huge set of concepts that contain

[3]We find POS information for a majority of concepts contained in ConceptNet, as used in specific tuples. In cases where this information is not given, we do not apply any filtering.

[4]This holds as long as the lemmas identified in the textual phrases can be identified within ConceptNet's concept nodes.

not only this lemma, but many other content words not present in the candidate phrase – possibly conceptually unrelated nodes that we want to omit. For example, if the candidate phrase is "dog", we map it to the ConceptNet nodes *dog* and *dogs*, but also conceptually not strictly related nodes such as *feeding my dogs, dogs are my favourite animals, it's raining cats and dogs*, etc. We therefore establish a method that allows us to filter out nodes that are not similar enough to the candidate phrase, and hence are assumed to be conceptually unrelated, which we describe in the following.

We filter the nodes (values) for each lemma (key) by calculating the similarity between the ConceptNet concepts and the extracted candidate phrase. We calculate similarity in terms of length (by token or char length) and in terms of semantic similarity (using word embeddings and similarity metrics). We experimented with different similarity metrics: we tried Dice Coefficient (Sørensen, 1948), Jaccard Coefficient (Jaccard, 1902), Minimum Edit Distance, Word Mover's Distance (Kusner et al., 2015), and Cosine Distance, with different similarity thresholds. For the metrics that require word representations in vector space (Word Mover's Distance and and Cosine Distance), we tried different embeddings (Numberbatch (Speer et al., 2017), Word2Vec trained on GoogleNews (Mikolov et al., 2013), and GloVe (Pennington et al., 2014)), where we compute representations for multiword terms by averaging their embeddings. We also consider differences in phrase lengths: here we compare the length of the ConceptNet nodes' concept phrases to the length of the candidate phrase – by number of tokens and of characters. E.g. when comparing the candidate phrase "my dog" to the nodes (a) *dogs* and (b) *many dogs*, we obtain for (a) a difference in the number of tokens by 1 and of characters by 1, and for (b) in the number of tokens by 0 and of characters by 3.

We evaluated the output of several configurations manually in terms of how well the filtered nodes fit the extracted candidate phrase, and found the following configurations to yield the highest coverage and lowest noise: we allow for a maximum token length difference of 1 and/or a maximum character difference of 10, and a minimum Dice coefficient of 0.85. The other configurations are implemented as well (as command line parameters), so users can experiment with different settings easily.

		Str-Match	CoCo-Ex
CommonsenseQA	Questions	99,217	88,631
	Answers	106,681	116,941
OpenBookQA	Questions	38,415	38,485
	Answers	53,748	61,313

Table 1: Number of concepts linked to ConceptNet by simple string matching vs. using CoCo-Ex. CommonsenseQA contains 12,247 questions with 5 answer choices each, and OpenBookQA provides 6,000 4-way multiple-choice questions.

3 Applications

Recent approaches that map natural language text to nodes in ConceptNet apply simple string matching. Wang et al. (2020) for example use ConceptNet in order to retrieve multi-hop knowledge paths as background information for improving the task of question answering. They map concepts that appear in questions and answers from the two benchmark datasets, CommonsenseQA (Talmor et al., 2019) and OpenBookQA (Mihaylov et al., 2018), to ConceptNet using plain string matching.

Irrespective of the question answering task, we want to evaluate the two methods of linking concepts from texts to ConceptNet (plain string matching vs. CoCo-Ex) by comparing the **number of concepts** that could be retrieved from ConceptNet by both methods, respectively; and by evaluating the **quality** of the retrieved concepts, with regard to their coverage and informativity, as well as the amount of utilized relational knowledge from the ConceptNet knowledge graph.

We reimplement the string matching method and make it comparable to CoCo-Ex by retrieving all noun phrases, verb phrases and adjective phrases and their nested phrases (as we do for CoCo-Ex). Additionally, as in CoCo-Ex, we filter these phrases by removing articles, pronouns, adverbs, conjunctions, interjections and punctuation, and keep the original phrases and the chunked versions.

The **counts of concepts** retrieved by simple string matching vs. using CoCo-Ex are displayed in Table 1. We find that for the CommonsenseQA dataset, more concepts are linked to ConceptNet from the questions when using string matching, while with CoCo-Ex we can link more concepts from the answers (Table 1). For OpenBookQA, the number of extracted concepts for the questions are similar for both methods, while again we can link more concepts from the answers with CoCo-Ex.

For evaluating **concept quality**, we set up a

	Str-Matching	CoCo-Ex
CommonsenseQA		
Coverage (binary)	17 of 25 (68%)	20 of 25 (80%)
Ratio of Informative (*Wanted*) Concepts (total and %)	152 of 220 (69%)	190 of 192 (99%)
Connecting Edges of Informative Concepts (total/avg-question)	151,526/6,061	185,663/7,427
OpenBookQA		
Coverage (binary)	16 of 25 (64%)	14 of 25 (56%)
Ratio of Informative (*Wanted*) Concepts (total and %)	92 of 148 (62%)	104 of 145 (72%)
Connecting Edges of Informative Concepts (total/avg-question)	91,938/3,678	110,039/4,402

Table 2: Manual evaluation of linked concepts from 25 questions for each dataset. For each question, our annotators evaluated if all meaningful concepts were extracted (*Coverage*; in a binary evaluation setup *yes/no*); and how many of the extracted concepts are informative (*wanted*) (*Ratio wanted/wanted+unwanted*). For all informative (*wanted*) concepts, we then looked up the number of edges connecting these nodes in ConceptNet (in- and outgoing *edges*).

small annotation experiment where we provided our annotators with 50 questions randomly sampled from CommonsenseQA and OpenBookQA. For each question, our annotators evaluated whether all meaningful concepts were extracted (coverage, in a binary setting (yes/no)); and if/how many informative (and thus, *wanted*) concepts are among the extracted concepts (which can be interpreted as reverse precision).[5] For each dataset, two annotators with linguistic background performed annotations. We measure annotator agreement in terms of Cohen's Kappa and achieve an agreement of 78%. Remaining conflicts were resolved by an expert annotator (one of the authors). The number of concepts that could be accessed in ConceptNet we evaluate automatically, in terms of the number of in- and outgoing edges connecting the node(s) which have been annotated as informative (*wanted*), identified by simple string matching vs. all nodes obtained by CoCo-Ex through keys and values.

The results of our manual evaluation experiment are displayed in Table 2. We find that the coverage (if all meaningful concepts were extracted, evaluated in a binary setting: yes/no) is higher for CommonsenseQA when using CoCo-Ex and higher for OpenBooksQA when applying string matching.

Next, we evaluate the informativeness of the extracted concepts. We find that the ratio between informative (*wanted*) and uninformative concepts (*unwanted*) is much better when using CoCo-Ex opposed to simple string matching on both datasets (cf. Table 2). Finally, we also evaluate the amount of relational information stored in the ConceptNet knowledge graph which can be retrieved by looking up in- and outgoing nodes from the nodes rated as informative. Here we find that with CoCo-Ex, much more relational information of ConceptNet can be accessed, indicating again the superiority of this method compared to simple string matching.

4 Conclusion

In this paper we presented CoCo-Ex, a tool for **Ex**tracting **Co**ncepts from texts and linking them to the **Co**nceptNet knowledge graph. As opposed to the common shortcut method of simply matching strings from texts to ConceptNet nodes, CoCo-Ex extracts *meaningful* concepts from texts and maps them to *collections of* concept nodes in ConceptNet, which enables us to assess the maximum of relational information stored in the ConceptNet knowledge graph. CoCo-Ex takes into account that concepts in ConceptNet are represented as non-canonicalized, free-form text and are often complex, noisy, uninformative, and/or over-specific. We evaluated CoCo-Ex against the method of simple string matching, which confirmed our hypotheses that (i) CoCo-Ex improves the precision of mapping by enabling the extraction of meaningful, important rather than overspecific or uninformative concepts, and (ii) allows to utilize the maximum of relational information stored in the knowledge graph, a step towards overcoming the well-known sparsity issue of commonsense knowledge graphs such as ConceptNet.

Acknowledgements

This work was funded by the DFG within the project ExpLAIN as part of the Priority Program *RATIO* (SPP-1999). We thank our annotators for their contribution.

[5]Our annotation manual can be found here: `https://github.com/Heidelberg-NLP/CoCo-Ex/blob/master/CoCo-Ex_Annotation_Manual.pdf`

References

Maria Becker, Michael Staniek, Vivi Nastase, and Anette Frank. 2019. Assessing the difficulty of classifying ConceptNet relations in a multi-label classification setting. In *RELATIONS - Workshop on meaning relations between phrases and sentences*, pages 1–15, Gothenburg, Sweden. Association for Computational Linguistics.

Kurt Bollacker, Colin Evans, Praveen Paritosh, Tim Sturge, and Jamie Taylor. 2008. Freebase: A Collaboratively Created Graph Database for Structuring Human Knowledge. In *Proceedings of the 2008 ACM SIGMOD International Conference on Management of Data*, SIGMOD '08, pages 1247–1250, New York, NY, USA. ACM.

Antoine Bosselut, Hannah Rashkin, Maarten Sap, Chaitanya Malaviya, Asli Celikyilmaz, and Yejin Choi. 2019. COMET: Commonsense transformers for automatic knowledge graph construction. In *Proceedings of the 57th Annual Meeting of the Association for Computational Linguistics*, pages 4762–4779, Florence, Italy. Association for Computational Linguistics.

Jim Breen. 2004. JMdict: a Japanese-multilingual dictionary. In *Proceedings of the Workshop on Multilingual Linguistic Resources*, pages 65–72, Geneva, Switzerland. COLING.

A. Carlson, J. Betteridge, B. Kisiel, B. Settles, E.R. Hruschka Jr., and T.M. Mitchell. 2010. Toward an architecture for never-ending language learning. In *Proceedings of the Conference on Artificial Intelligence (AAAI)*, pages 1306–1313. AAAI Press.

Stefano Faralli, Paola Velardi, and Farid Yusifli. 2020. Multiple knowledge GraphDB (MKGDB). In *Proceedings of The 12th Language Resources and Evaluation Conference*, pages 2325–2331, Marseille, France. European Language Resources Association.

Christiane Fellbaum. 1998. *WordNet: An Electronic Lexical Database*. Bradford Books.

José-Ángel González, Lluís-F. Hurtado, and Ferran Pla. 2018. ELiRF-UPV at SemEval-2019 task 3: Snapshot ensemble of hierarchical convolutional neural networks for contextual emotion detection. In *Proceedings of the 13th International Workshop on Semantic Evaluation*, pages 195–199, Minneapolis, Minnesota, USA. Association for Computational Linguistics.

Matthew Honnibal and Ines Montani. 2017. spaCy 2: Natural language understanding with Bloom embeddings, convolutional neural networks and incremental parsing.

Paul Jaccard. 1902. *Lois de distribution florale dans la zone alpine*, volume 38. Bulletin de la Société Vaudoise des Sciences Naturelles.

Matt J. Kusner, Yu Sun, Nicholas Kolkin, and Kilian Weinberger. 2015. From Word Embeddings To Document Distances. In *Proceedings of the 32nd International Conference on Machine Learning (ICML)*, pages 957–966.

Xiang Li, Aynaz Taheri, Lifu Tu, and Kevin Gimpel. 2016. Commonsense Knowledge Base Completion. In *Proceedings of the 54th Annual Meeting of the Association for Computational Linguistics (Volume 1: Long Papers)*, pages 1445–1455, Berlin, Germany. Association for Computational Linguistics.

Henry Liebermann. 2008. Usable AI Requires Commonsense Knowledge. In *Workshop on Usable artificial intelligence, held in conjunction with the Conference on Human Factors in Computing Systems (CHI)*, pages 1–5.

Bill Yuchen Lin, Xinyue Chen, Jamin Chen, and Xiang Ren. 2019. KagNet: Knowledge-aware graph networks for commonsense reasoning. In *Proceedings of the 2019 Conference on Empirical Methods in Natural Language Processing and the 9th International Joint Conference on Natural Language Processing (EMNLP-IJCNLP)*, pages 2829–2839, Hong Kong, China. Association for Computational Linguistics.

Chaitanya Malaviya, Chandra Bhagavatula, Antoine Bosselut, and Choi Yejin. 2020. Commonsense knowledge base completion with structural and semantic context. In *Proceedings of the AAAI Conference on Artificial Intelligence*, pages 2925–2933.

Haitao Mi and Liang Huang. 2015. Shift-reduce constituency parsing with dynamic programming and POS tag lattice. In *Proceedings of the 2015 Conference of the North American Chapter of the Association for Computational Linguistics: Human Language Technologies*, pages 1030–1035, Denver, Colorado. Association for Computational Linguistics.

Todor Mihaylov, Peter Clark, Tushar Khot, and Ashish Sabharwal. 2018. Can a suit of armor conduct electricity? a new dataset for open book question answering. In *Proceedings of the 2018 Conference on Empirical Methods in Natural Language Processing*, pages 2381–2391, Brussels, Belgium. Association for Computational Linguistics.

Todor Mihaylov and Anette Frank. 2018. Knowledgeable reader: Enhancing cloze-style reading comprehension with external commonsense knowledge. In *Proceedings of the 56th Annual Meeting of the Association for Computational Linguistics (Volume 1: Long Papers)*, pages 821–832, Melbourne, Australia. Association for Computational Linguistics.

Tomas Mikolov, G.s Corrado, Kai Chen, and Jeffrey Dean. 2013. Efficient estimation of word representations in vector space. In *International Conference on Learning Representations*, pages 1–12.

Maximilian Nickel, Volker Tresp, and Hans-Peter Kriegel. 2012. Factorizing yago: Scalable machine learning for linked data. In *Proceedings of the 21st International Conference on World Wide Web*, WWW '12, page 271–280, New York, NY, USA. Association for Computing Machinery.

Simon Ostermann, Michael Roth, Ashutosh Modi, Stefan Thater, and Manfred Pinkal. 2018. SemEval-2018 task 11: Machine comprehension using commonsense knowledge. In *Proceedings of The 12th International Workshop on Semantic Evaluation*, pages 747–757, New Orleans, Louisiana. Association for Computational Linguistics.

Debjit Paul and Anette Frank. 2019. Ranking and Selecting Multi-Hop Knowledge Paths to Better Predict Human Needs. In *Proceedings of the Annual Conference of the North American Chapter of the Association for Computational Linguistics*, volume 1, pages 3671–3681, Minneapolis, Minnesota, USA.

Debjit Paul, Juri Opitz, Maria Becker, Jonathan Kobbe, Graeme Hirst, and Anette Frank. 2020. Argumentative Relation Classification with Background Knowledge. In *Proceedings of the 8th International Conference on Computational Models of Argument (COMMA 2020)*, pages 319–330.

Jeffrey Pennington, Richard Socher, and Christopher D. Manning. 2014. Glove: Global vectors for word representation. In *Empirical Methods in Natural Language Processing (EMNLP)*, pages 1532–1543.

Itsumi Saito, Kyosuke Nishida, Hisako Asano, and Junji Tomita. 2018. Commonsense knowledge base completion and generation. In *Proceedings of the 22nd Conference on Computational Natural Language Learning*, pages 141–150, Brussels, Belgium. Association for Computational Linguistics.

Cícero dos Santos, Bing Xiang, and Bowen Zhou. 2015. Classifying relations by ranking with convolutional neural networks. In *Proceedings of the 53rd Annual Meeting of the Association for Computational Linguistics and the 7th International Joint Conference on Natural Language Processing (Volume 1: Long Papers)*, pages 626–634, Beijing, China. Association for Computational Linguistics.

Robyn Speer, Joshua Chin, and Catherine Havasi. 2017. ConceptNet 5.5: An Open Multilingual Graph of General Knowledge. In *Proceedings of 31St AAAI Conference on Artificial Intelligence*, pages 444–451.

Robyn Speer, Catherine Havasi, and Henry Lieberman. 2008. AnalogySpace: Reducing the Dimensionality of Common Sense Knowledge. In *Proceedings of the 23rd National Conference on Artificial Intelligence - Volume 1*, pages 548–553. AAAI Press.

Robyn Speer and Joanna Lowry-Duda. 2017. ConceptNet at SemEval-2017 Task 2: Extending Word Embeddings with Multilingual Relational Knowledge. In *Proceedings of the 11th International Workshop on Semantic Evaluation (SemEval-2017)*, pages 85–89, Vancouver, Canada. Association for Computational Linguistics.

Thorvald Sørensen. 1948. *A method of establishing groups of equal amplitude in plant sociology based on similarity of species and its application to analyses of the vegetation on Danish commons.* Kongelige Danske Videnskabernes Selskab. 5 (4): 1–34.

Alon Talmor, Jonathan Herzig, Nicholas Lourie, and Jonathan Berant. 2019. CommonsenseQA: A question answering challenge targeting commonsense knowledge. In *Proceedings of the 2019 Conference of the North American Chapter of the Association for Computational Linguistics: Human Language Technologies, Volume 1 (Long and Short Papers)*, pages 4149–4158, Minneapolis, Minnesota. Association for Computational Linguistics.

Bayu Distiawan Trisedya, Gerhard Weikum, Jianzhong Qi, and Rui Zhang. 2019. Neural relation extraction for knowledge base enrichment. In *Proceedings of the 57th Annual Meeting of the Association for Computational Linguistics*, pages 229–240, Florence, Italy. Association for Computational Linguistics.

Liang Wang, Meng Sun, Wei Zhao, Kewei Shen, and Jingming Liu. 2018. Yuanfudao at SemEval-2018 task 11: Three-way attention and relational knowledge for commonsense machine comprehension. In *Proceedings of The 12th International Workshop on Semantic Evaluation*, pages 758–762, New Orleans, Louisiana. Association for Computational Linguistics.

Peifeng Wang, Nanyun Peng, Filip Ilievski, Pedro Szekely, and Xiang Ren. 2020. Connecting the dots: A knowledgeable path generator for commonsense question answering. In *Findings of the Association for Computational Linguistics: EMNLP 2020*, pages 4129–4140, Online. Association for Computational Linguistics.

Dirk Weissenborn, Tomas Kocisky, and Chris Dyer. 2018. Dynamic Integration of Background Knowledge in Neural NLU Systems. In *International Conference on Learning Representations (ICLR) 2018.*

Tom Young, Erik Cambria, Iti Chaturvedi, Hao Zhou, Subham Biswas, and Minlie Huang. 2018. Augmenting End-to-End Dialog Systems with Commonsense Knowledge. *Proceedings of the AAAI Conference on Artificial Intelligence*, pages 4970–4977.

Gap in pagination due to unavailable paper.

Pages 127-134

InterpreT: An Interactive Visualization Tool for Interpreting Transformers

Vasudev Lal[1], Arden Ma[1], Estelle Aflalo[1], Phillip Howard[1], Ana Paula Q Simoes[1], Daniel Korat[2], Oren Pereg[2], Gadi Singer[1], Moshe Wasserblat[2]
[1]Intel Labs, Cognitive Computing Research, USA
[2]Intel Labs, Artificial Intelligence Lab, Israel
`{firstname.lastname}@intel.com`

Abstract

With the increasingly widespread use of Transformer-based models for NLU/NLP tasks, there is growing interest in understanding the inner workings of these models, why they are so effective at a wide range of tasks, and how they can be further tuned and improved. To contribute towards this goal of enhanced explainability and comprehension, we present InterpreT, an interactive visualization tool for interpreting Transformer-based models. In addition to providing various mechanisms for investigating general model behaviours, novel contributions made in InterpreT include the ability to track and visualize token embeddings through each layer of a Transformer, highlight distances between certain token embeddings through illustrative plots, and identify task-related functions of attention heads by using new metrics. InterpreT is a task agnostic tool, and its functionalities are demonstrated through the analysis of model behaviours for two disparate tasks: Aspect Based Sentiment Analysis (ABSA) and the Winograd Schema Challenge (WSC).

1 Introduction

In recent years, Transformer-based models (Vaswani et al., 2017) such as BERT (Devlin et al., 2019), GPT-2 (Radford et al., 2019), XLNET (Yang et al., 2019) and RoBERTa (Liu et al., 2019) have demonstrated state-of-the-art performance in many NLP tasks and have become the gold standard. However, there are many open questions regarding the behavior of these models. Phenomena such as why Transformers perform well on specific examples but not others, as well as how their internal mechanisms facilitate their ability to generalize to new tasks and settings (or lack therof) are not yet fully understood. Observations and insights which help answer these questions will be pivotal in driving the construction of more powerful and robust models.

The pursuit of such answers have spurred the development of a wide variety of analytical studies and tools to enable the visualization of information encapsulated in Transformer-based models. Clark et al. (2019), studied the attention mechanisms of a pre-trained BERT model to find that certain heads correspond to specific linguistic patterns. Jawahar et al. (2019) investigated the distribution of phrase-level information throughout the layers of BERT using t-SNE (van der Maaten and Hinton, 2008). The visualization tools of Aken et al. (2020) and Reif et al. (2019) perform a layer-wise analysis of BERT's hidden states to understand the internal workings of Transformer-based models that are fine-tuned for question-answering tasks. Other tools, such as Vig (2019), focus on visualizations of the attention matrices of pre-trained Transformer models. In the work of Tenney et al. (2020), the authors introduce an interactive platform for the visualization and interpretation of NLP models. The tool includes, among other capabilities, attention visualizations, embedding space visualizations, and aggregate analysis. Other related tools include those by Wallace et al. (2019) and Hoover et al. (2020). The increasingly large body of work on the interpretability and evaluation of Transformer-based models reveals the growing need for the development of tools and systems to aid in the fine-grained analysis and understanding of these models and their performance on complex language understanding tasks.

With this goal in mind, we present **InterpreT**[1], a tool for **interpre**ting **T**ransformers. A key contribution of InterpreT is that it is a single system that enables users to track hidden representations

[1]The source code for InterpreT, along with a live demo and screencast describing its functionality is available at https://github.com/IntelLabs/nlp-architect/tree/master/solutions/InterpreT

Proceedings of the 16th Conference of the European Chapter of the Association for Computational Linguistics: System Demonstrations, pages 135–142
April 19 - 23, 2021. ©2021 Association for Computational Linguistics

of tokens throughout each layer of a Transformer model, as well as visualize and analyze attention head behaviors. Similarly to Tenney et al. (2020), InterpreT enables dynamic point selection, aggregation of attention head statistics, visualization of attention head matrices, and the ability to compare models. Novel contributions made in InterpreT include the ability to track and visualize token embeddings through each layer of a Transformer (Section 3.2), highlight distances between certain token embeddings through illustrative plots (Section 3.6), and identify task-related functions of attention heads by using new metrics (Section 3.3).

Section 4 demonstrates how the new features introduced in InterpreT can be used to obtain novel insights into the underlying mechanisms used by Transformers to tackle diverse tasks such as Aspect-Based Sentiment Analysis (ABSA) and the Winograd Schema Challenge (WSC). More generally, these demonstrations illustrate how such features enable rich, granular analysis of Transformer models.

2 System Design and Workflow

The system flow consists of two main stages: offline extraction of model specific and task specific information such as targets, predictions, relevant hidden states, and attention matrices (henceforth referred to as "collateral") and running the application itself. During the offline stage, the extracted hidden states are processed using t-SNE before being saved to a file. The collateral generated for a specific model and task is independent of collateral from other models and tasks, which enables the user to either run the app to examine a single model or to compare two different models that were evaluated on the same task and data. In this latter case, the collateral files for the two models are linked at runtime. A detailed specification for the collateral, along with the source code used to run InterpreT can be found in our GitHub.

3 Application Features

3.1 Overview

Key features of InterpreT include plots for the visualization and tracking of t-SNE representations of hidden states through the layers of a Transformer, a plot presenting summary statistics, custom metrics to quantify attention head behavior, and attention matrix visualizations. In addition, InterpreT includes a multi-select feature that enables groups of examples to be selected in the t-SNE plot and used as input to other plots in the application, as well as the flexibility to be used both for analyzing a single model and for visualizing the differences in behaviors between two models. In general, the core functionalities present in InterpreT are model and task agnostic, working for a wide-variety of architectures, sequence lengths, and tasks.

3.2 t-SNE Embeddings

A central component of InterpreT is the ability to visualize the contextualized embeddings of specific tokens throughout the layers of a Transformer. Following van Aken et al. (2019) and Jawahar et al. (2019), we use t-SNE to project hidden representations of tokens after each Transformer layer onto a two-dimensional space, creating disjoint t-SNE spaces for each layer of each model. In the resulting t-SNE plot, token embeddings can be visualized for a specific model and layer, and colored using various color schemes (Figure 1d). An example selected in the t-SNE plot is tracked and continues to be highlighted in the new t-SNE space when the model or the layer is changed.

3.3 Head Summary

InterpreT includes a head summary plot that displays attention head summary statistics for each head and layer (Figure 1b). For a given sentence, all attention weights are obtained in a matrix of size $(num\_layers \times num\_heads \times sentence\_length \times sentence\_length)$ and compute statistics over the final two dimensions, yielding a summary plot of size $(num\_layers \times num\_heads)$. The following statistics are currently supported:

The **Standard Deviation** of an attention head is generated by calculating the standard deviation of the corresponding attention matrix weights. Intuitively, the standard deviation of an attention head increases as the attention patterns become less uniform, allowing a user to easily identify heads that exhibit interesting behaviors.

The **Attention Matrix Correlation** is obtained by computing the correlation between an attention matrix and an arbitrary, same-size matrix. In Section 4.1.2, this correlation is computed using a binary matrix that encodes syntactic dependency relations, analogous to the parse matrix used in

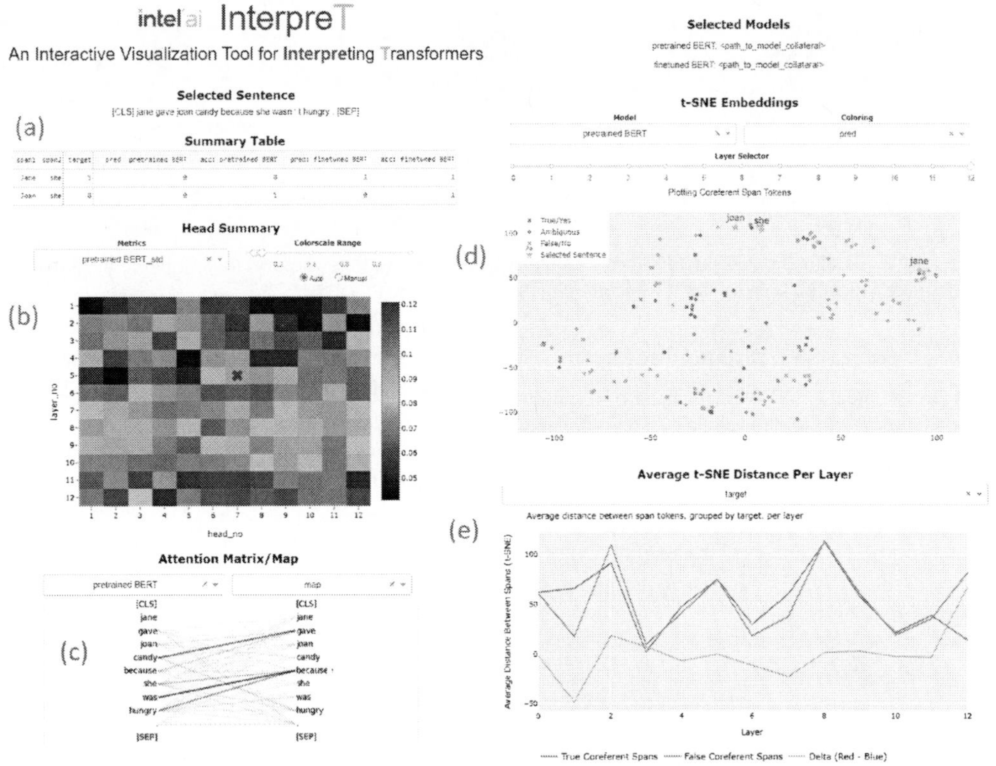

Figure (1) The InterpreT user interface (rearranged for print) for the task of coreference resolution (see Section 4.2). The UI includes a short description of the currently selected models and example at the top, along with the main features (a-e) described in Section 3.

Pereg et al. (2020). This formulation of a "grammar correlation" metric provides an indicator of an attention head's ability to identify syntactic relations in a sentence.

The **Task-Specific Attention Intensity** option allows a user to define and display custom metrics that highlight specific attention patterns. In Section 4.2.2, a "coreference intensity" metric is devised to pinpoint attention heads with an affinity for identifying coreference relationships. For this metric, each entry in the summary plot represents the attention weight between the coreferent spans being evaluated (if the span contains more than one token, the maximum is taken), for each head of each layer.

When running InterpreT with two models, the head summary plot can be used to visualize differences in the summary statistics between both models. As mentioned previously, the multi-select feature can be used with any of the summary statistic options. When using multi-select, the statistics are averaged over the selected examples, enabling the user to analyze general trends in attention behavior.

3.4 Attention Matrix/Map

Similarly to other systems, InterpreT provides the ability to display the attention patterns and weights exhibited by specific attention heads, which can be selected by clicking on a specific head and layer in the head summary plot. These attention patterns can be displayed as either a heatmap ("matrix" view) or a token "map" ("map" view) visualization used in Clark et al. (2019). There is an option to switch between the two views in-app (Figure 1c). These visualizations can become unwieldy when using large sequence lengths, but this will not affect the functionality of the rest of the system.

3.5 Summary Table

A short summary table is provided, which contains task-specific information such as predicted token classifications and the gold (target) labels for the selected sentence/example (Figure 1a).

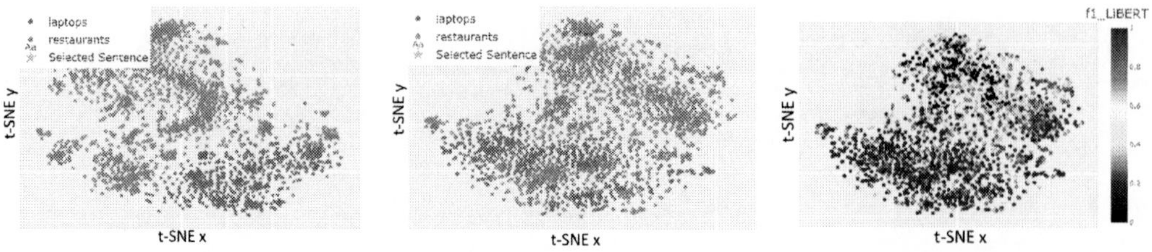

(a) (b) (c)

Figure (2) Baseline (a) and LIBERT (b,c) final layer t-SNE embeddings of aspect terms colored by domain (a,b) and aspect extraction sentence level F1 score (c) as seen in InterpreT.

3.6 Average t-SNE Distance Per Layer

To complement t-SNE visualization of the hidden states, InterpreT also introduces a novel plot showing the average t-SNE space distance between specific groups of terms across all of the Transformers' layers (Figure 1e). Section 4.2.1 demonstrates how information conveyed in this plot contributes towards novel interpretations of the inner workings of BERT.

4 Use Cases

The examples presented in this section focus on the analysis of bidirectional encoders using InterpreT, however the system can be applied to generative models or encoder-decoder architectures as well, so long as the appropriate collateral can be generated. Further examples of use cases along with instructions on how to use InterpreT for custom applications is detailed in our GitHub.

4.1 Cross-Domain Aspect Based Sentiment Analysis (ABSA)

A fundamental task in fine-grained sentiment analysis is the extraction of aspect and opinion terms. For example, in the sentence *"The chocolate cake was incredible"*, the aspect term is *chocolate cake* and the opinion term is *incredible*. Supervised learning approaches have shown promising results in single-domain setups where the training and the testing data are from the same domain. However, these approaches typically do not scale across domains, where only unlabeled data is available for the target domain. It has been shown that syntax, which is a basic trait of language and is therefore domain invariant, can help bridge the gap between domains (Ding et al., 2017; Wang and Jialin Pan, 2018).

In a recent work (Pereg et al., 2020), externally generated dependency relations are integrated into a pre-trained BERT model through the addition of a 13th attention head which incorporates the dependency relations into its Syntactically-Aware Self-Attention Mechanism. This model is referred to as Linguistically Informed BERT (LIBERT). InterpreT is used to analyze LIBERT and a Baseline model that shares the same size and structure as LIBERT but does not incorporate syntactic information for the cross-domain ABSA task, where both models are fine-tuned on laptop reviews and are evaluated on restaurant reviews (Pontiki et al., 2014, 2015; Wang et al., 2016). LIBERT and the Baseline model achieved aspect extraction F1 scores of 0.5143 and 0.4254 respectively on validation data from the restaurant domain.

4.1.1 Visualizing the Domain Gap

InterpreT is used to visualize how the incorporation of dependency relations in LIBERT contributes to bridging the gap between domains. Figure 2 depicts the final layer aspect term t-SNE embeddings from the restaurant and laptop domains produced by LIBERT and Baseline. The plot of the Baseline embeddings (2a) gives a prototypical depiction of the "domain gap" challenge present in cross-domain setups, through the clear separation of in-domain (blue) and out-of-domain (red) aspects. Conversely, the plot of LIBERT's embeddings (2b) demonstrates how LIBERT has learned to push the embeddings of some aspect terms from the out-of-domain region into the in-domain region, effectively overcoming the "domain gap" challenge for these examples. Furthermore, in the plot colored by the aspect extraction F1 score (2c), it is seen that LIBERT achieves a high F1 score on the out-of-domain examples that now overlap with in-domain examples, highlighting the usefulness of such visualizations for analyzing model performance and extensibility.

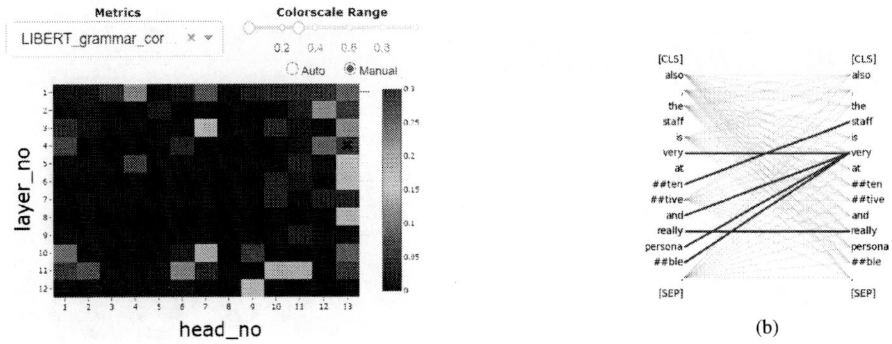

(a)

(b)

Figure (3) InterpreT's Head Summary plot displaying aggregated grammar correlation using multi-selection for LIBERT (a) along with an example of the the attention matrix of selected attention head (head 13 in layer 4) (b).

4.1.2 Grammar Correlation

A key feature of InterpreT is the addition of metrics to help identify attention heads which carry out specific functions. For analyzing LIBERT, the "grammar correlation" metric described in Section 3.3 is used to identify attention heads with an affinity for detecting syntactic relations. Figure 3a demonstrates the result of using multi-selection to compute the average grammar correlation in each of LIBERT's attention heads aggregated over multiple examples.

As expected, the Syntactically-Aware Self Attention head (head 13) tends to show much higher grammar correlation than the regular Self Attention heads. Utilizing the granularity provided in the head summary plot, it is observed that LIBERT's 13th head seems to only express an affinity for parsing syntactic relations in layers 2,3,4, and 11. This is unexpected behavior, as the syntax information is relayed identically to the 13th head across all layers. To investigate further, InterpreT can be used to display attention matrices from head 13 in layers that have high grammar correlation. One such attention matrix, for an out-of-domain example, is displayed in Figure 3b. In this attention matrix visualization, it can be seen how LIBERT's 13th head identifies syntactic relations such as the *adjectival modifier* relation between "staff" and "attentive", and how this can be useful for the cross-domain ABSA task where "staff" and "attentive" are aspect and opinion terms (respectively) in an out-of-domain example.

4.2 Coreference Resolution in the Winograd Schema Challenge (WSC)

In this section, the utility of InterpreT is showcased for a markedly different task: coreference resolution. Coreference resolution is a challenging NLP task that often requires a nuanced understanding of context and sentence semantics. This task is the basis of the Winograd Schema Challenge (WSC) from the SuperGLUE benchmark (Alex Wang, 2020), where the goal is to determine whether or not a pronoun is the correct referent of a given noun phrase. In this analysis of WSC, InterpreT demonstrates how information in the attention matrices and the hidden states of a Transformer can be used to understand the implicit mechanisms contributing to its ability to identify coreferent terms. BERT-base (uncased) is chosen for this analysis and is fine-tuned using the WSC task training set.

Example	Coreference Candidates (Fred, he)	(George, he)
"... got back"	**False**	**True**
"... got up"	**True**	True

Table (1) Predictions of the fine-tuned BERT model for the two examples. The values in bold are correct predictions.

4.2.1 Spatial Convergence of Coreferent Terms

While analyzing WSC with InterpreT, the system's wide-ranging capabilities gave rise to a novel observation, wherein it was discovered that a fine-tuned BERT model pushes closer together the embeddings of terms it predicts to be coreferent. Figure 4a displays the average distance per layer

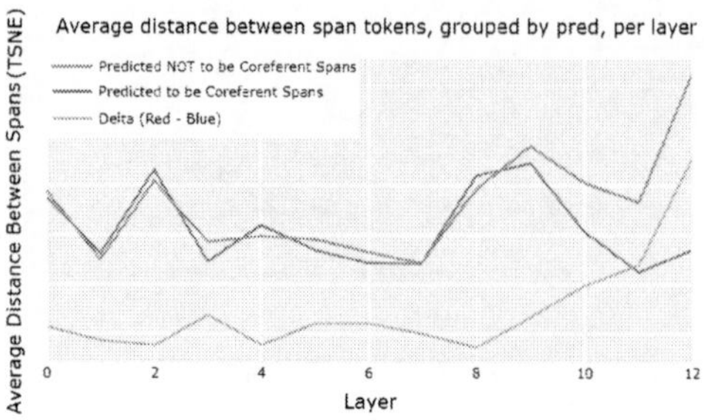

(a)

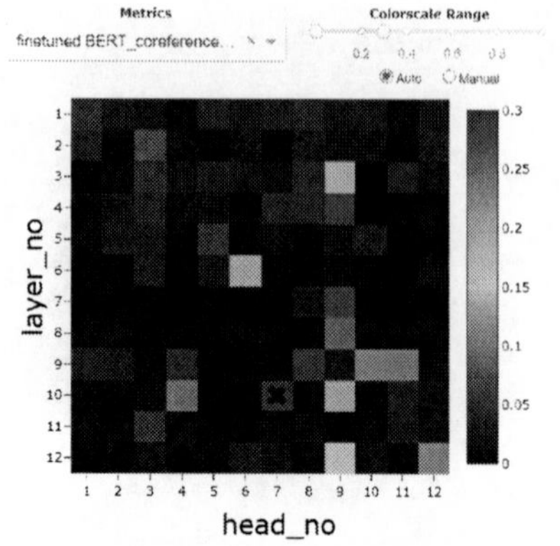

(b)

Figure (4) InterpreT summary plots for WSC. These plots display summary statistics for the average predicted span token distance per layer (a) and coreference intensity metric (b) for fine-tuned BERT aggregated over the full dataset.

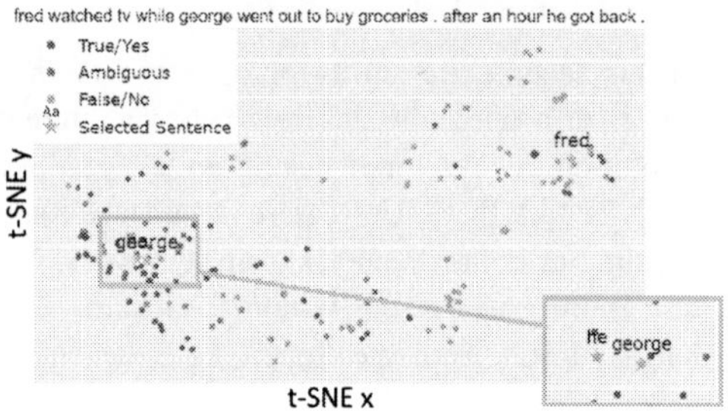

(a)

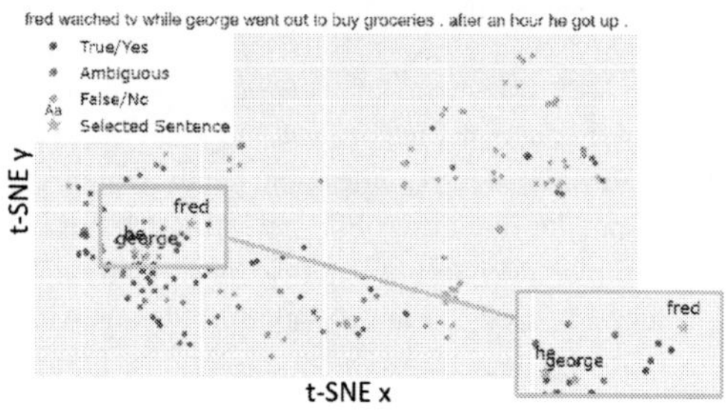

(b)

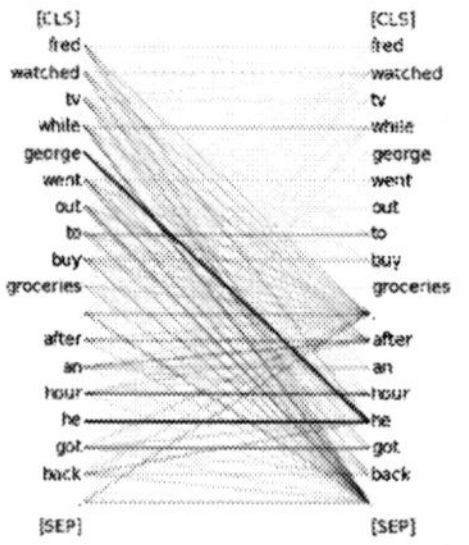

(c)

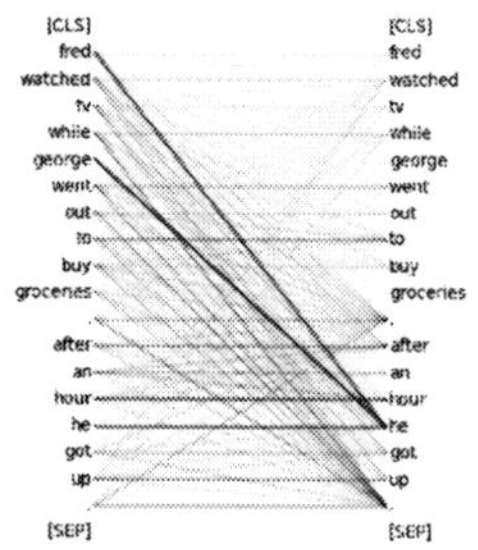

(d)

Figure (5) InterpreT plots tracking specific examples in WSC. These plots depict the final layer t-SNE embeddings and attention map visualizations of head 10 layer 7 for the following examples: "Fred watched TV while George went out to buy groceries. After an hour he got **back**" (a,c), and "Fred watched TV while George went out to buy groceries. After an hour he got **up**." (b,d). In (a) and (b), the yellow stars indicate candidate mention spans, and "He" and "George" are almost overlapping.

between terms which BERT predicts to be coreferent (blue) and terms which BERT predicts to not be coreferent (red), aggregated over the full WSC dataset. It is observed that in BERT's final layers, the model learns to modify the hidden representations of terms to increase or decrease the distance between them based on whether or not it predicts they are coreferents. This behavior can also be seen in the green trace, which measures the difference in the average distance of terms predicted to be coreferent and those that are not predicted to be coreferent.

Additionally, Figures 5a and 5b show a specific example of this phenomenon with the sentences:

"Fred watched TV while George went out to buy groceries. After an hour he got **back**" (Figure 5a and Table 1) and "Fred watched TV while George went out to buy groceries. After an hour he got **up**." (Figure 5b and Table 1). These two examples show how changing a single token ("**back**" became "**up**") significantly alters the sentence semantics, as in the first example, "he" refers to "George", and in the second example "he" refers to "Fred". InterpreT enables us to visualize this behavior using the t-SNE plots. Figure 5a show how for the first example, "he" and "George" are much closer together than "he" and "Fred" are. Figure 5b shows how in the second example, the change from "he got back" to "he got up" is reflected in BERT's behavior, where the representation of "Fred" to be pushed much closer to "he" than in the first example.

4.2.2 Attention Patterns between Coreferent Terms

Another feature of InterpreT is the ability to utilize custom metrics, such as the "coreference intensity" metric described in Section 3.3. Coreference intensity is visualized using the head summary plot in Figure 4b. The figure shows that the fine-tuned model highlights attention heads that seem to perform well as coreferent predictors. Darker shades of red correspond to higher attention between the two coreferents being evaluated. It appears that the heads which are the most involved in the coreference resolution task after fine-tuning are the 7th head of layer 10 and the 3rd head of layer 11.

This new metric is used to examine the example previously presented with "Fred", "George", and "he". Figures 5c and 5d show the attention matrix visualizations for the head selected in Figure 4b (head 7 in layer 10). The token map visualization depicts how "he" attends heavily to "George" in the first example (5c) while attending to both "Fred" and "George" in the second example (5d).

5 Conclusion and Future Work

InterpreT is a generic system for interpreting Transformers, as evident through its suite of tools for understanding general model behaviors and for enabling granular analysis of attention patterns and hidden states for individual examples. The capabilities provided by InterpreT empower users with new insights into what their models are learning, as illustrated in the visualization of the mitigation of the "domain gap" for ABSA and in the novel discovery of the spatial convergence of coreferent terms in WSC. These examples showcase how the fine-grained analysis enabled by InterpreT affords a higher level of insight that is indispensable for interpreting model behavior for complex language understanding tasks.

InterpreT is an ongoing development effort. Future work will include support for additional use cases as well as additional analysis and interactivity features, such as the ability to dynamically add and modify examples while the app is running.

6 Acknowledgements

We thank the anonymous reviewers for their comments and suggestions.

References

Betty van Aken, Benjamin Winter, Alexander Löser, and Felix A. Gers. 2019. How does bert answer questions? *Proceedings of the 28th ACM International Conference on Information and Knowledge Management.*

Betty van Aken, Benjamin Winter, Alexander Löser, and Felix A. Gers. 2020. Visbert: Hidden-state visualizations for transformers. In *Companion Proceedings of the Web Conference 2020*, WWW '20, page 207–211, New York, NY, USA. Association for Computing Machinery.

Nikita Nangia Amanpreet Singh Julian Michael Felix Hill Omer Levy Samuel R. Bowman Alex Wang, Yada Pruksachatkun. 2020. Superglue: A stickier benchmark for general-purpose language understanding systems.

Kevin Clark, Urvashi Khandelwal, Omer Levy, and Christopher D. Manning. 2019. What does bert look at? an analysis of bert's attention. In *BlackBoxNLP@ACL.*

Jacob Devlin, Ming-Wei Chang, Kenton Lee, and Kristina Toutanova. 2019. BERT: Pre-training of deep bidirectional transformers for language understanding. In *Proceedings of the 2019 Conference of the North American Chapter of the Association for Computational Linguistics: Human Language Technologies, Volume 1 (Long and Short Papers)*, pages 4171–4186, Minneapolis, Minnesota. Association for Computational Linguistics.

Ying Ding, Jianfei Yu, and Jing Jiang. 2017. Recurrent neural networks with auxiliary labels for cross-domain opinion target extraction. In *Association for the Advancement of Artificial Intelligence*, pages 3436—3442.

Benjamin Hoover, Hendrik Strobelt, and Sebastian Gehrmann. 2020. exBERT: A Visual Analysis Tool to Explore Learned Representations in Transformer Models. In *Proceedings of the 58th Annual Meeting of the Association for Computational Linguistics: System Demonstrations*, pages 187–196, Online. Association for Computational Linguistics.

Ganesh Jawahar, Benoît Sagot, and Djamé Seddah. 2019. What does BERT learn about the structure of language? In *Proceedings of the 57th Annual Meeting of the Association for Computational Linguistics*, pages 3651–3657, Florence, Italy. Association for Computational Linguistics.

Yinhan Liu, Myle Ott, Naman Goyal, Jingfei Du, Mandar Joshi, Danqi Chen, Omer Levy, Mike Lewis, Luke Zettlemoyer, and Veselin Stoyanov. 2019. Roberta: A robustly optimized BERT pretraining approach. *CoRR*, abs/1907.11692.

Laurens van der Maaten and Geoffrey Hinton. 2008. Visualizing data using t-sne. *Journal of Machine Learning Research*, 9(86):2579–2605.

Oren Pereg, Daniel Korat, and Moshe Wasserblat. 2020. Syntactically aware cross-domain aspect and opinion terms extraction. In *Proceedings of the 28th International Conference on Computational Linguistics*, pages 1772–1777, Barcelona, Spain (Online). International Committee on Computational Linguistics.

Maria Pontiki, Dimitris Galanis, Haris Papageorgiou, Suresh Manandhar, and Ion Androutsopoulos. 2015. SemEval-2015 task 12: Aspect based sentiment analysis. In *Proceedings of the 9th International Workshop on Semantic Evaluation (SemEval 2015)*, pages 486–495, Denver, Colorado. Association for Computational Linguistics.

Maria Pontiki, Dimitris Galanis, John Pavlopoulos, Harris Papageorgiou, Ion Androutsopoulos, and Suresh Manandhar. 2014. SemEval-2014 task 4: Aspect based sentiment analysis. In *Proceedings of the 8th International Workshop on Semantic Evaluation (SemEval 2014)*, pages 27–35, Dublin, Ireland. Association for Computational Linguistics.

A. Radford, Jeffrey Wu, R. Child, David Luan, Dario Amodei, and Ilya Sutskever. 2019. Language models are unsupervised multitask learners.

Emily Reif, Ann Yuan, Martin Wattenberg, Fernanda B Viegas, Andy Coenen, Adam Pearce, and Been Kim. 2019. Visualizing and measuring the geometry of bert. In *Advances in Neural Information Processing Systems*, volume 32, pages 8594–8603. Curran Associates, Inc.

Ian Tenney, James Wexler, Jasmijn Bastings, Tolga Bolukbasi, Andy Coenen, Sebastian Gehrmann, Ellen Jiang, Mahima Pushkarna, Carey Radebaugh, Emily Reif, and Ann Yuan. 2020. The language interpretability tool: Extensible, interactive visualizations and analysis for nlp models. In *Proceedings of the 2020 Conference on Empirical Methods in Natural Language Processing: System Demonstrations*.

Ashish Vaswani, Noam Shazeer, Niki Parmar, Jakob Uszkoreit, Llion Jones, Aidan N. Gomez, Lukasz Kaiser, and Illia Polosukhin. 2017. Attention is all you need.

Jesse Vig. 2019. Visualizing attention in transformer-based language representation models.

Eric Wallace, Jens Tuyls, Junlin Wang, Sanjay Subramanian, Matt Gardner, and Sameer Singh. 2019. AllenNLP interpret: A framework for explaining predictions of NLP models. In *Proceedings of the 2019 Conference on Empirical Methods in Natural Language Processing and the 9th International Joint Conference on Natural Language Processing (EMNLP-IJCNLP): System Demonstrations*, pages 7–12, Hong Kong, China. Association for Computational Linguistics.

Wenya Wang and Sinno Jialin Pan. 2018. Recursive neural structural correspondence network for cross-domain aspect and opinion co-extraction. In *Proceedings of the 56th Annual Meeting of the Association for Computational Linguistics*, pages 1—-11.

Wenya Wang, Sinno Jialin Pan, Daniel Dahlmeier, and Xiaokui Xiao. 2016. Recursive neural conditional random fields for aspect-based sentiment analysis. In *Proceedings of the 2016 Conference on Empirical Methods in Natural Language Processing*, pages 616–626, Austin, Texas. Association for Computational Linguistics.

Zhilin Yang, Zihang Dai, Yiming Yang, Jaime Carbonell, Ruslan Salakhutdinov, and Quoc V. Le. 2019. Xlnet: Generalized autoregressive pretraining for language understanding. Cite arxiv:1906.08237Comment: Pretrained models and code are available at https://github.com/zihangdai/xlnet.

Representing ELMo embeddings as two-dimensional text online

Andrey Kutuzov
University of Oslo
andreku@ifi.uio.no

Elizaveta Kuzmenko
University of Trento
lizaku77@gmail.com

Abstract

We describe a new addition to the *WebVectors* toolkit which is used to serve word embedding models over the Web. The new *ELMoViz* module adds support for contextualized embedding architectures, in particular for ELMo models. The provided visualizations follow the metaphor of 'two-dimensional text' by showing lexical substitutes: words which are most semantically similar in context to the words of the input sentence. The system allows the user to change the ELMo layers from which token embeddings are inferred. It also conveys corpus information about the query words and their lexical substitutes (namely their frequency tiers and parts of speech). The module is well integrated into the rest of the *WebVectors* toolkit, providing lexical hyperlinks to word representations in static embedding models. Two web services have already implemented the new functionality with pre-trained ELMo models for Russian, Norwegian and English.

1 Introduction

In this demo paper we describe a new module recently added to the free and open-source *WebVectors* toolkit (Kutuzov and Kuzmenko, 2017)[1]. *WebVectors* allows to easily deploy services to demonstrate the abilities of static distributional word representations (word embeddings) (Bengio et al., 2003; Mikolov et al., 2013) via web browsers. It currently powers at least two embedding model hubs:

- *NLPL WebVectors*[2], featuring models for English, Norwegian and other languages, trained within the Nordic Language Processing Laboratory initiative.

[1]A screencast is available at https://www.youtube.com/watch?v=dDugoV1r_wk.

[2]http://vectors.nlpl.eu/explore/embeddings/

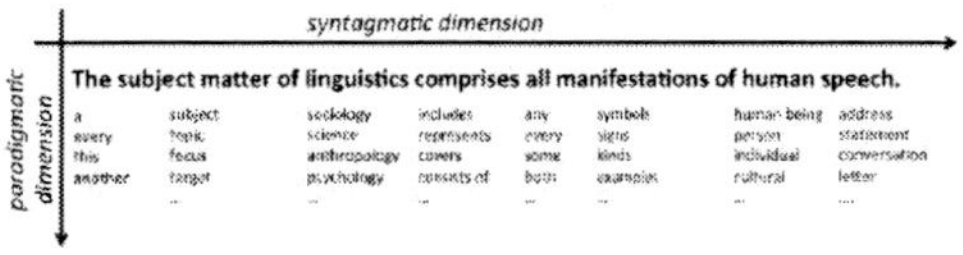

Figure 1: Metaphor of two-dimensional text; borrowed from (Biemann and Riedl, 2013).

- *RusVectōrēs*[3], featuring models for the Russian language.

The new module (we name it *ELMoViz*) adds the functionality to study, probe and compare recently introduced contextualized embedding (or 'token-based') models (Melamud et al., 2016). In particular, at this point we provide support for the ELMo architecture (Peters et al., 2018a) based on deep recurrent neural networks. In the future, we plan to add support for Transformer-based models like BERT (Devlin et al., 2019) and GPT-3 (Brown et al., 2020). ELMo architecture is significantly less computationally expensive than Transformers, while being almost on par in terms of performance. Thus, it yields rich possibilities in the context of non-commercial web services.

For analyzing ELMo representations of an arbitrary input text, we offer the metaphor of 'two-dimensional text' first proposed in (Biemann and Riedl, 2013) (see Figure 1). This allows a sort of 'visualization' for contextualized embeddings through finding words which are most semantically similar to the input words in their current contexts. From the linguistic point of view, these are 'paradigmatic replacements' (Saussure, 1916) – words that can to some extent substitute target words. The two dimensions here are the *syntagmatic* one (horizontal) which describes the linear order of the sentence, and the *paradigmatic* one (vertical) which describes semantic classes to which

[3]https://rusvectores.org/

Proceedings of the 16th Conference of the European Chapter of the Association for Computational Linguistics: System Demonstrations, pages 143–148
April 19 - 23, 2021. ©2021 Association for Computational Linguistics

the words in the sentence belong to. The generated substitutes in the vertical axis can also be thought of as 'semantic variations' of the input sentence.

The rest of the paper is organized as follows. In Section 2 we describe the background for this work, including the *WebVectors* framework, and explain the need to develop additional functionality in order to handle contextualized embeddings. Section 3 describes in detail this functionality, both from the point of view of the end user and from the point of view of deployment logistics. In Section 4, we conclude and outline future work.

2 Background

Since the widespread adoption of prediction-based word embeddings (Mikolov et al., 2013) started, there has always been a need to efficiently serve and demonstrate these representations over the Web. Researchers and practitioners need this for quick experimentation and testing hypotheses by comparing different distributional models. Those who teach natural language processing and computational linguistics need ways to show the students how dense distributional representations capture lexical semantics without installing any software or downloading any models (often it is desirable that this is shown for a particular language or domain).

In turn, language teachers value tools to demonstrate lexical variety and degrees of similarity for words in a foreign language. To this extent, serving word embeddings over the Web can help both the teachers with preparing educational materials and the students with grasping the concepts in a foreign language.

The *WebVectors* framework we presented in (Kutuzov and Kuzmenko, 2017) is aimed at all these purposes. It allows to quickly deploy a stable and robust web service featuring operations on vector semantic models, including querying, visualization and comparison, all available to users of any computer literacy level. It extended already existing embedding visualization services like Embedding Projector[4] by providing users with the ability to find nearest semantic neighbors of query words, perform vector math operations over embeddings, etc. Since being first presented in 2016, *WebVectors* keeps adding new functionality, and now it offers filtering nearest associates by part of speech tags or corpus frequency, and can generate semantic ego graphs, among other features (see Figure 2).

[4]`https://projector.tensorflow.org/`

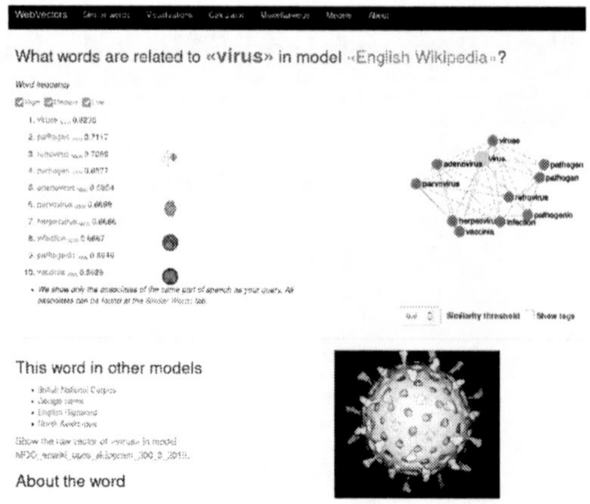

Figure 2: Screenshot of a *WebVectors* instance at `http://vectors.nlpl.eu/explore/embeddings/`

Until the introduction of *ELMoViz*, these features were limited to the so-called 'static word embeddings', that is, architectures like *word2vec* (Mikolov et al., 2013), *fastText* (Bojanowski et al., 2017) or *GloVe* (Pennington et al., 2014). In these architectures, after the training is finished, each word type in the vocabulary is rigidly associated with a single dense vector. However, in the recent years NLP saw a surge of pre-trained 'contextualized' embedding architectures, like ELMo (Peters et al., 2018a), BERT (Devlin et al., 2019), GPT-3 (Brown et al., 2020) and many others. One of the changes these deep learning models brought was that even at inference time, each word token representation (embedding) depends on its immediate context. This means that ambiguous words will receive different representations depending on the sense in which they are used, which opens rich new possibilities for natural language understanding.

Libraries used in *WebVectors* to deal with static word embeddings (*Gensim*, (Řehůřek and Sojka, 2010)) were not fit to power operations on contextualized models. That is why we decided to implement an entirely new *WebVectors* module, which would take a query phrase as an input, and produce paradigmatic replacements (lexical substitutions) for each content word in this phrase, based on a given pre-trained contextualized ELMo language model.

One can find a number of existing frameworks for online experimentation with contextualized models: among others, we should mention Language Interpretability Tool (Tenney et al., 2020), exBert by (Hoover et al., 2019) and the hosted inference API at the HuggingFace Community Model Hub (Wolf et al., 2020). However, these projects are aimed exclusively at the Transformer-based architectures. The system we present in this demo paper, on the other hand, is aimed more towards RNN-based architectures like ELMo. As it was shown, for example, in the field of semantic change detection (Kutuzov and Giulianelli, 2020), ELMo can often outperform BERT or be on par with it, while requiring significantly less computational resources. We believe it is especially important for teaching activities.

Additionally, our system is more lexically oriented and is integrated with the existing *WebVectors* functionality, as we will show in the next section.

3 System description

After turning on the contextualized embedding related functionality in the *WebVectors* configuration file,[5] the person deploying the service has to provide three data sources for each ELMo model:

1. a pre-trained *ELMo model* itself in the standard format (`*.HDF5` file with the weights and `options.json` file with the model architecture description);

2. a tab-separated *frequency dictionary* file to use when determining the frequency tier of word types (it is recommended to derive it from the same corpus the ELMo model was trained on, but technically this is not required);

3. a set of *static (type-based) word embeddings* produced by averaging contextualized token embeddings inferred with the same ELMo model.

The last item of this list requires some explanation. Our aim is to provide the end user with a set of lexical substitutes for each word token in context from the input sentence (see Figure 3). With static embedding architectures, this boils down to looking up the vector of the target word x and then finding n other words in the model vocabulary with the vectors closest to x. However, this is obviously impossible with contextualized language models: there are no static vector lookup tables to begin with. One can easily infer contextualized representations for each word in the input sentence: but

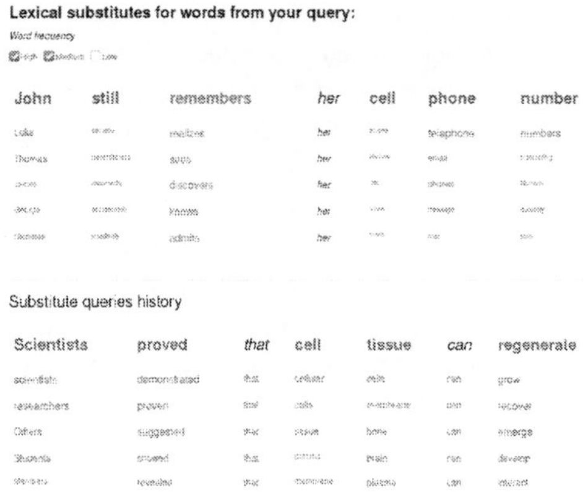

Figure 3: Examples of two-dimensional text inferred from an ELMo model ($n = 5$).

what to compare them with in order to illustrate their meaning?

To cope with this issue, we adopted the approach described in (Liu et al., 2019). They employed the so called type-level context averaging in order to align pre-trained contextualized models cross-linguistically. In our case, we needed only the first stage of their workflow. The idea is to obtain static type-level word representations located in the same vector space as the contextualized embeddings. Given a large enough reference text corpus and a pre-trained contextualized language model, one takes the average of all token representations for each target word occurrence in the corpus. This averaged type embedding is comparable to contextualized token embeddings routinely produced by the model.

In practice, we found that one does not even need to *average* token embeddings: it is enough to *sum* them, and then unit-normalize the resulting summed vector. As for the list of target words, we simply use top 10 000 (or any other amount found suitable) most frequent words from the corresponding ELMo model vocabulary or from a reference corpus (excluding functional parts of speech and digits). Low frequent words are usually not needed in this case anyway, since the quality of their embeddings is also lower. We provide a simple script to extract type embeddings from an ELMo model and a given corpus in our GitHub repository.[6]

As a result, when an end user enters an input phrase or sentence (typically from 5 to 15 words),

[5] In principle, it is also possible to use only ELMoViz, without other *WebVectors* modules.

[6] `https://github.com/akutuzov/webvectors/tree/master/elmo/`

WebVectors produces contextualized token embeddings for each token in the query, and finds top n words in the *type embedding* model, which are the closest (by cosine similarity) to each of the *token embeddings*. These predictions are *lexical substitutes* or *paradigmatic replacements*; they demonstrate what other words could fill these positions in the query, depending on the context.

Another option to produce such substitutes would be to feed the input sentence to the ELMo model and then for each word token choose the strongest activations at the final softmax layer of the language model and map them to words in the model vocabulary. However, in practice we found that this approach is slightly slower than the one described above. Additionally, ELMo models are often published online without the vocabulary they were trained on. Since the input layer of ELMo is purely character-based, it does not hinder inferring token embeddings, but it effectively blocks using these weights as language models *per se*. Our approach allows one to use any given ELMo model with any desired corpus to produce a set of reference type embeddings.

System maintainers can provide several models for the service to work with, including models for different languages; one of the models should be specified in the configuration files as the default one. When entering the query sentence, users can choose the model which will process the input.

Apart from choosing between different models, *WebVectors* also allows users to choose the exact ELMo layer from which token representations will be inferred; it was shown in (Peters et al., 2018b) that different neural network layers convey information related to different linguistic tiers: syntax, semantics, pragmatics, etc. At this point, one can choose between the top ELMo layer and the average of all layers. Note that for all operations with pre-trained ELMo models we use `simple_elmo`: a lightweight TensorFlow-based Python package also developed by us.[7] If need be, `simple_elmo` can also be used as a standalone library to handle ELMo models.

Both the words from the input sentence and the lexical substitutes are colored according to their frequency tier in the reference corpus (green for 'high', blue for 'mid' and red for 'low'), in accordance with other *WebVectors* components. Similarly, each word is hyperlinked to its 'landing page' bound to one of the static embedding models served by a particular *WebVectors* installation (like the one in Figure 2), allowing easy and playful exploration of the semantic space. The font size of the lexical substitute corresponds to cosine similarity between the token embedding and the substitute type embedding: thus, users can instantly see what word tokens the model is unsure about. The service performs fast under-the-hood part-of-speech tagging of the query,[8] so for functional words we always yield themselves as substitutes (see 'her', 'that' and 'can' in Figure 3). They are also uncolored and not hyperlinked, so that a user might focus on content words, while at the same time still having an impression of 'full sentence variations'.

The users should be aware that the lexical substitutes potentially contain all the biases inherited from the corpus the model was trained on. Thus, the paradigmatic axis might include slander words and stereotypes, if they were frequent enough in the data. We did not address this issue in the present work, but we advise the users to take this into account when dealing with any unsupervised language models.

Importantly, we keep a short history of substitute queries, so that it is possible to see at a glance the changes brought by a different context, a different word order or a different contextualized model (if the web service offers several models). Figure 4 shows an example from our Russian live demo at the *RusVectōrēs* web service. In the first sentence, the word закладку '*zakladku*' is used in the newer sense of 'a secret place to store illegal drugs', while in the second sentence it is used in the older sense of 'the act of founding a building'. The generated substitutes reflect the differences in word meaning depending on the context. In the first example the substitutes include such words as 'meeting, sale, operation', and in the second example the substitutes are 'opening, building, repair'.

4 Conclusion

The described system for generating two-dimensional text using pre-trained ELMo models is now deployed at the two model hubs mentioned in Section 1. *NLPL WebVectors* features ELMo models trained on English Wikipedia and on Norwegian corpora[9], while *RusVectōrēs* features a

[7] `https://pypi.org/project/simple-elmo/`

[8] Using UDPipe (Straka and Straková, 2017).

[9] `http://vectors.nlpl.eu/explore/embeddings/en/contextual`

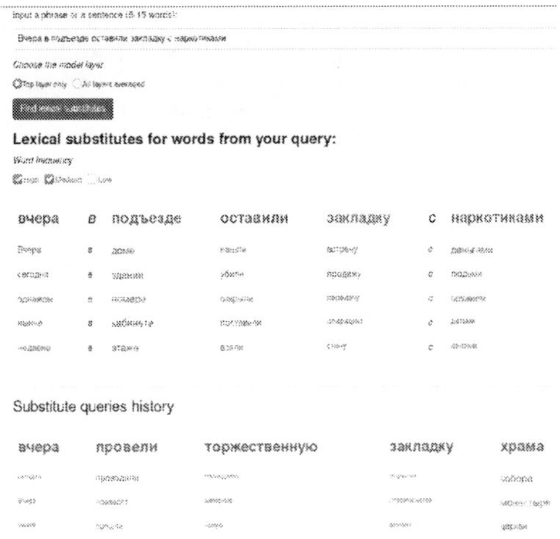

Figure 4: History of lexical substitute queries with a Russian ELMo model.

model trained on concatenated Russian Wikipedia and Russian National Corpus.[10]

The presented component for the *WebVectors* framework allows users to explore pre-trained ELMo models and to visualize contextualized embeddings as a two-dimensional text for faster analysis of early research prototypes. While previously the framework provided interface only to static vector semantic models, introducing support for contextualized architectures allows for more intricate exploration of linguistic phenomena, such as lexical ambiguity and contextual semantic change.

We hope that the new functionality will provide language teachers, NLP researchers and practitioners with a powerful tool to study word meaning in context and at the same time keep the audience up-to-date with recent advances in the field of distributional semantics and deep learning based NLP. A separate important contribution is our `simple_elmo` library which makes using ELMo models in Python much easier, especially for researchers with linguistic background.

In the future, we plan to add support for other contextualized embedding architectures like BERT, to allow inter-architectural comparisons. Another interesting room for future work is integrating with other exploratory services for neural NLP models, like the ones mentioned in Section 2.

[10] `https://rusvectores.org/en/contextual/`

References

Yoshua Bengio, Rejean Ducharme, and Pascal Vincent. 2003. A neural probabilistic language model. *Journal of Machine Learning Research*, 3:1137–1155.

Chris Biemann and Martin Riedl. 2013. Text: Now in 2d! a framework for lexical expansion with contextual similarity. *Journal of Language Modelling*, 1(1):55–95.

Piotr Bojanowski, Edouard Grave, Armand Joulin, and Tomas Mikolov. 2017. Enriching word vectors with subword information. *Transactions of the Association for Computational Linguistics*, 5:135–146.

Tom B Brown, Benjamin Mann, Nick Ryder, Melanie Subbiah, Jared Kaplan, Prafulla Dhariwal, Arvind Neelakantan, Pranav Shyam, Girish Sastry, Amanda Askell, et al. 2020. Language models are few-shot learners. *arXiv preprint arXiv:2005.14165*.

Jacob Devlin, Ming-Wei Chang, Kenton Lee, and Kristina Toutanova. 2019. BERT: Pre-training of deep bidirectional transformers for language understanding. In *Proceedings of the 2019 Conference of the North American Chapter of the Association for Computational Linguistics: Human Language Technologies, Volume 1 (Long and Short Papers)*, pages 4171–4186, Minneapolis, Minnesota. Association for Computational Linguistics.

Benjamin Hoover, Hendrik Strobelt, and Sebastian Gehrmann. 2019. exbert: A visual analysis tool to explore learned representations in transformers models. *arXiv preprint arXiv:1910.05276*.

Andrey Kutuzov and Mario Giulianelli. 2020. UiO-UvA at SemEval-2020 task 1: Contextualised embeddings for lexical semantic change detection. In *Proceedings of the Fourteenth Workshop on Semantic Evaluation*, pages 126–134, Barcelona (online). International Committee for Computational Linguistics.

Andrey Kutuzov and Elizaveta Kuzmenko. 2017. Building web-interfaces for vector semantic models with the webvectors toolkit. In *Proceedings of the Software Demonstrations of the 15th Conference of the European Chapter of the Association for Computational Linguistics*, pages 99–103.

Qianchu Liu, Diana McCarthy, Ivan Vulić, and Anna Korhonen. 2019. Investigating cross-lingual alignment methods for contextualized embeddings with token-level evaluation. In *Proceedings of the 23rd Conference on Computational Natural Language Learning (CoNLL)*, pages 33–43, Hong Kong, China. Association for Computational Linguistics.

Oren Melamud, Jacob Goldberger, and Ido Dagan. 2016. context2vec: Learning generic context embedding with bidirectional LSTM. In *Proceedings of The 20th SIGNLL Conference on Computational Natural Language Learning*, pages 51–61, Berlin, Germany. Association for Computational Linguistics.

Tomas Mikolov, Wen-tau Yih, and Geoffrey Zweig. 2013. Linguistic regularities in continuous space word representations. In *Proceedings of the 2013 Conference of the North American Chapter of the Association for Computational Linguistics: Human Language Technologies*, pages 746–751, Atlanta, Georgia. Association for Computational Linguistics.

Jeffrey Pennington, Richard Socher, and Christopher Manning. 2014. Glove: Global vectors for word representation. In *Proceedings of the 2014 Conference on Empirical Methods in Natural Language Processing (EMNLP)*, pages 1532–1543, Doha, Qatar. Association for Computational Linguistics.

Matthew Peters, Mark Neumann, Mohit Iyyer, Matt Gardner, Christopher Clark, Kenton Lee, and Luke Zettlemoyer. 2018a. Deep contextualized word representations. In *Proceedings of the 2018 Conference of the North American Chapter of the Association for Computational Linguistics: Human Language Technologies, Volume 1 (Long Papers)*, pages 2227–2237, New Orleans, Louisiana. Association for Computational Linguistics.

Matthew Peters, Mark Neumann, Luke Zettlemoyer, and Wen-tau Yih. 2018b. Dissecting contextual word embeddings: Architecture and representation. In *Proceedings of the 2018 Conference on Empirical Methods in Natural Language Processing*, pages 1499–1509, Brussels, Belgium. Association for Computational Linguistics.

Radim Řehůřek and Petr Sojka. 2010. Software Framework for Topic Modelling with Large Corpora. In *Proceedings of the LREC 2010 Workshop on New Challenges for NLP Frameworks*, pages 45–50, Valletta, Malta. ELRA.

Ferdinand de Saussure. 1916. *Course in general linguistics*. Duckworth.

Milan Straka and Jana Straková. 2017. Tokenizing, POS tagging, lemmatizing and parsing UD 2.0 with UDPipe. In *Proceedings of the CoNLL 2017 Shared Task: Multilingual Parsing from Raw Text to Universal Dependencies*, pages 88–99, Vancouver, Canada. Association for Computational Linguistics.

Ian Tenney, James Wexler, Jasmijn Bastings, Tolga Bolukbasi, Andy Coenen, Sebastian Gehrmann, Ellen Jiang, Mahima Pushkarna, Carey Radebaugh, Emily Reif, and Ann Yuan. 2020. The language interpretability tool: Extensible, interactive visualizations and analysis for NLP models. In *Proceedings of the 2020 Conference on Empirical Methods in Natural Language Processing: System Demonstrations*, pages 107–118. Association for Computational Linguistics.

Thomas Wolf, Lysandre Debut, Victor Sanh, Julien Chaumond, Clement Delangue, Anthony Moi, Pierric Cistac, Tim Rault, Rémi Louf, Morgan Funtowicz, Joe Davison, Sam Shleifer, Patrick von Platen, Clara Ma, Yacine Jernite, Julien Plu, Canwen Xu, Teven Le Scao, Sylvain Gugger, Mariama Drame, Quentin Lhoest, and Alexander M. Rush. 2020. Transformers: State-of-the-art natural language processing. In *Proceedings of the 2020 Conference on Empirical Methods in Natural Language Processing: System Demonstrations*, pages 38–45, Online. Association for Computational Linguistics.

LOME: Large Ontology Multilingual Extraction

Patrick Xia[1]*, Guanghui Qin[1]*, Siddharth Vashishtha[2]
Yunmo Chen[1], Tongfei Chen[1], Chandler May[1], Craig Harman[1]
Kyle Rawlins[1], Aaron Steven White[2], Benjamin Van Durme[1]
[1] Johns Hopkins University, [2] University of Rochester
{paxia,qin,vandurme}@jhu.edu

Abstract

We present LOME, a system for performing multilingual information extraction. Given a text document as input, our core system identifies spans of textual entity and event mentions with a FrameNet (Baker et al., 1998) parser. It subsequently performs coreference resolution, fine-grained entity typing, and temporal relation prediction between events. By doing so, the system constructs an event and entity focused knowledge graph. We can further apply third-party modules for other types of annotation, like relation extraction. Our (multilingual) first-party modules either outperform or are competitive with the (monolingual) state-of-the-art. We achieve this through the use of multilingual encoders like *XLM-R* (Conneau et al., 2020) and leveraging multilingual training data. LOME is available as a Docker container on Docker Hub. In addition, a lightweight version of the system is accessible as a web demo.

1 Introduction

As information extraction capabilities continue to improve due to advances in modeling, encoders, and data collection, we can now look (back) toward making richer predictions at the document-level, with a large ontology, and across multiple languages. Recently, Li et al. (2020) noted that despite a growth of open-source NLP software in general, there is still a lack of available software for knowledge extraction. We wish to provide a starting point that allows others to build increasingly comprehensive document-level knowledge graphs of events and entities from text in many languages.[1]

Therefore, we demonstrate LOME, a system for multilingual information extraction with large ontologies. Figure 1 shows the high-level pipeline by following a multilingual input example. A sentence-level parser identifies both INGESTION events and their arguments. To connect these events cross-sententially, the system clusters coreferent mentions and predicts the temporal relations between the events. LOME, which supports fine-grained entity types, additionally labels entities like **the rabbit** with LIVING_THING/ANIMAL.

Several prior packages have also used advances in state-of-the-art models to build comprehensive information extraction systems. Li et al. (2019) present an event, relation, and entity extraction and coreference system for three languages: English, Russian, and Ukrainian. Li et al. (2020, GAIA) extend that work to support cross-media documents. However, both of these systems consist of language-specific models that operate on monolingual documents after first identifying the language. On the other hand, work prioritizing coverage across tens or hundreds of languages is limited in their scope in extraction (Akbik and Li, 2016; Pan et al., 2017).

Like prior work, LOME is focused on extracting entities and events from raw text documents. However, LOME is language-agnostic; all components prioritize multilinguality. Using *XLM-R* (Conneau et al., 2020) as the underlying encoder paves the way for both training on multilingual data (where it exists) and inference in many languages.[2] Our pipeline includes a full FrameNet parser for events and their arguments, neural coreference resolution, an entity typing model over large ontologies, and temporal resolution between events.

Our system is designed to be modular: each component is trained independently and tuned on task-specific data. To communicate between modules, we use CONCRETE (Ferraro et al., 2014), a data schema used in other text processing systems (Peng et al., 2015). One advantage of using a stan-

*Equal Contribution

[1]Information on using the Docker container, web demo, and demo video at https://nlp.jhu.edu/demos.

[2]*XLM-R* itself is trained on CommonCrawl data spanning one hundred languages.

Proceedings of the 16th Conference of the European Chapter of the Association for Computational Linguistics: System Demonstrations, pages 149–159
April 19 - 23, 2021. ©2021 Association for Computational Linguistics

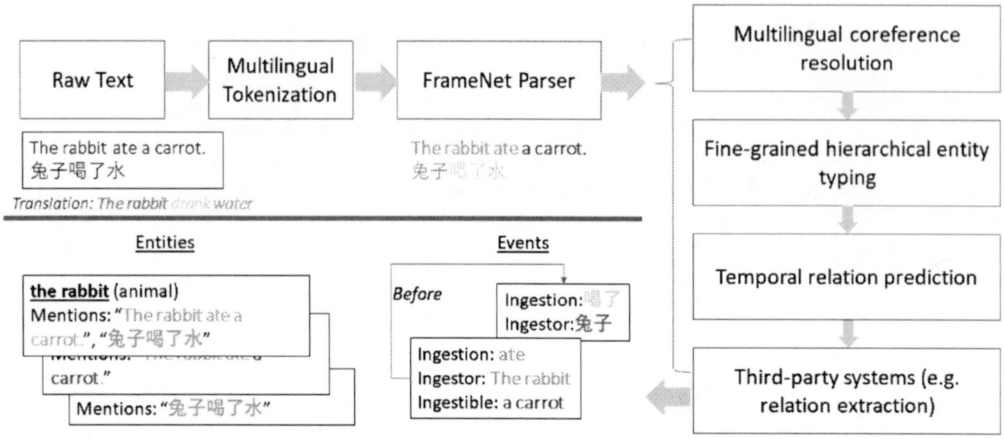

Figure 1: Architecture of LOME. The system processes text documents as input and first uses a FrameNet parser to detect entities and events. Then, a suite of models enrich the entities and events with additional predictions. Each individual model can be trained and tuned independently, ensuring modularity of the pipeline. Annotations between models are transferred using CONCRETE, a data schema for NLP.

dardized data schema is that it enables modularization and extension. Unless there are annotation dependencies, individual modules can be inserted, replaced, merged, or bypassed depending on the application. We discuss two example applications of our CONCRETE-based modules, one of which further extracts relations and the other performs cross-sentence argument linking for events.

2 Tasks

The overarching application of LOME is to extract an entity- and event-centric knowledge graph from a textual document. In particular, we are interested in using these graphs to support a multilingual schema learning task (KAIROS[3]) for which data has been annotated by the LDC (Cieri et al., 2020). As a result, some parts of LOME are designed for compatibility with the KAIROS event and entity ontology. Nonetheless, there is significant overlap with publicly available datasets, which we describe for those tasks.

Figure 1 presents the architecture of our pipeline. Besides the FrameNet parser, which is run first, the remaining modules can be run in any order, if at all. In addition, our use of a standardized data schema for communication allows for the integration of third-party systems. In this section, we will go into further detail for each task.

2.1 FrameNet Parsing

FrameNet parsing is a semantic role labeling style task. The goal is to find all the frames and their roles, as well as the trigger spans associated with them in a sentence. Frames are concepts, such as events or entities, in a sentences. Every frame is associated with some roles, and both of them are triggered by spans in the sentence.

Unlike most previous work (Yang and Mitchell, 2017; Peng et al., 2018; Swayamdipta et al., 2018), our system is not conditioned on the trigger spans or frames. We perform "full parsing" (Das et al., 2014), where the input is a raw sentence, and the output is the complete structure predictions.

As the first model in the whole pipeline system, the trigger spans found by the FrameNet parser will be used as candidate spans for all other tasks.

2.2 Entity Coreference Resolution

In coreference resolution, the goal is to cluster spans in the text that refer to the same entity. Neural models for doing so typically encode the text first before identifying possible mentions (Lee et al., 2017; Joshi et al., 2019, 2020). These spans are scored pairwise to determine whether two spans refer to each other. These scores then determine coreference clusters by decoding under a variety of strategies (Lee et al., 2018; Xu and Choi, 2020).

In this work, we choose a constant-memory variant of that model which also achieves high per-

[3]This goal is to develop a system that identifies, links, and temporally sequences complex events. More information at `https://www.darpa.mil/program/knowledge-directed-artificial-intelligence-reasoning-over-schemas`.

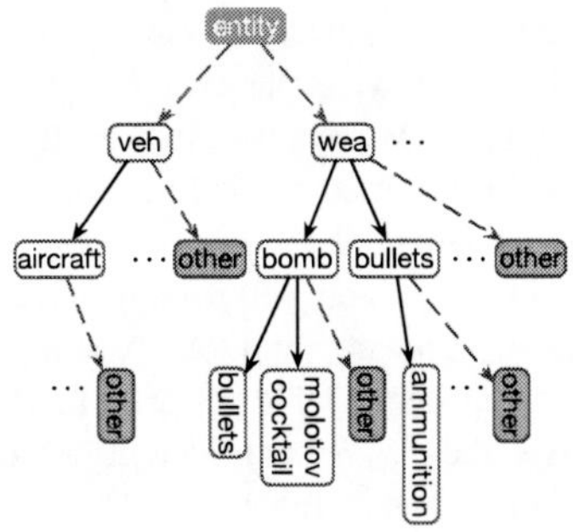

Figure 2: A portion of the AIDA entity type ontology.

formance (Xia et al., 2020). The motivation here is robustness: we prioritize the ability to soundly run on all document lengths over slightly better performing but fragile systems. In addition, because this coreference resolution model is part of a broader entity-centric system, the module used in this system does not perform the mention detection step (which is left to the FrameNet parser). Instead, both training and inference assumes given mentions, and the task we are concerned about in this paper is mention *linking*.

2.3 Entity Typing

Entity typing assigns a fine-grained semantic label to a span of text, where the span is a *mention* of some entity found by the FrameNet parser. Traditionally, labels include `PER`, `GPE`, `ORG`, etc., but recent work in *fine-grained* entity typing seek to classify spans into types defined by hierarchical type *ontologies* (e.g. BBN (Weischedel and Brunstein, 2005), FIGER (Ling and Weld, 2012), UltraFine[4] (Choi et al., 2018), COLLIE (Allen et al., 2020)). Such ontologies refine coarse types like `PER` to fine-grained types such as `/person/artist/singer` that sits on a type hierarchy. A portion of the AIDA ontology (LDC2019E07) is illustrated in Figure 2.

To support fine-grained ontologies, we employ a recent coarse-to-fine-decoding entity typing model (Chen et al., 2020a) that is specifically designed to assign types that are defined by hierarchical ontologies. The use of a coarse-to-fine model also allows users to select between coarse- and fine-grained types. We swap the underlying encoder from ELMo (Peters et al., 2018) to *XLM-R* to be able to assign types over mentions in different languages using a single multilingual model, and to enable transfer between languages.

The base typing model in Chen et al. (2020a) supports entity typing on entity *mentions*. We extend this model to gain the ability to perform entity typing on *entities*, i.e. clusters of entity mentions. Since our decoder is coarse-to-fine and predicts a type at each level of the type hierarchy, we employ Borda voting on each level. Specifically, given a coreference chain comprising mentions $m_{1,\cdots,n}$, and the score for mention m_i being typed as type t as $s_{i,t}$, we perform Borda counting to select the most confident type $t^* = \arg\max_t \sum_i r(i,t)$ over all t's in a specific type level, where $r(i,t) = 1/\text{rank}_t(s_{i,t})$ is the ranking relevance score used in Borda counting.

2.4 Temporal Relation Extraction

The task of temporal relation extraction focuses on finding the chronology of events (e.g., *Before*, *After*, *Overlaps*) in text. Extracting temporal relation is useful for various downstream tasks – curating structured clinical data (Savova et al., 2010; Soysal et al., 2018), text summarization (Glavaš and Šnajder, 2014; Kedzie et al., 2015), question-answering (Llorens et al., 2015; Zhou et al., 2019), etc. The task is most commonly viewed as a classification task where given a pair of events and its textual context, the temporal relation between them needs to be identified.

The construction of the TimeBank corpus (Pustejovsky et al., 2003) largely spurred the research in temporal relation extraction. It included 14 temporal relation labels. Other corpora (Verhagen et al., 2007, 2010; Sun et al., 2013; Cassidy et al., 2014) reduced the number of labels to a smaller number owing to lower inter-annotator agreements and sparse annotations. Various types of models (Chambers et al., 2014; Cheng and Miyao, 2017; Leeuwenberg and Moens, 2017; Ning et al., 2017; Vashishtha et al., 2019; Zhou et al., 2021) have been used in the recent years to extract temporal relations from text.

In this work, we use Vashishtha et al. (2019)'s best model and retrain it using *XLM-R*. We evaluate their model using the transfer learning approach described in their work and retrain it on TimeBank-Dense (TBD) (Cassidy et al., 2014). TBD uses a reduced set of 5 temporal relation labels – *before*, *after*, *includes*, *is_included*, and *vague*.

[4] UltraFine is slightly different in that the types are bucketed into 3 categories of different granularity, but without explicit subtyping relations.

3 System Design

3.1 Modularization

Our system is modularized into separate models and libraries that communicate with each other using CONCRETE, a data format for richly annotating natural language documents (Ferraro et al., 2014). Each component is independent of each other, which allows for both inserting additional modules or deleting those provided in the default pipeline. We choose this loosely-affiliated design to enable both faster and independent prototyping of individual components, as well as better compartmentalization of our models.

We emphasize that the system is a pipeline: while individual modules can be further improved, the system is not designed to be trained end-to-end and benchmarking the richly-annotated output depends on the application and priorities. In this paper, we only benchmark individual components and describe a couple of applications.

3.2 System Inputs and Outputs

The system can consume, as input, either tokenized or untokenized text, which is first tokenized either by whitespace or with a multilingual tokenizer, PolyGlot.[5] However, this tokenization is not necessarily used by all modules, which may choose to either operate on the raw text itself or on a SentencePiece (Kudo and Richardson, 2018) retokenization.

The system outputs a CONCRETE communication file for each input document. This output file contains annotations including entities, events, coreference, entity types, and temporal relations. This schema used is entirely self-contained and the well-documented library also contains tools for visualizing and inspecting CONCRETE files.[6] For the web demo, the output is displayed in the browser.

4 Evaluation Benchmarks

4.1 FrameNet Span Finding

The FrameNet parser is comprised of an *XLM-R* encoder, a BIO tagger, and a typing module. It encodes the input sentences into a list of vectors, used by both the BIO tagger and the typing module. The goal of BIO tagger is to find trigger spans, which are then labeled by the typing module. To parse a sentence, we run the model to find all frames, and then find their roles conditioned on the frames.

[5]`https://github.com/aboSamoor/polyglot`

[6]`http://hltcoe.github.io/concrete/`

We train the FrameNet parser on the FrameNet v1.7 corpus following Das et al. (2014), with statistics in Table 1. We evaluate the results with exact matching as our metric,[7] and get 56.34 labeled F1 or 66.41 unlabeled F1. Since we are not aware of previous work on both full parsing and a metric for its evaluation, we do not have a baseline. However, we can force the model to perform frame identification given the trigger span, like prior work. These results are shown in Table 2.

	# Sentences	# Frames	# Roles
train	3120	18604	32419
dev	311	2209	3853
test	1333	6687	11277

Table 1: Statistics of FrameNet v1.7

Model	Accuracy
Yang and Mitchell (2017)	88.2
Hermann et al. (2014)	88.4
Peng et al. (2018)	90.0
This work	**91.3**

Table 2: Result on frame identification

4.2 Coreference Resolution

We retrain the model by Xia et al. (2020) with *XLM-R* (large) as the underlying encoder and with additional multilingual data. The model is a constant-memory variant of neural coreference resolution models. We refer the reader to Xia et al. (2020) for model and training details.

Unlike that work, we operate under the assumption that we are provided gold spans. This is motivated by the location of coreference in LOME. In addition, while they use a frozen encoder, we found that finetuning improves performance.[8] Finally, we train on the full OntoNotes 5.0 (Weischedel et al., 2013; Pradhan et al., 2013), a subset of SemEval 2010 Task 1 (Recasens et al., 2010), and two additional sources of Russian data, RuCor (Toldova et al., 2014) and AnCor (Budnikov et al., 2019).

We benchmark the performance of our model on each language. We report the average F1 of MUC (Vilain et al., 1995), B^3 (Bagga and Baldwin, 1998), and $CEAF_{\phi_4}$ (Luo, 2005) by language in Table 3. We can compare the model's performance to monolingual gold-only baselines, where they exist. For

[7]A role is considered to be correctly predicted only when its frame is precisely predicted.

[8]We use AdamW and a learning rate of 5×10^{-6}.

English, we trained an identical model but instead use SpanBERT (Joshi et al., 2020), an English-only encoder finetuned for English OntoNotes coreference. That model achieves 92.2 average (dev.) F1, compared to our 92.7. There is also a comparable system for Russian AnCor from Le et al. (2019), which achieves 79.9 F1 using the model from Lee et al. (2018) and RuBERT (Kuratov and Arkhipov, 2019). This shows that our single, multilingual model, can perform similarly to monolingual models, with the advantage that our model does not need to perform language ID. This finding mirrors prior findings showing multilingual encoders are strong cross-lingually (Wu and Dredze, 2019).

Language	# Training	# Eval Docs	Avg. F1
Arabic[O]	359	44	71.3
Catalan[S]	829	142	58.7
Chinese[O]	1810	252	90.8
Dutch[S]	145	23	63.5
English[O]	2802	343	92.7
Italian[S]	80	17	47.2
Russian[A]	573	127	77.3
Spanish[S]	875	140	63.5

Table 3: Average F1 scores by language with gold mentions. The superscripts O indicates data from OntoNotes 5.0 (dev), S indicates data from SemEval 2010 Task 1 (dev), and A is the AnCor data (test).

4.3 Entity Typing

We retrain the coarse-to-fine entity typer by Chen et al. (2020a) with *XLM-R* as the underlying encoder, and using the AIDA ontology as the type label inventory. The dataset annotated from AIDA is relatively small. To make the model more robust, we pre-train the model using extra training data from GAIA (Li et al., 2020), where they obtained YAGO fine-grained types (Suchanek et al., 2008) from the results of Freebase entity linking, and mapped these types to the AIDA ontology. After pre-training, we fine-tune the model using the AIDA M18 and M36 data with 3-fold cross-validation, where each fold is distinct in the topics of these documents. The sizes of these datasets are shown in Table 4.

Our models perform well in these datasets. Using one third of the AIDA M36 data as dev, our method obtained 60.1% micro-F_1 score;[9] with pre-training using GAIA extra data, we get 76.5%.

Our system can also be extended to support other

Data source	Language	# of entities
AIDA M18 LDC2019E07	English	4,433
	Russian	4,826
	Ukrainian	4,261
AIDA M36 LDC2020E29	English	703
	Spanish	557
	Russian	729
GAIA	English	42.8M
	Spanish	11.1M
	Russian	2.4M

Table 4: Statistics of the datasets used for training our entity typing model.

commonly used fine-grained entity type ontologies. We report the results in micro-F_1 in Table 5.

Ontology	Prior state-of-the-art	Ours
BBN	78.1 (Lin and Ji, 2019)	**80.5**
FIGER	79.8 (Lin and Ji, 2019)	**80.8**
UltraFine	40.1 (Onoe and Durrett, 2019)	**41.5**

Table 5: Performance of our hierarchical entity typing model across several typing ontologies.

4.4 Temporal Relation Extraction

We retrain Vashishtha et al. (2019)'s best fine-grained temporal relation model on UDS-T (Vashishtha et al., 2019) using *XLM-R* (large). We then use their transfer learning approach and train an SVM model on event-event relations in TimeBank-Dense (TBD) to predict categorical temporal relation labels. With this approach, we see a micro-F1 score of 56 on the test set of TBD.[10]

For better performance, we train the same model on additional TempEval3 (TE3) dataset (UzZaman et al., 2013). Since TE3 and TBD use a different set of temporal relations, we consider only those instances that are labeled with 4 temporal relations from both TE3 and TBD for joint training – *before*, *after*, *includes* (*container*), and *is_included* (*contained*). We retrain Vashishtha et al. (2019)'s transfer learning model on the combined TE3 and TBD dataset considering only these 4 relations and evaluate on their combined test set.[11] Results on the combined test set are reported in Table 6. We use this model as the default temporal relation extraction model in LOME.

[9] Please refer to Chen et al. (2020a) for the exact definitions of the evaluation metric.

[10] The train and dev set of TBD has a total of 4,590 instances and the test set has 1,405 instances of event-event relations.

[11] We consider only event-event relations and the combined dataset has 5,987 (1,249) instances in the train (test) set.

We also test our default model on a Chinese temporal relation extraction dataset (Li et al., 2016).[12] In the zero-shot setting, we get a micro F1 score of 52.6 on the provided dataset, as compared to a majority baseline of 37.5.[13] Similar to the default temporal system in LOME, we use the *XLM-R* version of Vashishtha et al. (2019)'s model obtaining relation embeddings for the Chinese dataset and train an SVM model using the transfer learning approach to get a micro F1 score of 64.4.[14]

Relation	Precision	Recall	F1
before	68	89	77
after	74	69	71
includes	83	5	10
is_included	44	15	22

Table 6: Result on the combined test set of TempEval3 and TimeBank-Dense when trained with just 4 temporal relation labels

5 Extensions

5.1 Incorporating third-party systems

Besides the core components described above, we also discuss the viability of including additional modules that may not fit directly in the core pipeline but can be included depending on the downstream application. For example, the system described above does not predict any relation information, which is needed for the motivating application of downstream schema inference. To do so, we wrote a CONCRETE and Docker wrapper around OneIE (Lin et al., 2020) and attached it at the end of the pipeline. With our CONCRETE based design, the integration of any third-party module can be done via implementing the *AnnotateCommunicationService* service interface, which can ensure compatibility between LOME and external modules. The OneIE wrapper is one example of an external module.

5.2 Mix and Match Modules: SM-KBP

As another example application, we reconfigured our pipeline for the NIST SM-KBP 2020 Task 1 evaluation, which aims to produce document-level knowledge graphs.[15] Each given document may be in English, Russian, or Spanish. On a development set consisting solely of text-only documents,[16] we started with initial predictions made by GAIA (Li et al., 2020), for entity clusters, entity types, events and relations. Our goal was to recluster and relabel the a dataset for knowledge extraction.

Our pipeline consisted of the multilingual coreference resolution (using the predetermined mention from GAIA) and hierarchical entity typing models discussed in this paper, followed by a separate state-of-the-art argument linking model (Chen et al., 2020b). We found improved performance[17] with entity coreference (from 29.1 F1 to 33.3 F1), especially in Russian (from 26.2 F1 to 33.3 F1), likely due to our use of multilingual data and contextualized encoders. The improved entity clusters also led to downstream improvements in entity typing and argument linking. This example highlights the ability to pick out subcomponents of LOME and customize according to the downstream task.

6 Usage

We present two methods to interact with the pipeline. The first is a Docker container which contains the libraries, code, and trained models of our pipeline. This is intended to run on batches of documents. As a lighter demo of some of the system capabilities, we also have a web demo intended to interactively run on shorter documents.

Docker Our Docker image[18] consists of the four core modules: FrameNet parser, coreference resolution, entity typing, and temporal resolution. Furthermore, there are two options for entity typing: a fine-grained hierarchical model (with the AIDA typing ontology) and a coarse-grained model (with the KAIROS typing ontology). The container and documentation is available on Docker Hub.

As some modules depend on GPU libraries, the image also requires NVIDIA-Docker support. Since there is a high start-up (time) cost for using Docker and loading models, we recommend using this container for batch processing of documents. Further instructions for running can be found on the LOME Docker Hub page.

[12] We remove the instances with *unknown* relation from the dataset and convert the predictions with *includes* and *is_included* relations to the *overlaps* relation to match the label set of their dataset with our system.

[13] The authors were able to provide only half of the dataset with 10,476 event-event pairs, from which we ignore instances with *unknown* relation, resulting into 9,362 instances.

[14] The results are the average of the 5-fold cross validation splits provided by Li et al. (2016).

[15] `https://tac.nist.gov/2020/KBP/SM-KBP/index.html`

[16] AIDA M36, `LDC2020E29`.

[17] This evaluation metric is specific to the NIST SM-KBP 2020 task. It takes entity types into account.

[18] `https://hub.docker.com/r/hltcoe/lome`

Web Demo We make a few changes for the web demo.[19] To reduce latency, we preload the models into memory and we do not write the CONCRETE communications to disk. At the cost of modularity, this makes the demo lightweight and fast, allowing us to run it on a single 16GB CPU-only server. To present the predictions, our front-end uses `AllenNLP-demo`.[20]

In addition, the web demo is currently limited to FrameNet parsing and coreference resolution, as other models will increase latency and may impede usability. The web demo is intended to highlight only some of the system's capabilities, like its ability to process multilingual documents.

7 Conclusions

To facilitate increased interest in multilingual document-level knowledge extraction with large ontologies, we create and demonstrate LOME, a system for event and entity knowledge graph creation. Given input text documents, LOME runs a full FrameNet parser, coreference resolution, fine-grained entity typing, and temporal relation prediction. Furthermore, each component uses *XLM-R*, allowing our system to support a broader set of languages than previous systems. The pipeline uses a standardized data schema, which invites extending the pipeline with additional modules. By releasing both a Docker image and presenting a lightweight web demo, we hope to enable the community to build on top of LOME for even more comprehensive information extraction.

Acknowledgments

We thank Anton Belyy, Kenton Murray, Manling Li, Varun Iyer, and Zhuowan Li for helpful discussions and feedback. This work was supported in part by DARPA AIDA (FA8750-18-2-0015) and KAIROS (FA8750-19-2-0034). The views and conclusions contained in this work are those of the authors and should not be interpreted as necessarily representing the official policies, either expressed or implied, or endorsements of DARPA or the U.S. Government. The U.S. Government is authorized to reproduce and distribute reprints for governmental purposes notwithstanding any copyright annotation therein.

[19] `https://nlp.jhu.edu/demos/lome/`

[20] `https://github.com/allenai/allennlp-demo`.

References

Alan Akbik and Yunyao Li. 2016. POLYGLOT: Multilingual semantic role labeling with unified labels. In *Proceedings of ACL-2016 System Demonstrations*, pages 1–6, Berlin, Germany. Association for Computational Linguistics.

James Allen, Hannah An, Ritwik Bose, Will de Beaumont, and Choh Man Teng. 2020. A broad-coverage deep semantic lexicon for verbs. In *Proceedings of the 12th Language Resources and Evaluation Conference*, pages 3243–3251, Marseille, France. European Language Resources Association.

Amit Bagga and Breck Baldwin. 1998. Algorithms for scoring coreference chains. In *The First International Conference on Language Resources and Evaluation Workshop on Linguistics Coreference*, pages 563–566.

Collin F. Baker, Charles J. Fillmore, and John B. Lowe. 1998. The Berkeley FrameNet project. In *36th Annual Meeting of the Association for Computational Linguistics and 17th International Conference on Computational Linguistics, Volume 1*, pages 86–90, Montreal, Quebec, Canada. Association for Computational Linguistics.

A. E. Budnikov, S Yu Toldova, D. S. Zvereva, D. M. Maximova, and M. I. Ionov. 2019. Ru-eval-2019: Evaluating anaphora and coreference resolution for russian. In *Computational Linguistics and Intellectual Technologies - Supplementary Volume*.

Taylor Cassidy, Bill McDowell, Nathanael Chambers, and Steven Bethard. 2014. An annotation framework for dense event ordering. In *Proceedings of the 52nd Annual Meeting of the Association for Computational Linguistics (Volume 2: Short Papers)*, pages 501–506, Baltimore, Maryland. Association for Computational Linguistics.

Nathanael Chambers, Taylor Cassidy, Bill McDowell, and Steven Bethard. 2014. Dense event ordering with a multi-pass architecture. *Transactions of the Association for Computational Linguistics*, 2:273–284.

Tongfei Chen, Yunmo Chen, and Benjamin Van Durme. 2020a. Hierarchical entity typing via multi-level learning to rank. In *Proceedings of the 58th Annual Meeting of the Association for Computational Linguistics*, pages 8465–8475, Online. Association for Computational Linguistics.

Yunmo Chen, Tongfei Chen, and Benjamin Van Durme. 2020b. Joint modeling of arguments for event understanding. In *Proceedings of the First Workshop on Computational Approaches to Discourse*, pages 96–101, Online. Association for Computational Linguistics.

Fei Cheng and Yusuke Miyao. 2017. Classifying temporal relations by bidirectional LSTM over dependency paths. In *Proceedings of the 55th Annual*

Meeting of the Association for Computational Linguistics (Volume 2: Short Papers), pages 1–6, Vancouver, Canada. Association for Computational Linguistics.

Eunsol Choi, Omer Levy, Yejin Choi, and Luke Zettlemoyer. 2018. Ultra-fine entity typing. In *Proceedings of the 56th Annual Meeting of the Association for Computational Linguistics (Volume 1: Long Papers)*, pages 87–96, Melbourne, Australia. Association for Computational Linguistics.

Christopher Cieri, James Fiumara, Stephanie Strassel, Jonathan Wright, Denise DiPersio, and Mark Liberman. 2020. A progress report on activities at the Linguistic Data Consortium benefitting the LREC community. In *Proceedings of the 12th Language Resources and Evaluation Conference*, pages 3449–3456, Marseille, France. European Language Resources Association.

Alexis Conneau, Kartikay Khandelwal, Naman Goyal, Vishrav Chaudhary, Guillaume Wenzek, Francisco Guzmán, Edouard Grave, Myle Ott, Luke Zettlemoyer, and Veselin Stoyanov. 2020. Unsupervised cross-lingual representation learning at scale. In *Proceedings of the 58th Annual Meeting of the Association for Computational Linguistics*, pages 8440–8451, Online. Association for Computational Linguistics.

Dipanjan Das, Desai Chen, André F. T. Martins, Nathan Schneider, and Noah A. Smith. 2014. Frame-semantic parsing. *Computational Linguistics*, 40(1):9–56.

Francis Ferraro, Max Thomas, Matthew R. Gormley, Travis Wolfe, Craig Harman, and Benjamin Van Durme. 2014. Concretely annotated corpora. In *4th Workshop on Automated Knowledge Base Construction (AKBC)*.

Goran Glavaš and Jan Šnajder. 2014. Event graphs for information retrieval and multi-document summarization. *Expert Systems with Applications*, 41(15):6904–6916.

Karl Moritz Hermann, Dipanjan Das, Jason Weston, and Kuzman Ganchev. 2014. Semantic frame identification with distributed word representations. In *Proceedings of the 52nd Annual Meeting of the Association for Computational Linguistics (Volume 1: Long Papers)*, pages 1448–1458, Baltimore, Maryland. Association for Computational Linguistics.

Mandar Joshi, Danqi Chen, Yinhan Liu, Daniel S. Weld, Luke Zettlemoyer, and Omer Levy. 2020. SpanBERT: Improving pre-training by representing and predicting spans. *Transactions of the Association for Computational Linguistics*, 8:64–77.

Mandar Joshi, Omer Levy, Luke Zettlemoyer, and Daniel Weld. 2019. BERT for coreference resolution: Baselines and analysis. In *Proceedings of the 2019 Conference on Empirical Methods in Natural Language Processing and the 9th International Joint Conference on Natural Language Processing (EMNLP-IJCNLP)*, pages 5803–5808, Hong Kong, China. Association for Computational Linguistics.

Chris Kedzie, Kathleen McKeown, and Fernando Diaz. 2015. Predicting salient updates for disaster summarization. In *Proceedings of the 53rd Annual Meeting of the Association for Computational Linguistics and the 7th International Joint Conference on Natural Language Processing (Volume 1: Long Papers)*, pages 1608–1617, Beijing, China. Association for Computational Linguistics.

Taku Kudo and John Richardson. 2018. SentencePiece: A simple and language independent subword tokenizer and detokenizer for neural text processing. In *Proceedings of the 2018 Conference on Empirical Methods in Natural Language Processing: System Demonstrations*, pages 66–71, Brussels, Belgium. Association for Computational Linguistics.

Yuri Kuratov and Mikhail Arkhipov. 2019. Adaptation of deep bidirectional multilingual transformers for russian language. In *Computational Linguistics and Intellectual Technologies*, pages 333–339.

T. A. Le, M. A. Petrov, Y. M. Kuratov, and M. S. Burtsev. 2019. Sentence level representation and language models in the task of coreference resolution for russian. In *Computational Linguistics and Intellectual Technologies*, pages 364–373.

Kenton Lee, Luheng He, Mike Lewis, and Luke Zettlemoyer. 2017. End-to-end neural coreference resolution. In *Proceedings of the 2017 Conference on Empirical Methods in Natural Language Processing*, pages 188–197, Copenhagen, Denmark. Association for Computational Linguistics.

Kenton Lee, Luheng He, and Luke Zettlemoyer. 2018. Higher-order coreference resolution with coarse-to-fine inference. In *Proceedings of the 2018 Conference of the North American Chapter of the Association for Computational Linguistics: Human Language Technologies, Volume 2 (Short Papers)*, pages 687–692, New Orleans, Louisiana. Association for Computational Linguistics.

Artuur Leeuwenberg and Marie-Francine Moens. 2017. Structured learning for temporal relation extraction from clinical records. In *Proceedings of the 15th Conference of the European Chapter of the Association for Computational Linguistics: Volume 1, Long Papers*, pages 1150–1158, Valencia, Spain. Association for Computational Linguistics.

Manling Li, Ying Lin, Joseph Hoover, Spencer Whitehead, Clare Voss, Morteza Dehghani, and Heng Ji. 2019. Multilingual entity, relation, event and human value extraction. In *Proceedings of the 2019 Conference of the North American Chapter of the Association for Computational Linguistics (Demonstrations)*, pages 110–115, Minneapolis, Minnesota. Association for Computational Linguistics.

Manling Li, Alireza Zareian, Ying Lin, Xiaoman Pan, Spencer Whitehead, Brian Chen, Bo Wu, Heng Ji, Shih-Fu Chang, Clare Voss, Daniel Napierski, and Marjorie Freedman. 2020. GAIA: A fine-grained multimedia knowledge extraction system. In *Proceedings of the 58th Annual Meeting of the Association for Computational Linguistics: System Demonstrations*, pages 77–86, Online. Association for Computational Linguistics.

Peifeng Li, Qiaoming Zhu, Guodong Zhou, and Hongling Wang. 2016. Global inference to Chinese temporal relation extraction. In *Proceedings of COLING 2016, the 26th International Conference on Computational Linguistics: Technical Papers*, pages 1451–1460, Osaka, Japan. The COLING 2016 Organizing Committee.

Ying Lin and Heng Ji. 2019. An attentive fine-grained entity typing model with latent type representation. In *Proceedings of the 2019 Conference on Empirical Methods in Natural Language Processing and the 9th International Joint Conference on Natural Language Processing (EMNLP-IJCNLP)*, pages 6197–6202, Hong Kong, China. Association for Computational Linguistics.

Ying Lin, Heng Ji, Fei Huang, and Lingfei Wu. 2020. A joint neural model for information extraction with global features. In *Proceedings of the 58th Annual Meeting of the Association for Computational Linguistics*, pages 7999–8009, Online. Association for Computational Linguistics.

Xiao Ling and Daniel S. Weld. 2012. Fine-grained entity recognition. In *Proceedings of the Twenty-Sixth AAAI Conference on Artificial Intelligence, July 22-26, 2012, Toronto, Ontario, Canada.*, pages 94–100.

Hector Llorens, Nathanael Chambers, Naushad UzZaman, Nasrin Mostafazadeh, James Allen, and James Pustejovsky. 2015. SemEval-2015 task 5: QA TempEval - evaluating temporal information understanding with question answering. In *Proceedings of the 9th International Workshop on Semantic Evaluation (SemEval 2015)*, pages 792–800, Denver, Colorado. Association for Computational Linguistics.

Xiaoqiang Luo. 2005. On coreference resolution performance metrics. In *Proceedings of Human Language Technology Conference and Conference on Empirical Methods in Natural Language Processing*, pages 25–32, Vancouver, British Columbia, Canada. Association for Computational Linguistics.

Qiang Ning, Zhili Feng, and Dan Roth. 2017. A structured learning approach to temporal relation extraction. In *Proceedings of the 2017 Conference on Empirical Methods in Natural Language Processing*, pages 1027–1037, Copenhagen, Denmark. Association for Computational Linguistics.

Yasumasa Onoe and Greg Durrett. 2019. Learning to denoise distantly-labeled data for entity typing. In *Proceedings of the 2019 Conference of the North American Chapter of the Association for Computational Linguistics: Human Language Technologies, Volume 1 (Long and Short Papers)*, pages 2407–2417, Minneapolis, Minnesota. Association for Computational Linguistics.

Xiaoman Pan, Boliang Zhang, Jonathan May, Joel Nothman, Kevin Knight, and Heng Ji. 2017. Cross-lingual name tagging and linking for 282 languages. In *Proceedings of the 55th Annual Meeting of the Association for Computational Linguistics (Volume 1: Long Papers)*, pages 1946–1958, Vancouver, Canada. Association for Computational Linguistics.

Hao Peng, Sam Thomson, Swabha Swayamdipta, and Noah A. Smith. 2018. Learning joint semantic parsers from disjoint data. In *Proceedings of the 2018 Conference of the North American Chapter of the Association for Computational Linguistics: Human Language Technologies, Volume 1 (Long Papers)*, pages 1492–1502, New Orleans, Louisiana. Association for Computational Linguistics.

Nanyun Peng, Francis Ferraro, Mo Yu, Nicholas Andrews, Jay DeYoung, Max Thomas, Matthew R. Gormley, Travis Wolfe, Craig Harman, Benjamin Van Durme, and Mark Dredze. 2015. A concrete Chinese NLP pipeline. In *Proceedings of the 2015 Conference of the North American Chapter of the Association for Computational Linguistics: Demonstrations*, pages 86–90, Denver, Colorado. Association for Computational Linguistics.

Matthew Peters, Mark Neumann, Mohit Iyyer, Matt Gardner, Christopher Clark, Kenton Lee, and Luke Zettlemoyer. 2018. Deep contextualized word representations. In *Proceedings of the 2018 Conference of the North American Chapter of the Association for Computational Linguistics: Human Language Technologies, Volume 1 (Long Papers)*, pages 2227–2237, New Orleans, Louisiana. Association for Computational Linguistics.

Sameer Pradhan, Alessandro Moschitti, Nianwen Xue, Hwee Tou Ng, Anders Björkelund, Olga Uryupina, Yuchen Zhang, and Zhi Zhong. 2013. Towards robust linguistic analysis using OntoNotes. In *Proceedings of the Seventeenth Conference on Computational Natural Language Learning*, pages 143–152, Sofia, Bulgaria. Association for Computational Linguistics.

James Pustejovsky, Patrick Hanks, Roser Sauri, Andrew See, Robert Gaizauskas, Andrea Setzer, Dragomir Radev, Beth Sundheim, David Day, Lisa Ferro, et al. 2003. The Timebank corpus. In *Corpus linguistics*, volume 2003, page 40. Lancaster, UK.

Marta Recasens, Lluís Màrquez, Emili Sapena, M. Antònia Martí, Mariona Taulé, Véronique Hoste, Massimo Poesio, and Yannick Versley. 2010. SemEval-2010 task 1: Coreference resolution in multiple languages. In *Proceedings of the 5th International Workshop on Semantic Evaluation*, pages 1–8, Uppsala, Sweden. Association for Computational Linguistics.

Guergana K Savova, James J Masanz, Philip V Ogren, Jiaping Zheng, Sunghwan Sohn, Karin C Kipper-Schuler, and Christopher G Chute. 2010. Mayo clinical text analysis and knowledge extraction system (ctakes): architecture, component evaluation and applications. *Journal of the American Medical Informatics Association*, 17(5):507–513.

Ergin Soysal, Jingqi Wang, Min Jiang, Yonghui Wu, Serguei Pakhomov, Hongfang Liu, and Hua Xu. 2018. Clamp–a toolkit for efficiently building customized clinical natural language processing pipelines. *Journal of the American Medical Informatics Association*, 25(3):331–336.

Fabian M. Suchanek, Gjergji Kasneci, and Gerhard Weikum. 2008. YAGO: A large ontology from wikipedia and wordnet. *Journal of Web Semantics*, 6(3):203–217.

Weiyi Sun, Anna Rumshisky, and Ozlem Uzuner. 2013. Evaluating temporal relations in clinical text: 2012 i2b2 challenge. *Journal of the American Medical Informatics Association*, 20(5):806–813.

Swabha Swayamdipta, Sam Thomson, Kenton Lee, Luke Zettlemoyer, Chris Dyer, and Noah A. Smith. 2018. Syntactic scaffolds for semantic structures. In *Proceedings of the 2018 Conference on Empirical Methods in Natural Language Processing*, pages 3772–3782, Brussels, Belgium. Association for Computational Linguistics.

S Toldova, A. Roytberg, Alina Ladygina, Maria Vasilyeva, Ilya Azerkovich, Matvei Kurzukov, G. Sim, D.V. Gorshkov, A. Ivanova, Anna Nedoluzhko, and Y. Grishina. 2014. Ru-eval-2014: Evaluating anaphora and coreference resolution for russian. *Computational Linguistics and Intellectual Technologies*, pages 681–694.

Naushad UzZaman, Hector Llorens, Leon Derczynski, James Allen, Marc Verhagen, and James Pustejovsky. 2013. SemEval-2013 task 1: TempEval-3: Evaluating time expressions, events, and temporal relations. In *Second Joint Conference on Lexical and Computational Semantics (*SEM), Volume 2: Proceedings of the Seventh International Workshop on Semantic Evaluation (SemEval 2013)*, pages 1–9, Atlanta, Georgia, USA. Association for Computational Linguistics.

Siddharth Vashishtha, Benjamin Van Durme, and Aaron Steven White. 2019. Fine-grained temporal relation extraction. In *Proceedings of the 57th Annual Meeting of the Association for Computational Linguistics*, pages 2906–2919, Florence, Italy. Association for Computational Linguistics.

Marc Verhagen, Robert Gaizauskas, Frank Schilder, Mark Hepple, Graham Katz, and James Pustejovsky. 2007. SemEval-2007 task 15: TempEval temporal relation identification. In *Proceedings of the Fourth International Workshop on Semantic Evaluations (SemEval-2007)*, pages 75–80, Prague, Czech Republic. Association for Computational Linguistics.

Marc Verhagen, Roser Saurí, Tommaso Caselli, and James Pustejovsky. 2010. Semeval-2010 task 13: Tempeval-2. In *Proceedings of the 5th International Workshop on Semantic Evaluation*, pages 57–62, Uppsala, Sweden. Association for Computational Linguistics.

Marc Vilain, John Burger, John Aberdeen, Dennis Connolly, and Lynette Hirschman. 1995. A model-theoretic coreference scoring scheme. In *Sixth Message Understanding Conference (MUC-6): Proceedings of a Conference Held in Columbia, Maryland, November 6-8, 1995*.

Ralph Weischedel and Ada Brunstein. 2005. BBN pronoun coreference and entity type corpus. *Philadelphia: Linguistic Data Consortium.*

Ralph Weischedel, Martha Palmer, Mitchell Marcus, Eduard Hovy, Sameer Pradhan, Lance Ramshaw, Nianwen Xue, Ann Taylor, Jeff Kaufman, Michelle Franchini, et al. 2013. OntoNotes release 5.0. *Linguistic Data Consortium, Philadelphia, PA.*

Shijie Wu and Mark Dredze. 2019. Beto, bentz, becas: The surprising cross-lingual effectiveness of BERT. In *Proceedings of the 2019 Conference on Empirical Methods in Natural Language Processing and the 9th International Joint Conference on Natural Language Processing (EMNLP-IJCNLP)*, pages 833–844, Hong Kong, China. Association for Computational Linguistics.

Patrick Xia, João Sedoc, and Benjamin Van Durme. 2020. Incremental neural coreference resolution in constant memory. In *Proceedings of the 2020 Conference on Empirical Methods in Natural Language Processing (EMNLP)*, pages 8617–8624, Online. Association for Computational Linguistics.

Liyan Xu and Jinho D. Choi. 2020. Revealing the myth of higher-order inference in coreference resolution. In *Proceedings of the 2020 Conference on Empirical Methods in Natural Language Processing (EMNLP)*, pages 8527–8533, Online. Association for Computational Linguistics.

Bishan Yang and Tom Mitchell. 2017. A joint sequential and relational model for frame-semantic parsing. In *Proceedings of the 2017 Conference on Empirical Methods in Natural Language Processing*, pages 1247–1256, Copenhagen, Denmark. Association for Computational Linguistics.

Ben Zhou, Daniel Khashabi, Qiang Ning, and Dan Roth. 2019. "Going on a vacation" takes longer than "going for a walk": A study of temporal commonsense understanding. In *Proceedings of the 2019 Conference on Empirical Methods in Natural Language Processing and the 9th International Joint Conference on Natural Language Processing (EMNLP-IJCNLP)*, pages 3363–3369, Hong Kong, China. Association for Computational Linguistics.

Yichao Zhou, Yu Yan, Rujun Han, J Harry Caufield, Kai-Wei Chang, Yizhou Sun, Peipei Ping, and Wei Wang. 2021. Clinical temporal relation extraction with probabilistic soft logic regularization and global inference. In *Proceedings of AAAI 2021*.

MadDog:
A Web-based System for Acronym Identification and Disambiguation

Amir Pouran Ben Veyseh[1], **Franck Dernoncourt**[2],
Walter Chang[2], **and Thien Huu Nguyen**[1]
[1] Department of Computer and Information Science, University of Oregon,
Eugene, OR 97403, USA
[2] Adobe Research, San Jose, CA, USA
{apouranb,thien}@cs.uoregon.edu,
{franck.dernoncourt,wachang}@adobe.com

Abstract

Acronyms and abbreviations are the short-form of longer phrases and they are ubiquitously employed in various types of writing. Despite their usefulness to save space in writing and time in reading, they also provide challenges for understanding the text especially if the acronym is not defined in the text or if it is used far from its definition in long texts. To alleviate this issue, there are considerable efforts both from the research community and software developers to build systems for identifying acronyms and finding their correct meanings in the text. However, none of the existing works provide a unified solution capable of processing acronyms in various domains and to be publicly available. Thus, we introduce MadDog, the first web-based acronym identification and disambiguation system which can process acronyms from various domains including scientific, biomedical, and general domains. The web-based system is publicly available at `http://iq.cs.uoregon.edu:5000` and a demo video is available at `https://youtu.be/IkSh7LqI42M`. The system source code is also available at `https://github.com/amirveyseh/MadDog`.

1 Introduction

Textual contents such as books, articles, reports, and web-blogs in various domains are replete with phrases that are commonly used by people in that field. In order to save space in text writing and also facilitate communication among people who are already familiar with these phrases, the shorthanded form of long phrases, known as acronyms and abbreviations, are frequently used. However, the use of acronyms could also introduce challenges to understand the text, especially for newcomers. More specifically, two types of challenges might hinder reading text with acronyms. First, in long documents, e.g., a book chapter, an acronym might be defined somewhere in the text and used several times throughout the document. For someone who is not familiar with the definition of the acronym and interested in reading a part of the document, it might be time-consuming to find the definition of the acronym in the document. To solve this problem, an automatic acronym identification tool is required whose goal is to find all acronyms and their definitions that are locally provided in the same document. Second, some of the acronyms might not be even defined in the document itself. These acronyms are commonly used by writers in a specific domain. To find the correct meaning of them, a reader must look-up the acronym in a dictionary of acronyms. However, due to the shorter length of acronyms compared to their long-form, multiple phrases might be shortened with the same acronym, thereby, they will be ambiguous. In these cases, a deep understanding of the domain is required to recognize the correct meaning of the acronym among all possible long-forms. To solve this issue, a system capable of disambiguating an acronym based on its context is necessary.

Each of the aforementioned problems, i.e., acronym identification (AI) and acronym disambiguation (AD), has been extensively studied by the research community or software developers. One of the methods which are widely used in acronym identification research is proposed by Schwartz and Hearst (2002). This is a rule-based model that utilizes character-match between acronym letters and their context to find the acronym and its long-form in text. Later, some feature-based models have been also used for acronym identification (Kuo et al., 2009; Liu et al., 2017). In addition, some of the existing software employs regular expressions for acronym identification in the biomedical domain (Gooch, 2011). Acronym disambiguation is also approached with feature-based models (Wang et al., 2016) or more advanced deep learning meth-

Proceedings of the 16th Conference of the European Chapter of the Association for Computational Linguistics: System Demonstrations, pages 160–167

ods (Wu et al., 2015; Ciosici et al., 2019). The majority of deep models employ word embeddings to compute the similarity between the candidate long-form and the acronym context. In addition to the existing research for AD, there is some web-based software that employ dictionary look-up to expand an acronym to its long-form (ABBREX2018). Note that the methods based on dictionary look-up are not able to disambiguate the acronym if it has multiple meanings.

Despite the progress made on the AI and AD task in the last two decades, there are some limitations in the prior works that prevent achieving a functional system to be used in practice. More specifically, considering the research on the AD task, all of the prior works employ a small-size dataset covering a few hundred to a few thousand long-forms in a specific domain. Therefore, the models trained in these works are not capable to expand all acronyms of a domain or acronyms in other domains other than the one used in the training set. Although in the recent work (Wen et al., 2020), authors proposed a big dataset for acronym disambiguation in the medical domain with more than 14 million samples, it is still limited to a specific domain (i.e., medical domain). Another limitation in prior works is that they do not provide a unified system capable of performing both tasks in various domains and to be publicly available. To our knowledge, the only exiting web-based system for AI and AD is proposed by Ciosici and Assent (2018). For acronym identification, this system employs the rule-based model introduced by (Schwartz and Hearst, 2002). To handle corner cases, they add extra rules in addition to Schwartz's rules in their system. Unfortunately, they do not provide detailed information about these corner cases and extra rules or any evaluation to assess the performance of the model. For acronym disambiguation, they resort to a statistical model in which a pre-computed vector representation for each candidate long-form is employed to compute the similarity between candidate long-form with the context of the ambiguous acronym represented using another vector. However, there are two limitations with this approach: first, the pre-computed long-form vectors are obtained via only Wikipedia, thus limiting this system to the general domain and incapable of disambiguating acronyms in other domains such as scientific papers or biomedical texts; Second, the AD model based on the pre-computed vectors is a statistical model and is not benefiting from the advanced deep architectures, thereby it might have inferior performance compared to a deep AD model.

To address the shortcomings and limitations of the prior research works or systems for AI and AD, in this work, we introduce a web-based system for acronym identification and disambiguation that is capable of recognizing and expanding acronyms in multiple domains including general (e.g., Wikipedia articles), scientific (e.g., computer science papers), biomedical (e.g., Medline abstracts), or financial (e.g., financial discussions in Reddit). Note that the proposed system is capable to identify acronyms and their long-forms in all Latin-script languages. More specifically, for acronym identification, we propose a rule-based model by extending the set of rules proposed by (Schwartz and Hearst, 2002). We empirically show that the proposed model outperforms both the previous rule-based model and also the existing state-of-the-art deep learning models for acronym identification on the recent benchmark dataset SciAI (Pouran Ben Veyseh et al., 2020d). Next, we use a large dataset created from corpora in various domains for acronym disambiguation to train a deep model for this task. Specifically, we employ a sequential deep model to encode the context of the ambiguous acronym and solve the AD task using a feed-forward multi-class classifier. We also evaluate the performance of the proposed acronym disambiguation model on the recent benchmark dataset SciAD (Pouran Ben Veyseh et al., 2020d).

To summarize, our contributions are:

- The first web-based multi-domain acronym identification and disambiguation system
- Extensive evaluation of the proposed model on the two benchmark datasets SciAI and SciAD

2 System Description

The proposed system is a web-based system consisting of two major components: (i) Acronym Identification which consists of a set of prioritized rules to recognize the mentions of acronyms and their long-forms in the text; (ii) Acronym Expansion which involves a dictionary look-up to expand acronyms with only one possible long-form and a pre-trained deep learning model to predict the long-form of an ambiguous acronym using its context. The system takes as input a piece of text and returns the text with highlighted acronyms in which the user can click on the acronyms and their long-form will be shown in a pop-up window. The acronym glossary extracted from the text is also shown at the end of the text. Note that users can also enable/disable the acronym expansion component. This section studies the details of the aforementioned components.

2.1 Acronym Identification

Acronym Identification aims to find the mentions of acronyms and their long-forms in text. This is the first stage in the proposed system to identify the acronyms and their immediate definitions. Generally, this task is modeled as a sequence labeling problem. In our system, we employ a rule-based model to extract acronyms and their meanings from a given text. In particular, the proposed AI model is a collection of rules mainly inspired by the rule introduced in (Schwartz and Hearst, 2002). More specifically, the following rules are employed in the proposed AI model:

- **Acronym Detector**: This rule identifies all acronyms in text, regardless of having an immediate definition or not. Specifically, all words that at least 60% of their characters are upper-cased letters and the number of their characters is between 2 and 10 are recognized as an acronym (i.e., short-form).

- **Bounded Schwartz's**: Similar to (Schwartz and Hearst, 2002), we look for immediate definitions of detected acronyms if they follow one of the templates *long-form (short-form)* or *short-form (long-form)*. In particular, considering the first template, we take the $min(|A| + 5, 2 * |A|)$ words, where $|A|$ is the number of characters in the acronym, that appear immediately before the parentheses as the candidate long-form[1]. Then, a sub-sequence of the candidate long-form that some of its characters could form the acronym is selected as the long-form. However, despite the original Schwartz's rule that does not restrict the first and last word of the long-form to be used in the acronym, we enforce this restriction. This modification could fix erroneous long-form detection by Schwartz's rule. For instance, in the phrase *User-guided Social Media Crawling method (USMC)*, the modified rule identifies the long-form *User-guided Social Media Crawling*, excluding the leading word *method*.

- **Character Match**: While the Bounded Schwartz' rule could identify the majority of the long-forms, it might also introduce some noisy meanings. For instance, in the phrase *Analyzing Avatar Boundary Matching (AABM)*, the Bounded Schwartz's rule identifies *Avatar Boundary Matching* as the long-form of *AABM*, missing the starting word *Analyzing*. To solve this issue and increase the model's accuracy, we also employ a character match rule that assesses if the initials of the words in the candidate long-form could form the acronym. In the given example, it identifies the full phrase *Analyzing Avatar Boundary Matching* as the long-form. Since this rule is more restricted and it has higher precision than Bounded Schwartz's rule, in our system, it has a higher priority than the Bounded Schwartz's rule.

- **Initial Capitals**: One issue with the proposed Character Matching rule is that if there is a word in the long-form that is not used in the acronym, the rule fails to correctly identify the long-form. For instance, in the phrase *Analysis of Avatar Boundary Matching (AABM)* the Character Matching rule fails due to the existence of the word *of*. To mitigate this issue, we propose another high-precision rule, Initial Capitals. In this rule, if the concatenation of the initials of the words of the candidate long-form which are upper-cased could form the acronym, the candidate is selected as the expanded form of the acronym. This rule has the highest priority in our system.

In addition to the mentioned general rules, we also add some other rules to handle the special cases, e.g., acronyms with a hyphen, roman numbers, definitions provided in some templates, for example, CNN stands for convolution neural network.

In the web-based system, the user could enter the text and the system recognizes both acronyms without any definition in text and also acronyms that are locally defined with their identified long-forms. Users could also click on each detected acronym to see its definition in a pop-up window. Also, a

[1] Note that we use the same candidate long-form in other rules too.

Acronym	Long-form	Rule
AABM	Analyzing Avatar Boundary Matching	Character Match
ABBREX	Abbreviation Expander	Bounded Schwartz's
AD	acronym disambiguation	Character Match
AI	Acronym identification	Character Match
BADREX	Biomedical Abbreviations using Dynamic Regular Expressions	Bounded Schwartz's
BiLSTM	Bi - directional Long ShortTerm Memory	Bounded Schwartz's
DOG	Diverse acrOnym Glossary	Bounded Schwartz's
MAD	Massive Acronym Disambiguation	Capital Initials
MF	most frequent	Character Match
USMC	User - guided Social Media Crawling	Capital Initials

Table 1: The acronym glossary extracted from the text of this paper using MadDog.

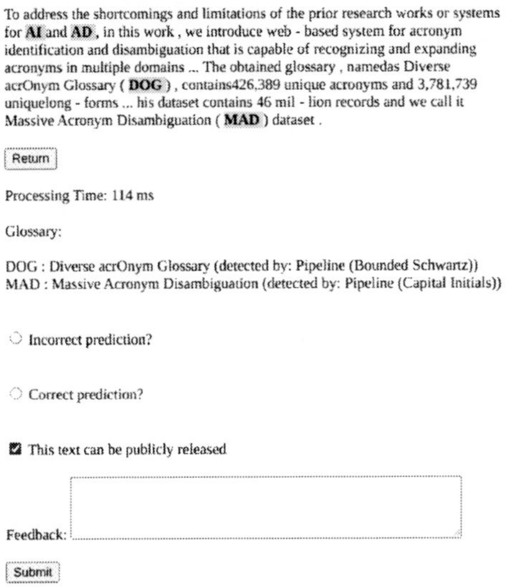

Figure 1: A screenshot of acronym identification by MadDog. It identifies all acronyms and their local-long forms. This interface highlights the detected acronyms and by clicking on them, a pop-up window shows the recognized meaning of the acronym.

glossary of detected acronyms and their long-forms is shown at the bottom of the page. A screenshot of the output of the system is shown in Figure 1. Moreover, Table 1 shows the glossary extracted from the text of this paper using the rule-based component of the system. In section 3 we compare the performance of the proposed rule-based model with the existing state-of-the-art models for AI (Pouran Ben Veyseh et al., 2020d).

2.2 Acronym Expansion

Although the proposed rule-based model is effective to recognize locally defined acronyms, it might not be able to expand acronyms that don't have any immediate definition in the text itself. To alleviate this issue and expand acronyms even without local definition, two resources are required: (i) A dictionary that provides the list of possible expansion for a given acronym; (ii) A model to exploit the context of the given acronym and choose the most likely expansion for a given acronym. For the acronym dictionary, we employ the glossary obtained by exploiting our proposed rule-based AI model on corpora in various domains (i.e., Wikipedia, Arxiv papers, Reddit submissions, Medline abstracts, and PMC OA subset). The obtained glossary, named as Diverse acrOnym Glossary (DOG), contains 426,389 unique acronyms and 3,781,739 unique long-forms. Note that the previously available web-based acronym disambiguation system (Ciosici and Assent, 2018) employed only Wikipedia corpus, therefore, it covers limited domains and acronyms compared to our system.

In DOG, the average number of long-forms per acronym is 6.9 and 81,372 ambiguous acronyms exist. Due to this ambiguity, a simple dictionary look-up is not sufficient for acronym expansion in the web-based system that uses DOG to expand acronyms with non-local definitions. In order to tackle this problem, we propose to train a supervised model in which the input is the text and the position of the ambiguous acronym in it and the model predicts the correct long-form among all possible candidates. To train this model, we use an automatically labeled dataset obtained by extracting samples from large corpora for each long-form in DOG. This dataset contains 46 million records and we call it the Massive Acronym Disambiguation (MAD) dataset. To split the dataset into train/dev/test splits, we use 80% of samples of each long-form for training, 10% for the development set, and 10% for the test set. It is noteworthy that to facilitate training, before splitting the dataset into train/dev/test splits, we first create chunks of size 100,000 samples in which all samples of an acronym are assigned to the same chunk. Since each acronym appears only in one chuck, we train a separate acronym disambiguation model for each chunk. During inference, we first identify which chuck the ambiguous acronym belongs to, then, we use the corresponding model to predict the expanded form of the acronym.

In this work, we use a deep sequential model to be trained on the MAD dataset for acronym disambiguation. More specifically, given the input text $T = [w_1, w_2, \ldots, w_n]$ with the ambiguous acronym w_a, we first represent each word using the corresponding GloVe embedding, i.e., $X = [x_1, x_2, \ldots, x_n]$. Afterward, the vectors

Model	Acronym			Long Form			
	P	R	F1	P	R	F1	Macro F1
NOA	80.31	18.08	29.51	88.97	14.01	24.20	26.85
ADE	79.28	86.13	82.57	98.36	57.34	72.45	79.37
UAD	86.11	91.48	88.72	96.51	64.38	77.24	84.09
BIOADI	83.11	87.21	85.11	90.43	73.79	77.49	82.35
LNCRF	84.51	90.45	87.37	95.13	69.18	80.10	83.73
LSTM-CRF	88.58	86.93	87.75	85.33	85.38	85.36	86.55
MadDog	89.98	87.56	88.75	96.45	79.53	87.18	88.12

Table 2: Performance of models for acronym identification (AI)

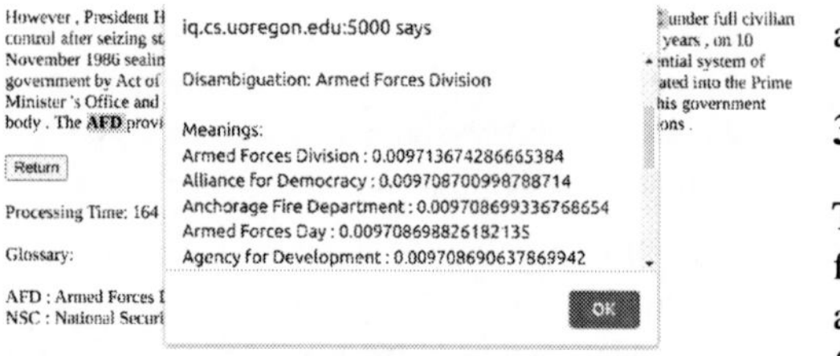

Figure 2: Sorted list of candidate long-forms along with their scores for the acronym *AFD* in the sentence *After 1991, the presidential system of government by Act of Parliament was abolished, and by October 1994, the AFD was integrated into the Prime Minister's Office and concurrently the combined armed forces authority was transferred to this government body.*

X are consumed by a Bi-directional Long Short-Term Memory network (BiLSTM) to encode the sequential order of the words. Next, we take the hidden states of the BiLSTM neurons, i.e., $H = [h_1, h_2, \ldots, h_n]$, and compute the text representation by computing the max-pool of the vectors H, i.e., $\bar{h} = MAX\_POOL(h_1, h_2, \ldots, h_n)$. Finally, the concatenation of the text representation, i.e., $\bar{h}$, and the acronym representation, i.e., h_a, is fed into a 2-layer feed-forward neural network whose final layer dimension is equal to the total number of long-forms in the dataset (i.e., dataset chunks explained above).

In the proposed system, the long-form of acronyms predicted by the acronym disambiguation model is presented in the glossary at the end of the page (See Figure 1). Moreover, by clicking on the acronym word in text, a pop-up window shows the model's prediction and also the sorted list of other candidate long-forms for the selected acronym. An example is shown in Figure 2. In the provided example, the system correctly predicts *Gross Domestic Production* as the long-form of the ambiguous acronym *GDP*. We name the proposed acronym identification and disambiguation system as MadDog.

3 Evaluation

This section provides more insight into the performance of the proposed acronym identification and disambiguation models. To evaluate the performance of the models in comparison with other state-of-the-art AI and AD models, we report the performance of the proposed models on SciAI and SciAD benchmark datasets (Pouran Ben Veyseh et al., 2020d). We also compare the performance of the proposed model with the baselines provided in the recent work (Pouran Ben Veyseh et al., 2020d). More specifically, on SciAI, we compare our model with rule-based models NOA (Charbonnier and Wartena, 2018), ADE (Li et al., 2018) and UAD (Ciosici et al., 2019); and also the feature-based models BIOADI (Kuo et al., 2009) and LNCRF (Liu et al., 2017); and finally the SOTA deep model LSTM-CRF (Pouran Ben Veyseh et al., 2020d). For evaluation metrics, following prior work, we report precision, recall, and F1 score for the acronym and long-form prediction and also their macro-averaged F1 score. The results are shown in Table 2. This table shows that our model outperforms both rule-based and more advanced feature-based or deep learning models. More interestingly, while the proposed model has comparable precision with the existing rule-based models, it enjoys higher recall.

To assess the performance of the proposed acronym disambiguation model, we evaluate its performance on the benchmark dataset SciAD (Pouran Ben Veyseh et al., 2020d) and compare it with the existing state-of-the-art models. Specifically, we compare the model with non-deep learning models including most frequent (MF) meaning (Pouran Ben Veyseh et al., 2020d), feature-based model (i.e., ADE (Li et al., 2018)), and deep learning models including NOA (Charbonnier and Wartena, 2018), UAD (Ciosici et al., 2019), BEM (Blevins

Model	P	R	F1
MF	89.03	42.2	57.26
ADE	86.74	43.25	57.72
NOA	78.14	35.06	48.40
UAD	89.01	70.08	78.37
BEM	86.75	35.94	50.82
DECBAE	88.67	74.32	80.86
GAD	89.27	76.66	81.90
MadDog	92.27	85.01	88.49

Table 3: Performance of models for acronym disambiguation (AD)

and Zettlemoyer, 2020), DECBAE (Jin et al., 2019) and GAD (Pouran Ben Veyseh et al., 2020d). The results are shown in Table 3. This table demonstrates the effectiveness of the proposed model compared with the baselines. Our hypothesis for the higher performance of the proposed model is the massive number of training examples for all acronyms which results in low generalization error.

4 Related Work

Acronym identification (AI) and acronym disambiguation (AD) are two well-known tasks with several prior works in the past two decades. For AI, both rule-based models (Park and Byrd, 2001; Wren and Garner, 2002; Schwartz and Hearst, 2002; Adar, 2004; Nadeau and Turney, 2005; Ao and Takagi, 2005; Kirchhoff and Turner, 2016) and supervised feature-based or deep learning models (Kuo et al., 2009; Liu et al., 2017; Pouran Ben Veyseh et al., 2020d, 2021) are utilized. Due to the higher accuracy of rule-based models, they are dominantly used in the majority of the related works, especially to automatically create acronym dictionary (Ciosici et al., 2019; Li et al., 2018; Charbonnier and Wartena, 2018). However, the existing works prepare a small-size dictionary in a specific domain. In contrast, in this work, we first improve the existing rules for acronym identification, then, we use a diverse acronym glossary in our system. For acronym disambiguation, prior works employ either feature-based models (Wang et al., 2016; Li et al., 2018) or deep learning methods (Wu et al., 2015; Antunes and Matos, 2017; Charbonnier and Wartena, 2018; Ciosici et al., 2019; Pouran Ben Veyseh et al., 2021). In this work, we also employ a sequential deep learning model for AD. However, unlike prior work that proposes an acronym disambiguation model for a specific domain and limited acronyms, our proposed model covers more acronyms and it is able to expand an acronym in various domains.

Another common limitation of the existing research-based models for AI and AD is that they do not provide any publicly available system that could be quickly incorporated into a text-processing application. Although there is some software for acronym identification such as expanding Biomedical Abbreviations using Dynamic Regular Expressions (BADREX) (Gooch, 2011) or Abbreviation Expander (ABBREX) (ABBREX2018), unfortunately, they are incapable of acronym disambiguation. To our knowledge, the most similar work to ours is proposed by Ciosici and Assent (2018). Specifically, similar to our work, this web-based system is able to identify and expand acronym in text. A rule-based model is employed for AI and this model is also used to create a dictionary of acronyms. For AD, unlike our work that trains a deep model, they use word embedding similarity to predict the most likely expansion. However, there are some limitations to this previous system. Firstly, it is restricted to the general domain (i.e., Wikipedia) and it covers a limited number of acronyms. Second, it does not provide any analysis and evaluations of the performance of the proposed model. Lastly, it is not publicly available anymore. The proposed MadDog system could be useful for many downstream applications including definition extraction (Pouran Ben Veyseh et al., 2020a; Spala et al., 2020, 2019), information extraction (Pouran Ben Veyseh et al., 2019, 2020b,c) or question answering (Perez et al., 2020)

5 System Deployment

MadDog is purely written in Python 3 and could be run as a FLASK (Grinberg, 2018) server. For text toknization, it employs SpaCy 2 (Honnibal and Montani, 2017). Also, the trained acronym expansion model requires PyTorch 1.7 and 64 GB of disk space. Note that all acronyms with their long-forms are encoded in the trained model so they can perform both the dictionary look-up operation and the disambiguation task. Moreover, the trained models could be loaded both on GPU and CPU.

6 Conclusion

In this work, we propose a new web-based system for acronym identification and disambiguation. For AI, we employ a refined set of rules which is shown to be more effective than the previous rule-based and deep learning models. Moreover, using a massive acronym disambiguation dataset with more than 46 million records in various domains, we train a supervised model for acronym disambiguation. The experiments on the existing benchmark datasets reveal the efficacy of the proposed AD model. In future, we aim to prepare the proposed model to be integrated into an e-reader where the readers can quickly hover the acronym and find the correct meaning for that. This system could help save time for reading technical documents that are replete with acronyms.

Acknowledgments

This work has been supported by Adobe Research Gifts and the Army Research Office (ARO) grant W911NF-17-S-0002. This research is also based upon work supported by the Office of the Director of National Intelligence (ODNI), Intelligence Advanced Research Projects Activity (IARPA), via IARPA Contract No. 2019-19051600006 under the Better Extraction from Text Towards Enhanced Retrieval (BETTER) Program. The views and conclusions contained herein are those of the authors and should not be interpreted as necessarily representing the official policies, either expressed or implied, of ARO, ODNI, IARPA, the Department of Defense, or the U.S. Government. The U.S. Government is authorized to reproduce and distribute reprints for governmental purposes notwithstanding any copyright annotation therein. This document does not contain technology or technical data controlled under either the U.S. International Traffic in Arms Regulations or the U.S. Export Administration Regulations.

References

ABBREX2018. Abbrex. 2018. abbrex - the abbreviation expander. In *BMC bioinformatics*.

Eytan Adar. 2004. Sarad: A simple and robust abbreviation dictionary. In *Bioinformatics*.

Rui Antunes and Sérgio Matos. 2017. Biomedical word sense disambiguation with word embeddings. In *International Conference on Practical Applications of Computational Biology & Bioinformatics*.

Hiroko Ao and Toshihisa Takagi. 2005. Alice: an algorithm to extract abbreviations from medline. In *Journal of the American Medical Informatics Association*.

Terra Blevins and Luke Zettlemoyer. 2020. Moving down the long tail of word sense disambiguation with gloss informed bi-encoders. In *Proceedings of the 58th Annual Meeting of the Association for Computational Linguistics*, pages 1006–1017, Online. Association for Computational Linguistics.

Jean Charbonnier and Christian Wartena. 2018. Using word embeddings for unsupervised acronym disambiguation. In *Proceedings of the 27th International Conference on Computational Linguistics*, pages 2610–2619, Santa Fe, New Mexico, USA. Association for Computational Linguistics.

Manuel R. Ciosici and Ira Assent. 2018. Abbreviation expander - a web-based system for easy reading of technical documents. In *Proceedings of the 27th International Conference on Computational Linguistics: System Demonstrations*, pages 1–4, Santa Fe, New Mexico. Association for Computational Linguistics.

Manuel R Ciosici, Tobias Sommer, and Ira Assent. 2019. Unsupervised abbreviation disambiguation. In *arXiv preprint arXiv:1904.00929*.

Phil Gooch. 2011. Badrex: In situ expansion and coreference of biomedical abbreviations using dynamic regular expressions.

Miguel Grinberg. 2018. *Flask web development: developing web applications with python.* " O'Reilly Media, Inc.".

Matthew Honnibal and Ines Montani. 2017. spaCy 2: Natural language understanding with Bloom embeddings, convolutional neural networks and incremental parsing. To appear.

Qiao Jin, Jinling Liu, and Xinghua Lu. 2019. Deep contextualized biomedical abbreviation expansion. In *arXiv preprint arXiv:1906.03360*.

Katrin Kirchhoff and Anne M Turner. 2016. Unsupervised resolution of acronyms and abbreviations in nursing notes using document-level context models. In *Proceedings of the Seventh International Workshop on Health Text Mining and Information Analysis*.

Cheng-Ju Kuo, Maurice HT Ling, Kuan-Ting Lin, and Chun-Nan Hsu. 2009. Bioadi: a machine learning approach to identifying abbreviations and definitions in biological literature. In *BMC bioinformatics*.

Yang Li, Bo Zhao, Ariel Fuxman, and Fangbo Tao. 2018. Guess me if you can: Acronym disambiguation for enterprises. In *Proceedings of the 56th Annual Meeting of the Association for Computational Linguistics (Volume 1: Long Papers)*, pages 1308–1317, Melbourne, Australia. Association for Computational Linguistics.

Jie Liu, Caihua Liu, and Yalou Huang. 2017. Multi-granularity sequence labeling model for acronym expansion identification. In *Information Sciences*.

David Nadeau and Peter D Turney. 2005. A supervised learning approach to acronym identification. In *Conference of the Canadian Society for Computational Studies of Intelligence*.

Youngja Park and Roy J. Byrd. 2001. Hybrid text mining for finding abbreviations and their definitions. In *Proceedings of the 2001 Conference on Empirical Methods in Natural Language Processing*.

Ethan Perez, Patrick Lewis, Wen-tau Yih, Kyunghyun Cho, and Douwe Kiela. 2020. Unsupervised question decomposition for question answering. In *Proceedings of the 2020 Conference on Empirical Methods in Natural Language Processing (EMNLP)*, pages 8864–8880, Online. Association for Computational Linguistics.

Amir Pouran Ben Veyseh, Franck Dernoncourt, Dejing Dou, and Thien Huu Nguyen. 2020a. A joint model for definition extraction with syntactic connection and semantic consistency. In *AAAI*.

Amir Pouran Ben Veyseh, Franck Dernoncourt, Dejing Dou, and Thien Huu Nguyen. 2020b. Exploiting the syntax-model consistency for neural relation extraction. In *Proceedings of the 58th Annual Meeting of the Association for Computational Linguistics*, pages 8021–8032, Online. Association for Computational Linguistics.

Amir Pouran Ben Veyseh, Franck Dernoncourt, Thien Huu Nguyen, Walter Chang, and Leo Anthony Celi. 2021. Acronym identification and disambiguation shared tasks for scientific document understanding. In *Proceedings of the 1st workshop on Scientific Document Understanding*.

Amir Pouran Ben Veyseh, Franck Dernoncourt, My Thai, Dejing Dou, and Thien Nguyen. 2020c. Multi-view consistency for relation extraction via mutual information and structure prediction. In *AAAI*.

Amir Pouran Ben Veyseh, Franck Dernoncourt, Quan Hung Tran, and Thien Huu Nguyen. 2020d. What does this acronym mean? introducing a new dataset for acronym identification and disambiguation. In *Proceedings of the 28th International Conference on Computational Linguistics*, pages 3285–3301, Barcelona, Spain (Online). International Committee on Computational Linguistics.

Amir Pouran Ben Veyseh, Thien Nguyen, and Dejing Dou. 2019. Improving cross-domain performance for relation extraction via dependency prediction and information flow control. In *IJCAI*.

Ariel S Schwartz and Marti A Hearst. 2002. A simple algorithm for identifying abbreviation definitions in biomedical text. In *Biocomputing 2003*.

Sasha Spala, Nicholas Miller, Franck Dernoncourt, and Carl Dockhorn. 2020. SemEval-2020 task 6: Definition extraction from free text with the DEFT corpus. In *Proceedings of the Fourteenth Workshop on Semantic Evaluation*.

Sasha Spala, Nicholas A. Miller, Yiming Yang, Franck Dernoncourt, and Carl Dockhorn. 2019. DEFT: A corpus for definition extraction in free- and semi-structured text. In *Proceedings of the 13th Linguistic Annotation Workshop*.

Yue Wang, Kai Zheng, Hua Xu, and Qiaozhu Mei. 2016. Clinical word sense disambiguation with interactive search and classification. In *AMIA Annual Symposium Proceedings*.

Zhi Wen, Xing Han Lu, and Siva Reddy. 2020. MeDAL: Medical abbreviation disambiguation dataset for natural language understanding pretraining. In *Proceedings of the 3rd Clinical Natural Language Processing Workshop*, pages 130–135, Online. Association for Computational Linguistics.

Jonathan D Wren and Harold R Garner. 2002. Heuristics for identification of acronym-definition patterns within text: towards an automated construction of comprehensive acronym-definition dictionaries. In *Methods of information in medicine*.

Yonghui Wu, Jun Xu, Yaoyun Zhang, and Hua Xu. 2015. Clinical abbreviation disambiguation using neural word embeddings. In *Proceedings of BioNLP 15*, pages 171–176, Beijing, China. Association for Computational Linguistics.

Graph Matching and Graph Rewriting: GREW tools for corpus exploration, maintenance and conversion

Bruno Guillaume
Université de Lorraine, CNRS, Inria, LORIA, F-54000 Nancy, France
Bruno.Guillaume@inria.fr

Abstract

This article presents a set of tools built around the Graph Rewriting computational framework which can be used to compute complex rule-based transformations on linguistic structures. Application of the graph matching mechanism for corpus exploration, error mining or quantitative typology are also given.

1 Introduction

The motivation of GREW is to have an effective tool to design rule-based transformations of linguistic structures. When designing GREW, our goal was to be able to manipulate at least syntactic and semantic representations of natural language (one of the first application of GREW was the modeling of a syntax-semantics interface). In a naive view, we can say that syntactic structures are trees and semantic ones are graphs. Then, if we want to work with both kinds of structures in a common framework, we can use the fact that a tree can be considered as a graph and hence consider that all structures are graphs.[1]

Now, if we consider all structures as graphs, how to describe rule-based transformation on these structures? In practice, these transformations can of course be computed with some programs but when it becomes complex and implies many rules, it is difficult to maintain and to debug. To deal with this, we propose to use the graph rewriting formalism to describe these transformations.

Graph rewriting is a well-defined mathematical formalism and we know that any computable transformation can be expressed by a graph rewriting system. In this approach, a global transformation is decomposed in a successive application of small and local transformations which are described by rules; linguistic transformations can be decomposed in a modular way in atomic steps which are easier to manage.

Several graph rewriting tools already exist but some specificities of NLP made it useful to build a system dedicated to this domain. In GREW tools, a built-in notion of feature structure is available and rules can be parametrised by lexical information. Moreover, transformations on dependency structures often requires to change head of substructures and a dedicated command ease this kind of operation (see Section 3.5).

In Section 2, we give a more precise definition of our graphs and graph rewriting framework and the next parts present examples about rewriting (Section 3) and about matching (Section 4).

2 Graphs and graph rewriting

The book (Bonfante et al., 2018) gives a complete description of the graphs and graph rewriting system used in GREW. We give here a short description on the main aspects.

In our framework, a graph is defined by a set of nodes labelled by non-recursive feature structure and a set of labelled edges (note that edges encode relations and hence, we do not consider multiple edges with the same label on the same pair of nodes). In addition to the usual graph mathematical definition of graphs, we also add a notion of order on nodes. For each graph, a sub-part of the nodes are ordered. The subset of ordered nodes can contains all the nodes (for instance in dependency structures like in Figure 1); it can be empty (for instance in semantic graphs like AMR structures shown in Section 4.2); but we can also have structures where a strict subpart is ordered, for instance with phrase structure trees where lexical nodes are ordered following the tokens order in the input sentence whereas non-lexical nodes are unordered.

[1]We may lose information if the order between the child nodes of a given node (see Section 2).

Proceedings of the 16th Conference of the European Chapter of the Association for Computational Linguistics: System Demonstrations, pages 168–175
April 19 - 23, 2021. ©2021 Association for Computational Linguistics

Global transformations of graphs are decomposed in small steps; each step is described as a rule. A rule encodes a local transformation and is composed in two parts: the left-hand side which expresses the conditions for the application of the rule and the right-hand part which describes the modifications to be done on the graph.

Formally, the conditions of application are described by a pattern which is itself a graph. Graph matching is used to decide if a pattern can be found in a graph. The pattern can be refined by a set of NAP (negative application patterns) which are used to filter out some occurrences given by the first pattern. The main pattern is introduced by the keyword `pattern` and NAPs are introduced with the keyword `without` (see examples in the next section).

To avoid complex mathematical definitions and to propose an operational way to modify graph, GREW describes the modifications of the graph through a sequence of atomic commands for edge deletion, edge creation, feature updating...

When the number of rules increases, it may become tricky to control the order in which they should be applied; a dedicated notion of rewriting strategies was design to let the user control these applications.

When using rewriting, confluence and termination are important aspects. These questions are discussed on examples in the next section.

3 Graph rewriting in practice

The goal of this section is to present through examples the usage of the rewriting part of GREW. Some important concepts like confluence and termination will be also discussed.

3.1 First rules

The conversion between different formats is one the common usage of GREW. We will use the example of the conversion from one dependency annotation format (used in the Sequoia project (Candito and Seddah, 2012)) to Universal Dependencies (UD) (Nivre et al., 2016). The Figure 1 shows the annotations of a French sentence in both formats.

The whole transformation is decomposed into small steps which are described by rules. When GREW is used to rewrite an input graph, a strategy describes how rules should be applied. In the first examples below, the strategy consists in just one rule.

In our conversion example, we need a rule to change the POS for adjectives: `A` is used in Sequoia and `ADJ` in UD. The GREW rule for this transformation is:

```
rule adj {
  pattern { N [upos=A] }
  commands { N.upos = ADJ }
}
```

The application of this rule on the input graph produces, as expected the graph below:

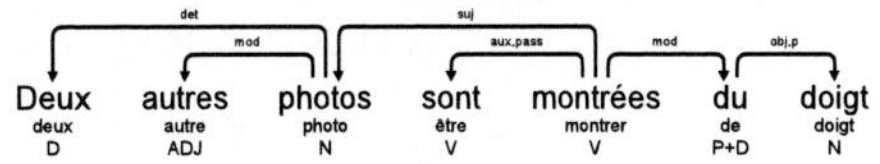

We can then imagine others similar rules for other POS tags: `P` is Sequoia becomes `ADP` in UD, `N` is Sequoia becomes `NOUN` in UD.

```
rule prep {
  pattern { N [upos=P] }
  commands { N.upos = ADP }
}
rule noun {
  pattern { N [upos=N] }
  commands { N.upos = NOUN }
}
```

But applying the rule `prep` to the input graph produces an empty set and the application of `noun` the input graph produced two different graphs (one with *photos* tagged as `NOUN`, the other with *doigt* tagged as `NOUN`)!

In fact, the result of the application of a rule on a graph is a set of graphs, one for each occurence of the pattern found in the input graph. This set is then empty if the pattern is not found (like `pattern {N [upos=P]}`) or contains two graphs if the pattern if found twice (like `pattern {N [upos=N]}`). To iterate the application of a rule, one has to use more complex strategies.

The strategy `Onf(noun)`[2] iterates the application of the strategy `noun` on the input graph. With the same input graph (of Figure 1), the application of GREW with the strategy `Onf(noun)` produces a graph where the two nouns have the new tag `NOUN`.

Note that `Onf(...)` always outputs exactly one graph. With the strategy `Onf(prep)` for instance, the rewriting process will output one graph, identical to the input graph, obtained after 0 application of the `prep` rule.

In previous examples, we considered rules separately, but in a global transformation all the previous rules must be used in the same global transformation. A solution to use several rules in the

[2] `Onf` stands for "one normal form"; it will be explained more in detail later with other strategies.

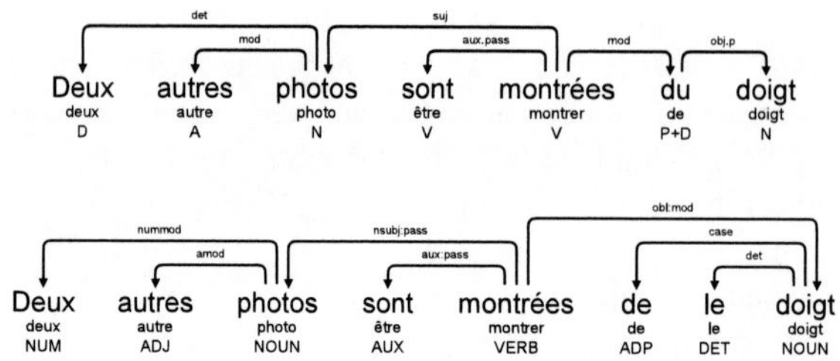

Figure 1: Annotation of the sentence *Deux autres photos sont montrées du doigt* [en: *Two other photos are pointed out*] in Sequoia (above) and in UD (below)

same rewriting process is to put them in the same `package` construction, for instance with the 3 rules above:

```
package POS {
  rule adj { ... }
  rule prep { ... }
  rule noun { ... }
}
```

The package name `POS` can be used as a strategy name for rewriting. Applying the package `POS` corresponds to the application of one of the rules of the package. With our input graph, it produces three different graphs, obtained either by the application of the rule `adj` or by the two possible applications of the rule `noun`.

In order to iterate the package, we need the strategy `Onf(POS)`. As before with `Onf`, exactly one graph is produced with three successive applications of the rules:

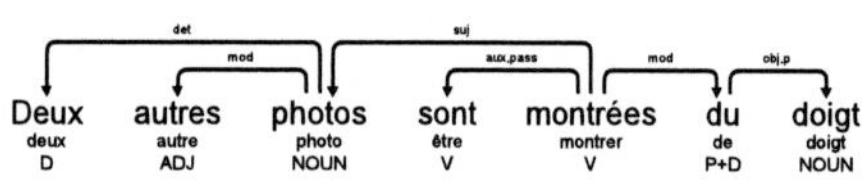

3.2 Termination

One key problem that may arise when using rewriting is the non-termination of the process. If we go on with the previous example about POS and consider verbs: the same tag `V` should be converted to `AUX` or to `VERB`. One way to decide that the new POS must be `AUX` is the presence of the relation `aux.pass`. We can propose the rule:

```
rule aux_1 {
  pattern { M -[aux.pass]-> N }
  commands { N.upos = AUX }
}
```

But the process of rewriting with strategy `Onf(aux_1)` is not terminating because nothing prevents the rule to be applied again and again, the pattern is still present after the application of the rule. In practice, a bound can be set on the number of rules applied[3] and an error is thrown when this bound is reached, in order to avoid non-terminating computation.

A way to solve this problem is to make the pattern stricter. With the rule below and the strategy `Onf(aux_2)`, the expected output is obtained after one application of the rule.

```
rule aux_2 {
 pattern { M -[aux.pass]-> N; N[upos=V] }
 commands { N.upos = AUX }
}
```

Of course, in a more general setting, we can have loops which imply more than one rule and which are more difficult to manage. Unfortunately, it is not possible to decide algorithmically if some rewriting system is terminating or not.

Anyway, in NLP applications like conversions from format A to format B, it is often easy to ensure termination be defining measure which stands for the fact that we are "closer" to the B format after each rule application. For instance, in all the non-looping rules above, if we count the number of Sequoia POS tag in the graph, it is strictly decreasing at each rule application.

3.3 Confluence

Another well-known issue with rewriting is the problem of confluence. As said earlier, the Sequoia tag V may be converted to AUX or VERB. A naive way to encode this in rules is to write the package:

```
package v_1 {
  rule aux {
    pattern { N [upos = V] }
    commands { N.upos = AUX }
  }
  rule verb {
    pattern { N [upos = V] }
    commands { N.upos = VERB }
  }
}
```

[3] 10,000 by default

The two rules overlap: each time a POS `V` is found, both rules can be used and produces a different output! We call this kind of system non-confluent. Anyway, the strategy `Onf(v_1)` still produced exactly one graph by choosing (in a way which cannot be controlled) one of the possible ways to rewrite.

What should we do with non-confluent system? There are two possible situations: (1) The two rules are correct and there is a real (linguistic) ambiguity and all solutions must be considered or (2) There is no ambiguity, the rules must be corrected.

In our example, we are clearly in the second case, but we consider briefly the other case for the explanation on how to deal with really non-confluent setting. Let us suppose that we are interested in all possible solutions. GREW provides a strategy `Iter(v_1)` to do this: this strategy applied to the same input graph produces 4 different graphs with different combinations of either `AUX` or `VERB` for the two words *sont* and *montrées*.

Of course, in our POS tags conversion example, the correct solution is to design more carefully our two rules, in order to produce the correct output:

```
package v_2 {
 rule aux {
  pattern {N[upos=V]; M -[aux.pass]-> N}
  commands { N.upos=AUX } }
 rule verb {
  pattern { N [upos=V] }
  without { M -[aux.pass]-> N }
  commands { N.upos=VERB } }
}
```

Here, the two rules are clearly exclusive: the same clause `M -[aux.pass]-> N` is used first in the `pattern` part of rule `aux` and in the `without` part of rule `verb`. With these two new rules, the system is confluent, and there is only one possible output. This can be tested with the `Iter(v_2)` strategy which produces all possible graphs, exactly one in this case.

Of course, the strategy `Onf(v_2)` produces the same output in this setting. When a package `p` is confluent, the two strategies `Onf(p)` and `Iter(p)` give the same result. In practice, the strategy `Onf(p)` must be preferred because it is much more efficient to compute.

3.4 More commands

In Figure 1, we can observe that in addition to a different POS tagset, the UD format also uses a different tokenisation. The word *du* of the input sentence is a token with a POS `P+D` in Sequoia but this is in fact an amalgam of two lexical units: a preposition and a determiner[4]. In UD, such combined tag are not allowed and the sentence is annotated with two tokens *de* and *le* for the word *du*. Hence, we have to design a rule to make this new tokenisation. The rule below computes this transformation:

```
rule amalgam {
  pattern {
    N [form = "du", upos = "P+D"];
    N -[obj.p]-> M }
  commands {
    add_node D :> N;
    N.form = "de"; N.upos = ADP;
    D.form = "le"; D.upos = DET;
    add_edge M -[det]-> D }
}
```

This is our first rule with more than one commands. In general, the transformation is described by a sequence of commands which are applied successively to the current graph. The application of this rule to our input graph builds:

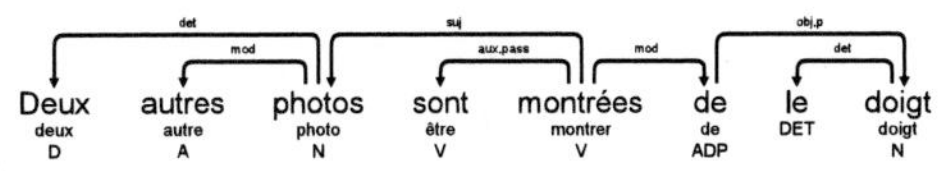

Note that `N -[obj.p]-> M` is not required to find a place where the rule must be applied, but we need it to get access to the node with identifier `M` and to define properly the command `add_edge`.

3.5 Changing head

For transformation between different syntactic annotation frameworks, we often have to deal with the fact that heads of constituents may change. For instance, with the sentence *je vois que tu es malade* [en: *I see that you are sick*]. The head of the clause *que tu es malade* is *es* in Sequoia and *malade* in UD. In practice, we have to realise the transformation between the two graphs described by Figure 2.

We can use what was presented before to remove the edge `ats`, to add a new edge `cop` and to change the POS of *es*; but we need something more: moving all other edges incident to the old head *es* towards the new head *malade*. GREW provides a dedicated command `shift` to compute this. In the rule below, the command `shift V ==> ATS` means: change all edges starting (resp. ending) on the node `V` to make them start (resp. end) on `ATS`.

```
rule ats {
  pattern {
    V[upos=VERB];
    e: V -[ats]-> ATS }
```

[4]This is exactly what the tag `P+D` means.

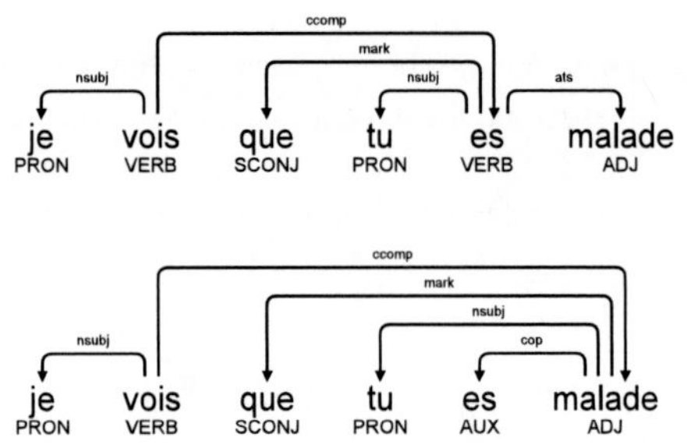

Figure 2: Graph transformation for head changes

```
  commands {
    del_edge e;
    shift V ==> ATS;
    add_edge ATS -[cop]-> V;
    V.upos = AUX }
}
```

3.6 More strategies

Above, we have seen how to handle atomic transformations through rules. But, in order to define a complete transformation system, some larger set of rules are needed. It is important to be able to control the order in which subset of rules should applied. In practice, large transformation system are divided in several steps and sub-systems are applied successively. In our example (Sequoia to UD), the global transformation can be divided into: 1) change POS and tokenisation, 2) change relation labels, 3) make needed head changes. The can be expressed in GREW by a strategy `Seq(POS, relations, heads)`, where `POS`, `relations` and `heads` correspond to dedicated subset of rules.

4 Application of graph matching

Graph matching is a subpart of the system used to describe left part of rewriting rules, but it is also useful alone as a way to make requests on a graph or a set of graphs. In practice, it can be used for searching examples of a given construction, for checking consistencies of annotations or for error mining. This subpart of GREW is now proposed as a separate tool, named GREW-MATCH and freely available as a web service[5]. This graph matching system is also available in the ARBORATORGREW tool (Guibon et al., 2020)[6].

A screenshot of the GREW-MATCH interface is shown in Figure 3. With the top bar and the list on the left, the user can chose a corpus (all 183 UD and SUD 2.7 corpora and a few other freely available corpora can be requested). A Request is entered and the user can visualise the occurrences found in the corpora with elements of the pattern highlighted in the sentence.

4.1 Error mining

It is difficult in general to ensure consistent annotations in large corpora. GREW-MATCH can be used to detect this kind of inconsistencies by making linguistic observation on some corpus. The Figure 3 illustrates the first step of such usage with the request: find `nsubj` relations where there is a `Number` disagreement (the head and the dependant of the relation both have a `Number` feature but with different values). In version 2.7 of UD_ENGLISH-GUM, 120 occurrences of the pattern are found, but there are not all errors, as the example of the figure shows. We can then refine the request by adding some negative patterns (with the `without` keyword), for instance to exclude occurrences with a copula linked to the head:

```
pattern {
  M -[nsubj]-> N;
  M.Number <> N.Number; }
without { M -[cop]-> C }
```

The new request returns 25 occurrences which can be manually inspected: we have found a mix of annotation errors, irregularities (institution plural name used as a singular *the United Nations rates...*) or misspelled sentences. The same approach can be used for many aspect: searching for verbs without subjects, for unwanted multiple relation (more than one `obj` on the same node).

4.2 data exploration

More generally, GREW-MATCH can be used for any kind of data exploration. Here, we use the example of AMR (Banarescu et al., 2013) annotations, this will allow us to show examples where the graph matching used cannot be reduced as a tree matching. Two corpora are available from the AMR website[7]: the English translation of the Saint-Exupéry's novel *The Little Prince* and some PubMed articles. With the pattern below, we search for a node which is the `ARG0` argument of two different related concepts.

```
pattern { P1 -> P2;
 P1 -[ARG0]-> N; P2 -[ARG0]-> N; }
```

[5] http://match.grew.fr

[6] https://arborator.github.io

[7] https://amr.isi.edu/

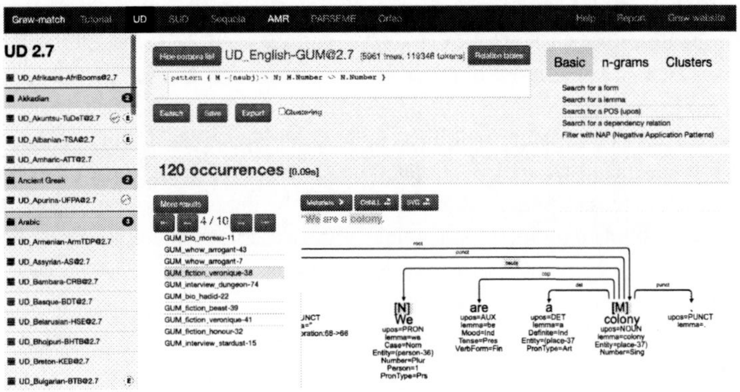

Figure 3: GREW-MATCH main interface

211 occurrences of this pattern are found in *The Little Prince*. Two of them are showed below, for the two sentences: *"What are you trying to say?"* and *"I administer them," replied the businessman.*

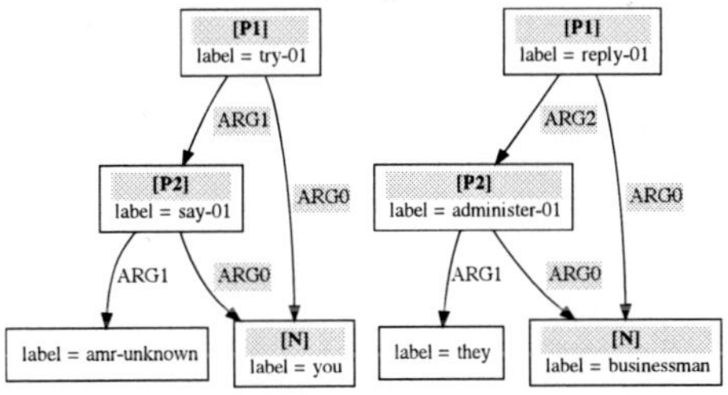

4.3 Typology

The pattern matching mechanism is also available in a `count` subcommand for GREW. Given a set of corpora and a set of requests, a table with the number of occurrences of each pattern on each corpora is returned. For instance, with the two patterns below, we can compute the ratio of `nsubj` relations which are use with or without a copula construction.

```
pattern { M -[nsubj]-> N; M -[cop]-> *}
```

and

```
pattern { M -[nsubj]-> N }
without { M -[cop]-> * }
```

The chart below shows these ratios, sorted by increasing values on the 141 corpora of UD 2.7 with more than 1000 sentences. Most corpora have a ratio between 0% and 25% with all value represented and a few corpora have a significantly higher proportion. 3 are above 30%: FAROESE-OFT with 67%, FRENCH-FQB with 43% and PERSIAN-SERAJI with 34%.

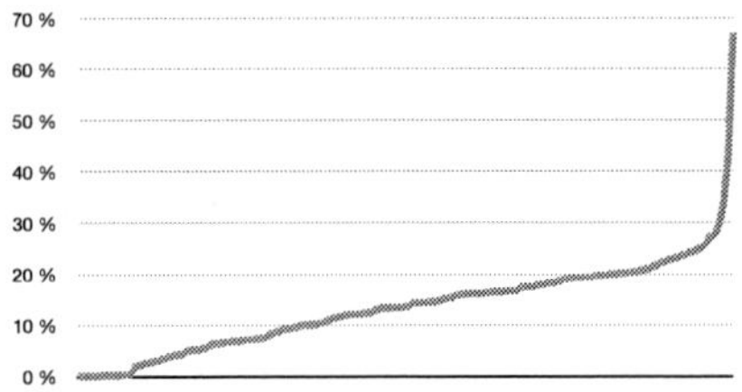

5 Related works

5.1 Rule-based transformations of linguistic structures

Many implementations of graph rewriting or graph transformation exist in other research areas. But the massive usage of feature structures in linguistic unit description, the usage of dedicated technical formats like CoNLL-U or the need for specific kinds of transformations (like the `shift` operation described above) make general graph transformation system difficult to use in NLP applications. Such applications would require several encodings of the data and they will not allow for a straightforward expression of linguistic transformations. Among existing rule-based software for transformations of linguistic structures, we can cite OGRE[8](Ribeyre, 2016) and Depedit[9].

[8]`https://gitlab.etermind.com/cribeyre/OGRE`

[9]`https://corpling.uis.georgetown.edu/depedit`

OGRE uses a notion of rules which is very closed to the ones used in GREW, but it does not provide interface with lexicons and there is no notion of strategies for the description of complex graph transformations which imply a large number of rules.

Depedit can be used as a separate tool or as a Python library. It is specifically designed to manipulate only dependency trees. Contrary to GREW, it does not proposed a built-in notion of strategies and does not handle not confluent rewriting processing. Moreover, the notion of rules is also more restricted: there are no NAP and it is not possible to express additional contraints on morphological features like the one we used in Section 4.1: `M.Number <> N.Number`.

5.2 Tools for corpora querying

A large number of online query tools are available online. Some of them have a more restrictive query language like SETS[10] or Kontext[11]. In these two tool, there is no notion of NAP and the kind of contraints that can be expressed is limited.

The PML Tree Query[12] and INESS[13] offers a query language with the same expressive power as the one proposed in GREW. An advantage of GREW is that it is interfaced in the larger annotation tool ARBORATORGREW[14]. With ARBORATOR-GREW, the user may query on his own treebank and then have access to a manual editing mode on the query output or to automatic updating through GREW rules.

6 Conclusion

GREW was used in many tasks of corpus conversion. It is used for instance for conversion between UD and SUD (Gerdes et al., 2018, 2019): all UD corpora are converted into SUD with it. GREW is implemented in Ocaml and is quite efficient: for instance the conversion of UD 2.7 (1.48M sentences, 26.5M tokens) into SUD uses 100 rules and takes 5,500 seconds on a labtop (around 267 graphs rewritten by second).

GREW is available as a command line program or through a Python library. Installation procedures and usage documentation are given on the GREW website: `https://grew.fr`. A web-based interface for the usage of the rewriting part of the software will be provided soon.

In this article, examples are given on dependency syntax and on semantic representations like AMR. A more complete set of examples is given in (Bonfante et al., 2018). Many other linguistic structures can be encoded as graphs and we plan to extend the experiments to other kind of semantic representations.

Acknowledgments

Thanks to all GREW users for their feedback and their requests which helps improve the software.

References

Laura Banarescu, Claire Bonial, Shu Cai, Madalina Georgescu, Kira Griffitt, Ulf Hermjakob, Kevin Knight, Philipp Koehn, Martha Palmer, and Nathan Schneider. 2013. Abstract meaning representation for sembanking. In *Proceedings of the 7th Linguistic Annotation Workshop and Interoperability with Discourse*, pages 178–186.

Guillaume Bonfante, Bruno Guillaume, and Guy Perrier. 2018. *Application of Graph Rewriting to Natural Language Processing*, volume 1 of *Logic, Linguistics and Computer Science Set*. ISTE Wiley.

Marie Candito and Djamé Seddah. 2012. Le corpus Sequoia : annotation syntaxique et exploitation pour l'adaptation d'analyseur par pont lexical. In *TALN 2012 - 19e conférence sur le Traitement Automatique des Langues Naturelles*, Grenoble, France.

Kim Gerdes, Bruno Guillaume, Sylvain Kahane, and Guy Perrier. 2018. SUD or Surface-Syntactic Universal Dependencies: An annotation scheme near-isomorphic to UD. In *Universal Dependencies Workshop 2018*, Brussels, Belgium.

Kim Gerdes, Bruno Guillaume, Sylvain Kahane, and Guy Perrier. 2019. Improving Surface-syntactic Universal Dependencies (SUD): surface-syntactic relations and deep syntactic features. In *TLT 2019 - 18th International Workshop on Treebanks and Linguistic Theories*, Paris, France.

Gaël Guibon, Marine Courtin, Kim Gerdes, and Bruno Guillaume. 2020. When Collaborative Treebank Curation Meets Graph Grammars. In *LREC 2020 - 12th Language Resources and Evaluation Conference*, Marseille, France.

Joakim Nivre, Marie-Catherine de Marneffe, Filip Ginter, Yoav Goldberg, Jan Hajic, Christopher D Manning, Ryan McDonald, Slav Petrov, Sampo Pyysalo, Natalia Silveira, et al. 2016. Universal dependencies

[10] `http://depsearch-depsearch.rahtiapp.fi/ds_demo`

[11] `http://lindat.mff.cuni.cz/services/kontext`

[12] `http://lindat.mff.cuni.cz/services/pmltq`

[13] `http://clarino.uib.no/iness`

[14] `https://arborator.github.io`

v1: A multilingual treebank collection. In *Proceedings of LREC 2016*, pages 1659–1666.

Corentin Ribeyre. 2016. *Méthodes d'analyse supervisée pour l'interface syntaxe-sémantique : De la réécriture de graphes à l'analyse par transitions*. Ph.D. thesis, Université Paris 7 Diderot & Inria.

Massive Choice, Ample Tasks (MaChAmp): A Toolkit for Multi-task Learning in NLP

Rob van der Goot **Ahmet Üstün** **Alan Ramponi** **Ibrahim Sharaf**
Barbara Plank

IT University of Copenhagen University of Groningen University of Trento
Fondazione the Microsoft Research - University of Trento COSBI Factmata
robv@itu.dk, a.ustun@rug.nl, alan.ramponi@unitn.it
ibrahim.sharaf@factmata.com, bapl@itu.dk

Abstract

Transfer learning, particularly approaches that combine multi-task learning with pre-trained contextualized embeddings and fine-tuning, have advanced the field of Natural Language Processing tremendously in recent years. In this paper we present MaChAmp, a toolkit for easy fine-tuning of contextualized embeddings in multi-task settings. The benefits of MaChAmp are its flexible configuration options, and the support of a variety of natural language processing tasks in a uniform toolkit, from text classification and sequence labeling to dependency parsing, masked language modeling, and text generation.[1]

1 Introduction

Multi-task learning (MTL) (Caruana, 1993, 1997) has developed into a standard repertoire in natural language processing (NLP). It enables neural networks to learn tasks in parallel (Caruana, 1993) while leveraging the benefits of sharing parameters. The shift—or "tsunami" (Manning, 2015)—of deep learning in NLP has facilitated the wide-spread use of MTL since the seminal work by Collobert et al. (2011), which has led to a multi-task learning "wave" (Ruder and Plank, 2018) in NLP. It has since been applied to a wide range of NLP tasks, developing into a viable alternative to classical pipeline approaches. This includes early adoption in Recurrent Neural Network models, e.g. (Lazaridou et al., 2015; Chrupała et al., 2015; Plank et al., 2016; Søgaard and Goldberg, 2016; Hashimoto et al., 2017), to the use of large pre-trained language models with multi-task objectives (Radford et al., 2019; Devlin et al., 2019). MTL comes in many flavors, based on the type of sharing, the weighting of losses, and the design and relations of tasks and layers. In general though, outperforming single-task settings remains a challenge (Martínez Alonso and Plank, 2017; Clark et al., 2019). For an overview of MTL in NLP we refer to Ruder (2017).

As a separate line of research, the idea of language model pre-training and contextual embeddings (Howard and Ruder, 2018; Peters et al., 2018; Devlin et al., 2019) is to pre-train rich representation on large quantities of monolingual or multilingual text data. Taking these representations as a starting point has led to enormous improvements across a wide variety of NLP problems. Related to MTL, recent research effort focuses on fine-tuning contextualized embeddings on a variety of tasks with supervised objectives (Kondratyuk and Straka, 2019; Sanh et al., 2019; Hu et al., 2020).

We introduce MaChAmp, a flexible toolkit for multi-task learning and fine-tuning of NLP problems. The main advantages of MaChAmp are:

- Ease of configuration, especially for dealing with multiple datasets and multi-task setups;
- Support of a wide range of NLP tasks, including a variety of sequence labeling approaches, text classification, dependency parsing, masked language modeling, and text generation (e.g., machine translation);
- Support of the initialization and fine-tuning of any contextualized embeddings from Hugging Face (Wolf et al., 2020).

As a result, the flexibility of MaChAmp supports up-to-date, general-purpose NLP (see Section 2.2). The backbone of MaChAmp is AllenNLP (Gardner et al., 2018), a PyTorch-based (Paszke et al., 2019) Python library containing modules for a variety of deep learning methods and NLP tasks. It is designed to be modular, high-

[1] The code is available at: https://github.com/machamp-nlp/machamp (v0.2), and an instructional video at https://www.youtube.com/watch?v=DauTEdMhUDI.

Proceedings of the 16th Conference of the European Chapter of the Association for Computational Linguistics: System Demonstrations, pages 176–197
April 19 - 23, 2021. ©2021 Association for Computational Linguistics

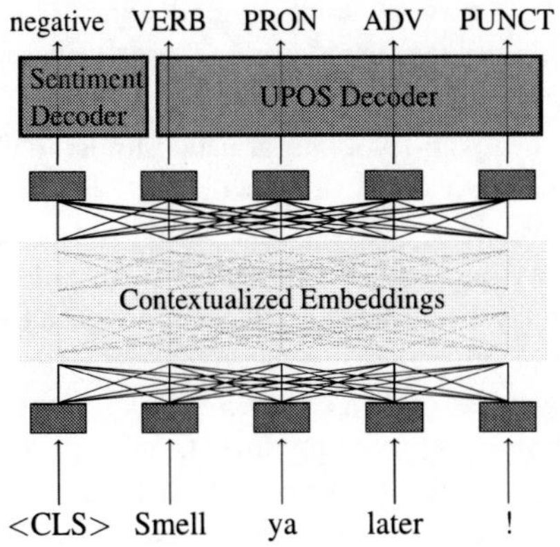

Figure 1: Overview of MaChAmp, when training jointly for sentiment analysis and POS tagging. A shared encoding representation and task-specific decoders are exploited to accomplish both tasks.

level and flexible. It should be noted that contemporary to MaChAmp, `jiant` (Pruksachatkun et al., 2020) was developed, and AllenNLP included multi-task learning as well since release 2.0. MaChAmp distinguishes from the other toolkits by supporting simple configurations, and a variety of multi-task settings.

2 Model

In this section we will discuss the model, its supported tasks, and possible configuration settings.

2.1 Model overview

An overview of the model is shown in Figure 1. MaChAmp takes a pre-trained contextualized model as initial encoder, and fine-tunes its layers by applying an inverse square root learning rate decay with linear warm-up (Howard and Ruder, 2018), according to a given set of downstream tasks. For the task-specific predictions, each task has its own decoder, which is trained for the corresponding task. The model defaults to the embedding-specific tokenizer in Hugging Face (Wolf et al., 2020).[2]

When multiple datasets are used for training, they are first separately split into batches so that each batch only contains instances from one dataset. Batches are then concatenated and shuffled before training. This means that small datasets will be underrepresented, which can be overcome by smoothing the dataset sampling (Section 3.2.2). During decoding, the loss function is only activated for tasks which are present in the current batch. By default, all tasks have an equal weight in the loss function. The loss weight can be tuned (Section 3.2.1).

2.2 Supported task types

We here describe the tasks MaChAmp supports.

SEQ For traditional token-level sequence prediction tasks, like part-of-speech tagging. MaChAmp uses greedy decoding with a softmax output layer on the output of the contextual embeddings.

STRING2STRING An extension to SEQ, which learns a conversion for each input token to its label. Instead of predicting the labels directly, the model can now learn to predict the conversion. This strategy is commonly used for lemmatization (Chrupała, 2006; Kondratyuk and Straka, 2019), where it greatly reduces the label vocabulary. We use the transformation algorithm from UDPipe-Future (Straka, 2018), which was also used by Kondratyuk and Straka (2019).

SEQ_BIO A variant of SEQ which exploits conditional random fields (Lafferty et al., 2001) as decoder, masked to enforce outputs following the BIO tagging scheme.

MULTISEQ An extension to SEQ which supports the prediction of multiple labels per token. Specifically, for some sequence labeling tasks it is unknown beforehand how many labels each token should get. We compute a probability score for each label, employing binary cross-entropy as loss, and outputting all the labels that exceed a certain threshold. The threshold can be set in the dataset configuration file.

DEPENDENCY For dependency parsing, MaChAmp uses the deep biaffine parser (Dozat and Manning, 2017) as implemented by AllenNLP (Gardner et al., 2018), with the Chu-Liu/Edmonds algorithm (Chu, 1965; Edmonds, 1967) for decoding the tree.

MLM For masked language modeling, our implementation follows the original BERT settings (Devlin et al., 2019). The chance that a token is masked is 15%, of which 80% are masked with a `[MASK]` token, 10% with a random token, and 10% are left unchanged. We do not include the next sentence prediction task following Liu et al. (2019), for simplicity and efficiency. We use a cross entropy loss,

[2] This includes both the pre-tokenization (in the traditional sense) and the subword segmentation.

```
smell	VERB
ya	PRON
later	ADV
!	PUNCT
```

(a) Example of a token-level file format (e.g., for POS tagging), where words are in column `word_idx`=0, and a single layer of corresponding annotations is in column `column_idx`=1.

```
smell ya later !	negative
```

(b) Example of a sentence-level file format (e.g., for sentiment classification), where only a sentence is required and is defined in column 0 (i.e., `sent_idxs`=[0]) and a single layer of annotation is in the second column (`column_idx`=1).

Figure 2: Examples of data file formats.

and the language model heads from the defined Hugging Face embeddings (Wolf et al., 2020). It assumes raw text files as input, so no `column_idx` has to be defined (See Section 3.1).

CLASSIFICATION For text classification, it predicts a label for every text instance by using the embedding of the first token, which is commonly a special token (e.g. `[CLS]` or <s>). For tasks which model a relation between multiple sentences (e.g., textual entailment), a special token (e.g. `[SEP]`) is automatically inserted between the sentences to inform the model about the sentence boundaries.

SEQ2SEQ For text generation, MACHAMP employs the sequence to sequence (encoder-decoder) paradigm (Sutskever et al., 2014). We use a recurrent neural network decoder, which suits the auto-regressive nature of the machine translation tasks (Cho et al., 2014) and an attention mechanism to avoid compressing the whole source sentence into a fixed-length vector (Bahdanau et al., 2015).

3 Usage

To use MACHAMP, one needs a configuration file, input data and a command to start the training or prediction. In this section we will describe each of these requirements.

3.1 Data format

MACHAMP supports two types of data formats for annotated data,[3] which correspond to the level of annotation (Section 2.2). For token-level tasks, we will use the term "token-level file format", whereas for sentence-level task, we will use "sentence-level file format".

The token-level file format is similar to the tab-separated CoNLL format (Tjong Kim Sang and De Meulder, 2003). It assumes one token per line (on a column index `word_idx`), with each annotation layer following each token separated by a tab character (each on a column index `column_idx`) (Figure 2a). Token sequences (e.g., sentences) are delimited by an empty line. Comments are lines on top of the sequence (which have a different number of columns with respect to "token lines").[4] It should be noted that for dependency parsing, the format assumes the relation label to be on the `column_idx` and the head index on the following column. Further, we also support the UD format by removing multi-word tokens and empty nodes using the UD-conversion-tools (Agić et al., 2016).

The sentence-level file format (used for text classification and text generation) is similar (Figure 2b), and also supports multiple inputs having the same annotation layers. A list of one or more column indices can be defined (i.e., `sent_idxs`) to enable modeling the relation between any arbitrary number of sentences.

3.2 Configuration

The model requires two configuration files, one that specifies the datasets and tasks, and one for the hyperparameters. For the hyperparameters, a default option is provided (`configs/params.json`, see Section 4).

3.2.1 Dataset configuration

An example of a dataset configuration file is shown in Figure 3. On the first level, the dataset names are specified (i.e., "UD" and "RTE"), which should be unique identifiers. Each of these datasets needs at least a `train_data_path`, a `validation_data_path`, a `word_idx` or `sent_idxs`, and a list of `tasks` (corresponding to the layers of annotation, see Section 3.1).

For each of the defined tasks, the user is required to define the `task_type` (Section 2.2), and the column index from which to read the relevant labels (i.e., `column_idx`). On top of this template, the following options can be passed on the task level:

[3]The MLM task does not require annotation, thus a raw text file can be provided.

[4]We do not identify comments based on lines starting with a '#', because datasets might have tokens that begin with '#'.

```
{ "UD": {
    "train_data_path": "data/ewt.train",
    "validation_data_path": "data/ewt.dev",
    "word_idx": 1,
    "tasks": {
      "lemma": {
        "task_type": "string2string",
        "column_idx": 2
      },
      "upos": {
        "task_type": "seq",
        "column_idx": 3
  } } }
  "RTE": {
    "train_data_path": "data/RTE.train",
    "validation_data_path": "data/RTE.dev",
    "sent_idxs": [0,1],
    "tasks": {
      "rte": {
        "task_type": "classification",
        "column_idx": 2
} } } }
```

Figure 3: Example dataset configuration file to predict UPOS, lemmas, and textual entailment simultaneously.

Metric For each task type, a commonly used metric is set as default metric. However, one can override the default by specifying a different metric at the task level. Supported metrics are 'acc', 'las', 'micro-f1', 'macro-f1', 'span_f1', 'multi_span_f1', 'bleu' and 'perplexity'.

Loss weight In multi-task settings, not all tasks might be equally important, or some tasks might just be harder to learn, and therefore should gain more weight during training. This can be tuned by setting the `loss_weight` parameter on the task level (by default the value is 1.0 for all tasks).

Dataset embedding Ammar et al. (2016) have shown that embedding which language an instance belongs to can be beneficial for multilingual models. Later work (Stymne et al., 2018; Wagner et al., 2020) has also shown that more fine-grained distinctions on the dataset level[5] can be beneficial when training on multiple datasets within the same language (family). In previous work, this embedding is usually concatenated to the word embedding before the encoding. However, in contextualized embeddings, the word embeddings themselves are commonly used as encoder, hence we concatenate the dataset embeddings in between the encoder and the decoder. This parameter is set on the dataset

[5]These are called treebank embeddings in their work. We will use the more general term "dataset embeddings", which would often roughly correspond to languages and/or domains/genres.

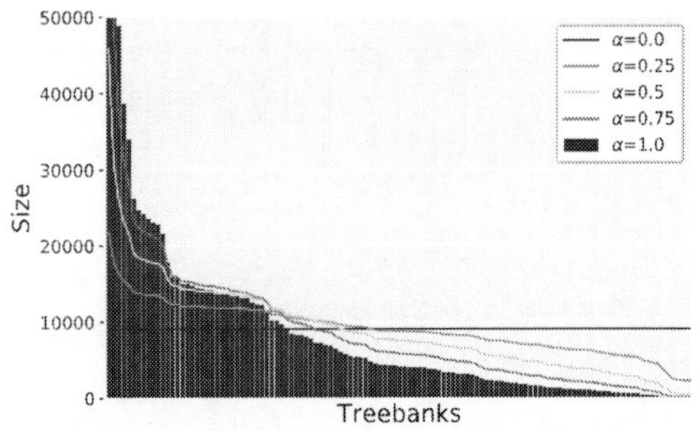

Figure 4: Effect of the sampling parameter α on the training sets of Universal Dependencies 2.6 data.

level with `dataset_embed_idx`, which specifies the column to read the dataset ID from. Setting `dataset_embed_idx` to -1 will use the dataset name as specified in the json file as ID.

Max sentences In order to limit the maximum number of sentences that are used during training, `max_sents` is used. This is done before the sampling smoothing (Section 3.2.2), if both are enabled. It should be noted that the specified number will be taken from the top of the dataset.

3.2.2 Hyperparameter configuration

Whereas most of the hyperparameters can simply be changed from the default configuration provided in `configs/params.json`, we would like to highlight two main settings.

Pre-trained embeddings The name/path to pre-trained Hugging Face embeddings[6] can be set in the configuration file at the `transformer_model` key; `transformer_dim` might be adapted accordingly to reflect the embeddings dimension.

Dataset sampling To avoid larger datasets from overwhelming the model, MACHAMP can re-sample multiple datasets according to a multinomial distribution, similar as used by Conneau and Lample (2019). MACHAMP performs the sampling on the batch level, and shuffles after each epoch (so it can see a larger variety of instances for downsampled datasets). The formula is:

$$\lambda = \frac{1}{p_i} * \frac{p_i^\alpha}{\sum_i p_i^\alpha} \quad (1)$$

where p_i is the probability that a random sample is from dataset i, and α is a hyperparameter that can be set. Setting α=1.0 means using the default sizes,

[6]`https://huggingface.co/models`

Parameter	Value	Range
Optimizer	Adam	
β_1, β_2	0.9, 0.99	
Dropout	0.2	0.1, 0.2, 0.3
Epochs	20	
Batch size	32	
Learning rate (LR)	1e-4	1e-3, 1e-4, 1e-5
LR scheduler	slanted triangular	
Weight decay	0.01	
Decay factor	0.38	.35, .38, .5
Cut fraction	0.2	.1, .2, .3

Table 1: Final parameter settings, incl. tested ranges.

and α=0.0 results in one average amount of batches for each dataset, similar to Sanh et al. (2019). The effect of different settings of α for the Universal Dependencies 2.6 data is shown in Figure 4. Smoothing can be enabled in the hyperparameters configuration file at the `sampling_smoothing` key.

3.3 Training

Given the setup illustrated in the previous sections, a model can be trained via the following command. It assumes the configuration (Figure 3) is saved in `configs/upos-lemma-rte.json`.

```
python3 train.py --dataset_config \
  configs/upos-lemma-rte.json
```

By default, the model and the logs will be written to `logs/<JSONNAME>/<DATE>`. The name of the directory can be set manually by providing `--name <NAME>`. Further, `--device <ID>` can be used to specify which GPU to use, otherwise the CPU will be used. As a default, `train.py` uses `configs/params.json` for the hyperparameters, but this can be overridden by using `--parameters_config <CONFIG FILE>`.

3.4 Inference

Prediction can be done with:

```
python3 predict.py \
  logs/<NAME>/<DATE>/model.tar.gz \
  <INPUT FILE> <OUTPUT FILE>
```

It requires the path to the best model (serialized during training) stored as `model.tar.gz` in the logs directory as specified above. By default, the data is assumed to be in the same format as the training data (i.e., with the same number of `column_idx` columns), but `--raw_text` can be specified to read a data file containing raw texts with one sentence per line. For models trained on multiple datasets (as "UD" and "RTE" in Figure 3), `--dataset <NAME>` can be used to specify which dataset to use in order to predict all tasks within that dataset.

Task	Reference	MaChAmp
EWT2.2	Kondratyuk et al. (2019)	
UPOS*	96.82	**97.07**
Lemma*	97.97	**98.14**
Feats*	97.27	**97.41**
LAS*	89.38	**89.80**
GLUE	Devlin et al. (2019)	
CoLA	**60.5**	53.7
MNLI	**86.7**	83.9
MNLI-mis	**85.9**	82.7
MRPC	**89.3**	87.2
QNLI	**92.7**	90.8
QQP	**72.1**	69.1
RTE	**70.1**	60.0
SST-2	**94.9**	92.5
WMT14	Liu et al. (2020)	
EN-DE	**30.1**	24.7
IWSLT15	Zaheer et al. (2018)	
EN-VI	**29.27**	24.72

Table 2: Scores of single task models on test data for three popular datasets and a variety of tasks. *one joint model. For the GLUE data, BERT-large (English) and tokenized BLEU are used for fair comparison.

4 Hyperparameter Tuning

In this section we describe the procedure how we determined robust default parameters for MaChAmp; note that the goal is not to beat the state-of-the-art, but to reach competitive performance for multiple tasks simultaneously.[7]

For the tuning of hyperparameters, we used the GLUE classification datasets (Wang et al., 2018; Warstadt et al., 2019; Socher et al., 2013; Dolan and Brockett, 2005; Cer et al., 2017; Williams et al., 2018; Rajpurkar et al., 2018; Bentivogli et al., 2009; Levesque et al., 2012) and the English Web Treebank (EWT 2.6) (Silveira et al., 2014) with multilingual BERT[8] (mBERT) as embeddings.[9] For each of these setups, we averaged the scores over all datasets/tasks and perform a grid search. The best hyperparameters across all datasets are reported in Table 1 and are the defaults values for MaChAmp.

[7]Compared to MaChAmp v0.1 (van der Goot et al., 2020) we removed parameters with negligible effects (word dropout, layer dropout, adaptive softmax, and layer attention).

[8]`https://github.com/google-research/bert/blob/master/multilingual.md`

[9]We capped the dataset sizes to a maximum of 20,000 sentences for efficiency reasons.

Setup	UD (LAS)	GLUE (Acc)
Single	72.22	**82.38**
All	72.82	80.96
Smoothed	**73.74**	81.87
Dataset embed.*	72.76	–
Sep. decoder*	73.69	–

Table 3: Average results over all development sets. Dataset embeddings and a separate decoder have not been tested in GLUE, because each dataset is annotated for a different task. *includes dataset smoothing.

Model\Size	0	<1k	<10k	>10k
Single	43.5	15.1	57.9	80.1
All	44.5	37.1	66.4	80.3
Smoothed	44.3	**45.4**	67.1	80.3
Dataset embed.*	43.9	36.5	**67.8**	**81.0**
Sep. decoder*	**45.1**	37.7	66.5	80.9

Table 4: Average LAS scores on test splits of UD treebanks grouped by training size (in number of sentences). *includes dataset smoothing.

5 Evaluation

5.1 Single task evaluation

As a starting point, we evaluate single task models to ensure our implementations are competitive with the state-of-the-art. We report scores on dependency parsing (EWT), the GLUE classification tasks, and machine translation (WMT14 DE-EN (Bojar et al., 2014), IWSLT15 EN-VI (Cettolo et al., 2014)) using mBERT as our embeddings.[10] Table 2 reports our results on the test sets compared to previous work. For all UD tasks, we score slightly higher, whereas for GLUE tasks we score consistently lower compared to the references. This is mostly due to differences in fine-tuning strategies, as implementations themselves are highly similar. Scores on the machine translation tasks show the largest drops, indicating that task-specific finetuning and pre-processing might be necessary.

5.2 Multi-dataset evaluation

We evaluate the effect of a variety of multi-dataset settings on all GLUE and UD treebanks (v2.7) on the test splits. It should be noted that the UD treebanks all have the same tasks, as opposed to GLUE. First, we jointly train on all datasets (ALL), then we attempt to improve performance on smaller sets by enabling the sampling smoothing (SMOOTHED, Section 3.2.2, we set $\alpha = 0.5$). Furthermore, we attempt to improve the performance by informing the decoder of the dataset through dataset embeddings (DATASET EMBED., Section 3.2.1) or by giving each dataset its own decoder (SEP. DECODER). Results (Table 3) show that multi-task learning is only beneficial for performance when training on the same set of tasks (i.e., UD), dataset smoothing is helpful, dataset embeddings and separate decoders do not improve upon smoothing on average.

For analysis purposes, we group the UD treebanks based on training size, and also evaluate UD treebanks which have no training split (zero-shot). For the zero-shot experiments, we select a proxy parser based on word overlap of the first 10 sentences of the target test data and the source training data.[11] Results on the UD data (Table 4) show that multi-task learning is mostly beneficial for medium-sized datasets (<1k and <10k). For these datasets, the combination of smoothing and dataset embeddings are the most promising settings. Perhaps surprisingly, the zero-shot datasets (<1k) have a higher LAS as compared to the small datasets and using a separate decoder based on the proxy treebank is the best setting; this is mainly because for many small datasets there is no other in-language training treebank. For the GLUE tasks (Table 5, Appendix), multi-task learning is only beneficial for the RTE data. This is to be expected, as the tasks are different in this setup, and training data is generally larger. Dataset smoothing here prevents the model from dropping too much in performance, as it outperforms ALL for 7 out of 9 tasks.

6 Conclusion

We introduced MACHAMP, a powerful toolkit for multi-task learning supporting a wide range of NLP tasks. We also provide initial experiments demonstrating the usefulness of some of its options. We learned that multi-task learning is mostly beneficial for setups in which multiple datasets are annotated for the same set of tasks, and that dataset embeddings can still be useful when employing contextualized embeddings. However, the current experiments are just scratching the surface of MACHAMP's capabilities, as a wide variety of tasks and multi-task settings is supported.

[10] For the sake of comparison we use BERT-large for GLUE, and EWT version 2.2.

[11] Scores on individual sets and proxy treebanks can be found in the Appendix.

Acknowledgments

We would like to thank Anouck Braggaar, Max Müller-Eberstein and Kristian Nørgaard Jensen for testing development versions. Furthermore, we thank Rik van Noord for his participation in the video, and providing an early use-case for MACHAMP (van Noord et al., 2020). This research was supported by an Amazon Research Award, an STSM in the Multi3Generation COST action (CA18231), a visit supported by COSBI, grant 9063-00077B (Danmarks Frie Forskningsfond), and Nvidia corporation for sponsoring Titan GPUs. We thank the NLPL laboratory and the HPC team at ITU for the computational resources used in this work.

References

Anne Abeillé, Lionel Clément, and Alexandra Kinyon. 2000. Building a treebank for French. In *Proceedings of the Second International Conference on Language Resources and Evaluation (LREC'00)*, Athens, Greece. European Language Resources Association (ELRA).

Noëmi Aepli and Simon Clematide. 2018. Parsing approaches for Swiss German. In *Proceedings of the 3rd Swiss Text Analytics Conference (SwissText), Winterthur, Switzerland.*

Željko Agić, Anders Johannsen, Barbara Plank, Héctor Martínez Alonso, Natalie Schluter, and Anders Søgaard. 2016. Multilingual projection for parsing truly low-resource languages. *Transactions of the Association for Computational Linguistics*, 4:301–312.

Željko Agić and Nikola Ljubešić. 2015. Universal Dependencies for Croatian (that work for Serbian, too). In *The 5th Workshop on Balto-Slavic Natural Language Processing*, pages 1–8, Hissar, Bulgaria. INCOMA Ltd. Shoumen, BULGARIA.

Lars Ahrenberg. 2015. Converting an English-Swedish parallel treebank to Universal Dependencies. In *Proceedings of the Third International Conference on Dependency Linguistics (Depling 2015)*, pages 10–19, Uppsala, Sweden. Uppsala University, Uppsala, Sweden.

Linda Alfieri and Fabio Tamburini. 2016. (almost) automatic conversion of the Venice Italian Treebank into the merged Italian Dependency Treebank format. In *CLiC-it/EVALITA*.

Ika Alfina, Indra Budi, and Heru Suhartanto. 2020. Tree rotations for dependency trees: Converting the head-directionality of noun phrases. *Journal of Computer Science*, 16(11):1585–1597.

Héctor Martínez Alonso and Daniel Zeman. 2016. Universal Dependencies for the AnCora treebanks. *Procesamiento del Lenguaje Natural*, 57:91–98.

Waleed Ammar, George Mulcaire, Miguel Ballesteros, Chris Dyer, and Noah A. Smith. 2016. Many languages, one parser. *Transactions of the Association for Computational Linguistics*, 4:431–444.

Angelina Aquino, Franz de Leon, and Mary Ann Bacolod. 2020. UD_Tagalog-Ugnayan. `https://github.com/UniversalDependencies/UD_Tagalog-Ugnayan`.

Carolina Coelho Aragon. 2018. Variações estilísticas e sociais no discurso dos falantes akuntsú. *Polifonia*, 25(38.1):90–103.

Maria Jesus Aranzabe, Aitziber Atutxa, Kepa Bengoetxea, Arantza Diaz de Ilarraza, Iakes Goenaga, Koldo Gojenola, and Larraitz Uria. 2015. Automatic conversion of the Basque dependency treebank to universal dependencies. In *Proceedings of the fourteenth international workshop on treebanks an linguistic theories (TLT14)*, pages 233–241.

Masayuki Asahara, Hiroshi Kanayama, Takaaki Tanaka, Yusuke Miyao, Sumire Uematsu, Shinsuke Mori, Yuji Matsumoto, Mai Omura, and Yugo Murawaki. 2018. Universal Dependencies version 2 for Japanese. In *Proceedings of the Eleventh International Conference on Language Resources and Evaluation (LREC 2018)*, Miyazaki, Japan. European Language Resources Association (ELRA).

Elena Badmaeva and Francis M. Tyers. 2017. Dependency treebank for Buryat. In *Proceedings of the 15th International Workshop on Treebanks and Linguistic Theories (TLT15)*, pages 1–12.

Dzmitry Bahdanau, Kyunghyun Cho, and Yoshua Bengio. 2015. Neural machine translation by jointly learning to align and translate. In *3rd International Conference on Learning Representations, ICLR 2015, Conference Track Proceedings*, San Diego, CA, USA.

David Bamman and Gregory Crane. 2011. The ancient Greek and Latin dependency treebanks. In *Language technology for cultural heritage*, pages 79–98. Springer.

Verginica Barbu Mititelu, Radu Ion, Radu Simionescu, Elena Irimia, and Cenel-Augusto Perez. 2016. The Romanian treebank annotated according to Universal Dependencies. In *Proceedings of the tenth international conference on natural language processing (hrtal2016)*.

Colin Batchelor. 2019. Universal dependencies for Scottish Gaelic: syntax. In *Proceedings of the Celtic Language Technology Workshop*, pages 7–15, Dublin, Ireland. European Association for Machine Translation.

Shabnam Behzad and Amir Zeldes. 2020. A cross-genre ensemble approach to robust Reddit part of speech tagging. In *Proceedings of the 12th Web as Corpus Workshop*, pages 50–56, Marseille, France. European Language Resources Association.

Eduard Bejček, Eva Hajičová, Jan Hajič, Pavlína Jínová, Václava Kettnerová, Veronika Kolářová, Marie Mikulová, Jiří Mírovský, Anna Nedoluzhko, Jarmila Panevová, et al. 2013. Prague dependency treebank 3.0.

Luisa Bentivogli, Ido Dagan, Hoa Trang Dang, Danilo Giampiccolo, and Bernardo Magnini. 2009. The fifth PASCAL recognizing textual entailment challenge. In *Proceedings of the Second Text Analysis Conference, TAC 2009*, Gaithersburg, Maryland, USA.

Yevgeni Berzak, Jessica Kenney, Carolyn Spadine, Jing Xian Wang, Lucia Lam, Keiko Sophie Mori, Sebastian Garza, and Boris Katz. 2016. Universal Dependencies for learner English. In *Proceedings of the 54th Annual Meeting of the Association for Computational Linguistics (Volume 1: Long Papers)*, pages 737–746, Berlin, Germany. Association for Computational Linguistics.

Irshad Bhat, Riyaz A. Bhat, Manish Shrivastava, and Dipti Sharma. 2018. Universal Dependency parsing for Hindi-English code-switching. In *Proceedings of the 2018 Conference of the North American Chapter of the Association for Computational Linguistics: Human Language Technologies, Volume 1 (Long Papers)*, pages 987–998, New Orleans, Louisiana. Association for Computational Linguistics.

Riyaz Ahmad Bhat, Rajesh Bhatt, Annahita Farudi, Prescott Klassen, Bhuvana Narasimhan, Martha Palmer, Owen Rambow, Dipti Misra Sharma, Ashwini Vaidya, Sri Ramagurumurthy Vishnu, et al. 2016. The hindi/urdu treebank project. In *Handbook of Linguistic Annotation*. Springer Press.

Agne Bielinskiene, Loic Boizou, and Jolanta Kovalevskaite. 2016. Lithuanian dependency treebank. In *Human Language Technologies–The Baltic Perspective: Proceedings of the Seventh International Conference Baltic HLT 2016*, volume 289, page 107. IOS Press.

Su Lin Blodgett, Johnny Wei, and Brendan O'Connor. 2018. Twitter Universal Dependency parsing for African-American and mainstream American English. In *Proceedings of the 56th Annual Meeting of the Association for Computational Linguistics (Volume 1: Long Papers)*, pages 1415–1425, Melbourne, Australia. Association for Computational Linguistics.

Ondřej Bojar, Christian Buck, Christian Federmann, Barry Haddow, Philipp Koehn, Johannes Leveling, Christof Monz, Pavel Pecina, Matt Post, Herve Saint-Amand, Radu Soricut, Lucia Specia, and Aleš Tamchyna. 2014. Findings of the 2014 workshop on statistical machine translation. In *Proceedings of the Ninth Workshop on Statistical Machine Translation*, pages 12–58, Baltimore, Maryland, USA. Association for Computational Linguistics.

Guillaume Bonfante, Bruno Guillaume, and Guy Perrier. 2018. *Application of Graph Rewriting to Natural Language Processing*. Wiley Online Library.

Emanuel Borges Völker, Maximilian Wendt, Felix Hennig, and Arne Köhn. 2019. HDT-UD: A very large Universal Dependencies treebank for German. In *Proceedings of the Third Workshop on Universal Dependencies (UDW, SyntaxFest 2019)*, pages 46–57, Paris, France. Association for Computational Linguistics.

Cristina Bosco, Felice Dell'Orletta, Simonetta Montemagni, Manuela Sanguinetti, and Maria Simi. 2014. The EVALITA 2014 dependency parsing task. In *EVALITA 2014 Evaluation of NLP and Speech Tools for Italian*, pages 1–8. Pisa University Press.

Gosse Bouma and Gertjan van Noord. 2017. Increasing return on annotation investment: The automatic construction of a Universal Dependency treebank for Dutch. In *Proceedings of the NoDaLiDa 2017 Workshop on Universal Dependencies (UDW 2017)*, pages 19–26, Gothenburg, Sweden. Association for Computational Linguistics.

Anouck Braggaar and Rob van der Goot. 2021. Challenges in annotating and parsing spoken, code-switched, Frisian-Dutch data. In *Proceedings of the Second Workshop on Domain Adaptation for Natural Language Processing*.

Sabine Brants, Stefanie Dipper, Peter Eisenberg, Silvia Hansen-Schirra, Esther König, Wolfgang Lezius, Christian Rohrer, George Smith, and Hans Uszkoreit. 2004. TIGER: Linguistic interpretation of a german corpus. *Research on language and computation*, 2(4):597–620.

Bernard Caron, Marine Courtin, Kim Gerdes, and Sylvain Kahane. 2019. A surface-syntactic UD treebank for Naija. In *Proceedings of the 18th International Workshop on Treebanks and Linguistic Theories (TLT, SyntaxFest 2019)*, pages 13–24, Paris, France. Association for Computational Linguistics.

Rich Caruana. 1993. Multitask learning: A knowledge-based source of inductive bias. In *Proceedings of the Tenth International Conference on Machine Learning*, pages 41–48, Amherst, MA, USA.

Rich Caruana. 1997. Multitask learning. In *Learning to learn*, pages 95–133. Springer.

Flavio Massimiliano Cecchini, Marco Passarotti, Paola Marongiu, and Daniel Zeman. 2018. Challenges in converting the index Thomisticus treebank into Universal Dependencies. In *Proceedings of the Second Workshop on Universal Dependencies (UDW 2018)*, pages 27–36, Brussels, Belgium. Association for Computational Linguistics.

Slavomír Čéplö. 2018. Constituent order in Maltese: A quantitative analysis.

Daniel Cer, Mona Diab, Eneko Agirre, Iñigo Lopez-Gazpio, and Lucia Specia. 2017. SemEval-2017 task 1: Semantic textual similarity multilingual and crosslingual focused evaluation. In *Proceedings of the 11th International Workshop on Semantic Evaluation (SemEval-2017)*, pages 1–14, Vancouver, Canada. Association for Computational Linguistics.

Özlem Çetinoğlu and Çağrı Çöltekin. 2019. Challenges of annotating a code-switching treebank. In *Proceedings of the 18th International Workshop on Treebanks and Linguistic Theories (TLT, SyntaxFest 2019)*, pages 82–90, Paris, France. Association for Computational Linguistics.

Mauro Cettolo, Niehues Jan, Stüker Sebastian, Luisa Bentivogli, Roldano Cattoni, and Marcello Federico. 2014. The IWSLT 2014 evaluation campaign. In *International Workshop on Spoken Language Translation*, Lake Tahoe, CA, USA.

Kyunghyun Cho, Bart van Merriënboer, Caglar Gulcehre, Dzmitry Bahdanau, Fethi Bougares, Holger Schwenk, and Yoshua Bengio. 2014. Learning phrase representations using RNN encoder–decoder for statistical machine translation. In *Proceedings of the 2014 Conference on Empirical Methods in Natural Language Processing (EMNLP)*, pages 1724–1734, Doha, Qatar. Association for Computational Linguistics.

Grzegorz Chrupała, Ákos Kádár, and Afra Alishahi. 2015. Learning language through pictures. In *Proceedings of the 53rd Annual Meeting of the Association for Computational Linguistics and the 7th International Joint Conference on Natural Language Processing (Volume 2: Short Papers)*, pages 112–118, Beijing, China. Association for Computational Linguistics.

Grzegorz Chrupała. 2006. Simple data-driven context-sensitive lemmatization. *SEPLN*, 37:121–127.

Yoeng-Jin Chu. 1965. On the shortest arborescence of a directed graph. *Scientia Sinica*, 14:1396–1400.

Jayeol Chun, Na-Rae Han, Jena D. Hwang, and Jinho D. Choi. 2018. Building Universal Dependency treebanks in Korean. In *Proceedings of the Eleventh International Conference on Language Resources and Evaluation (LREC 2018)*, Miyazaki, Japan. European Language Resources Association (ELRA).

Alessandra Teresa Cignarella, Cristina Bosco, and Paolo Rosso. 2019. Presenting TWITTIRÒ-UD: An Italian Twitter treebank in Universal Dependencies. In *Proceedings of the Fifth International Conference on Dependency Linguistics (Depling, SyntaxFest 2019)*, pages 190–197, Paris, France. Association for Computational Linguistics.

Kevin Clark, Minh-Thang Luong, Urvashi Khandelwal, Christopher D. Manning, and Quoc V. Le. 2019. BAM! born-again multi-task networks for natural language understanding. In *Proceedings of the 57th Annual Meeting of the Association for Computational Linguistics*, pages 5931–5937, Florence, Italy. Association for Computational Linguistics.

Ronan Collobert, Jason Weston, Léon Bottou, Michael Karlen, Koray Kavukcuoglu, and Pavel Kuksa. 2011. Natural language processing (almost) from scratch. *Journal of Machine Learning Research*, 12:2493–2537.

Cagrı Cöltekin. 2015. A grammar-book treebank of Turkish. In *Proceedings of the 14th workshop on Treebanks and Linguistic Theories (TLT 14)*, pages 35–49.

Alexis Conneau and Guillaume Lample. 2019. Cross-lingual language model pretraining. In *Advances in Neural Information Processing Systems*, pages 7059–7069, Vancouver, Canada.

Sam Davidson, Dian Yu, and Zhou Yu. 2019. Dependency parsing for spoken dialog systems. In *Proceedings of the 2019 Conference on Empirical Methods in Natural Language Processing and the 9th International Joint Conference on Natural Language Processing (EMNLP-IJCNLP)*, pages 1513–1519, Hong Kong, China. Association for Computational Linguistics.

Mehmet Oguz Derin. 2020. UD_Old_Turkish-Tonqq. `https://github.com/UniversalDependencies/UD_Old_Turkish-Tonqq`.

Jacob Devlin, Ming-Wei Chang, Kenton Lee, and Kristina Toutanova. 2019. BERT: Pre-training of deep bidirectional transformers for language understanding. In *Proceedings of the 2019 Conference of the North American Chapter of the Association for Computational Linguistics: Human Language Technologies, Volume 1 (Long and Short Papers)*, pages 4171–4186, Minneapolis, Minnesota. Association for Computational Linguistics.

Cheikh Bamba Dione. 2019. Developing Universal Dependencies for Wolof. In *Proceedings of the Third Workshop on Universal Dependencies (UDW, SyntaxFest 2019)*, pages 12–23, Paris, France. Association for Computational Linguistics.

Peter Dirix, Liesbeth Augustinus, Daniel van Niekerk, and Frank Van Eynde. 2017. Universal Dependencies for Afrikaans. In *Proceedings of the NoDaLiDa 2017 Workshop on Universal Dependencies (UDW 2017)*, pages 38–47, Gothenburg, Sweden. Association for Computational Linguistics.

Kaja Dobrovoljc, Tomaž Erjavec, and Simon Krek. 2017. The Universal Dependencies treebank for Slovenian. In *Proceedings of the 6th Workshop on Balto-Slavic Natural Language Processing*, pages

33–38, Valencia, Spain. Association for Computational Linguistics.

Kaja Dobrovoljc and Joakim Nivre. 2016. The Universal Dependencies treebank of spoken Slovenian. In *Proceedings of the Tenth International Conference on Language Resources and Evaluation (LREC'16)*, pages 1566–1573, Portorož, Slovenia. European Language Resources Association (ELRA).

William B. Dolan and Chris Brockett. 2005. Automatically constructing a corpus of sentential paraphrases. In *Proceedings of the Third International Workshop on Paraphrasing (IWP2005)*, pages 9–16, Jeju Island, Korea.

Timothy Dozat and Christopher D Manning. 2017. Deep biaffine attention for neural dependency parsing. In *Proceedings of 5th International Conference on Learning Representations, ICLR 2017, Conference Track Proceedings*, Toulon, France.

Kira Droganova, Olga Lyashevskaya, and Daniel Zeman. 2018. Data conversion and consistency of monolingual corpora: Russian UD treebanks. In *Proceedings of the 17th international workshop on treebanks and linguistic theories (tlt 2018)*, 155, pages 53–66.

Puneet Dwivedi and Guha Easha. 2017. Universal Dependencies for Sanskrit. *International Journal of Advance Research, Ideas and Innovations in Technology*, 3(4).

Hanne Eckhoff, Kristin Bech, Gerlof Bouma, Kristine Eide, Dag Haug, Odd Einar Haugen, and Marius Jøhndal. 2018. The PROIEL treebank family: a standard for early attestations of Indo-European languages. *Language Resources and Evaluation*, 52(1):29–65.

Hanne Martine Eckhoff and Aleksandrs Berdičevskis. 2015. Linguistics vs. digital editions: The Tromsø Old Russian and OCS treebank. *Scripta & e-Scripta*, 14(15):9–25.

Jack Edmonds. 1967. Optimum branchings. *Journal of Research of the national Bureau of Standards B*, 71(4):233–240.

Marhaba Eli, Weinila Mushajiang, Tuergen Yibulayin, Kahaerjiang Abiderexiti, and Yan Liu. 2016. Universal dependencies for Uyghur. In *Proceedings of the Third International Workshop on Worldwide Language Service Infrastructure and Second Workshop on Open Infrastructures and Analysis Frameworks for Human Language Technologies (WLSI/OIAF4HLT2016)*, pages 44–50, Osaka, Japan. The COLING 2016 Organizing Committee.

Marília Fernanda Pereira de Freitas. 2017. A posse em apurinã: Descrição de construções atributivas e predicativas em comparação com outras línguas aruák. *Belém: Programa de Pós-Graduação em Letras, Universidade Federal do Pará (Tese de Doutorado)*.

Marcos Garcia. 2016. Universal dependencies guidelines for the Galician-TreeGal treebank. Technical report, Technical Report, LyS Group, Universidade da Coruna.

Matt Gardner, Joel Grus, Mark Neumann, Oyvind Tafjord, Pradeep Dasigi, Nelson F. Liu, Matthew Peters, Michael Schmitz, and Luke Zettlemoyer. 2018. AllenNLP: A deep semantic natural language processing platform. In *Proceedings of Workshop for NLP Open Source Software (NLP-OSS)*, pages 1–6, Melbourne, Australia. Association for Computational Linguistics.

Fabrìcio Ferraz Gerardi. 2020. UD_Tupinamba-TuDeT. `https://github.com/UniversalDependencies/UD_Tupinamba-TuDeT`.

Fabrìcio Ferraz Gerardi. 2021. The structure of Mundurukú.

Memduh Gökırmak and Francis M. Tyers. 2017. A dependency treebank for Kurmanji Kurdish. In *Proceedings of the Fourth International Conference on Dependency Linguistics (Depling 2017)*, pages 64–72, Pisa,Italy. Linköping University Electronic Press.

Xavier Gómez Guinovart. 2017. Recursos integrados da lingua galega para a investigación lingüística. *Gallaecia. Estudos de lingüística portuguesa e galega. Santiago de Compostela: Universidade de Santiago*, pages 1037–1048.

Rob van der Goot and Gertjan van Noord. 2018. Modeling input uncertainty in neural network dependency parsing. In *Proceedings of the 2018 Conference on Empirical Methods in Natural Language Processing*, pages 4984–4991, Brussels, Belgium. Association for Computational Linguistics.

Rob van der Goot, Ahmet Üstün, Alan Ramponi, and Barbara Plank. 2020. Massive choice, ample tasks (MaChAmp): A toolkit for multi-task learning in NLP. *arXiv preprint arXiv:2005.14672v2*.

Normunds Gruzitis, Lauma Pretkalnina, Baiba Saulite, Laura Rituma, Gunta Nespore-Berzkalne, Arturs Znotins, and Peteris Paikens. 2018. Creation of a balanced state-of-the-art multilayer corpus for NLU. In *Proceedings of the Eleventh International Conference on Language Resources and Evaluation (LREC 2018)*, Miyazaki, Japan. European Language Resources Association (ELRA).

Bruno Guillaume, Marie-Catherine de Marneffe, and Guy Perrier. 2019. Conversion et améliorations de corpus du Français annotés en Universal Dependencies. *Traitement Automatique des Langues*, 60(2):71–95.

Jan Hajič, Otakar Smrž, Petr Zemánek, Petr Pajas, Jan Šnaidauf, Emanuel Beška, Jakub Krácmar, and Kamila Hassanová. 2009. Prague Arabic dependency treebank 1.0.

Kazuma Hashimoto, Caiming Xiong, Yoshimasa Tsuruoka, and Richard Socher. 2017. A joint many-task model: Growing a neural network for multiple NLP tasks. In *Proceedings of the 2017 Conference on Empirical Methods in Natural Language Processing*, pages 1923–1933, Copenhagen, Denmark. Association for Computational Linguistics.

Dag TT Haug and Marius Jøhndal. 2008. Creating a parallel treebank of the old Indo-European Bible translations. In *Proceedings of the second workshop on language technology for cultural heritage data (LaTeCH 2008)*, pages 27–34.

Johannes Heinecke and Francis M. Tyers. 2019. Development of a Universal Dependencies treebank for Welsh. In *Proceedings of the Celtic Language Technology Workshop*, pages 21–31, Dublin, Ireland. European Association for Machine Translation.

Oliver Hellwig, Salvatore Scarlata, Elia Ackermann, and Paul Widmer. 2020. The treebank of Vedic Sanskrit. In *Proceedings of the 12th Language Resources and Evaluation Conference*, pages 5137–5146, Marseille, France. European Language Resources Association.

Barbora Hladká, Jan Hajič, Jirka Hana, Jaroslava Hlaváčová, Jiří Mírovský, and Jan Raab. 2008. The Czech academic corpus 2.0 guide. *The Prague Bulletin of Mathematical Linguistics*, 89(1):41–96.

Jeremy Howard and Sebastian Ruder. 2018. Universal language model fine-tuning for text classification. In *Proceedings of the 56th Annual Meeting of the Association for Computational Linguistics (Volume 1: Long Papers)*, pages 328–339, Melbourne, Australia. Association for Computational Linguistics.

Junjie Hu, Sebastian Ruder, Aditya Siddhant, Graham Neubig, Orhan Firat, and Melvin Johnson. 2020. XTREME: A massively multilingual multitask benchmark for evaluating cross-lingual generalization. In *Proceedings of the 37th International Conference on Machine Learning*, volume 119, pages 4411–4421.

Anton Karl Ingason, Eiríkur Rögnvaldsson, Einar Freyr Sigurosson, and Joel C. Wallenberg. 2020. The Faroese parsed historical corpus. CLARIN-IS, Stofnun Árna Magnússonar.

Olájídé Ishola and Daniel Zeman. 2020. Yorùbá dependency treebank (YTB). In *Proceedings of the 12th Language Resources and Evaluation Conference*, pages 5178–5186, Marseille, France. European Language Resources Association.

Tomás Jelínek. 2017. FicTree: A manually annotated treebank of Czech fiction. In *ITAT*, pages 181–185.

Anders Johannsen, Héctor Martínez Alonso, and Barbara Plank. 2015. Universal dependencies for Danish. In *International Workshop on Treebanks and Linguistic Theories (TLT14)*, page 157.

Hildur Jónsdóttir and Anton Karl Ingason. 2020. Creating a parallel Icelandic dependency treebank from raw text to Universal Dependencies. In *Proceedings of the 12th Language Resources and Evaluation Conference*, pages 2924–2931, Marseille, France. European Language Resources Association.

Jenna Kanerva. 2020. UD_Finnish-OOD. `https://github.com/UniversalDependencies/UD_Finnish-OOD`.

Dan Kondratyuk and Milan Straka. 2019. 75 languages, 1 model: Parsing universal dependencies universally. In *Proceedings of the 2019 Conference on Empirical Methods in Natural Language Processing and the 9th International Joint Conference on Natural Language Processing (EMNLP-IJCNLP)*, pages 2779–2795, Hong Kong, China. Association for Computational Linguistics.

Kamil Kopacewicz. 2018. UD_Akkadian-PISANDUB. `https://github.com/UniversalDependencies/UD_Akkadian-PISANDUB`.

Natalia Kotsyba, Bohdan Moskalevskyi, Mykhailo Romanenko, Halyna Samoridna, Ivanka Kosovska, Olha Lytvyn, Oksana Orlenko, Hanna Brovko, Bohdana Matushko, Natalia Onyshchuk, Valeriia Pareviazko, Yaroslava Rychyk, Anastasiia Stetsenko, Snizhana Umanets, and Larysa Masenko. 2018. UD_Ukrainian-IU. `https://github.com/UniversalDependencies/UD_Ukrainian-IU`.

Vincent Kríž, Barbora Hladká, and Zdenka Uresova. 2016. Czech legal text treebank 1.0. In *Proceedings of the Tenth International Conference on Language Resources and Evaluation (LREC'16)*, pages 2387–2392.

Anne Lacheret-Dujour, Sylvain Kahane, and Paola Pietrandrea. 2019. *Rhapsodie: A prosodic and syntactic treebank for spoken French*, volume 89. John Benjamins Publishing Company.

John D. Lafferty, Andrew McCallum, and Fernando C. N. Pereira. 2001. Conditional random fields: Probabilistic models for segmenting and labeling sequence data. In *Proceedings of the Eighteenth International Conference on Machine Learning*, ICML '01, page 282–289, San Francisco, CA, USA.

Angeliki Lazaridou, Nghia The Pham, and Marco Baroni. 2015. Combining language and vision with a multimodal skip-gram model. In *Proceedings of the 2015 Conference of the North American Chapter of the Association for Computational Linguistics: Human Language Technologies*, pages 153–163, Denver, Colorado. Association for Computational Linguistics.

John Lee, Herman Leung, and Keying Li. 2017. Towards Universal Dependencies for learner Chinese. In *Proceedings of the NoDaLiDa 2017 Workshop on Universal Dependencies (UDW 2017)*, pages 67–71, Gothenburg, Sweden. Association for Computational Linguistics.

Hector Levesque, Ernest Davis, and Leora Morgenstern. 2012. The Winograd schema challenge. In *Thirteenth International Conference on the Principles of Knowledge Representation and Reasoning*, Rome, Italy.

Xiaodong Liu, Kevin Duh, Liyuan Liu, and Jianfeng Gao. 2020. Very deep transformers for neural machine translation. *arXiv preprint arXiv:2008.07772v2*.

Yijia Liu, Yi Zhu, Wanxiang Che, Bing Qin, Nathan Schneider, and Noah A. Smith. 2018. Parsing tweets into Universal Dependencies. In *Proceedings of the 2018 Conference of the North American Chapter of the Association for Computational Linguistics: Human Language Technologies, Volume 1 (Long Papers)*, pages 965–975, New Orleans, Louisiana. Association for Computational Linguistics.

Yinhan Liu, Myle Ott, Naman Goyal, Jingfei Du, Mandar Joshi, Danqi Chen, Omer Levy, Mike Lewis, Luke Zettlemoyer, and Veselin Stoyanov. 2019. RoBERTa: A robustly optimized BERT pretraining approach. *arXiv preprint arXiv:1907.11692*.

Mikko Luukko, Aleksi Sahala, Sam Hardwick, and Krister Lindén. 2020. Akkadian treebank for early neo-assyrian royal inscriptions. In *Proceedings of the 19th International Workshop on Treebanks and Linguistic Theories*, pages 124–134, Düsseldorf, Germany. Association for Computational Linguistics.

Olga Lyashevskaya. 2019. A reusable tagset for the morphologically rich language in change: A case of Middle Russian. In *Proceedings of the International Conference Dialogue 2019*, pages 422–434.

Olga Lyashevskaya, Angelika Peljak-Łapińska, and Daria Petrova. 2017. UD_Belarusian-HSE. `https://github.com/UniversalDependencies/UD_Belarusian-HSE`.

Olga Lyashevskaya and Dmitry Sichinava. 2017. UD_Lithuanian-HSE. `https://github.com/UniversalDependencies/UD_Lithuanian-HSE`.

Teresa Lynn and Jennifer Foster. 2016. Universal dependencies for irish. In *CLTW*.

Aibek Makazhanov, Aitolkyn Sultangazina, Olzhas Makhambetov, and Zhandos Yessenbayev. 2015. Syntactic annotation of Kazakh: Following the Universal Dependencies guidelines. a report. In *3rd International Conference on Turkic Languages Processing, (TurkLang 2015)*, pages 338–350.

Christopher D Manning. 2015. Computational linguistics and deep learning. *Computational Linguistics*, 41(4):701–707.

Cătălina Mărănduc, Cenel-Augusto Perez, and Radu Simionescu. 2016. Social media-processing Romanian chat and discourse analysis. *Computación y Sistemas*, 20(3):405–414.

Héctor Martínez Alonso and Barbara Plank. 2017. When is multitask learning effective? semantic sequence prediction under varying data conditions. In *Proceedings of the 15th Conference of the European Chapter of the Association for Computational Linguistics: Volume 1, Long Papers*, Valencia, Spain. Association for Computational Linguistics.

Héctor Martínez Alonso, Djamé Seddah, and Benoît Sagot. 2016. From noisy questions to Minecraft texts: Annotation challenges in extreme syntax scenario. In *Proceedings of the 2nd Workshop on Noisy User-generated Text (WNUT)*, pages 13–23, Osaka, Japan. The COLING 2016 Organizing Committee.

Ryan McDonald, Joakim Nivre, Yvonne Quirmbach-Brundage, Yoav Goldberg, Dipanjan Das, Kuzman Ganchev, Keith Hall, Slav Petrov, Hao Zhang, Oscar Täckström, Claudia Bedini, Núria Bertomeu Castelló, and Jungmee Lee. 2013. Universal Dependency annotation for multilingual parsing. In *Proceedings of the 51st Annual Meeting of the Association for Computational Linguistics (Volume 2: Short Papers)*, pages 92–97, Sofia, Bulgaria. Association for Computational Linguistics.

Maria Mitrofan, Verginica Barbu Mititelu, and Grigorina Mitrofan. 2019. MoNERo: a biomedical gold standard corpus for the Romanian language. In *Proceedings of the 18th BioNLP Workshop and Shared Task*, pages 71–79, Florence, Italy. Association for Computational Linguistics.

Foroushani Mojiri, Hossein Amir, Hamid Aghaei, and Amir Ahmadi. 2020. UD_Soi-AHA. `https://github.com/UniversalDependencies/UD_Soi-AHA`.

AmirHossein Mojiri Foroushani, Hamid Aghaei, and Amir Ahmadi. 2020a. UD_Khunsari-AHA. `https://github.com/UniversalDependencies/UD_Khunsari-AHA`.

AmirHossein Mojiri Foroushani, Hamid Aghaei, and Amir Ahmadi. 2020b. UD_Nayini-AHA. `https://github.com/UniversalDependencies/UD_Nayini-AHA`.

Kadri Muischnek, Kaili Müürisep, Tiina Puolakainen, Eleri Aedmaa, Riin Kirt, and Dage Särg. 2014. Estonian dependency treebank and its annotation scheme. In *Proceedings of 13th workshop on treebanks and linguistic theories (TLT13)*, pages 285–291.

Kadri Muischnek, Kaili Müürisep, and Dage Dage Särg. 2019. CG roots of UD treebank of Estonian web language. In *Proceedings of the NoDaLiDa 2019 Workshop on Constraint Grammar-Methods, Tools and Applications, 30 September 2019, Turku, Finland*, 168, pages 23–26. Linköping University Electronic Press.

Robert Munro. 2020. Human-in-the-loop machine learning. *Sl: O'REILLY MEDIA*.

Phuong-Thai Nguyen, Xuan-Luong Vu, Thi-Minh-Huyen Nguyen, Van-Hiep Nguyen, and Hong-Phuong Le. 2009. Building a large syntactically-annotated corpus of Vietnamese. In *Proceedings of the Third Linguistic Annotation Workshop (LAW III)*, pages 182–185, Suntec, Singapore. Association for Computational Linguistics.

Rik van Noord, Antonio Toral, and Johan Bos. 2020. Character-level representations improve DRS-based semantic parsing Even in the age of BERT. In *Proceedings of the 2020 Conference on Empirical Methods in Natural Language Processing (EMNLP)*, pages 4587–4603, Online. Association for Computational Linguistics.

Atul Kr. Ojha and Daniel Zeman. 2020. Universal Dependency treebanks for low-resource Indian languages: The case of Bhojpuri. In *Proceedings of the WILDRE5– 5th Workshop on Indian Language Data: Resources and Evaluation*, pages 33–38, Marseille, France. European Language Resources Association (ELRA).

Mai Omura, Yuta Takahashi, and Masayuki Asahara. 2017. Universal dependency for modern Japanese. In *Proceedings of the 7th Conference of Japanese Association for Digital Humanities (JADH2017)*, pages 34–36.

Robert Östling, Carl Börstell, Moa Gärdenfors, and Mats Wirén. 2017. Universal Dependencies for Swedish Sign Language. In *Proceedings of the 21st Nordic Conference on Computational Linguistics*, pages 303–308, Gothenburg, Sweden. Association for Computational Linguistics.

Lilja Øvrelid and Petter Hohle. 2016. Universal Dependencies for Norwegian. In *Proceedings of the Tenth International Conference on Language Resources and Evaluation (LREC'16)*, pages 1579–1585, Portorož, Slovenia. European Language Resources Association (ELRA).

Lilja Øvrelid, Andre Kåsen, Kristin Hagen, Anders Nøklestad, Per Erik Solberg, and Janne Bondi Johannessen. 2018. The LIA treebank of spoken Norwegian dialects. In *Proceedings of the Eleventh International Conference on Language Resources and Evaluation (LREC 2018)*, Miyazaki, Japan. European Language Resources Association (ELRA).

Martha Palmer, Rajesh Bhatt, Bhuvana Narasimhan, Owen Rambow, Dipti Misra Sharma, and Fei Xia. 2009. Hindi syntax: Annotating dependency, lexical predicate-argument structure, and phrase structure. In *The 7th International Conference on Natural Language Processing*, pages 14–17.

Niko Partanen, Rogier Blokland, KyungTae Lim, Thierry Poibeau, and Michael Rießler. 2018. The first Komi-Zyrian Universal Dependencies treebanks. In *Proceedings of the Second Workshop on Universal Dependencies (UDW 2018)*, pages 126–132, Brussels, Belgium. Association for Computational Linguistics.

Adam Paszke, Sam Gross, Francisco Massa, Adam Lerer, James Bradbury, Gregory Chanan, Trevor Killeen, Zeming Lin, Natalia Gimelshein, Luca Antiga, Alban Desmaison, Andreas Kopf, Edward Yang, Zachary DeVito, Martin Raison, Alykhan Tejani, Sasank Chilamkurthy, Benoit Steiner, Lu Fang, Junjie Bai, and Soumith Chintala. 2019. PyTorch: An imperative style, high-performance deep learning library. In *Advances in Neural Information Processing Systems 32*, pages 8026–8037. Vancouver, Canada.

Agnieszka Patejuk and Adam Przepiórkowski. 2018. *From Lexical Functional Grammar to Enhanced Universal Dependencies: Linguistically informed treebanks of Polish*. Institute of Computer Science, Polish Academy of Sciences, Warsaw.

Matthew Peters, Mark Neumann, Mohit Iyyer, Matt Gardner, Christopher Clark, Kenton Lee, and Luke Zettlemoyer. 2018. Deep contextualized word representations. In *Proceedings of the 2018 Conference of the North American Chapter of the Association for Computational Linguistics: Human Language Technologies, Volume 1 (Long Papers)*, pages 2227–2237, New Orleans, Louisiana. Association for Computational Linguistics.

Jussi Piitulainen and Hanna Nurmi. 2017. UD_Finnish-FTB. `https://github.com/UniversalDependencies/UD_Finnish-FTB`.

Tommi A Pirinen. 2019. Building minority dependency treebanks, dictionaries and computational grammars at the same time—an experiment in Karelian treebanking. In *Proceedings of the Third Workshop on Universal Dependencies (UDW, SyntaxFest 2019)*, pages 132–136, Paris, France. Association for Computational Linguistics.

Barbara Plank, Anders Søgaard, and Yoav Goldberg. 2016. Multilingual part-of-speech tagging with bidirectional long short-term memory models and auxiliary loss. In *Proceedings of the 54th Annual Meeting of the Association for Computational Linguistics (Volume 2: Short Papers)*, pages 412–418, Berlin, Germany. Association for Computational Linguistics.

Prokopis Prokopidis and Haris Papageorgiou. 2017. Universal Dependencies for Greek. In *Proceedings of the NoDaLiDa 2017 Workshop on Universal Dependencies (UDW 2017)*, pages 102–106, Gothenburg, Sweden. Association for Computational Linguistics.

Yada Pruksachatkun, Phil Yeres, Haokun Liu, Jason Phang, Phu Mon Htut, Alex Wang, Ian Tenney, and Samuel R. Bowman. 2020. jiant: A software toolkit for research on general-purpose text understanding models. In *Proceedings of the 58th Annual Meeting of the Association for Computational Linguistics:*

System Demonstrations, pages 109–117, Online. Association for Computational Linguistics.

Sampo Pyysalo, Jenna Kanerva, Anna Missilä, Veronika Laippala, and Filip Ginter. 2015. Universal Dependencies for Finnish. In *Proceedings of the 20th Nordic Conference of Computational Linguistics (NODALIDA 2015)*, pages 163–172, Vilnius, Lithuania. Linköping University Electronic Press, Sweden.

Peng Qi and Koichi Yasuoka. 2019. UD_Chinese-GSDSimp. `https://github.com/UniversalDependencies/UD_Chinese-GSDSimp`.

Alexandre Rademaker, Fabricio Chalub, Livy Real, Cláudia Freitas, Eckhard Bick, and Valeria de Paiva. 2017. Universal Dependencies for Portuguese. In *Proceedings of the Fourth International Conference on Dependency Linguistics (Depling 2017)*, pages 197–206, Pisa,Italy. Linköping University Electronic Press.

Alec Radford, Jeffrey Wu, Rewon Child, David Luan, Dario Amodei, and Ilya Sutskever. 2019. Language models are unsupervised multitask learners. *OpenAI blog*.

Pranav Rajpurkar, Robin Jia, and Percy Liang. 2018. Know what you don't know: Unanswerable questions for SQuAD. In *Proceedings of the 56th Annual Meeting of the Association for Computational Linguistics (Volume 2: Short Papers)*, pages 784–789, Melbourne, Australia. Association for Computational Linguistics.

Taraka Rama and Sowmya Vajjala. 2017. A Telugu treebank based on a grammar book. In *Proceedings of the 16th International Workshop on Treebanks and Linguistic Theories*, pages 119–128, Prague, Czech Republic.

Loganathan Ramasamy and Zdeněk Žabokrtský. 2012. Prague dependency style treebank for Tamil. In *Proceedings of Eighth International Conference on Language Resources and Evaluation (LREC 2012)*, pages 1888–1894, İstanbul, Turkey.

Vinit Ravishankar. 2017. A Universal Dependencies treebank for Marathi. In *Proceedings of the 16th International Workshop on Treebanks and Linguistic Theories*, pages 190–200, Prague, Czech Republic.

Ines Rehbein, Josef Ruppenhofer, and Bich-Ngoc Do. 2019. tweeDe – a Universal Dependencies treebank for German tweets. In *Proceedings of the 18th International Workshop on Treebanks and Linguistic Theories (TLT, SyntaxFest 2019)*, pages 100–108, Paris, France. Association for Computational Linguistics.

Eiríkur Rögnvaldsson, Anton Karl Ingason, Einar Freyr Sigurosson, and Joel Wallenberg. 2012. The Icelandic parsed historical corpus (IcePaHC). In *Proceedings of the Eighth International Conference on Language Resources and Evaluation (LREC'12)*, pages 1977–1984, Istanbul, Turkey. European Language Resources Association (ELRA).

Sebastian Ruder. 2017. An overview of multi-task learning in deep neural networks. *arXiv preprint arXiv:1706.05098*.

Sebastian Ruder and Barbara Plank. 2018. Strong baselines for neural semi-supervised learning under domain shift. In *Proceedings of the 56th Annual Meeting of the Association for Computational Linguistics (Volume 1: Long Papers)*, pages 1044–1054, Melbourne, Australia. Association for Computational Linguistics.

Jack Rueter and Niko Partanen. 2019. Survey of Uralic Universal Dependencies development. In *Workshop on Universal Dependencies*, page 78. The Association for Computational Linguistics.

Jack Rueter, Niko Partanen, and Larisa Ponomareva. 2020. On the questions in developing computational infrastructure for Komi-permyak. In *Proceedings of the Sixth International Workshop on Computational Linguistics of Uralic Languages*, pages 15–25, Wien, Austria. Association for Computational Linguistics.

Jack Rueter and Francis Tyers. 2018. Towards an open-source universal-dependency treebank for Erzya. In *Proceedings of the Fourth International Workshop on Computational Linguistics of Uralic Languages*, pages 106–118.

Jack Michael Rueter. 2018. Mordva. In *The Uralic Languages*. Routledge.

Mohammad Sadegh Rasooli, Pegah Safari, Amirsaeid Moloodi, and Alireza Nourian. 2020. The Persian dependency treebank made universal. *arXiv e-prints*, pages arXiv–2009.

Alessio Salomoni. 2019. UD_German-LIT. `https://github.com/UniversalDependencies/UD_German-LIT`.

Tanja Samardžić, Mirjana Starović, Željko Agić, and Nikola Ljubešić. 2017. Universal Dependencies for Serbian in comparison with Croatian and other Slavic languages. In *Proceedings of the 6th Workshop on Balto-Slavic Natural Language Processing*, pages 39–44, Valencia, Spain. Association for Computational Linguistics.

Stephanie Samson and Cagrı Cöltekin. 2020. UD_Tagalog-TRG. `https://github.com/UniversalDependencies/UD_Tagalog-TRG`.

Manuela Sanguinetti and Cristina Bosco. 2014. Towards a Universal Stanford Dependencies parallel treebank. In *Proceedings of the 13th Workshop on Treebanks and Linguistic Theories (TLT-13)*. Springer.

Manuela Sanguinetti, Cristina Bosco, Alberto Lavelli, Alessandro Mazzei, Oronzo Antonelli, and Fabio Tamburini. 2018. PoSTWITA-UD: an Italian Twitter treebank in Universal Dependencies. In *Proceedings of the Eleventh International Conference on Language Resources and Evaluation (LREC 2018)*, Miyazaki, Japan. European Language Resources Association (ELRA).

Victor Sanh, Thomas Wolf, and Sebastian Ruder. 2019. A hierarchical multi-task approach for learning embeddings from semantic tasks. In *Proceedings of the AAAI Conference on Artificial Intelligence*, volume 33, pages 6949–6956, Honolulu, Hawaii, USA.

Kengatharaiyer Sarveswaran and Gihan Dias. 2020. ThamizhiUDp: A dependency parser for Tamil. *arXiv preprint arXiv:2012.13436*.

Kevin Scannell. 2020. Universal Dependencies for Manx Gaelic. In *Proceedings of the Fourth Workshop on Universal Dependencies (UDW 2020)*, pages 152–157, Barcelona, Spain (Online). Association for Computational Linguistics.

Djamé Seddah and Marie Candito. 2016. Hard time parsing questions: Building a QuestionBank for French. In *Proceedings of the Tenth International Conference on Language Resources and Evaluation (LREC'16)*, pages 2366–2370, Portorož, Slovenia. European Language Resources Association (ELRA).

Mojgan Seraji, Filip Ginter, and Joakim Nivre. 2016. Universal Dependencies for Persian. In *Proceedings of the Tenth International Conference on Language Resources and Evaluation (LREC'16)*, pages 2361–2365, Portorož, Slovenia. European Language Resources Association (ELRA).

Binyam Ephrem Seyoum, Yusuke Miyao, and Baye Yimam Mekonnen. 2018. Universal Dependencies for Amharic. In *Proceedings of the Eleventh International Conference on Language Resources and Evaluation (LREC 2018)*, Miyazaki, Japan. European Language Resources Association (ELRA).

Tatiana Shavrina and Olga Shapovalova. 2017. To the methodology of corpus construction for machine learning:"Taiga" syntax tree corpus and parser. In *Proceedings of "CORPORA-2017" International Conference*, pages 78–84.

Mo Shen, Ryan McDonald, Daniel Zeman, and Peng Qi. 2016. UD_Chinese-GSD. `https://github.com/UniversalDependencies/UD_Chinese-GSD`.

Timothy Shopen. 2018. UD_Warlpiri-UFAL. `https://github.com/UniversalDependencies/UD_Lithuanian-HSE`.

Natalia Silveira, Timothy Dozat, Marie-Catherine de Marneffe, Samuel Bowman, Miriam Connor, John Bauer, and Chris Manning. 2014. A gold standard dependency corpus for English. In *Proceedings of the Ninth International Conference on Language Resources and Evaluation (LREC'14)*, pages 2897–2904, Reykjavik, Iceland. European Language Resources Association (ELRA).

Kiril Simov, Petya Osenova, Alexander Simov, and Milen Kouylekov. 2005. Design and implementation of the Bulgarian HPSG-based treebank. *Journal of Research on Language and Computation. Special Issue*, pages 495–522.

Richard Socher, Alex Perelygin, Jean Wu, Jason Chuang, Christopher D. Manning, Andrew Ng, and Christopher Potts. 2013. Recursive deep models for semantic compositionality over a sentiment treebank. In *Proceedings of the 2013 Conference on Empirical Methods in Natural Language Processing*, pages 1631–1642, Seattle, Washington, USA. Association for Computational Linguistics.

Anders Søgaard and Yoav Goldberg. 2016. Deep multi-task learning with low level tasks supervised at lower layers. In *Proceedings of the 54th Annual Meeting of the Association for Computational Linguistics (Volume 2: Short Papers)*, pages 231–235, Berlin, Germany. Association for Computational Linguistics.

Achim Stein and Sophie Prévost. 2013. Syntactic annotation of medieval texts. *New methods in historical corpora*, 3:275.

Milan Straka. 2018. UDPipe 2.0 prototype at CoNLL 2018 UD shared task. In *Proceedings of the CoNLL 2018 Shared Task: Multilingual Parsing from Raw Text to Universal Dependencies*, pages 197–207, Brussels, Belgium. Association for Computational Linguistics.

Sara Stymne, Miryam de Lhoneux, Aaron Smith, and Joakim Nivre. 2018. Parser training with heterogeneous treebanks. In *Proceedings of the 56th Annual Meeting of the Association for Computational Linguistics (Volume 2: Short Papers)*, pages 619–625, Melbourne, Australia. Association for Computational Linguistics.

Umut Sulubacak, Memduh Gokirmak, Francis Tyers, Çağrı Çöltekin, Joakim Nivre, and Gülşen Eryiğit. 2016. Universal Dependencies for Turkish. In *Proceedings of COLING 2016, the 26th International Conference on Computational Linguistics: Technical Papers*, pages 3444–3454, Osaka, Japan. The COLING 2016 Organizing Committee.

Ilya Sutskever, Oriol Vinyals, and Quoc V Le. 2014. Sequence to sequence learning with neural networks. In *Advances in Neural Information Processing Systems*, volume 27, pages 3104–3112, Montreal, Canada.

Guillaume Thomas. 2019. Universal Dependencies for Mbyá Guaraní. In *Proceedings of the Third Workshop on Universal Dependencies (UDW, SyntaxFest 2019)*, pages 70–77, Paris, France. Association for Computational Linguistics.

Erik F. Tjong Kim Sang and Fien De Meulder. 2003. Introduction to the CoNLL-2003 shared task: Language-independent named entity recognition. In *Proceedings of the Seventh Conference on Natural Language Learning at HLT-NAACL 2003*, pages 142–147.

Marsida Toska, Joakim Nivre, and Daniel Zeman. 2020. Universal Dependencies for Albanian. In *Proceedings of the Fourth Workshop on Universal Dependencies (UDW 2020)*, pages 178–188, Barcelona, Spain (Online). Association for Computational Linguistics.

Utku Türk, Furkan Atmaca, Şaziye Betül Özateş, Gözde Berk, Seyyit Talha Bedir, Abdullatif Köksal, Balkiz Öztürk Başaran, Tunga Güngör, and Arzucan Özgür. 2020. Resources for Turkish dependency parsing: Introducing the BOUN treebank and the BoAT annotation tool.

Francis Tyers and Karina Mishchenkova. 2020. Dependency annotation of noun incorporation in polysynthetic languages. In *Proceedings of the Fourth Workshop on Universal Dependencies (UDW 2020)*, pages 195–204, Barcelona, Spain (Online). Association for Computational Linguistics.

Francis Tyers, Mariya Sheyanova, Aleksandra Martynova, Pavel Stepachev, and Konstantin Vinogorodskiy. 2018. Multi-source synthetic treebank creation for improved cross-lingual dependency parsing. In *Proceedings of the Second Workshop on Universal Dependencies (UDW 2018)*, pages 144–150, Brussels, Belgium. Association for Computational Linguistics.

Francis M Tyers and Vinit Ravishankar. 2018. A prototype dependency treebank for Breton. In *Actes de la Conférence TALN. Volume 1 - Articles longs, articles courts de TALN*, pages 197–204, Rennes, France. ATALA.

Francis M. Tyers and Mariya Sheyanova. 2017. Annotation schemes in North Sámi dependency parsing. In *Proceedings of the Third Workshop on Computational Linguistics for Uralic Languages*, pages 66–75, St. Petersburg, Russia. Association for Computational Linguistics.

Veronika Vincze, Dóra Szauter, Attila Almási, György Móra, Zoltán Alexin, and János Csirik. 2010. Hungarian dependency treebank. In *Proceedings of the Seventh International Conference on Language Resources and Evaluation (LREC'10)*, Valletta, Malta. European Language Resources Association (ELRA).

Valentin Vydrin. 2013. Bamana Reference Corpus (BRC). *Procedia-Social and Behavioral Sciences*, 95:75–80.

Joachim Wagner, James Barry, and Jennifer Foster. 2020. Treebank embedding vectors for out-of-domain dependency parsing. In *Proceedings of the 58th Annual Meeting of the Association for Computational Linguistics*, pages 8812–8818, Online. Association for Computational Linguistics.

Alex Wang, Amanpreet Singh, Julian Michael, Felix Hill, Omer Levy, and Samuel Bowman. 2018. GLUE: A multi-task benchmark and analysis platform for natural language understanding. In *Proceedings of the 2018 EMNLP Workshop BlackboxNLP: Analyzing and Interpreting Neural Networks for NLP*, pages 353–355, Brussels, Belgium. Association for Computational Linguistics.

Hongmin Wang, Jie Yang, and Yue Zhang. 2019. From genesis to creole language: Transfer learning for Singlish Universal Dependencies parsing and pos tagging. *ACM Transactions on Asian and Low-Resource Language Information Processing (TALLIP)*, 19(1):1–29.

Alex Warstadt, Amanpreet Singh, and Samuel R Bowman. 2019. Neural network acceptability judgments. *Transactions of the Association for Computational Linguistics*, 7:625–641.

Adina Williams, Nikita Nangia, and Samuel Bowman. 2018. A broad-coverage challenge corpus for sentence understanding through inference. In *Proceedings of the 2018 Conference of the North American Chapter of the Association for Computational Linguistics: Human Language Technologies, Volume 1 (Long Papers)*, pages 1112–1122. Association for Computational Linguistics.

Thomas Wolf, Lysandre Debut, Victor Sanh, Julien Chaumond, Clement Delangue, Anthony Moi, Pierric Cistac, Tim Rault, Remi Louf, Morgan Funtowicz, Joe Davison, Sam Shleifer, Patrick von Platen, Clara Ma, Yacine Jernite, Julien Plu, Canwen Xu, Teven Le Scao, Sylvain Gugger, Mariama Drame, Quentin Lhoest, and Alexander Rush. 2020. Transformers: State-of-the-art natural language processing. In *Proceedings of the 2020 Conference on Empirical Methods in Natural Language Processing: System Demonstrations*, pages 38–45, Online. Association for Computational Linguistics.

Tak-sum Wong, Kim Gerdes, Herman Leung, and John Lee. 2017. Quantitative comparative syntax on the Cantonese-Mandarin parallel dependency treebank. In *Proceedings of the Fourth International Conference on Dependency Linguistics (Depling 2017)*, pages 266–275, Pisa,Italy. Linköping University Electronic Press.

Alina Wróblewska. 2018. Extended and enhanced Polish dependency bank in Universal Dependencies format. In *Proceedings of the Second Workshop on Universal Dependencies (UDW 2018)*, pages 173–182, Brussels, Belgium. Association for Computational Linguistics.

Mary Yako. 2019. UD_Assyrian-AS. `https://github.com/UniversalDependencies/UD_Assyrian-AS`.

Koichi Yasuoka. 2019. Universal dependencies treebank of the four books in Classical Chinese. In *DADH2019: 10th International Conference of Digital Archives and Digital Humanities*, pages 20–28. Digital Archives and Digital Humanities.

M Yavrumyan, H Khachatrian, A Danielyan, and G Arakelyan. 2017. ArmTDP: Eastern Armenian treebank and dependency parser. In *XI International Conference on Armenian Linguistics, Abstracts. Yerevan.*

Manzil Zaheer, Sashank Reddi, Devendra Sachan, Satyen Kale, and Sanjiv Kumar. 2018. Adaptive methods for nonconvex optimization. In *Advances in Neural Information Processing Systems*, volume 31, pages 9793–9803, Montreal, Canada.

Shorouq Zahra. 2020. Parsing low-resource Levantine Arabic: Annotation projection versus small-sized annotated data.

Amir Zeldes. 2017. The GUM corpus: Creating multilayer resources in the classroom. *Language Resources and Evaluation*, 51(3):581–612.

Amir Zeldes and Mitchell Abrams. 2018. The Coptic Universal Dependency treebank. In *Proceedings of the Second Workshop on Universal Dependencies (UDW 2018)*, pages 192–201, Brussels, Belgium. Association for Computational Linguistics.

Dan Zeman, Anna Nedoluzhko, and Martin Majliš. 2017. UD_Upper_Sorbian-UFAL. `https://github.com/UniversalDependencies/UD_Upper_Sorbian-UFAL`.

Daniel Zeman. 2017. Slovak dependency treebank in Universal Dependencies. *Journal of Linguistics/Jazykovedný casopis*, 68(2):385–395.

Dataset size	RTE 2k	MRPC 4k	CoLa 9k	SST-2 67k	QNLI 105k	QQP 364k	MNLI 393k	MNLI-mis 393k	SNLI 550k
Single	67.1	85.5	74.7	88.4	85.2	90.5	80.2	80.8	88.9
All	69.3	81.6	70.2	88.2	82.3	90.1	79.2	79.7	88.1
Smoothed	72.9	82.8	72.7	87.6	83.1	90.3	78.8	80.1	88.4

Table 5: The scores (accuracy) per dataset on the GLUE tasks (dev) for a variety of multi-task settings (ordered by size, indicated in number of sentences in training data).

Appendix

Multi-dataset evaluation on GLUE tasks Table 5 contains the per-dataset scores for the GLUE tasks for all our tested settings. Only for RTE the performance increases when using multi-task learning. Overall, smoothing helps to overcome some of the performance loss we get when training one model on all datasets simultaneously.

Multi-dataset evaluation on UD treebanks Table 6 (on the next four pages) shows the LAS scores for each treebank (UD2.7) for all of our settings. We pre-processed the data with the UD-conversion tools to remove all language-specific sub-labels, and the multi-word tokens and empty nodes. *However, we calculate the scores against the official files for fair comparison.*[12] We included as many datasets as we could find. In the top part of the table, we include all official UD datasets for which we could get the words (only UD_Arabic-NYUAD and UD_Japanese-BCCWJ are missing), and the last 12 treebanks are taken from other sources, some have undergone some specific pre-processing to pass the evaluation script; details about this process can be found in the repository in `scripts/udExtras`.

[12] This is why the scores for some datasets might seem low compared to previous work, which did either do tokenization or did not take it into account during evaluation. In our case the model is punished for not tokenizing.

						+smoothing		
dataset	citation	proxy	size	self	conc.	conc.	sepDec	dataEmb
af_afribooms	(Dirix et al., 2017)	—	33,894	86.7	85.9	86.6	**87.0**	85.9
aii_as	(Yako, 2019)	et_ewt	0	**9.7**	3.5	3.9	5.1	3.4
ajp_madar	(Zahra, 2020)	ar_padt	0	31.2	**33.8**	33.1	33.2	31.2
akk_pisandub	(Kopacewicz, 2018)	et_edt	0	3.0	4.3	**4.7**	3.6	3.3
akk_riao	(Luukko et al., 2020)	et_edt	0	4.0	**8.2**	7.6	7.3	8.1
am_att	(Seyoum et al., 2018)	et_ewt	0	**1.8**	0.8	0.8	0.5	0.8
apu_ufpa	(Freitas, 2017)	fi_ftb	0	6.1	13.3	13.1	8.1	**13.4**
aqz_tudet	(Aragon, 2018)	cs_pdt	0	6.7	9.6	9.6	9.2	**14.7**
ar_padt	(Hajič et al., 2009)	—	191,869	31.5	31.4	31.3	31.4	**31.5**
ar_pud	(McDonald et al., 2013)	ar_padt	0	62.8	64.5	63.9	64.0	**64.7**
be_hse	(Lyashevskaya et al., 2017)	—	249,897	81.0	83.6	83.1	81.8	**83.8**
bg_btb	(Simov et al., 2005)	—	124,336	92.5	92.7	92.5	92.7	**92.7**
bho_bhtb	(Ojha and Zeman, 2020)	hi_hdtb	0	**37.7**	36.1	36.2	36.5	36.3
bm_crb	(Vydrin, 2013)	qhe_hiencs	0	**8.8**	6.5	6.1	6.7	6.3
br_keb	(Tyers and Ravishankar, 2018)	fr_gsd	0	**54.9**	32.0	31.3	33.2	32.4
bxr_bdt	(Badmaeva and Tyers, 2017)	—	153	11.6	23.9	**29.0**	21.5	24.0
ca_ancora	(Alonso and Zeman, 2016)	—	416,659	92.1	**92.2**	91.8	91.9	92.2
ckt_hse	(Tyers and Mishchenkova, 2020)	ru_syntagrus	0	8.1	**15.3**	15.3	13.7	14.5
cop_scriptorium	(Zeldes and Abrams, 2018)	—	12,926	0.8	0.8	0.7	0.7	**0.9**
cs_cac	(Hladká et al., 2008)	—	471,594	91.2	**92.2**	91.0	90.8	92.0
cs_cltt	(Kríž et al., 2016)	—	27,752	83.9	89.6	88.7	87.7	**89.6**
cs_fictree	(Jelínek, 2017)	—	133,137	91.5	93.0	92.3	92.4	**93.3**
cs_pdt	(Bejček et al., 2013)	—	1,171,190	92.7	92.8	91.2	91.1	**92.8**
cs_pud	(McDonald et al., 2013)	cs_pdt	0	87.7	**88.4**	88.0	88.1	88.2
cu_proiel	(Haug and Jøhndal, 2008)	—	37,432	65.1	67.1	**68.0**	67.6	67.3
cy_ccg	(Heinecke and Tyers, 2019)	—	15,706	74.5	73.9	**76.2**	76.0	73.8
da_ddt	(Johannsen et al., 2015)	—	80,378	86.7	86.1	86.5	**86.8**	86.0
de_gsd	(Brants et al., 2004)	—	259,194	81.7	79.9	81.5	**82.0**	80.8
de_hdt	(Borges Völker et al., 2019)	—	2,753,627	**96.7**	96.6	90.0	94.8	96.6
de_lit	(Salomoni, 2019)	de_hdt	0	76.9	78.9	**79.8**	77.8	78.4
de_pud	(McDonald et al., 2013)	de_hdt	0	78.5	81.2	**82.3**	78.8	80.6
el_gdt	(Prokopidis and Papageorgiou, 2017)	—	41,212	86.9	89.0	88.9	88.8	**89.0**
en_ewt	(Silveira et al., 2014)	—	202,141	**87.6**	85.6	85.4	86.7	86.0
en_gum	(Zeldes, 2017)	—	81,861	**89.0**	87.3	87.3	88.9	88.1
en_lines	(Ahrenberg, 2015)	—	57,372	87.4	86.8	86.9	**88.0**	87.2
en_partut	(Sanguinetti and Bosco, 2014)	—	43,477	89.7	89.3	89.5	**90.7**	89.8
en_pronouns	(Munro, 2020)	en_ewt	0	81.8	85.5	86.8	84.9	**87.2**
en_pud	(McDonald et al., 2013)	en_ewt	0	89.3	87.8	87.7	**89.7**	89.1
es_ancora	(Alonso and Zeman, 2016)	—	443,086	**90.8**	89.0	88.7	90.5	90.4
es_gsd	(McDonald et al., 2013)	—	375,149	85.6	81.7	81.6	**85.8**	85.0
es_pud	(McDonald et al., 2013)	es_gsd	0	79.4	78.6	78.7	**79.7**	79.5
et_edt	(Muischnek et al., 2014)	—	344,646	86.7	86.7	85.5	85.5	**86.8**
et_ewt	(Muischnek et al., 2019)	—	34,287	74.6	82.4	81.6	80.9	**82.4**
eu_bdt	(Aranzabe et al., 2015)	—	72,974	**83.3**	82.3	82.4	82.4	82.3
fa_perdt	(Sadegh Rasooli et al., 2020)	—	445,587	**89.2**	88.9	84.2	87.8	89.2
fa_seraji	(Seraji et al., 2016)	—	119,945	**87.2**	81.8	84.8	86.9	86.4
fi_ftb	(Piitulainen and Nurmi, 2017)	—	127,359	**89.1**	80.4	80.1	88.6	88.8
fi_ood	(Kanerva, 2020)	fi_tdt	0	77.6	69.5	69.1	77.5	**78.1**
fi_pud	(McDonald et al., 2013)	fi_tdt	0	90.4	86.6	86.0	**90.5**	90.4
fi_tdt	(Pyysalo et al., 2015)	—	162,617	89.1	83.2	82.7	**89.5**	89.5

dataset	citation	proxy	size	self	conc.	+smoothing conc.	+smoothing sepDec	+smoothing dataEmb
fo_farpahc	(Ingason et al., 2020)	—	23,089	80.9	87.0	86.5	85.4	**87.1**
fo_oft	(Tyers et al., 2018)	fo_farpahc	0	49.8	62.1	62.2	61.6	**62.7**
fr_fqb	(Seddah and Candito, 2016)	fr_gsd	0	84.9	84.6	84.6	**85.2**	85.2
fr_gsd	(Guillaume et al., 2019)	—	344,975	**88.6**	86.0	85.3	88.5	88.2
fr_partut	(Sanguinetti and Bosco, 2014)	—	23,322	87.0	81.7	82.7	**87.7**	82.7
fr_pud	(McDonald et al., 2013)	fr_gsd	0	85.3	83.9	84.1	85.4	**85.5**
fr_sequoia	(Bonfante et al., 2018)	—	49,157	88.4	85.9	87.1	**89.6**	87.4
fr_spoken	(Lacheret-Dujour et al., 2019)	—	14,921	77.5	81.9	**83.1**	82.3	81.8
fro_srcmf	(Stein and Prévost, 2013)	—	136,020	**88.5**	87.6	87.3	87.4	87.6
ga_idt	(Lynn and Foster, 2016)	—	95,860	77.8	**78.1**	78.1	77.9	78.1
gd_arcosg	(Batchelor, 2019)	—	37,817	72.2	72.8	**73.7**	73.7	72.8
gl_ctg	(Gómez Guinovart, 2017)	—	71,928	**66.3**	65.6	65.4	66.0	65.5
gl_treegal	(Garcia, 2016)	—	14,158	65.9	56.7	63.5	**68.4**	58.5
got_proiel	(Haug and Jøhndal, 2008)	—	35,024	75.4	79.0	**79.7**	77.8	78.9
grc_perseus	(Bamman and Crane, 2011)	—	159,895	59.6	63.3	62.4	62.2	**63.4**
grc_proiel	(Eckhoff et al., 2018)	—	187,033	71.7	74.8	74.0	73.3	**74.9**
gsw_uzh	(Aepli and Clematide, 2018)	de_hdt	0	27.8	36.7	**37.1**	35.1	36.9
gun_thomas	(Thomas, 2019)	it_isdt	0	7.7	10.5	**11.1**	9.2	10.9
gv_cadhan	(Scannell, 2020)	en_singpar	0	2.9	12.2	**13.4**	6.3	12.5
he_htb	(McDonald et al., 2013)	—	98,348	**36.3**	36.0	35.9	36.1	36.2
hi_hdtb	(Palmer et al., 2009)	—	281,057	**92.0**	91.8	91.6	91.8	91.9
hi_pud	(McDonald et al., 2013)	hi_hdtb	0	59.6	**59.8**	59.5	59.6	59.7
hr_set	(Agić and Ljubešić, 2015)	—	152,857	89.1	89.5	88.9	89.7	**90.0**
hsb_ufal	(Zeman et al., 2017)	—	460	10.5	59.8	**65.9**	60.1	59.8
hu_szeged	(Vincze et al., 2010)	—	20,166	82.6	83.9	**85.1**	84.8	84.0
hy_armtdp	(Yavrumyan et al., 2017)	—	41,837	75.0	76.8	**77.3**	76.6	76.2
id_csui	(Alfina et al., 2020)	—	17,904	77.1	74.8	76.9	**79.2**	75.1
id_gsd	(McDonald et al., 2013)	—	97,531	**79.9**	79.7	79.3	79.5	79.9
id_pud	(McDonald et al., 2013)	id_gsd	0	59.6	**63.1**	62.9	61.0	63.1
is_icepahc	(Rögnvaldsson et al., 2012)	—	704,716	**83.5**	83.4	80.3	80.0	83.4
is_pud	(Jónsdóttir and Ingason, 2020)	is_icepahc	0	57.9	**59.3**	59.0	58.7	59.3
it_isdt	(Bosco et al., 2014)	—	257,616	81.1	81.0	80.8	81.0	**81.4**
it_partut	(Sanguinetti and Bosco, 2014)	—	45,477	79.2	80.0	80.1	**80.7**	80.3
it_postwita	(Sanguinetti et al., 2018)	—	95,308	74.0	**74.9**	74.8	74.8	74.7
it_pud	(McDonald et al., 2013)	it_isdt	0	80.1	80.3	80.3	**80.6**	80.6
it_twittiro	(Cignarella et al., 2019)	—	22,656	72.6	**77.3**	77.1	76.5	76.6
it_vit	(Alfieri and Tamburini, 2016)	—	208,795	78.6	78.0	77.6	**78.9**	78.8
ja_gsd	(Asahara et al., 2018)	—	167,482	**93.1**	92.7	92.4	92.4	92.6
ja_modern	(Omura et al., 2017)	ja_gsd	0	51.8	52.9	53.8	**53.8**	52.9
ja_pud	(McDonald et al., 2013)	ja_gsd	0	94.3	**94.3**	94.1	94.2	94.2
kfm_aha	(Mojiri Foroushani et al., 2020a)	fa_perdt	0	17.6	16.7	18.5	18.9	**22.1**
kk_ktb	(Makazhanov et al., 2015)	—	511	21.6	56.7	**59.1**	53.0	56.5
kmr_mg	(Gökırmak and Tyers, 2017)	—	242	12.0	15.8	**36.0**	28.4	16.1
ko_gsd	(Chun et al., 2018)	—	56,687	**85.6**	73.7	77.7	85.0	82.5
ko_kaist	(Chun et al., 2018)	—	296,446	**87.6**	85.0	80.3	86.2	87.1
ko_pud	(McDonald et al., 2013)	ko_kaist	0	47.7	46.1	43.6	48.2	**48.9**
koi_uh	(Rueter et al., 2020)	ru_syntagrus	0	12.2	19.1	**19.4**	18.0	18.4
kpv_ikdp	(Partanen et al., 2018)	ru_syntagrus	0	19.5	22.1	**22.2**	21.1	21.8
kpv_lattice	(Partanen et al., 2018)	ru_syntagrus	0	8.2	11.3	**11.7**	10.5	11.6
krl_kkpp	(Pirinen, 2019)	fi_tdt	0	45.9	42.1	44.9	46.0	**46.4**

dataset	citation	proxy	size	self	conc.	+smoothing		
						conc.	sepDec	dataEmb
la_ittb	(Cecchini et al., 2018)	—	390,785	90.5	**91.0**	89.5	89.8	91.0
la_llct	(Cecchini et al., 2018)	—	194,143	**94.6**	94.6	94.2	94.5	94.5
la_perseus	(Bamman and Crane, 2011)	—	18,184	63.3	68.4	69.1	**69.4**	68.3
la_proiel	(Haug and Jøhndal, 2008)	—	172,133	79.9	**81.6**	80.1	80.1	81.6
lt_alksnis	(Bielinskiene et al., 2016)	—	47,641	78.0	78.1	**78.3**	78.3	78.2
lt_hse	(Lyashevskaya and Sichinava, 2017)	—	3,210	47.8	63.7	64.2	**68.5**	64.3
lv_lvtb	(Gruzitis et al., 2018)	—	167,594	**86.8**	86.6	86.3	86.2	86.8
lzh_kyoto	(Yasuoka, 2019)	—	185,211	79.7	**79.8**	75.9	75.6	79.7
mdf_jr	(Rueter, 2018)	ru_syntagrus	0	16.8	17.7	17.5	**18.2**	17.8
mr_ufal	(Ravishankar, 2017)	—	2,730	50.3	65.9	**67.1**	64.6	64.6
mt_mudt	(Čéplö, 2018)	—	22,880	75.5	76.2	**78.9**	78.1	76.2
myu_tudet	(Gerardi, 2021)	ro_nonstandard	0	16.1	15.4	**17.4**	14.0	14.4
myv_jr	(Rueter and Tyers, 2018)	be_hse	0	**20.1**	18.9	19.1	18.6	18.6
nl_alpino	(Bouma and van Noord, 2017)	—	185,883	90.9	91.4	91.4	91.1	**91.5**
nl_lassysmall	(Bouma and van Noord, 2017)	—	75,080	89.4	91.0	91.0	90.7	**91.2**
no_bokmaal	(Øvrelid and Hohle, 2016)	—	243,886	92.2	**92.6**	92.2	92.3	92.5
no_nynorsk	(Øvrelid and Hohle, 2016)	—	245,330	91.8	92.1	92.0	91.9	**92.2**
no_nynorsklia	(Øvrelid et al., 2018)	—	35,207	74.1	75.6	**76.0**	75.4	75.8
nyq_aha	(Mojiri Foroushani et al., 2020b)	fa_perdt	0	30.8	29.1	37.2	34.2	**38.9**
olo_kkpp	(Pirinen, 2019)	—	144	8.4	40.4	**44.7**	26.3	43.1
orv_rnc	(Lyashevskaya, 2019)	—	10,156	58.3	70.6	**71.6**	69.6	70.5
orv_torot	(Eckhoff and Berdičevskis, 2015)	—	118,630	63.9	65.1	64.6	64.4	**65.4**
otk_tonqq	(Derin, 2020)	et_ewt	0	7.7	11.8	5.9	**11.9**	7.1
pcm_nsc	(Caron et al., 2019)	—	111,843	90.0	90.2	89.9	89.5	**90.2**
pl_lfg	(Patejuk and Przepiórkowski, 2018)	—	104,750	95.7	93.7	93.6	95.7	**95.8**
pl_pdb	(Wróblewska, 2018)	—	279,596	89.4	88.8	88.2	89.3	**89.7**
pl_pud	(Wróblewska, 2018)	pl_pdb	0	91.2	91.0	90.5	91.0	**91.4**
pt_bosque	(Rademaker et al., 2017)	—	191,406	**78.2**	74.1	73.8	78.1	77.1
pt_gsd	(McDonald et al., 2013)	—	238,714	**83.0**	80.8	80.6	82.7	82.7
pt_pud	(McDonald et al., 2013)	pt_gsd	0	68.5	**69.6**	69.3	68.8	68.8
qtd_sagt	(Çetinoğlu and Çöltekin, 2019)	—	4,761	46.4	58.0	**60.9**	59.9	57.7
ro_nonstandard	(Mărănduc et al., 2016)	—	532,881	86.8	87.0	86.0	85.7	**87.1**
ro_rrt	(Barbu Mititelu et al., 2016)	—	185,113	88.3	**88.6**	88.3	88.2	88.5
ro_simonero	(Mitrofan et al., 2019)	—	116,857	**91.3**	91.0	91.2	91.0	91.0
ru_gsd	(McDonald et al., 2013)	—	74,906	87.4	88.9	89.2	89.2	**89.7**
ru_pud	(McDonald et al., 2013)	ru_syntagrus	0	86.8	88.5	**89.0**	86.9	87.4
ru_syntagrus	(Droganova et al., 2018)	—	870,479	**93.7**	93.0	88.9	92.0	93.5
ru_taiga	(Shavrina and Shapovalova, 2017)	—	43,557	77.9	78.7	79.6	**81.0**	80.1
sa_ufal	(Dwivedi and Easha, 2017)	hi_hdtb	0	14.2	15.5	16.2	14.4	**16.5**
sa_vedic	(Hellwig et al., 2020)	—	17,445	54.9	57.9	**60.0**	57.5	57.8
sk_snk	(Zeman, 2017)	—	80,575	92.3	**94.3**	93.7	93.1	94.2
sl_ssj	(Dobrovoljc et al., 2017)	—	112,530	**93.4**	93.2	93.1	93.0	93.0
sl_sst	(Dobrovoljc and Nivre, 2016)	—	19,473	69.4	73.6	**74.7**	73.9	73.5
sme_giella	(Tyers and Sheyanova, 2017)	—	16,835	61.3	65.3	**68.5**	64.5	65.5
sms_giellagas	(Rueter and Partanen, 2019)	id_gsd	0	7.8	**14.9**	14.6	11.7	14.8
soj_aha	(Mojiri et al., 2020)	fa_perdt	0	27.9	37.6	27.3	32.1	**39.4**
sq_tsa	(Toska et al., 2020)	ga_idt	0	52.1	62.8	**64.0**	51.2	62.6
sr_set	(Samardžić et al., 2017)	—	74,259	91.9	91.4	91.9	92.4	**92.5**
sv_lines	(Ahrenberg, 2015)	—	55,451	86.5	**88.3**	88.1	88.2	88.2
sv_pud	(McDonald et al., 2013)	sv_lines	0	83.8	**86.9**	86.9	85.8	86.7

						+smoothing		
dataset	citation	proxy	size	self	conc.	conc.	sepDec	dataEmb
sv_talbanken	(McDonald et al., 2013)	—	66,645	89.1	89.8	89.7	**90.1**	89.7
swl_sslc	(Östling et al., 2017)	—	644	26.2	26.1	**37.7**	29.4	26.8
ta_mwtt	(Sarveswaran and Dias, 2020)	ta_ttb	0	65.4	**70.0**	66.1	67.1	69.9
ta_ttb	(Ramasamy and Žabokrtský, 2012)	—	5,734	40.8	44.7	44.7	**44.9**	44.3
te_mtg	(Rama and Vajjala, 2017)	—	5,082	82.8	84.2	84.5	**85.7**	84.7
th_pud	(McDonald et al., 2013)	en_ewt	0	**28.2**	25.7	25.4	22.2	26.2
tl_trg	(Samson and Cöltekin, 2020)	en_singpar	0	**34.8**	32.9	29.9	25.0	32.4
tl_ugnayan	(Aquino et al., 2020)	en_singpar	0	**28.4**	24.9	25.0	19.3	27.4
tpn_tudet	(Gerardi, 2020)	cs_pdt	0	**9.7**	5.1	4.2	6.5	3.2
tr_boun	(Türk et al., 2020)	—	97,257	69.6	68.8	67.1	69.9	**70.0**
tr_gb	(Cöltekin, 2015)	tr_boun	0	66.3	64.8	64.1	66.1	**66.6**
tr_imst	(Sulubacak et al., 2016)	—	36,822	62.5	59.1	61.2	**64.2**	63.8
tr_pud	(McDonald et al., 2013)	tr_boun	0	61.4	60.7	59.3	61.2	**61.6**
ug_udt	(Eli et al., 2016)	—	19,262	48.5	**50.3**	50.1	49.7	50.2
uk_iu	(Kotsyba et al., 2018)	—	92,355	88.0	90.2	89.7	89.6	**90.3**
ur_udtb	(Bhat et al., 2016)	—	108,690	81.6	82.4	82.3	82.2	**82.8**
vi_vtb	(Nguyen et al., 2009)	—	20,285	**66.1**	65.3	65.3	65.7	65.4
wbp_ufal	(Shopen, 2018)	id_gsd	0	5.5	6.8	**8.7**	7.6	8.0
wo_wtb	(Dione, 2019)	—	22,817	67.6	68.5	**72.6**	71.4	68.4
yo_ytb	(Ishola and Zeman, 2020)	ga_idt	0	16.0	17.2	14.4	12.7	**18.1**
yue_hk	(Wong et al., 2017)	zh_gsd	0	31.8	32.4	32.5	31.7	**32.7**
zh_cfl	(Lee et al., 2017)	zh_gsdsimp	0	47.4	**48.1**	47.6	46.9	47.9
zh_gsd	(Shen et al., 2016)	—	98,616	**85.9**	84.2	84.4	84.3	84.0
zh_gsdsimp	(Qi and Yasuoka, 2019)	—	98,616	**85.8**	84.1	84.5	84.3	84.2
zh_hk	(Wong et al., 2017)	zh_gsd	0	52.1	**53.7**	53.5	52.9	53.6
zh_pud	(McDonald et al., 2013)	zh_gsd	0	62.1	62.2	62.0	61.7	**62.3**
de_tweede	(Rehbein et al., 2019)	—	5,752	68.2	76.9	77.6	**79.6**	77.7
en_aae	(Blodgett et al., 2018)	en_ewt	0	51.5	55.1	55.9	**56.5**	56.1
en_convbank	(Davidson et al., 2019)	—	5,057	69.1	71.4	70.4	71.2	**71.9**
en_esl	(Berzak et al., 2016)	—	78,541	92.0	91.4	91.3	**92.1**	91.7
en_gumreddit	(Behzad and Zeldes, 2020)	—	10,831	75.9	84.9	84.8	**86.5**	85.5
en_monoise	(van der Goot and van Noord, 2018)	en_ewt	0	55.6	64.7	64.5	62.4	**64.7**
en_singpar	(Wang et al., 2019)	—	27,368	80.3	79.0	78.5	**82.2**	79.4
en_tweebank2	(Liu et al., 2018)	—	24,753	80.5	81.7	82.4	**82.6**	81.6
fr_extremeugc	(Martínez Alonso et al., 2016)	fr_gsd	0	56.2	55.7	56.6	**58.0**	54.4
fr_ftb	(Abeillé et al., 2000)	—	442,228	**83.1**	82.2	81.6	82.9	82.8
qfn_fame	(Braggaar and van der Goot, 2021)	nl_alpino	0	**54.0**	43.2	42.6	43.8	43.4
qhe_hiencs	(Bhat et al., 2018)	—	20,203	62.8	62.4	**65.5**	64.0	62.0

Table 6: LAS scores from official conll2018 script on test splits of all UD datasets we could obtain, averaged over 3 random seeds. Size refers to number of sentences in the training split. Results for single dataset trained models, and our 4 multi-task strategies. The last 12 rows contain datasets that are either available without words on the official Universal Dependencies website or are not officialy submitted.

SCoT: Sense Clustering over Time – a tool for analysing lexical change

Christian Haase[†], **Saba Anwar**[†], **Seid Muhie Yimam**[†], **Alexander Friedrich**[⋆], **Chris Biemann**[†]
[†] Language Technology group, Universität Hamburg, Germany
[⋆] Institute for Philosophy, TU Darmstadt, Germany
{haase,anwar,yimam,biemann}@informatik.uni-hamburg.de
friedrich@phil.tu-darmstadt.de

Abstract

We present Sense Clustering over Time (SCoT), a novel network-based tool for analysing lexical change. SCoT represents the meanings of a word as clusters of similar words. It visualises their formation, change, and demise. There are two main approaches to the exploration of dynamic networks: the discrete one compares a series of clustered graphs from separate points in time. The continuous one analyses the changes of one dynamic network over a time-span. SCoT offers a new hybrid solution. First, it aggregates time-stamped documents into intervals and calculates one sense graph per discrete interval. Then, it merges the static graphs to a new type of dynamic semantic neighbourhood graph over time. The resulting sense clusters offer uniquely detailed insights into lexical change over continuous intervals with model transparency and provenance. SCoT has been successfully used in a European study on the changing meaning of 'crisis'.

1 Introduction

Most real-world networks change over time. So do dynamic networks of word similarities that can be used to infer the meanings of a word. The noun 'crisis', for example, used to be strongly linked to the religious word 'doom' in English-language books in the early modern period. However, in the modern age 'crisis' has become more closely associated with terms denoting economic problems such as 'unemployment', 'depression' or 'inflation' (Biemann et al., 2020).

In the recent decade, the interest in dynamic networks has increased. (Rosetti and Cazabet, 2018). This has also stimulated new graph-based approaches to analysing vocabulary change (Mitra et al., 2015; Riedl et al., 2014). Such research is a key interest of linguists (Tahmasebi et al., 2018; Nulty, 2017) and scholars in the humanities (Koselleck, 1989; Mueller and Schmieder, 2016; Friedrich and Biemann, 2016).

Traditionally, scholars have determined such changes through close reading. However, the growing availability of ever larger digital corpora (Goldberg and Orwant, 2013) and the increasing speed of sense changes in social media (Stilo and Velardi, 2017) have boosted the significance of new research (Nulty, 2017).

Of particular importance in the research on lexical change is the unsupervised approach of word sense induction (WSI). WSI enables the development of data-driven hypotheses. The approach induces meaning from the bottom upwards and can be used with a diachronic angle. Several implementations for diachronic WSI exist (Tahmasebi et al., 2018). While many of them represent word meaning by dense vector embeddings, sparse models with network representations still play an important role. The use of sparse, human-readable models enables a better interpretation of meaning hypotheses by linguists and other researchers.

There are two main approaches to implement diachronic network-based WSI. Discrete approaches compare several networks that relate to discrete points in time. Continuous approaches analyse when specific nodes, edges or clusters appear in a single dynamic network that changes continuously over time (Rosetti and Cazabet, 2018).

Many applications in the field of diachronic network-based WSI fall into the discrete category. Mitra et al. (2015), for example, reduce the number of measuring points to single intervals, build one graph per discrete interval, cluster it and track the resulting sense clusters over intervals. While this approach is considered as less complex than the continuous one (Rosetti and Cazabet, 2018), it brings up complexity problems of its own. The clustering of graphs can namely lead to different

Proceedings of the 16th Conference of the European Chapter of the Association for Computational Linguistics: System Demonstrations, pages 198–204
April 19 - 23, 2021. ©2021 Association for Computational Linguistics

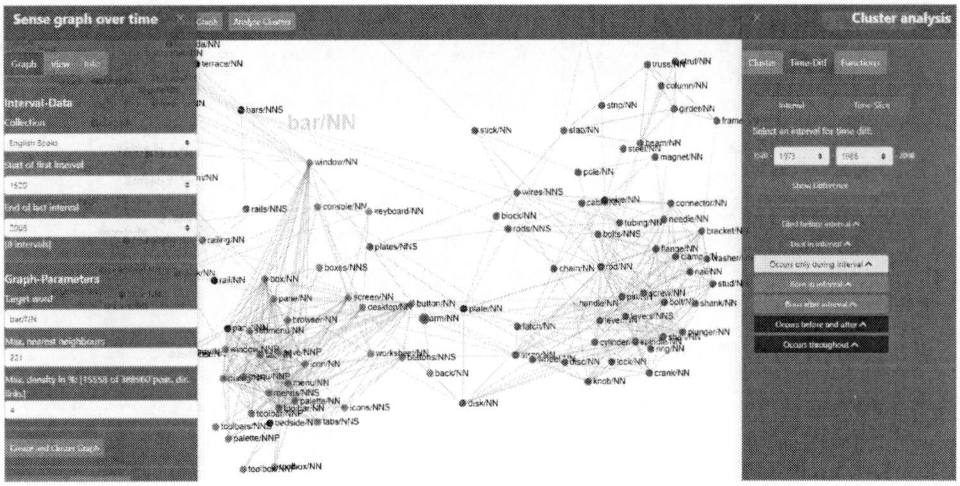

Figure 1: Analysis of the sense shifts of 'bar/NN' in Google Books (Goldberg and Orwant, 2013) with SCoT: the clusters of the neighbourhood graph over time show that the sense "a rigid piece of metal used as a fastening or obstruction" [top right] loses traction, while the sense "computer-menu" [bottom left] gains significance. The coloring is relative to the interval "1973-1986". Red indicates the disappearance of a node before 1986. Green indicates the emergence of a node after 1986.

solutions. Thus, the number of clustering combinations in a time-series of sense graphs can grow unpredictably. Another issue is the identification of corresponding clusters across time points.

Continuous representations are more fine-grained, but can lead to other issues. Since the clustering in such scenarios is mostly done in an incremental way, problems of costly reclusterings or very large clusters can emerge.

The application Sense Clustering over Time (SCoT) offers a new hybrid approach to network-based WSI that reduces complexity. SCoT works in two steps. In a first, 'discrete' step, the time-stamped documents are aggregated into intervals. Static graphs are built per interval. Then SCoT merges the static graphs to a new type of dynamic neighbourhood graph over time (NGoT). The encoded time-based information from the underlying continuous series of graphs enables a time-coloring of the sense clusters.

Haase (2020) has shown that there are different approaches to constructing such semantic NGoTs. The best known method for creating such a dynamic network consists of the merging of a series of equally-sized graphs from each interval, but it is also possible to aggregate nodes and links in different ways. These approaches exhibit different strengths and are explained in more detail below. Figure 1 shows how such a NGoT looks like. The graph shows sense clusters for the target word *bar*. It shows that words such as "button", "desktop" and "icon" became increasingly similar to each other and to the target *bar* in the 1990s, thereby forming the new sense of 'computer-menu'.

SCoT can be used for various tasks such as linguistic studies of polysemic words or research into the history of concepts, but also offers a general and new solution to the analysis of dynamic networks with the neighbourhood graph over time.

2 System description

The system enables an analysis of the lexical change of words in an interactive web-interface based on metrics calculated from large time-sliced corpora. This requires a division of the system into a web-front-end and a back-end that accesses the databases with the similarity scores. In addition, the system offers the user additional information on the syntagmatic features that have been used to calculate the similarity scores.

2.1 Computing distributional thesauri for time-sliced corpora

The calculation of the similarity scores that inform the graph is steeped in the de Saussurian notion of paradigms and syntagmatic contexts as implemented in JoBimText (Biemann and Riedl, 2013). The nodes represent the paradigms. The more syn-

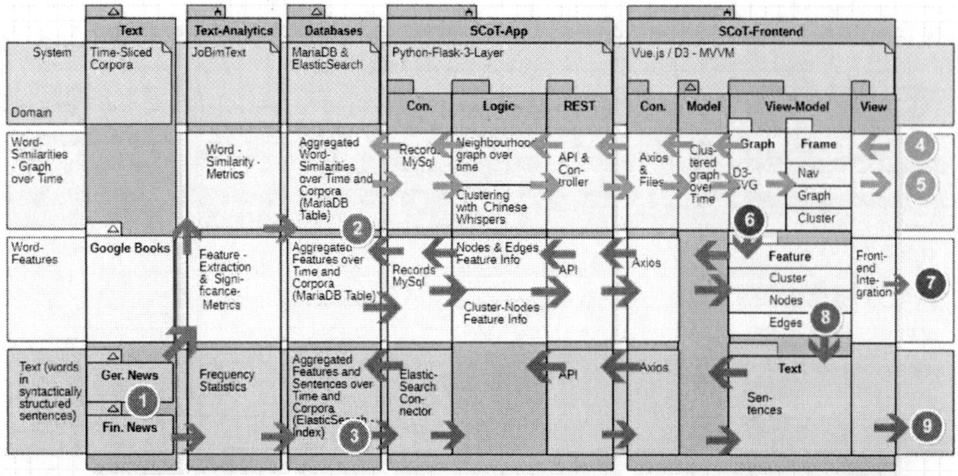

Figure 2: The SCoT-system consists of multiple layers and domain-specific components relating to the similarity graph (green), the underlying syntagmatic features (yellow) and the corpus (red). The system's four key processes are highlighted with numbers: the preprocessing (1-3), the graph-analysis (4-5), the feature-analysis (6-7) and the querying of example sentences for research (8-9). Arrows indicate the data-flow direction.

tagmatic contexts two paradigms share, the more similar they are (Miller and Charles, 1991). The contexts and words are extracted from the sentences of documents.

The raw texts, the syntagmatic features and the network representation of the relations between the paradigms require very different processing steps. They are thus handled by different groups of components of the SCoT application that constitute so-called sub-domains. They have been color-coded in Figure 2.

The current online demonstration version of SCoT uses three corpora. These include a large dataset of syntactic n-grams from Google Books (Goldberg and Orwant, 2013), a corpus of Finnish magazines and newspaper articles (University of Helsinki, 2017), and a corpus of German newspapers articles as described by (Biemann et al., 2007; Benikova et al., 2014). These corpora have been sliced into 7 to 9 time-based intervals which roughly contain the same amount of data.

The semantic similarity of words can be computed with different methods. For SCoT, we have opted for distributional thesauri (DT) due to their flexibility. They can be based upon different types of context features such as word n-grams, part-of-speech n-grams and syntactic dependencies. We have used syntactic dependencies.

We have calculated the DTs with the software JoBimText (Biemann and Riedl, 2013). It uses the Lexicographer's Mutual Information (LMI) to rank words and their context features. We have limited the computation to the top ranked 1000 features.

We have stored the scores in one SQL-database per corpus. Each database includes three tables: a table of intervals, a table of word pairs with their similarity scores and references to the intervals in which they occurred, and a table of words and their features with interval information. In addition, we have stored example sentences in an ElasticSearch server. This calculation and storage is highlighted with the numbers 1, 2 and 3 in Figure 2.

2.2 Creating the neighbourhood-graph over time

The system offers the user the possibility to select a target word and to enter parameters for building the NGoT. This is highlighted as number 4 in Figure 2. The user can select between three different types of NGoTs. These have repercussions for the resulting sense clusters (Haase, 2020). We have implemented the interval-, the dynamic and a mixed global/dynamic approach. The user can fine-tune them with three parameters: the number of intervals i, the number of nearest neighbour nodes n and the density d.

The interval-approach creates one static graph with n words and the density d per interval and then merges these. This results in a dynamically sized graph, which is often larger than a static single interval graph. This creates a very clear distinction between clusters and nodes that occur frequently over time and those that do not. The approach is optimal for getting an analytical overview of sense-shifts. We, thus, use it as a starting point for the analysis.

The dynamic approach fixes the number of unique words n and the density d of the resulting graph and expands the underlying data-points of the static graphs across intervals. This usually only creates partial graphs per interval. Since the dynamic approach fixes the number of links and nodes of the resulting graph it is better suited for comparisons across different graphs than the interval-approach.

The global approach fixes the number of static single word-nodes and edges in total across all intervals based on maximal values. The significance of the approach lies in the ability to tweak the number of single edges, which has an effect on the number of resulting clusters. For ease of use, we have implemented it as a mixed approach: the nodes are allocated according the dynamic approach. The edges can be tweaked globally.

The number of the edges in relation to the nodes is the key to creating a useful graph for clustering and the analysis of lexical change. In order to enhance the dynamic allocation of edges over time, we have relaxed the condition that each node in the resulting graph has a fixed limit of connected edges. This is the standard implementation in many neighbourhood graphs. In sum, SCoT offers a new type of neighbourhood graph that is different to all known implementations of neighbourhood or so-called ego graphs (Mitra et al., 2015).

The variants are implemented with a similar pattern: each algorithm first searches for the nodes and then for the edges. Then, the algorithm merges those nodes and edges that refer to the same words in different intervals. It encodes the time-based scores in the nodes and edges.

2.3 Sense clustering

The advantage of NGoTs is that they need to be clustered only once. For this, we use the Chinese Whispers algorithm (Biemann, 2006). The key characteristics of the algorithm are that it is non-deterministic, has a linear time-complexity and runs with a fixed number of iterations that result in a stable partition of the graph. We set the number of iterations to 15 in order to increase the chances of the algorithm of reaching a stable plateau. However, there may be more than one stable solution. We have thus implemented the possibility to recluster the graph in order to see whether multiple solutions exist. If one wants to break a tie, it is recommended to slightly reduce the density of the graph and to cluster again. This should remove less significant edges and thus provide a more nuanced clustering.

2.4 Displaying the sense clusters over time

During the creation process of the NGoT, the interval information is encoded in the nodes and edges. This information is used for the subsequent coloring of the nodes in the time-difference analysis in the front-end.

The front-end is based on a modern Model-View-View-Model (MVVM) framework, namely Vue. In MVVM frameworks, the main view of the web-page is rendered by several dynamic model-view components. SCoT has four main components. They render the navigation and side-bars, display the graph, show additional syntagmatic features and exhibit exemplary sentences. The graph-component uses the D3.js library to render the graph. In addition, the front-end includes a connection-layer that communicates with the RESTful SCoT API of the back-end.

2.5 Diachronic analysis with time-colouring

Since the sense clusters over time are the most important feature of SCoT and provide the starting point for the research, they are displayed by default when the graph has been created. In the cluster-view, the clusters are ordered by size.

The tool offers a wide range of advanced functions to analyse the sense clusters. One can use a hovering function over nodes and links to display the development of similarity scores over time for each node and edge. Furthermore, network metrics such as the betweenness centrality can be used to enlarge central nodes. Such central nodes play a significant role as centres of the clusters and bridges between clusters. Nodes between clusters, which can exhibit ambivalence, can also be highlighted.

Among the advanced functions, the time-difference mode is particularly noteworthy. The application offers two functions for the time-diff mode. The first color-codes the nodes in the sense clusters in relation to their occurrence to a set interval. Nodes can disappear before the interval, emerge in the interval or occur after the interval. They can also be stable. The second function offers a slider that

highlights all nodes that occur per time-interval (Kempfert et al., 2020).
Furthermore, the front-end offers the opportunity to change several view-parameters. These include charge strength, link distance, and the zoom-factor. It is also possible to drag the graph and individual nodes, add name labels to the clusters and manually change cluster assignments.

2.6 Model transparency

A key aim of SCoT is to enable a transparent interpretation of meaning hypotheses. Therefore, SCoT offers functions to drill into the syntagmatic features utilized in the representation of word meaning here. These are available in a count-based sparse model in the form of the DTs from JoBimText (Biemann and Riedl, 2013). This analysis can be triggered by clicking on a node or an edge. This has been labelled as step 6 in Figure 2. It results in the display syntagmatic contexts per selected word-nodes, including whole clusters, as ranked by LMI. E.g., for the 'rod/stick' sense of 'bar' in Google books, the most salient syntagmatic contexts are "-nn/platinum/NN, -dep/stumbling/NN, -dep/altar/JJ, -dep/electro/NN, -nn/vertebral/NN, -in_pobj/link/NN, -nn/crank/NN, -on_pobj/leaning/VBG, and_conj/key/NN", whereas the same query for the 'menu bar/button' sense yields "-nn/dialog/NN, -nn/edit/NNP, nn/publishing/NN, -nn/options/NNPS, -on_pobj/click/NN, -dobj/clicking/VBG, -on_pobj/button/NN, -nn/cardboard/NN, dep/sill/NN".
The displayed pairs of syntagmatic features and paradigms can serve as a starting point for further analyses: one can retrieve example sentences that include the paradigm and the selected syntagmatic context. This has been labelled as step 8 and 9 in Figure 2.

3 Use case: sense shifts of "crisis"

SCoT can be used in various research fields. Conceptual history is of particular relevance. It is used to produce lexicons of 'basic concepts' and thus encompasses aspects of linguistics and historical research.
Mueller and Schmieder (2016); Friedrich and Biemann (2016) have shown that the growing research field is in need of new unsupervised methods in order to deal with newly available large digital corpora. The research that was established by Koselleck places a particular emphasis on concepts that have changed in the transition to the modern age between 1750 and 1850. (Olsen, 2012)
Within this context, the noun 'crisis' takes centre-stage as the contemporaries perceived the transition into the modern age as a time of different crises. The analysis of the changing meanings of the noun is thus an ideal test case for the applicability of the tool in this interdisciplinary field.

3.1 The 'economic turn' and the changing concept of 'crisis'

The first step in most text-based research projects is the choice of the corpus. We have chosen English Google Books as a suitable corpus.
We start the analysis with a generalized overview over all eight intervals with the graph-type-mode 'interval'. We set the parameters n=100 and d=20 and render the graph. This results in a NGoT with 221 nodes. SCoT analyses three sense clusters over time.
After we have established the overview, we go into the time-diff mode. From the ongoing research, the prominent hypothesis about the changing meaning of 'crisis' between 1750 and 1850 has emerged. We test this hypothesis. We switch to the time-diff mode and color the nodes in relation to the interval 1908-1953. The resulting graph shows that one full sense cluster consists only of 'red' nodes that all disappeared in the first interval. We have thus found a candidate for a first sense shift.
We now follow up the analysis with a more specific look at the nodes. We find that the pre-modern sense of religious "doom" and "juncture of time" was replaced by modern political and economic senses of crisis centred on terms such as 'election', 'law' or 'class'. We then look at individual nodes to deepen the analysis. Each node in the clusters provides an important aspect of the development. The node 'class', for example, relates to Marxist philosophy that viewed the cyclic nature of capitalist 'crises' as the defining characteristic of the modern age.
Subsequently, we want to find out which changes occurred within the modern political and economic clusters in the subsequent intervals. With the help of the time-slider-mode and the individual graphs that are depicted in Figure 2, we can show that that the sense transformation of the term 'crisis' continued after the breakthrough of the modern age. An ever growing cluster with economic words can be observed. Terms, such as 'depression', 'boom', 'inflation' and 'unemployment' dominate the cluster,

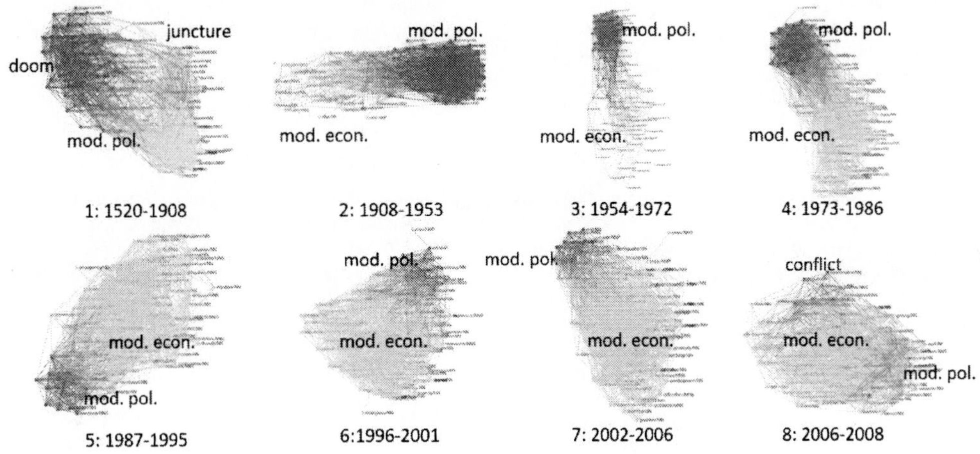

Figure 3: Analysis of sense-shifts of crisis/NN: The neighbourhood graph merges graphs from each interval. The underlying time-series shows that "crisis/NN" developed a modern political and an economic sense with an increasing dominance of economics between 1520 and 2008. Parameters: n=100, d=30, i=1, corpus: Google Books (English).

increasingly so after the 1950s, and in particular after the oil crisis in the 1970s.

This tallies with the research on the so-called "economic turn" in the 1950s and beyond. The argument by economic historians such as Nützenadel is that the cornerstone of the Western postwar-order was the diffusion of new economic and democratic thought, centred on the so-called consensus liberalism that was seen as the antidote to the 'crisis' of the great depression and the following political chaos. (Haase and Schildt, 2007) SCoT advances these findings by adding new details to them in a transparent and scientific manner.

The results of SCoT always need to be contextualised within the limits of the underlying corpus. Google Books contains primary and secondary material and has a strong "thematic" orientation. Since Google Books contains many books from libraries that serve universities, we need to test whether the 'economic turn' of the term 'crisis' has shown up so dramatically in the data due to the underlying basis of vast specialist economic literature stored in university libraries.

In order to check against the possible bias, we use a second corpus, namely German web-news. We find in this corpus a similar development and conclude that the 'economic turn' can be regarded as a wider phenomenon in Western countries after the 1950s. We have arrived at this analysis by the research steps of generalisation, specialisation and comparison that are well supported by SCoT.

4 Conclusion and future directions

This article describes SCoT, a new tool for the analysis of the changes of sense clusters in dynamic networks. SCoT reduces the complexity of this task through interval-aggregation and neighbourhood graphs over time. The dynamic network retains the time-based information. This enables advanced analyses that can be well visualised. The usage of a sparse approach to distributional semantic modeling provides model transparency and provenance. We have demonstrated the applicability of the solution in the domain of lexical and conceptual change. However, the general nature of the application make it transferable to other domains that use dynamic networks for analysis.

Future directions in the development of SCoT lie in the further refinement of neighbourhood graphs over time, the broadening of the usage of SCoT in various domains, including conceptual change, as well the research on the wider implications of the application for diachronic distributional semantics. ScoT is available open source under the MIT license[1] and as an online demo[2]. A video demonstrating many of the functionalities can be found at `https://youtu.be/SbmfA4hKjvg`.

[1] `https://github.com/uhh-lt/SCoT`

[2] `http://ltdemos.informatik.uni-hamburg.de/scot/`

References

Darina Benikova, Uli Fahrer, Alexander Gabriel, Manuel Kaufmann, Seid Muhie Yimam, Tatiana von Landesberger, and Chris Biemann. 2014. Network of the day: Aggregating and visualizing entity networks from online sources. In *Proceedings of the 12th Conference on Natural Language Processing, KONVENS*, pages 48–52, Hildesheim, Germany.

Chris Biemann. 2006. Chinese whispers - an efficient graph clustering algorithm and its application to natural language processing problems. In *Proceedings of TextGraphs: the First Workshop on Graph Based Methods for Natural Language Processing*, pages 73–80, New York City.

Chris Biemann, Christian Haase, Alexander Friedrich, and Antero Holmila. 2020. Sense induction of crisis/Krise/kriisi in English, German and Finnish text corpora with the Sense Clustering over Time (SCoT) tool: Contribution to the workshop "Crisis - a digital humanities perspective", University of Jyväskylä, Finland.

Chris Biemann, Gerhard Heyer, Uwe Quasthoff, and Matthias Richter. 2007. The Leipzig Corpora Collection: Monolingual corpora of standard size. In *Proceedings of Corpus Linguistics*, Birmingham, UK.

Chris Biemann and Martin Riedl. 2013. Text: Now in 2D! a framework for lexical expansion with contextual similarity. *Journal of Language Modelling*, 1(1):55–95.

Alexander Friedrich and Chris Biemann. 2016. Digitale Begriffsgeschichte? Methodologische Überlegungen und exemplarische Versuche am Beispiel moderner Netzsemantik". *Forum für interdisziplinäre Begriffsgeschichte*, 5(2):78–96.

Yoav Goldberg and Jon Orwant. 2013. A dataset of syntactic-ngrams over time from a very large corpus of English books. In *Second Joint Conference on Lexical and Computational Semantics (*SEM), Volume 1: Proceedings of the Main Conference and the Shared Task: Semantic Textual Similarity*, pages 241–247, Atlanta, Georgia, USA.

Christian Haase. 2020. Semantisches Clustern von Hashtags in Zeitintervallen. Master-Arbeit, Fachbereich Informatik, FernUniversität Hagen.

Christian Haase and Axel Schildt, editors. 2007. *Die Zeit und die Bonner Republik: Eine meinungsbildende Wochenzeitung zwischen Wiederbewaffnung und Wiedervereinigung*. Wallstein.

Inga Kempfert, Saba Anwar, Alexander Friedrich, and Chris Biemann. 2020. Digital History of Concepts: Sense Clustering over Time [42. Jahrestagung der Deutschen Gesellschaft für Sprachwissenschaft (DGfS), Universität Hamburg, 4.-6. März 2020.].

Reinhart Koselleck. 1989. Linguistic change and the history of events. *The Journal of Modern History*, 64:650–666.

George A. Miller and Walter G. Charles. 1991. Contextual correlates of semantic similarity. *Language and Cognitive Processes*, 6(1):1–28.

Sunny Mitra, Ritwik Mitra, Suman Maity, Martin Riedl, Chris Biemann, Pawan Goyal, and Animesh Mukerjee. 2015. An automatic approach to identify word sense changes in text media across timescales. *Natural Language Engineering*, 21(5):773–798.

Ernst Mueller and Falko Schmieder. 2016. *Begriffsgeschichte und historische Semantik*. Suhrkamp.

Paul Nulty. 2017. Semantic network analysis of contested political concepts. In *International Conference on Computational Semantics (IWCS 2017)*, Montpellier, France.

Niklas Olsen. 2012. *History in the plural: an introduction to the work of Reinhart Koselleck*. Berghahn.

Martin Riedl, Richard Steuer, and Chris Biemann. 2014. Distributed distributional similarities of Google Books over the centuries. In *Proceedings of the Ninth International Conference on Language Resources and Evaluation (LREC'14)*, pages 1401–1405, Reykjavik, Iceland.

Giulio Rosetti and Remy Cazabet. 2018. Community discovery in dynamic networks: A survey. *ACM Comput. Surv.*, 51(2):1–37.

Giovanni Stilo and Paola Velardi. 2017. Hashtag Sense Clustering Based on Temporal Similarity. *Computational Linguistics*, 43(1):181–200.

Nina Tahmasebi, Lars Borin, and Adam Jatowt. 2018. Survey of computational approaches to lexical semantic change. *CoRR abs/1811.06278*.

University of Helsinki. 2017. Corpus of Finnish Magazines and Newspapers from the 1990s and 2000s, Downloadable Version 2, http://urn.fi/urn:nbn:fi:lb-2017091902.

GCM: A Toolkit for Generating Synthetic Code-mixed Text

Mohd Sanad Zaki Rizvi **Anirudh Srinivasan** **Tanuja Ganu**
Monojit Choudhury **Sunayana Sitaram**

Microsoft Research India
{v-mori, t-ansrin, tanuja.ganu, monojitc, sunayana.sitaram}@microsoft.com

Abstract

Code-mixing is common in multilingual communities around the world, and processing it is challenging due to the lack of labeled and unlabeled data. We describe a tool that can automatically generate code-mixed data given parallel data in two languages. We implement two linguistic theories of code-mixing, the Equivalence Constraint theory and the Matrix Language theory to generate all possible code-mixed sentences in the language-pair, followed by sampling of the generated data to generate natural code-mixed sentences. The toolkit provides three modes: a batch mode, an interactive library mode and a web-interface to address the needs of researchers, linguists and language experts. The toolkit can be used to generate unlabeled text data for pre-trained models, as well as visualize linguistic theories of code-mixing. We plan to release the toolkit as open source and extend it by adding more implementations of linguistic theories, visualization techniques and better sampling techniques. We expect that the release of this toolkit will help facilitate more research in code-mixing in diverse language pairs. [1 2]

1 Introduction

Code-mixing, which is the alternation between two or more languages in a single conversation or utterance is prevalent in multilingual communities all over the world. Processing code-mixed language is challenging due to the lack of labeled as well as unlabeled data available for training NLP models. Since code-mixing is a spoken language phenomenon, it is more likely to occur in informal written text, such as social media and chat data. Such data may not as easily available as monolingual data for building models, and may also exhibit other issues such as cross-transcription and non-standard spellings.

To alleviate this problem and train language models that can use unlabeled data for pre-training, we see the generation of synthetic code-mixed data as a promising direction. Various linguistic theories have been proposed that can determine how languages are mixed together, and in prior work we presented the first computational implementation (Bhat et al., 2016) of the Matrix-language (Myers-Scotton, 1993) and Equivalence Constraint theories (Poplack, 1980). We also showed that generating synthetic data using our computational implementations improved word embeddings leading to better downstream performance on sentiment analysis and POS tagging (Pratapa et al., 2018b), as well as RNN language models (Pratapa et al., 2018a). The multilingual BERT (Devlin et al., 2019) model fine-tuned with synthetic code-mixed data outperformed all prior techniques on the GLUECoS benchmark (Khanuja et al., 2020) for code-switching, which spans 11 NLP tasks in two language pairs. The approach of generating synthetic code-mixed data has gained traction following our work, with other approaches including using Generative Adversarial Networks (Chang et al., 2019), an encoder-decoder framework with transfer learning (Gupta et al., 2020), using parallel data with a small amount of real code-mixed data to learn code-mixing patterns (Winata et al., 2019) and a novel two-level variational autoencoder approach (Samanta et al., 2019).

In this work, we present a tool GCM that can automatically generate synthetic code-mixed data given parallel data or a Machine Translation system between the languages that are being mixed. Our tool is intended for use by NLP practitioners who would like to generate training data to train models that can handle code-mixing, as well as linguists and language experts who would like to visualize how code-mixing occurs between languages given

[1]Screencast: `https://aka.ms/eacl21gcmdemo`
[2]Code: `https://aka.ms/eacl21gcmcode`

Proceedings of the 16th Conference of the European Chapter of the Association for Computational Linguistics: System Demonstrations, pages 205–211
April 19 - 23, 2021.

different linguistic theories. The toolkit provides three modes - a batch mode, that can run the data generation pipeline on servers, an interactive mode, that can be used for quick prototyping as well as a web interface that can be used to visualize code-mixed sentence generation. The GCM tool will be released as open source and we plan to improve it by adding more implementations of linguistic theories, visualization techniques and better algorithms for sampling. We expect that the release of this toolkit will spur research in code-mixing in diverse language pairs and enable many NLP applications that would not be possible to build due to the lack of code-mixed data.

2 Method

In this section we discuss the linguistic theories that we implement in the tool and the pipeline we use for generating code-mixed (hereafter referred to as CM) sentences.

2.1 Linguistic theories

Our tool currently contains implementations of two two linguistic theories for generating valid CM text: Equivalence Constraint Theory (Poplack, 1980) and Matrix Language Theory (Myers-Scotton, 1993).

The **Equivalence Constraint Theory** states that intra-sentential code-mixing can only occur at places where the surface structures of two languages map onto each other, thereby, implicitly following the grammatical rules of both the languages. The **Matrix Language Theory** deals with code-mixing by introducing the concept of "Matrix Language" or the base language into which pockets of the "Embedded Language" or second language are introduced in such a way that the former sets the grammatical structure of the sentence while the later "switches-in" at grammatically correct points of the sentence.

1E. With this the prescribed fee will be sent.
1H. इसके साथ निर्धारित शुल्क भेजा जाएगा।
Transliterated. iske saath nirdhaarith shulkh bheja jayega.

1CM. इसके साथ prescribed fee भेजा जाएगा।
Transliterated. iske saath prescribed fee bheja jayega.

2E. My husband is working on his master's degree.
1S. Mi marido está trabajando en su maestría.
2CM. Mi marido está working on his master's degree.

Figure 1: (a) Input sentences for Hindi-English (1E, 1H) and Spanish-English (2E, 1S) and (b) GCM output Code-Mixed sentences for Hindi-English (1CM) and Spanish-English (2CM).

Figure 1 shows example source sentences in Hindi, English and Spanish and their CM counterparts generated by the EC theory. Figures 2 and 3 show the parse trees of all the sentences above, illustrating how the sentences are generated by the theory.

2.2 Code-mixed (CM) Text Generation Process

The generation process is a sequential process (Figure 4), which requires parallel sentences in the two languages being mixed as input data. Three ma-

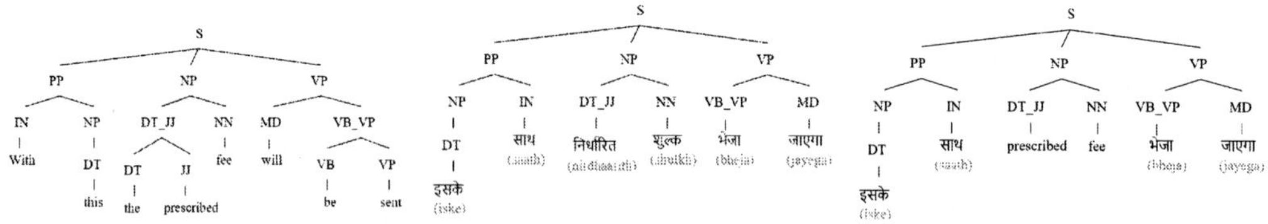

Figure 2: Parse-trees of (a) sentences [1E] and (b) [1H], and (c) of [1CM] according to the EC Theory

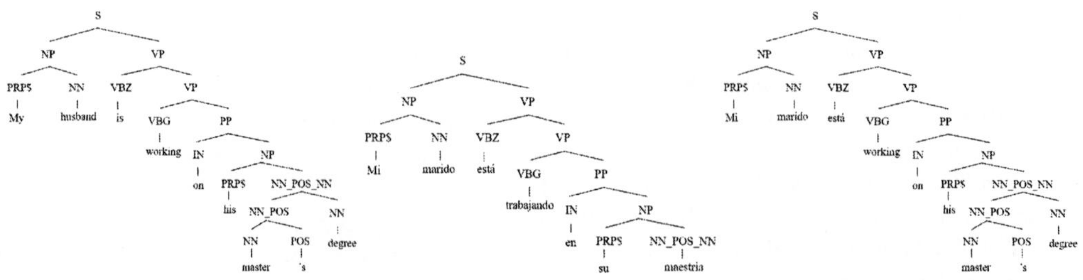

Figure 3: Parse-trees of (a) sentences [2E] and (b) [1S], and (c) of [2CM] according to the EC Theory

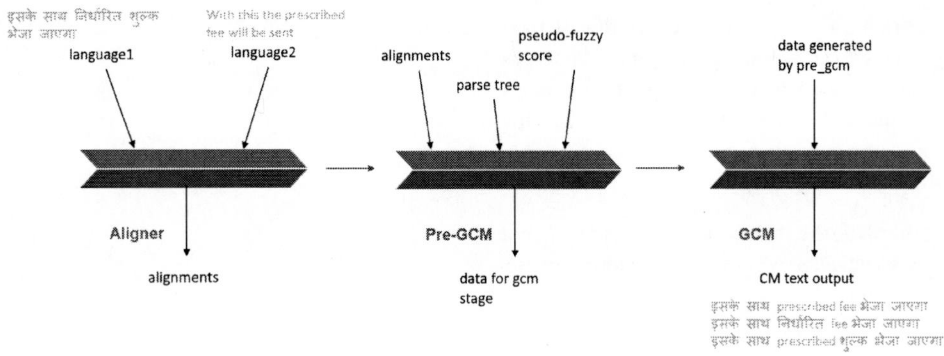

Figure 4: The CM Generation Process

jor components play a part in the process and the stages occur in the following order:

The first stage is the "Alignment stage". In this stage, the **Aligner** is used to generate word level alignments for input pair of sentences. We currently use "fast_align" (Dyer et al., 2013) which performs well compared to other aligners in terms of both speed and accuracy.

The second stage is the **Pre-GCM** stage which is responsible for pre-processing the input. This stage combines the aligner outputs along with constituent parse trees generated by the parser and "Pseudo Fuzzy-match Score" (Pratapa et al., 2018a) for each sentence pair to make one row of input data for the GCM stage. The **Parser** is used to generate a sentence level constituent parse tree for one of the source languages. Previously in (Pratapa et al., 2018a) we used the Stanford Parser (Klein and Manning, 2003) but we now also provide the option to use the Berkeley Neural Parser (Kitaev and Klein, 2018). This stage is also responsible for creating appropriate batches of data to be consumed by the next stage.

The final **GCM** stage, processes each batch of data, applying linguistic theories in order to generate CM sentences as output.

2.3 Sampling

Figure 5 shows some sentences generated by the EC theory for a pair of Hindi-English source sentences. Through manual observation and user studies, we find that the EC theory generates sentences that may be grammatically correct, but may not feel natural to bilingual speakers. In prior work we showed that sampling appropriately from the generated data is crucial. We experimented with various sampling techniques and showed that training an RNN Language Model with sampled synthetic data reduces the perplexity of the model by an amount which is equivalent to doubling the amount of real CM data available (Pratapa et al., 2018a). So, we add a sampling stage after the generation stage, for which we propose the following techniques.

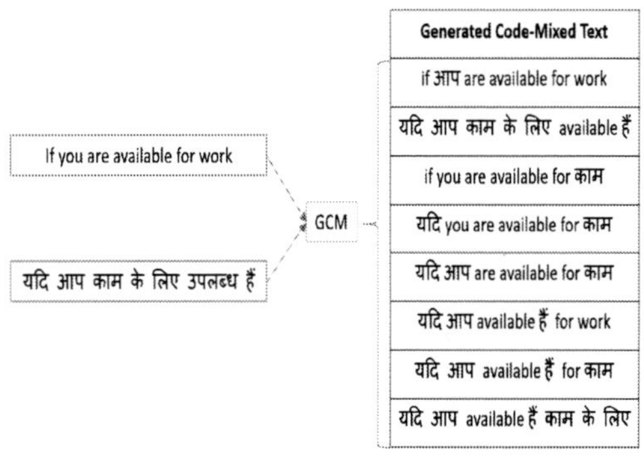

Figure 5: Need for Sampling: Not all generated CM sentences feel natural

- **Random**: For each parallel pair of input sentences, we arbitrarily pick a fixed number k of CM sentences from the generated corpus. The advantage of this method is that we are not dependent on having real CM data.
- **SPF-based**: The **Switch Point Fraction or SPF** is the number of switch points in a sentence divided by the total number of words in the sentence (Pratapa et al., 2018a). For each parallel pair of input sentences, we randomly pick k CM sentences such that the SPF distri-

bution of these is as close as possible to that of the real CM data. The benefit of this method is that we can generate a synthetic CM corpus that close to the real data distribution in terms of amount of switching, but this method imposes a requirement of having real CM data for the given language pair.

- **Linguistic Features-based**: Words do not get switched at random, and it would be useful to be able to learn patterns of switching from real CM data. For example, learning how nouns and verbs tend to get switched can create more realistic data. However, this method imposes additional requirements - in addition to real CM data, we also need POS taggers for CM data, which are not readily available.

Out of the above techniques, Random and SPF-based sampling are currently implemented in the system. In the future, we would like to add improved sampling techniques to the tool, since it is an important step to achieve high quality synthetic data.

3 System Overview

We provide three modes in the GCM tool: a batch mode, an interactive library mode and a web-interface to address the needs of NLP practitioners, researchers, linguists and language experts:

3.1 Batch Mode

This mode is primarily intended for those who want to generate CM data on servers given large parallel corpora of monolingual data. It operates via a configuration file that contains multiple options to customize CM text generation. We describe some of the options available in batch mode (Listing 1). The entire list of options can be found in the code documentation.

```
[GENERAL]
.
.
# choose which stages of the pipeline
    are going to be run; default: pregcm
    , gcm
stages_to_run =
# whether to run the pregcm and gcm
    stages parallely; default: 0 ; set
    to 1 to run parallely
parallel_run =

[ALIGNER]
.
.

[PREGCM]
.
# cut-off value for PFMS score
max_pfms =
# select the parser to be used from
    available parsers - stanford and
    benepar; default: benepar
parser =

[GCM]
.
# max number of sentences to generate
    per sentence; default: 5
k =

[OUTPUT]
# language tag at word level in each
    output code-mixed sentence
lid_ouput =
# visualize DFAs that were used to make
    generations
dfa_output =
# sampling technique to use - random or
    spf
sampling =
```

Listing 1: Options available in the configuration file in batch mode

In the `[GENERAL]` section, the option `stages_to_run` lets the user choose specific stages to be run on the data. When a large scale CM corpus is to be generated, it is useful to run the CM generator pipeline in parallel mode to speed up the process. The `parallel_run` options lets the user run the Pre-GCM and GCM stages asynchronously so that instead of waiting for all the data to be preprocessed, the GCM stage can start working on batch of data as and when ready.

The `max_pfms` option in `[PREGCM]` lets user select the "Pseudo Fuzzy-match Score" threshold for the input sentences. In order to prepare consistent input data, we perform back-translation as one of the steps. The Pseudo Fuzzy-match Score quantifies the quality of back-translation that directly impacts the quality of CM data generated, hence this feature is particularly important.

`parser` lets you choose between the Stanford Parser and Berkeley Natural Parser. The Stanford Parser contains support for parsing Arabic, Chinese, English, French, German and Spanish, while the Berkeley Natural Parser can parse English, Chinese, Arabic, German, Basque, French, Hebrew, Hungarian, Korean, Polish, Swedish. While we rely on one of these supported languages to be one of the two languages in the parallel corpus from which the CM text is generated, we generate the second parse tree using the alignments from the previous step. So, we can generate CM sentences in language pairs where one of the languages is supported by either of the two parsers.

The `k` option in `[GCM]` controls the maximum number of CM sentences to be generated per input sentence. Similarly, the `lid_output` and `dfa_output` options in the `[OUTPUT]` lets the user extract additional information in the form of word-level language tags and DFAs for each generated CM sentence. This can be used for debugging the CM generation process, since the user can see the language tags assigned to the generated CM sentence in case both languages are in the same script. The sampling option lets the user choose the kind of sampling technique they want for generating CM text: currently, the options available are Random or SPF based, as described earlier.

3.2 Library Mode

The library mode is a light weight interactive interface for a programmer to go back and forth with the output of various stages to adjust parameters. This mode was designed to be able to accommodate modules that the user may want to add to the pipeline to increase speed, accuracy and language coverage. The library is designed to be continuously extensible, for example, to add a new preprocessing sub-module or a parser in a language that the available parsers do not support. Below is an example of using the library mode to experiment with CM generation by utilizing the outputs of both the Stanford Parser and the Berkeley Neural Parser (Listing 2):

```
from gcm.aligners import fast_align
from gcm.parsers import benepar, stparser
from gcm.stages import pregcm, gcm


# code to generate alignments using fast_align
# assuming corpus is the variable storing data

aligns = fast_align.gen_aligns(corpus)

# code to use benepar to generate parse trees from the corpus
pt_benepar = benepar.parse(corpus)

# code to use stanford parser to generate parse trees from the corpus
pt_stanford = stparser.gen_parse(corpus)

# generating two set of CMs one based on the stanford parser and the other on benepar
# assuming pfms_scores to have PFS of the input sentences

pgcm_benepar = pregcm.process(corpus, aligns, pt_benepar)
pgcm_stanford = pregcm.process(corpus, aligns, pt_stanford)

gcm_stanford = gcm.gen(pgcm_stanford)
gcm_benepar = gcm.gen(pgcm_benepar)

# now both the generated CMs can be trained on downstream language-modeling tasks to compare their performance
```

Listing 2: Using library mode to generate CM text based on Benepar and Stanford Parser parse trees.

3.3 Web UI

In addition to the batch mode and library modes, which are targeted at users who want to either create large amounts of CM data or are proficient programmers, we also wanted to create a way for linguists and language experts to be able to visualize linguistic theories of code-mixing in an intuitive and easy to use interface. For this, we created a Web UI mode, which we describe next. The Web UI mode is meant to generate CM sentences for one pair of input sentences at a time.

The user can provide either a pair of parallel sentences, or can use the Translate option to translate a source sentence into another language using translation APIs. The user can choose the linguistic theory that they want to use to generate the CM text as can be seen in Figure 6.

Once the user has selected the options and clicks on the generate button, we generate the output of GCM which consists of all the parse trees and the generated CM sentences. As shown in Figure 7, we show all possible sentences generated by the linguistic theory and do not restrict the number of sentences or sample them. This is to enable users to see all the sentences that are generated by the linguistic theory, which can then be restricted or sampled by using the code in batch or library mode. We expect that the Web UI will be very useful as the support for more implementations of CM theories increases, as well as to visualize CM between different language pairs.

4 Conclusion and Future Work

Generating synthetic CM data has become a promising direction in research on code-mixing, due to the lack of available data and has proved to be successful in improving various CM NLP tasks.

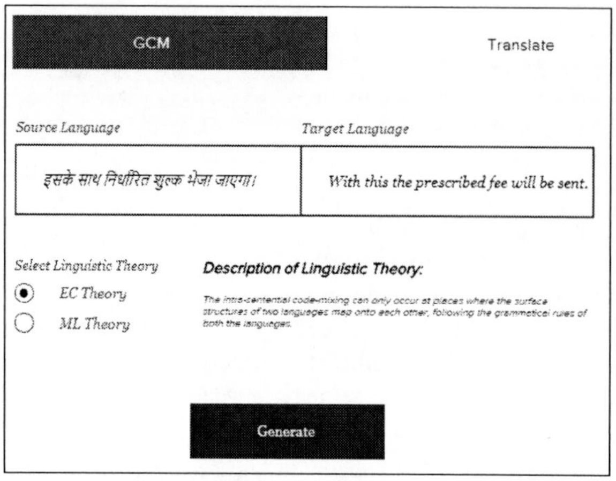

Figure 6: Selecting the linguistic theory and giving input sentences to GCM Web UI.

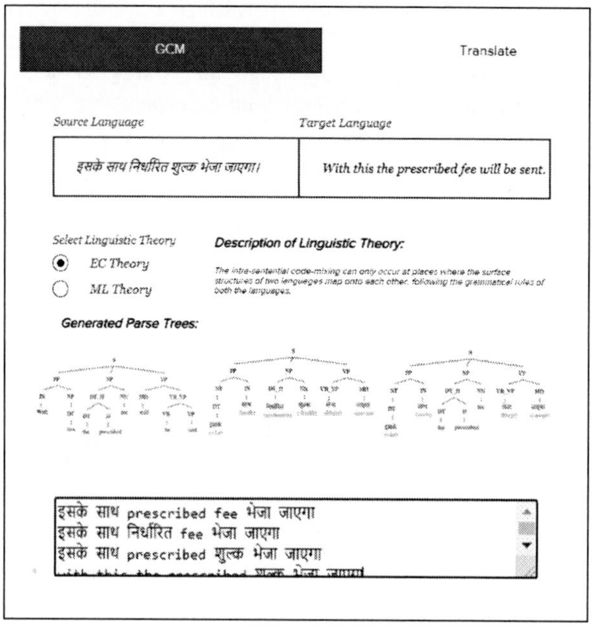

Figure 7: Code-Mixed sentences and the associated parse trees as output.

In this paper, we describe a tool for generating synthetic CM data given parallel data in two languages, or a translator between two languages. We implement two theories of code-mixing, the Equivalence Constraint (EC) theory and the Matrix-Language (ML) theory to generate CM data, followed by a sampling stage to sample sentences that are close to real code-mixing in naturalness. The GCM tool operates in three modes - a batch mode, which is meant for large scale generation of data, a library mode, which is meant to be customizable and extensible and a Web UI, which is meant as a visualization tool for linguists and language experts.

We plan to release the GCM tool as open source code and add more implementations of linguistic theories, generation techniques and sampling techniques. We believe that this tool will help address some of the problems of data scarcity in CM languages, as well as help evaluate linguistic theories for different language pairs and we expect that the release of this toolkit will spur research in diverse code-mixed language pairs.

References

Gayatri Bhat, Monojit Choudhury, and Kalika Bali. 2016. Grammatical constraints on intra-sentential code-switching: From theories to working models. *arXiv preprint arXiv:1612.04538*.

Ching-Ting Chang, Shun-Po Chuang, and Hung-Yi Lee. 2019. Code-switching sentence generation by generative adversarial networks and its application to data augmentation. *Proc. Interspeech 2019*, pages 554–558.

J. Devlin, Ming-Wei Chang, Kenton Lee, and Kristina Toutanova. 2019. Bert: Pre-training of deep bidirectional transformers for language understanding. In *NAACL-HLT*.

Chris Dyer, Victor Chahuneau, and Noah A. Smith. 2013. A simple, fast, and effective reparameterization of IBM model 2. In *Proceedings of the 2013 Conference of the North American Chapter of the Association for Computational Linguistics: Human Language Technologies*, pages 644–648, Atlanta, Georgia. Association for Computational Linguistics.

Deepak Gupta, Asif Ekbal, and Pushpak Bhattacharyya. 2020. A semi-supervised approach to generate the code-mixed text using pre-trained encoder and transfer learning. In *Proceedings of the 2020 Conference on Empirical Methods in Natural Language Processing: Findings*, pages 2267–2280.

Simran Khanuja, Sandipan Dandapat, Anirudh Srinivasan, Sunayana Sitaram, and Monojit Choudhury. 2020. Gluecos: An evaluation benchmark for code-switched nlp.

Nikita Kitaev and Dan Klein. 2018. Constituency parsing with a self-attentive encoder. In *Proceedings of the 56th Annual Meeting of the Association for Computational Linguistics (Volume 1: Long Papers)*, Melbourne, Australia. Association for Computational Linguistics.

Dan Klein and Christopher D. Manning. 2003. Accurate unlexicalized parsing. In *Proceedings of the 41st Annual Meeting of the Association for Computational Linguistics*, pages 423–430, Sapporo, Japan. Association for Computational Linguistics.

Carol Myers-Scotton. 1993. Duelling languages: Grammatical structure in code-switching. *Clarendon Press, Oxford*.

Shana Poplack. 1980. Sometimes i'll start a sentence in spanish y termino en espaÑol: toward a typology of code-switching 1. *Linguistics*, 18:581–618.

Adithya Pratapa, Gayatri Bhat, Monojit Choudhury, Sunayana Sitaram, Sandipan Dandapat, and Kalika Bali. 2018a. Language modeling for code-mixing: The role of linguistic theory based synthetic data. In *Proceedings of the 56th Annual Meeting of the Association for Computational Linguistics (Volume 1: Long Papers)*, pages 1543–1553.

Adithya Pratapa, Monojit Choudhury, and Sunayana Sitaram. 2018b. Word embeddings for code-mixed language processing. In *Proceedings of the 2018 Conference on Empirical Methods in Natural Language Processing*, pages 3067–3072.

Bidisha Samanta, Sharmila Reddy, Hussain Jagirdar, Niloy Ganguly, and Soumen Chakrabarti. 2019. A deep generative model for code-switched text. In *Proceedings of the 28th International Joint Conference on Artificial Intelligence*, pages 5175–5181. AAAI Press.

Genta Indra Winata, Andrea Madotto, Chien-Sheng Wu, and Pascale Fung. 2019. Code-switched language models using neural based synthetic data from parallel sentences. In *Proceedings of the 23rd Conference on Computational Natural Language Learning (CoNLL)*, pages 271–280.

T2NER: Transformers based Transfer Learning Framework for Named Entity Recognition

Saadullah Amin Günter Neumann

Department of Language Science and Technology, Saarland University, Saarbrücken
Multilinguality and Language Technology Lab, DFKI GmbH, Saarbrücken
{saadullah.amin, guenter.neumann}@dfki.de

Abstract

Recent advances in deep transformer models have achieved state-of-the-art in several natural language processing (NLP) tasks, whereas named entity recognition (NER) has traditionally benefited from long-short term memory (LSTM) networks. In this work, we present a **T**ransformers based **T**ransfer Learning framework for **N**amed **E**ntity **R**ecognition (T2NER) created in PyTorch for the task of NER with deep transformer models. The framework is built upon the *Transformers* library as the core modeling engine and supports several transfer learning scenarios from sequential transfer to domain adaptation, multi-task learning, and semi-supervised learning. It aims to bridge the gap between the algorithmic advances in these areas by combining them with the state-of-the-art in transformer models to provide a unified platform that is readily extensible and can be used for both the transfer learning research in NER, and for real-world applications. The framework is available at: `https://github.com/suamin/t2ner`.

1 Introduction

Named entity recognition (NER) is an important task in information extraction, benefiting the downstream applications such as entity linking (Cucerzan, 2007), relation extraction (Culotta and Sorensen, 2004) and question answering (Krishnamurthy and Mitchell, 2015). NER has been a challenging task in NLP due to large variations in entity names and flexibility in how entities are mentioned. These challenges are further enhanced in cross-lingual and cross-domain NER settings, where the added difficulty comes from the difference in text genre and entity names across languages and domains (Jia et al., 2019).

Furthermore, NER models have shown relatively high variance even when trained on the same data (Reimers and Gurevych, 2017). These models generalize poorly when tested on data from different domains and languages, and even more so when they contain unseen entity mentions (Augenstein et al., 2017; Agarwal et al., 2020; Wang et al., 2020). These challenges make transfer learning research an important and well studied area in NER.

Recent successes in transfer learning have mainly come from pre-trained language models (Devlin et al., 2019; Radford et al., 2019) with contextualized word embeddings based on deep transformer models (Vaswani et al., 2017). These models achieve state-of-the-art in several NLP tasks such as named entity recognition, document classification, and question answering. Due to their wide success and the community adoption, successful frameworks like *Transformers* have emerged. In NER, the existing frameworks like NCRF++ (Yang and Zhang, 2018) lack the core infrastructure to support such models directly with state-of-the-art transfer learning algorithms.

In this paper, we present an adaptable and user-friendly development framework for growing research in transfer learning with deep transformer models for NER, with underexplored areas such as semi-supervised learning. This is in contrast to the standard LSTM based approaches which have largely and successfully dominated the NER research. Our framework is aimed to bridge several gaps with core design principles that are discussed in next section.

2 Design Principles

T2NER is divided into several components as shown in Figure 1. The core design principle is to seamlessly integrate the *Transformers* (Wolf et al., 2020) library as the backend for modeling, while extending it to support different transfer learning scenarios with a range of existing algorithms. *Trans-*

Proceedings of the 16th Conference of the European Chapter of the Association for Computational Linguistics: System Demonstrations, pages 212–220
April 19 - 23, 2021. ©2021 Association for Computational Linguistics

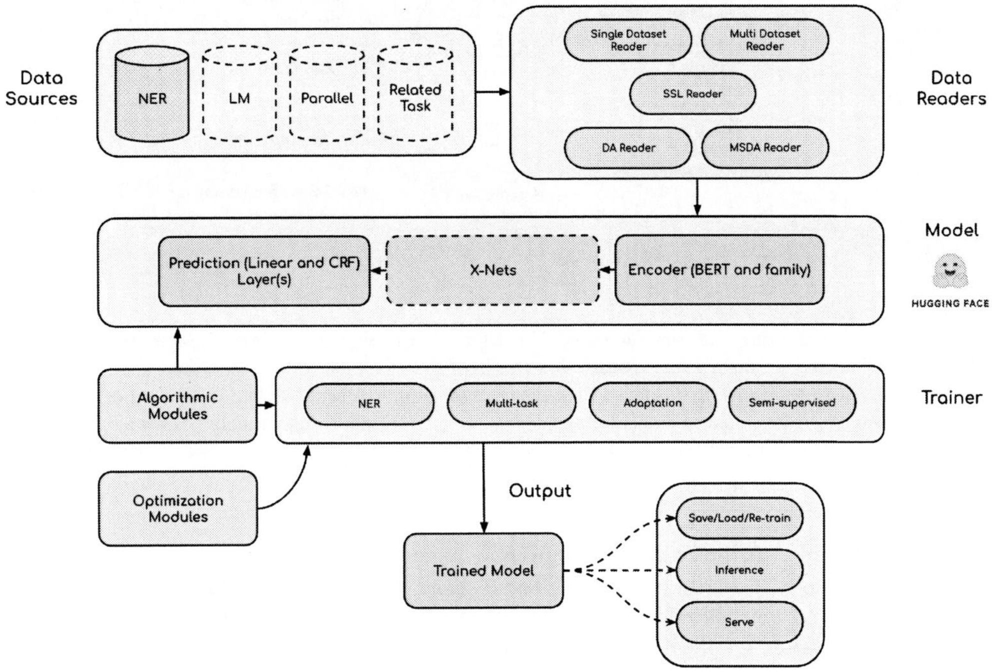

Figure 1: Overview of the T2NER framework.

formers offer optimized implementations of several deep transformer models, including BERT (Devlin et al., 2019), GPT (Radford et al., 2019), RoBERTa (Liu et al., 2019), and XLM (Conneau and Lample, 2019) among others, with multi-GPU, distributed, and mixed precision training.

The second design principle is inspired by previous pre-trained models in the computer vision: `Dassl.pytorch` (Zhou et al., 2020)[1] and `Trans-Learn` (Jiang et al., 2020)[2] that unify domain adaptation, domain generalization, and semi-supervised learning, thus allowing easy benchmarking, fair comparisons, and reproducibility. T2NER is the unification of these major algorithmic approaches to bridge the gap between the algorithms and advance transfer learning research in NER.

Lastly, the cross-lingual and cross-domain research in NER has itself proposed several advances, including multi-task and joint learning (Pan et al., 2017; Peng and Dredze, 2017; Lin et al., 2018; Jia et al., 2019; Wang et al., 2020), adversarial learning (Zhou et al., 2019; Keung et al., 2019), feature transfer (Daumé III, 2007; Kim et al., 2015; Wang et al., 2018), newer architectures (Lin et al., 2018; Jia and Zhang, 2020), parameter sharing (Lee et al., 2018; Yang et al., 2018; Lin and Lu, 2018), parameter generation (Jia et al., 2019), mixture-of-experts (Chen et al., 2018), and usage of external resources (Xie et al., 2018; Wang et al., 2019). Therefore, our final design principle aims to unify these researches and offer a framework to test them with deep transformer models, wherever such an algorithmic abstraction is possible, while exploring new paradigms.

3 The T2NER Framework

3.1 Data Sources

The main data source is the NER data, which is expected to be labeled or unlabeled in the CoNLL format. We adopt widely used BIO tagging scheme. In practice, the differences in results which arise due to different schemes are negligible (Ratinov and Roth, 2009). A simple preprocessing routine is provided to standardize the data files, along with the required metadata, that is used through-

[1]`https://github.com/KaiyangZhou/Dassl.pytorch`

[2]`https://github.com/thuml/Transfer-Learning-Library`

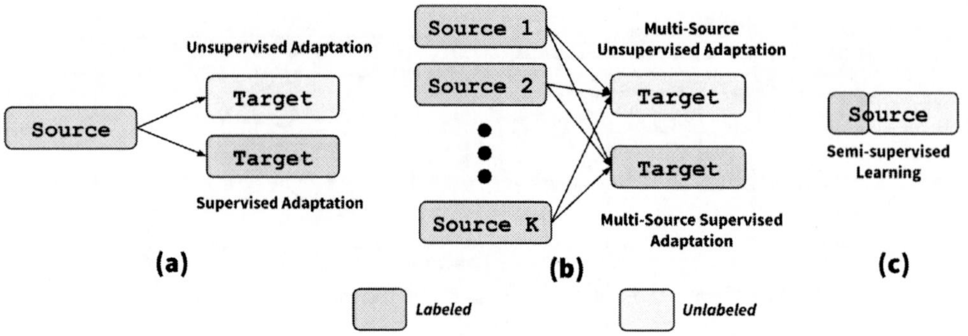

Figure 2: Transfer learning scenarios supported in T2NER. The adaptation scenarios apply to the *cross-domain*, *cross-lingual*, or a *mix* of both. These scenarios can further be complemented with multi-task learning. (a) Single source *supervised* or *unsupervised* domain or language adaptation (b) Multi-source *supervised* or *unsupervised* domain or language adaptation (c) Single source *semi-supervised* learning with partially labeled data. Further new directions in NER, such as multi-source adaptation with semi-supervised or few-shot learning of the target, are possible.

out the framework. In particular, for a given named collection as `domain.datasetname` (possibly split into train, development and test files), T2NER creates output data files named as `lang.domain.datasetname-split` and `lang.domain.datasetname.labels`, where language information is provided by the user. In case of missing metadata, a placeholder `xxx` can be used. For preprocessing, we tokenize via *Transformers* and split the sentences which are longer than the user-defined maximum length. An example output file could be `en.news.conll-train`, referring to the CoNLL 2003 data set (Tjong Kim Sang and De Meulder, 2003).

Besides NER data, additional task data can also be provided, such as that for language modeling, POS tagging, and alignment resources (e.g. bilingual dictionaries or parallel sentences).

3.2 Data Readers

These are classes that are designed to serve the data needs of a given transfer learning scenario in a modular and extensible way. The framework provides `SimpleData`, `SimpleAdaptationData`, `MultiData`, and `SemiSupervisedData` which are suitable for single dataset NER, cross- lingual and domain NER, multi-dataset NER, and single dataset semi-supervised NER, respectively. Each class is derived from a base class `BaseData` and can be extended for further scenarios. As a concrete example, consider a dataset reader class `SimpleAdaptationData` in T2NER, which can provide training data for *source* and *target* language or domain up to a requested number of copies.

3.3 Models

A model is composed of three main components: a base encoder from the *Transformers* (Wolf et al., 2020), any additional networks (X-nets) on top of the encoder, and the prediction layer(s).

Encoder is the main model component that takes as input tokenized text and returns hidden states such as those from BERT (Devlin et al., 2019) or RoBERTa (Liu et al., 2019). There are five encoder modes that we support:

- `finetune`: Fine-tunes the encoder and uses the last layer hidden states.
- `freeze`: Freezes the encoder and uses the last layer hidden states.
- `firstn`: Freezes only the first n layers of the encoder and uses the last layer hidden states (Wu and Dredze, 2019).
- `lastn`: Freezes the encoder and uses the aggregated hidden states by summing the outputs from the last n layers (Wang et al., 2019).
- `embedonly`: Uses and fine-tunes the embedding layer only of the encoder.

X-nets are additional neural architectures that can be used on top of the encoder to further function on the encoder hidden states. T2NER provides

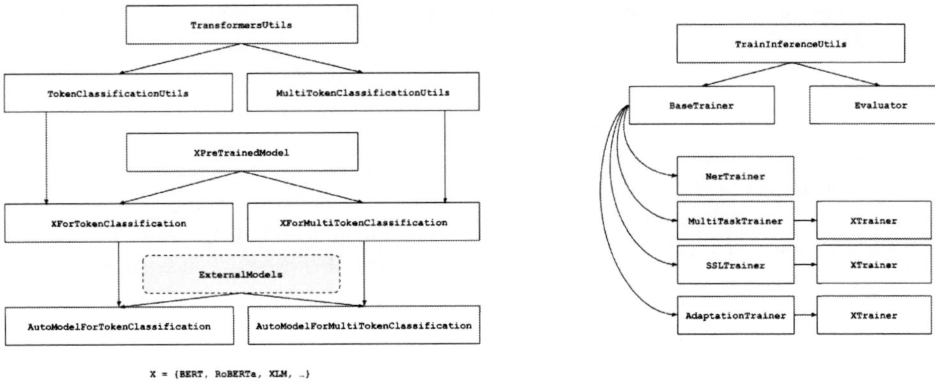

Figure 3: Class hierarchies in T2NER for two main class concepts: (**Left**) Main model architectures in single and multi-task settings with the adoption of `Auto` classes concepts from *Transformers* (Wolf et al., 2020), where customized functionality or new modeling concepts can easily be added. (**Right**) Main trainer classes that offer a particular transfer learning scenario and extend it to a specific transferring algorithm.

multi-layered Transformers and BiLSTM by default.

Prediction Layers offer the final classification layer for the sequence labeling. Following Devlin et al. (2019), the default prediction layer in T2NER is a linear layer, however support for linear-chain conditional random field (CRF) is included. In the multi-task setting, several output layers from different datasets in different domains or languages might be available with partial or exact entity types as outputs. To help the transfer across the tasks, **private** and **shared** prediction layers are also supported (Wang et al., 2020; Lin et al., 2018).

With these underlying components, models are mainly implemented as single or multi-task architectures. To support a wide range of encoders in a unified API, T2NER adopts the `Auto` classes design from the *Transformers*. Figure 3 shows the class hierarchies, outlining the customized extensions with further possibilities to extend with external model implementations.

3.4 Criterions

For a given sequence of length L with tokens $x = [x_1, x_2, ..., x_L]$, labels $y = [y_1, y_2, ..., y_L]$ with each $y_i \in \Delta^C$ a one-hot entity type vector with C types, and the linear prediction layer, the NER loss is defined as:

$$\mathcal{L}(y; x) = -\sum_{i=1}^{C}\sum_{j=1}^{L} y_{ij} \log p(h_j = i|x_j)$$

where $p(h_j = i|x_j)$ is the probability of token x_j being labeled as entity type i and h_j is the model output. When p is softmax, this becomes cross-entropy loss. To tackle class-imbalance in real-world applications, T2NER also offers two-class sensitive loss functions:

- **Focal Loss** adds a modulating factor to the standard softmax which reduces the loss contribution from easy examples and extends the range in which an example receives low loss (Lin et al., 2017).
- **LDAM Loss** is the label-distribution-aware loss function that encourages the model to have the optimal trade-off between per-class margins by promoting the minority classes to have larger margins (Cao et al., 2019).

3.5 Auxiliary Tasks

Multi-task learning has greatly benefited transfer learning in NER (Lin et al., 2018; Wang et al., 2020; Jia et al., 2019; Jia and Zhang, 2020). Several auxiliary tasks are supported in a multi-task model by default:

- *Language Classification*: In the cross-lingual setting, this task provides an additional classification signal over the languages (e.g., English and Spanish) used in the training data (Keung et al., 2019).
- *Domain Classification*: In the cross-domain setting, this task provides an additional clas-

sification signal over the domains (e.g., News and Biomedical) used in the training data (Wang et al., 2020).

- *Adversarial Classification*: In the cross- lingual or domain setting, this task provides an additional adversarial classification signal over the languages or domains to learn invariant features used in the training data (Keung et al., 2019; Chen et al., 2018).
- *Language Modeling*: While pre-trained transformer models are already tuned on a specific corpora, additional causal language modeling signal is supported during fine-tuning over the raw texts (Rei, 2017; Jia et al., 2019; Jia and Zhang, 2020).
- *Entity Type Classification*: To better extract entity type knowledge, an additional linear classifier is added. This performs classification over entity types such as [PER, LOC, O, ...] without the segmentation tags such as B/I/E (Jia and Zhang, 2020).
- *Shared Tagging*: In NER settings where the entity types might differ, a shared prediction layer across all the entity types provides an additional signal to the base NER tasks.
- *All-Outside Classification*: This is a binary classification task which predicts if the sentence has entity types other than the outside (O) type.

3.6 Optimization Modules

T2NER provides thin wrappers around the optimizers and learning rate schedulers from the PyTorch (Paszke et al., 2019) and the *Transformers* (Wolf et al., 2020) libraries.

3.7 Trainers

Trainer is the main class concept that glues together all the components and provides a unified setup to develop, test, and benchmark the algorithms. Figure 3 shows the organization of trainer classes. Each transfer learning scenario inherits from the `BaseTrainer` class, where each scenario can further be extended to create an algorithm-specific training regime. This allows the researchers to focus mainly on the algorithms' logic while the framework fulfills the requirements of a chosen transfer scenario. Following (Zhou et al., 2020; Jiang et al., 2020), a few training algorithms are implemented by default which we briefly describe. In the following, a feature extractor is referred to as the base encoder with any X-nets. An optional pooling strategy {`mean`, `sum`, `max`, `attention`, ...} can be applied to aggregate the hidden states. In what follows, domain and language can be used interchangeably. For consistency, we use the word domain.

Gradient Reversal Layer (GRL) adds a domain classifier which is trained to discriminate whether input features come from the source or target domain, whereas the feature extractor is trained to deceive the domain classifier to match feature distributions.

Earth Mover Distance (EMD) adds a critic that maximizes the difference between unbounded scores of source and target features. This effectively returns the approximation of Wasserstein distance between source and target feature distributions (Arjovsky et al., 2017). The overall objective jointly minimizes NER cross-entropy loss and Wasserstein distance. Theoretically, GRL is effectively minimizing Jensen-Shannon (JS) divergence which suffers from discontinuities and thus provide poor gradients for feature extractor. In contrast Wasserstein distance is stable and less prone to hyperparamter selection (Chen et al., 2018). For stable training, the gradient penalty is also provided (Gulrajani et al., 2017).

Keung Adversarial is closely related to GRL but additionally uses the generator loss such that the features are difficult for the discriminator to classify correctly between source and target. The optimization is carried out in step-wise fashion for the feature extractor, discriminator, and generator (Keung et al., 2019).

Maximum Classifier Discrepancy (MCD) adds a second classifier to measure the discrepancy between the predictions of two classifiers on target samples. It is noted that the target samples outside the support of the source can be measured by two different classifiers. Overall, MCD solves a *minimax* problem in which the goal is to find two classifiers that maximize the discrepancy on the target sample, and a features generator that minimizes this discrepancy (Saito et al., 2018).

Minimax Entropy (MME) decreases the entropy on unlabeled target features in adversarial manner by using GRL to obtain high quality discriminative features (Saito et al., 2019). Besides unsupervised domain adaptation, the method can

```
{
    "train_datasets": ["en.news.conll", "es.news.conll"],
    "valid_datasets": ["es.news.conll"],
    "eval_datasets": ["de.news.conll","nl.news.conll"],
    "output_dir": "...",
    "do_train": true,
    "do_eval": true,
    "do_predict": true,
    "encoder_mode": "fintune",
    "use_private_clf": true,
    "use_shared_clf": false,
    "use_all_shared_clf": false,
    "ignore_metadata": false,
    "add_lang_clf": true,
    "add_domain_clf": false,
    "add_type_clf": false,
    "add_all_outside_clf": true,
    "add_lm": false,
    "pooling": "mean",
    "aux_lmbda": 1.0,
    "max_num_train_examples": -1,
    "learning_rate": 3e-5,
    "lr_scheduler": "linear",
    "per_device_train_batch_size": 32,
    "per_device_eval_batch_size": 32,
    "num_train_epochs": 2.0,
    "loss_fct": "ce",
    "evaluate_during_training": true,
    "valid_metric": "f1",
    "ignore_heads": false,
    "warmup_steps": 0.1
}
```

Figure 4: An example of the configuration file that allows the user to specify their choices. It shows an instantiation of the multi-task learning scenario.

additionally be used in semi-supervised and few-shot learning scenarios when some labeled target samples are available.

Further algorithms, such as classical conditional entropy minimization (CEM) for semi-supervised learning (Grandvalet and Bengio, 2004) or recent works based on maximum mean discrepancy (MMD) for multi-source domain adaptation (Peng et al., 2019), are provided. In general, extending T2NER for newer algorithms is simple and flexible.

4 Usage

T2NER offers a single entry point to the framework which relies on a base JSON configuration file, an experiment-specific JSON configuration file with an optional algorithm name to run. An example experiment-specific configuration file is shown in Figure 4. The command below shows an example run:

```
$ python t2ner/run.py \
    --exp_type unsup_adapt \
    --base_json configs/base.json \
    --exp_json configs/grl.json \
    --method grl
```

Like other frameworks, it can be further developed and used as a standard Python library.

5 Conclusion and Future Work

In this work we presented a transformer based framework for transfer learning research in named entity recognition (NER). We laid out the design principles, detailed out the architecture, and presented the transfer scenarios and some of the representative algorithms. T2NER offers to bridge the gap between growing research in deep transformer models, NER transfer learning, and domain adaptation. T2NER has the potential to serve as a unified benchmark for existing and newer algorithms with state-of-the-art models.

For future work, we consider the following:

- We would like to create a benchmark data and perform comparison of the transfer learning algorithms (Ramponi and Plank, 2020; Kashyap et al., 2020).
- We would like to investigate adding support for few-shot (Huang et al., 2020), nested (Jue et al., 2020) and document-level (Schweter and Akbik, 2020) NER.
- Assess the performance of framework in terms of speed and efficiency and compare with other tools[3].
- While we focused on the task of NER here, we would also like to add related tasks such as relation extraction, entity linking, and question answering.

Acknowledgments

The work was partially funded by the European Union's Horizon 2020 research and innovation programme under grant agreement No. 777107 through the project Precise4Q and by the German Federal Ministry of Education and Research (BMBF) through the project CoRA4NLP (01IW20010).

References

Oshin Agarwal, Yinfei Yang, Byron C Wallace, and Ani Nenkova. 2020. Interpretability analysis for named entity recognition to understand system predictions and how they can improve. *arXiv preprint arXiv:2004.04564*.

[3]https://github.com/JayYip/bert-multitask-learning

Martin Arjovsky, Soumith Chintala, and Léon Bottou. 2017. Wasserstein generative adversarial networks. In *International Conference on Machine Learning*, pages 214–223.

Isabelle Augenstein, Leon Derczynski, and Kalina Bontcheva. 2017. Generalisation in named entity recognition: A quantitative analysis. *Computer Speech & Language*, 44:61–83.

Kaidi Cao, Colin Wei, Adrien Gaidon, Nikos Arechiga, and Tengyu Ma. 2019. Learning imbalanced datasets with label-distribution-aware margin loss. In *Advances in Neural Information Processing Systems*, pages 1567–1578.

Xilun Chen, Yu Sun, Ben Athiwaratkun, Claire Cardie, and Kilian Weinberger. 2018. Adversarial deep averaging networks for cross-lingual sentiment classification. *Transactions of the Association for Computational Linguistics*, 6:557–570.

Alexis Conneau and Guillaume Lample. 2019. Cross-lingual language model pretraining. In *Advances in Neural Information Processing Systems*, pages 7059–7069.

Silviu Cucerzan. 2007. Large-scale named entity disambiguation based on wikipedia data. In *Proceedings of the 2007 joint conference on empirical methods in natural language processing and computational natural language learning (EMNLP-CoNLL)*, pages 708–716.

Aron Culotta and Jeffrey Sorensen. 2004. Dependency tree kernels for relation extraction. In *Proceedings of the 42nd Annual Meeting of the Association for Computational Linguistics (ACL-04)*, pages 423–429.

Hal Daumé III. 2007. Frustratingly easy domain adaptation. In *Proceedings of the 45th Annual Meeting of the Association of Computational Linguistics*, pages 256–263.

Jacob Devlin, Ming-Wei Chang, Kenton Lee, and Kristina Toutanova. 2019. Bert: Pre-training of deep bidirectional transformers for language understanding. In *Proceedings of the 2019 Conference of the North American Chapter of the Association for Computational Linguistics: Human Language Technologies, Volume 1 (Long and Short Papers)*, pages 4171–4186.

Yves Grandvalet and Yoshua Bengio. 2004. Semi-supervised learning by entropy minimization. *Advances in neural information processing systems*, 17:529–536.

Ishaan Gulrajani, Faruk Ahmed, Martin Arjovsky, Vincent Dumoulin, and Aaron C Courville. 2017. Improved training of wasserstein gans. In *Advances in neural information processing systems*, pages 5767–5777.

Jiaxin Huang, Chunyuan Li, Krishan Subudhi, Damien Jose, Shobana Balakrishnan, Weizhu Chen, Baolin Peng, Jianfeng Gao, and Jiawei Han. 2020. Few-shot named entity recognition: A comprehensive study. *arXiv preprint arXiv:2012.14978*.

Chen Jia, Xiaobo Liang, and Yue Zhang. 2019. Cross-domain ner using cross-domain language modeling. In *Proceedings of the 57th Annual Meeting of the Association for Computational Linguistics*, pages 2464–2474.

Chen Jia and Yue Zhang. 2020. Multi-cell compositional lstm for ner domain adaptation. In *Proceedings of the 58th Annual Meeting of the Association for Computational Linguistics*, pages 5906–5917.

Junguang Jiang, Bo Fu, and Mingsheng Long. 2020. Transfer-learning-library. `https://github.com/thuml/Transfer-Learning-Library`.

WANG Jue, Lidan Shou, Ke Chen, and Gang Chen. 2020. Pyramid: A layered model for nested named entity recognition. In *Proceedings of the 58th Annual Meeting of the Association for Computational Linguistics*, pages 5918–5928.

Abhinav Ramesh Kashyap, Devamanyu Hazarika, Min-Yen Kan, and Roger Zimmermann. 2020. Domain divergences: a survey and empirical analysis. *arXiv preprint arXiv:2010.12198*.

Phillip Keung, Vikas Bhardwaj, et al. 2019. Adversarial learning with contextual embeddings for zero-resource cross-lingual classification and ner. In *Proceedings of the 2019 Conference on Empirical Methods in Natural Language Processing and the 9th International Joint Conference on Natural Language Processing (EMNLP-IJCNLP)*, pages 1355–1360.

Young-Bum Kim, Karl Stratos, Ruhi Sarikaya, and Minwoo Jeong. 2015. New transfer learning techniques for disparate label sets. In *Proceedings of the 53rd Annual Meeting of the Association for Computational Linguistics and the 7th International Joint Conference on Natural Language Processing (Volume 1: Long Papers)*, pages 473–482.

Jayant Krishnamurthy and Tom M Mitchell. 2015. Learning a compositional semantics for freebase with an open predicate vocabulary. *Transactions of the Association for Computational Linguistics*, 3:257–270.

Ji Young Lee, Franck Dernoncourt, and Peter Szolovits. 2018. Transfer learning for named-entity recognition with neural networks. In *Proceedings of the Eleventh International Conference on Language Resources and Evaluation (LREC 2018)*.

Bill Yuchen Lin and Wei Lu. 2018. Neural adaptation layers for cross-domain named entity recognition. In *Proceedings of the 2018 Conference on Empirical Methods in Natural Language Processing*, pages 2012–2022.

Tsung-Yi Lin, Priya Goyal, Ross Girshick, Kaiming He, and Piotr Dollár. 2017. Focal loss for dense object detection. In *Proceedings of the IEEE international conference on computer vision*, pages 2980–2988.

Ying Lin, Shengqi Yang, Veselin Stoyanov, and Heng Ji. 2018. A multi-lingual multi-task architecture for low-resource sequence labeling. In *Proceedings of the 56th Annual Meeting of the Association for Computational Linguistics (Volume 1: Long Papers)*, pages 799–809.

Yinhan Liu, Myle Ott, Naman Goyal, Jingfei Du, Mandar Joshi, Danqi Chen, Omer Levy, Mike Lewis, Luke Zettlemoyer, and Veselin Stoyanov. 2019. Roberta: A robustly optimized bert pretraining approach. *arXiv preprint arXiv:1907.11692*.

Xiaoman Pan, Boliang Zhang, Jonathan May, Joel Nothman, Kevin Knight, and Heng Ji. 2017. Cross-lingual name tagging and linking for 282 languages. In *Proceedings of the 55th Annual Meeting of the Association for Computational Linguistics (Volume 1: Long Papers)*, pages 1946–1958.

Adam Paszke, Sam Gross, Francisco Massa, Adam Lerer, James Bradbury, Gregory Chanan, Trevor Killeen, Zeming Lin, Natalia Gimelshein, Luca Antiga, et al. 2019. Pytorch: An imperative style, high-performance deep learning library. In *Advances in neural information processing systems*, pages 8026–8037.

Nanyun Peng and Mark Dredze. 2017. Multi-task domain adaptation for sequence tagging. In *Proceedings of the 2nd Workshop on Representation Learning for NLP*, pages 91–100.

Xingchao Peng, Qinxun Bai, Xide Xia, Zijun Huang, Kate Saenko, and Bo Wang. 2019. Moment matching for multi-source domain adaptation. In *Proceedings of the IEEE International Conference on Computer Vision*, pages 1406–1415.

Alec Radford, Jeffrey Wu, Rewon Child, David Luan, Dario Amodei, and Ilya Sutskever. 2019. Language models are unsupervised multitask learners. *OpenAI blog*, 1(8):9.

Alan Ramponi and Barbara Plank. 2020. Neural unsupervised domain adaptation in nlp—a survey. In *Proceedings of the 28th International Conference on Computational Linguistics*, pages 6838–6855.

Lev Ratinov and Dan Roth. 2009. Design challenges and misconceptions in named entity recognition. In *Proceedings of the Thirteenth Conference on Computational Natural Language Learning (CoNLL-2009)*, pages 147–155.

Marek Rei. 2017. Semi-supervised multitask learning for sequence labeling. In *Proceedings of the 55th Annual Meeting of the Association for Computational Linguistics (Volume 1: Long Papers)*, pages 2121–2130.

Nils Reimers and Iryna Gurevych. 2017. Reporting score distributions makes a difference: Performance study of lstm-networks for sequence tagging. In *Proceedings of the 2017 Conference on Empirical Methods in Natural Language Processing*, pages 338–348.

Kuniaki Saito, Donghyun Kim, Stan Sclaroff, Trevor Darrell, and Kate Saenko. 2019. Semi-supervised domain adaptation via minimax entropy. In *Proceedings of the IEEE International Conference on Computer Vision*, pages 8050–8058.

Kuniaki Saito, Kohei Watanabe, Yoshitaka Ushiku, and Tatsuya Harada. 2018. Maximum classifier discrepancy for unsupervised domain adaptation. In *Proceedings of the IEEE Conference on Computer Vision and Pattern Recognition*, pages 3723–3732.

Stefan Schweter and Alan Akbik. 2020. Flert: Document-level features for named entity recognition. *arXiv preprint arXiv:2011.06993*.

Erik F Tjong Kim Sang and Fien De Meulder. 2003. Introduction to the conll-2003 shared task: language-independent named entity recognition. In *Proceedings of the seventh conference on Natural language learning at HLT-NAACL 2003-Volume 4*, pages 142–147.

Ashish Vaswani, Noam Shazeer, Niki Parmar, Jakob Uszkoreit, Llion Jones, Aidan N Gomez, Łukasz Kaiser, and Illia Polosukhin. 2017. Attention is all you need. In *Advances in neural information processing systems*, pages 5998–6008.

Jing Wang, Mayank Kulkarni, and Daniel Preoţiuc-Pietro. 2020. Multi-domain named entity recognition with genre-aware and agnostic inference. In *Proceedings of the 58th Annual Meeting of the Association for Computational Linguistics*, pages 8476–8488.

Zhenghui Wang, Yanru Qu, Liheng Chen, Jian Shen, Weinan Zhang, Shaodian Zhang, Yimei Gao, Gen Gu, Ken Chen, and Yong Yu. 2018. Label-aware double transfer learning for cross-specialty medical named entity recognition. In *Proceedings of the 2018 Conference of the North American Chapter of the Association for Computational Linguistics: Human Language Technologies, Volume 1 (Long Papers)*, pages 1–15.

Zirui Wang, Jiateng Xie, Ruochen Xu, Yiming Yang, Graham Neubig, and Jaime G Carbonell. 2019. Cross-lingual alignment vs joint training: A comparative study and a simple unified framework. In *International Conference on Learning Representations*.

Thomas Wolf, Julien Chaumond, Lysandre Debut, Victor Sanh, Clement Delangue, Anthony Moi, Pierric Cistac, Morgan Funtowicz, Joe Davison, Sam Shleifer, et al. 2020. Transformers: State-of-the-art natural language processing. In *Proceedings of the 2020 Conference on Empirical Methods in Natural Language Processing: System Demonstrations*, pages 38–45.

Shijie Wu and Mark Dredze. 2019. Beto, bentz, becas: The surprising cross-lingual effectiveness of bert. In *Proceedings of the 2019 Conference on Empirical Methods in Natural Language Processing and the 9th International Joint Conference on Natural Language Processing (EMNLP-IJCNLP)*, pages 833–844.

Jiateng Xie, Zhilin Yang, Graham Neubig, Noah A Smith, and Jaime G Carbonell. 2018. Neural cross-lingual named entity recognition with minimal resources. In *Proceedings of the 2018 Conference on Empirical Methods in Natural Language Processing*, pages 369–379.

Jie Yang, Shuailong Liang, and Yue Zhang. 2018. Design challenges and misconceptions in neural sequence labeling. In *Proceedings of the 27th International Conference on Computational Linguistics*, pages 3879–3889.

Jie Yang and Yue Zhang. 2018. Ncrf++: An open-source neural sequence labeling toolkit. In *Proceedings of ACL 2018, System Demonstrations*, pages 74–79.

Joey Tianyi Zhou, Hao Zhang, Di Jin, Hongyuan Zhu, Meng Fang, Rick Siow Mong Goh, and Kenneth Kwok. 2019. Dual adversarial neural transfer for low-resource named entity recognition. In *Proceedings of the 57th Annual Meeting of the Association for Computational Linguistics*, pages 3461–3471.

Kaiyang Zhou, Yongxin Yang, Yu Qiao, and Tao Xiang. 2020. Domain adaptive ensemble learning. *arXiv preprint arXiv:2003.07325*.

European Language Grid:
A Joint Platform for the European Language Technology Community

Georg Rehm[1], Stelios Piperidis[2], Kalina Bontcheva[3], Jan Hajič[4], Victoria Arranz[5], Andrejs Vasiļjevs[6], Gerhard Backfried[7], José Manuel Gómez-Pérez[8], Ulrich Germann[9], Rémi Calizzano[1], Nils Feldhus[1], Stefanie Hegele[1], Florian Kintzel[1], Katrin Marheinecke[1], Julián Moreno-Schneider[1], Dimitrios Galanis[2], Penny Labropoulou[2], Miltos Deligiannis[2], Katerina Gkirtzou[2], Athanasia Kolovou[2], Dimitris Gkoumas[2], Leon Voukoutis[2], Ian Roberts[3], Jana Hamrlová[4], Dušan Variš[4], Lukáš Kačena[4], Khalid Choukri[5], Valérie Mapelli[5], Mickaël Rigault[5], Jūlija Meļņika[6], Miroslav Jánošík[7], Katja Prinz[7], Andrés García-Silva[8], Cristian Berrío[8], Ondrej Klejch[9], Steve Renals[9]

[1]DFKI GmbH, Berlin, Germany; [2]R. C. Athena, ILSP, Greece; [3]University of Sheffield, UK; [4]Charles University, Czechia; [5]ELDA, France; [6]Tilde, Latvia; [7]HENSOLDT Analytics, Austria; [8]Expert System, Spain; [9]University of Edinburgh, UK

Corresponding author: georg.rehm@dfki.de

Abstract

Europe is a multilingual society, in which dozens of languages are spoken. The only option to enable and to benefit from multilingualism is through Language Technologies (LT), i. e., Natural Language Processing and Speech Technologies. We describe the European Language Grid (ELG), which is targeted to evolve into the primary platform and marketplace for LT in Europe by providing one umbrella platform for the European LT landscape, including research and industry, enabling all stakeholders to upload, share and distribute their services, products and resources. At the end of our EU project, which will establish a legal entity in 2022, the ELG will provide access to approx. 1300 services for all European languages as well as thousands of data sets.

1 Introduction

Europe is a multilingual society with 24 EU Member State languages and dozens of additional languages including regional and minority languages and languages spoken by immigrants, trade partners and tourists. The only option to enable and to benefit from multilingualism is through Language Technologies (LT) including Natural Language Processing (NLP) and Speech Technologies (Rehm, 2017). While the European LT landscape is world class, it is also massively fragmented (Vasiljevs et al., 2019; Rehm et al., 2020d).

We describe Release 2 of the European Language Grid (ELG) cloud platform.[1] This scalable system is targeted to evolve into the primary platform for LT in Europe. It will provide one umbrella platform for all LTs developed by the European LT landscape, including research and industry, addressing a gap that has been repeatedly raised by the European LT community for many years (Rehm and Uszkoreit, 2013; Rehm et al., 2016b; STOA, 2017; Rehm, 2017; Rehm and Hegele, 2018; European Parliament, 2018). ELG is meant to be a virtual home and marketplace for all products, services and organisations active in the LT space in Europe (Rehm et al., 2020a). The platform can be used by all stakeholders to showcase, share and distribute their products, services, tools and resources. At the end of the EU project ELG (2019-2022), which will establish a legal entity in early 2022, the platform will provide access to approx. 1300 commercial and non-commercial tools and services for all European languages, as well as thousands of language resources (LRs). ELG will enable the European LT community to deposit and upload their technologies and data sets and to deploy them through the grid. The ELG is also meant to support *digital language equality* in Europe (STOA, 2017; European Parliament, 2018), i. e., to create a situation in which all languages are supported through technologies equally well. The current imbalance is characterised by a stark predominance of LTs for English, while almost all other languages are only marginally supported and, thus, in danger of digital language extinction (Rehm and Uszkoreit, 2012; Kornai, 2013; Rehm et al., 2014, 2016a; ELRC, 2019).

Section 2 gives an overview of the ELG platform and related activities. Section 3 touches upon related work. Section 4 concludes the paper.

[1]https://www.european-language-grid.eu. We provide a screencast demo video at https://youtu.be/LD6QadkkZiM.

2 The European Language Grid

The European LT community has been demanding a dedicated LT platform for years. ELG concentrates on *commercial* and *non-commercial* LTs, both *functional* (processing and generation, written and spoken language) and *non-functional* (corpora, data sets etc.). We want to establish the ELG as the primary market place for the fragmented European LT landscape (Rehm et al., 2020d) to connect demand and supply. The ELG is based on robust, scalable and reliable open source technologies, enabling it to scale with the growing demand and supply. It contains records of all resources, service and application types, languages as well as LT companies, research organisations, projects, etc. (see Figure 1 and Figure 4 in the appendix).

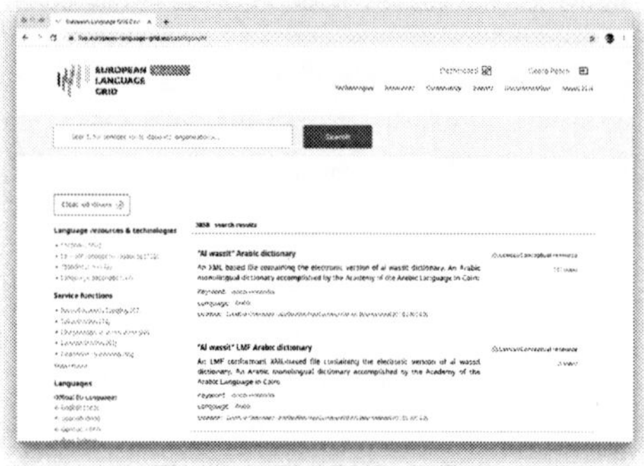

Figure 1: The ELG platform

2.1 Architectural Overview

ELG is a scalable platform with a web user interface, backend components and REST APIs. It offers access (search, discovery, etc.) to various kinds of LT-related resources such as functional services as well as corpora and data sets and organisations. An ELG functional service is an LT tool wrapped with the ELG LT Service API[2] and packaged in a Docker container; both steps have to be carried out by the LT provider. Then, the LT service container is integrated into the ELG (Section 2.7) so that it can be used through the web UI or APIs. The architecture consists of three layers: *base infrastructure*, *platform backend*, *platform frontend* (Figure 2).

The *base infrastructure* is operated on a Kubernetes[3] cluster in the data centre of a cloud provider located in Berlin, Germany, where all platform components and all LT functional services run as Docker containers. The only components outside the cluster are the S3 storage, ReadtheDocs (ELG documentation), and any LT services deployed through external servers.

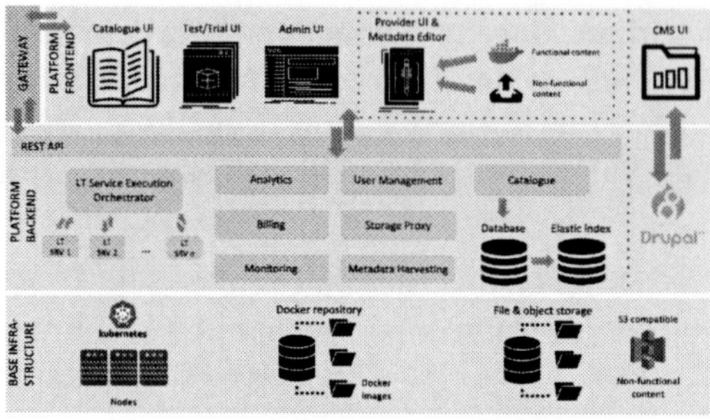

Figure 2: Technical architecture

The *platform backend* consists of (1) the *backend components* of the ELG catalogue, i. e., an inventory of all metadata records (Section 2.3). Users can browse and search the catalogue through queries or by utilising filters (e. g., language, service type, domain etc.). Users with the "LT provider" role can create new entries either by uploading XML descriptions or through a graphical metadata editor. The catalogue backend is implemented using Django, PostgreSQL and ElasticSearch. (2) The LT Service Execution Server offers a common REST API for executing functional services, also handling failures, time-outs etc. (3) The user management and authentication module is based on Keycloak, an identity and access management solution. (4) The Storage Proxy is used for interacting with the S3-compatible storage. (5) All integrated LT services. Additional components, especially for billing and monitoring purposes, are currently work in progress.

The *platform frontend* consists of UIs for the different types of users, e. g., LT providers, potential buyers and administrators (Section 2.6.2). These include (1) catalogue UIs (browse, search, view), provider and metadata editor UIs for uploading and registering functional and non-functional resources. They are implemented using React and packaged in the same container. (2) The administration pages are implemented using Django. (3) The test/trial UIs for functional services run in separate containers. The UIs are powered by the catalogue REST API, e. g., a resource's metadata record is returned as a JSON object and rendered as HTML. The frontend also includes a Drupal-based CMS for additional content (Section 2.6.2).

[2]https://gitlab.com/european-language-grid/platform/
[3]https://kubernetes.io

All core components of the ELG platform are built with robust, scalable, reliable and widely used technologies, e. g., Django, Angular and React. For managing LT service containers, ELG makes use of Knative[4], a layer on top of Kubernetes that handles auto-scaling.

2.2 Base Infrastructure

The base infrastructure consists of the nodes running the ELG platform, volume storage, networking facilities and S3-compatible object storage. We use *managed* Kubernetes, i. e., the maintenance and operation of Kubernetes itself is taken care of by the provider. The infrastructure also consists of a large set of Git repositories and Docker registries, hosted in a common group on GitLab[5] for all ELG source and configuration files. Many external registries are used to pull in third-party components, like database servers (MariaDB[6], PostgreSql[7]), authentication and identity management (Keycloak[8]), monitoring (Prometheus[9]), among others. Most LT services offered by the ELG platform are pulled from the Docker registries of their respective developers.

ELG uses a GitOps approach to deployment, with the cluster configuration stored in a dedicated Git repository as a set of Helm charts[10]. A continuous integration pipeline triggers a deployment with each check-in to this repository.

Eventually hosting more than one thousand LT services with different hardware needs, we are unable to keep all of them up concurrently as this would require hundreds of Gigabyte of RAM. KNative is used to automatically scale down services not currently in use to zero replicas. A service is scaled up further if a certain threshold of requests is exceeded. This setup is suitable for services with little traffic. For services intended to power actual applications, however, the time to spin up a container is likely too long. ELG will, later on, offer scaling profiles, which will keep a specific number of replicas online at all times.

Non-functional LT resources uploaded to the platform are made persistent to an S3 compatible object storage and can be downloaded from there.

[4]https://knative.dev
[5]https://gitlab.com/european-language-grid/
[6]https://mariadb.org
[7]https://www.postgresql.org
[8]https://www.keycloak.org
[9]https://prometheus.io
[10]https://helm.sh

2.3 Catalogue

The metadata records stored in the catalogue enable access to services and data resources. They are described using the ELG metadata schema (Labropoulou et al., 2020) and can be browsed and explored. The catalogue also includes a registry of stakeholders who develop LT services or products, and relevant projects, thus providing an overview of the whole European LT landscape. The ELG metadata schema builds upon, consolidates and updates the META-SHARE schema (Gavrilidou et al., 2012; Piperidis et al., 2018; Labropoulou et al., 2018), taking into account ELG's requirements, recent developments in the metadata domain (e. g., FAIR[11]), and the need for creating a common pool of resources through exchange mechanisms with collaborating initiatives.

The metadata schema caters for the description of the ELG core entities, i. e., Language Technologies (*tools/services*), including functional services and non-functional ones, and Data Language Resources, comprising *data sets* (corpora), *language descriptions* (i. e., models) and *lexical/-conceptual resources* (e. g., gazetteers, ontologies, etc.). It also provides for related entities involved in the production, namely *actors* (*organizations*, *groups* and *persons*), *projects*, *documents*, and *licences/terms of use*. Metadata records are created by providers using the online editor (Section 2.6.1), or from other sources through harvesting and conversion APIs (Section 2.5), gradually enriched through (semi-)automatic processes and curated by persons who rightfully claim them.

2.4 Functional Services

The European LT landscape is broad and varied, with many providers of different classes of services and tools, exposed through different APIs and data formats. We attempt to bring more order to this varied landscape by identifying classes of related services, and providing a generic API for each class. So far, we have identified three classes. (1) *Machine Translation (MT)* services take text in one language and translate it into text in another language, possibly with additional metadata associated with each segment. (2) *Information Extraction (IE)* services take text and annotate it with metadata on specific segments. This class can cover a wide variety of services from basic NER through to complex sentiment analysis

[11]https://www.force11.org/group/fairgroup/fairprinciples

and domain-specific tools. (3) *Automatic Speech Recognition (ASR)* services take audio as input and produce text (e. g., a transcription) as output, possibly with metadata associated with each segment.

	A	B	C	D
ASR				
Speech Recognition	12	3	9	
IE & Text Analysis				
Dependency Parsing	24	7	13	
Lemmatisation	24	7	13	
Morphological analyser	24	7	13	
Part of Speech tagging	24	7	13	
Tokenization	24	7	13	
Language identification	22	6	14	13
Named Entity Recognition	16	5	11	
Keyword extraction	9	3	9	
Sentiment Analysis	8		4	
Key phrase Extraction	7		5	
Polarity detection	7		4	
Summarization	7		5	
Other services (not shown here)	30			
MT (Source ↓ / Target →)				
A	30		2	1
C	1			
Other				
Text to Speech	7	1	1	2

Table 1: Language coverage per category of the services to integrate in ELG

Other clusters are emerging as we are preparing more services for integration, e. g., text-to-speech and text classification. Our goal is to provide services of all classes for all official EU languages and for other EU and non-EU languages that are of social or strategic interest in the EU. Table 1 shows the overall language coverage of each category of services across all consortium partners; languages have been divided into four groups: (A) EU official languages; (B) other EU languages without official status, plus languages from candidate countries and free trade partners; (C) languages spoken by immigrants or important trade and political partners; (D) languages that do not fit (A), (B), (C).

Release 1 of the platform (April 2020) targeted the languages spoken in the countries of the ELG consortium, with 141 IE and text analysis services, 24 MT, nine ASR, four TTS and two text categorisation services. Further services are being added on a regular basis with 200+ additional IE and text analysis services, 21 MT, eight ASR and nine TTS scheduled to be included by the time of ELG Release 2 in February 2021.

We aim to make it as simple as possible for LT providers to integrate their services, but in a way that avoids the proliferation of incompatible APIs for the same task, allowing users to access the widest range of services without being locked in to a single vendor. Our generic APIs use HTTP as the transport protocol and specific schemas of JSON-based messages as the payload. Providers who want to integrate their services into the ELG need to provide a Docker image that presents an HTTP endpoint that can receive requests and return responses in the specified format (user authentication, authorisation, etc. are handled by the platform). Once a service is integrated, it can be used via the public APIs and UIs (Section 2.6).

2.5 Data Sets and Language Resources

Already now ELG provides access to more than 2700 language resources. We ingested substantial resources from existing repositories, especially ELDA/ELRA, ELRC-SHARE (Lösch et al., 2018; Piperidis et al., 2018; Smal et al., 2020) and META-SHARE (Piperidis, 2012; Piperidis et al., 2014). We have also been working on 'external' repositories, about 220 of which have been identified so far. Some (e. g., Zenodo, Quantum Stat) are already being ingested together with two repositories related to ELG, LINDAT/CLARIAH-CZ and ELRA-SHARE-LRs (LRs published at LREC).

2.6 Access Methods and User Interfaces

Our main groups of users are: (1) LT/LR providers – companies or research organisations with tools, services or data that can be provided through the ELG; (2) Developers and integrators – companies and research institutions interested in using LT; (3) General LT information seekers; (4) Stakeholders who wish to provide information about events etc.; (5) Casual visitors. We provide three ways of access: REST APIs, web UIs, Python package.

2.6.1 REST APIs

The ELG exposes several REST APIs, which are used by all clients. They are exposed for (1) browsing and searching the catalogue, (2) creating, updating and retrieving metadata records, (3) executing services, (4) downloading resources. Authentication is performed through OAuth2 (OpenID-Connect) using JSON Web Tokens.

The catalogue API is based on a JSON serialisation of the metadata schema. The entry point is the search operation, which supports free text search as well as faceted browsing. The metadata record creation, update and retrieval API is controlled by the catalogue module and associates each record with a creator and curator. The curator can edit and update the record until it is published.

The functional service API (internal LT API) provides a way of executing any functional service deployed in the ELG. *All* functional services of a given class (MT, ASR, etc.) are presented under a common API for that class, allowing the user to choose the best service for their requirements without being locked in to a single vendor.[12] The public-facing LT service API mirrors the internal LT service provider API (see above), being based around the same JSON message formats, but also offers simplified options. It is possible to HTTP POST plain text to an MT service, or binary audio to an ASR service, without having to wrap it in the full JSON envelope or multi-part MIME structure used by the internal API. Since the public and internal APIs are conceptually distinct, we can add and offer public APIs that use other technologies (e. g., gRPC). The LT Service Execution Server component translates requests between the public and internal APIs. An asynchronous interaction style is offered for services that require a longer run time to process a request, this works by returning an immediate response that directs the caller to another URL, which it can then poll to request the result.

2.6.2 Web Interface (GUI)

Angular 9.0 and Typescript were adopted for developing the Drupal CMS front-end which is used for presenting content such as news or conferences. For the catalogue UI we use React. Currently, both web applications (CMS and catalogue frontend) use client-side-rendering, i. e., they deliver a single HTML file, the rest of the application comes as Javascript files. User authorisation is ensured by adding a JSON Web Token (JWT) to data requests, where the user identity data is encoded and sent as an encrypted JSON object.

For LT services the catalogue record detail page includes a trial GUI, allowing users to experiment with the service in the browser. Generic trial UIs have been developed for the principal service types (ASR, MT, TTS, text annotation and classification services) but LT service providers can also supply their own GUI if the standard ones are not suitable. An example is the family of UDPipe dependency parser services, where the provider has created a custom UI to visualise dependency graphs.[13]

The web GUI also includes a metadata editor that supports different entities (LTs, organisations, etc.). It provides validation rules, lookup mechanisms that use values from previously filled-in metadata elements and an online help.

```python
from elg import Catalog, Service
# Search for cz/en MT services
catalog = Catalog()
results = catalog.search(
    function='Machine Translation',
    languages=['en', 'cz'])
print(results)
# Create Service object from first result
service = Service.from_entity(results[0])
# Translate plain text input from English to Czech
translated = service(
    "Did Nikola Tesla live in Berlin?")
print(translated)
```

Figure 3: Python Client Package – code example

2.6.3 Python Client Package

The Python Client Package, available through the Python package manager pip[14], comprises a command line interface and utility scripts for querying the ELG catalogue and executing ELG-hosted services via REST API calls. For features that require authentication, e. g., calling services, the client prompts the user to enter a token which is received after successful authentication in a browser window (Figure 3). This simplifies the integration of ELG-hosted services into Python projects.

2.7 Contribution of Services and Resources

We want to enable commercial and non-commercial providers to adapt their LT services so that they can be integrated into the ELG and also to make this ingestion as simple as possible. Currently, the process consists of six steps: (1) adapt the service to fit the ELG API; (2) create a Docker image; (3) push the image into a Docker registry; (4) deploy the service by creating a Kubernetes configuration file; (5) create an ELG provider account; (6) register the service by creating a metadata record. For some of the ELG services, the integration took a few days, for others only a few hours. This effort was recently brought further down by adding Docker templates for the most common cases and introducing the metadata editor. Two alternative

[12] While workflows that consist of multiple services are currently not addressed by ELG, we do experiment with workflow composition and platform interoperability (Rehm et al., 2020b,c; Moreno-Schneider et al., 2020a,b).

[13] Trial UIs can include third-party code. They are sandboxed using an iframe and configured via JavaScript message passing.

[14] https://pypi.org/project/elg/

ways of integrating a service exist. It is possible to package the LT tool in a container that does not implement the ELG LT service API. In this case, a second container is required as an adapter, which implements the ELG LT service API and communicates with the LT tool container. It is also possible to run an LT service outside the cluster: here, a proxy container that implements the ELG LT service API is required and deployed in the cluster for accessing the external service. Libraries are available that produce skeleton code.

2.8 Key Stakeholders

The ELG is meant to be a joint umbrella platform for the whole European LT landscape including industry and research. ELG caters for *commercial LT providers* who want to showcase their products, services and their organisation. We want to provide *the* marketplace for European LT, which requires coverage of, ideally, all European provider companies. In December 2020 we populated the ELG catalogue with a list of 900 LT companies. Representatives of these organisations can claim (or delete) their record and take over maintenance of their ELG page, including upload of services or data sets. *Research centres and universities* are also LT providers but their interest is research-driven, providing data sets and experimental software. *LT users* are, e. g., organisations who want to make use of LT. They interact with the ELG in the role of a consumer or potential customer. ELG also collaborates with a number of EU-funded projects and initiatives (Rehm et al., 2020c,d) and set up a network of 32 National Competence Centres (NCCs), which function as bridges between the national and regional communities and the ELG.

2.9 Open Calls: Pilot Projects

ELG provides approx. 30% of its project budget to a number of pilot projects. The pilots either broaden ELG's portfolio (by developing services or resources), or demonstrate the ELG's usefulness. Financial support is awarded following an open, transparent and expert-driven evaluation process. The first call was published in March 2020, the second one in October 2020. The first set of projects started in July 2020, the second set starts in February 2021 with a duration of 9-12 months. In the first call, 110 proposals were accepted for evaluation with applicants from 29 countries. We received more proposals from SMEs (62) than research organisations (48). While 79 proposals focused on contributing services or resources, 31 proposals concentrated on developing applications using the ELG. We selected ten projects for funding, amounting to a sum of 1,363,915€ in total.[15] We received a total of 106 proposals to the second call with applicants from 28 countries. Again, we had more proposals from SMEs (61) than from research organisations (45). In February 2021, five projects were selected for funding.

2.10 Legal Entity

We will establish a not-for-profit legal entity in early 2022, which will take over operation of the ELG platform after the end of the current EU project (June 2022). The long-term operational model is currently under development.

3 Related Work

ELG builds upon previous work of the ELG consortium and the wider European LT community, especially META-NET/META and ELRC.

In addition, we have collected more than 30 platforms, projects or initiatives that can be considered relevant for ELG including, among others, UIMA (Ferrucci and Lally, 2003), CLARIN (Hinrichs and Krauwer, 2014), DKPro (Gurevych et al., 2007); Rehm et al. (2020a) provide an exhaustive comparison. They share at least one of the following goals with ELG, i. e., they provide: 1) a collection of LT/NLP tools or data sets; 2) a platform, which harvests metadata records from distributed sources, 3) a platform for the sharing of tools or data sets. While related projects do exist, the approach of ELG is unique. The platform that most closely resembles ELG is the National Platform for LT, operated by the Ministry of Electronics and Information Technology in India.[16]

Several global technology enterprises offer LT services. Among these are Amazon Comprehend[17] and Microsoft Azure Cognitive Services (Del Sole, 2018). Furthermore, Google recently (Sept. 2018) released a search platform for data sets.[18] Intento[19] offers commercial LT services from different providers for selected tasks.

[15] https://www.european-language-grid.eu/open-calls/
[16] https://nplt.in
[17] https://aws.amazon.com/en/comprehend/
[18] https://toolbox.google.com/datasetsearch
[19] https://inten.to

4 Conclusions and Future Work

It has been argued that Europe should not outsource its multilingual communication and language infrastructure to other continents since the European demands are unique and complex (Rehm and Uszkoreit, 2013; Rehm, 2017; Rehm et al., 2020d). Instead, Europe should make use of and support its own LT community. One of the obstacles to overcome is the creation of a joint technology platform. The ELG will foster LTs *for Europe* built *in Europe*. In its first two years, the ELG project has seen the demo of the MVP in October 2019, Release 1 in early 2020 and two successfully completed open calls for pilot projects. We have been improving and extending the platform and continuously added services and data sets. While Release 2 of the platform will follow in March 2021, Release 3 is foreseen for early 2022.

Acknowledgments

The work presented in this paper has received funding from the European Union's Horizon 2020 research and innovation programme under grant agreement no. 825627 (European Language Grid) and from the German Federal Ministry of Education and Research (BMBF) through the project QURATOR (Wachstumskern no. 03WKDA1A). The inclusion of LINDAT/CLARIAH-CZ resources and tools has been in part funded by the Ministry of Education, Youth and Sports of the Czech Republic, project no. LM2018101.

References

Alessandro Del Sole. 2018. Introducing Microsoft Cognitive Services. In *Microsoft Computer Vision APIs Distilled*, pages 1–4. Springer.

ELRC. 2019. ELRC White Paper: Sustainable Language Data Sharing to Support Language Equality in Multilingual Europe. https://lr-coordination.eu/sites/default/files/Documents/ELRCWhitePaper.pdf. European Language Resource Coordination (ELRC), Second online edition.

European Parliament. 2018. Report on language equality in the digital age. http://www.europarl.europa.eu/doceo/document/A-8-2018-0228_EN.html. (2018/2028(INI)). Committee on Culture and Education (CULT), Committee on Industry, Research and Energy (ITRE); Rapporteur: Jill Evans.

David Ferrucci and Adam Lally. 2003. Accelerating Corporate Research in the Development, Application, and Deployment of Human Language Technologies. In *Proceedings of the HLT-NAACL 2003 Workshop on Software Engineering and Architecture of Language Technology Systems (SEALTS)*, pages 67–74. ACL.

Maria Gavrilidou, Penny Labropoulou, Elina Desipri, Stelios Piperidis, Haris Papageorgiou, Monica Monachini, Francesca Frontini, Thierry Declerck, Gil Francopoulo, Victoria Arranz, and Valerie Mapelli. 2012. The META-SHARE Metadata Schema for the Description of Language Resources. In *Proceedings of the Eighth International Conference on Language Resources and Evaluation (LREC 2012)*. European Language Resources Association (ELRA).

Iryna Gurevych, Max Mühlhäuser, Christof Müller, Jürgen Steimle, Markus Weimer, and Torsten Zesch. 2007. Darmstadt Knowledge Processing Repository based on UIMA. In *Proceedings of the First Workshop on Unstructured Information Management Architecture at Biannual Conference of the Society for Computational Linguistics and Language Technology, Tübingen, Germany*, page 89.

Erhard Hinrichs and Steven Krauwer. 2014. The CLARIN Research Infrastructure: Resources and Tools for eHumanities Scholars. In *Proceedings of the Ninth International Conference on Language Resources and Evaluation (LREC-2014)*, pages 1525–1531.

Andras Kornai. 2013. Digital Language Death. *PLoS ONE*, 8(10). https://doi.org/10.1371/journal.pone.0077056.

Penny Labropoulou, Dimitris Galanis, Antonis Lempesis, Mark Greenwood, Petr Knoth, Richard Eckart de Castilho, Stavros Sachtouris, Byron Georgantopoulos, Stefania Martziou, Lucas Anastasiou, Katerina Gkirtzou, Natalia Manola, and Stelios Piperidis. 2018. OpenMinTeD: A Platform Facilitating Text Mining of Scholarly Content. In *WOSP 2018 Workshop Proceedings, Eleventh International Conference on Language Resources and Evaluation (LREC 2018)*, pages 7–12, Miyazaki, Japan. European Language Resources Association (ELRA).

Penny Labropoulou, Katerina Gkirtzou, Maria Gavriilidou, Miltos Deligiannis, Dimitris Galanis, Stelios Piperidis, Georg Rehm, Maria Berger, Valérie Mapelli, Michael Rigault, Victoria Arranz, Khalid Choukri, Gerhard Backfried, José Manuel Gómez Pérez, and Andres Garcia-Silva. 2020. Making Metadata Fit for Next Generation Language Technology Platforms: The Metadata Schema of the European Language Grid. In *Proceedings of the 12th Language Resources and Evaluation Conference (LREC 2020)*, pages 3421–3430, Marseille, France. European Language Resources Association (ELRA).

Andrea Lösch, Valérie Mapelli, Stelios Piperidis, Andrejs Vasiļjevs, Lilli Smal, Thierry Declerck, Eileen

Schnur, Khalid Choukri, and Josef Van Genabith. 2018. European Language Resource Coordination: Collecting Language Resources for Public Sector Multilingual Information Management. In *Proceedings of the Eleventh International Conference on Language Resources and Evaluation (LREC 2018)*, Miyazaki, Japan. European Language Resources Association (ELRA).

Julián Moreno-Schneider, Peter Bourgonje, Florian Kintzel, and Georg Rehm. 2020a. A Workflow Manager for Complex NLP and Content Curation Workflows . In *1st International Workshop on Language Technology Platforms (IWLTP 2020)*, Marseille. Submitted to IWLTP 2020.

Julián Moreno-Schneider, Georg Rehm, Elena Montiel-Ponsoda, Víctor Rodriguez-Doncel, Artem Revenko, Sotirios Karampatakis, Maria Khvalchik, Christian Sageder, Jorge Gracia, and Filippo Maganza. 2020b. Orchestrating NLP Services for the Legal Domain. In *Proceedings of the 12th Language Resources and Evaluation Conference (LREC 2020)*, Marseille, France. European Language Resources Association (ELRA). Accepted for publication.

Stelios Piperidis. 2012. The META-SHARE Language Resources Sharing Infrastructure: Principles, Challenges, Solutions. In *Proceedings of the Eight International Conference on Language Resources and Evaluation (LREC'12)*, Istanbul, Turkey. European Language Resources Association (ELRA).

Stelios Piperidis, Penny Labropoulou, Miltos Deligiannis, and Maria Giagkou. 2018. Managing Public Sector Data for Multilingual Applications Development. In *Proceedings of the Eleventh International Conference on Language Resources and Evaluation (LREC 2018)*, Miyazaki, Japan. European Language Resources Association (ELRA).

Stelios Piperidis, Harris Papageorgiou, Christian Spurk, Georg Rehm, Khalid Choukri, Olivier Hamon, Nicoletta Calzolari, Riccardo Del Gratta, Bernardo Magnini, and Christian Girardi. 2014. META-SHARE: One Year After. In *Proceedings of the Ninth International.Conference on Language Resources and Evaluation (LREC'14)*, Reykjavik, Iceland. European Language Resources Association (ELRA).

Georg Rehm, editor. 2017. *Language Technologies for Multilingual Europe: Towards a Human Language Project. Strategic Research and Innovation Agenda.* CRACKER and Cracking the Language Barrier federation. Version 1.0. Unveiled at META-FORUM 2017 in Brussels, Belgium, on November 13/14, 2017. Prepared by the Cracking the Language Barrier federation, supported by the EU-funded project CRACKER.

Georg Rehm, Maria Berger, Ela Elsholz, Stefanie Hegele, Florian Kintzel, Katrin Marheinecke, Stelios Piperidis, Miltos Deligiannis, Dimitris Galanis, Katerina Gkirtzou, Penny Labropoulou, Kalina Bontcheva, David Jones, Ian Roberts, Jan Hajic, Jana Hamrlová, Lukáš Kačena, Khalid Choukri, Victoria Arranz, Andrejs Vasiļjevs, Orians Anvari, Andis Lagzdiņš, Jūlija Meļņika, Gerhard Backfried, Erinç Dikici, Miroslav Janosik, Katja Prinz, Christoph Prinz, Severin Stampler, Dorothea Thomas-Aniola, José Manuel Gómez Pérez, Andres Garcia Silva, Christian Berrío, Ulrich Germann, Steve Renals, and Ondrej Klejch. 2020a. European Language Grid: An Overview. In *Proceedings of the 12th Language Resources and Evaluation Conference (LREC 2020)*, pages 3359–3373, Marseille, France. European Language Resources Association (ELRA).

Georg Rehm, Kalina Bontcheva, Khalid Choukri, Jan Hajic, Stelios Piperidis, and Andrejs Vasiljevs, editors. 2020b. *Proceedings of the 1st International Workshop on Language Technology Platforms.* Marseille, France. 16 May 2020, https://www.european-language-grid.eu/iwltp-2020/.

Georg Rehm, Dimitrios Galanis, Penny Labropoulou, Stelios Piperidis, Martin Welß, Ricardo Usbeck, Joachim Köhler, Miltos Deligiannis, Katerina Gkirtzou, Johannes Fischer, Christian Chiarcos, Nils Feldhus, Julián Moreno-Schneider, Florian Kintzel, Elena Montiel, Víctor Rodríguez Doncel, John P. McCrae, David Laqua, Irina Patricia Theile, Christian Dittmar, Kalina Bontcheva, Ian Roberts, Andrejs Vasiļjevs, and Andis Lagzdiņš. 2020c. Towards an Interoperable Ecosystem of AI and LT Platforms: A Roadmap for the Implementation of Different Levels of Interoperability. In *Proceedings of the 1st International Workshop on Language Technology Platforms (IWLTP 2020, co-located with LREC 2020)*, pages 96–107, Marseille, France. 16 May 2020.

Georg Rehm, Jan Hajic, Josef van Genabith, and Andrejs Vasiļjevs. 2016a. Fostering the Next Generation of European Language Technology: Recent Developments – Emerging Initiatives – Challenges and Opportunities. In *Proceedings of the 10th Language Resources and Evaluation Conference (LREC 2016)*, pages 1586–1592, Portorož, Slovenia. European Language Resources Association (ELRA).

Georg Rehm and Stefanie Hegele. 2018. Language Technology for Multilingual Europe: An Analysis of a Large-Scale Survey regarding Challenges, Demands, Gaps and Needs. In *Proceedings of the 11th Language Resources and Evaluation Conference (LREC 2018)*, pages 3282–3289, Miyazaki, Japan. European Language Resources Association (ELRA).

Georg Rehm, Katrin Marheinecke, Stefanie Hegele, Stelios Piperidis, Kalina Bontcheva, Jan Hajic, Khalid Choukri, Andrejs Vasiļjevs, Gerhard Backfried, Christoph Prinz, José Manuel Gómez Pérez, Luc Meertens, Paul Lukowicz, Josef van Genabith, Andrea Lösch, Philipp Slusallek, Morten Irgens, Patrick Gatellier, Joachim Köhler, Laure Le Bars, Dimitra Anastasiou, Albina Auksoriūtė, Núria Bel, António Branco, Gerhard Budin, Walter Daelemans,

Koenraad De Smedt, Radovan Garabík, Maria Gavriilidou, Dagmar Gromann, Svetla Koeva, Simon Krek, Cvetana Krstev, Krister Lindén, Bernardo Magnini, Jan Odijk, Maciej Ogrodniczuk, Eiríkur Rögnvaldsson, Mike Rosner, Bolette Pedersen, Inguna Skadina, Marko Tadić, Dan Tufiş, Tamás Váradi, Kadri Vider, Andy Way, and François Yvon. 2020d. The European Language Technology Landscape in 2020: Language-Centric and Human-Centric AI for Cross-Cultural Communication in Multilingual Europe. In *Proceedings of the 12th Language Resources and Evaluation Conference (LREC 2020)*, pages 3315–3325, Marseille, France. European Language Resources Association (ELRA).

Georg Rehm and Hans Uszkoreit, editors. 2012. *META-NET White Paper Series "Europe's Languages in the Digital Age"*. Springer, Heidelberg, New York, Dordrecht, London. 31 volumes on 30 European languages. http://www.meta-net.eu/whitepapers.

Georg Rehm and Hans Uszkoreit, editors. 2013. *The META-NET Strategic Research Agenda for Multilingual Europe 2020*. Springer, Heidelberg, New York, Dordrecht, London.

Georg Rehm, Hans Uszkoreit, Sophia Ananiadou, Núria Bel, Audronė Bielevičienė, Lars Borin, António Branco, Gerhard Budin, Nicoletta Calzolari, Walter Daelemans, Radovan Garabík, Marko Grobelnik, Carmen García-Mateo, Josef van Genabith, Jan Hajič, Inma Hernáez, John Judge, Svetla Koeva, Simon Krek, Cvetana Krstev, Krister Lindén, Bernardo Magnini, Joseph Mariani, John McNaught, Maite Melero, Monica Monachini, Asunción Moreno, Jan Odjik, Maciej Ogrodniczuk, Piotr Pęzik, Stelios Piperidis, Adam Przepiórkowski, Eiríkur Rögnvaldsson, Mike Rosner, Bolette Sandford Pedersen, Inguna Skadiņa, Koenraad De Smedt, Marko Tadić, Paul Thompson, Dan Tufis, Tamás Váradi, Andrejs Vasiļjevs, Kadri Vider, and Jolanta Zabarskaite. 2016b. The Strategic Impact of META-NET on the Regional, National and International Level. *Language Resources and Evaluation*, 50(2):351–374. 10.1007/s10579-015-9333-4.

Georg Rehm, Hans Uszkoreit, Ido Dagan, Vartkes Goetcherian, Mehmet Ugur Dogan, Coskun Mermer, Tamás Váradi, Sabine Kirchmeier-Andersen, Gerhard Stickel, Meirion Prys Jones, Stefan Oeter, and Sigve Gramstad. 2014. An Update and Extension of the META-NET Study "Europe's Languages in the Digital Age". In *Proceedings of the Workshop on Collaboration and Computing for Under-Resourced Languages in the Linked Open Data Era (CCURL 2014)*, pages 30–37, Reykjavik, Iceland.

Lilli Smal, Andrea Lösch, Josef van Genabith, Maria Giagkou, Thierry Declerck, and Stephan Busemann. 2020. Language Data Sharing in European Public Services – Overcoming Obstacles and Creating Sustainable Data Sharing Infrastructures. In *Proceedings of the 12th Language Resources and Evaluation Conference (LREC 2020)*, page 3443–3448, Marseille, France. European Language Resources Association (ELRA).

STOA. 2017. Language equality in the digital age – Towards a Human Language Project. STOA study (PE 598.621), IP/G/STOA/FWC/2013-001/Lot4/C2, March 2017. Carried out by Iclaves SL (Spain) at the request of the Science and Technology Options Assessment (STOA) Panel, managed by the Scientific Foresight Unit (STOA), within the Directorate-General for Parliamentary Research Services (DG EPRS) of the European Parliament. http://www.europarl.europa.eu/stoa/.

Andrejs Vasiljevs, Khalid Choukri, Luc Meertens, and Stefania Aguzzi. 2019. Final study report on CEF Automated Translation value proposition in the context of the European LT market/ecosystem. DOI 10.2759/142151. A study prepared for the European Commission, DG Communications Networks, Content & Technology by Crosslang, Tilde, ELDA, IDC.

A Selected Screenshots

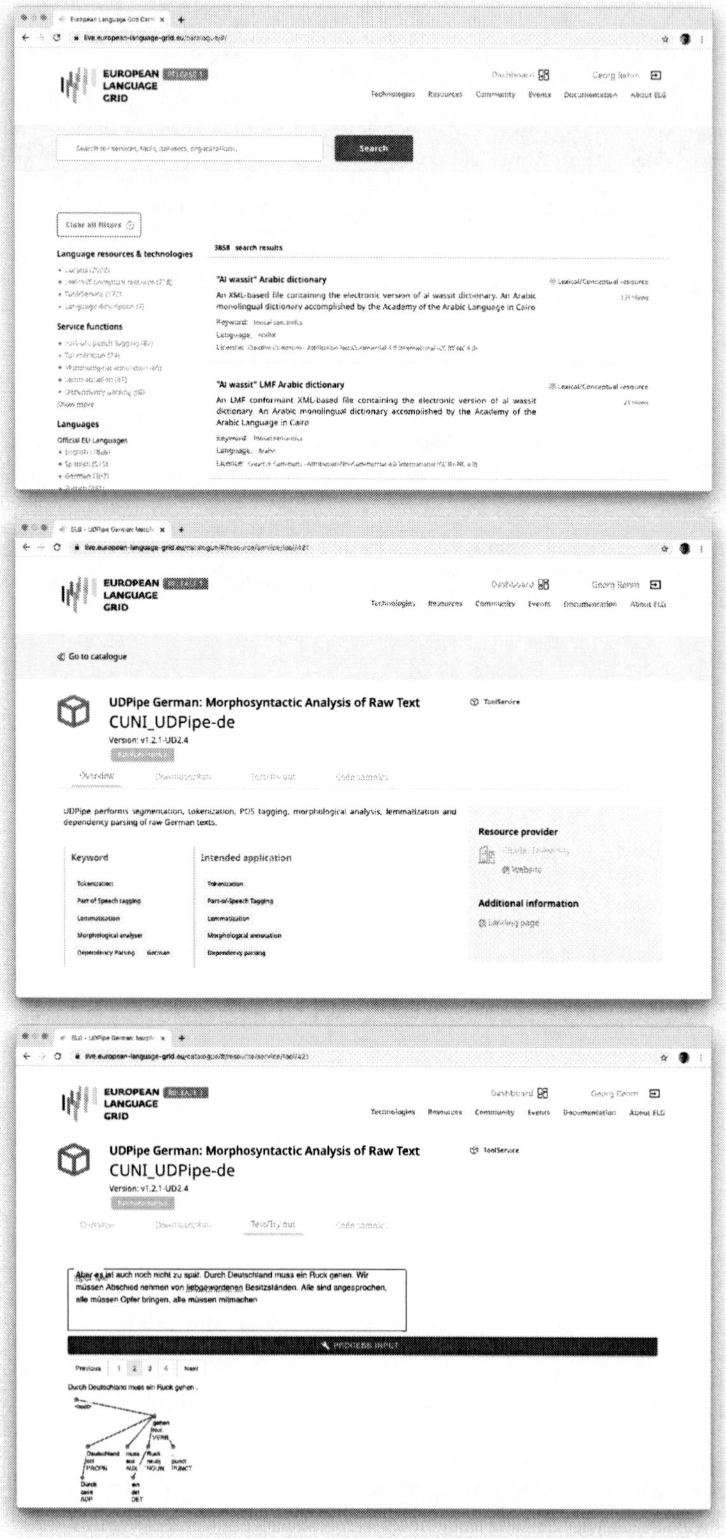

Figure 4: Selected screenshots of the European Language Grid (ELG)

A New Surprise Measure for Extracting Interesting Relationships between Persons

Hidetaka Kamigaito[1]**, Jingun Kwon**[1]**, Young-In Song**[2] **and Manabu Okumura**[1]
[1]Tokyo Institute of Technology
[2]Naver Corporation
kwon.j.ad@m.titech.ac.jp
{kamigaito,oku}@lr.pi.titech.ac.jp
song.youngin@navercorp.com

Abstract

One way to enhance user engagement in search engines is to suggest interesting facts to the user. Although relationships between persons are important as a target for text mining, there are few effective approaches for extracting the interesting relationships between persons. We therefore propose a method for extracting interesting relationships between persons from natural language texts by focusing on their surprisingness. Our method first extracts all personal relationships from dependency trees for the texts and then calculates surprise scores for distributed representations of the extracted relationships in an unsupervised manner. The unique point of our method is that it does not require any labeled dataset with annotation for the surprising personal relationships. The results of the human evaluation show that the proposed method could extract more interesting relationships between persons from Japanese Wikipedia articles than a popularity-based baseline method. We demonstrate our proposed method as a chrome plugin on google search.

Ex.1: **Tim Burton** and **Johnny Depp**
When Tim Burton met Johnny Depp for the first time, he had the impression that Johnny Depp was a hopelessly poor actor.

Ex.2: **Chien-Ming Wang** and **Suzuki Ichiro**
Chien-Ming Wang, a major-leaguer from Taiwan, asked Suzuki Ichiro three autographs before the start of the game.

Ex.3: **Ringo Starr** and **Beatles' members**
In the film Yellow Submarine, after hearing about the crisis in Pepper Land, Ringo Starr, along with Beatles companions John Lennon, George Harrison, and Paul McCartney, went to the bottom of the sea in a Yellow Submarine to save Pepper Land.

Figure 1: Example sentences that contain interesting relationships between persons.

1 Introduction

Interesting facts are useful information for a variety of important tasks. For example, in data mining, the interesting facts can enhance user engagement in search engines (Fatma et al., 2017). In natural language processing, the interesting facts can improve user experience with automatic conversation systems (Niina and Shimada, 2018). However, if we rely on experts to gather the interesting facts, the cost becomes quite high.

As a solution, several approaches have been developed to extract interesting facts automatically. Lin and Chalupsky (2003) proposed a set of unsupervised link discovery methods that can compute interestingness on graph data represented as a set of entities connected by a set of binary relations. Prakash et al. (2015) extracted interesting sentences about movie entities from Wikipedia articles and ordered them based on their interestingness by utilizing Rank-SVM, trained in a supervised manner. Tsurel et al. (2017) proposed an algorithm that automatically mines trivia facts from Wikipedia by utilizing its category structure. Their approach can rank categories for an entity based on their trivia quality induced from the categories. Fatma et al. (2017) proposed a method for automatically mining trivia facts for an entity of a given domain in knowledge graphs by utilizing deep convolutional neural networks, trained in a supervised manner. Korn et al. (2019) mined trivia facts from superlative tables in Wikipedia articles. Kwon et al. (2020) proposed a method to obtain sentences including trivia facts with utilizing paragraph structures in Wikipedia articles.

However, some of these approaches work only on structured datasets such as knowledge graphs or Wikipedia categories. In addition, while supervised approaches can work on unstructured natural language texts, the applicable domain is restricted due to the lack of annotated datasets. Hence, the current approaches for extracting interesting facts

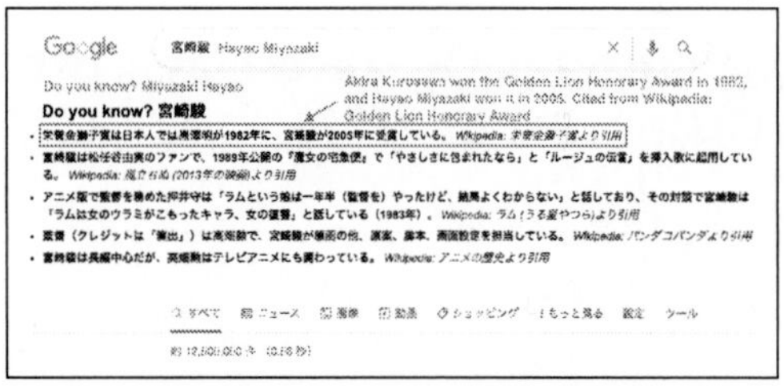

Figure 2: A screenshot of our chrome plugin. For the Japanese search query Hayao Miyazaki, top five interesting relationships are presented at the top of the search results. The red texts are translations of them.

are considered limited. In particular, although relationships between persons are important as a target for text mining, there are few effective approaches for extracting interesting relationships between persons.

Figure 1 shows examples of interesting relationships between persons.[1] The first example is a famous film director who initially had a fairly low regard for an actor who is now extremely famous and successful. The second example is about a famous baseball player who asked another famous baseball player for an autograph. The third example relates to famous musicians engaged in something completely unrelated to music. These examples illustrate that surprisingness is an important factor in interesting personal relationships.

In this paper, to extract such interesting relationships, we focus on surprising relationships between persons. We propose a method that extracts relationships between persons from natural language texts and then scores their surprise scores based on the Mahalanobis distance (De Maesschalck et al., 2000), which has been used in the outlier detection task. Our proposed method first extracts all personal relationships from dependency trees for each sentence and then calculates the surprise scores of the extracted relationships on a continuous vector space in an unsupervised manner. As such, our method does not require any labeled dataset for extracting the surprising personal relationships.

The results of our human evaluation show that the proposed method could extract more interesting relationships between persons from Japanese Wikipedia articles than a popularity-based baseline method. Furthermore, as shown in Figure 2, we incorporated our method into a google chrome plugin. You can watch our demo video for this plugin at a shared directory in our google drive.

[1]These examples were extracted from Japanese Wikipedia articles and then were translated into English.

2 Extracting Interesting Relationships between Persons

Figure 3 provides an overview of the entire process of extracting sentences that may include interesting personal relationships about a target person from given documents. The extraction procedure is as follows:

1. Construct dependency trees from sentences in the target documents through an automatic dependency parser.
2. Extract personal relationships that are represented as tuples of persons and their relationships from the obtained dependency trees.
3. Calculate scores for whether the extracted personal relationships are interesting or not.
4. Select top-k personal relationships and sentences that include the target person based on the calculated scores.

The details of each step are described in the following subsections.

2.1 Extracting Personal Relationships

We use a dependency parser for extracting personal relationships from sentences. First, we parse given sentences with the parser and obtain their dependency trees. Next, if a sentence includes more than one person name, we extract pairs of two names e_i and e_j. We also extract a set p_k that includes words $\{w_1, \cdots, w_n\}$ in the shortest path between e_i and e_j on the dependency tree. These elements are represented as a tuple r_l as follows:

$$r_l = (e_i, e_j, p_k). \tag{1}$$

Because r_l is a tuple, it satisfies $r_{l,0} = e_i$, $r_{l,1} = e_j$, and $r_{l,2} = p_k$.

2.2 Representation of Personal Relationships

For calculating a score of interestingness for r_l, we encode e_i, e_j, and p_k into fixed-dimensional continuous vectors by utilizing the skip-gram model (Mikolov et al., 2013). When training the model, we treat a person name as a single word. Hereafter, we represent the vector of a word w_i as E_{w_i}. Thus, the person names e_i and e_j are represented as E_{e_i} and E_{e_j}, respectively.

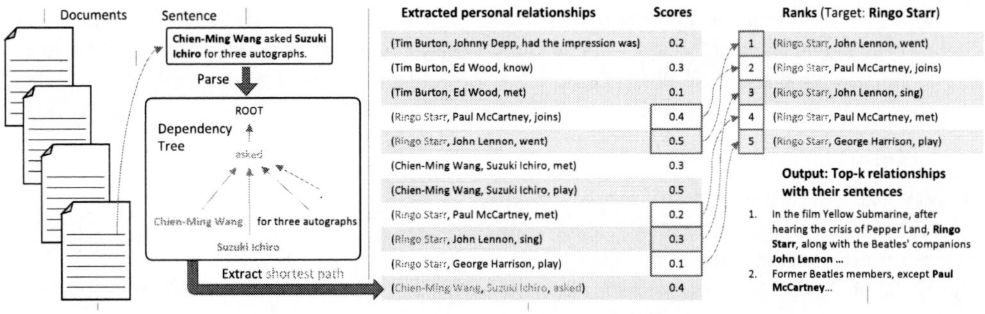

Figure 3: Overview of our proposed method for extracting interesting relationships between persons from given documents.

To cope with person names e_i with few occurrences, that might cause the sparseness problem, we map person names e_i to clusters, whose number is smaller than the number of person names. We represent a cluster that e_i is assigned to as C_{e_i}. We use k-means as a clustering method to ensure that these clusters are based on the cosine similarity between the vectors.

Unlike the person names, the relationship between two persons, p_k, is represented as a set of words. For encoding the set of words representing the relationship into the continuous vector space, we use smooth inverse frequency (SIF) (Arora et al., 2017),[2] which can encode a sequence of words into a continuous vector by utilizing the frequencies of the words for calculating the weighted sum of the word vectors. Algorithm 1 describes the details of the procedure for obtaining the vector representation of each personal relationship. Through this procedure, we can get V_{p_k}, which is the vector representation of p_k in r_l included in Rel, where Rel is a set of all personal relationships in the corpus.

Algorithm 1 Vector representation for each relationship.

Input: All personal relationships Rel.
Output: Vectors for each personal relationship $\{V_{p_k} | p_k = r_{l,0}, r_{l,0} \in Rel\}$.
Calculate a weighted sum of the word vectors for each r_l based on a word frequency $f(w_{m'})$ of a word $w_{m'}$ and hyper-parameter a.
for all relation p_k in Rel **do**
  $V_{p_k} \leftarrow \frac{1}{|p_{k'}|} \sum_{w_{m'} \in p_{k'}} \frac{a}{a+f(w_{m'})} E_{w_{m'}}$
end for
Form a matrix A whose columns are $\{V_{p_k} | p_k = r_{l,0}, r_{l,0} \in Rel\}$ and then obtain left singular vector u through singular value decomposition (SVD).
$u \leftarrow SVD(A)$
Transform the original vectors V_{p_k} with the obtained u.
for all relation p_k in Rel **do**
  $V_{p_k} \leftarrow uu^{\top} V_{p_k}$
end for

2.3 Scoring Personal Relationships

In this section, we describe our scoring method for extracting interesting relationships between persons. Our method tries to take into account the following three aspects of the interestingness: **Popularity**, **Surprisingness**, and **Commonness**. The scoring method is based on our assumption that an unusual relationship in a commonly observed pair of two famous persons increases the interestingness, and thus, such a relationship is interesting. The popularity calculates the fame of the persons, the surprisingness calculates the rareness of the relationship, and the commonness calculates how often the pair of the persons commonly appears. The next subsections explain the scores for each aspect in detail.

2.3.1 Popularity

To judge whether the relationships between persons are interesting or not, the reader must know them in advance. From this viewpoint, we consider that the popularity of each person is an important factor in judging whether the relationship between the persons is interesting. Taking this assumption into account, we define $S_{ppl}(e_j)$, the popularity for e_j, as follows:

$$S_{ppl}(e_j) = log(1 + freq(e_j)), \quad (2)$$

[2]https://github.com/PrincetonML/SIF

where $freq(\cdot)$ is a function that returns the frequency of the input element. $S_{ppl}(e_i)$ can be similarly defined. Note that we use Wikipedia articles for counting the frequency of entities.

2.3.2 Surprisingness

We assume that a surprising personal relationship is a kind of outlier in a set of personal relationships. We use the Mahalanobis distance (De Maesschalck et al., 2000) in the outlier detection task for defining the surprisingness of a personal relationship. Since both the persons and their relationships are represented as continuous vectors, we use a multivariate normal distribution to handle them. If the dimensions of continuous vectors are independent with each other, the variance-covariance matrix of the multivariate normal distribution becomes a diagonal matrix. Under this condition, the Mahalanobis distance is defined as follows:

$$Outlier(\mathbf{x}_i; X) = \sqrt{\sum_{j=1}^{D} \frac{(\mathbf{x}_{i,j} - \hat{\mu}_j)^2}{\hat{\sigma}_j^2}}, \quad (3)$$

where D is a dimension size of $\mathbf{x}$. As explained later, while we consider vector representations of entities as elements of X for the commonness, we consider vector representations of relationships between persons as elements of X for the surprisingness. Both the elements are based on co-occurrence of persons. Thus, these may encounter the sparseness problem.

To deal with the sparseness problem of the elements in X, we use a maximum a posterior probability (MAP) estimation to calculate the mean $\hat{\mu}$ and variance $\hat{\sigma}$. Assuming that each dimension of the continuous vectors obey a normal distribution whose prior distribution of the mean is also a normal distribution $N(\alpha, \beta^2)$ with mean α and variance β^2, the mean $\hat{\mu}$ and the standard deviation $\hat{\sigma}$ is estimated as follows:

$$\hat{\mu} = \frac{\alpha \odot \sigma \odot \sigma + \beta \odot \beta \odot \sum_{i=1}^{|X|} x_i}{|X|\beta \odot \beta + \sigma \odot \sigma}, \quad (4)$$

$$\hat{\sigma} = \sqrt{\frac{1}{|X|} \sum_{i=1}^{|X|} (\hat{\mu} - x_i) \odot (\hat{\mu} - x_i)}, \quad (5)$$

where $|X|$ is the number of elements in X, and $\odot$ is an element-wise product. To use Eq. (3) for calculating surprisingness for a given personal relationship, we need to consider a set $Set_{e_i,e_j,*}$ whose elements are relationships between persons e_i and e_j. However, considering a pair of entities may cause the sparseness problem. To avoid the problem, we use clusters again (as explained in Section 2.2) for representing e_i and e_j to define $Set_{e_i,e_j,*}$ as follows:

$$\begin{aligned} Set_{e_i,e_j,*} =& \{p_k = r_{n,2} | C_{r_{n,0}} = C_{e_i} \\ & \wedge C_{r_{n,1}} = C_{e_j} \wedge r_n \in Rel\}. \end{aligned} \quad (6)$$

By using $Set_{e_i,e_j,*}$, the surprisingness of a relationship p_k between e_i and e_j, S_{sup}, is calculated as follows:

$$\begin{aligned} & S_{sup}(e_i, e_j, p_k) \\ =& Outlier(V_{p_k}; \{V_{p_{k'}} | p_{k'} \in Set_{e_i,e_j,*}\}). \end{aligned} \quad (7)$$

When calculating the outlier scores in Eq. (7), we estimate the prior mean α and prior variance β^2 through a maximum likelihood estimation, based on the whole vector representation of personal relationships in the corpus.

2.3.3 Commonness

To determine whether relationships between persons are surprising or not, people must know the ordinary relationships between them in advance.

For example, in Ex.3 of Figure 1, to be surprised by this sentence, the readers must know the common relationships between Ringo Starr and the other members of The Beatles. Since they know that singing, playing a music, etc. are the common relationship among the members of The Beatles, they can be surprised by the phrase "went to the bottom of the sea" in the sentence. Thus, considering how often a pair of persons have a relationship can support our surprisingness. Based on the assumption, our commonness measures how common a pair of two persons.

Since counting the co-occurrence between two persons may cause the sparseness problem, we use continuous vectors for calculating this score. Specifically, we use the minus valued score of Eq.(3), based on the assumption that a pair of two persons is the common pair if it is not an outlier. To use Eq.(3) for calculating commonness, we need to use a set $Set_{e_i,*}$ whose elements are a person who has a relationship with a person e_i. To avoid the sparseness problem, we represent e_i as a cluster again (as explained in Section 2.2) and define $Set_{e_i,*}$ as follows:

$$Set_{e_i,*} = \{e_j = r_{n,1} | C_{r_{n,0}} = C_{e_i} \wedge r_n \in Rel\}, \quad (8)$$

where Rel is a set that includes all relationships between persons in the corpus. By using $Set_{e_i,*}$, commonness S_{com} from e_j to e_i is calculated as follows:

$$S_{com}(e_i|e_j) \tag{9}$$
$$= -\,Outlier(E_{e_i}; \{E_{e_{i'}}|e_{i'} \in Set_{e_j,*}\}). \tag{10}$$

$S_{com}(e_j|e_i)$ is defined similarly. Because $S_{com}(e_i|e_j)$ and $S_{com}(e_j|e_i)$ do not return the same score, we simply use their average for our final score. When calculating the outlier scores in Eq.(10) , we estimate the prior mean α and prior variance β^2 through a maximum likelihood estimation based on the whole word vectors.

2.4 Selecting Top-k Personal Relationships

For ranking personal relationships, we combine all the above three scores. Because these scores have different ranges with each other, we scale them with z-score normalization (Kreyszig, 1979). Let the mean of S_{ppl}, S_{com}, and S_{sup} on all relationships be respectively μ_{ppl}, μ_{com}, and μ_{sup}, and let the variance of S_{ppl}, S_{com}, and S_{sup} on all relationships be respectively σ_{ppl}, σ_{com}, and σ_{sup}. The final score of the interestingness for the target entity e_i is defined as follows:

$$S_{int}(e_i, e_j, p_k) \tag{11}$$
$$= \lambda_{ppl} \cdot \frac{S_{ppl}(e_j) - \mu_{ppl}}{\sigma_{ppl}} \tag{12}$$
$$+ \lambda_{com} \cdot \frac{1}{2} \cdot \left(\frac{S_{com}(e_i|e_j) - \mu_{com}}{\sigma_{com}} + fracS_{com}(e_j|e_i) - \mu_{com}\sigma_{com} \right) \tag{13}$$
$$+ \lambda_{sup} \cdot \frac{S_{sup}(e_i, e_j, p_k) - \mu_{sup}}{\sigma_{sup}}, \tag{14}$$

where λ_{ppl}, λ_{com} and λ_{sup} are weights for adjusting the importance of each score. We tune these weights by using our validation dataset (explained in the next section). Based on $S_{int}(e_i, e_j, p_k)$, we extract top-k relationships that include the target person e_i.

3 Experiments

We conducted human evaluation to determine how well our proposed method can extract interesting relationships between persons. The next subsections describe the details of our experimental settings and the evaluation results.

3.1 Experimental Settings

3.1.1 Dataset

We used sentences in Japanese Wikipedia as our evaluation dataset. We listed articles whose category includes the word "person" as person names and then selected the persons who have more than five relationships from various domains (e.g., anime, manga, novel, actor, music, movie, sports, comedy, and talent) based on their frequencies in Japanese Wikipedia. To remove historical persons, we selected only those who are categorized as "living persons". Finally, we obtained a total of 50 persons for the test dataset and 12 persons for the validation dataset through this process. We next extracted sentences that include personal relationships for the selected persons by using each of the compared methods, that we will describe in the next subsection. We put the top five sentences ranked by each method that include personal relationships for each selected person in the test dataset. If the same sentence was already included in the dataset, we skip it. After this procedure, for each of the compared methods, 250 sentences were included in the test dataset. To provide contextual information, we added the title of the article where the sentences were found to the sentences in the test dataset. The validation dataset was constructed in the same way for the 12 persons.

All personal relationships were extracted with CaboCha,[3] a chunk-based Japanese dependency parser, with the NEologd dictionary (Sato et al., 2017).[4] To filter the personal relationships in compound sentences, we ignored any personal relationships that include multiple predicates. When a sentence lacks its subject, we complement it with the title of the article that contains the sentence. Furthermore, we filtered any sentences starting with a pronoun or conjugation because such sentences are not understandable without the surrounding sentences.

3.1.2 Compared Methods

We evaluated the performance of the proposed methods and several baselines on our test dataset. The following methods were used as the baselines:

- **Rand**: This method randomly selects five personal relationships for each person.

[3] `https://github.com/taku910/cabocha`
[4] `https://github.com/neologd/mecab-ipadic-neologd`

- **Pop**: This method selects five personal relationships on the basis of only the popularity score (Eq.(2)).

We used the following as our proposed methods:

- **Pop+Com**: This method selects five personal relationships on the basis of the combined score of the popularity (Eq.(12)) and the commonness (Eq.(13)). Similar to Eq.(11), we tuned the weight parameters λ_{ppl} and λ_{com} on the validation dataset.

- **Pop+Sup**: This method selects five personal relationships on the basis of the combined score of the popularity (Eq.(12)) and the surprisingness (Eq.(14)). Similar to Eq.(11), we tuned the weight parameters λ_{ppl} and λ_{sup} on the validation dataset.

- **Pop+Com+Sup**: This method selects five personal relationships on the basis of a combination of the popularity, the commonness, and the surprisingness (Eq.(11)).

Prior to running these baselines and proposed methods, we obtained word vectors from Japanese Wikipedia articles by utilizing word2vec.[5] In this step, all sentences were tokenized using MeCab[6] with the NEologd dictionary. We further tuned the word vectors by utilizing a retrofitting approach (Faruqui et al., 2015)[7] with Wikipedia's category information to consider similarities between persons. The retrofitting approach can refine word vectors using graph information by making word vectors close to each other when they have a link in the graph. To construct a graph for personal similarities, we linked two words if a Wikipedia category includes the words. Because some person names have several articles due to their ambiguity, we skipped such words in this step.[8] In the end, we reran the retrofitting with the default hyperparameters. Then, we mapped the obtained word vectors of person names to 300 clusters estimated by k-means. When calculating the vectors for each personal relationship, we set a in SIF to 1.0.

	$k=1$	$k=2$	$k=3$	$k=4$	$k=5$
Rand	49.3	51.4	51.3	51.5	51.1
Pop	51.2	52.5	52.9	52.5	**52.0**
Pop+Com	52.1	52.8	53.3	52.1	51.8
Pop+Sup	54.7†	52.7	53.2	**52.6**	**52.0**
Pop+Com+Sup	**54.9**†	**52.8**	**53.8**	52.0	51.6

Table 1: Evaluation results of rescaled 5-scale scores (%). The bold values indicate the best scores. † indicates that the difference of the score from the best baseline is statistically significant.[10]

We tuned weight parameters in our methods on our validation dataset, which were created for 12 person names in Japanese Wikipedia, and which are not overlapped with the test dataset. We gathered 123 relationships related to the selected persons. Because ranking the degree of interestingness for the gathered relationships would be very costly, we simply attached a label of whether it is interesting or not to them. After that, we estimated the weight parameters by utilizing logistic regression. In Pop+Com, estimated λ_{pop} and λ_{com} were respectively 0.79 and 0.21; in Pop+Sup, estimated λ_{pop} and λ_{sup} were respectively 0.80 and 0.20; and in Pop+Com+Sup, estimated λ_{pop}, λ_{com}, and λ_{sup} were respectively 0.67, 0.17, and 0.16.

3.1.3 Evaluation Metrics

The extracted top five sentences for each method were evaluated in terms of interestingness by six human raters, who rated them on a five-point Likert scale ranging from one to five (Larger is better.). For this rating, we used Lancers,[9] a Japanese cloud sourcing service. We showed personal relationships and their sentences to the raters. For interpretability, we rescaled the rating in the range from 0.0 to 1.0 (Preston and Colman, 2000). In this rescaling, the five scales, 1, 2, 3, 4, and 5, are respectively mapped to 0.0, 0.25, 0.5, 0.75, and 1.0. We averaged the scores of all k-best results for each method.

3.2 Results

Table 1 shows the results of the five-scale scores. Pop+Sup achieved statistically significant improvement over the baselines when $k = 1$. This result can support our expectation that the surprisingness has a strong correlation to the interesting-

[5] https://code.google.com/archive/p/word2vec/

[6] http://taku910.github.io/mecab/

[7] https://github.com/mfaruqui/retrofitting

[8] Note that in Wikipedia, to disambiguate such words, brackets in article titles indicate their ambiguity. Thus, we can skip ambiguous titles based on the brackets.

[9] https://www.lancers.jp/

[10] We used paired-bootstrap-resampling (Koehn, 2004) with 10,000 random samples ($p < 0.05$).

ness of relationships between persons. In addition, Pop+Com+Sup achieved statistically significant improvement over the baselines when $k = 1$, and outperformed the scores of Pop+Sup when $k = 1, 2, 3$. These results indicate that the commonness can also support the interestingness, especially for a small number of k. When k is larger than 2, all scores are close compared with the scores at $k = 1$. This tendency may suggest that the number of interesting personal relationships is limited for each person.

4 Demonstration System

As shown in Figure 2, our demonstration system presents the top five interesting relationships between persons at the top of the search results based on the current search query. This demonstration system consists of server and client sides. The working process of the system follows the order:

1. In the client side, our google chrome plugin makes a query based on the name of the person input in the google search form.
2. The server-side distributes personal relationships of the person included in the given query to the client-side by loading from the pre-computed personal relationships and their scores.
3. After receiving the result, the client-side shows the result below the search form. If the server does not return any personal relationship, the plugin does not have any action for the search result.

The client-side was implemented on jQuery libraries, and the server-side was implemented on python 3.0 with utilizing http.server module. We chose Pop+Com+Sup as our demonstration system because this model achieved the best result in the human evaluation in the cases of $k = 1, 2$, and 3.

5 Related Work

There have been several approaches for extracting interesting facts. We can divide them into supervised and unsupervised approaches.

The unsupervised approaches have been commonly used for this type of extraction. Merzbacher (2002) proposed a method that mines good trivia questions from a relational database based on predefined rules. Lin and Chalupsky (2003) proposed a set of unsupervised link discovery methods that can compute interestingness on graph data that is represented as a set of entities connected by a set of binary relations. Tsurel et al. (2017) proposed an algorithm that automatically mines trivia facts from Wikipedia by utilizing its category structure. Their approach can rank the entity's categories by their trivia quality, which is induced by the category. Korn et al. (2019) mined trivia facts from superlative tables in Wikipedia articles. They utilized a template-based approach for semi-automatically generating natural language statements as fun facts. Their work had actually been incorporated into the search engine by Google. Kwon et al. (2020) proposed a method to obtain sentences including trivia facts by focusing on a tendency of the Wikipedia article structure that a paragraph containing trivial facts is not similar to other paragraphs in a article.

The supervised approaches have also been used for extracting interesting facts. Gamon et al. (2014) proposed models that predict the level of interest a user gives to various text spans in a document by observing the user's browsing behavior via clicks from one page to another. Prakash et al. (2015) constructed a labeled dataset for movie entities and proposed a method for extracting interesting sentences from Wikipedia articles and ordering them based on interestingness by utilizing Rank-SVM trained with the constructed dataset. Fatma et al. (2017) proposed a method for automatically mining trivia facts for an entity of a given domain in knowledge graphs by utilizing deep convolutional neural networks trained in a supervised manner.

6 Conclusion

In this paper, we proposed a method for extracting interesting relationships between persons from natural language texts in an unsupervised manner.

Human evaluation of the personal relationships extracted from Japanese Wikipedia articles showed that the proposed method improved the interestingness compared to a popularity-based baseline. Through the result, we can conclude that considering the surprisingness of relationships between persons is effective in improving the interestingness of the extracted results.

Furthermore, to demonstrate our proposed method, we incorporated the method into a google chrome plugin, which can work on google search.

As future work, we will investigate ways to extract personal relationships based on more detailed information about a dependency tree.

Acknowledgement

We are thankful to the research group at Naver Corporation for supporting our research.

References

Sanjeev Arora, Yingyu Liang, and Tengyu Ma. 2017. A simple but tough-to-beat baseline for sentence embeddings.

Roy De Maesschalck, Delphine Jouan-Rimbaud, and Désiré L Massart. 2000. The mahalanobis distance. *Chemometrics and intelligent laboratory systems*, 50(1):1–18.

Manaal Faruqui, Jesse Dodge, Sujay K. Jauhar, Chris Dyer, Eduard Hovy, and Noah A. Smith. 2015. Retrofitting word vectors to semantic lexicons. In *Proceedings of NAACL*.

Nausheen Fatma, Manoj K. Chinnakotla, and Manish Shrivastava. 2017. The unusual suspects: Deep learning based mining of interesting entity trivia from knowledge graphs. In *Proceedings of the Thirty-First AAAI Conference on Artificial Intelligence*, AAAI'17, page 1107–1113. AAAI Press.

Michael Gamon, Arjun Mukherjee, and Patrick Pantel. 2014. Predicting interesting things in text. In *Proceedings of COLING 2014, the 25th International Conference on Computational Linguistics: Technical Papers*, pages 1477–1488, Dublin, Ireland. Dublin City University and Association for Computational Linguistics.

Philipp Koehn. 2004. Statistical significance tests for machine translation evaluation. In *Proceedings of the 2004 Conference on Empirical Methods in Natural Language Processing*, pages 388–395, Barcelona, Spain. Association for Computational Linguistics.

Flip Korn, Xuezhi Wang, You Wu, and Cong Yu. 2019. Automatically generating interesting facts from wikipedia tables. In *Proceedings of the 2019 International Conference on Management of Data*, SIGMOD '19, page 349–361, New York, NY, USA. Association for Computing Machinery.

Erwin. Kreyszig. 1979. *Advanced engineering mathematics /*, 4th ed. edition. Wiley,, New York :.

Jingun Kwon, Hidetaka Kamigaito, Young-In Song, and Manabu Okumura. 2020. Hierarchical trivia fact extraction from Wikipedia articles. In *Proceedings of the 28th International Conference on Computational Linguistics*, pages 4825–4834, Barcelona, Spain (Online). International Committee on Computational Linguistics.

Shou-de Lin and Hans Chalupsky. 2003. Using unsupervised link discovery methods to find interesting facts and connections in a bibliography dataset. *SIGKDD Explor. Newsl.*, 5(2):173–178.

Matthew Merzbacher. 2002. Automatic generation of trivia questions. In *Proceedings of the 13th International Symposium on Foundations of Intelligent Systems*, ISMIS '02, page 123–130, Berlin, Heidelberg. Springer-Verlag.

Tomas Mikolov, Ilya Sutskever, Kai Chen, Greg Corrado, and Jeffrey Dean. 2013. Distributed representations of words and phrases and their compositionality. In *Proceedings of the 26th International Conference on Neural Information Processing Systems - Volume 2*, NIPS'13, page 3111–3119, Red Hook, NY, USA. Curran Associates Inc.

Kazuya Niina and Kazutaka Shimada. 2018. Trivia score and ranking estimation using support vector regression and RankNet. In *Proceedings of the 32nd Pacific Asia Conference on Language, Information and Computation*, Hong Kong. Association for Computational Linguistics.

Abhay Prakash, Manoj Kumar Chinnakotla, Dhaval Patel, and Puneet Garg. 2015. Did you know? - mining interesting trivia for entities from wikipedia. In *Proceedings of the Twenty-Fourth International Joint Conference on Artificial Intelligence, IJCAI 2015, Buenos Aires, Argentina, July 25-31, 2015*, pages 3164–3170.

Carolyn Preston and Andrew Colman. 2000. Optimal number of response categories in rating scales: Reliability, validity, discriminating power, and respondent preferences. *Acta psychologica*, 104:1–15.

Toshinori Sato, Taiichi Hashimoto, and Manabu Okumura. 2017. Implementation of a word segmentation dictionary called mecab-ipadic-neologd and study on how to use it effectively for information retrieval (in japanese). In *NLP*, pages NLP2017–B6–1. The Association for Natural Language Processing.

David Tsurel, Dan Pelleg, Ido Guy, and Dafna Shahaf. 2017. Fun facts: Automatic trivia fact extraction from wikipedia. In *Proceedings of the Tenth ACM International Conference on Web Search and Data Mining*, WSDM '17, page 345–354, New York, NY, USA. Association for Computing Machinery.

This page intentionally left blank.

Paladin: an annotation tool based on active and proactive learning

Minh-Quoc Nghiem[1,2], **Paul Baylis**[2], **Sophia Ananiadou**[1]
[1] National Centre for Text Mining
School of Computer Science, The University of Manchester, United Kingdom
[2] Bott and Co Solicitors
{minh-quoc.nghiem, sophia.ananiadou}@manchester.ac.uk
p.baylis@bottonline.co.uk

Abstract

In this paper, we present Paladin, an open-source web-based annotation tool for creating high-quality multi-label document-level datasets. By integrating active learning and proactive learning to the annotation task, Paladin makes the task less time-consuming and requiring less human effort. Although Paladin is designed for multi-label settings, the system is flexible and can be adapted to other tasks in single-label settings.

1 Introduction

Labelled data is essential in many NLP tasks based on Machine Learning. Manually annotating such data is time-consuming, and require a lot of human effort. *Active learning* has been used to ease this process by choosing the data points for annotation instead of annotating all instances of the unlabeled data (Settles, 2009). Some recent research has also utilized *proactive learning*, in which the system is allowed to assign specific unlabeled instances to specific annotators (Li et al., 2019). The annotators, in these scenarios, only have to annotate a small set of representative and informative data which they can provide reliable labels. It helps reduce the labelling effort and at the same time makes the best use of available annotators.

To date, there are many tools available for active learning, such as the TexNLP (Baldridge and Palmer, 2009), the Active-Learning-Scala (Santos and Carvalho, 2014), the JCLAL (Reyes et al., 2016), the LibAct (Yang et al., 2017) libraries, the Vowpal Wabbit[1]. These tools, however, focus only on the active learning algorithms and provide no user interface thus making it difficult to use for the end-users. On the other hand, several tools have been made with user-friendly interface such as BRAT (Stenetorp et al., 2012), WebAnno (Yimam et al., 2013), PubAnnotation (Kim and Wang, 2012), doccano[2]. Some of the tools offer active/proactive learning such as APLenty (Nghiem and Ananiadou, 2018), DUALIST (Settles and Zhu, 2012), AlpacaTag (Lin et al., 2019), Discrete Active Learning Coref (Li et al., 2020a). Currently, these tools support sequence labelling/coreference resolution tasks but not document classification tasks. To the best of our knowledge, there is no such tool for document classification which supports active/proactive learning. Prodigy[3] supports active learning for both sequence labelling and document classification tasks but it is a commercial product.

To compensate for the lack of available document-level annotation tool, we develop **Paladin** (**Pro**active **l**earning **a**nnotator for **d**ocument **in**stances), an open-source web-based system for creating labelled data using active/proactive learning[4]. The main innovation of Paladin is the combination of a user-friendly annotation tool with active/proactive learning. Specifically:

1. Active/proactive learning integration: Paladin makes annotation easy, time-efficient, and require less human effort by offering active and proactive learning.

2. An easy-to-use interface for annotators: Paladin adapts the interface of doccano, making annotation intuitive and easy to use.

3. Suitable for multi-label document annotation tasks: Paladin is best used for multi-label document annotation tasks, although it can be used for other single-label classification problems.

[1] http://hunch.net/~vw/

[2] https://github.com/doccano

[3] https://prodi.gy/

[4] The source code is publicly available at https://github.com/bluenqm/Paladin

Proceedings of the 16th Conference of the European Chapter of the Association for Computational Linguistics: System Demonstrations, pages 238–243
April 19 - 23, 2021. ©2021 Association for Computational Linguistics

The remainder of this paper is organized as follows. Section 2 presents details of Paladin. Section 3 describes a case study of using Paladin for a multi-label document annotation task. Section 4 concludes the paper and points to avenues for future work.

2 System Descriptions

Paladin is a web-based tool implemented in Python using Django web framework and Vue.js. The main user interface consists of a project management page and an annotation page. Below, this section describes Paladin in detail.

2.1 Project management

In Paladin, there are two main types of user role: the project manager role and the annotator role. A project manager can create/customise annotation projects and add annotators to the projects. The annotators can annotate text assigned to them. The interface allows the project manager to: 1. create a project 2. define the tagset 3. upload the seeding and unlabelled data to the webserver 4. assign annotators to a project 5. choose the active/proactive learning strategy. The project manager can additionally set how the batch is allocated, the sampling and proficiency thresholds, the steps before retraining and samples per session as illustrated in Figure 1.

Figure 1: Project Settings

When creating a new annotation project, the project manager needs to upload two datasets (in Tab Separated Values format) to the server. The first dataset is the seeding dataset, which will be used by the system to train the classifier and estimate the annotators' proficiency. The second dataset is the unlabelled dataset, on which the system chooses the text to assign to the annotators. If there is no seeding data, the system will select random text from the unlabelled dataset for annotation in the first batch. Figure 2 shows the text when successfully uploaded to the system.

Figure 2: Dataset/Seed Dataset

2.2 Annotation interface

For annotation and visualization of annotated documents, we adapted the doccano annotation interface. The annotation interface displays a set of documents that are assigned to the annotator, one at a time as illustrated in Figure 3. The annotator can navigate to next or previous documents during annotation using the "Prev" or "Next" buttons. When working on Paladin, the annotator uses the mouse or keyboard shortcut to select label(s) for the current document. When finishing the assigned documents, the annotator can click on "Finish Annotation". The system will validate the annotated documents, retrain the classifier, and assign new documents to the annotator. Each annotator can only see the documents assigned to him/her in the current batch.

2.3 Active learning

Depending on the project manager's settings, the system chooses different document instances to send to the annotators. The project manager can choose to prioritise the most informative instances for the classifier or to maintain the balance between the number of instances in each class. With the first option, the system prioritises the most

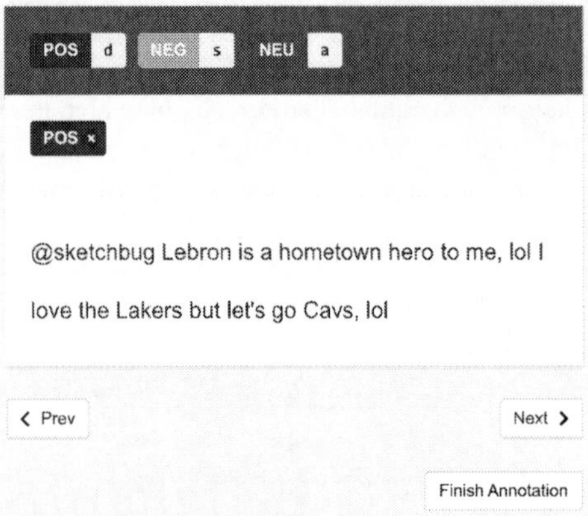

Figure 3: Annotation interface. The displayed sentence was taken from the Sentiment140 dataset. All labels are shown in the blue rectangle box with the shortcut keys next to them. Annotated labels are shown above the sentence.

informative documents, regardless of the class. Paladin currently employs the least confidence uncertainty-based strategy (Culotta and McCallum, 2005) based on the classification outputs from a Transformer model (Devlin et al., 2019). A linear model is added to the embedding output to predict the score for the labels. Previous research has established that active learning can increase the performance of Transformer-based text classifiers (Grießhaber et al., 2020). With the second option, the system uses the same classification outputs but unlabelled instances are taken from each class in equal amounts. The default option in Paladin is the second one. This setting aims to minimise the unbalanced data problems where we have unequal instances for different classes.

Paladin uses pool-based sampling scenario, where the data samples are chosen for labeling from the unlabeled dataset. The project manager, however, can upload additional unlabeled data to an existing annotation project at anytime.

2.4 Proactive learning

In many annotation tasks, we assume that the annotators are experts who always provide correct annotations. But in reality, different annotators have different levels of expertise in different domains. It has been demonstrated that proactive learning is helpful for task allocation in crowdsourcing setting where the level of expertise varies from annotator to annotator (Donmez and Carbonell, 2010; Li et al., 2017, 2019, 2020b). Proactive learning is useful in modelling the annotator reliability which can be used to assign the unlabelled instances to the best possible annotators.

Before any annotation, Paladin estimates the proficiency of the annotators for each class by assigning the documents in the seed dataset to all annotators. When the annotators finish labelling these seed documents, the system calculates the likelihood that a particular annotator provides a correct label for a particular label. Then, when assigning new documents to the annotators, Paladin will assign the documents to the best possible annotators by combining the predicted label(s) and the likelihood that the annotator provides a correct label for a particular label. The system will update the estimation after every annotation batch.

3 Use cases

The typical use cases of Paladin are as following:

1. A user wishes to add more data to an existing dataset to improve model performance: the user can use the existing labelled dataset as the seed to train the initial model, the labels will be automatically extracted from the labelled dataset. The model will select instances from the unlabelled dataset and then distribute them to the annotators for annotation.

2. A user wishes to create a labelled dataset from scratch: the user needs to provide the tag set and the unlabelled data. The first iteration will select unlabelled instances for annotation randomly. After the first iteration, the process is the same as the previous use case.

3. A user wishes to add more data to an existing unbalanced dataset: the user can choose "maintain class balance" option in Settings. With this option, the model will try to select more data from the potential minority classes for annotation.

4 Experiments and Results

4.1 Simulated Annotators

We used the Toxic Comment Classification Challenge dataset[5] for this experiment. The dataset contains Wikipedia comments which have been manually labelled for toxic behaviour. There are

[5] https://www.kaggle.com/c/jigsaw-toxic-comment-classification-challenge/data

six classes: toxic, severe toxic, obscene, threat, insult, and identity hate. In the experiment, we used 60 comments as the initial training data (seed), 600 comments as test data, and 18,000 for unlabelled data. The instances forming the seed and test data are randomly taken from the original data but we make sure that each class has at least 10 instances and 100 instances in the seed and test data respectively.

We compare three settings in this case study. The first one is Random Sampling: the system randomly chooses the next documents for annotation. The second one is Active Learning: the system uses the output of the trained model to assign new documents to an expert (annotator who always provide correct labels). The third one is Proactive Learning: same as Active Learning, but we have two annotators, one expert, and one fallible annotator (annotator who makes mistakes with a probability of 0.1). Figure 4 shows the F1 scores on the test set. In all cases, active/proactive learning setting outperformed Random Sampling setting.

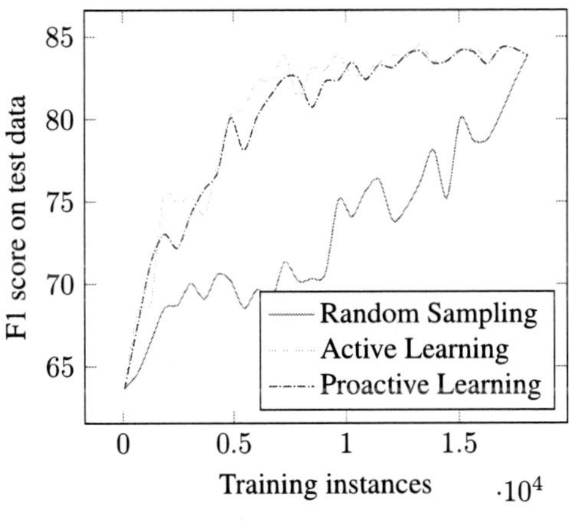

Figure 4: Learning curve

4.2 Real-World Annotators

For this experiment, we worked with a consumer law firm analysing 6,880 emails. Each email can have one or more labels from a predefined list which consist of 15 labels. Some examples are "update query", "payment query", and "fee query". Given an email, the annotator had to annotate all labels that are applicable to that email. There are a total of 2,000 emails which were already annotated.

This dataset is an unbalanced dataset where nearly two-thirds of the emails belong to the 5 most common labels while less than 7 percent of the emails come from the 5 least common labels. In the experiment, we used 1,000 emails as the initial training data, 1,000 emails as test data, and the rest (4,880) as unlabelled data. The purpose of the experiment was to investigate the performance of Paladin with an unbalanced seed dataset.

Using Paladin, we created an annotation project with four annotators and in each annotation session, an annotator must annotate 20 emails. All annotators are members of the law firm with legal background. We used "maintain class balance" and "best annotators first" for active learning strategy and proactive learning strategy respectively. We stopped when a total of 1,000 emails were annotated. Figure 5 shows the F1 scores and the stacking percentages of label instance count. The results showed that the F1 score and percentage of minority classes were gradually increased after each annotation batch.

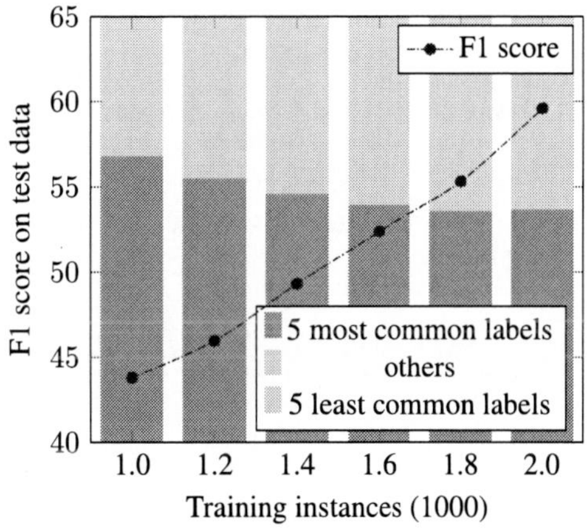

Figure 5: F1 scores and percentages of label instance count. We grouped 5 labels together for readability.

We used an Intel Core i9 9820X Linux server with 64GB RAM and a Titan RTX GPU. When allocating a new annotation batch (retraining the model, predicting the unlabelled instances, selecting new instances for annotation), Paladin runs consistently at the rate of around 0.01 to 0.02 seconds per document and it takes less than two minutes to get results. The average level of satisfaction (with ratings from 1 to 5 of three aspects: responsiveness, easy to annotate, easy to navigate) of the annotators with the annotation tool is 4.5/5.

5 Conclusion

We introduced Paladin, a web-based open environment for constructing multi-label document-level datasets using active and proactive learning. Paladin can support the quick development of high-quality labelled data needed to train and evaluate NLP tools for different applications.

Considerably more work will need to be done to further enhance Paladin to work with other active/proactive learning algorithms. Besides that, a natural progression of this work is to evaluate Paladin in a large scale annotation project.

Acknowledgments

This research has been carried out with funding from KTP11612. We would like to thank the anonymous reviewers for their helpful comments.

References

Jason Baldridge and Alexis Palmer. 2009. How well does active learning actually work?: Time-based evaluation of cost-reduction strategies for language documentation. In *Proceedings of the 2009 Conference on Empirical Methods in Natural Language Processing: Volume 1-Volume 1*, pages 296–305. Association for Computational Linguistics.

Aron Culotta and Andrew McCallum. 2005. Reducing labeling effort for structured prediction tasks. In *AAAI*, volume 5, pages 746–751.

Jacob Devlin, Ming-Wei Chang, Kenton Lee, and Kristina Toutanova. 2019. BERT: Pre-training of deep bidirectional transformers for language understanding. In *Proceedings of the 2019 Conference of the North American Chapter of the Association for Computational Linguistics: Human Language Technologies, Volume 1 (Long and Short Papers)*, pages 4171–4186, Minneapolis, Minnesota. Association for Computational Linguistics.

Pinar Donmez and Jaime G Carbonell. 2010. From active to proactive learning methods. In *Advances in Machine Learning I*, pages 97–120. Springer.

Daniel Grießhaber, Johannes Maucher, and Ngoc Thang Vu. 2020. Fine-tuning BERT for low-resource natural language understanding via active learning. In *Proceedings of the 28th International Conference on Computational Linguistics*, pages 1158–1171, Barcelona, Spain (Online). International Committee on Computational Linguistics.

Jin-Dong Kim and Yue Wang. 2012. Pubannotation: a persistent and sharable corpus and annotation repository. In *Proceedings of the 2012 Workshop on Biomedical Natural Language Processing*, pages 202–205. Association for Computational Linguistics.

Belinda Z. Li, Gabriel Stanovsky, and Luke Zettlemoyer. 2020a. Active learning for coreference resolution using discrete annotation. In *Proceedings of the 58th Annual Meeting of the Association for Computational Linguistics*, pages 8320–8331, Online. Association for Computational Linguistics.

Maolin Li, Arvid Fahlström Myrman, Tingting Mu, and Sophia Ananiadou. 2019. Modelling instance-level annotator reliability for natural language labelling tasks. In *Proceedings of the 2019 Conference of the North American Chapter of the Association for Computational Linguistics: Human Language Technologies, Volume 1 (Long and Short Papers)*, pages 2873–2883, Minneapolis, Minnesota. Association for Computational Linguistics.

Maolin Li, Nhung Nguyen, and Sophia Ananiadou. 2017. Proactive learning for named entity recognition. In *BioNLP 2017*, pages 117–125, Vancouver, Canada,. Association for Computational Linguistics.

Maolin Li, Hiroya Takamura, and Sophia Ananiadou. 2020b. A neural model for aggregating coreference annotation in crowdsourcing. In *Proceedings of the 28th International Conference on Computational Linguistics*, pages 5760–5773, Barcelona, Spain (Online). International Committee on Computational Linguistics.

Bill Yuchen Lin, Dong-Ho Lee, Frank F. Xu, Ouyu Lan, and Xiang Ren. 2019. AlpacaTag: An active learning-based crowd annotation framework for sequence tagging. In *Proceedings of the 57th Annual Meeting of the Association for Computational Linguistics: System Demonstrations*, pages 58–63, Florence, Italy. Association for Computational Linguistics.

Minh-Quoc Nghiem and Sophia Ananiadou. 2018. APLenty: annotation tool for creating high-quality datasets using active and proactive learning. In *Proceedings of the 2018 Conference on Empirical Methods in Natural Language Processing: System Demonstrations*, pages 108–113, Brussels, Belgium. Association for Computational Linguistics.

Oscar Reyes, Eduardo Pérez, María Del Carmen Rodríguez-Hernández, Habib M Fardoun, and Sebastián Ventura. 2016. JCLAL: a Java framework for active learning. *The Journal of Machine Learning Research*, 17(1):3271–3275.

Davi P Santos and André CPLF Carvalho. 2014. Comparison of active learning strategies and proposal of a multiclass hypothesis space search. In *Hybrid Artificial Intelligence Systems*, pages 618–629. Springer.

Burr Settles. 2009. Active learning literature survey. Computer Sciences Technical Report 1648, University of Wisconsin–Madison.

Burr Settles and Xiaojin Zhu. 2012. Behavioral factors in interactive training of text classifiers. In *Proceedings of the 2012 Conference of the North*

American Chapter of the Association for Computational Linguistics: Human Language Technologies, pages 563–567. Association for Computational Linguistics.

Pontus Stenetorp, Sampo Pyysalo, Goran Topić, Tomoko Ohta, Sophia Ananiadou, and Jun'ichi Tsujii. 2012. BRAT: a web-based tool for NLP-assisted text annotation. In *Proceedings of the Demonstrations at the 13th Conference of the European Chapter of the Association for Computational Linguistics*, pages 102–107. Association for Computational Linguistics.

Yao-Yuan Yang, Shao-Chuan Lee, Yu-An Chung, Tung-En Wu, Si-An Chen, and Hsuan-Tien Lin. 2017. libact: Pool-based active learning in Python. Technical report, National Taiwan University. Available as arXiv preprint `https://arxiv.org/abs/1710.00379`.

Seid Muhie Yimam, Iryna Gurevych, Richard Eckart de Castilho, and Chris Biemann. 2013. WebAnno: A flexible, web-based and visually supported system for distributed annotations. In *Proceedings of the 51st Annual Meeting of the Association for Computational Linguistics: System Demonstrations*, pages 1–6.

Story Centaur: Large Language Model Few Shot Learning as a Creative Writing Tool

Ben Swanson, Kory W. Mathewson[2], Ben Pietrzak,
Sherol Chen, Monica Dinalescu
Google, [2]DeepMind
pwnr, korymath, bpietrzak, sherol, noms@google.com

Abstract

Few shot learning with large language models has the potential to give individuals without formal machine learning training the access to a wide range of text to text models. We consider how this applies to creative writers and present STORY CENTAUR, a user interface for prototyping few shot models and a set of recombinable web components that deploy them. STORY CENTAUR's goal is to expose creative writers to few shot learning with a simple but powerful interface that lets them compose their own co-creation tools that further their own unique artistic directions. We build out several examples of such tools, and in the process probe the boundaries and issues surrounding generation with large language models.

1 Introduction

One of the most promising possibilities for large language models (LLMs) is *few-shot learning* (Brown et al., 2020) in which it is possible to create text to text models with little or no training data. Few shot learning with LLMs relies on the ease at which the desired Input/Output (I/O) behavior can be effectively translated into the text continuation problem at which these models excel. In recent years, LLMs have progressed to the level where this translation requires only familiarity with the natural (e.g. English) language on which the model was trained.

We present STORY CENTAUR, a Human-Computer Interface that closes the gap between non-technical users and the power and possibilities of few shot learning, with the intended audience of writers of creative text. It is our intention that by giving writers a tool for building generative text models unique to their process and vision that these artists will experience genuine feelings of co-creation.

STORY CENTAUR consists of a prototyping UI as well as a set of Angular web components that interact via a central pub-sub synchronization mechanism[1]. Due to the non-trivial monetary cost of inference and the requirement of specialized hardware, the LLM that underlies our tool is not included in this release; instead we dependency inject the LLM with a simple (string) $\rightarrow$ string interface to be provided by an arbitrary service.

As the ethical implications of LLMs (Bender et al., 2021) are an important and unsolved problem in NLP, we highlight this design choice to decouple the LLM itself from STORY CENTAUR, a web based user interface that prepares the LLM's inputs and processes its outputs. To put it another way, the text generated is no more or less biased than the LLM and user themselves, as STORY CENTAUR's purpose is not to enhance or change the abilities of a LLM, but instead to democratize its use to non-technical users.

2 Related Work

The observation that simple "fill-in-the-blank" neural network models trained on large quantities of text can be used for problems beyond their primary learning objective dates back to word2vec (Mikolov et al., 2013) in which word embeddings were able to perform some SAT style analogies. While this ability captured many researchers' fascination, these models' dual function as a representation learner from which other models could be initialized and/or fine-tuned took center stage in the following years.

Representation learning techniques made steady advances, expanding to sentence level contextually sensitive word embedding with ELMo (Peters et al., 2018), the introduction of Transformers and MLM objectives with BERT (Devlin et al., 2018),

[1]source code: https://chonger.github.io/centaur/

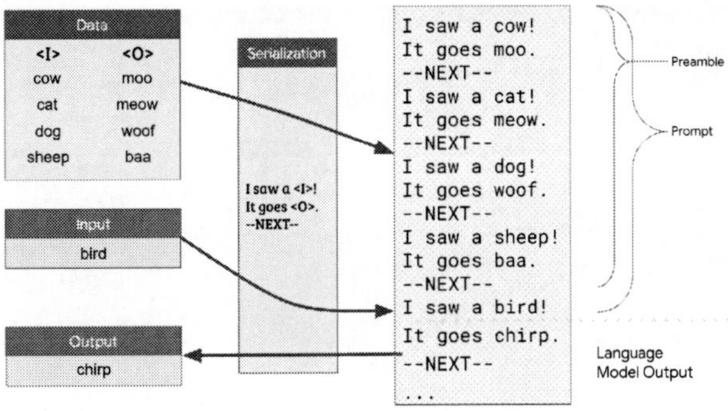

Figure 1: A Few Shot Formula in action. The Data and Serialization are used to create the Prompt, which along with the serialized inference time Input becomes the Preamble. The LM generates a continuation, from which the Serialization extracts the output. The Sentinels used (with newlines omitted) are "I saw a", "! It goes ", and ". –NEXT–".

and the menagerie of similar systems that followed. While most work concerned itself primarily with topping each other's GLUE and SUPERGLUE scores (Wang et al., 2019), work from OpenAI kept the torch lit for investigating the emergent abilities of representation learning (Radford et al., 2017, 2018, 2019; Brown et al., 2020). Their most recent work undeniably shows that sufficiently large LMs enable few shot models that approach and sometimes surpass state of the art performance on a wide range of NLP tasks.

Human + AI co-creation has existed in both practice and theory for several years. To highlight some examples in practice that relate to creative writing, as opposed to music or visual art of which there are many, we refer the reader to browse the Electronic Literature Collection[2] a longstanding community of artist-technologists who have blazed this trail since the days of hypertext. A number of publications of AI co-creation exist as well on a diverse range of artistic applications (Martin et al., 2016; Mathewson and Mirowski, 2017; Oh et al., 2018; Mirowski and Mathewson, 2019; Kreminski et al., 2019; Sloan, 2019; Tsioustas et al., 2020).

For a lighter introduction, Case (2018) gives some examples of AI + Human collaborations, or Centaurs[3], but primarily presents the argument that the HCI that connects the Human and Computer is of paramount importance, a sentiment that is in line with our own work. We also resonate with the opinion of Llano et al. (2020), which argues for explainability as a catalyst for fruitful co-creation, as it is central to our design that the artist be given the tools to create and iterate on NLP models.

[2]https://collection.eliterature.org/

[3]Case (2018) also explains this term's etymology

3 Few Shot Formulas

The core contribution of this work is a UI for the creation of few shot text generation models (Figure 2). We first define terms for the components of LM based few shot modeling as it is decomposed in our system: The few shot learning system as a whole is represented as a **Formula** which when used with a large LM provides arbitrary text to text I/O behavior.

We note that while generally LMs refer to any probability distribution over a sequence of tokens, in this work we use the term to refer to the subset model class that factorizes the joint probability into conditional $P(w_t|\mathbf{w_{1...t-1}})$ terms. Put simply, we are referring to the "predict the next word given all words so far" variety of LM, which includes all of the GPT models.

A Formula is composed of **Data** and **Serialization**. Each item in the Data consists of lists of string inputs and outputs that exemplify the desired I/O. The Serialization defines a reversible transformation between the Data and the raw text handled by the LM.

STORY CENTAUR uses a Serialization template of fixed text **Sentinels** that interleave the inputs and outputs; a Sentinel is defined to precede each input and output, as well as one that separates inputs and outputs and one that comes after the final output (See Figure 2 for an example). Carefully chosen sentinels are powerful tools for nudging the language model in desired directions (see the

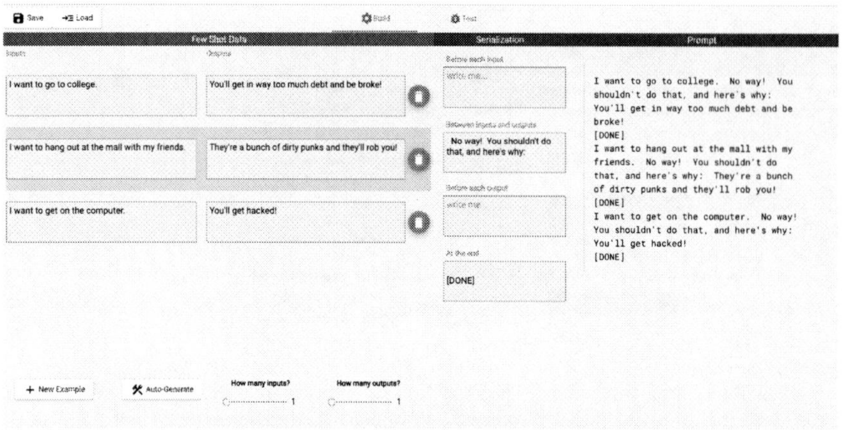

Figure 2: STORY CENTAUR's Formula Development User Interface.

Appendices for examples), but must also be designed so as not to be confused with model input or outputs.

A Formula is used by first invoking the Serialization on the Data, creating the **Preamble**. Then, the new inputs are converted using the Serialization and concatenated to the Preamble, creating the **Prompt**. The LM is asked to continue the text in the Prompt, and the Serialization is used to extract the output(s) from the result. The LM cannot explicitly enforce the Serialization format and as such will often produce non-conformant results, in which case it must be rejected. In practice, if the LM is sufficiently capable and the task well suited then a simple rejection sampler suffices to produce several acceptable options, as decoding is parallelizable.

3.1 Formula Development

STORY CENTAUR's user interface for Formula design is shown in Figure 2, with supplemental screenshots in the appendices. While there is no fixed workflow, we have found the following process to be effective. We assume only that the user is proficient in English and has a strong concept of their desired I/O.

First, the user must enter at least two examples of I/O pairs into the Data panel and take a pass at defining a Serialization, relying on the live updated Preamble panel to preview their progress. With a few examples in place, the Auto-Generate button can then be used to suggest new candidate IO pairs by passing the Preamble to the LM and allowing the user to prune these suggestions. This process can be repeated, quickly converging to several (10 or more) solid examples and clear evidence that the Serialization is being captured by the LM. As a final evaluation technique, we provide a Test mode that takes inference inputs and applies the current Formula, also reporting the rate at which the LM output respects the Serialization.

4 Writing Tool Experiments

We showcase the potential of Formulas that one might create using STORY CENTAUR in several Experiments. These experiments all rely on one or more Formulas that were built using the development tool and workflow described above, and are each motivated by a different artistic scenario. When possible, we present the I/O specifications for each Experiment and invite the reader to view full Experiment screenshots as well as the underlying Formulas' Data and Serialization in the Appendices.

4.1 Magic Word

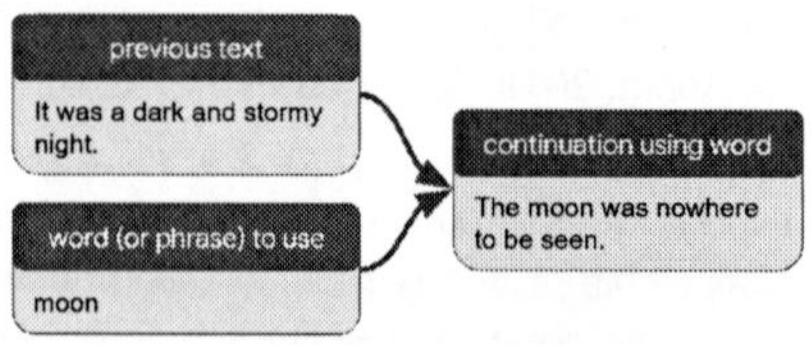

Figure 3: Formula I/O for Magic Word.

Perhaps the most obvious application of generative language models to creative writing is overcoming writer's block. Specifically, we consider the scenario in which the writer has some existing seed text and wants to be presented with possible continuations.

Generative LMs are ripe for this task as they can reliably continue short text; for the definition of LM used in this work (see Section 3) this is indeed exactly the task they were trained on. In this pure use of the LM the author is only able to provide the seed text, and so in this experiment we use a few shot Formula to provide an additional input of a word or phrase that is required to appear in the generated text.

The Magic Word formula takes two inputs: the seed text that must be continued by the model and the "Magic Word" that must be used in the continuation. In this Experiment, the generated outputs are not only discarded if they do not conform to the Serialization but also if the Magic Word does not appear as a substring. The UI allows editing of both the magic word and seed text, and on generation the user is given a maximum of three sentences that they can click to append to the editable main text box.

From an academic perspective, it is worth noting that this I/O paradigm has been explored in several examples of previous work, often with the same motivation as a writer's aid (Ippolito et al., 2019).

4.2 Say It Again

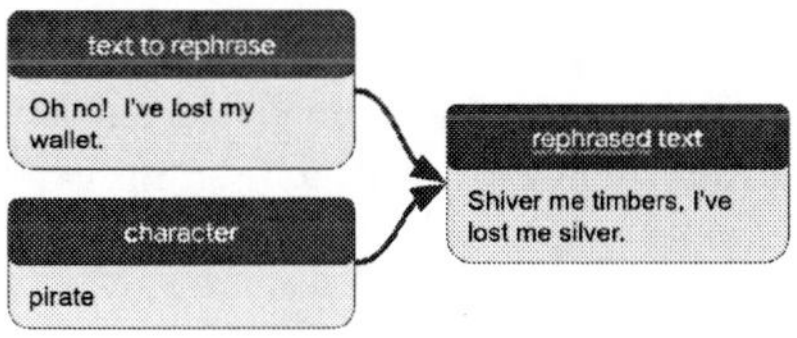

Figure 4: Formula I/O for Say It Again's CUSTOM Formula.

Many literary characters have their own peculiar way of speaking; Yoda, Tolkein's dwarves, Treasure Island's Pirates. In this Experiment we address the scenario where a writer has a clear idea of *what* they want the character to say and want suggestions as to *how* their character might actually say it.

We phrase this problem as a Formula with one input and one output in which the input is in neutral style and the output is a paraphrase with the desired style applied. This works nicely with few shot learning, as it is relatively easy to invent (or generate) a simple unstyled statement and then to imagine how a character might say it. We showcase several such Formulas in this experiment, selectable in a menu. For unstyled source text, there are three editable areas for text to rephrase that can be restyled individually or all at once.

We provide one additional Formula that might be considered zero shot style transfer, although it is still performed using a few shot Formula. When the style "CUSTOM" is selected, an input box appears where the user can enter any raw text they wish. This text is then used in a Formula with two inputs, the text to be restyled and the name or description of the character whose style to use. The surprising result is that this is often possible with no examples of the requested style itself, only the proper Serialization and a few example of the full I/O shown in Figure 4 with other custom characters. As this information most likely comes from patterns and associations encoded into the LMs parameters during training, this method works best with fictional characters from major movies or celebrities.

We encourage the further examination of large LMs for style transfer, as we were anecdotally impressed with the output of this experiment in particular. As some recently successful work in style transfer (Riley et al., 2020) already follows a label free approach that might itself be considered few shot in nature, interesting experimental comparisons are likely possible.

4.3 Story Spine

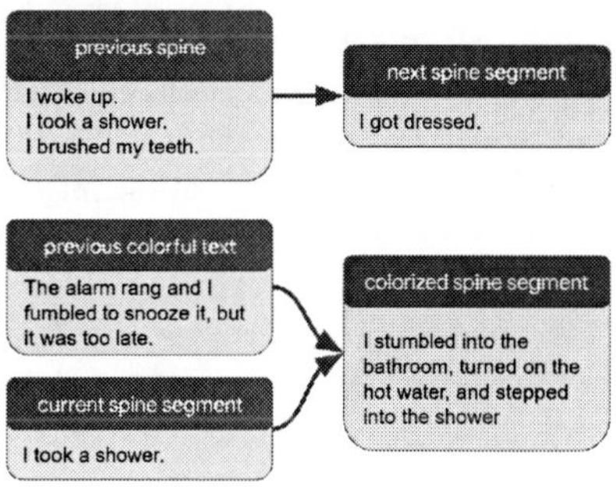

Figure 5: Story Spine's two formulas for spine continuation (top) and spine colorizing (bottom).

Modern LMs excel at producing text that is coherent, grammatical, and at times interesting, and frequently amusing. However, cracks begin to show in coherence as generations grow longer (Cho et al., 2018). A common mitigating technique has been to construct hierarchical generation systems in which a high level representation that is focused on common sense story structure which is then transformed into narrative text (Fan et al., 2018; Ammanabrolu et al.). This trend inspires this experiment, whose goal is the co-creation of a short story that is both coherent and detailed.

One ubiquitous quality of such hierarchical systems is that the high level representation is a structural and/or semantic abstraction chosen to be amenable to plot coherence modeling. This experiment poses the question: what if the high level representation was itself natural language? To explain our setup we make the distinction between *simple* text and *colorful* text, where the former is a grammatically bare bones statement of fact and the latter is more linguistically interesting, as a sentence might actually appear.

We use two Formulas to accomplish this goal, shown in Figure 5. The first takes a simple short plot point sentence as input and returns a plausible following simple plot point as output; this is used in a loop to generate the *spine*. The second is a context conditional paraphrasing formula with two inputs; the first is a simple plot point and the second is the "story so far" which is written in colorful text. The Formula's output is a paraphrase of the simple plot point, *colorized* to both respect the factual information of the plot point and the context of the story so far.

The user is presented with an interface that lets them write and edit custom spine plot points as well as use the first Formula to generate up to five candidates for plot points to continue the story. Each spine plot point is connected to its colorized paraphrase, which appear as a whole on the right side. In order to maintain a model of the mapping between the spine and colorized text, the colorized text is not editable.

4.4 Character Maker

Super-Objective	to write a novel
Sub-Objective	to invent a main character
Scene Objective	to find inspiration
Internal Obstacles	is bored and tired
External Obstacles	can't find a pen
Tactics	trying tech tools
Physical Attributes	frizzy hair
Backstory	from Sandusky, Ohio

Figure 6: The eight character creation points used in Character Maker, with examples.

Interesting characters are at the heart of much creative writing, and various template filling exercises exist to create them. Often this comes down to filling out a template containing fields that flesh out the character, as shown in Figure 6. In this experiment, the user is presented with an editable template containing each of these fields, with the option to edit or clear any of the fields' values. Once a value has been cleared, it can be filled in by the LM conditioned on all current non-empty fields.

We take this experiment in a direction that goes beyond our own Formula development tools to define a flexible Few Shot model for data completion. Our generalized problem statement is as follows: given a set of fields of which an arbitrary subset are blank, for one such blank field generate a plausible value conditioned on the non-blank fields. We build a dynamic Formula creation system that fulfills this generalized contract, and apply it to the filling of character creation exercise forms.

Our few shot solution naturally relies on a small number of fully filled out and plausibly consistent fields (e.g. complete character descriptions). At inference time, we extract the subset of non-blank fields in the inference item from each of these few shot examples and stitch together a Formula on the spot with precisely these inputs and the single output of the desired inference output field. This dynamic creation of Formulas requires a flexible Serialization that can accommodate any field name and value in any order, which for this experiment we simple simply use "name : value".

4.5 Improv Prompts

In improvisational acting (improv) one of the primary pleasures is to see actors bring a set of constraints provided by the audience to life in a coherent story. We see the potential for the sometimes wildly creative suggestions of large language models to supply these constraints, either as a tool for practitioners to hone their craft or as a way to spice up (or speed up) a live performance itself.

Improv constraints must be both open ended and subject to specific categories; for example the popular "Party Quirks" game requires a personal quirk for each actor attending a dinner party. We build Formulas and UIs for several improv games, and note their distinction from the other Formulas in this work in that they require no user input at all.

In constructing such zero input few shot learning

models it became apparent that beyond controlling the grammatical form and semantic intent of the outputs we could also control their tone, as it would mimic the tone of the Formula's Data. Crucially, this allows easy adaptation of these tools to different audiences (children versus adults, for example) and an implicit nudge towards whimsical outputs.

5 Discussion

While the experiments presented above demonstrate how few shot learning can be used to create interesting tools for writers, the real power of STORY CENTAUR is its unlocking of rapid experimentation. Not only were we able to probe the boundary of what "works" efficiently, but also to engage individuals regardless of formal machine learning training to help us to do so. Needless to say, in the course of this work many attempted Formulas did not produce compelling results.

Perhaps our most interesting failure was to build a Formula that would produce the second half of a rhyming couplet given the first half, a task that would require understanding of both phonetics and meter as well as linguistic coherence. This was disappointing given the compelling examples of GPT-3 poetry available online[4]. One possible explanation is that while general poetry and specifically rhyming couplets are in our minds connected closely with a subset relationship rooted in human culture, the hard constraint of rhyme and meter in fact divides them into very different problems for an LM. It is certainly the case that recent successful work in rhyming metered poetry generation has needed to resort to fixed rhyme words and syllable counting(Ghazvininejad et al., 2017).

In terms of larger themes, we found that constructing Formulas in which any of the inputs or outputs were much longer than a few sentences were hard to construct. We speculate that it is more difficult for the models to latch on to the Serialization in this case, as the observed symptom was often that no generated text passed the de-serialization filter. On the positive side we observed that few shot tasks that rely on paraphrasing (such as those used Say It Again) were surprisingly easy to construct successfully.

It is a common and intuitively plausible observation that the design of the Serialization is crucial to the performance of few shot learning with large LMs. Our Formulas can only be evaluated qualitatively and so we leave to future work the human studies that would be necessary to investigate this hypothesis. Our Magic Word experiment does offer the promise of a good test bed for Serialization design; even after considerable iteration we found the rate at which outputs pass both the de-Serialization filter to be surprisingly low given the relative simplicity of the task and the model's innate ability to generate coherent text continuation.

Finally we note that our true goal is to empower artists with no technical training to imagine a Formula, construct it in our development mode, and then produce experiments as we have. In our current process, such an artist could indeed construct their Formula, but would at some point require a programmer to build it into an experiment, requiring e.g. a WYSIWG editor. While this was beyond the scope of our work, we did construct our system using Angular, a modern web development framework whose core premise is modularity, dependency injection, and reuse of components. Not only do our experiments make use of a small set of these reusable components for functionality like editable text fields and clickable suggestion lists, but also all text and Formulas are synchronized by a global pub-sub service with simple string keys.

6 Conclusion

We present STORY CENTAUR, a tool for the creation and tuning of text based few shot learning Formulas powered by large language models and several experiments using Formulas built with our tool that are focused around the topic of creative writing.

The emergence of large language models has shaped the course of NLP research in the late 2010's but the question remains as to what, if any, is a viable use case for these models in their raw, un-finetuned, form. Additionally, while some claim that scaling these models is a viable path to Artificial General Intelligence, others disagree (Bender and Koller, 2020), and learning what is easy, hard, and impossible for them is crucial this debate. The answers to these questions will undoubtedly reveal themselves in the coming years and we are particularly excited to see their impact on the fine arts. In particular, we see great potential in tools built with this technology when there is a human, in this case an artist, in the loop to complement the natural deficiencies of a simple but powerful text generator that lacks editorial control and responsibility.

[4] https://www.gwern.net/GPT-3#transformer-poetry

References

Prithviraj Ammanabrolu, Ethan Tien, Wesley Cheung, Zhaochen Luo, William Ma, Lara J Martin, and Mark O Riedl. Story realization: Expanding plot events into sentences.

Emily M Bender, Timnit Gebru, Angelina McMillan-Major, and Shmargaret Shmitchell. 2021. On the dangers of stochastic parrots: Can language models be too big. In *Proceedings of the 2020 Conference on Fairness, Accountability, and Transparency; Association for Computing Machinery: New York, NY, USA*.

Emily M. Bender and Alexander Koller. 2020. Climbing towards NLU: On meaning, form, and understanding in the age of data. In *Proceedings of the 58th Annual Meeting of the Association for Computational Linguistics*, pages 5185–5198, Online. Association for Computational Linguistics.

Tom B Brown, Benjamin Mann, Nick Ryder, Melanie Subbiah, Jared Kaplan, Prafulla Dhariwal, Arvind Neelakantan, Pranav Shyam, Girish Sastry, Amanda Askell, et al. 2020. Language models are few-shot learners. *arXiv preprint arXiv:2005.14165*.

Nicky Case. 2018. How to become a centaur. *Journal of Design and Science*.

Woon Sang Cho, Pengchuan Zhang, Yizhe Zhang, Xiujun Li, Michel Galley, Chris Brockett, Mengdi Wang, and Jianfeng Gao. 2018. Towards coherent and cohesive long-form text generation. *arXiv preprint arXiv:1811.00511*.

Jacob Devlin, Ming-Wei Chang, Kenton Lee, and Kristina Toutanova. 2018. Bert: Pre-training of deep bidirectional transformers for language understanding. *arXiv preprint arXiv:1810.04805*.

Angela Fan, Mike Lewis, and Yann Dauphin. 2018. Hierarchical neural story generation. *arXiv preprint arXiv:1805.04833*.

Marjan Ghazvininejad, Xing Shi, Jay Priyadarshi, and Kevin Knight. 2017. Hafez: an interactive poetry generation system. In *Proceedings of ACL 2017, System Demonstrations*, pages 43–48.

Daphne Ippolito, David Grangier, Chris Callison-Burch, and Douglas Eck. 2019. Unsupervised hierarchical story infilling. In *Proceedings of the First Workshop on Narrative Understanding*, pages 37–43.

Max Kreminski, Devi Acharya, Nick Junius, Elisabeth Oliver, Kate Compton, Melanie Dickinson, Cyril Focht, Stacey Mason, Stella Mazeika, and Noah Wardrip-Fruin. 2019. Cozy mystery construction kit: Prototyping toward an ai-assisted collaborative storytelling mystery game. In *Proceedings of the 14th International Conference on the Foundations of Digital Games*, pages 1–9.

Maria Teresa Llano, Mark d'Inverno, Matthew Yee-King, Jon McCormack, Alon Ilsar, Alison Pease, and Simon Colton. 2020. Explainable computational creativity. In *Proc. ICCC*.

Lara J Martin, Brent Harrison, and Mark O Riedl. 2016. Improvisational computational storytelling in open worlds. In *International Conference on Interactive Digital Storytelling*, pages 73–84. Springer.

Kory Mathewson and Piotr Mirowski. 2017. Improvised theatre alongside artificial intelligences. In *Proceedings of the AAAI Conference on Artificial Intelligence and Interactive Digital Entertainment*, volume 13.

Tomas Mikolov, Ilya Sutskever, Kai Chen, Greg S Corrado, and Jeff Dean. 2013. Distributed representations of words and phrases and their compositionality. *Advances in neural information processing systems*, 26:3111–3119.

Piotr Mirowski and Kory Wallace Mathewson. 2019. Human improvised theatre augmented with artificial intelligence. In *Proceedings of the 2019 on Creativity and Cognition*, pages 527–530.

Changhoon Oh, Jungwoo Song, Jinhan Choi, Seonghyeon Kim, Sungwoo Lee, and Bongwon Suh. 2018. I lead, you help but only with enough details: Understanding user experience of co-creation with artificial intelligence. In *Proceedings of the 2018 CHI Conference on Human Factors in Computing Systems*, pages 1–13.

Matthew E Peters, Mark Neumann, Mohit Iyyer, Matt Gardner, Christopher Clark, Kenton Lee, and Luke Zettlemoyer. 2018. Deep contextualized word representations. *arXiv preprint arXiv:1802.05365*.

Alec Radford, Rafal Jozefowicz, and Ilya Sutskever. 2017. Learning to generate reviews and discovering sentiment. *arXiv preprint arXiv:1704.01444*.

Alec Radford, Karthik Narasimhan, Tim Salimans, and Ilya Sutskever. 2018. Improving language understanding by generative pre-training.

Alec Radford, Jeffrey Wu, Rewon Child, David Luan, Dario Amodei, and Ilya Sutskever. 2019. Language models are unsupervised multitask learners. *OpenAI blog*, 1(8):9.

Parker Riley, Noah Constant, Mandy Guo, Girish Kumar, David Uthus, and Zarana Parekh. 2020. Textsettr: Label-free text style extraction and tunable targeted restyling. *arXiv preprint arXiv:2010.03802*.

Robin Sloan. 2019. Writing with the machine: Gpt-2 and text generation. In *Roguelike Celebration*.

Charalampos Tsioustas, Daphne Petratou, Maximos Kaliakatsos-Papakostas, Vassilis Katsouros, Apostolos Kastritsis, Konstantinos Christantonis, Konstantinos Diamantaras, and Michael Loupis. 2020.

Innovative applications of natural language processing and digital media in theatre and performing arts. In *Proceedings of the ENTRENOVA-ENTerprise REsearch InNOVAtion Conference*, volume 6, pages 84–96.

Alex Wang, Yada Pruksachatkun, Nikita Nangia, Amanpreet Singh, Julian Michael, Felix Hill, Omer Levy, and Samuel R. Bowman. 2019. Superglue: A stickier benchmark for general-purpose language understanding systems. *CoRR*, abs/1905.00537.

A Appendices

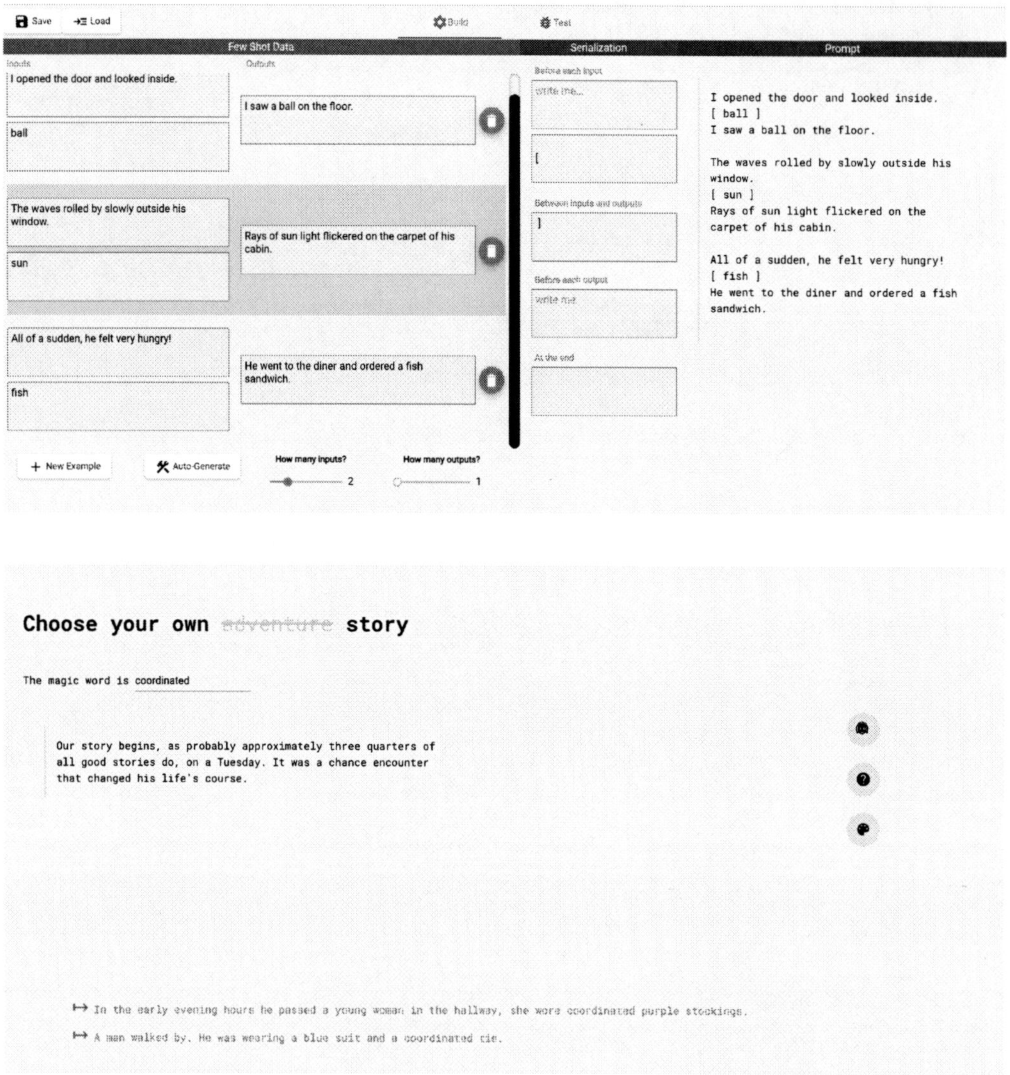

Figure 7: A Screenshot of the Magic Word Formula and Experiment.

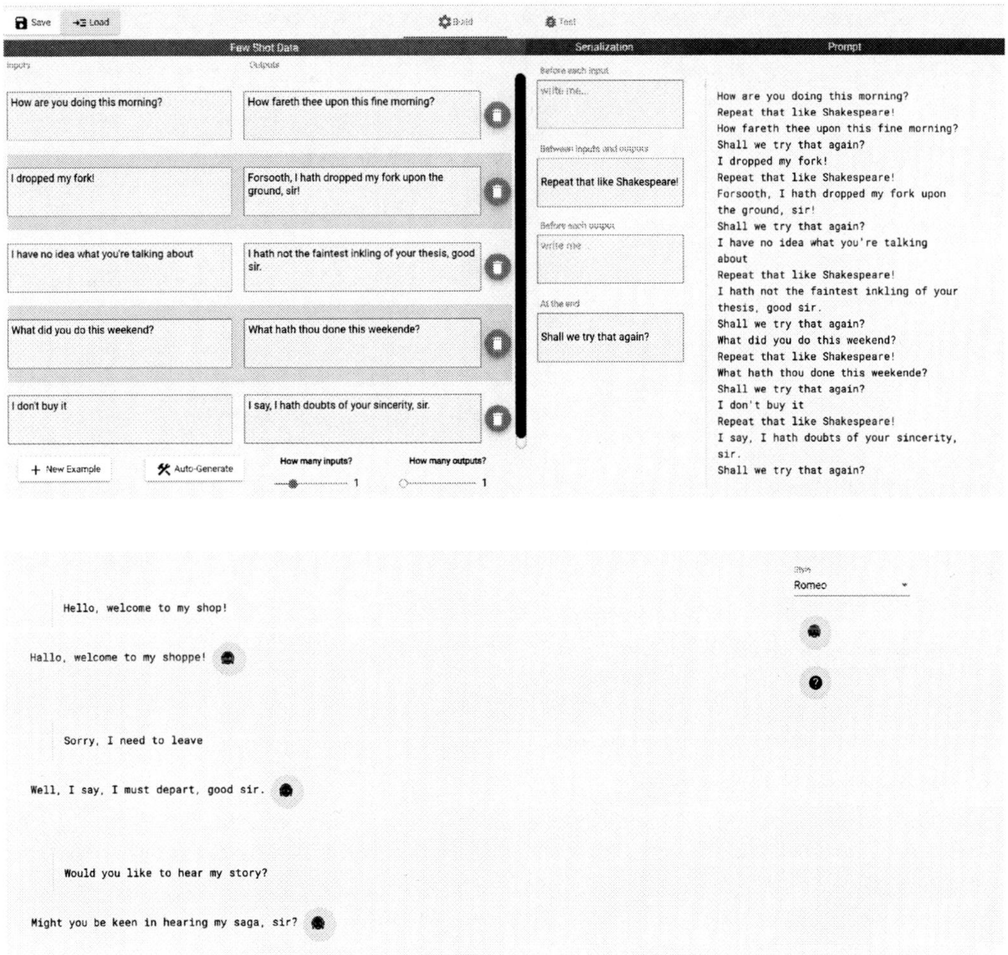

Figure 8: Say It Again in the style of a Shakespearean character using 5 Few Shot Examples.

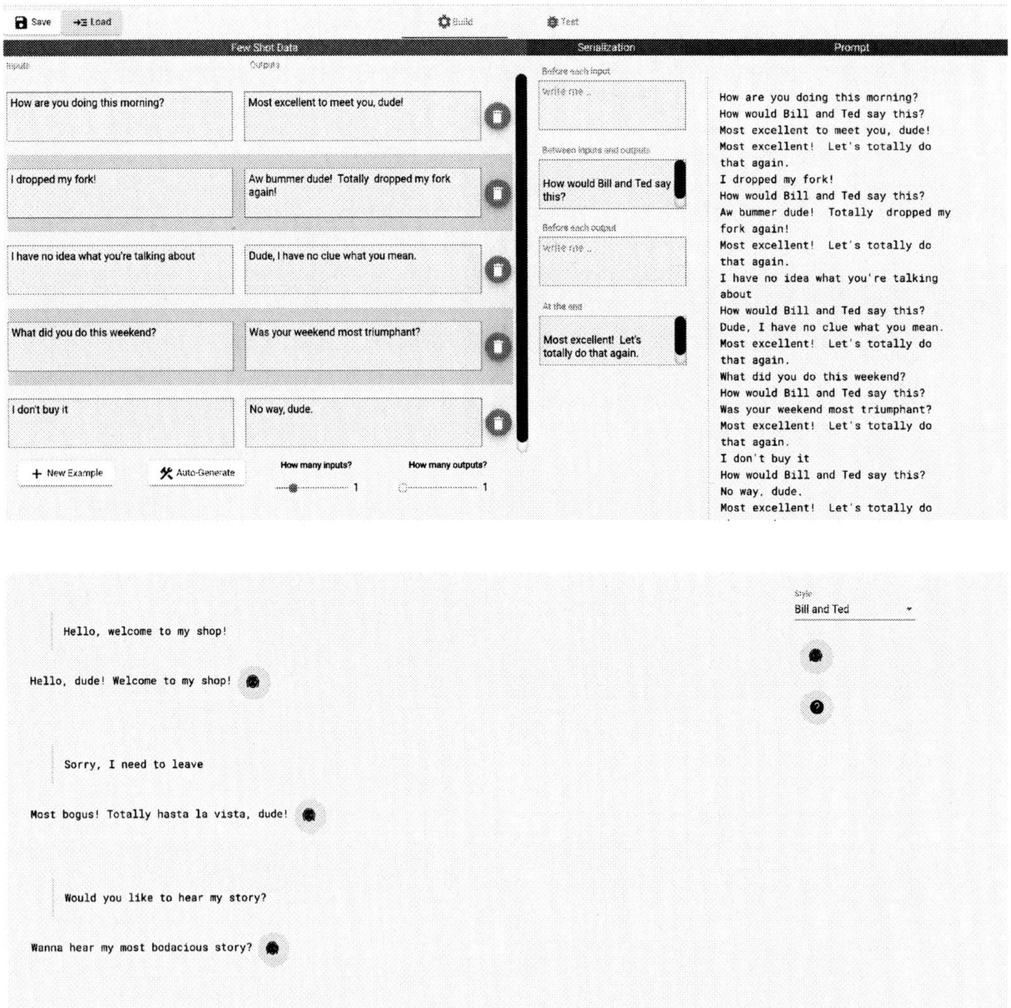

Figure 9: Say It Again in the style of Bill and Ted using 5 Few Shot Examples.

Figure 10: Say It Again in the style of Data from Star Trek using 5 Few Shot Examples of style transfer, but no examples of Data's actual style.

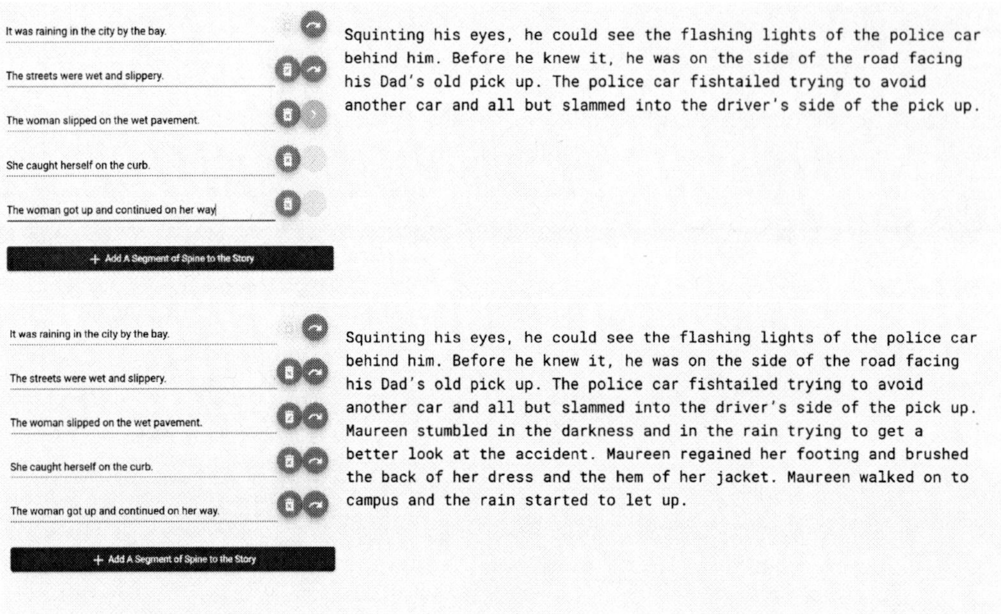

Figure 11: Story Spine screenshots. In the top screenshot, a five segment spine has been constructed, but only two spine segments have been colorized. The bottom image shows the result of colorizing the final three segments.

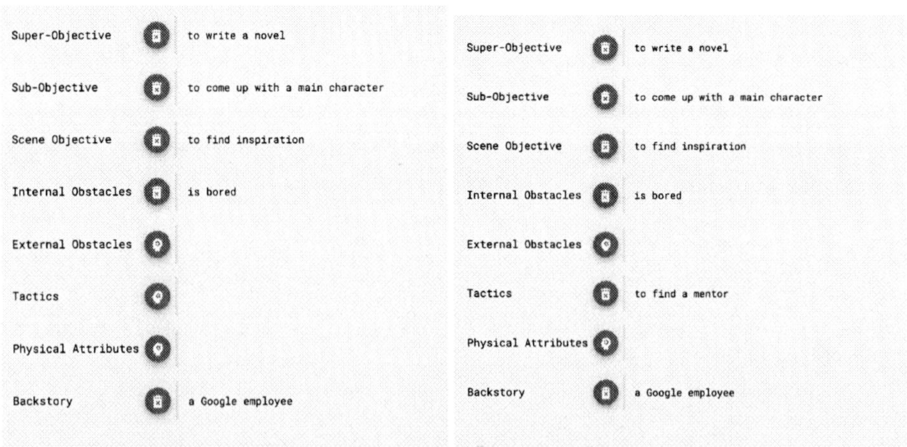

Figure 12: Character Maker, before and after generation of the Tactics field. In this case, generation was performed by constructing a few shot Formula dynamically with Super-Objective, Sub-Objective, Scene Objective, and Backstory as input, and Tactics as output, using 4 examples of full templates to create the Data.

FrameForm: An Open-source Annotation Interface for FrameNet

Büşra Marşan
Starlang Yazılım Danışmanlık
busra@starlangyazilim.com

Olcay Taner Yıldız
Özyeğin University
olcay.yildiz@ozyegin.edu.tr

Abstract

In this paper, we introduce FrameForm[1], an open-source annotation tool designed to accommodate predicate annotations based on Frame Semantics (Fillmore et al., 1976). FrameForm is a user-friendly tool for creating, annotating and maintaining computational lexicography projects like FrameNet and has been used while building the Turkish FrameNet (Marşan et al., 2021). Responsive and open-source, FrameForm can be easily modified to answer the annotation needs of a wide range of different languages.

1 Introduction

FrameNet (Lowe, 1997; Baker et al., 1998; Fillmore and Atkins, 1998; Johnson et al., 2001) is a growing NLP resource developed by the International Computer Science Institute in Berkeley, California. Having its theoretical background in Fillmore's Frame Semantics notion (Fillmore et al., 1976), FrameNet is a coherent and exhaustive computational lexicography that provides in-depth semantic information regarding the argument structure and thematic relations of a predicate.

In FrameNet, predicates are annotated into their respective frames. A frame refers to a schematic representation that brings lemmas together based on their semantic properties and syntactic features (for a more detailed definition and discussion of the frame notion, see (Fillmore et al., 1976)). For instance, Motion frame brings frames that denote a motion between two points or on a path, and it has the following definition[2]:

> Some entity (Theme) starts out in one place (Source) and ends up in some other place (Goal), having covered some space between the two (Path). Alternatively, the Area or Direction in which the Theme moves or the Distance of the movement may be mentioned.

Predicates (Lexical Units or LUs, as called in FrameNet) that fit the definition above are annotated to this frame. Here we must point out that each sense of a Lexical Unit pertains to a different frame. For instance, "blow" (as an intransitive verb) has several meanings[3]:

1. to move or be carried by or as if by wind
2. erupt, explode
3. to send forth a current of air or other gas

With its first meaning, "blow" is annotated to Move frame.

Following the framework put forward by English FrameNet team, many other researchers re-created this resource in different languages. In order to ease building process and streamline the maintenance of FrameNet resources, we developed an open-source annotation interface called FrameForm[4].

We will discuss the creation process of FrameForm in Section 2 and introduce its features in Section 3. Finally, we will offer a brief discussion regarding the future work in Section 4.

2 Developing the FrameForm

Development process of FrameForm is closely tied to the creation process of Turkish FrameNet (Marşan et al., 2021): While gathering data for Turkish FrameNet, our team needed an easy-to-use tool that allowed frame annotation, semantic annotation and morphologic analysis. First we did a thorough research to see what software and tools

[1] https://github.com/StarlangSoftware/SemanticRoleLabeling
[2] https://framenet.icsi.berkeley.edu/fndrupal/frameIndex
[3] https://www.merriam-webster.com/dictionary/blow
[4] https://github.com/StarlangSoftware/SemanticRoleLabeling

Proceedings of the 16th Conference of the European Chapter of the Association for Computational Linguistics: System Demonstrations, pages 257–262
April 19 - 23, 2021. ©2021 Association for Computational Linguistics

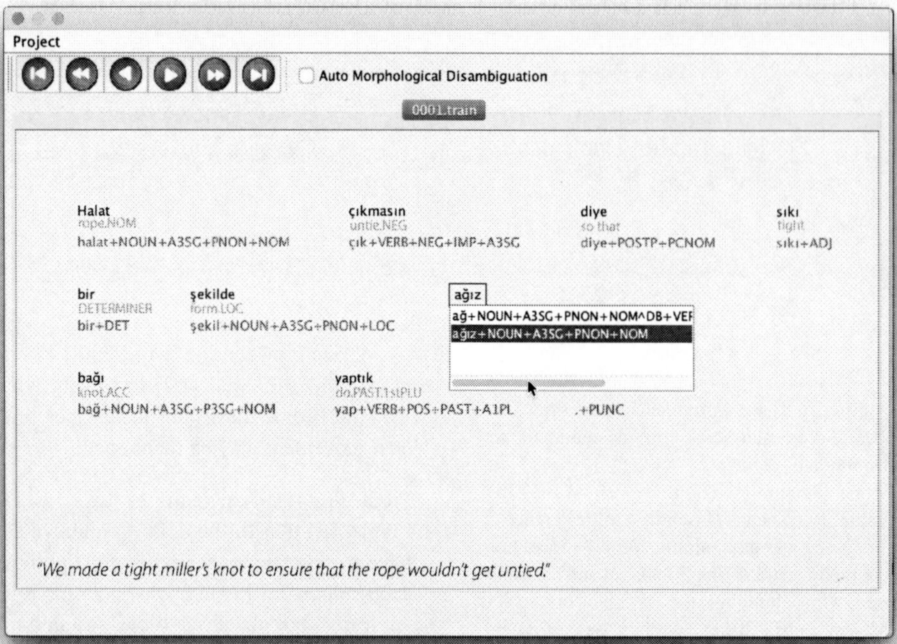

Figure 1: Morphologic analysis interface of FrameForm

were used for building other FrameNets. In their articles covering the process of building and/or expanding their FrameNets, many teams don't mention the tools or interface they use, that is why we were able to find only few resources regarding the annotation of FrameNets in various languages:

- FrameNet Brasil team uses a web-based annotation tool called FrameNet Brasil WebTool (Matos and Torrent, 2016). The same tool is also used for Global FrameNet annotations. It allows the users to create language specific tags to accommodate typological features of different languages but it does not allow an in-depth morphological analysis. That is why our team was unable to use FrameNet Brasil WebTool.

- The team behind German FrameNet SALSA uses two main tools for annotation: SALTO (Burchardt et al., 2006) and FrameNet Transformer (Ruppenhofer et al., 2010). Although very practical, these tools fell short of satisfying our needs regarding morphological analysis and semantic annotation.

- Swedish FrameNet team uses Karp, "the open lexical infrastructure of Sprakbanken (the Swedish Language Bank)" (Borin et al., 2013), which cannot be used for annotating other languages.

- Spanish FrameNet team uses the same annotation software as Berkeley team (Fillmore et al., 2002), which, again, does not allow us to do a semantic annotation and morphological analysis as detailed as we desire.

After our thorough research, we found ourselves in a position where we had to develop our own annotation interface. Thus, we created FrameForm. It is written in Java and can be found on GitHub. Since it is an open-source program, it is possible to change or further develop FrameForm freely. That is why we believe that it can be easily integrated into many other FrameNet projects in different languages.

Thus far, mostly Indo-European languages followed suit with the English FrameNet. These languages are relatively poorer in morphology compared to agglutinative languages like Turkish. That

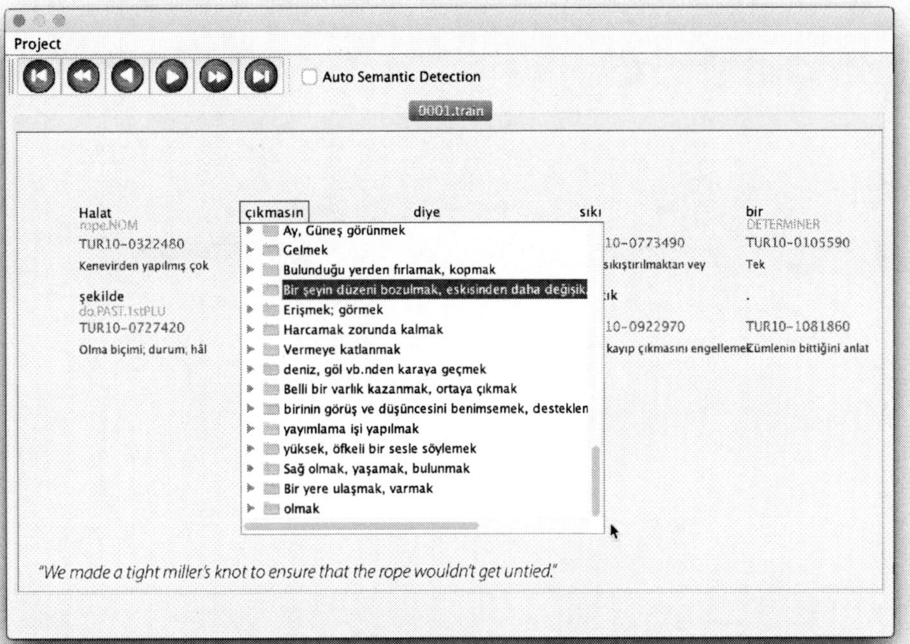

Figure 2: Semantic annotation interface of FrameForm

is why the annotation tools we discussed above do not offer a morphologic analyser component which is essential for morphologically richer languages. Our annotation tool, FrameForm allows adding a new morphological analyser and introducing a new dictionary and/or WordNet. That is why different languages can utilise FrameForm for their annotation processes simply by making some minor adjustments in the back-end.

3 Features

FrameForm saves every annotation pertaining to a Lexical Unit in a single file: Morphologic analysis, predicate analysis (shows which word or group of words is the predicate), semantic analysis (maps the related meaning to the word), frame information and frame elements. This way, one can find all the necessary information regarding a Lexical unit with one click.

The annotation process starts with the morphologic analysis of the sample sentence (see Figure 1). For this analysis, we incorporated our own morphological analysis library for Turkish, which can be accessed freely on GitHub [5]. Using this library, FrameForm offers an automatic morphologic analysis to speed up the process. The annotator can change auto-generated annotation if it is not correct.

Using the Starlang Turkish Morphological Analysis library, FrameForm processes roots and suffixes separately. It chooses the longest possible root (including derivational suffixes but excluding inflectional suffixes). If the longest possible root yields a plausible analysis, the algorithm goes with that. Otherwise, it refers to a set of predetermined set of rules (see (Yıldız et al., 2019) for a detailed discussion). In order to use the morphological analysis feature of FrameForm in a different language, Starlang's Turkish Morphological Analysis library can be replaced with a different library pertaining to the target language.

Next step involves the semantic annotation. In this step, the annotator should select the correct meaning of the Lexical Unit in regard to the frame, and appropriate meanings of the other elements in the sample sentence as well (see Figure 2). Au-

[5] https://github.com/StarlangSoftware/TurkishMorphologicalAnalysis

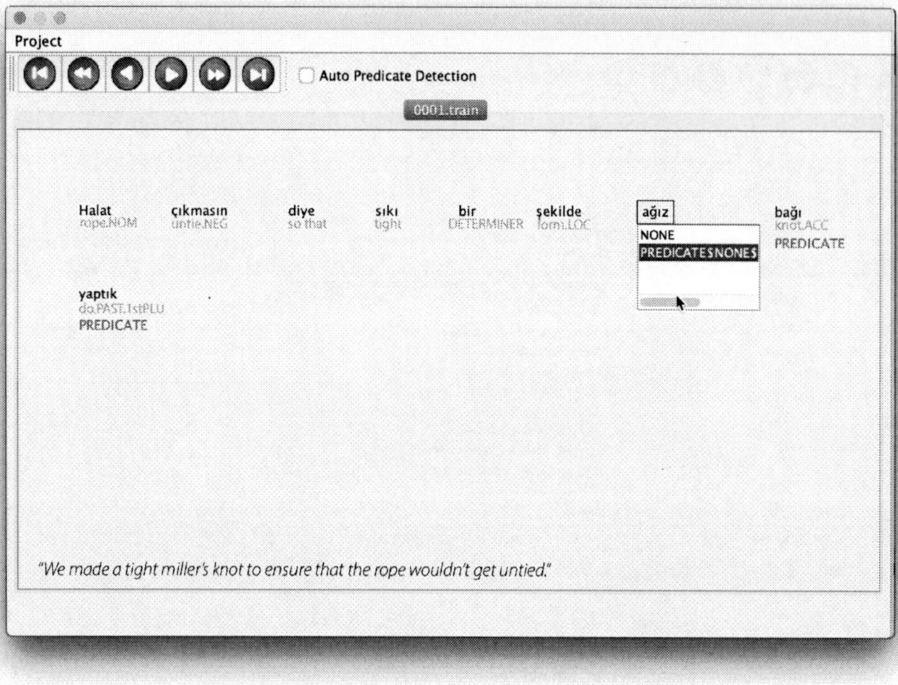

Figure 3: Predicate annotation interface of FrameForm

tomatic semantic annotation is possible in order to make annotation process more seamless but the annotator can always change or manually select the meanings. For the certain multi-word expressions (such as phrasal verbs, idioms, etc.) or the words that have only one meaning, the annotation is done automatically. The rest of the words are annotated by human annotators.

For the semantic annotation step, FrameForm refers to a dictionary or WordNet. For the purposes of Turkish FrameNet, we used Turkish WordNet KeNet (Bakay et al., 2021) in order to make Turkish FrameNet compatible with other resources in Turkish (such as Turkish PropBank (Kara et al., 2020)) yet it is possible to introduce different dictionaries or WordNets in order to use FrameForm in different languages.

After the semantic annotation, the annotator should move on to predicate selection screen where they need to mark the predicate/Lexical Unit in the sample sentence (see Figure 3).

Final step is annotating the Frame Elements where the annotator can see all the FEs within that frame and match them with related sentence elements (see Figure 4).

One of the most important features of the FrameForm is the fact that it significantly facilitates to ensure inter-annotator agreement and coherency. FrameForm allows all annotators to see each others' annotations, that is why the annotators can discuss specific cases or annotations and notify one another regarding potential agreement issues. In addition, FrameForm groups together the Lexical Units and Frame Elements of a single Frame. This way, the annotators can only see and select the Frame Elements pertaining to the Frame they are annotating. Thus, the annotators cannot use or mark down Frame Elements of other frames.

3.1 Interfaces

FrameForm has 4 different screens for the each step of the annotation process: Morphologic analysis screen (see Figure 1), semantic annotation screen (see Figure 2), predicate marking screen (see Figure 3) and frame element annotation screen (see Figure 4).

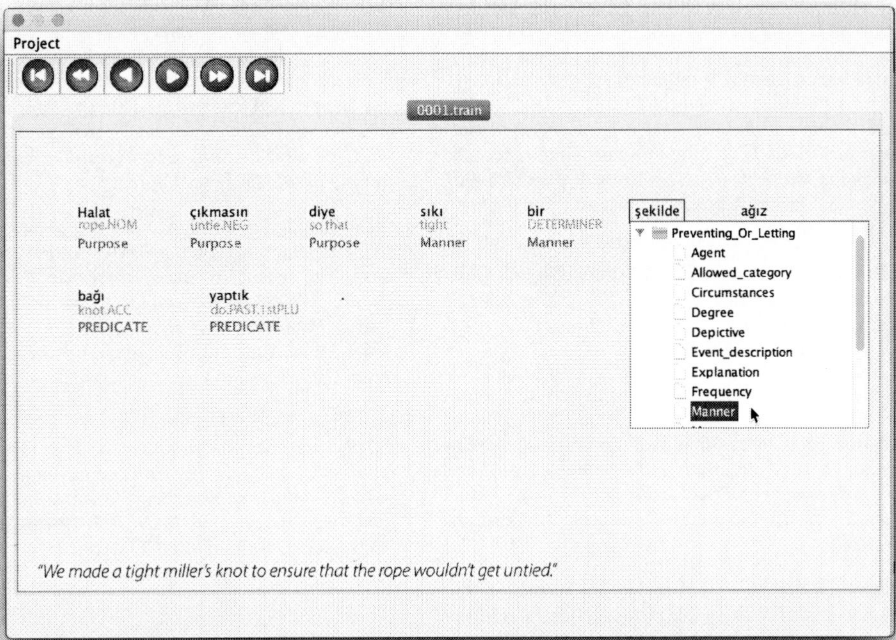

Figure 4: Frame element annotation interface of FrameForm

3.2 What can be annotated with FrameForm?

FrameForm is a very potent tool for annotation. It allows the user to:

- Create new frames,
- Transfer data between the frames,
- Manually edit or change sample sentences,
- Delete Lexical Units,
- Do morphologic analysis, semantic annotation, predicate marking and frame element annotation.

4 Conclusion and Future Studies

With FrameForm, we aimed to create a potent, flexible, easy-to-use annotation tool. In order to ensure that FrameForm alone is enough for every step of the FrameNet annotation and maintenance processes, we equipped our tool with a wide range of features including semantic annotation and Frame Element annotation. Thus it is possible to create a FrameNet from scratch, grow it and maintain it using only FrameForm.

FrameForm can be downloaded freely on GitHub. Being easy to access and distribute, a crowded team of annotators can use FrameForm for their annotation needs. Since annotators can see progress made by other members of the team, FrameForm makes it easier to ensure inter-annotator agreement.

One of our main goals was to make FrameForm capable of answering the needs of other FrameNet teams. That is why it is an open-source tool that can be modified or advanced in accordance with the unique needs and typologies of other languages. Further studies can focus on the compatibility of FrameForm with other languages and what should be improved.

References

Özge Bakay, Özlem Ergelen, Elif Sarmış, Selin Yıldırım, Bilge Nas Arıcan, Atilla Kocabalcıoğlu, Merve Özçelik, Ezgi Sanıyar, Oğuzhan Kuyrukçu, Begüm Avar, and Olcay Taner Yıldız. 2021. Turkish WordNet KeNet. In *Proceedings of the 11th*

Global Wordnet Conference, pages 166–174, University of South Africa (UNISA). Global Wordnet Association.

Collin F. Baker, Charles J. Fillmore, and John B. Lowe. 1998. The Berkeley FrameNet project. In *36th Annual Meeting of the Association for Computational Linguistics and 17th International Conference on Computational Linguistics, Volume 1*, pages 86–90, Montreal, Quebec, Canada. Association for Computational Linguistics.

Lars Borin, Markus Forsberg, Leif-Jöran Olsson, Olof Olsson, and Jonatan Uppström. 2013. The lexical editing system of karp. In *Proceedings of the eLex 2013 conference*, pages 503–516.

Aljoscha Burchardt, Katrin Erk, Anette Frank, Andrea Kowalski, and Sebastian Pado. 2006. SALTO - a versatile multi-level annotation tool. In *Proceedings of the Fifth International Conference on Language Resources and Evaluation (LREC'06)*, Genoa, Italy. European Language Resources Association (ELRA).

Charles J Fillmore and Beryl TS Atkins. 1998. Framenet and lexicographic reference. In *First International Conference on language resources & evaluation: Granada, Spain, 28-30 May 1998*, pages 417–426. European Language Resources Association.

Charles J. Fillmore, Collin F. Baker, and Hiroaki Sato. 2002. The FrameNet database and software tools. In *Proceedings of the Third International Conference on Language Resources and Evaluation (LREC'02)*, Las Palmas, Canary Islands - Spain. European Language Resources Association (ELRA).

Charles J Fillmore et al. 1976. Frame semantics and the nature of language. In *Annals of the New York Academy of Sciences: Conference on the origin and development of language and speech*, volume 280, pages 20–32. New York.

Christopher Johnson, Charles J Fillmore, E Wood, Josef Ruppenhofer, Margaret Urban, MIRIAM Petruck, and COLLIN Baker. 2001. The framenet project: Tools for lexicon building. *Manuscript. Berkeley, CA, International Computer Science Institute*.

Neslihan Kara, Deniz Baran Aslan, Büşra Marşan, Özge Bakay, Koray Ak, and Olcay Taner Yıldız. 2020. TRopBank: Turkish PropBank v2.0. In *Proceedings of the 12th Language Resources and Evaluation Conference*, pages 2763–2772, Marseille, France. European Language Resources Association.

John B Lowe. 1997. A frame-semantic approach to semantic annotation. In *Tagging Text with Lexical Semantics: Why, What, and How?*

Büşra Marşan, Neslihan Kara, Merve Özçelik, Bilge Nas Arıcan, Neslihan Cesur, Aslı Kuzgun, Ezgi Sanıyar, Oğuzhan Kuyrukçu, and Olcay Taner Yildiz. 2021. Building the Turkish FrameNet. In *Proceedings of the 11th Global Wordnet Conference*, pages 118–125, University of South Africa (UNISA). Global Wordnet Association.

Ely Matos and Tiago Torrent. 2016. A flexible tool for an enriched framenet. In *Proceedings of the 9th International Conference on Construction Grammar (ICCG9), Juiz de Fora, Brazil, october. Federal University of Juiz de Fora (UFJF).*

Josef Ruppenhofer, Jonas Sunde, and Manfred Pinkal. 2010. Generating FrameNets of various granularities: The FrameNet transformer. In *Proceedings of the Seventh International Conference on Language Resources and Evaluation (LREC'10)*, Valletta, Malta. European Language Resources Association (ELRA).

Olcay Taner Yıldız, Begüm Avar, and Gökhan Ercan. 2019. An open, extendible, and fast Turkish morphological analyzer. In *Proceedings of the International Conference on Recent Advances in Natural Language Processing (RANLP 2019)*, pages 1364–1372, Varna, Bulgaria. INCOMA Ltd.

OCTIS: Comparing and Optimizing Topic Models is Simple!

Silvia Terragni
University of Milano-Bicocca
Viale Sarca 336, 20126
Milan, Italy
s.terragni4@campus.unimib.it

Elisabetta Fersini*
University of Milano-Bicocca
Viale Sarca 336, 20126
Milan, Italy
elisabetta.fersini@unimib.it

Bruno Galuzzi
University of Milano-Bicocca
Viale Sarca 336, 20126
Milan, Italy
bruno.galuzzi@unimib.it

Pietro Tropeano
University of Milano-Bicocca
Viale Sarca 336, 20126
Milan, Italy
p.tropeano1@campus.unimib.it

Antonio Candelieri
University of Milano-Bicocca
Viale Sarca 336, 20126
Milan, Italy
antonio.candelieri@unimib.it

Abstract

In this paper, we present OCTIS, a framework for training, analyzing, and comparing Topic Models, whose optimal hyper-parameters are estimated using a Bayesian Optimization approach. The proposed solution integrates several state-of-the-art topic models and evaluation metrics. These metrics can be targeted as objective by the underlying optimization procedure to determine the best hyper-parameter configuration. OCTIS allows researchers and practitioners to have a fair comparison between topic models of interest, using several benchmark datasets and well-known evaluation metrics, to integrate novel algorithms, and to have an interactive visualization of the results for understanding the behavior of each model. The code is available at the following link: `https://github.com/MIND-Lab/OCTIS`.

1 Introduction

Topic models are promising statistical methods that aim to extract the hidden topics underlying a collection of documents. Although researchers have proposed several models across the years (Blei, 2012; Vayansky and Kumar, 2020), their evaluation and comparison is still a hard task. The evaluation of a topic model usually involves different datasets (with non-standard pre-processing) (Schofield and Mimno, 2016; Schofield et al., 2017) and several evaluation metrics (Lau et al., 2014; Wallach et al., 2009; Terragni et al., 2020a). Furthermore, topic models are usually compared by fixing their hyper-parameters. However, choosing the optimal hyper-parameter configuration for a given dataset and a given evaluation metric is fundamental to induce each model at the best of its capabilities, and therefore to guarantee a fair comparison with other models.

Current topic modeling frameworks (McCallum et al., 2005; Qiang et al., 2018; Lisena et al., 2020) typically focus on the release of topic modeling algorithms while ignoring one or more critical aspects of the topic modeling pipeline, such as pre-processing, evaluation, comparison of the models, and visualization. Most importantly, they disregard the hyper-parameter selection.

In this paper, we present OCTIS (Optimizing and Comparing Topic models Is Simple)[1], a unified and open-source evaluation framework for training, analyzing, and comparing Topic Models, over several datasets and evaluation metrics. Their optimal hyper-parameter configuration is determined according to a Bayesian Optimization (BO) strategy (Archetti and Candelieri, 2019; Snoek et al., 2012; Galuzzi et al., 2020).

In the following, we summarize the main contributions of the proposed framework:

- several open-source topic models have been integrated into a *unified framework*, providing a common interface that allows the users to easily experiment with topic models;
- a single-objective BO approach has been integrated to determine the *optimal hyper-parameter* values of each model, for a given dataset and a specific evaluation metric of interest;
- an *interactive visualization* of the results for inspecting the details of the models, providing

* Corresponding author.

[1]The video demonstration is available at `https://youtu.be/nPmiWBFFJ8E`.

Proceedings of the 16th Conference of the European Chapter of the Association for Computational Linguistics: System Demonstrations, pages 263–270
April 19 - 23, 2021.

insights about the optimization strategy, word and topic distributions, and robustness of the estimated configuration;

- a *python library* for advanced exploitation of the framework for integrating novel algorithms, with their training and inference algorithms.

2 System design and architecture

OCTIS is an open-source evaluation framework for the comparison of a set of state-of-the-art topic models, that allows the user to optimize the models' hyper-parameters for a fair experimental comparison. The proposed framework follows an object-oriented paradigm, providing all the tools for running a topic modeling pipeline.

The main functionalities of the proposed OCTIS are related to dataset pre-processing, training topic models, estimating evaluation metrics, hyper-parameter optimization, and interactive web dashboard visualization. Figure 1 summarizes the workflow involving the first four modules (the dashboard interacts with all of them).

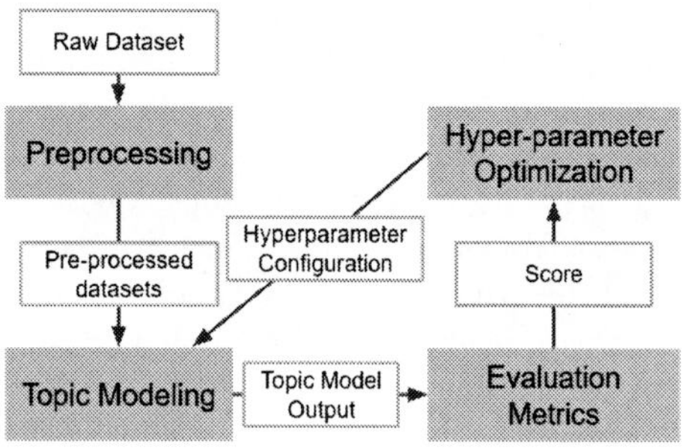

Figure 1: Workflow of the OCTIS framework

The framework can be used both as a python library and as a dashboard. The python library offers more advanced functionalities than the ones available in the dashboard. The modules that comprise the OCTIS framework are detailed in the following sections.

2.1 Datasets and Pre-processing

The first step of the topic modeling pipeline is the pre-processing of the input dataset. OCTIS includes the following pre-processing utilities:

- reducing the text to lowercase;
- punctuation removal;
- lemmatization;
- stop-words removal;
- removal of unfrequent and most frequent words (according to a specified frequency threshold);
- removal of documents with few words (according to a specified frequency threshold).

These utilities include the most common techniques for pre-processing text for topic modeling. However, some of these features may not be appropriate for specific domains and languages, e.g. requiring language-specific or domain-specific stop-words.

OCTIS currently provides 4 pre-processed datasets, i.e. 20 NewsGroups [2], M10 (Lim and Buntine, 2014), DBLP [3] and BBC News (Greene and Cunningham, 2006), different in nature and length.

The datasets already available in OCTIS, and accessible through the web dashboard, have been pre-processed according to the length of the documents. In particular, we removed the punctuation, we lemmatized the text, filtered out the stop-words (using the English stop-words list provided by MALLET), and removed the words that have a word frequency less than 0.5% for 20 Newsgroups and BBC News and less than 0.05% for DBLP and M10. Subsequently, we removed the documents with less than 5 words for 20 Newsgroups and BBC News and less than 3 words for the other datasets.

Table 1 reports some statistics about the currently available pre-processed.

Dataset	Domain	# Docs	Avg # words in docs	# Unique words
20 Newsgroups	Forum posts	16309	48	1612
BBC News	News	2225	150	3106
M10	Scientific papers	8355	6	1696
DBLP	Scientific papers	54595	5	1513

Table 1: Statistics of the pre-processed datasets.

[2] http://people.csail.mit.edu/jrennie/20Newsgroups/

[3] https://github.com/shiruipan/TriDNR/tree/master/data

Although OCTIS already provides some datasets, a user can upload and pre-process any dataset (using the python library) according to its needs.

2.2 Topic Modeling

OCTIS integrates both classical topic models and neural topic models. In particular, the following traditional and neural approaches are available to be trained, optimized, analyzed, and compared (the models that are available in the web dashboard are marked with $\star$):

- Latent Dirichlet Allocation* (Blei et al., 2003, LDA);[4]
- Non-negative Matrix Factorization* (Lee and Seung, 2000, NMF);[4]
- Latent Semantic Analysis* (Hofmann, 1999, LSI);[4]
- Hierarchical Dirichlet Process (Teh et al., 2004, HDP);[4]
- Neural LDA* (Srivastava and Sutton, 2017);[5]
- Product-of-Experts LDA* (Srivastava and Sutton, 2017, ProdLDA);[5]
- Embedded Topic Models* (Dieng et al., 2019, ETM);[6]
- Contextualized Topic Models (Bianchi et al., 2021, CTM).[7]

Moreover, we defined a standard interface for allowing a user to integrate their topic model's implementation. A topic model is indeed a black-box, a system solely viewed in terms of its inputs and outputs and whose internal workings are invisible. This black-box topic model takes as input a dataset and a set of hyperparameters values and returns the top-t topic words, the document-topic distributions, and the topic-word distribution in a specified format.

[4]https://radimrehurek.com/gensim/

[5]https://github.com/estebandito22/PyTorchAVITM

[6]https://github.com/adjidieng/ETM

[7]https://github.com/MilaNLProc/contextualized-topic-models

2.3 Evaluation Metrics

The proposed framework provides several evaluation metrics. A metric can be used as the objective targeted by a Bayesian Optimization strategy, or to monitor the behavior of a topic model while the model is optimized on a different objective. The performance of a topic model can be evaluated by investigating different aspects, according to the following evaluation metrics:

- Topic coherence metrics (Lau et al., 2014; Röder et al., 2015) that compute how the top-k words of a topic are related to each other;
- Topic significance metrics (AlSumait et al., 2009; Terragni et al., 2020b) that focus on the document-topic and topic-word distributions to discover high-quality and junk topics;
- Diversity metrics (Dieng et al., 2019; Bianchi et al., 2020) that measure how diverse the top-k words of a topic are to each other;
- Classification metrics (Phan et al., 2008; Terragni et al., 2020a) where the document-topic distribution of each document is used as the K-dimensional representation to train a classifier that predicts the document's class.

OCTIS provides 10 evaluation metrics directly available in the web dashboard, and 13 accessible through the python library.

2.4 Hyper-parameter Optimization

The proposed framework uses Bayesian Optimization (Snoek et al., 2012; Shahriari et al., 2015) to tune the hyper-parameters of the topic models. If any of the available hyper-parameters is selected to be optimized for a given evaluation metric, BO explores the search space to determine the optimal settings. Since the performance estimated by the evaluation metrics can be affected by noise, the objective function is computed as the median of a given number of *model runs* (i.e., topic models run with the same hyperparameter configuration) computed for the selected evaluation metric.

BO is a sequential model-based optimization strategy for expensive and noisy black-box functions (e.g. topic models). The basic idea consists of using all the model's configurations evaluated so far to approximate the value of the performance metric and then selects a new promising configuration to evaluate.

Features	OCTIS	Gensim	STTM	PyCARET	MALLET	TOMODAPI
Pre-processing tools	√	√		√	√	√
Pre-processed datasets	√	√	√	√		√
Classical topic models	√	√	√	√	√	√
Neural topic models	√					√
Coherence metrics	√	√	√	√	√	
Diversity metrics	√					
Significance metrics	√					
Classification metrics	√		√	√	√	√
Hyper-parameters tuning	BO	MLE		grid-search	MLE	
Usage	import in script, web dashboard	import in script	command line	import in script	command line	import in script, API
Programming Language	Python	Python	Java	Python	Java	Python

Table 2: Comparison between OCTIS and the most well-known topic modeling libraries.

The approximation is provided by a probabilistic *surrogate model*, which describes the prior belief over the objective function using the observed configurations. The next configuration to evaluate is selected through the optimization of an *acquisition function*, which leverages the uncertainty in the posterior to guide the exploration.

We integrated into OCTIS most of the BO algorithms of the Scikit-Optimize library (Head et al., 2018) to provide a robust and efficient BO implementation. We integrated Gaussian Process and Random Forest as surrogate models, while we included Probability of Improvement, Expected Improvement, and Upper Confidence Bound as acquisition functions. See (Snoek et al., 2012; Candelieri and Archetti, 2019) for more details about the use of BO for hyper-parameter optimization.

Instead of performing BO, a user can also use a random search technique to find the best hyper-parameter configuration. Since the Bayesian Optimization requires some initial configurations to fit the surrogate model, the user can provide the initial configurations, according to their domain knowledge. Alternatively, a user can perform a pure exploration of the search space using a random sampling strategy. Different algorithms are available (e.g. Uniform Random Sampling or Latin Hypercube sequence) for sampling the initial configurations.

3 Existing frameworks

The existing topic modeling frameworks usually provide topic modeling algorithms, while disregarding other essential aspects of the whole topic modeling pipeline: pre-processing, evaluation, comparison, and visualization of the results and, most importantly, the hyper-parameter selection. In the following, we outline the existing frameworks, highlighting their advantages and limitations.

MALLET(McCallum, 2002) and gensim[4] are the most known topic modeling libraries and include several classical topic models. They provide pre-processing methods and the estimation of the hyper-parameters using maximum likelihood estimation (MLE) techniques. These libraries do not include the recently proposed neural topic models, and they just provide topic coherence metrics.

STTM (Qiang et al., 2018) is a java library that provides a set of topic models that are specifically designed for short texts, providing several evaluation metrics.

ToModAPI (Lisena et al., 2020) is a python API that allows for training, inference, and evaluating different topic models, also including some of the most recent. However, it does not provide a method for finding the best hyper-parameter configuration of topic models. Instead, a tool that allows for optimizing the hyper-parameter of a machine learning model is PyCARET (Ali, 2020). However, it employs a grid-search technique to tune the hyper-parameters. This approach can be very time-consuming if the number of hyperparameters is high and the search space is huge (Bergstra and Bengio, 2012).

OCTIS stands at the union of the features of the existing frameworks: we integrated both classical and recent neural topic models, providing pre-processing methods, evaluation metrics, and the possibility of optimizing the hyper-parameters. Finally, a user-friendly graphical interface to launch one or more hyper-parameter optimization experiments on a given topic model and on a specific dataset has been provided.

Table 2 summarizes the main features of the

existing topic modeling frameworks and compares them with OCTIS.

4 System usage

OCTIS has been designed to be used as a python library by advanced users, as well as a simple web dashboard by anyone.

4.1 Example of use case for the python library

```
# loading of a pre-processed dataset
dataset = Dataset()
dataset.load("path/to/dataset")

#model instantiation
lda = LDA(num_topics=25)

#definition of the metric
td = TopicDiversity()

#definition of the search space
search_space = {
  "eta": Real(low=0.01, high=5.0),
  "alpha": Real(low=0.01, high=5.0)
}

#define and launch optimization
optimizer=Optimizer()
opt_result = optimizer.optimize(model,
     dataset, td, search_space)
```

The above lines of code will execute an optimization experiment that will provide an optimal configuration of the hyperparameters α and β for LDA with 25 topics by maximizing the diversity of the topics.

4.2 Web-based dashboard

The dashboard includes a set of simple but useful operations to conduct an experimental campaign on different topic models. Here we briefly explain the four main functionalities of the dashboard.

Experiment creation. First, a user can define an optimization experiment by selecting the dataset, the topic model, the corresponding hyperparameter to optimize, the evaluation metric to be considered by the BO (possibly other extra metrics to evaluate), and the settings of the optimization process.

Management of the experiments' queue. The user can monitor the queue of the experiments and see the corresponding progress. The user can also pause, restart, or delete an experiment that has been launched before. Additionally, the user can easily change the order of the queue of the experiments, by allowing a given run to be executed before others.

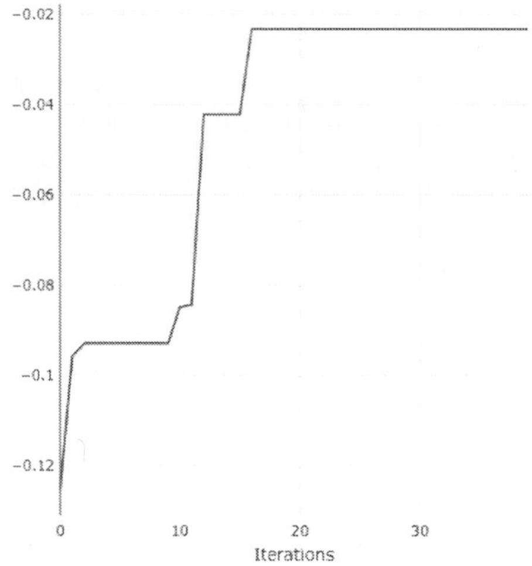

Figure 2: Example of the best-seen evolution for an optimization experiment.

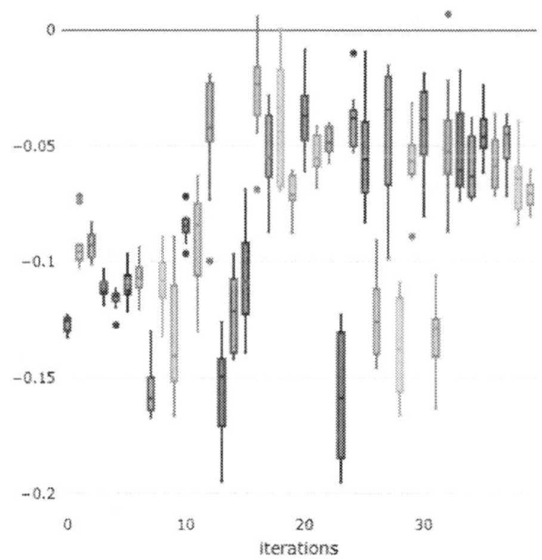

Figure 3: Example of box plot of an optimization experiment.

Comparison of the Topic Models. The user can select the models to be analyzed and compared. At the first stage, one can observe the progress of the BO iterations, observing a plot that contains at each iteration the best-seen evaluation, i.e. the median at each iteration of the metric that has been optimized (see Figure 2). Alternatively, a user can visualize a box plot at each iteration (see Figure 3) to understand if a given hyper-parameter configuration is noisy (high variance) or not.

Analysis of a single experiment. A user can further inspect the results of a specific topic model on a given dataset with respect to the considered metrics, by analyzing a single experiment.

Here, a user can visualize all the information and statistics related to the experiment, including the best hyper-parameter configuration and the best value of the optimized metric. They can also have an outline of the statistics of the other extra metrics that they had chosen to evaluate.

Figure 4: Example of word cloud of a topic.

We provide three different plots for inspecting the output of a single run of a topic model. Figure 4 shows the word cloud obtained from the most relevant words of a given topic, scaled by their probability. Focusing on the distributions inferred by a topic model, Figure 5 shows the topic distribution of a document, and Figure 6 represents an example of the weight of a selected word of the vocabulary for each topic.

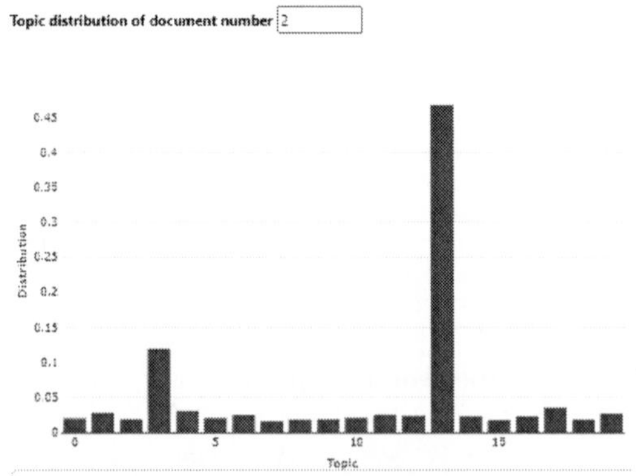

Figure 5: Example of distribution of the topics in a selected document.

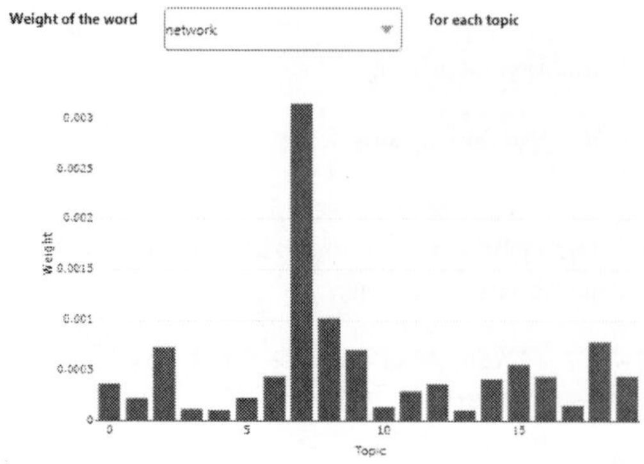

Figure 6: Example of the weight of the word "network" for each document.

5 Conclusions

In this paper, we presented the framework OCTIS for training, analyzing, and comparing Topic Models. The proposed framework is composed of a python library and a web dashboard and integrates several state-of-the-art topic models (both traditional and neural). These models can be trained by searching for their optimal hyperparameter configuration, for a given metric and dataset, exploiting a BO strategy. OCTIS allows researchers to train existing models, integrate new training and inference algorithms, and fairly compare the topic models of interest. On the other hand, practitioners could use OCTIS to boost the performance of Topic Models for their preferred downstream task or a wide range of practical applications, such as data exploratory analysis (Boyd-Graber et al., 2017).

Regarding future work, OCTIS could integrate a multi-objective optimization strategy to optimize multiple metrics in the same BO procedure (Paria et al., 2020). For example, this could allow a user to find an optimal hyper-parameter configuration for both topic coherence and document classification.

References

Moez Ali. 2020. *PyCaret: An open source, low-code machine learning library in Python*. PyCaret version 2.3.

Loulwah AlSumait, Daniel Barbará, James Gentle, and Carlotta Domeniconi. 2009. Topic significance ranking of LDA generative models. In *Machine Learning and Knowledge Discovery in Databases, European Conference, ECML PKDD 2009*, volume 5781 of *Lecture Notes in Computer Science*, pages 67–82. Springer.

Francesco Archetti and Antonio Candelieri. 2019. *Bayesian Optimization and Data Science*. Springer International Publishing.

James Bergstra and Yoshua Bengio. 2012. Random search for hyper-parameter optimization. *Journal of Machine Learning Research*, 13:281–305.

Federico Bianchi, Silvia Terragni, and Dirk Hovy. 2020. Pre-training is a hot topic: Contextualized document embeddings improve topic coherence. *arXiv preprint arXiv:2004.03974*.

Federico Bianchi, Silvia Terragni, Dirk Hovy, Debora Nozza, and Elisabetta Fersini. 2021. Cross-lingual Contextualized Topic Models with Zero-shot Learning. In *Proceedings of the 16th Conference of the European Chapter of the Association for Computational Linguistics*.

David M. Blei. 2012. Probabilistic topic models. *Commun. ACM*, 55(4):77–84.

David M. Blei, Andrew Y. Ng, and Michael I. Jordan. 2003. Latent dirichlet allocation. *Journal of Machine Learning Research*, 3:993–1022.

Jordan L. Boyd-Graber, Yuening Hu, and David M. Mimno. 2017. Applications of topic models. *Found. Trends Inf. Retr.*, 11(2-3):143–296.

Antonio Candelieri and Francesco Archetti. 2019. Global optimization in machine learning: the design of a predictive analytics application. *Soft Comput.*, 23(9):2969–2977.

Adji B. Dieng, Francisco J. R. Ruiz, and David M. Blei. 2019. Topic modeling in embedding spaces. *CoRR*, abs/1907.04907.

BG Galuzzi, I Giordani, A Candelieri, R Perego, and F Archetti. 2020. Hyperparameter optimization for recommender systems through bayesian optimization. *Computational Management Science*, pages 1–21.

Derek Greene and Pádraig Cunningham. 2006. Practical solutions to the problem of diagonal dominance in kernel document clustering. In *Proceedings of the 23rd International Conference on Machine learning (ICML'06)*, pages 377–384. ACM Press.

Tim Head, Gilles Louppe MechCoder, Iaroslav Shcherbatyi, et al. 2018. scikit-optimize/scikit-optimize: v0. 5.2.

Thomas Hofmann. 1999. Probabilistic latent semantic indexing. In *SIGIR '99: Proceedings of the 22nd Annual International ACM SIGIR Conference on Research and Development in Information Retrieval*, pages 50–57. ACM.

Jey Han Lau, David Newman, and Timothy Baldwin. 2014. Machine reading tea leaves: Automatically evaluating topic coherence and topic model quality. In *Proceedings of the 14th Conference of the European Chapter of the Association for Computational Linguistics, EACL 2014*, pages 530–539.

Daniel D. Lee and H. Sebastian Seung. 2000. Algorithms for non-negative matrix factorization. In *Advances in Neural Information Processing Systems 13, Papers from Neural Information Processing Systems (NIPS) 2000*, pages 556–562. MIT Press.

Kar Wai Lim and Wray L. Buntine. 2014. Bibliographic analysis with the citation network topic model. In *Proceedings of the Sixth Asian Conference on Machine Learning, ACML 2014*.

Pasquale Lisena, Ismail Harrando, Oussama Kandakji, and Raphael Troncy. 2020. ToModAPI: A Topic Modeling API to Train, Use and Compare Topic Models. In 2nd *International Workshop for Natural Language Processing Open Source Software (NLP-OSS)*.

Andrew McCallum, Andrés Corrada-Emmanuel, and Xuerui Wang. 2005. Topic and role discovery in social networks. In *IJCAI-05, Proceedings of the Nineteenth International Joint Conference on Artificial Intelligence*, pages 786–791.

Andrew Kachites McCallum. 2002. Mallet: A machine learning for language toolkit. *http://mallet. cs. umass. edu.*

Biswajit Paria, Kirthevasan Kandasamy, and Barnabás Póczos. 2020. A flexible framework for multi-objective bayesian optimization using random scalarizations. In *Uncertainty in Artificial Intelligence*, pages 766–776. PMLR.

Xuan Hieu Phan, Minh Le Nguyen, and Susumu Horiguchi. 2008. Learning to classify short and sparse text & web with hidden topics from large-scale data collections. In *Proceedings of the 17th International Conference on World Wide Web, WWW 2008*, pages 91–100. ACM.

Jipeng Qiang, Yun Li, Yunhao Yuan, Wei Liu, and Xindong Wu. 2018. Sttm: A tool for short text topic modeling. *arXiv preprint arXiv:1808.02215*.

Michael Röder, Andreas Both, and Alexander Hinneburg. 2015. Exploring the space of topic coherence measures. In *Proceedings of the Eighth ACM International Conference on Web Search and Data Mining, WSDM 2015, Shanghai, China, February 2-6, 2015*, pages 399–408. ACM.

Alexandra Schofield, Måns Magnusson, and David Mimno. 2017. Pulling out the stops: Rethinking stopword removal for topic models. In *Proceedings of the 15th Conference of the European Chapter of the Association for Computational Linguistics: Volume 2, Short Papers*, pages 432–436.

Alexandra Schofield and David Mimno. 2016. Comparing apples to apple: The effects of stemmers on topic models. *Transactions of the Association for Computational Linguistics*, 4:287–300.

Bobak Shahriari, Kevin Swersky, Ziyu Wang, Ryan P Adams, and Nando De Freitas. 2015. Taking the human out of the loop: A review of bayesian optimization. *Proceedings of the IEEE*, 104(1):148–175.

Jasper Snoek, Hugo Larochelle, and Ryan P. Adams. 2012. Practical bayesian optimization of machine learning algorithms. In *Advances in Neural Information Processing Systems 25: 26th Annual Conference on Neural Information Processing Systems 2012*, pages 2960–2968.

Akash Srivastava and Charles Sutton. 2017. Autoencoding variational inference for topic models. In *5th International Conference on Learning Representations, ICLR 2017*.

Yee Whye Teh, Michael I. Jordan, Matthew J. Beal, and David M. Blei. 2004. Sharing clusters among related groups: Hierarchical dirichlet processes. In *Advances in Neural Information Processing Systems, 17*, pages 1385–1392.

Silvia Terragni, Elisabetta Fersini, and Enza Messina. 2020a. Constrained relational topic models. *Information Sciences*, 512:581 – 594.

Silvia Terragni, Debora Nozza, Elisabetta Fersini, and Messina Enza. 2020b. Which matters most? comparing the impact of concept and document relationships in topic models. In *Proceedings of the First Workshop on Insights from Negative Results in NLP*, pages 32–40.

Ike Vayansky and Sathish A. P. Kumar. 2020. A review of topic modeling methods. *Information Systems*, 94:101582.

Hanna M Wallach, Iain Murray, Ruslan Salakhutdinov, and David Mimno. 2009. Evaluation methods for topic models. In *Proceedings of the 26th annual international conference on machine learning*, pages 1105–1112.

ELITR Multilingual Live Subtitling: Demo and Strategy

Ondřej Bojar and **Dominik Macháček** and **Sangeet Sagar** and **Otakar Smrž** and
Jonáš Kratochvíl and **Peter Polák** and **Ebrahim Ansari** and **Mohammad Mahmoudi** and **Rishu Kumar**
Charles University; `<surname>@ufal.mff.cuni.cz` except `jkratochvil@ufal.mff.cuni.cz`

Dario Franceschini and **Chiara Canton** and **Ivan Simonini**
PerVoice

Thai-Son Nguyen and **Felix Schneider** and **Sebastian Stüker** and **Alex Waibel**
Karlsruhe Institute of Technology; `<firstname>.<lastname>@kit.edu`

Barry Haddow and **Rico Sennrich** and **Philip Williams**
University of Edinburgh

Abstract

This paper presents an automatic speech translation system aimed at live subtitling of conference presentations. We describe the overall architecture and key processing components. More importantly, we explain our strategy for building a complex system for end-users from numerous individual components, each of which has been tested only in laboratory conditions.

The system is a working prototype that is routinely tested in recognizing English, Czech, and German speech and presenting it translated simultaneously into 42 target languages.

1 Introduction

With the tremendous gains observed recently in automatic speech recognition (ASR) and machine translation (MT) quality, including methods of joint learning of both of the tasks, the goal of a practically usable simultaneous spoken language translation (SLT[1]) system is getting closer.

In this paper, we introduce the SLT system developed in the EU project ELITR (European Live Translator[2]) (Bojar et al., 2020) which aims at a distinct setting: real-time speech translation into many target languages.

2 Motivation

In the current globalized world, meetings with participants from a very wide spectrum of nations are common. Many multinational organizations, public or private, regularly run congresses and conferences where attendees do not have any language in common. Interpretation is a must at such meetings and the cost of interpretation services consumes a considerable portion of the budget. The number of provided languages is then kept as low as possible, even in cases when some of the attendees are not sufficiently fluent in any of them.

We primarily focus on the setting of such multinational congresses where one source speech needs to be translated into many target languages. While we are aware of the quality limitations of speech recognition and machine translation, we strongly believe that the technology has reached the level where it is becoming practically usable and related systems confirm that belief, see Section 3 below.

Even if the automatic translation of recognized speech is not perfect, it can serve as a valuable supportive material. For instance, a Czech attendee may have a fair knowledge of English and French, but may easily get lost due to pronunciation difficulties to follow, gaps in his or her grammar knowledge, general vocabulary or specific terminology. Following live subtitles in mother tongue while listening to the foreign language could be of great help. Some level of errors in the subtitles is acceptable *if* the subtitles are sufficiently simultaneous. Our main goal is thus *gist interpretation*, i.e. live supportive translation of speech into text.

Within the ELITR project, we focus on ASR for English, Czech, German, French, Spanish and later Russian and Italian, and targetting the set of 43 languages spoken in member countries of EUROSAI, the association of supreme audit institu-

[1] We use the term SLT to refer primarily to simultaneous systems, although off-line spoken language systems can also fall under the same acronym.

[2] `http://elitr.eu/`

Proceedings of the 16th Conference of the European Chapter of the Association for Computational Linguistics: System Demonstrations, pages 271–277
April 19 - 23, 2021.

tions of the EU and nearby countries. Experimentally, we include also other languages based on available systems among the research partners in our project, e.g. Hindi.

The scientific motivation for our efforts is to find an approach that allows to assemble laboratory system components to a practically usable product and to document the problems on this journey.

3 Related Systems

Live spoken language translation has been continuously studied for decades, see e.g. Osterholtz et al. (1992); Fügen et al. (2008); Bangalore et al. (2012). Recent systems differ in whether they provide revisions to their previous output (Müller et al., 2016; Niehues et al., 2016; Dessloch et al., 2018; Niehues et al., 2018; Arivazhagan et al., 2020), or whether they only append output tokens (Grissom II et al., 2014; Gu et al., 2017; Arivazhagan et al., 2019; Press and Smith, 2018; Xiong et al., 2019; Ma et al., 2019; Zheng et al., 2019).

Müller et al. (2016) were probably the first to allow output revision when they find a better translation. Zenkel et al. (2018) released a simpler setup as an open-source toolkit consisting of a neural speech recognition system, a sentence segmentation system, and an attention-based translation system providing also some pre-trained models for their tasks. (Zenkel et al., 2018) evaluated only the quality of the output translations using BLEU and WER metrics.

Zheng et al. (2019) proposed a new approach with a delay-based heuristic. The model decides to read more input (or wait for it) or write the translation to the output. Ma et al. (2019) introduced a simple wait-k heuristic: output is emitted after k words of input. Both works are limited to simultaneous *translation*, i.e. they start from text and only simulate the speech-like input by processing input word by word.

Arivazhagan et al. (2020) combine industry-grade ASR and MT and allow output revisions by re-translating the source from scratch as it grows to decrease the latency, providing acceptable translation quality at the price of a higher number of text revisions.

4 ELITR Flexible Architecture

We always strive for the best performance for each considered language pair. With the perpetual competition in ASR and MT research, it is not surprising that there is no universally best solution. The interplay of available data, underlying method, the actual implementation as well as its adaptability to the domain of interest requires different choices for different languages.

Furthermore, the top-performing components are often available only at universities or research labs, as more or less stable research prototypes. Releasing any such system, let alone their combination so that they could be easily deployed by lay users is surely possible, but it would require considerable additional implementation resources.

The ELITR architecture (Franceschini et al., 2020) tackles this integration problem by means of a distributed connection-based client-server application. Research labs provide their components by connecting to a central point (the "mediator") which in turn uses these "workers" to satisfy users' stream processing requests. A technical benefit is that worker connection is issued *from* the secured networks of the labs so it usually does not run into firewall issues.

5 System Components

All our workers, except recent online sequence-to-sequence ASRs, have been described in our IWSLT 2020 shared task submission (Macháček et al., 2020). We briefly summarize them in following sections.

5.1 ASR Systems in ELITR

All our ASR systems provide online processing with low latency and hypotheses updates, as in KIT Lecture Translator (Müller et al., 2016). We use the hybrid ASR models based on Janus from KIT Lecture Translator, for German and English, as well as recent neural sequence-to-sequence ASR models trained on the same data (Nguyen et al., 2020). For Czech ASR, we use a Kaldi hybrid model trained on a Corpus of Czech Parliament Plenary Hearings (Kratochvíl et al., 2019). Czech sequence-to-sequence ASR is a work in progress.

5.2 MT Systems in ELITR

We use bilingual NMT models for some high resource and well-studied language pairs e.g. for English-Czech (Popel et al., 2019; Wetesko et al., 2019). For other targets, we use multi-target models, e.g. an English-centric universal model for

Index Name	Worker	Source Lang	Target Lang	sacreBLEU	WER	Words	Lines
auto-iwslt2020-antrecorp(ASR)	en-EU-lecture_KIT-s2s	EN	–	–	0.46	6634	571
auto-iwslt2020-antrecorp(MT)	rb-EU_fromEN-en_to_41_all	EN	CS	13.66	–	5345	571
auto-iwslt2020-antrecorp(MT)	rb-EU_fromEN-en_to_41_all	EN	DE	17.95	–	6119	571
auto-asr-english-auditing(ASR)	en-EU-lecture_KIT-s2s	EN	–	–	0.37	24530	2220
auto-asr-english-auditing(MT)	rb-EU_fromEN-en_to_41_all	EN	CS	16.45	–	43146	2170
auto-asr-english-auditing(MT)	rb-EU_fromEN-en_to_41_all	EN	DE	19.60	–	18616	2220
auto-iwslt2020-khanacademy(ASR)	en-EU-lecture_KIT-s2s	EN	–	–	0.55	4470	538

Table 1: An overview of WER, sacreBLEU scores on the ELITR test set domain and the size of gold transcript for reference.

42 languages (Johnson et al., 2017). The models are mostly Transformers (Vaswani et al., 2017) but we improve their performance in massively multilingual setting by extra depth (Zhang et al., 2020).

5.3 Interplay of ASR and MT

Connecting ASR and MT systems is not straightforward because MT systems assume input in the form of complete sentences. We follow the strategy of Niehues et al. (2016), first inserting punctuation into the stream of tokens coming from ASR (Tilk and Alumäe, 2016), breaking it up at full stops and sending individual sentences to MT, either as unfinished sentence prefixes, or complete sentences. We are using re-translation, as ASR or punctuation updates are received.

Currently, the main problem is that punctuation prediction does not have access to the sound any more, so intonation cannot be considered. Another problem is the information structure of translated sentences, where MT systems tend to "normalize" word order. The loss of topicalization reduces understandability of the stream of uttered sentences.

For the future, we consider three approaches: (1) training MT on sentence chunks, (2) including sound input in punctuation prediction, or (3) end-to-end neural SLT.

6 Evaluation

We evaluate our systems in multiple ways:

- The individual components are evaluated in isolation during deployment, and on a comparable test set. compared with baseline by the MT quality.
- English to Czech and German simultaneous translation of non-native speech was evaluated on a shared task at IWSLT 2020 (Ansari et al., 2020). We validated our candidate systems, and submitted the best one as Macháček et al. (2020). The results showed that the speech recognition of the non-native speech in the test set was problematic, and resulted to inadequate translations. However, the systems were not yet adapted to non-natives or for the domain. It is a challenge for future work. It can be achieved by speaker adaptation of the ASR from a small sample of the speaker, by multi-lingual ASR, and by collecting non-native speech training data, as AMI corpus.
- We regurarly test our system end-to-end on linguistic seminars in Czech or English. The participants are Czech or English speakers and do not need any assistance with the language, so we can not receive relevant feedback about adequacy and fluency. However, we test our system in end-to-end fashion and face engineering problems and technical issues on all layers from sound acquisition through network connections, worker configuration to subtitle presentation.
- We are currently running a user study with non-German speakers watching German videos with our online subtitles, see Section 7.1. We aim to measure the comprehension loss caused by different subtitling options, latency or flicker.

For comparability across our project partners but also across external research labs, we publicly released a tool for evaluation, SLTev[3] (Ansari et al., 2021) and a test set.[4] The results of our currently best candidates on the testset are in Table 1.

It is important to realize that the evaluation for quality, latency and stability on a speech-to-text test set in lab conditions is necessary, but not sufficient for assessing the practical usability of the system. Practical usability has to include the presentation layer (Section 7) and tests in live sessions or rigorously controlled conditions.

[3]https://github.com/ELITR/SLTev
[4]https://github.com/ELITR/elitr-testset

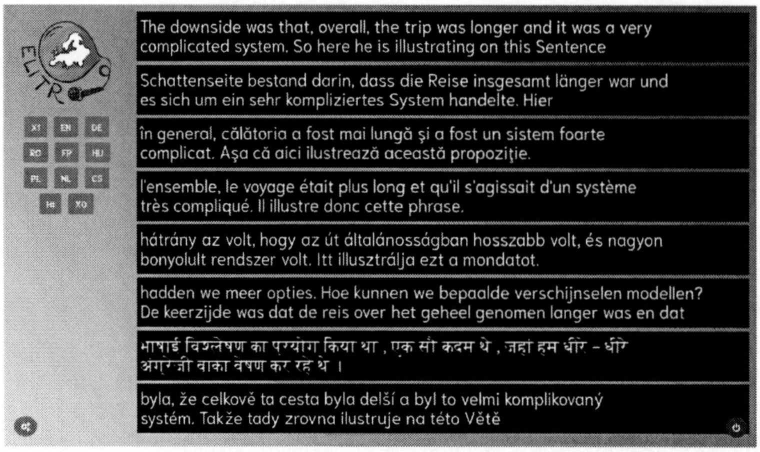

Figure 1: A screenshot of subtitle view from a presentation given in Czech (last row), automatically transcribed and translated to English (first row) and then from English into several other languages. The various processing and network delays lead to slightly different timing of each of the languages.

7 Presentation Techniques

The last step in an SLT system is the delivery of the translated content to the user. Our goal stops at the textual representation, i.e. we do not include speech synthesis and delivery of the sound, which would bring yet another set of design decisions and open problems, see e.g. Zheng et al. (2020).

We experiment with two different views for our text output, both implemented as web applications. The "subtitle view" is optimized toward minimal use of screen space. Only two lines of text are available which leaves room either for e.g. a streamed video of the session or the slides, or for many languages displayed at once, if the screen is intended for a multi-lingual audience. The "paragraph view" provides more textual context to the user.

7.1 Subtitle View

The subtitle view offers a simple interface with a HLS stream of the video or slides and one or more subtitles streams.

Section 7.1 presents one screenshot of this view, selected from a screencast. Instead of presenting the video, we use the screen space to show seven target languages, in addition to the live transcript of the source Czech.

We are probably the first to combine re-translation strategy with the presentation in such limited space. To limit text flicker as re-translations are arriving, we had to introduce a critical component after the MT output called Subtitler (Macháček and Bojar, 2020). The subtitler allows us to choose the level of updates, trading simultaneity for stability. A user study on the impact of this choice on comprehensibility is currently running. We believe that the ideal choice will depend also on the users' knowledge of the source and target languages and their reading speed.

Even if the flicker is avoided, there remains the main drawback of the subtitle view, the limited context. Both ASR and MT suffer from natural errors. Following the output of ASR (subtitles of the speakers' language) is easier, the erroneous hypotheses still somehow resemble the original sound, so the user can recover from recognition errors.

The output of MT causes a substantially bigger challenge for the user because the sentences are mostly rendered as fully fluent but containing unexpected words or information structure. With only two lines of text available, the user does not see sufficient number of words to let the brain "make up" or reconstruct the original meaning from pieces. The short-term memory of recently processed text does not seem to be sufficient for this type recovery, while seeing the words in larger context gives the user a better chance.

7.2 Paragraph View

We created the paragraph view primarily to improve the chances of recovery from translation errors. The added benefit is a clearer indication of which sentences are finished and which may still

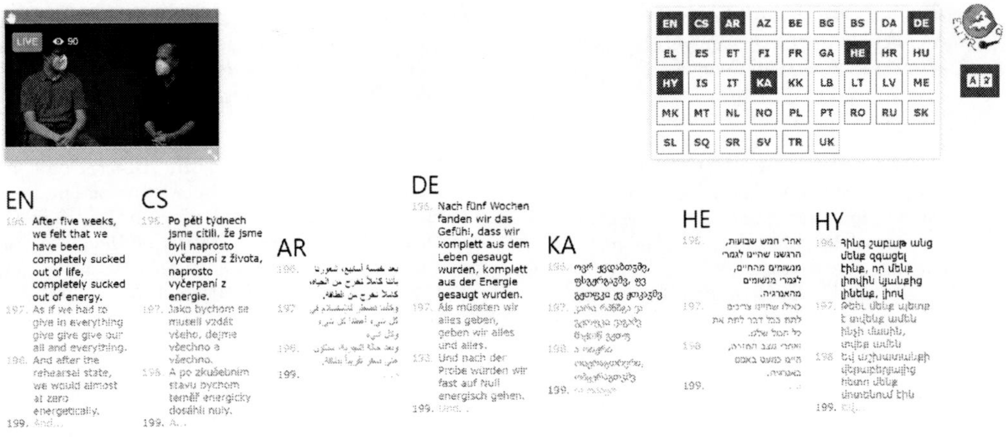

Figure 2: Sample screenshot from the paragraph view of simultaneous translation output on a live discussion of THEaiTRE project. The talk was given in Czech, interpreted into English by a human interpreter, automatically recognized (the leftmost EN column) and translated into 41 languages. Sentence indices correspond to each other across languages in all columns. Sentences in black are "stable", no update will arrive. Sentences in dark gray and with yellow index number are tentative, the segmentation (and thus translation) still may change. The last sentence (light gray) is still being uttered and is thus highly unstable.

change. Without any settings, users can simply decide if they want to read the less stable gray output, or rather wait for the stable segments.

The view is illustrated in Figure 2, with Czech as source and two more languages shown. More than three languages can be presented as well but they generally do not fit. The scrolling of the languages is not fully parallel by our design decision to prefer contiguous columns within each language over tabular synchronous presentation. One important aspect is however synchronized, and that is the stable "level" for finalized sentences: the completed text (shown in black) is aligned at the bottom across languages while the unstable hypotheses flicker below the level, varying in their length as needed.

A drawback of this interface is that all errors such as laughable or obscene words in MT output remain on screen for a long time, needlessly distracting the user.

8 Conclusion

We presented a complex system for live subtitling of conference speech into many target languages, composed of research prototype components but still serving in close-to-production setting. New and updated models and other components can be easily plugged in and tested in practice.

As of now, we are at a good starting point for gradual model improvement and field tests. One of them is very likely to be the META-FORUM 2021 but we are also searching for suitable events with more than one official communication language.

Demonstration videos from past sessions can be found in the blogposts at `https://elitr.eu/blog/`.

Acknowledgments

This work has received funding from the European Union's Horizon 2020 Research and Innovation Programme under Grant Agreement No 825460 (ELITR). The Charles University team is grateful to Karel Veselý for his great help with the Czech Kaldi model.

References

Ebrahim Ansari, Amittai Axelroad, Nguyen Bach, Ondrej Bojar, Roldano Cattoni, Fahim Dalvi, Nadir Durrani, Marcello Federico, Christian Federmann, Jiatao Gu, Fei Huang, Kevin Knight, Xutai Ma, Ajay Nagesh, Matteo Negri, Jan Niehues, Juan Pino, Elizabeth Salesky, Xing Shi, Sebastian Stüker, Marco Turchi, and Changhan Wang. 2020. Findings of the IWSLT 2020 Evaluation Campaign. In *Proceedings of the 17th International Conference on Spoken Language Translation (IWSLT 2020)*, Seattle, USA.

Ebrahim Ansari, Ondřej Bojar, Barry Haddow, and Mohammad Mahmoudi. 2021. SLTev: Comprehensive evaluation of spoken language translation. In *Proceedings of the System Demonstrations of the 16th Conference of the European Chapter of the Association for Computational Linguistics*, Kyiv, Ukraine. Association for Computational Linguistics.

Naveen Arivazhagan, Colin Cherry, Wolfgang Macherey, Chung-Cheng Chiu, Semih Yavuz, Ruoming Pang, Wei Li, and Colin Raffel. 2019. Monotonic infinite lookback attention for simultaneous machine translation. In *Proceedings of the 57th Annual Meeting of the Association for Computational Linguistics*, pages 1313–1323, Florence, Italy. Association for Computational Linguistics.

Naveen Arivazhagan, Colin Cherry, Wolfgang Macherey, and George Foster. 2020. Re-translation versus streaming for simultaneous translation. In *Proceedings of the 17th International Conference on Spoken Language Translation*, pages 220–227, Online. Association for Computational Linguistics.

Srinivas Bangalore, Vivek Kumar Rangarajan Sridhar, Prakash Kolan, Ladan Golipour, and Aura Jimenez. 2012. Real-time incremental speech-to-speech translation of dialogs. In *Proceedings of the 2012 Conference of the North American Chapter of the Association for Computational Linguistics: Human Language Technologies*, pages 437–445, Montréal, Canada. Association for Computational Linguistics.

Ondřej Bojar, Dominik Macháček, Sangeet Sagar, Otakar Smrž, Jonáš Kratochvíl, Ebrahim Ansari, Dario Franceschini, Chiara Canton, Ivan Simonini, Thai-Son Nguyen, Felix Schneider, Sebastian Stücker, Alex Waibel, Barry Haddow, Rico Sennrich, and Philip Williams. 2020. ELITR: European live translator. In *Proceedings of the 22nd Annual Conference of the European Association for Machine Translation*, pages 463–464, Lisboa, Portugal. European Association for Machine Translation.

Florian Dessloch, Thanh-Le Ha, Markus Müller, Jan Niehues, Thai-Son Nguyen, Ngoc-Quan Pham, Elizabeth Salesky, Matthias Sperber, Sebastian Stüker, Thomas Zenkel, and Alexander Waibel. 2018. KIT lecture translator: Multilingual speech translation with one-shot learning. In *Proceedings of the 27th International Conference on Computational Linguistics: System Demonstrations*, pages 89–93, Santa Fe, New Mexico. Association for Computational Linguistics.

Dario Franceschini, Chiara Canton, Ivan Simonini, Armin Schweinfurth, Adelheid Glott, Sebastian Stüker, Thai-Son Nguyen, Felix Schneider, Thanh-Le Ha, Alex Waibel, Barry Haddow, Philip Williams, Rico Sennrich, Ondřej Bojar, Sangeet Sagar, Dominik Macháček, and Otakar Smrž. 2020. Removing European language barriers with innovative machine translation technology. In *Proceedings of the 1st International Workshop on Language Technology Platforms*, pages 44–49, Marseille, France. European Language Resources Association.

Christian Fügen, Alex Waibel, and Muntsin Kolss. 2008. Simultaneous translation of lectures and speeches. *Springer Netherlands, Machine Translation, MTSN 2008, Springer, Netherland*, 21(4).

Alvin Grissom II, He He, Jordan Boyd-Graber, John Morgan, and Hal Daumé III. 2014. Don't until the final verb wait: Reinforcement learning for simultaneous machine translation. In *Proceedings of the 2014 Conference on Empirical Methods in Natural Language Processing (EMNLP)*, pages 1342–1352, Doha, Qatar. Association for Computational Linguistics.

Jiatao Gu, Graham Neubig, Kyunghyun Cho, and Victor O.K. Li. 2017. Learning to translate in real-time with neural machine translation. In *Proceedings of the 15th Conference of the European Chapter of the Association for Computational Linguistics: Volume 1, Long Papers*, pages 1053–1062, Valencia, Spain. Association for Computational Linguistics.

Melvin Johnson, Mike Schuster, Quoc V. Le, Maxim Krikun, Yonghui Wu, Zhifeng Chen, Nikhil Thorat, Fernanda Viégas, Martin Wattenberg, Greg Corrado, Macduff Hughes, and Jeffrey Dean. 2017. Google's multilingual neural machine translation system: Enabling zero-shot translation. *Transactions of the Association for Computational Linguistics*, 5:339–351.

Jonáš Kratochvíl, Peter Polák, and Ondřej Bojar. 2019. Large corpus of czech parliament plenary hearings. LINDAT/CLARIN digital library at the Institute of Formal and Applied Linguistics (ÚFAL), Faculty of Mathematics and Physics, Charles University.

Mingbo Ma, Liang Huang, Hao Xiong, Renjie Zheng, Kaibo Liu, Baigong Zheng, Chuanqiang Zhang, Zhongjun He, Hairong Liu, Xing Li, Hua Wu, and Haifeng Wang. 2019. STACL: Simultaneous translation with implicit anticipation and controllable latency using prefix-to-prefix framework. In *Proceedings of the 57th Annual Meeting of the Association for Computational Linguistics*, pages 3025–3036, Florence, Italy. Association for Computational Linguistics.

Dominik Macháček and Onřej Bojar. 2020. Presenting simultaenous translation in limited space. In *Proceedings of the 20th Conference ITAT 2020: Workshop on Automata, Formal and Natural Languages (WAFNL 2020)*. To be published.

Dominik Macháček, Jonáš Kratochvíl, Sangeet Sagar, Matúš Žilinec, Ondřej Bojar, Thai-Son Nguyen, Felix Schneider, Philip Williams, and Yuekun Yao. 2020. ELITR non-native speech translation at IWSLT 2020. In *Proceedings of the 17th International Conference on Spoken Language Translation*, pages 200–208, Online. Association for Computational Linguistics.

Markus Müller, Thai Son Nguyen, Jan Niehues, Eunah Cho, Bastian Krüger, Thanh-Le Ha, Kevin Kilgour, Matthias Sperber, Mohammed Mediani, Sebastian

Stüker, and Alex Waibel. 2016. Lecture translator - speech translation framework for simultaneous lecture translation. In *Proceedings of the 2016 Conference of the North American Chapter of the Association for Computational Linguistics: Demonstrations*, pages 82–86, San Diego, California. Association for Computational Linguistics.

Thai-Son Nguyen, Ngoc-Quan Pham, Sebastian Stueker, and Alex Waibel. 2020. High performance sequence-to-sequence model for streaming speech recognition. *arXiv preprint arXiv:2003.10022*.

Jan Niehues, Thai Son Nguyen, Eunah Cho, Thanh-Le Ha, Kevin Kilgour, Markus Müller, Matthias Sperber, Sebastian Stüker, and Alex Waibel. 2016. Dynamic transcription for low-latency speech translation. In *17th Annual Conference of the International Speech Communication Association, INTERSPEECH 2016*, volume 08-12-September-2016 of *Proceedings of the Annual Conference of the International Speech Communication Association. Ed. : N. Morgan*, pages 2513–2517. International Speech and Communication Association, Baixas.

Jan Niehues, Ngoc-Quan Pham, Thanh-Le Ha, Matthias Sperber, and Alex Waibel. 2018. Low-latency neural speech translation. In *Interspeech 2018*, Hyderabad, India.

L. Osterholtz, C. Augustine, A. McNair, I. Rogina, H. Saito, T. Sloboda, J. Tebelskis, and A. Waibel. 1992. Testing generality in janus: a multi-lingual speech translation system. In *[Proceedings] ICASSP-92: 1992 IEEE International Conference on Acoustics, Speech, and Signal Processing*, volume 1, pages 209–212 vol.1.

Martin Popel, Dominik Macháček, Michal Auersperger, Ondřej Bojar, and Pavel Pecina. 2019. English-czech systems in wmt19: Document-level transformer. In *Proceedings of the Fourth Conference on Machine Translation (Volume 2: Shared Task Papers, Day 1)*, pages 342–348, Florence, Italy. Association for Computational Linguistics.

Ofir Press and Noah A. Smith. 2018. You may not need attention.

Ottokar Tilk and Tanel Alumäe. 2016. Bidirectional recurrent neural network with attention mechanism for punctuation restoration. In *Interspeech 2016*.

Ashish Vaswani, Noam Shazeer, Niki Parmar, Jakob Uszkoreit, Llion Jones, Aidan N Gomez, Ł ukasz Kaiser, and Illia Polosukhin. 2017. Attention is all you need. In I. Guyon, U. V. Luxburg, S. Bengio, H. Wallach, R. Fergus, S. Vishwanathan, and R. Garnett, editors, *Advances in Neural Information Processing Systems 30*, pages 6000–6010. Curran Associates, Inc.

Joanna Wetesko, Marcin Chochowski, Pawel Przybysz, Philip Williams, Roman Grundkiewicz, Rico Sennrich, Barry Haddow, Antonio Valerio Miceli Barone, and Alexandra Birch. 2019. Samsung and University of Edinburgh's System for the IWSLT 2019. In *IWSLT*.

Hao Xiong, Ruiqing Zhang, Chuanqiang Zhang, Zhongjun Hea, Hua Wu, and Haifeng Wang. 2019. Dutongchuan: Context-aware translation model for simultaneous interpreting.

Thomas Zenkel, Matthias Sperber, Jan Niehues, Markus Müller, Ngoc-Quan Pham, Sebastian Stüker, and Alex Waibel. 2018. Open source toolkit for speech to text translation. *The Prague Bulletin of Mathematical Linguistics, NUMBER 11, p. 125-135.*

Biao Zhang, Philip Williams, Ivan Titov, and Rico Sennrich. 2020. Improving massively multilingual neural machine translation and zero-shot translation. In *Proceedings of the 58th Annual Meeting of the Association for Computational Linguistics*, pages 1628–1639, Online. Association for Computational Linguistics.

Baigong Zheng, Renjie Zheng, Mingbo Ma, and Liang Huang. 2019. Simpler and faster learning of adaptive policies for simultaneous translation. In *Proceedings of the 2019 Conference on Empirical Methods in Natural Language Processing and the 9th International Joint Conference on Natural Language Processing (EMNLP-IJCNLP)*, pages 1349–1354, Hong Kong, China. Association for Computational Linguistics.

Renjie Zheng, Mingbo Ma, Baigong Zheng, Kaibo Liu, Jiahong Yuan, Kenneth Church, and Liang Huang. 2020. Fluent and low-latency simultaneous speech-to-speech translation with self-adaptive training. In *Findings of the Association for Computational Linguistics: EMNLP 2020*, pages 3928–3937, Online. Association for Computational Linguistics.

Breaking Writer's Block:
Low-cost Fine-tuning of Natural Language Generation Models

Alexandre Duval
CentraleSupelec

Thomas Lamson
CentraleSupelec

Gaël de Léséleuc de Kérouara
CentraleSupelec

{alexandre.duval, thomas.lamson, gael.de-leseleuc}@student-cs.fr

Matthias Gallé
Naver Labs Europe
matthias.galle@naverlabs.com

Abstract

It is standard procedure these days to solve Information Extraction task by fine-tuning large pre-trained language models. This is not the case for generation task, which relies on a variety of techniques for controlled language generation.

In this paper, we describe a system that fine-tunes a natural language generation model for the problem of solving *Writer's Block*. The fine-tuning changes the conditioning to also include the right context in addition to the left context, as well as an optional list of entities, the size, the genre and a summary of the paragraph that the human author wishes to generate.

Our proposed fine-tuning obtains excellent results, even with a small number of epochs and a total cost of USD 150. The system can be accessed as a web-service,[1] and all the code is released.[2] A video showcasing the interface and the model is also available.[3]

1 Introduction

Thanks to the powerful capacity of large neural networks based on the attention mechanism (Vaswani et al., 2017), the current practice in NLP is to start from pre-trained models, which were trained to predict words in context (Devlin et al., 2018; Dai et al., 2019) or to perform various other tasks (Raffel et al., 2019). These pre-trained models are then fine-tuned to solve the task at hand: all top entries of the SuperGLUE benchmark[4] for instance follow this trend.

Concerning generation however, the standard methods are very different. Approaches to *controlled generation* are mostly focused on nudging the model to generate text about a certain topic (Keskar et al., 2019; Dathathri et al., 2019), or on using distributional models (Khalifa et al., 2021). Fine-tuning is often dismissed as too expensive as it would require to modify the ensemble of the number of parameters, often measured in the billions. This is considered impractical, because either too slow, expensive or ecologically not responsible (Strubell et al., 2019). Brown et al. (2020) state clearly that "GPT-3 could also in principle be evaluated in the traditional fine-tuning setting, but we leave this to future work."

In this paper, we show that it is possible to fine-tune a language model not only to generate text of a certain type, but also to condition it easily on more than a one-sided context. In particular, we propose to fine-tune GPT-2 to generate paragraphs based on surrounding (previous and next) sections, a summary of the target content, the entities that should appear, the genre and the desired length. The resulting model is then used for a web-based system demonstration[5] that allows authors to break *Writer's Block*, meaning the "the condition of being unable to create a piece of written work".[6] Our experiments show that it is possible to obtain excellent results (as measured by a variety of metrics benchmarking the control capacity) with a very limited budget. The complete training cost of our model, performed on a commercial cloud provider, is around USD 150. Our demo introduces the following contribution:

[1] http://textgen.thomas-lamson.com/

[2] https://github.com/ThomasLamsonFr/AITextGenerator

[3] https://www.youtube.com/watch?v=zwezKGrahK0

[4] https://super.gluebenchmark.com/leaderboard

[5] http://textgen.thomas-lamson.com/

[6] https://dictionary.cambridge.org/dictionary/english/writer-s-block

Proceedings of the 16th Conference of the European Chapter of the Association for Computational Linguistics: System Demonstrations, pages 278–287
April 19 - 23, 2021. ©2021 Association for Computational Linguistics

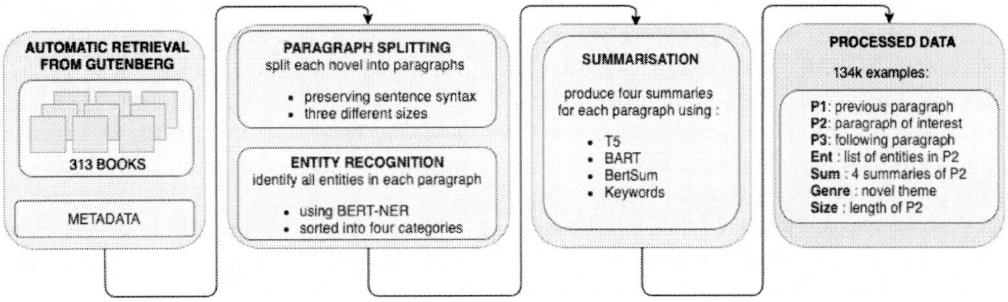

Figure 1: Data Preprocessing Pipeline, shows the extracted meta-data that can be used to control the generated text

- An open-source writing tool that can help creative authors break *Writer's Block*, by proposing novel paragraphs.
- A fine-tuned GPT-2 model that respects the context of surrounding paragraphs and allows to control entities, desired output length, the genre as well as the content summary.
- Experiments showing that even with a reduced budget, the fine-tuned model diverges from the starting model while generating coherent text.

2 Related Work

Recent progress in transfer-learning has shown that large pre-trained models are powerful enough to be quickly fine-tuned to solve natural language understanding tasks.

Diverging from this, current approaches to adapt generation models are generally based on picking carefully the *prompt* on which the text is to be generated. This was popularized by Brown et al. (2020) and has since then seen steady growth by different proposals aiming to find good prompts (Schick and Schütze, 2020a,b; Gao et al., 2020; Li and Liang, 2021).

A related approach is to adapt the model so that it presents desired biases. This can be done by training with control tokens (Arivazhagan et al., 2019; Keskar et al., 2019) or by adapting an existing model with additional layers (Wang et al., 2020) or sampling techniques (Dathathri et al., 2019; Khalifa et al., 2021). Those methods allow generating style variations of the same form. However, they are less well suited to changes in the conditioned text, such as providing not only a prefix but also a continuation of the text to be generated. We are particularly interested in conditioning on categorical variables, like GROVER (Zellers et al., 2019), but without retraining. Our experiments show that fine-tuning is surprisingly effective for this.

Several research directions have explored the use of languages models for creative writing and interactive story-telling (Peng et al., 2018; Luo et al., 2019). This also includes online tools such as *plot generator*[7] or *talk to transformers*,[8] where the control that can be exerted over the text remains quite rudimentary. Of special inspiration for this work was *AI Dungeon*.[9]

3 Method

In our approach, the model will be trained to regenerate each book's paragraph (called P2) using the previous and following paragraphs (P1 and P3) as well as information concerning P2: its size, the genre of the book it belongs to, the entities it should include and a summary of its content. Instead of training a model from scratch, we leverage a pre-trained GPT-2 117M model and fine-tune it on 313 pre-processed novels. We teach it to predict the next word using the above contextual information as well as already generated words.

Our approach is separated into three main steps: (i) data preparation (ii) transformation of the data and (iii) fine-tuning:

3.1 Data

We emphasise key aspects of the data generation phase, an often overlooked aspect in research projects that however proved essential in our demo.

Novels data Our paper focuses on text generation for novels and thus requires adequate data. We

[7] https://www.plot-generator.org.uk/story/
[8] https://talktotransformer.com/
[9] https://aidungeon.io/

select books from the Gutenberg Project,[10] which we clean and filter based on the associated metadata. Only English books corresponding to novels are kept, and the genre (used for fine-tuning later) is defined using a manual mapping from the fine-grained tags provided by Gutenberg. Due to limited computational resources, we only consider 500 books and ultimately retain 313 after filtering. We then split the text of each book into paragraphs of different lengths, with a minimum and maximum bound, being careful not to cut a sentence in the middle, nor to separate core parts like chapters or even to split big paragraphs into uneven pieces. This step is essential for the later reconstruction within our training phase. The size of each paragraph is used to categorise them into *Small* (400-800 characters), *Medium* (800-1400) or *Large* (1400-1700).

Entity extraction Once each book is preprocessed, we detect entities for each paragraph using a pre-trained BERT NER Large model.[11] Entities are classified into four categories: persons, locations, organisations and miscellaneous. This allows for authors later to control the generation by specifying the entities they wish to incorporate.

Summary Similarly, in order for authors to be able to guide the generation by giving information on the desired content, we use different summarization models taken from distinct families. This tends to make our model more robust to the possible ways authors could provide this type of information. In this sense, we use four different models, covering:

- One extractive model (in case authors provide key sentences): BertSum (Liu, 2019).
- Two abstractive models (to allow rich rephrases): BART (Lewis et al., 2019) and T5 (Raffel et al., 2019).
- One graph-based non-neural model that extracts keyword phrases: TextRank (Mihalcea and Tarau, 2004, Kw)

The full data processing pipeline is shown in Fig. 1.

3.2 Preparation step

The resulting documents are split into paragraphs enriched with the related metadata (author, title, language, genre, theme) as well as the four summaries (Bart, T5, BertSum, Kw) and a list of the entities appearing in the text. All entities and one summary chosen at random are fed to the GPT-2 model, alongside metadata information (size and genre) and pure text (P1, P2, P3) to help it control and contextualise the generation.

The training corpus therefore consists of pairs (x, y) (predict y from prefix x), where y is the middle paragraph $P2$ and x is

```
[P3] P3 [Sum] Sum [T] Theme
[Ent] Entities [Size]
[P1] P1 [P2]
```

where $[P1]$, $[P2]$, $[P3]$, $[Sum]$, $[T]$ and $[Ent]$ indicate the type of input received by the model (special tokens). $[Size]$ is either $[S]$, $[M]$ or $[L]$ and gives information about the paragraph's length. Note that the order of the input is not essential. We only put $P1$ at the end so that GPT-2 can continue from there, as it has been trained to do so.

The pre-trained model (small GPT-2) has a maximum window size of 1024 tokens. If x exceeds that length we truncate $P1$ on the left and $P3$ on the right. As a heuristic we allocate $2/3$ of the remaining space[12] to $P1$ and $1/3$ to $P3$, as we consider $P1$ to be more important than P3.

All the text is segmented using the corresponding pre-trained BPE tokenizer. Special tokens are created for the separators ($[P1]$, $[P2]$, etc.) and a segment embedding is added on top of the token and position embeddings. It has the same dimension and serves to distinguish the segment each token corresponds to (P1, P2, P3, theme, size, summary and entities).

3.3 Fine-tuning

We fine-tuned the pre-trained GPT2LMHeadModel (small) from HuggingFace (Wolf et al., 2020), using a customised version of the given training script.[13] x is provided as prefix, and only the cross-entropy error over y (and $P2$) is back-propagated to fine-tune the weights. The training procedure is shown in Fig. 2. One of the goals of this demo is to show that this type of fine-tuning can be done with limited resources: here we used an AWS's *p3.2xlarge instance* (using one Nvidia Tesla V100 GPU). In total, the model received 134k samples

[10] https://www.gutenberg.org/

[11] https://github.com/kamalkraj/BERT-NER

[12] once everything except $P1$ and $P3$ has been fed as input

[13] `https://huggingface.co/transformers/model_doc/GPT-2.html`

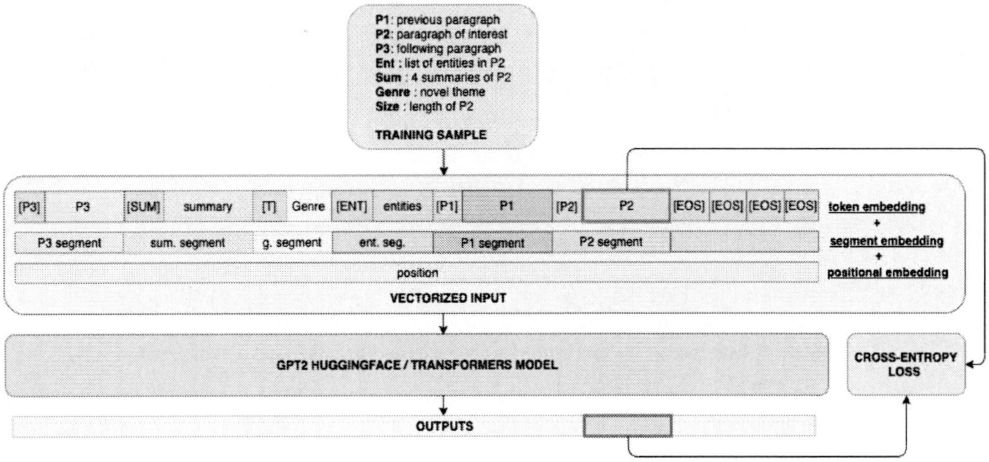

Figure 2: Training framework. The loss over the prefix is masked out, and only the cross-entropy loss over P2 is used for fine-tuning.

for each epoch, and was trained for 10 epochs. However, we believe that fewer epochs might be enough to reach good performances although the loss did not converge (Fig. 3).

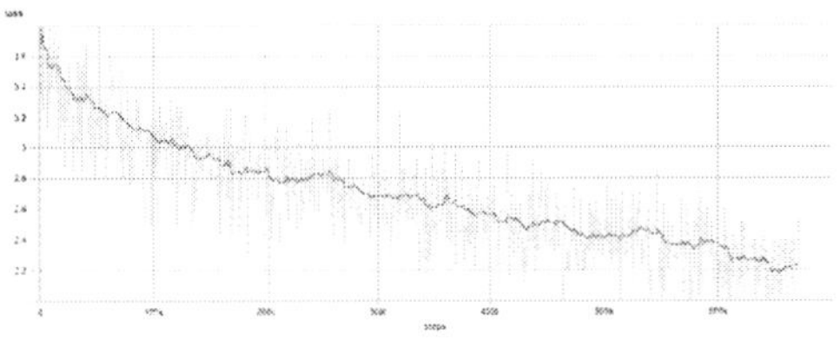

Figure 3: Loss function during training (smoothed).

4 Web Service Architecture

The model was enriched with a user interface, and opened to a small targeted public (online community of authors), to gather relevant feedback on both model generation and user-friendliness of the interface.

To gain in flexibility in the choice of instances, to perform the heavy computations and to allow load balancing on several instances, we uncoupled the *master* instance – serving the JavaScript front-end and general data – from the computational instances, performing NER and text generation on demand. It is also possible for the client to run the servers locally to avoid delays and server overloads. Fig. 4 shows the general architecture of our service.

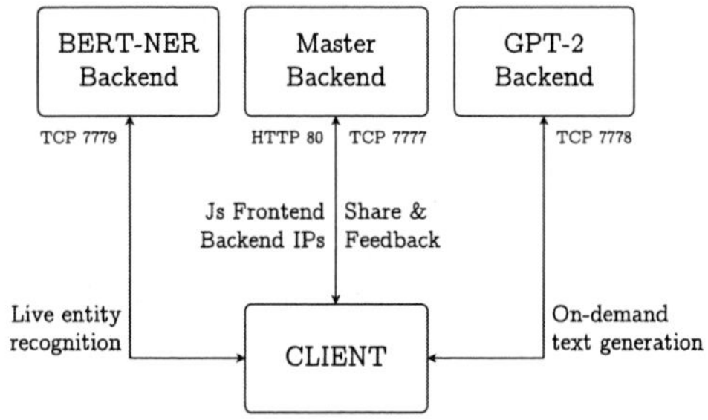

Figure 4: Webservice architecture

The interface allows users to write some text in a simple editor. Named entities of the four types (characters, locations, organisations and others) are detected on the fly by the NER backend and displayed on the left panel. They can be manually edited.

Users have the possibility to select several options: length of the desired paragraph, genre of their work and list of entities they want to see appear in the generation. They can also highlight a small part of the text that will act as a summary (or a list of keywords). A snapshot of the interface is shown in Fig. 5.

5 Generation and Evaluation

At inference time we provide the prefix x and generate until reaching the end-of-sentence symbol, using Nucleus Sampling (Holtzman et al., 2019) with $p = 0.9$.

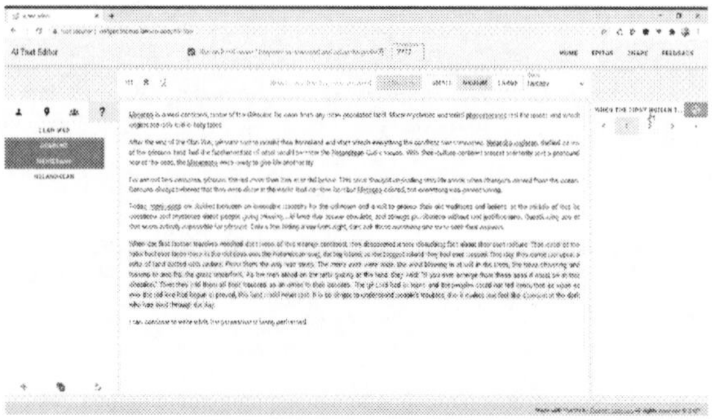

Figure 5: Interface of the text editor, highlightening the generated text in green.

5.1 Evaluation

The final model was evaluated after ten epochs of training, on some unseen novels. We focused the evaluation on the degree of control and contextualization, as well as the impact of different types of summaries. Due to space constraints, we report the results obtained when providing 10 keywords as summaries (extracted with TextRank), but the trend for other summarization techniques is similar. For the evaluation we focus on

- Divergence of the original model, as measured through perplexity of the original GPT-2. (Fig. 6).
- Similarity to the true P2, measured through (i) the similarity of the [CLS] tokens of a pre-trained BERT model (Devlin et al., 2018) (Fig. 6) and (ii) BLEU[14] and ROUGE[15] (Fig. 7).
- Control capabilities, by measuring the number of entities and keywords given as prefix that occur in the resulting text. (Fig. 8)

To evaluate the model, we focus on the distribution of the above metrics across all paragraphs and compare our trained model with a raw GPT-2 model.

Our experiments show that even with the reduced amount of fine-tuning the model deviates strongly from the base one and is able to learn to produce *middle paragraphs*.

Fig 6 shows that our approach leads to a decrease in perplexity (less fluent generation). Nevertheless, this is compensated (of course, those values are

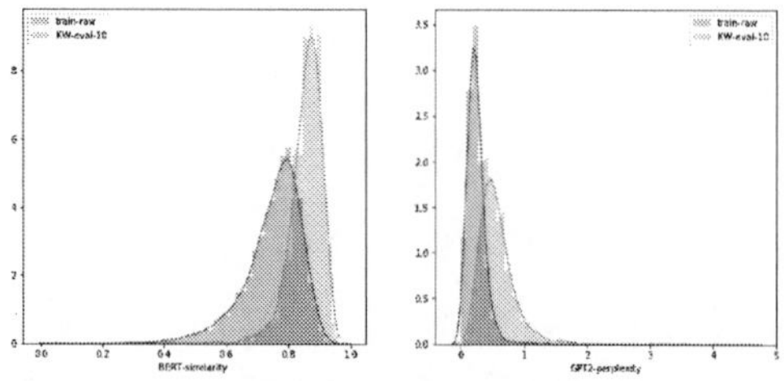

Figure 6: BertSimilarity (left) and Perplexity (right) of the base (not fine-tuned) GPT-2 model and our fine-tuned one. Fluency decreases slightly, but the generated text is more similar to the gold middle paragraph.

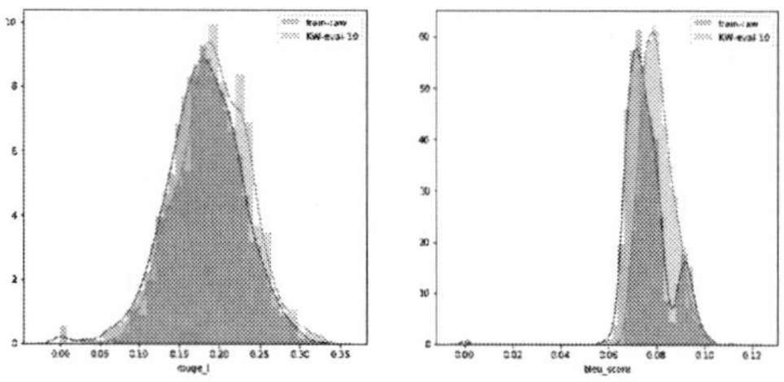

Figure 7: ROUGE (left) and BLEU (right) scores: a small but consistent increase of both metrics.

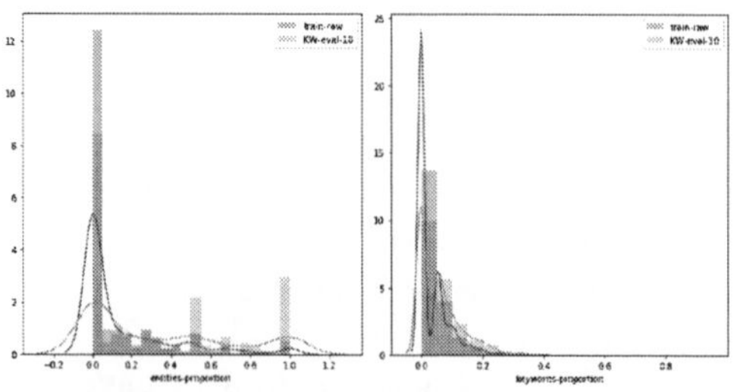

Figure 8: EntitiesCount (left) and KwCount (right). There is a significantly higher proportion of specified entities and keywords appearing in the generated text.

not directly comparable) by a better reconstruction

[14]we used nltk's version: `https://www.nltk.org/_modules/nltk/translate/bleu_score.html`

[15]`https://pypi.org/project/rouge/`

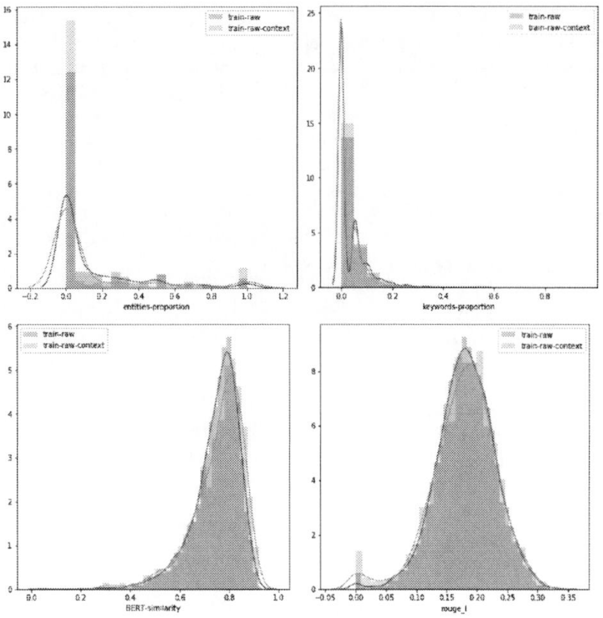

Figure 9: Evaluation metrics on vanilla GPT-2, when providing as prefix only P1 – *train-raw* – and the full context (all of x) – *train-raw-context*.

of the middle paragraph P2, as shown by the histograms of BERT similarity as well as precision and recall of n-gram overlap Fig. 7–all significantly shifted to the right. Finally, the model clearly learns to control the generated output (Fig. 8) with the desired entities occurring most often in the generated text (the shift is weaker with keywords).

As baseline, we also experimented with providing x to the vanilla GPT-2 model. This allows measuring the added benefit of training with respect to prompting. The resulting histograms are shown in Fig. 9, they reveal that GPT-2 cannot control and contextualise the generation (when taking x as input) if not fine-tuned.

6 Conclusion

In this paper, we present an end-to-end pipeline allowing authors to break *Writer's Block*. The objective is to allow users – at any point during the creative writing process – to generate new paragraphs that are consistent with the rest of the writing, especially previous and following paragraphs. The presented tool gives the possibility to select entities (characters, locations, etc.) that have been previously introduced in the novel and that should appear in the target paragraph. Similarly, the author can specify the size of the desired text, its content via a small summary or keywords and even the genre of the book. In the end, the tool proposes several suggestions that users can choose from and edit. The aim is to produce creative outputs that give new ideas to the writers.

The underlying model is obtained by fine-tuning a GPT-2 model on a carefully designed dataset, obtained through a selection and cleaning of books from the Project Gutenberg library. Our experiments show that the generated text is significantly more similar to the gold paragraphs on a variety of metrics and is able to successfully take into consideration the context specified by the user.

Fine-tuning is often discarded for natural language generation in favour of other cheaper methods, such as prompt engineering or adapter layers. This work shows a use-case where a pre-trained neural language generation model can be fine-tuned with a reduced economic and ecological cost: the complete training (including preliminary experiments as well as the final mode) was done with a budget of USD 150.

References

Naveen Arivazhagan, Ankur Bapna, Orhan Firat, Dmitry Lepikhin, Melvin Johnson, Maxim Krikun, Mia Xu Chen, Yuan Cao, George Foster, Colin

Cherry, et al. 2019. Massively multilingual neural machine translation in the wild: Findings and challenges. *arXiv preprint arXiv:1907.05019*.

Tom B Brown, Benjamin Mann, Nick Ryder, Melanie Subbiah, Jared Kaplan, Prafulla Dhariwal, Arvind Neelakantan, Pranav Shyam, Girish Sastry, Amanda Askell, et al. 2020. Language models are few-shot learners. *arXiv preprint arXiv:2005.14165*.

Zihang Dai, Zhilin Yang, Yiming Yang, Jaime Carbonell, Quoc V Le, and Ruslan Salakhutdinov. 2019. Transformer-xl: Attentive language models beyond a fixed-length context. *arXiv preprint arXiv:1901.02860*.

Sumanth Dathathri, Andrea Madotto, Janice Lan, Jane Hung, Eric Frank, Piero Molino, Jason Yosinski, and Rosanne Liu. 2019. Plug and play language models: a simple approach to controlled text generation. *arXiv preprint arXiv:1912.02164*.

Jacob Devlin, Ming-Wei Chang, Kenton Lee, and Kristina Toutanova. 2018. Bert: Pre-training of deep bidirectional transformers for language understanding. *arXiv preprint arXiv:1810.04805*.

Tianyu Gao, Adam Fisch, and Danqi Chen. 2020. Making pre-trained language models better few-shot learners.

Ari Holtzman, Jan Buys, Li Du, Maxwell Forbes, and Yejin Choi. 2019. The curious case of neural text degeneration. *arXiv preprint arXiv:1904.09751*.

Nitish Shirish Keskar, Bryan McCann, Lav R Varshney, Caiming Xiong, and Richard Socher. 2019. Ctrl: A conditional transformer language model for controllable generation. *arXiv preprint arXiv:1909.05858*.

Muhammad Khalifa, Hady Elsahar, and Marc Dymetman. 2021. A distributional approach to controlled text generation. In *ICLR*.

Mike Lewis, Yinhan Liu, Naman Goyal, Marjan Ghazvininejad, Abdelrahman Mohamed, Omer Levy, Ves Stoyanov, and Luke Zettlemoyer. 2019. Bart: Denoising sequence-to-sequence pre-training for natural language generation, translation, and comprehension. *arXiv preprint arXiv:1910.13461*.

Xiang Lisa Li and Percy Liang. 2021. Prefix-tuning: Optimizing continuous prompts for generation. *arXiv preprint arXiv:2101.00190*.

Yang Liu. 2019. Fine-tune bert for extractive summarization. *arXiv preprint arXiv:1903.10318*.

Fuli Luo, Damai Dai, Pengcheng Yang, Tianyu Liu, Baobao Chang, Zhifang Sui, and Xu Sun. 2019. Learning to control the fine-grained sentiment for story ending generation. In *Proceedings of the 57th Annual Meeting of the Association for Computational Linguistics*, pages 6020–6026, Florence, Italy. Association for Computational Linguistics.

Rada Mihalcea and Paul Tarau. 2004. Textrank: Bringing order into text. In *Proceedings of the 2004 conference on empirical methods in natural language processing*, pages 404–411.

Nanyun Peng, Marjan Ghazvininejad, Jonathan May, and Kevin Knight. 2018. Towards controllable story generation. In *Proceedings of the First Workshop on Storytelling*, pages 43–49, New Orleans, Louisiana. Association for Computational Linguistics.

Colin Raffel, Noam Shazeer, Adam Roberts, Katherine Lee, Sharan Narang, Michael Matena, Yanqi Zhou, Wei Li, and Peter J Liu. 2019. Exploring the limits of transfer learning with a unified text-to-text transformer. *arXiv preprint arXiv:1910.10683*.

Timo Schick and Hinrich Schütze. 2020a. Few-shot text generation with pattern-exploiting training. *arXiv preprint arXiv:2012.11926*.

Timo Schick and Hinrich Schütze. 2020b. It's not just size that matters: Small language models are also few-shot learners. *arXiv preprint arXiv:2009.07118*.

Emma Strubell, Ananya Ganesh, and Andrew McCallum. 2019. Energy and policy considerations for deep learning in nlp. *arXiv preprint arXiv:1906.02243*.

A Vaswani, N Shazeer, N Parmar, J Uszkoreit, L Jones, AN Gomez, L Kaiser, and I Polosukhin. 2017. Attention is all you need. arxiv 2017. *arXiv preprint arXiv:1706.03762*.

Ruize Wang, Duyu Tang, Nan Duan, Zhongyu Wei, Xuanjing Huang, Cuihong Cao, Daxin Jiang, Ming Zhou, et al. 2020. K-adapter: Infusing knowledge into pre-trained models with adapters. *arXiv preprint arXiv:2002.01808*.

Thomas Wolf, Julien Chaumond, Lysandre Debut, Victor Sanh, Clement Delangue, Anthony Moi, Pierric Cistac, Morgan Funtowicz, Joe Davison, Sam Shleifer, et al. 2020. Transformers: State-of-the-art natural language processing. In *Proceedings of the 2020 Conference on Empirical Methods in Natural Language Processing: System Demonstrations*, pages 38–45.

Rowan Zellers, Ari Holtzman, Hannah Rashkin, Yonatan Bisk, Ali Farhadi, Franziska Roesner, and Yejin Choi. 2019. Defending against neural fake news. In *Advances in Neural Information Processing Systems*, pages 9051–9062.

A Appendix

A.1 Interface

Fig. 10 shows the landing page of the online demo.

A.2 Samples of Generated Text

We show here some samples generated with the demo:

Sample 1

Keywords: face - glenure - murder
Genre: biography, history
Size: M
Persons: Glenure, Appin, God, Catriona
Organisations: Appin
Locations: Scotland, Appin, Dean

P1: "What is this you say?" she asked. "What are you talking of?" "It is my testimony which may save an innocent life," said I, "and they will not suffer me to bear it. What would you do yourself? You know what this is, whose father lies in danger. Would you desert the poor soul? They have tried all ways with me. They have sought to bribe me; they offered me hills and valleys.

Generated P2: But they have not been in the least afraid of me, although they have known me as the murderer." "There is something I would have left to have," she said; "if they had taken me from their hands. You shall die." "O my soul!" she cried. "What am I to die at that?" Her father, who had a mother's love, would have killed a slave in the bush; and that was the case. "If you see me here, you'll know the difference between us." He had gone, at least, and she would have heard from him again. There was something he had not understood. "Well," he said, "if that is, then I shall die; if it were not for my sake, I should have been a free man. And if I had done it, I would have died from my father's grave, and taken my money from the country." I had no more idea of his feelings than he had of their manners. On the night appointed, we started for Scotland. The men left us a good cabin, and entered, to their great delight.

Original P2: And to-day that sleuth-hound told me how I stood, and to what a length he would go to butcher and disgrace me. I am to be brought in a party to the murder; I am to have held Glenure in talk for money and old clothes; I am to be killed and shamed. If this is the way I am to fall, and me scarce a man - if this is the story to be told of me in all Scotland - if you are to believe it too, and my name is to be nothing but a by-word - Catriona, how can I go through with it? The thing's not possible; it's more than a man has in his heart." I poured my words out in a whirl, one upon the other; and when I stopped I found her gazing on me with a startled face. "Glenure! It is the Appin murder," she said softly, but with a very deep surprise. I had turned back to bear her company, and we were now come near the head of the brae above Dean village. At this word I stepped in front of her like one suddenly distracted. "For God's sake!" I cried, "for God's sake, what is this that I have done?" and carried my fists to my temples.

P3: "What made me do it? Sure, I am bewitched to say these things!" "In the name of heaven, what ails you now!" she cried. "I gave my honour," I groaned, "I gave my honour and now I have broke it. O, Catriona!" "I am asking you what it is," she said; "was it these things you should not have spoken? And do you think I have no honour, then? or that I am one that would betray a friend?"

Sample 2

Genre: Science-Fiction
Size: L
Organisations: Council
Locations: Council House

P1: Along this a disorderly swarm of people marched shouting. They were singing snatches of the song of the revolt, most of them out of tune. Here and there torches flared creating brief hysterical shadows. He asked his way and was twice puzzled by that same thick dialect. His third attempt won an answer he could understand. He was two miles from the wind-vane offices in Westminster, but the way was easy to follow. When at last he did approach the district of the wind-vane offices it seemed to him, from the cheering processions that came marching along the Ways, from the tumult of rejoicing, and finally from the restoration of the lighting of the city, that the overthrow of the Council must already be accomplished. And still no news of his absence came to his ears. The re-illumination of the city came with startling abruptness. Suddenly he stood blinking, all about him men halted dazzled, and the world was incandescent. The light found him already upon the outskirts of the excited crowds that choked the Ways near the wind-vane offices, and the sense of visibility and exposure that came with it turned his colourless intention of joining Ostrog to a keen anxiety.

Generated P2: He could not conceive how he was to get within the unbroken facade of this place till he reached the street by a great open space of marble pavement to take hold of an afternoon train. For a moment he could not see the crowding. Then another group was seen, then another. He made his way slowly into the crowding in the central path. This way he was most eager to know. He had no desire to enter the city in order to get hold of some one else, to whom he could apply as little as possible to information; and so he went at once on the long platform, hoping to reach the Council House before he was in time to receive any information that he had received from his brother or his wife. After waiting several minutes for that, the expressman, who had been most unwilling to return to the city, said that he would join the Council on the way to meet the new manager, and was even more delighted to have taken possession of his money than he had been when he went to see the London cable office and asked about the interview he had held during the afternoon. The cable service had been decided after he had left it.

Original P2: For a time he was jostled, obstructed, and endangered by men hoarse and weary with cheering his name, some of them bandaged and bloody in his cause. The frontage of the wind-vane offices was illuminated by some moving picture, but what it was he could not see, because in spite of his strenuous attempts the density of the crowd prevented his approaching it. From the fragments of speech he caught, he judged it conveyed news of the fighting about the Council House. Ignorance and indecision made him slow and ineffective in his movements. For a time he could not conceive how he was to get within the unbroken facade of this place. He made his way slowly into the midst of this mass of people, until he realised that the descending staircase of the central Way led to the interior of the buildings. This gave him a goal, but the crowding in the central path was so dense that it was long before he could reach it. And even then he encountered intricate obstruction, and had an hour of vivid argument first in this guard room and then in that before he could get a note taken to the one man of all men who was most eager to see him.

P3: His story was laughed to scorn at one place, and wiser for that, when at last he reached a second stairway he professed simply to have news of extraordinary importance for Ostrog. What it was he would not say. They sent his note reluctantly. For a long time he waited in a little room at the foot of the lift shaft, and thither at last came Lincoln, eager, apologetic, astonished. He stopped in the doorway scrutinising Graham, then rushed forward effusively. "Yes," he cried. "It is you. And you are not dead!" Graham made a brief explanation. "My brother is waiting," explained Lincoln. "He is alone in the wind-vane offices. We feared you had been killed in the theatre. He doubted - and things are very urgent still in spite of what we are telling them there - or he would have come to you." They ascended a lift, passed along a narrow passage, crossed a great hall, empty save for two hurrying messengers, and entered a comparatively little room, whose only furniture was a long settee

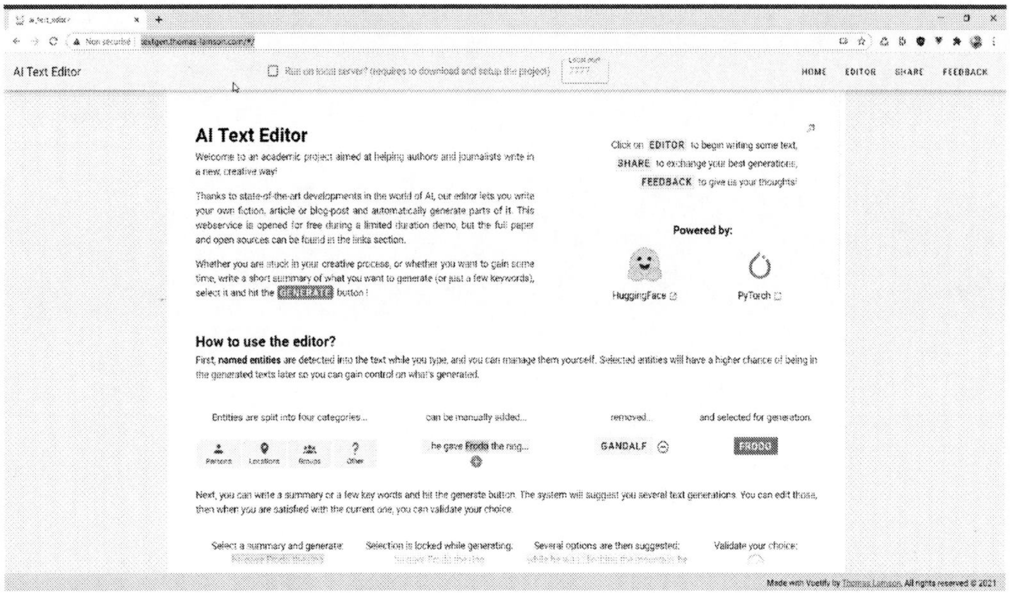

Figure 10: Menu interface

and a large oval disc of cloudy, shifting grey, hung by cables from the wall.

BART: He could not conceive how he was to get within the unbroken facade of this place. He made his way slowly into The crowding in a central path prevented him from reaching it until after an hour's argument with one man who had been most eager for information about what happened at Council House, and then another

Gap in pagination due to unavailable paper.

Pages 288-294

Domain Expert Platform for Goal-Oriented Dialogue Collection

Didzis Gosko **Arturs Znotins** **Inguna Skadina**
Normunds Gruzitis **Gunta Nespore-Berzkalne**
Institute of Mathematics and Computer Science,
University of Latvia
Raina bulv. 29, Riga, Latvia
firstname.lastname@lumii.lv

Abstract

Today, most dialogue systems are fully or partly built using neural network architectures. A crucial prerequisite for the creation of a goal-oriented neural network dialogue system is a dataset that represents typical dialogue scenarios and includes various semantic annotations, e.g. intents, slots and dialogue actions, that are necessary for training a particular neural network architecture. In this demonstration paper, we present an easy to use interface and its back-end which is oriented to domain experts for the collection of goal-oriented dialogue samples. The platform not only allows to collect or write sample dialogues in a structured way, but also provides a means for simple annotation and interpretation of the dialogues. The platform itself is language-independent; it depends only on the availability of particular language processing components for a specific language. It is currently being used to collect dialogue samples in Latvian (a highly inflected language) which represent typical communication between students and the student service.

1 Introduction

Modeling of human-computer interaction through dialogue systems and chatbots has raised a great interest among researchers and industry already since the time when the first chatbot Eliza (Weizenbaum, 1966) was created. This interest has become viral after the successful introduction of Siri (Bellegarda, 2013). Today, virtual assistants, virtual agents and chatbots are present everywhere: on mobile devices, on different social networking platforms, on many websites and through smart home devices and robots.

The virtual conversational agents are usually implemented as end-to-end neural network models, or their components are implemented through neural network architectures (Louvan and Magnini, 2020). Such architectures require creation of datasets that represent various dialogue scenarios, as well as knowledge of the specific domain. This information has to be provided in specific data formats that in many cases are too complicated for domain experts. Moreover, the required training datasets usually include various annotation layers, such as named entities, dialogue acts, intents, etc. The creation of such datasets is a complex task, and the datasets are not completely isolated and abstracted from the particular dialogue system. Thus, domain experts that are involved in the creation of the datasets must have a high-level understanding of the overall structure of the dialogue system and its components, and how it is reflected in the annotated dialogue samples.

This demonstration paper address this issue by presenting a web-based platform for the creation and maintenance of dialogue datasets [1]. The interface of the platform is very simple and high-level: it allows a domain expert without detailed technical knowledge of the underlying dialogue system to create and update a representative training dataset, as well as to maintain the underlying database of domain- and organisation-specific information that will be used for question answering. The platform provides tools for the creation of goal-oriented dialogue systems, in particular:

- creation of datasets for dialogue systems that provide (or generate) responses depending on user input, intents and on the previous actions of the dialogue system;
- creation of datasets for dialogue systems that cover one or several topics;
- slot filling, including slot filler (e.g. named entity) normalization and annotation;
- creation and maintenance of slot filler aliases;

[1] http://bots.ailab.lv/

Proceedings of the 16th Conference of the European Chapter of the Association for Computational Linguistics: System Demonstrations, pages 295–301
April 19 - 23, 2021. ©2021 Association for Computational Linguistics

- creation and maintenance of knowledge base and interactive response selection;
- response generation, including the generation of inflectional forms for syntactic agreement.

Our platform not only supports collection of dialogue scenarios, but also simulates prototypical interaction between human and computer. The tool has been successfully used for the creation of a dialogue dataset for the virtual assistant that supports the work of the student service in relation to three frequently asked topics: working hours and contacts of the personnel and structural units (e.g. libraries), issues regarding academic leave, as well as enrollment requirements and documents to be submitted (Skadina and Gosko, 2020).

In the next chapters of this paper, we describe our motivation to develop the platform, its overall architecture and main components, and the domain expert interface and its main components.

2 Background and Motivation

For English and several other widely used languages, many publicly available dialogue datasets have been created and are reused for different research and development needs (e.g., Budzianowski et al. (2018), Zeng et al. (2020)). However, in the case of less-resourced languages, only few or no training datasets are available (Serban et al., 2018). To our knowledge, there is no publicly available dataset for Latvian, that could be used for goal-oriented dialogue system modelling. To overcome this obstacle, some research groups machine-translate existing English datasets into the low-resourced languages, while others try to build training datasets from scratch. When possible, crowdsourcing, including gamification (Ogawa et al., 2020), is used as well. However, there in no best recipe for obtaining or collecting dialogue samples for a specific NLP task (in our case, dialogue modeling) for a less-resourced language with a relatively small number of speakers.

The motivation of our work is the necessity to build virtual assistants in less-resourced settings. The practical use case to test the platform has been the everyday communication between students and the student service of the University of Latvia. Since this communication has never been intentionally recorded, we started with the analysis of data retrieved from an online student forum to identify the most common topics, question and answer templates, and the typical dialogue scenarios. For the demonstration purposes, we have chosen three common topics: working hours, academic leave, and enrollment requirements. Elaborated and annotated sample dialogues constituting the training dataset have been specified by a domain expert using the dialogue management platform presented in this paper.

Since we focus on goal-oriented virtul assistants, the Hybrid Code Networks (HCN) architecture has been selected for the implementation (Williams et al., 2017) allowing us to combine recursive neural networks (RNN) with the domain-specific knowledge and action templates of the dialogue system. The concrete dialogue system is implemented within the DeepPavlov framework[2].

3 Overall Architecture and Components

The platform presented in this paper is designed to support three use cases:

1. To create and gradually improve a collection of dialogue samples necessary for developing and testing a goal-oriented dialogue system.
2. To support (re-)training of a goal-oriented dialogue system.
3. To support dialogue testing in the inference mode. Training and running a dialogue system in the inference mode is performed through the DeepPavlov framework by passing the goal-oriented bot model configuration along with relations to other objects that are specific to the platform.

Figure 1 illustrates the architecture of the platform. Apart from the domain expert user interface described in detail in Section 4, key components of the platform are four databases for storing the dialogue scenarios, the relevant entities and their aliases for slot filling, the required external knowledge for question answering, and reusable templates for response generation.

3.1 Dialogue Database

Dialogues created by the users of the platform (i.e., by domain experts not end-users) are stored in the SQLite database *Dialogues* to support concurrent modification. The dialogue database stores potential end-user utterances together with the respective

[2]`https://deeppavlov.ai/`

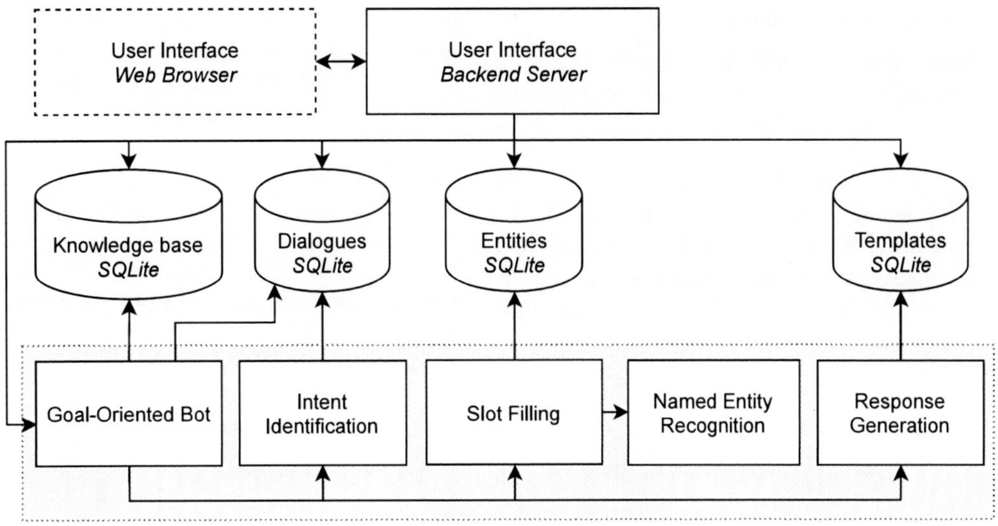

Figure 1: Architecture of the platform. The selected (grey) part of the diagram is language-specific and can be replaced or removed entirely.

intents, slot values and the corresponding bot actions.

Intents for the particular dialogue dataset are defined in a separate view of the platform's interface. The predefined intents are linked to utterances during the dialogue writing process (for details, see Section 4) and later used for training. In our demonstration dialogue system, we use a Keras classification model with Latvian fastText word embeddings for intent detection.

The configurator of the platform uses a custom data reader that reads training data from a custom-schema SQLite database. The reason why SQLite is used is the high modification rate produced by the platforms's user interface for dialogue editing.

3.2 Knowledge Base

The database *Knowledge base* stores the external knowledge that is necessary for the dialogue system to provide the answers to the end-users. Such knowledge is usually dynamic and can change while the dialogue system is deployed (e.g. working hours of the university personnel in our demonstration case).

3.3 Entity Database

For our use case, the named entity recognition (NER) model combines a neural network model and a rule-based model.

The neural network model is based on Latvian BERT word embeddings (Znotins and Barzdins, 2020). To support entity classes of a particular domain, the NER model is trained on a larger general-domain dataset (Gruzitis et al., 2018; Paikens et al., 2020) and a smaller domain-specific dataset. The combined model allows to recognize not only commonly used entity classes like persons, locations and organizations, but also domain specific entities like job positions and working hours.

The rule-based NER is based on the Aho-Corasick algorithm (Aho and Corasick, 1975) with additional regular expression rules to ensure entity detection in various inflectional forms, as well as detection of very specific domain entities like room names and specific job positions that would not be recognised otherwise due to the limited amount of training data.

In our demonstration dialogue system, a custom slot filler is implemented, which relies on normalized entities returned by the NER module to be directly filled in the respective slots.

The normalization is done in two steps. First, after the recognition of named entities (NE), an external NE normalization service is called, which provides base forms for both single-word entities and multi-word entities. Second, the database *Entities* is consulted to align the recognised and normalised entities (entered by the end-user) with the corresponding entities in the database. This also includes resolving NE aliases (for more details see Subsection 4.5).

3.4 Template Database

Responses to the end-user are generated using a template-based approach which depends on the recognised intent and slots. The response templates support additional markup for slot filler inflection that are replaced with the correctly inflected word forms during the response generation step. In our demonstration system, word forms are inflected using a Latvian morphological analyser (Paikens et al., 2013) as an external service. All template data are stored in and reused from the database *Templates*.

4 User Interface

In this section we present overall interface and constituents (sub-windows) of our dialogue data preparation platform: the window for dialogue collection, the action template editing window, the knowledge base preparation and management window, the window for intent definition and the window for creation and maintenance of slot filler aliases (see Figure 2)[3].

The user interface for data editing is powered by Python HTTP backend that serves static files and API calls. The backend modifies all four databases directly and uses slotfiller to retrieve slots from user interface. Frontend is written in Javascript and VueJS, and is running inside a web browser.

4.1 Dialogue Collection Window

The central part of the dialogue collection platform is the dialog collection window. The dialogue collection window contains all dialogues submitted by the user. The dialogues could be changed any time:

- by adding or deleting one or several utterances,
- changing text of the utterance and corresponding slot and intent values,
- changing corresponding dialogue act.

To enter a new dialogue user have to push "Add dialogue" button and write an utterance (Figure 3). By pushing button "Extract", entities (slots) in user's utterance are automatically identified by the named entity recognizer, they are extracted and grammatically normalised (see Subsection 3.3), and, if necessary, semantically normalised (for details, see Subsection 4.5). Then user can specify an intent and select an action that needs to be performed by the dialogue system. When the action of the dialogue system is selected, the expected response from the bot is displayed to the user, allowing to check the possible answer and change it, in case a mistake has been identified (for details see Subsection 4.2). The utterance entering process continues until dialogue writing is completed. After pushing "Done" button the dialogue is being add to the *Dialogues* SQLite database.

[3]Although the platform is currently being used to collect dialogue samples in Latvian, in this paper we followed recommendations from reviewers and included prototypical English dialogue samples.

4.2 Action Definition and Editing

The action template window is used to define the action performed by the dialogue system. For our purposes we have introduced two types of actions: (1) templates of bot answers for particular action and (2) information retrieval request from the knowledge base depending on identified slot values.

In the simplest case system's action is a fixed utterance, specified in action template window. However, in most cases dialogue action and answer depends on previous actions and information gathered from the user. Therefore we introduced mechanisms allowing to generate context dependent grammatically correct slot values identified during the dialogue. The slot values used for answer generation could be from the last utterance or previous ones, as well as from bot's previous answers.

For example, the template for action 'info_working_hours', contains utterance template '*Working hours for #position of the #ORG #PERSON: #time*', where '#position', '#ORG', '#PERSON' and '#time' represent slot values (entities), identified during the dialogue or retrieved from the knowledge base.

Action templates can also include form generation instructions which are very important for fluent output generation in case of inflected languages. For example, in the Latvian template *'Kuras fakultātes position@g darbalaiku Jūs vēlētos noskaidrot?'* (*Which faculty #position@g working hours you would like to know?*) item *#position* represents slot (entity), identified during the dialogue (e.g., *dekāns* (*dean*)), while '@g' requests generation of the genitive form of this entity (e.g., *dekāna* instead of lemma *dekāns*).

When action requires information retrieval from the database (template api_call), the previously extracted information from user's input (slots) is used

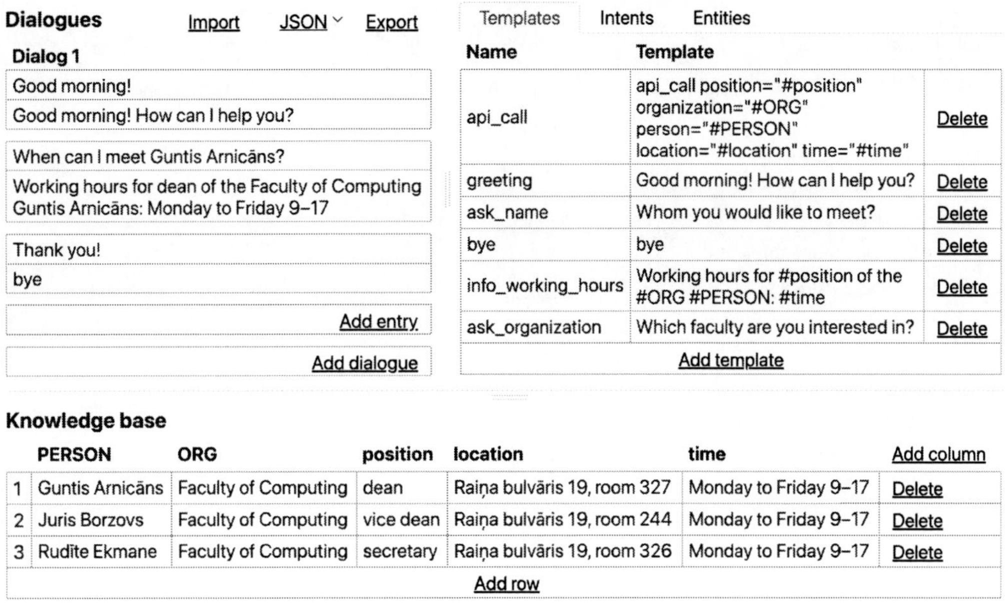

Figure 2: Overview of interface

to form request to the database (see Subsection 4.3). For example, if answer to the previous question is *"Faculty of Computing"*, then query to database will ask for working hours of the dean of the Faculty of Computing.

Similarly to dialogue utterances, actions and their templates could be easily modified during the dialogue writing process, new actions could be added and unnecessary actions removed.

4.3 Knowledge Base Preparation

Goal-oriented dialogue systems often include means for knowledge retrieval from database or any other type of knowledge base. In some cases database already exist, while often creation of knowledge base is part of the dialog system building process. To ensure consistency between dialogues and information in database, the database could be created, filled and modified during dialogue collection process.

The Knowledge base preparation and maintenance window has very simple interface allowing user to enter new entries, change the existing ones or even modify database structure. To ensure consistency between different information pieces of the dialogue system, names of columns in database needs to correspond to the entity types of the dialogue system.

4.4 Intents

For intent management, small and simple window is created, allowing to add, modify and delete intents. Intents defined in this window, are used during dialogue writing process: they can be assigned to each user's utterance (for details see Subsection 4.1).

4.5 Creation and Maintenance of Slot Filler Aliases

The common problem in dialogue systems that include knowledge retrieval, is incoherence between entity in utterance submitted by user and correct and normalised entity fixed in database. For instance, when dialogue system asks to specify name of particular organization, user can enter its abbreviation (e.g., "DF" or "FC" instead of *Faculty of Computing*), commonly used shortened form, use jargon or make spelling errors (e.g., errors in capitalization - *faculty of computing* instead of *Faculty of Computing*). To overcome this bottleneck we introduce entity alias management window, where user can specify official (normalised) form of the entity which has been stored in knowledge base and its typical aliases (see Figure 4).

Similarly to other windows of this platform, the entity editing window allows to add, edit and delete entities and their aliases. Each "official" entity could have several aliases (synonyms). We also

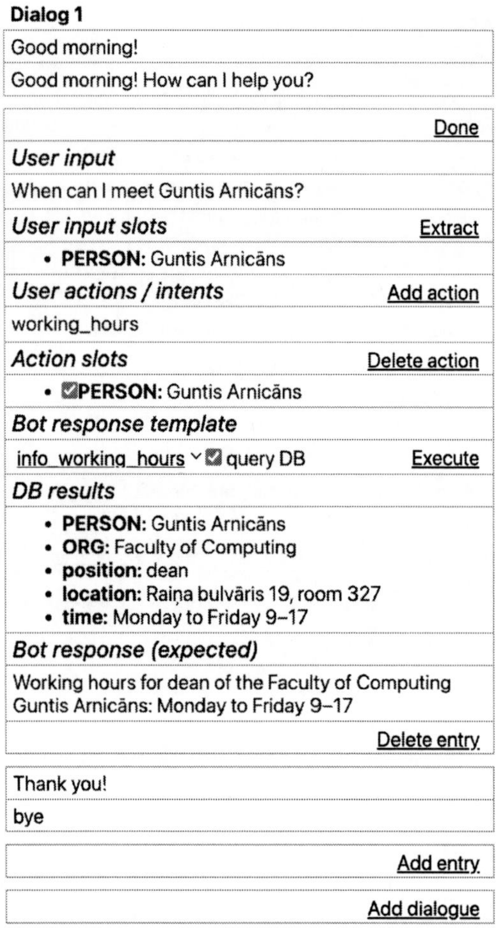

Figure 3: Demonstration of dialogue preparation - utterance writing, slot filling, intent identification and retrieval from the database

keep entity type, in case the same string belongs to several types.

5 Conclusion

In this paper, we have presented a configurable platform for dialogue collection that supports synchronization of information necessary for building a goal-oriented dialogue system, besides specification of dialogue scripts.

The presented platform is publicly available[4]. It has been used for creation of Latvian-specific dataset of dialogues between students and a student service. Following recommendations from reviewers the platform is currently demonstrated on prototypical English dialogue samples, demonstrating its scalability to other languages. We will add a short walkthrough video demonstrating the main features of the platform.

[4]`http://bots.ailab.lv/`

ID	Entity	Category	Alias		
1	Faculty of Computing	ORG	the Faculty of Computing	Delete Alias	Add Alias Delete Entity
2	Faculty of Humanities	ORG	the Faculty of Humanities	Delete Alias	Add Alias Delete Entity
3	Faculty of Humanities	ORG	FH	Delete Alias	Add Alias Delete Entity
			HZF	Delete Alias	
			faculty of humanities	Delete Alias	
4	Faculty of Computing	ORG	FC	Delete Alias	Add Alias Delete Entity
			faculty of computing	Delete Alias	
			DF	Delete Alias	
5	Juris Borzovs	PERSON	Borzovs	Delete Alias	Add Alias Delete Entity
Add Entity					

Figure 4: Window for creation and maintenance of slot filler aliases

The next development tasks include simple export of dialogue data in commonly used formats to facilitate experiments with various neural dialogue system architectures, and support for a one-click re-training process which currently is implemented as separate background process.

Acknowledgments

This research is funded by the Latvian Council of Science project "Latvian Language Understanding and Generation in Human-Computer Interaction", project No. lzp2018/2-0216.

References

AV Aho and MJ Corasick. 1975. Fast pattern matching: an aid to bibliographic search. *Communications of ACM*, 18(6):333–340.

Jerome R. Bellegarda. 2013. Large-Scale Personal Assistant Technology Deployment: The Siri Experience. In *INTERSPEECH 2013, 14th Annual Conference of the International Speech Communication Association, Lyon, France, August 25-29, 2013*, pages 2029–2033. ISCA.

Paweł Budzianowski, Tsung-Hsien Wen, Bo-Hsiang Tseng, Iñigo Casanueva, Ultes Stefan, Ramadan Osman, and Milica Gašić. 2018. MultiWOZ - A Large-Scale Multi-Domain Wizard-of-Oz Dataset for Task-Oriented Dialogue Modelling. In *Proceedings of the 2018 Conference on Empirical Methods in Natural Language Processing (EMNLP)*.

Normunds Gruzitis, Lauma Pretkalnina, Baiba Saulite, Laura Rituma, Gunta Nespore-Berzkalne, Arturs Znotins, and Peteris Paikens. 2018. Creation of a Balanced State-of-the-Art Multilayer Corpus for NLU. In *Proceedings of the 11th International Conference on Language Resources and Evaluation (LREC)*, pages 4506–4513.

Samuel Louvan and Bernardo Magnini. 2020. Recent Neural Methods on Slot Filling and Intent Classification for Task-Oriented Dialogue Systems: A Survey. In *Proceedings of the 28th International Conference on Computational Linguistics*, pages 480–496, Barcelona, Spain (Online). International Committee on Computational Linguistics.

Haruna Ogawa, Hitoshi Nishikawa, Takenobu Tokunaga, and Hikaru Yokono. 2020. Gamification platform for collecting task-oriented dialogue data. In *Proceedings of the 12th Language Resources and Evaluation Conference*, pages 7084–7093, Marseille, France. European Language Resources Association.

Peteris Paikens, Laura Rituma, and Lauma Pretkalnina. 2013. Morphological analysis with limited resources: Latvian example. In *Proceedings of the 19th Nordic Conference of Computational Linguistics (NODALIDA)*.

Peteris Paikens, Arturs Znotins, and Guntis Barzdins. 2020. Human-in-the-Loop Conversation Agent for Customer Service. In *Natural Language Processing and Information Systems*, volume 12089, pages 277–284. Springer.

Iulian Serban, Ryan Lowe, Peter Henderson, Laurent Charlin, and Joelle Pineau. 2018. A Survey of Available Corpora for Building Data-Driven Dialogue Systems. *ArXiv*, abs/1512.05742.

Inguna Skadina and Didzis Gosko. 2020. Towards Hybrid Model for Human-Computer Interaction in Latvian. In *Human Language Technologies - The Baltic Perspective*, volume 328, pages 103 – 110. IOS Press.

Joseph Weizenbaum. 1966. ELIZA—a Computer Program for the Study of Natural Language Communication between Man and Machine. *Commun. ACM*, 9(1):36–45.

Jason D Williams, Kavosh Asadi, and Geoffrey Zweig. 2017. Hybrid code networks: practical and efficient end-to-end dialog control with supervised and reinforcement learning. *arXiv preprint arXiv:1702.03274*.

Guangtao Zeng, Wenmian Yang, Zeqian Ju, Yue Yang, Sicheng Wang, Ruisi Zhang, Meng Zhou, Jiaqi Zeng, Xiangyu Dong, Ruoyu Zhang, Hongchao Fang, Penghui Zhu, Shu Chen, and Pengtao Xie. 2020. MedDialog: Large-scale medical dialogue datasets. In *Proceedings of the 2020 Conference on Empirical Methods in Natural Language Processing (EMNLP)*, pages 9241–9250, Online. Association for Computational Linguistics.

Arturs Znotins and Guntis Barzdins. 2020. LVBERT: Transformer-Based Model for Latvian Language Understanding. In *Human Language Technologies - The Baltic Perspective*, volume 328, pages 111–115. IOS Press.

Which is Better for Deep Learning: Python or MATLAB? Answering Comparative Questions in Natural Language

Viktoriia Chekalina[1,2], **Alexander Bondarenko**[3], **Chris Biemann**[4], **Meriem Beloucif**[4], **Varvara Logacheva**[2], **and Alexander Panchenko**[2]

[1]Philips Research Russia
[2]Skolkovo Institute of Science and Technology, Russia
[3]Martin-Luther-Universität Halle-Wittenberg, Germany
[4]Universität Hamburg, Germany
{viktoriia.chekalina, v.logacheva, a.panchenko}@skoltech.ru
alexander.bondarenko@informatik.uni-halle.de
{biemann, beloucif}@informatik.uni-hamburg.de

Abstract

We present a system for answering comparative questions (*Is X better than Y with respect to Z?*) in natural language. Answering such questions is important for assisting humans in making informed decisions. The key component of our system is a natural language interface for comparative QA that can be used in personal assistants, chatbots, and similar NLP devices. Comparative QA is a challenging NLP task, since it requires collecting support evidence from many different sources, and direct comparisons of rare objects may be not available even on the entire Web. We take the first step towards a solution for such a task offering a testbed for comparative QA in natural language by probing several methods, making the three best ones available as an online demo.

1 Introduction

Comparison of objects of a particular class (e.g., holiday destinations, mobile phones, programming languages) is an essential daily task that many individuals require every day. According to Bondarenko et al. (2020a), comparative questions constitute around 3% of queries submitted to major search engines—a non-negligible amount. Answering a comparative question (*What is better, X or Y?*) requires collecting and combining facts and opinions about compared objects from various sources. This challenges general-purpose question answering (QA) systems that rely on finding a direct answer in some existing datasets or extracting from web documents.

Nowadays, many websites (e.g. Diffen, WolphramAlpha, or Versus) provide users with a comparison functionality. Furthermore, the task of answering comparative questions has recently attracted the attention of the research community (Kessler and Kuhn, 2014; Arora et al., 2017; Yang et al., 2018). Most of the current research suggests that an answer to a comparative question not only should indicate the "winner" of comparison but also provide arguments in favor of this decision and arguments that support the alternative choice.

Therefore, we argue that a comparative QA system should be a combination of an argument mining engine and a dialogue system that mimics a human expert in the field. In this work, we make the first step towards the development of such technology. Namely, we develop a Comparative Question Answering System (CoQAS), an application that consists of a Natural Language Understanding (NLU) module that identifies comparative structures (objects, aspects, predicates) in free input questions and a Natural Language Generation (NLG) module that constructs an answer. We tested various options for both NLU and NLG parts ranging from a simple template-based generation to Transformers-based language models.

The main contributions of our work are threefold: (i) we design an evaluation framework for comparative QA, featuring a dataset based on Yahoo! Answers; (ii) we test several strategies for identification of comparative structures and for answer generation; (iii) we develop an online demo using three answer generation approaches. A demo of the system is available online.[1] Besides, we release our code and data.

2 Related Work

Text Generation Most of the current text natural language generation tasks (Dušek and Jurčíček, 2016; Freitag and Roy, 2018) are based on se-

[1]`https://skoltech-nlp.github.io/coqas`

Proceedings of the 16th Conference of the European Chapter of the Association for Computational Linguistics: System Demonstrations, pages 302–311
April 19 - 23, 2021. ©2021 Association for Computational Linguistics

quence to sequence model architecture (Sutskever et al., 2014). The existing generation methods are developed by employing attention mechanism (Bahdanau et al., 2015) and pointer-generator network (See et al., 2017). More recent work on text generation focus on generating natural language using multitask learning from multi-document or multi-passage sources (Hsu et al., 2018; Nishida et al., 2019). However, in our generation task, we have a list of arguments used to build the final answer. This makes our task similar to unsupervised summarization. There exist several approaches for tackling the latter task, e.g. graph-based (Litvak and Last, 2008) and neural models (Isonuma et al., 2019; Coavoux et al., 2019). A common approach to summarization is based on the TextRank graph algorithm (Mihalcea, 2004; Fan and Fang, 2017).

Comparative QA According to Li and Roth (2006), questions can be divided into 6 coarse and 50 fine-grained categories, such as factoid questions, list questions, or definition questions: we focus on comparative questions. Sun et al. (2006) proposed one of the first works on automatic comparative web search, where each object was submitted as a separate query, then obtained results were compared. Opinion mining of comparative sentences is discussed by Ganapathibhotla and Liu (2008) and Jindal and Liu (2006), yet with no connection to argumentation mining. Instead, comparative information needs are partially satisfied by several kinds of industrial systems mentioned above. Schildwächter et al. (2019) proposed Comparative Argumentative Machine (CAM)[2], which a comparison system based on extracting and ranking arguments from the web. The authors have conducted a user study on 34 comparison topics, showing that the system is faster and more confident at finding arguments when answering comparative questions in contrast to a keyword-based search. Wachsmuth et al. (2017) presented args.me, a search engine for retrieving pro and con arguments given for a given controversial topic. The input to this system is not structured but rather a query in a free textual form. The Touché shared task on argument retrieval at CLEF (Bondarenko et al., 2020b, 2021) featured a related track. The task was to retrieve from a large web corpus documents answering comparative question queries like "What IDE is better for Java: NetBeans or Eclipse?".

[2]https://ltdemos.informatik.uni-hamburg.de/cam

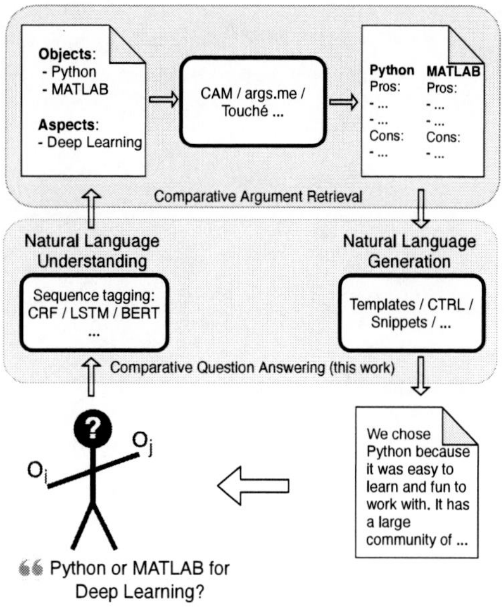

Figure 1: The comparative QA workflow. A user submits a comparative question, the NLU module identifies compared objects and aspects and transfers them to CAM to retrieves comparative arguments. Then, the NLG module represents the arguments in textual form.

3 System Design

Our system is designed to help the user make a proper choice by fully and reasonably describing the possible advantages and disadvantages of each of the matching options. For this purpose, we have defined structures that contain significant information about the desired comparison: compared *objects*, comparison *aspects*, and *predicates*.

In the example "Which is better for Deep Learning: Python or MATLAB?", the objects are entities that the user wants to compare (*Python, MATLAB*). The predicate is the entity that frames the comparison (*better*); it introduces a comparison relation between the objects and is often represented by a comparative adjective or adverb. Finally, the comparison aspects are shared properties along which the two objects are compared, e.g., *Deep Learning.*

Our comparative question answering system is based on CAM (Schildwächter et al., 2019), which retrieves pro/con arguments for a pair of compared objects. We extend CAM by enabling it to process natural language questions and generate coherent human-like answers as depicted in Figure 1.

Comparative Argument Mining CAM mines sentences in favor or against two compared objects

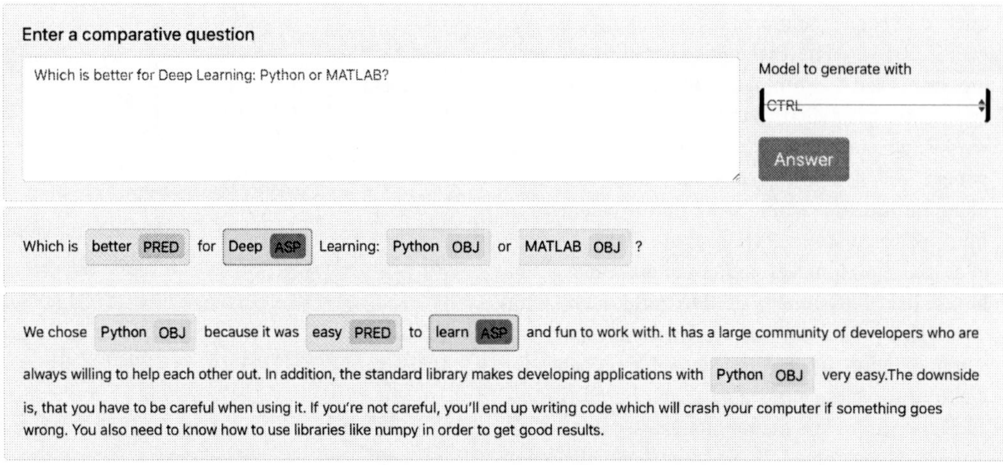

Figure 2: The interface of the Comparative Question Answering System (CoQAS).

with respect to an aspect specified by the user. First, using the Elasticsearch BM25, CAM retrieves sentences containing the two compared objects and the comparison aspect from the Common Crawl-based corpus featuring 14.3 billion sentences (Panchenko et al., 2018). Then, CAM classifies the sentences as comparative or not and identifies the "winner" of the two compared objects in the sentence context. Besides, it extracts aspects and predicates from the retrieved comparative sentences (Panchenko et al., 2019). Finally, CAM outputs a list of argumentative pro/con sentences and shows the "winner" of the comparison along with the comparison aspects.

Comparative Question Answering We extend CAM with natural language question understanding (described in Section 4) and natural language answer generation (described in Section 5) modules. The first module is developed to automatically identify the compared objects and the comparison aspect in a user-provided natural-language comparative question. This information is passed to CAM, which queries DepCC for comparative sentences. The NLG module receives the output of CAM and transforms the retrieved argumentative sentences into a short text, the generated answer. The structure of our modular system is presented in Figure 1.

The user interface (Figure 2) contains an input form for submitting a comparative question and an output box for a generated answer. To improve the readability of the answer and help find the arguments in it, NLU module also labels the output with identified objects, aspects, and predicates. In Figure 2, we present an example of the system's web interface in action.

In the NLG module, we use several approaches to response generation: an information retrieval-based approach and an approach built upon pre-trained language models. These techniques provide different answers: the first is more structured, and the second one is based on experience and opinions. Therefore, we allow a user to choose a generation model from different types: CAM, CTRL, and Snippets (cf. Figure 2).

Finally, for integration into NLP applications, e.g., personal assistants and chatbots, we also provide a RESTful API for our comparative QA.

4 Natural Language Understanding

The goal of the NLU module is to identify the objects to compare and comparison structure aspects and predicates if they were specified. We cast this as a sequence labeling task.

Training Dataset To train the NLU, we created *Comparely*, a dataset with comparative sentences manually labeled with objects, aspects, and predicates. First, we extracted comparative sentences for 270 object pairs from the dataset of (not) comparative sentences by Panchenko et al. (2019). We extracted them from DepCC corpus (Panchenko et al., 2018) using CAM. We then performed manual labeling (two annotators) using WebAnno (Yimam et al., 2013). Some of the extracted sentences were not comparative, so the annotators were instructed to discard them. The majority of sentences were labeled once, but we also labeled 200 of them multiple times to compute the inter-annotator agree-

Table 1: Statistics of the NLU dataset.

	Object	Aspect	Predicate
# occurrences	7,555	2,593	3,990
# per sentence	2.51	1.35	1.34
Avg. # words	1.04	1.37	1.16

Table 2: Evaluation in terms of F1 of the NLU tagger.

Model	Objects	Aspects	Predicates
RoBERTa	**0.925**	**0.685**	**0.894**
BERT	0.829	0.563	0.869
ELMO	0.654	0.487	0.825
BiLSTM-CRF	0.631	0.475	0.766
BiLSTM	0.582	0.328	0.730

ment. The Cohen's κ for the aspect labeling is 0.71 (substantial agreement). For predicates and objects, the values are 0.90 and 0.93, respectively—perfect agreement. The dataset consists of 3,004 sentences, each of them has a comparison of two or more distinct objects and at least one aspect or predicate. The average length of sentence is 26.7 words (Table 1). The majority of sentences compare more than one pair of objects across multiple parameters (i.e., sentences often contain more than one aspect or predicate). As the NLU processed not statements but questions, for the further improvement of the dataset, we could use comparative questions from (Bondarenko et al., 2020a).

This dataset is essentially similar to the ones by (Arora et al., 2017; Kessler and Kuhn, 2014). They also contain comparative statements labeled with objects, aspects, and predicates. The primary difference of our dataset is domain diversity. The mentioned datasets are drawn from a single domain, namely, camera reviews. The information contained in such sentences is difficult to generalize. Thus, they demonstrate a proof of concept rather than a resource that can be used for real-world tasks. On the other hand, *Comparely* features objects of different domains. It was created based on real-world objects that are frequently compared. It contains data from three domains: brands, generic objects, and computer science. The two former domains are more numerous: 41% and 46% sentences deal with objects of brands and generic domains, respectively. The remaining 13% are devoted to objects of the computer science domain.

Method Identification of comparative question components (objects, aspects, predicates, or none) is a sequence-labeling task, where the classifier should tag respective tokens in an input question. We test several common baselines starting with simple one-layer bidirectional LSTM described by (Arora et al., 2017) where the input is encoded with GloVe (Pennington et al., 2014) embeddings. For some further improvements, we add Conditional Random Field (Sutton and McCallum, 2012) to LSTM and use context-based ELMO (Peters et al., 2018) embeddings for token representations. We also experiment with Transformers (Vaswani et al., 2017) using a pre-trained BERT model (Devlin et al., 2019) and RoBERTa (Liu et al., 2019), which is its modification yielding better performance. For every classifier, during training, we tune hyperparameters by varying a batch size (from 16 to 100) and a learning rate (from 10^{-6} to 10^{-2}). To find a proper converge of the training process, we apply two types of learning rate schedulers: Linear With Warmup and Slanted Triangular.

For the model with the highest achieved F1 (RoBERTa), we employ stochastic weight ensembling (Goodfellow et al., 2015; Garipov et al., 2018), i.e., we interpolate between the weights obtained by training a certain model with different random seeds. All models were trained on the *Comparely* dataset and tested on its manually relabeled subset of 400 sentences. The overview of the classifiers' effectiveness is shown in Table 2.

Results and Discussion The evaluation shows that comparison aspect classification is the hardest task: the baseline one-layer BiLSTM achieves an F1 of 0.33, and the most effective RoBERTa-based classifier achieves an F1 of 0.69. The most reliable classification was achieved for predicting the compared objects with an F1 of 0.58 for the baseline and an F1 of 0.93 for RoBERTa. An addition of a CRF layer and the use of pre-trained ELMo embeddings to the BiLSTM classifier slightly improved the results. Transformers demonstrated significant improvement in classification effectiveness over the baseline. Finally, we choose to deploy a RoBERTa-based classifier in the NLU module of our system.

5 Comparative Answer Generation

Based on comparative sentences retrieved by CAM, we develop several generation approaches to construct a human-like concise answer: (1) genera-

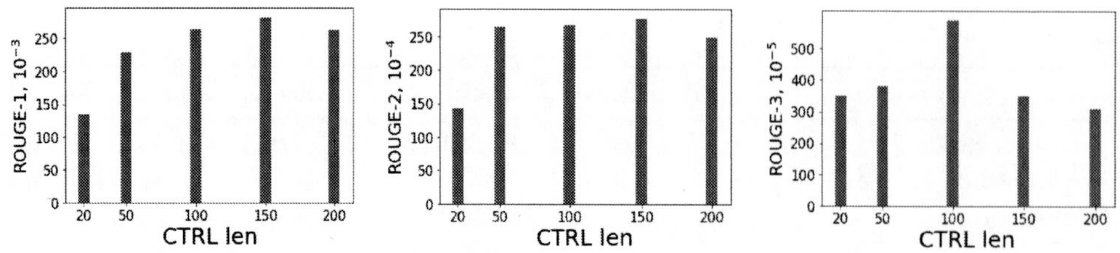

Figure 3: Dependence of ROUGE metrics on the maximum length of the generated sequence (CTRL model).

tion with pre-trained Transformers-based language models, (2) retrieval of argumentative sentences ranked by CAM or TextRank, (3) extracting context of sentence retrieved by CAM as support for the "winning" object, and (4) entering extracted comparative structures in templates.

5.1 Generation Methods

Pre-trained Language Models Pre-trained language models have been shown to contain commonsense knowledge, so they can be successfully used for question answering (Andrews and Witteveen, 2019) and for generating sensible and coherent continuation of text. Therefore, we use Transformers-based CTRL (Keskar et al., 2019) models for answering comparative questions.

CTRL allows explicit control codes to vary the domain and the content of the text. We use the Links control code, which forces the model to produce text similar to online news and reports. We feed into CTRL phrase "Links Which is better in respect to the aspect: $object_1$ or $object_2$?" and a row question from the input.

We also vary the maximum number of tokens generated by CTRL. We experiment with different length set, including: 20, 50, 100, 150, and 200 and generate answers to questions from the Yahoo! Answers dataset (cf. Section 5.2). For the evaluation part, we calculate ROUGE-1, ROUGE-2, ROUGE-3 scores between generated texts and corresponding Yahoo!'s "best answers". According to the results (cf. Figure 3), a model with a maximum length of 100 tokens gives the highest ROUGE-3 score (we select this length parameter for our further experiments).

Sentence-Retrieval-Based Methods The CAM output contains a list of the argumentative sentences ranked by the BM25 inverted index-based score. Every sentence is a supportive argument for the superiority of the respective compared object. Sentence-retrieval-based methods try to extract the most representative sentences and display it in the proper form. To create an answer, CAM: Bullet points mentions a "winner" defined by CAM with respect to aspects if they exist. It also takes the top-3 sentences supporting each of the objects and produces a list for highlighting the advantages and disadvantages of each object in comparison.

An alternative way of retrieving the most relevant sentences is clustering. This approach is used in TextRank: Bullet points. TextRank is a graph-based summarization algorithm. We use the version proposed by Mallick et al. (2019). We represent sentences with hidden states of a LSTM network pre-trained on Wikipedia. TextRank iteratively updates the weights of edges and sets the node weights to be proportional to the importance of adjacent edges. To make the graph sparse, we remove the edges with a score below average.

We create separate graphs for sentences supporting each of the objects. We apply TextRank to each of them and then cluster them. Clustering divides the nodes in graphs by semantic similarity and thus allows identifying groups of sentences supporting a particular idea. Then, we apply TextRank again to each of the clusters separately and select the three most characteristic sentences from each cluster as produced by Chinese Whispers (Biemann, 2006), an iterative clustering algorithm, which assigns vertices to the most common class among their neighbors. Argumentative sentences selected in this way are displayed as a bullet-list after declaring the "winner" object of comparison.

Document-Retrieval-Based Method To compose an answer, CAM: First snippets takes the first sentence related to the "winner" object in CAM output. Then it finds a document corresponding to this sentence and extracts the surrounding context. The obtained context consists of 3 sentences and is considered to be a system answer.

Table 3: Evaluation of generation methods on the Yahoo! Answers. The best models of each type are highlighted.

Method	Type	ROUGE-1	ROUGE-2	ROUGE-3
CTRL: Question, len≤100	Language Model	0.2423	**0.0226**	**0.0023**
CTRL: Which-better-x-y-for-z, len≤100	Language Model	**0.2454**	0.0200	0.0021
CAM: First snippets	Doc.Retrieval	**0.2162**	**0.0167**	**0.0017**
CAM: Bullet points	Sent.Retrieval + Slots	**0.2298**	**0.0328**	**0.0040**
TextRank: Bullet points	Sent.Retrieval + Slots	0.2203	0.0238	0.0036
Templates	Object/Aspect Slots	0.1969	0.0195	0.0016

Template-Based Answer Besides the argumentative sentences, CAM extracts aspects and predicates from them. The predicates are adjectives or adverbs, which allows using templates of the following form: "I would prefer to use $Object_1$ because it is $Predicate_1$ and $Predicate_2$. In addition, it is $Predicate_3$, ..., and $Predicate_i$. However, you should also take into account that $Object_2$ is $Predicate_{i+1}$, ..., and $Predicate_k$". Here $Object_1$ is the winner of comparison.

5.2 Experiments

Evaluation Dataset To evaluate the answer generation module of our system, we use information extracted from Yahoo! Answers. Namely, we get a subset of L6–Yahoo! Answers Comprehensive Questions and Answers version 1.0 (multi-part) retrieved from Yahoo! Webscope. We take pairs of objects that we used for generating *Comparely* and extract a subset of questions from the Yahoo! Answers dataset which contains these objects, yielding 1,200 questions.

Additionally, we extract the answers to these questions, which are labeled by users as "best answer", and use them to evaluate our NLG methods.

Evaluation Metric Generated and reference texts are usually compared by a number of matched N-grams: BLUE (precision), ROUGE (recall), METEOR (F-score). For the all-round representation of the similarity of the text, we select F1 score from ROUGE-N outputs as an evaluation metric. We evaluate our generation models on the Yahoo! Answers dataset using the "best answer" (defined by users) as the reference.

Discussion of Results Evaluation results are provided in Table 3. CTRL models receive the highest ROUGE-1 scores that describe overlapping of single words, and CTRL's high performance relative to it can be explained by the fact that the pre-trained language model stores information about a vast dictionary and, with some probability, yields the words that are placed in the standard answer. While the language-model-based system may yield grammatically correct answers, they may not necessarily satisfy the information need of the user. For example, the CTRL answers the question "What should I eat an orange or an apple?" with "It is simple: eat what you like and don't worry about it."

Despite having low ROUGE-1, sentence retrieval-based approaches (Text Rank: Bullet points, CAM: Bullet points) have consistently higher ROUGE-2 and ROUGE-3. The generated answers are more structured and built on sentences marked by the system as comparative. They often contain typical 2-gram and 3-gram sequences as found in explanations. Answers from CAM: First snippets, consisting of a single comparative sentences only, perform worse on all metrics. Interestingly, CAM: Bullet points has better performance than TextRank: Bullet points. It could indicate that modeling relevance by a standard index provides more accurate results than clustering. Meanwhile, template-based generation performs poorly. This indicates that the grammatical structure is essential for the answer generation task.

We choose 50 random sentences from the Yahoo! Answers dataset as described in Section 6 and calculate ROUGE-N scores for every generation method and Yahoo!'s "best answers". For each group of methods, we select one providing the best result—CTRL: Question 100, CAM: First snippets, and CAM: Bullet points—and add them to the system demonstration engine.

6 User Study

To additionally evaluate the proposed answer generation methods, we also collect human assessments in a small user study for the three models with the highest ROUGE scores (CTRL: Question 100,

Table 4: User study results for answer completeness and fluency (30 questions, 3-point Likert scales).

Method	Answers a question (%)			Answer fluency (%)		
	Complete	Partial	Does not	Complete	Partial	Not fluent
Yahoo! Best Answer	62	28	10	86	6	8
CTRL: Question 100	30	37	33	80	12	8
CAM: Bullet points	28	58	14	22	48	30
CAM: First snippets	23	49	28	27	38	35

CAM: Bullet points, and CAM: First snippets).

Experimental Setup For our study, we randomly sampled 30 comparative questions from the Yahoo! Answers dataset and generated answers using three methods: CTRL: Question 100, CAM: Bullet points, and CAM: First snippets. Additionally, since we used Yahoo!'s "best answers" as ground truth for automatic evaluation, we asked our participants to also assess the quality of the human "best answers". For the user study, we internally recruited five (under-)graduate students. We focused on the two answer evaluation criteria: (1) Whether an answer is complete ("Does it answer the question?") and (2) how fluently it is written. The 120 question–answer pairs (3 generated answers and Yahoo!'s "best answer" for 30 questions) were randomly ordered, and the participants had to rate the answer completeness and fluency on a three-point Likert scale (3: fully answers/fluent, 2: partially answers/fluent, and 1: does not answer/not fluent at all).

Results and Discussion The inter-annotator agreement shows a slight overall agreement between the five annotators (Fleiss' $\kappa = 0.20$ for answer completeness and $\kappa = 0.13$ for fluency) such that we decided to increase the reliability by calculating the κ-scores for all combinations of three or four annotators. We then decided to include only the three participants with the highest agreement (κ = 0.32 for answer completeness and 0.30 for fluency; both fair agreement) and to remove the two "outlier" participants from the study.

Table 4 summarizes the study results as the ratio of votes collected from the three annotators (we cannot use majority voting since about 60% of the question-answer pairs do not have a majority vote). Not surprisingly, the human-written answers are perceived as the most complete and fluent. The participants were almost equally satisfied with the answers generated by CTRL: Question 100 and CAM: Bullet points. However, they assessed the CTRL answers as much more fluent. Interestingly, the relatively low inter-annotator agreement might indicate that humans have different perceptions of answer completeness and fluency (even some "best answers" were rated as incomplete and not fluent). For completeness, we calculated the statistical significance of the user study results using Bonferroni corrected p-values. For the pair CTRL: Question 100 (our best NLG model) and the Yahoo! Best Answer: $p \ll 0.05$ for the answer completeness and $p \gg 0.05$ for the answer fluency. For the CTRL model, Pearson's $r = 0.121$ between the answer completeness and fluency (small correlation), and for the "best answers", $r = 0.407$ (medium correlation). The results show that our proposed system is almost as fluent as the human-written answers but still needs some improvement in terms of adequacy.

7 Conclusion

We present a comparative question answering system targeted at answering comparative questions, such as "Is X better than Y with respect to Z?". Our system is based on the Comparative Argument Mining (CAM) system—a tool that retrieves from a large corpus textual comparative arguments for two to-be-compared objects. We extend CAM with an NLU module that identifies objects and aspects in a user textual query and highlights them in the answer, and a generation module that gives a concise and coherent answer based on the retrieved information. Evaluation of generation methods showed that a CTRL-based answer generation has a better performance with respect to ROUGE-1, and Sentence Retrieval Methods provide superior ROUGE-2 and ROUGE-3 scores. We hope that the presented testbed for comparative QA and the set of baseline approaches will pave the way for further research.

Acknowledgments

This work was partially supported by the DFG through the project "ACQuA: Answering Comparative Questions with Arguments" (grants BI 1544/7-1 and HA 5851/2-1) as part of the priority program "RATIO: Robust Argumentation Machines" (SPP 1999). The demo is hosted using the Zhores supercomputer infrastructure (Zacharov et al., 2019). We thank the following Skoltech students who conducted several preliminary experiments related to this work as a part of their research assignments: Anna Shalova, Nikita Borovkov, Filipp Furaev, and Anton Razzhigaev. Finally, we thank Artem Shelmanov for providing a training script for the RoBERTa-based sequence tagger.

References

Martin Andrews and Sam Witteveen. 2019. Unsupervised natural question answering with a small model. In *Proceedings of the Second Workshop on Fact Extraction and VERification (FEVER)*, pages 34–38, Hong Kong, China.

Jatin Arora, Sumit Agrawal, Pawan Goyal, and Sayan Pathak. 2017. Extracting entities of interest from comparative product reviews. In *Proceedings of the 2017 ACM on Conference on Information and Knowledge Management*, CIKM '17, pages 1975–1978, New York, NY, USA. Association for Computing Machinery.

Dzmitry Bahdanau, Kyunghyun Cho, and Yoshua Bengio. 2015. Neural machine translation by jointly learning to align and translate. In *3rd International Conference on Learning Representations, ICLR 2015, San Diego, CA, USA, May 7-9, 2015, Conference Track Proceedings*.

Chris Biemann. 2006. Chinese whispers - an efficient graph clustering algorithm and its application to natural language processing problems. In *Proceedings of TextGraphs: the First Workshop on Graph Based Methods for Natural Language Processing*, pages 73–80, New York City. Association for Computational Linguistics.

Alexander Bondarenko, Pavel Braslavski, Michael Völske, Rami Aly, Maik Fröbe, Alexander Panchenko, Chris Biemann, Benno Stein, and Matthias Hagen. 2020a. Comparative web search questions. In *Proceedings of the 13th ACM International Conference on Web Search and Data Mining (WSDM 2020)*, pages 52–60, Houston, USA. Association for Computing Machinery.

Alexander Bondarenko, Maik Fröbe, Meriem Beloucif, Lukas Gienapp, Yamen Ajjour, Alexander Panchenko, Chris Biemann, Benno Stein, Henning Wachsmuth, Martin Potthast, and Matthias Hagen. 2020b. Overview of Touché 2020: Argument retrieval. In *Working Notes Papers of the CLEF 2020 Evaluation Labs*, volume 2696 of *CEUR Workshop Proceedings*.

Alexander Bondarenko, Lukas Gienapp, Maik Fröbe, Meriem Beloucif, Yamen Ajjour, Alexander Panchenko, Chris Biemann, Benno Stein, Henning Wachsmuth, Martin Potthast, and Matthias Hagen. 2021. Overview of Touché 2021: Argument retrieval. In *Proceedings of the 43rd European Conference on IR Research (ECIR 2021)*, volume 12036 of *Lecture Notes in Computer Science*, Berlin Heidelberg New York. Springer.

Maximin Coavoux, Hady Elsahar, and Matthias Gallé. 2019. Unsupervised aspect-based multi-document abstractive summarization. In *Proceedings of the 2nd Workshop on New Frontiers in Summarization*, pages 42–47, Hong Kong, China. Association for Computational Linguistics.

Jacob Devlin, Ming-Wei Chang, Kenton Lee, and Kristina Toutanova. 2019. BERT: Pre-training of deep bidirectional transformers for language understanding. In *Proceedings of the 2019 Conference of the North American Chapter of the Association for Computational Linguistics: Human Language Technologies, NAACL-HLT 2019*, pages 4171–4186. Association for Computational Linguistics.

Ondřej Dušek and Filip Jurčíček. 2016. A context-aware natural language generator for dialogue systems. In *Proceedings of the 17th Annual Meeting of the Special Interest Group on Discourse and Dialogue*, pages 185–190, Los Angeles, CA, USA. Association for Computational Linguistics.

Qiaoqing Fan and Yu Fang. 2017. An answer summarization method based on keyword extraction. In *BIO Web of Conferences*, volume 8, pages 30–37. EDP Sciences.

Markus Freitag and Scott Roy. 2018. Unsupervised natural language generation with denoising autoencoders. In *Proceedings of the 2018 Conference on Empirical Methods in Natural Language Processing*, pages 3922–3929, Brussels, Belgium. Association for Computational Linguistics.

Murthy Ganapathibhotla and Bing Liu. 2008. Mining opinions in comparative sentences. In *Proceedings of the 22nd International Conference on Computational Linguistics (Coling 2008)*, pages 241–248, Manchester, UK. Coling 2008 Organizing Committee.

Timur Garipov, Pavel Izmailov, Dmitrii Podoprikhin, Dmitry P Vetrov, and Andrew G Wilson. 2018. Loss surfaces, mode connectivity, and fast ensembling of dnns. In *Advances in Neural Information Processing Systems*, volume 31, Montreal, Quebec, Canada. Curran Associates, Inc.

Ian J. Goodfellow, Oriol Vinyals, and Andrew M. Saxe. 2015. Qualitatively characterizing neural network optimization problems.

Wan-Ting Hsu, Chieh-Kai Lin, Ming-Ying Lee, Kerui Min, Jing Tang, and Min Sun. 2018. A unified model for extractive and abstractive summarization using inconsistency loss. In *Proceedings of the 56th Annual Meeting of the Association for Computational Linguistics*, volume 1, pages 132–141, Melbourne, Australia. Association for Computational Linguistics.

Masaru Isonuma, Junichiro Mori, and Ichiro Sakata. 2019. Unsupervised Neural Single-Document Summarization of Reviews via Learning Latent Discourse Structure and its Ranking. In *Proceedings of the 57th Conference of the Association for Computational Linguistics, ACL 2019*, pages 2142–2152, Florence, Italy. Association for Computational Linguistics.

Nitin Jindal and Bing Liu. 2006. Mining comparative sentences and relations. In *Proceedings, The Twenty-First National Conference on Artificial Intelligence and the Eighteenth Innovative Applications of Artificial Intelligence Conference*, pages 1331–1336, Boston, Massachusetts. Innovative Applications of Artificial Intelligence (AAAI) Press.

Nitish Shirish Keskar, Bryan McCann, Lav R. Varshney, Caiming Xiong, and Richard Socher. 2019. CTRL: A conditional transformer language model for controllable generation. *CoRR*, abs/1909.05858.

Wiltrud Kessler and Jonas Kuhn. 2014. A corpus of comparisons in product reviews. In *Proceedings of the Ninth International Conference on Language Resources and Evaluation (LREC'14)*, pages 2242–2248, Reykjavik, Iceland. European Language Resources Association (ELRA).

Xin Li and Dan Roth. 2006. Learning question classifiers: the role of semantic information. *Natural Language Engineering*, 12(3):229–249.

Marina Litvak and Mark Last. 2008. Graph-based keyword extraction for single-document summarization. In *Coling 2008: Proceedings of the workshop Multi-source Multilingual Information Extraction and Summarization*, pages 17–24, Manchester, UK. Coling 2008 Organizing Committee.

Yinhan Liu, Myle Ott, Naman Goyal, Jingfei Du, Mandar Joshi, Danqi Chen, Omer Levy, Mike Lewis, Luke Zettlemoyer, and Veselin Stoyanov. 2019. Roberta: A robustly optimized BERT pretraining approach. *CoRR*, abs/1907.11692.

Chirantana Mallick, Ajit Kumar Das, Madhurima Dutta, Asit Kumar Das, and Apurba Sarkar. 2019. Graph-based text summarization using modified textrank. In *Soft Computing in Data Analytics*, pages 137–146. Springer.

Rada Mihalcea. 2004. Graph-based ranking algorithms for sentence extraction, applied to text summarization. In *Proceedings of the ACL Interactive Poster and Demonstration Sessions*, pages 170–173, Barcelona, Spain. Association for Computational Linguistics.

Kyosuke Nishida, Itsumi Saito, Kosuke Nishida, Kazutoshi Shinoda, Atsushi Otsuka, Hisako Asano, and Junji Tomita. 2019. Multi-style generative reading comprehension. In *Proceedings of the 57th Annual Meeting of the Association for Computational Linguistics*, pages 2273–2284, Florence, Italy. Association for Computational Linguistics.

Alexander Panchenko, Alexander Bondarenko, Mirco Franzek, Matthias Hagen, and Chris Biemann. 2019. Categorizing comparative sentences. In *Proceedings of the 6th Workshop on Argument Mining*, pages 136–145, Florence, Italy. Association for Computational Linguistics.

Alexander Panchenko, Eugen Ruppert, Stefano Faralli, Simone P. Ponzetto, and Chris Biemann. 2018. Building a web-scale dependency-parsed corpus from CommonCrawl. In *Proceedings of the Eleventh International Conference on Language Resources and Evaluation (LREC 2018)*, pages 1816–1823, Miyazaki, Japan. European Language Resources Association (ELRA).

Jeffrey Pennington, Richard Socher, and Christopher Manning. 2014. GloVe: Global vectors for word representation. In *Proceedings of the 2014 Conference on Empirical Methods in Natural Language Processing (EMNLP)*, pages 1532–1543, Doha, Qatar. Association for Computational Linguistics.

Matthew E. Peters, Mark Neumann, Mohit Iyyer, Matt Gardner, Christopher Clark, Kenton Lee, and Luke Zettlemoyer. 2018. Deep contextualized word representations. In *Proceedings of the 2018 Conference of the North American Chapter of the Association for Computational Linguistics: Human Language Technologies, NAACL-HLT 2018*, pages 2227–2237. Association for Computational Linguistics.

Matthias Schildwächter, Alexander Bondarenko, Julian Zenker, Matthias Hagen, Chris Biemann, and Alexander Panchenko. 2019. Answering comparative questions: Better than ten-blue-links? In *Proceedings of the 2019 Conference on Human Information Interaction and Retrieval (CHIIR 2019)*, pages 361–365. Association for Computing Machinery.

Abigail See, Peter J. Liu, and Christopher D. Manning. 2017. Get to the point: Summarization with pointer-generator networks. In *Proceedings of the 55th Annual Meeting of the Association for Computational Linguistics*, volume 1, pages 1073–1083, Vancouver, Canada. Association for Computational Linguistics.

Jian-Tao Sun, Xuanhui Wang, Dou Shen, Hua-Jun Zeng, and Zheng Chen. 2006. CWS: A comparative web search system. In *Proceedings of the 15th international conference on World Wide Web, WWW 2006, Edinburgh, Scotland, UK, May 23-26, 2006*, pages 467–476. Association for Computing Machinery.

Ilya Sutskever, Oriol Vinyals, and Quoc V. Le. 2014. Sequence to sequence learning with neural networks. In *Advances in Neural Information Processing Systems 27: Annual Conference on Neural Information Processing Systems*, pages 3104–3112, Montreal, Quebec, Canada.

Charles Sutton and Andrew McCallum. 2012. An introduction to conditional random fields. *Found. Trends Mach. Learn.*, 4(4):267–373.

Ashish Vaswani, Noam Shazeer, Niki Parmar, Jakob Uszkoreit, Llion Jones, Aidan N Gomez, Ł ukasz Kaiser, and Illia Polosukhin. 2017. Attention is all you need. In *Advances in Neural Information Processing Systems*, volume 30, pages 5998–6008, Long Beach, CA, USA. Curran Associates, Inc.

Henning Wachsmuth, Martin Potthast, Khalid Al-Khatib, Yamen Ajjour, Jana Puschmann, Jiani Qu, Jonas Dorsch, Viorel Morari, Janek Bevendorff, and Benno Stein. 2017. Building an argument search engine for the web. In *4th Workshop on Argument Mining (ArgMining 2017) at EMNLP*, pages 49–59, Copenhagen, Denmark. Association for Computational Linguistics.

Zhilin Yang, Peng Qi, Saizheng Zhang, Yoshua Bengio, William Cohen, Ruslan Salakhutdinov, and Christopher D. Manning. 2018. HotpotQA: A dataset for diverse, explainable multi-hop question answering. In *Proceedings of the 2018 Conference on Empirical Methods in Natural Language Processing*, pages 2369–2380, Brussels, Belgium. Association for Computational Linguistics.

Seid Muhie Yimam, Iryna Gurevych, Richard Eckart de Castilho, and Chris Biemann. 2013. WebAnno: A flexible, web-based and visually supported system for distributed annotations. In *Proceedings of the 51st Annual Meeting of the Association for Computational Linguistics: System Demonstrations*, pages 1–6, Sofia, Bulgaria. Association for Computational Linguistics.

Igor Zacharov, Rinat Arslanov, Maksim Gunin, Daniil Stefonishin, Andrey Bykov, Sergey Pavlov, Oleg Panarin, Anton Maliutin, Sergey Rykovanov, and Maxim Fedorov. 2019. "Zhores"—Petaflops supercomputer for data-driven modeling, machine learning and artificial intelligence installed in Skolkovo Institute of Science and Technology. *Open Engineering*, 9(1):512–520.

PunKtuator: A Multilingual Punctuation Restoration System for Spoken and Written Text

Varnith Chordia
Palo Alto Research Center
3333 Coyote Hill Road
Palo Alto, CA - 94034
vchordia@parc.com

Abstract

Text transcripts without punctuation or sentence boundaries are hard to comprehend for both humans and machines. Punctuation marks play a vital role by providing meaning to the sentence and incorrect use or placement of punctuation marks can often alter it. This can impact downstream tasks such as language translation and understanding, pronoun resolution, text summarization, etc. for humans and machines. An automated punctuation restoration (APR) system with minimal human intervention can improve comprehension of text and help users write better. In this paper we describe a multitask modeling approach as a system to restore punctuation in multiple high resource – Germanic (English and German), Romanic (French)– and low resource languages – Indo-Aryan (Hindi) Dravidian (Tamil) – that does not require extensive knowledge of grammar or syntax of a given language for both spoken and written form of text. For German language and the given Indic based languages this is the first towards restoring punctuation and can serve as a baseline for future work.

1 Introduction

Automatic speech recognition (ASR) has become ubiquitous these days and has wide applications in business and personal life. One of the drawbacks of ASR is it produces an unpunctuated stream of text. Restoring punctuation manually is a time-consuming task. Apart from spoken text a large amount of written text online - blogs, articles, social media,etc. - sometimes lack the appropriate punctuation marks due to human inconsistencies, which can alter the meaning of text. An APR system designed with an understanding of ASR and written forms of text can help resolve these issues. Transcriptions passed to an APR system, can improve the following machine learning tasks such as machine translation, conversational agents, co-reference resolution, etc. Further it can be used as an unsupervised auxiliary or pretext task, for training large scale transformer language models, as it would require understanding about global structure of the text.

Prior punctuation restoration methods have mostly been solved using lexical features, prosodic features or combination of both. Due to large availability of text data, majority of the methods have focused on using lexical features. Early methods (Christensen et al., 2001) used Hidden Markov Models (HMM) to model punctuation using acoustic features such as pause duration, pitch and intensity. Though the acoustic based models perform well on ASR system, they can perform better when combined with textual data. Liu et al. (2006); Batista et al. (2007); Kolář and Lamel (2012) proposed various methods that combined lexical features along with prosodic information thereby improving APR tasks. Tilk and Alumäe (2015, 2016) proposed unidirectional and bidirectional Long Short Term Memory (Bi-LSTM) based punctuation prediction model which did not require extensive feature engineering. Though the above method considered the long distant token dependencies, it ignored label dependencies. To address label dependencies (Klejch et al., 2017) made use of recurrent neural networks for sequence to sequence mapping using an encoder-decoder architecture. Recently the use of transformer based approaches combination of speech and pre-trained word embeddings have achieved state of art performance on IWSLT datasets (spoken transcripts from TED talks for ASR tasks, but often used as benchmark for comparison of punctuation restoration models). Yi et al. (2020) used pretrained BERT (Devlin et al., 2018) that is used to perform adversarial multi-task learning to restore punctuation. Alam et al. (2020) explored various transformer model architectures

Proceedings of the 16th Conference of the European Chapter of the Association for Computational Linguistics: System Demonstrations, pages 312–320
April 19 - 23, 2021. ©2021 Association for Computational Linguistics

Language	Total	Other (O)	Period	Comma	Question
English	48,334,765	43,855,115 **(90.7%)**	1,914,198 **(3.96%)**	2,492,124 **(5.15%)**	55,123 **(0.11%)**
French	22,315,779	20,223,881 **(90.6%)**	1,232,798 **(5.5%)**	815,123 **(3.6%)**	30,379 **(0.11%)**
German	41,269,527	36,438,630 **(88.2%)**	1,875,766 **(4.54%)**	2,816,425 **(6.82%)**	60216 **(0.14%)**
Hindi	3,388,500	3,135,290 **(92.5%)**	127,101 **(3.75%)**	100,710 **(2.97%)**	1246 **(0.03%)**
Tamil	906,271	791,6320 **(87.8%)**	58,963 **(6.50%)**	53,198 **(5.86%)**	1,496 **(0.09%)**

Table 1: Distribution of the High resource and long resource language datasets. The top-3 languages in the table are considered high Resource,while the bottom 2 are low resource languages

and used an augmentation strategy to make models more robust to ASR errors.

Though most approaches have shown considerable improvement in overcoming some of the challenges faced in terms of modeling and achieving the state of performance in spoken language transcripts in English, there are the following limitations:

- Restoring punctuation varies in spoken and written text due to differences in rules of writing and speaking. The frequent use of personal pronouns, colloquial words and usage of direct speech often results in more varied use of punctuation in spoken text as compared to written text. This often affects readability for humans and machines.

- Though there has been some research (Tilk and Alumäe, 2016; Kolář and Lamel, 2012; Alam et al., 2020) that has focused on developing non-english APR system, extensive research and baseline results have not been studied for other languages.

To overcome some of the challenges, we make the following contributions:

- We implemented a multi-task multilingual punctuation restoration model. Our technique implements punctuation restoration task as sequence labeling task, which is jointly trained with language classifiers and text mode classification ('Spoken' and 'Written'). We use the proposed technique to build two multilingual models for high resource and low resource languages, thereby reducing the dependency of multiple monolingual language models.

- We developed a web browser extension that can help multilingual spoken and written users to punctuate transcripts as a post-processing step. We have made a demo of the web extension available online. [1]

- We prepared training and test datasets and evaluated the performance of our proposed model. Further to evaluate the generalization of the model we evaluated across the benchmark IWSLT reference dataset. The code and models have been made publicly available.[2]

2 Punctuation restoration system

2.1 Data Gathering

Due to varying set of language data, we segregated the data sources according to the languages, which we gathered for spoken and written text. For Written text we considered data from news web sources.

2.1.1 High Resource Languages

For high resource European languages, we considered a parallel sentence corpus known as the *'EUROPARL'* corpus (Vanmassenhove and Hardmeier, 2018) for spoken text. This corpus is a collection of speeches made in the proceedings of European parliament from 1996 to 2012, transcribed as text. To gather written text we used news articles from Alexa's top-25 ranked news sources. These were publicly available[3] for every language.

[1] https://youtu.be/9FdkuENPhuY

[2] https://github.com/VarnithChordia/Multlingual_Punctuation_restoration

[3] https://webhose.io/

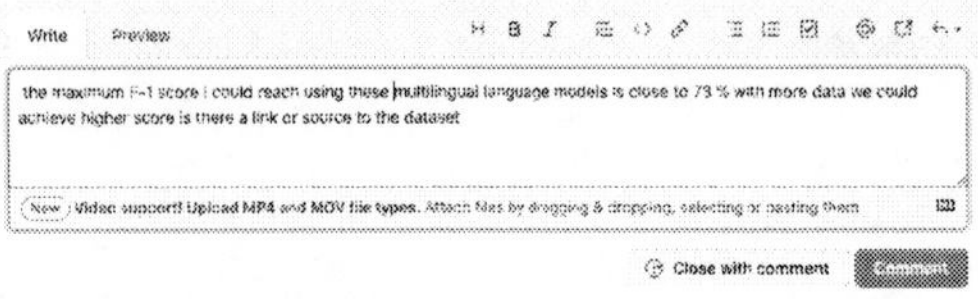

(a) Unpunctuated text transcripts within the editor window

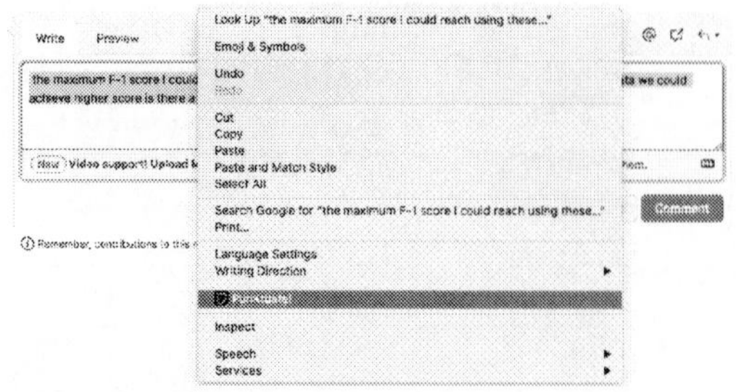

(b) Select the text to be punctuated and right click to punctuate

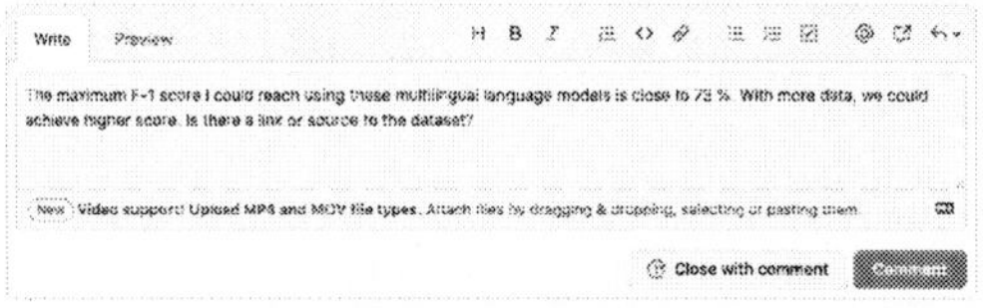

(c) Output punctuated text

Figure 1: Example of punctuation via web extension.
Source: www.github.com

2.1.2 Low Resource Languages

Due to lack of language resources available for indic languages for APR, we gather publicly released datasets. For Spoken text we used the Indian Prime Minister's address to the nation. These corpora manually translated into several Indian languages. Written text was obtained from Siripragada et al. (2020) who crawled articles articles released from the Press Information Bureau (PIB), an Indian government agency that provides information to news media.

2.2 Annotation

Due to lack of readily available annotated datasets and large size corpora, we used an automated approach to label the data. We analyzed languages and selected the three most common punctuation – 'PERIOD', 'COMMA' and 'QUESTION MARK' – that occurred across the languages for training our model. This was done to improve the readability of text so that could be easily understood by users, one of the goals of the system. Since we treat our task as a sequence labeling task, we annotated every word in the sequence according to the punctuation following it. We achieved this by tokenizing the input text into a stream of word tokens and punctuation tokens. We converted this into a set of pairs of (token, punctuation) where punctuation is the null punctuation ('O'), if there was no punctuation mark following in the text. To make our data set more diverse and training more robust, we ended sentences (10%) a few tokens before the 'PERIOD' tag and labeled the final token as 'EOS' (end of sentence). Further we converted all our text to lowercase to remove any signal while training the language model. The distribution of the labels can be seen in table 1.

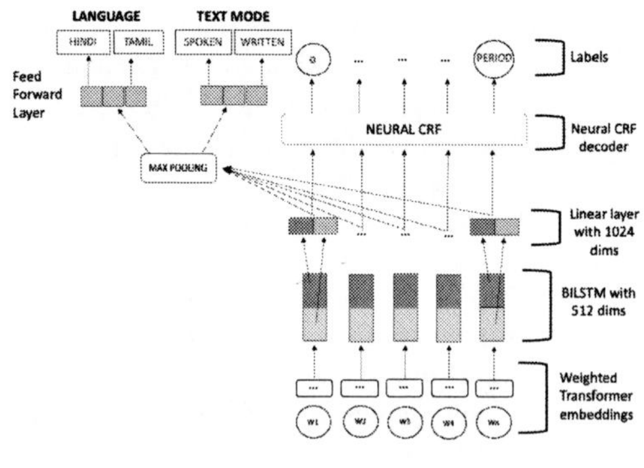

Figure 2: Joint Punctuation model on indic languages for spoken and written text.
Looks better when Zoomed.

2.3 Joint Multilingual Model-Architecture

The model consists of four main sub-parts as observed in Figure 2 – (i) Transformer Language Model (ii) BILSTM (iii) Neural Conditional Random Field (NCRF++) and (iv) Language and Text Mode classifiers. We use a pretrained transformer language model to generate word/sub-word embeddings, but do not fine tune this model to our specific task. A BILSTM on top of the transformer

Model	Language	TextMode	Period	Comma	Question	Overall
Joint - BILSTM NCRF + FastText	English	Spoken	92.3	66.7	65.2	74.8
		Written	83.3	57.6	32.5	57.7
	French	Spoken	88.9	64.2	30.8	61.3
		Written	77.0	56.7	33.9	55.9
	German	Spoken	93.2	88.6	48.0	76.6
		Written	77.3	71.0	31.0	64.1
Joint - XLMRoberta NCRF	English	Spoken	92.8	79.9	86.7	86.5
		Written	90.4	75.9	80.7	82.3
	French	Spoken	92.8	80.9	82.7	85.5
		Written	83.8	66.2	75.1	66.2
	German	Spoken	95.8	93.8	85.7	91.8
		Written	91.8	88.8	69.7	83.4
Joint - Multilingual-BERT NCRF	English	Spoken	95.8	80.6	92.8	**90.1**
		Written	96.0	82.7	79.7	**86.4**
	French	Spoken	94.8	80.8	88.1	**89.2**
		Written	93.5	78.5	73.0	**81.7**
	German	Spoken	97.0	95.0	90.7	**94.2**
		Written	96.0	74.3	90.0	**86.8**
Punctuation Restoration (Alam et al., 2020)	English	Spoken	80.8	75.0	78.7	78.1

Table 2: Results on High resource languages. The values in bold indicate the best perfoming model.

model is used to model token dependencies better, from forward and backward directions. NCRF (Yang and Zhang, 2018) relies on learning the high level features from the deep neural network and passes this information to a linear CRF layer for inference, which helps manage label dependencies. This architecture sequential in nature, is trained for APR task. The output sequence representation from the BILSTM is passed through a max pooling layer, the result of which passed through linear feed forward layer for language and text mode classification. We jointly trained our sequential language model, along with the classifiers.

2.4 Web Extension

We created a web extension that can be used to punctuate text within the text editors on web pages. It lets users to select text which could range from a few words to large paragraphs to entire documents to punctuate. The text does not have to be non punctuated as the system removes punctuation as a preprocessing step and punctuates again.The steps to punctuate are shown in Fig 1.

3 Experiments

3.1 Experimental setup

We used the pretrained transformer model and specific tokenizers available on HuggingFace[4]. The model architecture consists of the 12 hidden layer encoder, which is used to produce the embeddings. We used an optimized weighting technique (Peters et al., 2018) to sum all the hidden layers rather than use a common practice of using one single layer to generate embeddings. This showed an improvement in performance as seen under ablation studies in table 5. The weighting method is as defined:

$$O_{\text{i}} = \gamma \sum_{j=0}^{L-1} S_j H_j \quad (1)$$

where

- H_j is a trainable task weight for the jth layer. γ is another task trainable task parameter that aids the optimization process
- S_j is the normalized embedding output from the jth hidden layer of the transformer.
- O_j is the output vector.

[4]https://huggingface.co/

- L is the number of hidden layers.

To train the proposed model, we used a maximum sequence length of 505. We use a subword tokenization technique - sentence piece model (Kudo and Richardson, 2018) - which might result in token length exceeding the maximum sequence length, in such cases we exclude the tokens and start a new paragraph. For sequences less than the specified max sequence length, we pad the sequences to the maximum sequence length and mask the padded sequence to avoid performing attention on it. We used a batch size of 32, grouping similar sequence length prior to padding that enhances the speed while training the model. We do not fine tune the transformer model, but use it to embed the input text. A BILSTM stacked on top of the transformer model, is set to a dimension of 512, the layers are initialized with a uniform distribution in the range of (-.003, .003). A Neural CRF layer is trained with a maximum log-likelihood loss. Viterbi algorithm is used to search for the label sequence with the highest probability during decoding. The entire model was trained with an Adam optimization algorithm with a learning rate close to 1e-4 over 10 epochs. The proposed multitask network was trained via a dynamically weighted averaging (DWA) technique to balance each task. Thereby not allowing one task to dominate over the other or negatively impact the performance of the other. This approach was proposed and utilized for training a multi-task computer vision network (Liu et al., 2019), we followed a similar approach and implemented this on language processing task to show overall improvement in performance. Similar to Gradnorm (Chen et al., 2018) which learns to average tasks over time, the DWA method does not use the gradients of network rather uses numeric task loss. The weighting λ_j for task j is defined as:

$$\lambda_j = \frac{K \exp(w_j(n-1)/T)}{\sum_i \exp(w_i(n-1)/T)} \quad (2)$$

where

$$w_j(n-1) = \frac{L_j(n-1)}{L_j(n-2)} \quad (3)$$

L_j is the loss function of each task j, so w_j is the ratio of loss function over the last two epochs. T represents the temperature, which is used to represent the softness of task weighting. A higher value of T represents a more even distribution between the tasks, when T is high enough, the value of λ_j equals 1. K is the total number of the tasks that we are training for. The overall loss is the sum of the individual task loss averaged over each iteration.

$$L_{ovrl} = \frac{\lambda_1 L_{pr} + \lambda_2 L_{lc} + \lambda_3 L_{tm}}{batchsize} \quad (4)$$

where L_{pr} - Maximum Likelihood loss for Punctuation restoration, L_{lc} - Cross Entorpy loss for Language Classification and L_{tm} - Cross entropy loss for text mode classification.

3.2 Results

To evaluate the performance of our joint model, we built different multilingual neural models. We split our dataset into two parts — train set (80%),validation set (10%) and test set (10%). The performance for every model was evaluated on test set, after being trained on the train set. We chose F1-score to evaluate the performance of our model. We established a baseline using BILSTM-CRF and pretrained FastText word embeddings (Bojanowski et al., 2017) as features and trained jointly on language and text mode classification tasks. The FastText word embeddings used as features for training are monolingual. To train multilingual models, we developed cross lingual embeddings by aligning monolingual embeddings of different languages along a single dimension using unsupervised techniques (Chen and Cardie, 2018). The parameters and training setup of the baseline was similar to the proposed model, except we used FastText based word embeddings as input features. Further we make comparisons using MBERT and XLM-Roberta as pretrained models. Table 2 shows the performance of the various models on high resource European languages along with their F1 scores. To ensure a fairer comparison, we implemented the trained model by Alam et al. (2020) that achieved state of art performance on IWSLT datasets to evaluate on our test set. The Joint-Multilingual BERT NCRF as proposed in section 2.3 outperforms the other models across spoken and written text for all punctuations. We observe German language performs the best across spoken and written text. The performance of the German language can be attributed to a couple of reasons. In German multiple words can be condensed into a single word. This reduces ambiguity and thus there are fewer decision points for the machine to provide inference on. German is an inflected language i.e the word order changes according to the function in the sentence. Most word orders are

Model	Language	TextMode	Period	Comma	Question	Overall
Joint - BILSTM NCRF + FastText	Hindi	Spoken	84.8	47.0	47.6	59.6
		Written	89.2	34.7	55.2	59.7
	Tamil	Spoken	59.8	40.3	19.4	39.8
		Written	47.2	24.9	14.9	29.0
Joint - XLMRoberta NCRF	Hindi	Spoken	88.7	67.3	41.1	65.6
		Written	92.3	70.8	43.4	68.5
	Tamil	Spoken	75.9	58.7	20.3	56.6
		Written	70.5	43.6	20.3	44.8
Joint - Multilingual BERT NCRF	Hindi	Spoken	90.6	66.6	68.8	**75.3**
		Written	93.7	74.9	59.6	**76.1**
	Tamil	Spoken	85.3	71.8	66.6	**74.6**
		Written	74.8	50.1	43.1	**56.0**

Table 3: Results on low resource languages

defined in terms of finite verb (V), in combination with Subject (S), and object (O). In German, this can vary according to independent or dependent clauses. In cases of independent clauses, the main verb must be the second element in the sentence (SVO) and the past participle the final element. Under dependent clauses, the object must be the second element in the sentence (SOV). This may provide an additional signal to model and that can impact its performance.

Models	F1-Score
DRNN-LWMA-pre (Kim, 2019)	68.6
Self-Attention (Yi and Tao, 2019)	72.9
BERT-Adversarial (Yi et al., 2020)	77.8
Joint M-BERT (Our Model)	**80.3**
XLM-R Augmented (Alam et al., 2020)	82.9

Table 4: Performance of the Joint Model on the IWSLT Ref dataset in comparison with other models. The table indicates the average F1 Scores.

To asses the ability of our model to generalize, we evaluated our best performing model on the reference transcripts of the IWSLT dataset. Even though our model was not trained specifically using these datasets, but was able to outperform on some of the prior state of art models as shown in Table 4. The metrics shown refer to the average F1-score. The performance of our proposed models was carried out on the low resource languages for spoken and written transcripts, which can be observed in Table 3 . We obtained the best result using the Joint-Multilingual BERT NCRF model. For low resource languages the performance of *Question* is lower than the *Comma* and *Period*, due to lower number of questions in true label set.

3.3 Ablation Studies

Models	HRL	LRL
BILSTM-NCRF	66.3	32.3
M-BERT-NCRF	73.5	41.6
M-BERT-BILSTM	78.3	52.4
M-BERT-BILSTM NCRF W/O Weighting Layers	82.6	63.1
M-BERT-BILSTM NCRF W/O Classification layers	84.8	65.2
Our Model	**88.0**	**70.5**

Table 5: Ablation Study on our dataset. HRL - High Resource Languages, LRL - Low resource languages

We experimented with different ablations of the best performing model, as seen in table 5 .

- **BILSTM-NCRF** - We do not consider any embeddings and train a simple BILSTM-NCRF model.
- **MBERT-NCRF** - We removed the BILSTM layer and use only NCRF layer on top of transformers.
- **MBERT-BILSTM** - We remove the NCRF layer and model only the token dependencies.
- **Without weighted layers** - We removed the trainable weighing parameters and considered

only the top layer of the transformer as input to the BILSTM.

- **Without classification layers** - We removed the classification layers and trained the model without any auxillary information.

4 Conclusion

In this paper we described and implemented a joint modeling approach for restoring punctuation for High and low resource languages across spoken and written text. Joint language model trained with auxiliary language and text mode classification improved the performance of the APR task. We achieved reasonable performance on the benchmark IWSLT datasets without being trained on it. We also presented a web extension that can help multilingual users improve overall readability and coherence of text. Further we present baseline results on indic languages that can be used for future work. We have shown examples of punctuated text that was output from our system in the Appendix section.

5 Acknowledgement

We would like to thank Palo Alto Research Center for providing compute resources and Sebastian Safari for providing valuable help in developing the web extension.

References

Tanvirul Alam, Akib Khan, and Firoj Alam. 2020. Punctuation restoration using transformer models for high-and low-resource languages. In *Proceedings of the Sixth Workshop on Noisy User-generated Text (W-NUT 2020)*, pages 132–142, Online. Association for Computational Linguistics.

Fernando Batista, Diamantino Caseiro, Nuno Mamede, and Isabel Trancoso. 2007. Recovering punctuation marks for automatic speech recognition. In *Eighth Annual Conference of the International Speech Communication Association*.

Piotr Bojanowski, Edouard Grave, Armand Joulin, and Tomas Mikolov. 2017. Enriching word vectors with subword information. *Transactions of the Association for Computational Linguistics*, 5:135–146.

Xilun Chen and Claire Cardie. 2018. Unsupervised multilingual word embeddings. In *Proceedings of the 2018 Conference on Empirical Methods in Natural Language Processing*, pages 261–270, Brussels, Belgium. Association for Computational Linguistics.

Zhao Chen, Vijay Badrinarayanan, Chen-Yu Lee, and Andrew Rabinovich. 2018. Gradnorm: Gradient normalization for adaptive loss balancing in deep multitask networks. In *International Conference on Machine Learning*, pages 794–803. PMLR.

Heidi Christensen, Yoshihiko Gotoh, and Steve Renals. 2001. Punctuation annotation using statistical prosody models.

Jacob Devlin, Ming-Wei Chang, Kenton Lee, and Kristina Toutanova. 2018. Bert: Pre-training of deep bidirectional transformers for language understanding. *arXiv preprint arXiv:1810.04805*.

Seokhwan Kim. 2019. Deep recurrent neural networks with layer-wise multi-head attentions for punctuation restoration. In *ICASSP 2019-2019 IEEE International Conference on Acoustics, Speech and Signal Processing (ICASSP)*, pages 7280–7284. IEEE.

Ondřej Klejch, Peter Bell, and Steve Renals. 2017. Sequence-to-sequence models for punctuated transcription combining lexical and acoustic features. In *2017 IEEE International Conference on Acoustics, Speech and Signal Processing (ICASSP)*, pages 5700–5704. IEEE.

Jáchym Kolář and Lori Lamel. 2012. Development and evaluation of automatic punctuation for french and english speech-to-text. In *Thirteenth Annual Conference of the International Speech Communication Association*.

Taku Kudo and John Richardson. 2018. Sentencepiece: A simple and language independent subword tokenizer and detokenizer for neural text processing. *arXiv preprint arXiv:1808.06226*.

Shikun Liu, Edward Johns, and Andrew J Davison. 2019. End-to-end multi-task learning with attention. In *Proceedings of the IEEE Conference on Computer Vision and Pattern Recognition*, pages 1871–1880.

Yang Liu, Nitesh V Chawla, Mary P Harper, Elizabeth Shriberg, and Andreas Stolcke. 2006. A study in machine learning from imbalanced data for sentence boundary detection in speech. *Computer Speech & Language*, 20(4):468–494.

Matthew E Peters, Mark Neumann, Mohit Iyyer, Matt Gardner, Christopher Clark, Kenton Lee, and Luke Zettlemoyer. 2018. Deep contextualized word representations. *arXiv preprint arXiv:1802.05365*.

Shashank Siripragada, Jerin Philip, Vinay P Namboodiri, and CV Jawahar. 2020. A multilingual parallel corpora collection effort for indian languages. *arXiv preprint arXiv:2007.07691*.

Ottokar Tilk and Tanel Alumäe. 2015. Lstm for punctuation restoration in speech transcripts. In *Sixteenth annual conference of the international speech communication association*.

Ottokar Tilk and Tanel Alumäe. 2016. Bidirectional recurrent neural network with attention mechanism for punctuation restoration. In *Interspeech*, pages 3047–3051.

Eva Vanmassenhove and Christian Hardmeier. 2018. Europarl datasets with demographic speaker information.

Jie Yang and Yue Zhang. 2018. Ncrf++: An open-source neural sequence labeling toolkit. *arXiv preprint arXiv:1806.05626*.

Jiangyan Yi and J. Tao. 2019. Self-attention based model for punctuation prediction using word and speech embeddings. *ICASSP 2019 - 2019 IEEE International Conference on Acoustics, Speech and Signal Processing (ICASSP)*, pages 7270–7274.

Jiangyan Yi, Jianhua Tao, Ye Bai, Zhengkun Tian, and Cunhang Fan. 2020. Adversarial transfer learning for punctuation restoration. *arXiv preprint arXiv:2004.00248*.

A Example Appendix

We present a few examples of text passed to our system in Table 6 and Figure 3 as seen in the next page. It contains two columns - 'Input Text' & 'Output Text'. The 'Input Text' columns consists of unpunctuated examples that was passed to our system, while the 'Output Text' column is the punctuated text that was returned. The highlighted colors of punctuation marks indicate whether the punctuation was replaced correctly or not. Green indicates the correct punctuation restored, red indicates the incorrect punctuation mark and yellow indicates the missed punctuation mark.

Input Text	Output Text
japan then laid siege to the syrian penalty area for most of the game but rarely breached the syrian defence oleg shatskiku made sure of the win in injury time hitting an unstoppable left foot shot from just outside the area	Japan then laid siege to the syrian penalty area for most of the game ,but rarely breached the syrian defence .Oleg shatskiku made sure of the win in injury time ,hitting an unstoppable left foot shot from just outside the area .
russia's refusal to support emergency supply cuts would effectively and fatally undermine OPEC+'s ability to play the role of oil price stabilizing swing producer says Rapidan Energy's Bob McNally	Russia's refusal to support emergency supply cuts would effectively and fatally undermine OPEC +'s ability to play the role of oil price stabilizing | Swing producer , says Rapidan Energy's Bob McNally .
Romeo Romeo wherefore art thou Romeo	Romeo , Romeo | wherefore art thou Romeo ?
sans préjuger de l'efficacité de ce couvre-feu avancé ces données ne sont toutefois pas si facilement lisibles selon les experts suivant l'épidémie de Covid-19 Tout d'abord on manque encore de recul	Sans préjuger de l'efficacité de ce couvre-feu avancé, ces données ne sont toutefois pas si facilement lisibles , selon les experts | suivant l'épidémie de Covid-19 . Tout d'abord , on manque encore de recul .

Table 6: Examples of automatic punctuation restoration of text in our system for European languages.

Input	Output
आखिरी ओवर का खेल शेष था उससे ठीक पहले ऑस्ट्रेलियाई कप्तान टिम पेन ने हार मान ली भारत ने ऐतिहासिक ड्रॉ खेला यह ड्रॉ किसी जीत से कम नहीं चोट से जूझती हुए भारतीय खिलाड़ियों ने विषम हालातों में मैच बचाया	आखिरी ओवर का खेल शेष था, उससे ठीक पहले ऑस्ट्रेलियाई कप्तान टिम पेन ने हार मान ली। भारत ने ऐतिहासिक ड्रॉ खेला। यह ड्रॉ किसी जीत से कम नहीं। चोट से जूझती हुए भारतीय खिलाड़ियों ने विषम हालातों में मैच बचाया।
கோவிஷீல்டு கோவாக்சினை யார் யாருக்கு எந்த தடுப்பூசிகளை போடுவது என்பது பற்றி இதுவரை முடிவு செய்யவில்லை தடுப்பூசி தொடர்பாக மத்திய அரசு தொடர்ந்து வழிகாட்டு நெறிமுறைகள் வழங்கி வருகிறது புனேயில் இருந்து காலை 10:30 மணிக்கு கொரோனா தடுப்பு மருந்து சென்னை விமான நிலையம் வருகிறது	கோவிஷீல்டு, கோவாக்சினை யார் யாருக்கு எந்த தடுப்பூசிகளை போடுவது என்பது பற்றி இதுவரை முடிவு செய்யவில்லை. தடுப்பூசி தொடர்பாக மத்திய அரசு தொடர்ந்து வழிகாட்டு நெறிமுறைகள் வழங்கி வருகிறது புனேயில். இருந்து காலை 10:30 மணிக்கு கொரோனா தடுப்பு மருந்து சென்னை விமான நிலையம் வருகிறது.

Figure 3: Indic language example

Conversational Agent for Daily Living Assessment Coaching Demo

Aditya Gaydhani*
Dept. of Computer Science and Engineering
University of Minnesota
gaydh001@umn.edu

Raymond Finzel*
Dept. of Pharmaceutical Care & Health Systems
University of Minnesota
finze006@umn.edu

Sheena Dufresne
Dept. of Experimental and Clinical Pharmacology
University of Minnesota
gahmx008@umn.edu

Maria Gini
Dept. of Computer Science and Engineering
University of Minnesota
gini@umn.edu

Serguei VS Pakhomov
Dept. of Pharmaceutical Care & Health Systems
University of Minnesota
pakh0002@umn.edu

Abstract

Conversational Agent for Daily Living Assessment Coaching (CADLAC) is a multi-modal conversational agent system designed to impersonate "individuals" with various levels of ability in activities of daily living (ADLs: e.g., dressing, bathing, mobility, etc.) for use in training professional assessors how to conduct interviews to determine one's level of functioning. The system is implemented on the MindMeld platform for conversational AI and features a Bidirectional Long Short-Term Memory topic tracker that allows the agent to navigate conversations spanning 18 different ADL domains, a dialogue manager that interfaces with a database of over 10,000 historical ADL assessments, a rule-based Natural Language Generation (NLG) module, and a pre-trained open-domain conversational sub-agent (based on GPT-2) for handling conversation turns outside of the 18 ADL domains. CADLAC is delivered via state-of-the-art web frameworks to handle multiple conversations and users simultaneously and is enabled with voice interface. The paper includes a description of the system design and evaluation of individual components followed by a brief discussion of current limitations and next steps.

1 Introduction

A person's ability to function independently in everyday life depends on multiple factors including, but not limited to, intact physical and mental capacity. In the United States, significant public resources are dedicated to providing assistance to those in need. A key aspect of assistance programs is to provide ongoing assessment of individuals to determine their level of functioning (e.g. independent, needs supervision, needs physical assistance, or dependent) and their specific needs in order to provide assistance appropriately. These assessments are conducted by certified assessors specifically trained for this purpose. A challenge in the assessment process is to ensure consistency across large numbers of assessors with various degrees of experience and interview skills and to prepare novice assessors for the variety of interactions they will experience in the field. The Conversational Agent for Daily Living Assessment Coaching (CADLAC) is designed to coach certified assessors to conduct their assessment interviews in a natural conversational style that simulates real interactions. Previously, dialogue systems similar to CADLAC have been developed (Campillos Llanos et al., 2015; Nirenburg et al., 2008; Jaffe et al., 2015; Laleye et al., 2020). These systems simulate "Virtual Patients", which are used in healthcare education. CADLAC is tailored to support novel application domains of function and disability. An example of the interaction with the conversational agent is shown in Figure 1. The interface and a video highlighting the system can be found here [1] [2].

2 Data

We used two sources of data in order to inform CADLAC system design, train machine learning models, and to develop a database to support rule-based approaches used by the system. One source of data consisted of a survey that was administered to certified assessors, and the other consisted

*Equal contribution.

[1]Demo: https://rxinformatics.net/cadlac
[2]Video: https://vimeo.com/500734362

Proceedings of the 16th Conference of the European Chapter of the Association for Computational Linguistics: System Demonstrations, pages 321–328
April 19 - 23, 2021. ©2021 Association for Computational Linguistics

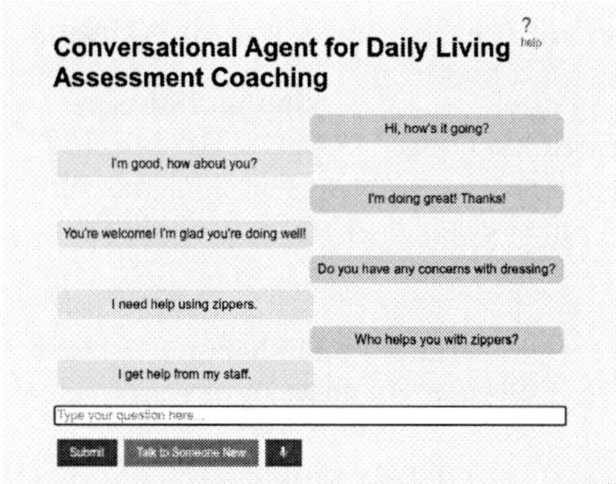

Figure 1: Example of interaction with the conversational agent.

Domain:	Grooming
Ability:	Physical Assistance
Assessor-1:	"Can you tell me about how you take care of your grooming needs?" *intent - generic*
Participant-1:	"I have a hard time."
Assessor-2:	"Can you brush your hair?" *intent - challenges*
Participant-2:	"No, I can't reach my hair to get it brushed in the back."
Assessor-3:	"Who helps you to brush your hair?" *intent - helper*
Participant-3:	"My daughter helps me to brush my hair."
Age:	65-84
Gender:	Female

Table 1: Example dialogue from the survey.

of anonymized historical assessment data shared by the Minnesota Department of Human Services (DHS).

2.1 Survey Data

We designed a survey to collect sample dialogues from certified assessors. This survey was administered to approximately 1,700 assessors statewide. The assessors were asked to recall some of their past assessments and provide examples of interactions that they had with people during the assessment interviews. Specifically, each example consists of up to 3 dialogue turns between the assessor and the person being interviewed, the gender and age category of the person, domain of the conversation, and the person's ability level within the domain. The data consists of assessments of activities of daily living (ADLs - e.g., walking) and instrumental activities of daily living (iADLS - e.g., paying bills) in 18 functional domains related to personal cares, movement, household management, and eating/meal preparation. We also manually annotated the assessor questions for 6 intents: challenges, preferences, equipment, helper, generic, and frequency. We were able to collect a total of 2,885 dialogues through the survey. A sample record from the resulting dataset, including the annotations for intents, is shown in Table 1.

2.2 Synthetic Profiles

CADLAC relies on a database of over 10,000 historical assessments, conducted by experienced certified assessors and managed by Minnesota DHS. Each historical assessment contains fields that indicate the person's ability to function in ADLs and iADLs in addition to basic demographic information such as age range and sex of the person being assessed. It also contains certified assessors' notes taken during the assessments. These notes represent very brief descriptions of the assessed person's challenges, preferences, and equipment they use to help them, among other information organized by the ADL and iADL domain.

Historical data was anonymized by DHS staff for inclusion in CADLAC by removing any individually identifiable information including individuals' names and exact age information that was converted to age ranges. Furthermore, sensitive personal information such as phone number, email, location, etc. was excluded from the historical data, keeping the privacy of the individuals protected.

These anonymized historical assessments are used to generate synthetic profiles of "individuals" that specify varying levels of independence in everyday functioning and specific needs. These profiles are created by mapping the categorical attributes related to the independence levels in the historical assessment to those levels specified for the conversational agent (CA). Additionally, assessor notes about challenges, preferences, and equipment from the historical data were populated in the synthetic profiles.

The profiles are used to customize the CA and generate natural language responses that are tailored to the question asked by the assessor and are as consistent as possible with all of the information in the profile. For example, if the synthetic profile states that the individual being assessed is completely dependent on external assistance in the mobility domain, the responses generated by CADLAC to a question about the ability to perform heavy housekeeping should not indicate any degree of independence in this domain either. The profiles include a numeric representation of the independence level of the "person" represented by the profile. These numeric representations are used to compare assessments produced by novice assessors using CADLAC for training to those produced by experienced assessors, and to provide summary feedback about the assessment.

Despite the fact that these profiles are based on data from real individuals assessed in the state of Minnesota, the profiles may potentially convey biases present in the underlying data. In order to minimize potential systematic bias, the historical data used to construct the profiles were randomly sampled from a diverse population of assessed individuals with equal proportions by sex and with the following race distribution: 17.1% African American; 2.4% American Indian; Asian or Pacific Islander 7.7%; Hispanic 2.6%; White 64.4%; Two or more races 1.1%; and Unknown race 4.6%. The current prototype of CADLAC does not use race information; however, this information is available in the underlying data and can be used to adjust the composition of the synthetic profile database as needed for assessor training purposes.

3 System Design

CADLAC is implemented on the MindMeld platform for conversational AI applications (Raghuvanshi et al., 2018) that relies on a commonly used modular dialogue system design consisting broadly of natural language understanding (NLU), natural language generation (NLG) and a dialogue state tracker/manager (DM) components. These components of CADLAC prototype have been developed using a hybrid machine learning and rule-based approaches. The prototype is currently deployed via a web service written in Python with the modern asynchronous web Responder framework. This web service is responsible for accepting requests from a user-facing web client, managing user sessions, and passing conversation objects into the Dialogue Parser. The web-based client supports text-only, voice-only or hybrid modalities. This demonstration will focus on showing the natural dialogue between human users and CADLAC aimed

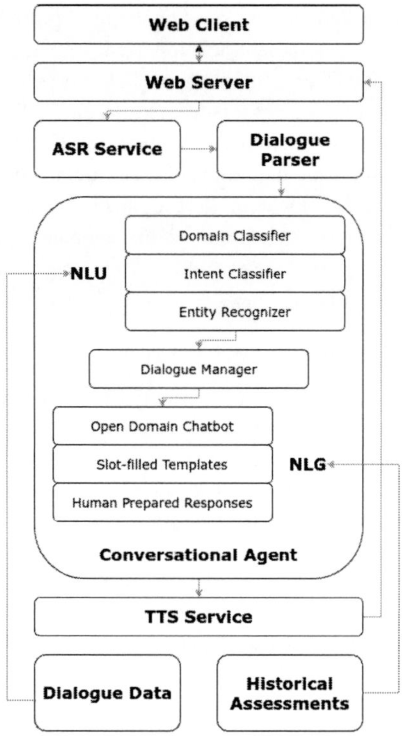

Figure 2: CADLAC system architecture.

at assessing the level of functioning of the "individual" impersonated by CADLAC and the feedback provided to the users regarding their assessments. The system architecture is shown in Figure 2.

4 Natural Language Understanding

4.1 Domain Classifier

The domain classifier (a.k.a. topic tracker) categorizes the input query into one of 18 domains related to ADLs and iADLs, as well as two additional domains: "generic follow-up question" and "unsupported". CADLAC's domain recognizer comprises a BiLSTM neural network (Hochreiter and Schmidhuber, 1997) that we trained on available survey data using GloVe embeddings (Pennington et al., 2014) to represent the semantics of input tokens. We evaluated this model using 10-fold cross-validation resulting in a mean f-score of 0.801 and an accuracy of 0.830 across all domains.

4.2 Intent Classifier

Next, the NLU module recognizes the intent of the user query. In our case, each domain has the following intents that reflect the nature of the questions asked by assessors: challenges, preferences, generic, equipment, unsupported, helper, and frequency. These intents specify the type of information that the assessor wants to elicit. We used the survey data to train an intent classifier for each domain using the same BiLSTM architecture that we used for the domain recognizer. The results of 10-fold cross-validation for this component consist of a range of f-scores from 0.704 to 0.927 that vary by domain.

4.3 Named Entity Recognizer

We also trained a Named Entity Recognizer to identify the words or phrases, referred to as "entities", present in the input query (e.g., shirt, shoes, pants are entities in the dressing domain). These entities are then used to fill the empty slots in the natural language response or select an appropriate response from the knowledge base. We also use a rule-based language parser within MindMeld to model the dependencies between the recognized entities.

4.4 Dialogue Manager

The dialogue manager consists of the dialogue state tracker, which maps the input query to appropriate dialogue states. Each dialogue state is responsible for handling a particular type of query. We use a rule-based and pattern matching procedure, which depends on the domain and the intent of the input query, to define the dialogue states. One of the important functionalities of the CA is to handle follow-up questions as illustrated in Figure 3. For this purpose, we use the domain of the previous turn and make a transition to the dialogue state specified by the intent of the current turn. If the intent of the question is unsupported, then we use the intent of the previous turn and the domain of the current turn, and make a transition to the corresponding dialogue state. The unsupported queries are handled by the neural model based on GPT-2 (Zhang et al., 2020) as illustrated in Figure 4.

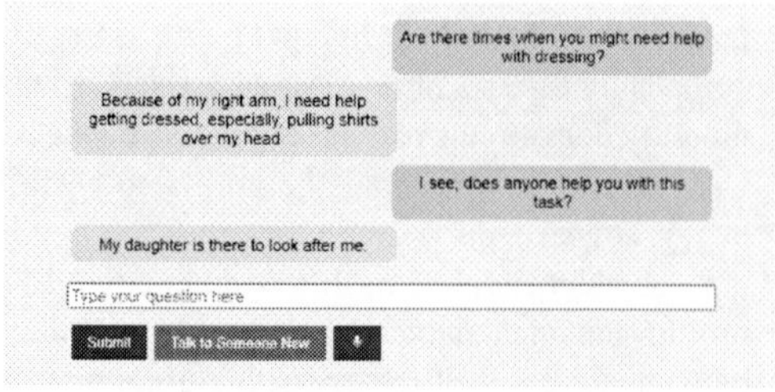

Figure 3: Response to a follow-up question. The second question of the conversation refers to the previous domain of dressing.

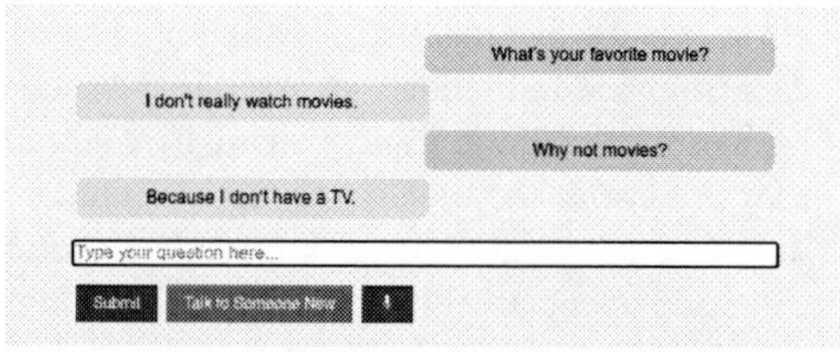

Figure 4: Response to off-topic questions.

5 Natural Language Generation

We use a rule-based approach in which we first look up a field in the knowledge-base of historical assessments that corresponds to the identified topic and intent for a specific synthetic profile (e.g., challenges[intent] with dressing[domain]). Information contained in historical assessments is underspecified and is not usable as a natural language response. For example, it may contain a note "Behavioral issues" for challenges with dressing. We manually annotated a subset of over 100 assessments, where the annotators were instructed to become familiar with the person's level of functioning in various domains and use that knowledge to convert the historical notes to a format that would sound more natural yet still consistent with the synthetic profile (e.g., "Behavioral issues" note for a 5 year old child's assessment would be converted to "He can't dress by himself because he throws a tantrum each time he has to change clothes.") The current prototype of CADLAC's dialogue manager queries the knowledge base for these manually converted responses and returns a response that most closely matches the named entities mentioned in the user's question. If no natural language response is found, CADLAC generates a generic response randomly chosen from a set of responses consistent with the synthetic profile (e.g., for a profile of a person who requires intermittent physical assistance with dressing, the response may be "I need someone to help me with this"). We are currently experimenting with transformer neural models used in machine translation in order to determine if they can "learn" the mapping between the original historical assessment notes and the natural language responses; however, the current demo does not include these models yet.

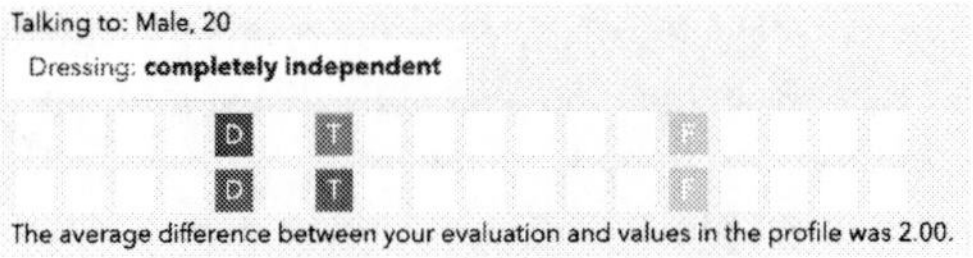

Figure 5: Assessment feedback. Top row shows values in the profile only for those domains assessed up to a checkpoint. Bottom row shows user-selected assessments.

6 Feedback

The feedback to users being trained to perform assessments is provided via a visual interface designed to compare users' assessments to those stored in synthetic profiles as illustrated in Figure 5.

7 Voice Services

In order to enable voice input-output capabilities in CADLAC we implemented a Automatic Speech Recognition (ASR) and a Text-to-Speech (TTS) web services. Both services are implemented using PyTorch.

Voice activity is streamed from the web client to the web server in real time using an implementation of WebRTC peer connections. The WebRTC protocols are available in most modern browsers, and include hooks to access media devices, standards for establishing peer connections, and asynchronous data channels. The implementation of WebRTC that was used for the python web server was AIORTC.

After voice data arrive at the server they are passed to the ASR service, which transcribes English words from the speech utterance. These words take the place of the text from the chat interface for the rest of the conversational turn.

7.1 ASR Service

We trained an ASR system based on Baidu's Deep Speech 2 architecture (Amodei et al., 2016) implemented in PyTorch [3] consisting of 3 convolutional neural network (CNN) layers, followed by 5 bidirectional recurrent neural network (RNN) layers with gated recurrent units (GRU), a single lookeahead convolution layer followed by a fully connected layer and a single softmax layer. The system was trained using the Connectionist Temporal Classification (CTC) loss function (Graves et al., 2006). In addition to the default greedy search decoding over the hypotheses produced by the softmax layer, the system's implementation also can use a beam search decoder with a standard n-gram language model. We used default hyperparameters: size of the RNN layers was set to 800 GRU units; starting learning rate was set to 0.0003 with the annealing parameter set to 1.1 and momentum of 0.9. Audio signal processing consisted of transforming the audio from the time to the frequency domain via Short-time Fourier transform as implemented by the Python librosa library. The signal was sampled in frames of 20 milliseconds overlapping by 10 miliseconds. The resulting input vectors to the first CNN layer of the Deep Speech 2 network consisted of 160 values representing the power spectrum of each frame.

A collection of speech corpora available from the Linguistic Data Consortium was used as training data. These corpora include the Wall Street Journal (WSJ: LDC93S6A, LDC94S13B), Resource Management (RM - LDC93S3A), TIMIT (LDC93S1), FFMTIMIT (LDC96S32), DCIEM/HCRC (LDC96S38), USC-SFI MALACH corpus (LDC2019S11), Switchboard-1 (LDC97S62), and Fisher (LDC2004S13, LDC2005S13). In addition to these corpora, we used the following publicly available data: TalkBank (CMU, ISL, SBCSAE collections) (MacWhinney and Wagner, 2010), Common Voice (CV: Version 1.0)) corpus [4], Voxforge corpus [5], TED-LIUM corpus (Release 2) (Rousseau et al., 2014), LibriSpeech(Panayotov et al., 2015), Flicker8K(Hodosh et al., 2013), CSTR VCTK corpus (Veaux et al., 2017), and the Spoken Wikipedia Corpus (SWC-English(Köhn et al., 2016)). Audio samples from all of these these data sources were split into pieces shorter than 25 seconds in duration. The total size of the resulting corpus was approximately 4,991 hours of audio (2,000 hours contributed by the Fisher corpus alone). Finally, we also used audio data from various prior studies that were conducted at the University of Minnesota consisting of story recall, verbal fluency, and spontaneous narrative tasks. With the exception of the Fisher and Switchboard corpora, all other data were recorded at a minimum of 16 kHz sampling frequency. The Fisher and Switchboard corpora contain narrow-band telephone conversations sampled

[3] https://github.com/SeanNaren/deepspeech.pytorch

[4] http://voice.mozilla.org

[5] http://www.voxforge.org/

at 8 KHz. All data were either downsampled or upsampled and converted using the SoX toolkit[6] to a single channel 16 bit 16 kHz PCM WAVE format.

The performance of the ASR service was evaluated off-line using the heldout portion of the TED-LIUM corpus. Without using a language model for rescoring the output of the neural model (greedy decoding), the word error rate (WER) and character error rate (CER) of our ASR system were 18.84 and 5.24, which are comparable to those previously reported for the same dataset also using a Deep Speech 2 system (WER: 28.1, CER: 9.2) (Hernandez et al., 2018). Using a 4-gram language model constructed with the SRILM Toolkit (Stolcke, 2002) from the English language portion of the 1 Billion words text corpus[7] model with Kneser-Ney smoothing (Ney et al., 1994) resulted in improving ASR accuracy to WER: 15.73 and CER: 4.57.

7.2 TTS Service

We used a pre-trained model based on Tacotron2 (Shen et al., 2017) and WaveGlow (Prenger et al., 2018) for the text-to-speech service. This model was implemented in PyTorch and is based on the NVIDIA's GitHub repositories for Tacotron2 [8] and WaveGlow [9]. The Tacotron2 model converts the input text to mel spectrograms and then the WaveGlow model uses the mel spectrograms to generate speech. The Tacotron2 implementation used here slightly differs from the one described in by Shen et al. (2017): it uses Dropout (Srivastava et al., 2014) regularization instead of Zoneout (Krueger et al., 2016) for the LSTM layers, and replaces the WaveNet model with the WaveGlow model. The models are trained on the LJ Speech (Ito and Johnson, 2017) dataset using mixed precision training (Micikevicius et al., 2017).

The above model generates speech in female voice since it is trained on the LJ Speech dataset, which has voice samples from a single female speaker. However, our system has synthetic profiles for both males and females. In order to generate speech for a male profile, the current implementation relies on pitch manipulation techniques. Specifically, we use the phonetics software Praat (Boersma and Weenink, 2018) through the library Parselmouth (Jadoul et al., 2018), which exposes the functionality and algorithms of Praat in Python. To change the female voice to a male voice, we set the parameter *formant shift ratio* to 0.85 and *new pitch median* to 100 Hz. The formant shift ratio determines the frequencies of the formants and the new pitch median determines the median pitch of the male voice. Using these specific values of the parameters gives us the best results. However, we are currently exploring ways to retrain the Tacotron2 and WaveGlow model on a male voice dataset to generate better quality outputs.

8 Limitations and Future Steps

One of the limitations of the current implementation of CADLAC is that it does not currently learn from user input. One of the next key steps in further development of this system is to implement active learning components for domain and intent classification, ASR, and other supervised components of the system. We are also currently developing a formal evaluation of the usability of this system with human end-users. Specifically, we plan to use metrics of sensibility and specificity for each system response as proposed by Adiwardana et al. (2020) in addition to overall subjective measures of dialogue success, conversation naturalness, and intelligibility of responses. We also plan to evaluate the system for any potential bias in responses generated by the system and develop ways of un-biasing the system via hybrid rule-based and data-driven approaches (Liu et al., 2020).

9 Acknowledgements

The work on this project was supported by funding from the Minnesota Department of Human Services. We would like to thank the people at DSD and MNIT for help with project specifications, gathering of historical data, and expert guidance on domain-specific aspects of the project. We would also like to thank Pamela Miller, Sidney Kiltie, and Elise Moore for help with transforming certified assessor notes to natural language format and Julia Garbuz for helping to develop and conduct the surveys of DHS assessors.

[6] `http://sox.sourceforge.net`

[7] `https://github.com/ciprian-chelba/1-billion-word-language-modeling-benchmark`

[8] `https://github.com/NVIDIA/tacotron2`

[9] `https://github.com/NVIDIA/waveglow`

References

Daniel Adiwardana, Minh-Thang Luong, David R. So, Jamie Hall, Noah Fiedel, Romal Thoppilan, Zi Yang, Apoorv Kulshreshtha, Gaurav Nemade, Yifeng Lu, and Quoc V. Le. 2020. Towards a human-like open-domain chatbot.

Dario Amodei, Sundaram Ananthanarayanan, Rishita Anubhai, Jingliang Bai, Eric Battenberg, Carl Case, Jared Casper, Bryan Catanzaro, Qiang Cheng, Guoliang Chen, Jie Chen, Jingdong Chen, Zhijie Chen, Mike Chrzanowski, Adam Coates, Greg Diamos, Ke Ding, Niandong Du, Erich Elsen, Jesse Engel, Weiwei Fang, Linxi Fan, Christopher Fougner, Liang Gao, Caixia Gong, Awni Hannun, Tony Han, Lappi Vaino Johannes, Bing Jiang, Cai Ju, Billy Jun, Patrick LeGresley, Libby Lin, Junjie Liu, Yang Liu, Weigao Li, Xiangang Li, Dongpeng Ma, Sharan Narang, Andrew Ng, Sherjil Ozair, Yiping Peng, Ryan Prenger, Sheng Qian, Zongfeng Quan, Jonathan Raiman, Vinay Rao, Sanjeev Satheesh, David Seetapun, Shubho Sengupta, Kavya Srinet, Anuroop Sriram, Haiyuan Tang, Liliang Tang, Chong Wang, Jidong Wang, Kaifu Wang, Yi Wang, Zhijian Wang, Zhiqian Wang, Shuang Wu, Likai Wei, Bo Xiao, Wen Xie, Yan Xie, Dani Yogatama, Bin Yuan, Jun Zhan, and Zhenyao Zhu. 2016. Deep speech 2: End-to-end speech recognition in english and mandarin. In *Proceedings of the 33rd International Conference on International Conference on Machine Learning - Volume 48*, ICML'16, page 173–182. JMLR.org.

Paul Boersma and David Weenink. 2018. Praat: doing phonetics by computer [Computer program]. Version 6.0.37, retrieved 3 February 2018 `http://www.praat.org/`.

Leonardo Campillos Llanos, Dhouha Bouamor, Éric Bilinski, Anne-Laure Ligozat, Pierre Zweigenbaum, and Sophie Rosset. 2015. Description of the PatientGenesys dialogue system. In *Proceedings of the 16th Annual Meeting of the Special Interest Group on Discourse and Dialogue*, pages 438–440, Prague, Czech Republic. Association for Computational Linguistics.

Alex Graves, Santiago Fernández, Faustino Gomez, and Jürgen Schmidhuber. 2006. Connectionist temporal classification: Labelling unsegmented sequence data with recurrent neural networks. In *Proceedings of the 23rd International Conference on Machine Learning*, ICML '06, pages 369–376, New York, NY, USA. ACM.

François Hernandez, Vincent Nguyen, Sahar Ghannay, Natalia Tomashenko, and Yannick Estève. 2018. Ted-lium 3: Twice as much data and corpus repartition for experiments on speaker adaptation. In *Speech and Computer*, pages 198–208, Cham. Springer International Publishing.

Sepp Hochreiter and Jürgen Schmidhuber. 1997. Long short-term memory. *Neural Computation*, 9(8):1735–1780.

M. Hodosh, P. Young, and J. Hockenmaier. 2013. Framing Image Description as a Ranking Task: Data, Models and Evaluation Metrics. *Journal of Artificial Intelligence Research*, 47:853–899.

Keith Ito and Linda Johnson. 2017. The lj speech dataset. `https://keithito.com/LJ-Speech-Dataset/`.

Yannick Jadoul, Bill Thompson, and Bart de Boer. 2018. Introducing Parselmouth: A Python interface to Praat. *Journal of Phonetics*, 71:1–15.

Evan Jaffe, Michael White, William Schuler, Eric Fosler-Lussier, Alex Rosenfeld, and Douglas Danforth. 2015. Interpreting questions with a log-linear ranking model in a virtual patient dialogue system. In *Proceedings of the Tenth Workshop on Innovative Use of NLP for Building Educational Applications*, pages 86–96, Denver, Colorado. Association for Computational Linguistics.

Arne Köhn, Florian Stegen, and Timo Baumann. 2016. Mining the spoken wikipedia for speech data and beyond. In *Proceedings of the Tenth International Conference on Language Resources and Evaluation (LREC 2016)*, Paris, France. European Language Resources Association (ELRA).

David Krueger, Tegan Maharaj, János Kramár, Mohammad Pezeshki, Nicolas Ballas, Nan Rosemary Ke, Anirudh Goyal, Yoshua Bengio, Aaron Courville, and Chris Pal. 2016. Zoneout: Regularizing rnns by randomly preserving hidden activations.

Fréjus A. A. Laleye, Gaël de Chalendar, Antonia Blanié, Antoine Brouquet, and Dan Behnamou. 2020. A French medical conversations corpus annotated for a virtual patient dialogue system. In *Proceedings of the 12th Language Resources and Evaluation Conference*, pages 574–580, Marseille, France. European Language Resources Association.

Haochen Liu, Jamell Dacon, Wenqi Fan, Hui Liu, Zitao Liu, and Jiliang Tang. 2020. Does gender matter? towards fairness in dialogue systems.

Brian MacWhinney and Johannes Wagner. 2010. Transcribing, searching and data sharing: The CLAN software and the TalkBank data repository. *Gesprachsforschung: Online-Zeitschrift Zur Verbalen Interaktion*, 11:154–173.

Paulius Micikevicius, Sharan Narang, Jonah Alben, Gregory Diamos, Erich Elsen, David Garcia, Boris Ginsburg, Michael Houston, Oleksii Kuchaiev, Ganesh Venkatesh, and Hao Wu. 2017. Mixed precision training.

Hermann Ney, Ute Essen, and Reinhard Kneser. 1994. On structuring probabilistic dependencies in stochastic language modelling. *Computer Speech and Language*, 8:1–38.

Sergei Nirenburg, Stephen Beale, Marjorie McShane, Bruce Jarrell, and George Fantry. 2008. Language understanding in Maryland virtual patient. In *Coling 2008: Proceedings of the workshop on Speech Processing for Safety Critical Translation and Pervasive Applications*, pages 36–39, Manchester, UK. Coling 2008 Organizing Committee.

V. Panayotov, G. Chen, D. Povey, and S. Khudanpur. 2015. Librispeech: An asr corpus based on public domain audio books. In *2015 IEEE International Conference on Acoustics, Speech and Signal Processing (ICASSP)*, pages 5206–5210.

Jeffrey Pennington, Richard Socher, and Christopher Manning. 2014. GloVe: Global vectors for word representation. In *Proceedings of the 2014 Conference on Empirical Methods in Natural Language Processing (EMNLP)*, pages 1532–1543, Doha, Qatar. Association for Computational Linguistics.

Ryan Prenger, Rafael Valle, and Bryan Catanzaro. 2018. Waveglow: A flow-based generative network for speech synthesis.

Arushi Raghuvanshi, Lucien Carroll, and Karthik Raghunathan. 2018. Developing production-level conversational interfaces with shallow semantic parsing. In *Proceedings of the 2018 Conference on Empirical Methods in Natural Language Processing: System Demonstrations*, pages 157–162.

Anthony Rousseau, Paul Deléglise, and Yannick Estève. 2014. Enhancing the ted-lium corpus with selected data for language modeling and more ted talks. In *LREC*.

Jonathan Shen, Ruoming Pang, Ron J. Weiss, Mike Schuster, Navdeep Jaitly, Zongheng Yang, Zhifeng Chen, Yu Zhang, Yuxuan Wang, RJ Skerry-Ryan, Rif A. Saurous, Yannis Agiomyrgiannakis, and Yonghui Wu. 2017. Natural tts synthesis by conditioning wavenet on mel spectrogram predictions.

Nitish Srivastava, Geoffrey Hinton, Alex Krizhevsky, Ilya Sutskever, and Ruslan Salakhutdinov. 2014. Dropout: A simple way to prevent neural networks from overfitting. *J. Mach. Learn. Res.*, 15(1):1929–1958.

Andreas Stolcke. 2002. Srilm - an extensible language modeling toolkit. In *INTERSPEECH*.

Christophe Veaux, Junichi Yamagishi, and Kirsten Macdonald. 2017. Cstr vctk corpus: English multi-speaker corpus for cstr voice cloning toolkit.

Yizhe Zhang, Siqi Sun, Michel Galley, Yen-Chun Chen, Chris Brockett, Xiang Gao, Jianfeng Gao, Jingjing Liu, and Bill Dolan. 2020. Dialogpt: Large-scale generative pre-training for conversational response generation. In *ACL, system demonstration*.

HULK: An Energy Efficiency Benchmark Platform for Responsible Natural Language Processing

Xiyou Zhou, Zhiyu Chen, Xiaoyong Jin, William Yang Wang
Department of Computer Science, University of California Santa Barbara
{xiyou, zhiyuchen, x_jin, william}@cs.ucsb.edu

Abstract

Computation-intensive pretrained models have been taking the lead of many natural language processing benchmarks such as GLUE (Wang et al., 2018). However, energy efficiency in the process of model training and inference becomes a critical bottleneck. We introduce HULK, a multi-task energy efficiency benchmarking platform for responsible natural language processing. With HULK, we compare pretrained models' energy efficiency from the perspectives of time and cost. Baseline benchmarking results are provided for further analysis. The fine-tuning efficiency of different pretrained models can differ significantly among different tasks, and fewer parameter number does not necessarily imply better efficiency. We analyzed such a phenomenon and demonstrated the method for comparing the multi-task efficiency of pretrained models. Our platform is available at https://hulkbenchmark.github.io/.

1 Introduction

Environmental concerns of machine learning research have been rising as the carbon emission of specific tasks like neural architecture search reached an exceptional "ocean boiling" level (Strubell et al., 2019). Increased carbon emission has been one of the key factors to aggravate global warming [1]. Research and development processes like parameter search further increase the environmental impact. When using cloud-based machines, the environmental impact is strongly correlated with the financial cost.

The recent emergence of leaderboards such as SQuAD (Rajpurkar et al., 2016), GLUE (Wang et al., 2018), and SuperGLUE (Wang et al., 2019) has greatly boosted the development of advanced models in the NLP community. Pretrained models have proven to be the key ingredient for achieving state-of-the-art in conventional metrics. However, such models can be costly to train. For example, XLNet-Large (Yang et al., 2019) was trained on 512 TPU v3 chips for 500K steps, which costs around 61,440 dollars[2], let alone staggeringly large carbon emission.

Moreover, despite impressive performance gain, the fine-tuning and inference efficiency of NLP models remain under-explored. As recently mentioned in a tweet[3], the popular AI text adventure game *AI Dungeon* has reached 100 million inferences. The energy efficiency of inference cost could be critical to both business planning and environmental impact.

Previous work (Schwartz et al., 2019; Dodge et al., 2019) on this topic proposed new metrics like FPO (floating-point operations) and other practices to report experimental results based on computing budget. Other benchmarks like (Coleman et al., 2017) and (Mattson et al., 2019) compare the efficiency of models on the classic reading comprehension task SQuAD and machine translation tasks. However, there has not been any concrete or practical reference for accurate estimation on NLP model pretraining, fine-tunning, and inference considering multi-task energy efficiency.

Energy efficiency can be reflected in many metrics, including carbon emission, electricity usage, time consumption, number of parameters, and FPO, as shown in (Schwartz et al., 2019). Carbon emission and electricity are intuitive measures yet either hard to track or hardware-dependent. The number of model parameters does not reflect the actual cost for model training and inference. FPO

[1]Source: https://climate.nasa.gov/causes/

[2]Source: The Staggering Cost of Training SOTA AI Models by Synced Global

[3]Source: Nick Walton's Tweet on Passing 100 Million Inferences on AI Dungeon.

Proceedings of the 16th Conference of the European Chapter of the Association for Computational Linguistics: System Demonstrations, pages 329–336
April 19 - 23, 2021. ©2021 Association for Computational Linguistics

Model	Hardware	Time	Cost	Params
BERT$_{BASE}$ (Devlin et al., 2018)	4 TPU v2 Pods	4 days	\$1,728	108M
BERT$_{LARGE}$ (Devlin et al., 2018)	16 TPU v2 Pods	4 days	\$6,912	334M
XLNet$_{BASE}$ (Yang et al., 2019)	–	–	–	117M
XLNet$_{LARGE}$ (Yang et al., 2019)	512 TPU v3	2.5 days	\$61,440	361M
RoBERTa$_{BASE}$ (Liu et al., 2019)	1024 V100 GPUs	1 day	\$75,203	125M
RoBERTa$_{LARGE}$ (Liu et al., 2019)	1024 V100 GPUs	1 day	\$75,203	356M
ALBERT$_{BASE}$ (Lan et al., 2019)	64 TPU v3	–	–	12M
ALBERT$_{XXLARGE}$ (Lan et al., 2019)	1024 TPU v3	32 hours	\$65,536	223M
DistilBERT* (Sanh et al., 2019)	8×16G V100 GPU	90 hours	\$2,203	66M
ELECTRA$_{SMALL}$ (Clark et al., 2020)	1 V100 GPU	96 hours	\$294	14M
ELECTRA$_{BASE}$ (Clark et al., 2020)	16 TPU v3	96 hours	\$3,072	110M

Table 1: Pretraining costs of baseline models. Hardware and pretraining time were collected from original papers, with which costs were estimated with the current TPU price at \$8 per hour with 4 core TPU v3 chips and V100 GPU at \$3.06 per hour. DistilBERT model was trained upon a pretrained BERT model. Parameter numbers are estimated using the pretrained models implemented in the Transformers (`https://github.com/huggingface/transformers`) library (Wolf et al., 2019), shown in millions. The RoBERTa model was trained for 100K steps.

is steady for models but cannot be directly used for cost estimation. Here, to provide a practical reference for model selection on real applications, especially model development outside academia, we keep track of the time consumption and actual financial cost for comparison. Cloud-based machines are employed for budget estimation as they are easily accessible and consistent in hardware configuration, price, and performance. In the following sections, we would use "time" and "cost" to denote the time elapsed and the actual budget in model pretraining, training, and inference.

In most NLP pretrained model settings, there are three phases: pretraining, fine-tuning, and inference. If a model is trained from scratch, we consider such a model has no pretraining phase but is fine-tuned from scratch. Typically pretraining takes several days and hundreds of dollars, according to Table 1. Fine-tuning takes a few minutes to hours, costing much less than the pretraining phase. Inference takes several milliseconds to seconds, similarly costing much less than the fine-tuning phase. Meanwhile, pretraining is done before fine-tuning once for all, while fine-tuning could be performed multiple times as training data updates. Inference is expected to be called numerous times for downstream applications. Such characteristics make it a natural choice to separate different phases during benchmarking.

Our HULK benchmark, as shown in Figure 1, utilizes several classic datasets that have been widely adopted in the community as benchmarking tasks to benchmark energy efficiency. The benchmark compares pretrained models in a multi-task fashion. The tasks include natural language inference task MNLI (Williams et al., 2017), sentiment analysis task SST-2 (Socher et al., 2013) and Named Entity Recognition Task CoNLL-2003 (Sang and De Meulder, 2003). Such tasks are selected to provide a thorough comparison of end-to-end energy efficiency in pretraining, fine-tuning, and inference.

With the HULK benchmark, we quantify the energy efficiency of model pretraining, fine-tuning, and inference phase by comparing the time and cost they require to reach a certain overall task-specific performance level on selected datasets. The design principle and benchmarking process are detailed in section 2. We also explore the relation between model parameters and fine-tuning efficiency and demonstrate energy efficiency consistency between different pretrained models' tasks.

2 Benchmark Overview

For the pretraining phase, the benchmark is designed to favor energy-efficient models in terms of time and cost that each model takes to reach specific multi-task performance pretrained from scratch. For example, we keep track of the time and cost of a BERT model in the following way: After every thousand pretraining steps, we clone the model for fine-tuning and see if the final performance can reach our cut-off performance on different tasks. When the level is reached, time and cost for pretraining are used for comparison. Mod-

	CoNLL 2003	MNLI	SST-2
Train Size	14,041	392,702	67,349
Dev Size	3,250	19,647	872
Cut-off	91	85	90
Metric	F1	Acc	Acc
SOTA	93.5	91.85	97.4

Table 2: Dataset Information

els faster or cheaper to pretrain are recommended.

We consider the time and cost each model takes to reach specific multi-task performance fine-tuned from given pretrained models for the fine-tuning phase. For each task with different difficulty and instance numbers, the fine-tuning characteristics may differ a lot. When pretrained models are used to deal with a non-standard downstream task, especially ad hoc application in industry, the task's fine-tuning time and cost cannot be estimated directly from any other standard task. Therefore, it is essential to compare the multi-task efficiency for model choice.

For the inference phase, each model's time and cost for making inference on a single instance on multiple tasks are compared similarly to the fine-tuning phase. Specially, we estimate the time elapsed for each inference by averaging thousands of inference samples.

2.1 Dataset Overview

The datasets we used are widely adopted in the NLP community. Quantitative details of datasets can be found in Table 2. The selected tasks are shown below:

CoNLL 2003 The Conference on Computational Natural Language Learning (CoNLL-2003) shared task concerns language-independent named entity recognition (Sang and De Meulder, 2003). The task concentrates on four types of named entities: persons, locations, organizations, and other miscellaneous entities. Here we only use the English dataset. The English data is a collection of news wire articles from the Reuters Corpus. The result is reflected as F1 score considering the label accuracy and recall on the dev set.

MNLI The Multi-Genre Natural Language Inference Corpus (Williams et al., 2017) is a crowdsourced collection of sentence pairs with textual entailment annotations. Given a premise sentence and a hypothesis sentence, the task is to predict whether the premise entails the hypothesis (entailment), contradicts the hypothesis (contradiction), or neither (neutral). The premise sentences are gathered from ten different sources, including transcribed speech, fiction, and government reports. The accuracy score is reported as the average of performance on matched and mismatched dev sets.

SST-2 The Stanford Sentiment Treebank (Socher et al., 2013) consists of sentences from movie reviews and human annotations of their sentiment. The task is to predict the sentiment of a given sentence. Following the setting of GLUE, we also use the two-way (positive/negative) class split and use only sentence-level labels.

The tasks are selected based on how representative the dataset is. CoNLL 2003 has been a widely used dataset for named entity recognition and requires the output of token-level labeling. NER is a core NLP task, and CoNLL 2003 has been a classic dataset in this area. SST-2 and MNLI are part of the GLUE benchmark, representing sentence-level labeling tasks. SST-2 has been frequently used in sentiment analysis across different generations of models. MNLI is a newly introduced large dataset for natural language inference. The training time for MNLI is relatively long, and the task requires a lot more training instances. We select the three tasks for a diverse yet practical benchmark for pretrained models without constraining the models on sentence-level classification tasks. Besides, their efficiency differs significantly in the fine-tuning and inference phase. Such a difference can still be reflected in the final score after normalization, as shown in Table 3. Provided with more computing resources, we can bring in more datasets for even more thorough benchmarking in the future. We illustrate the evaluation criteria in the following subsection.

2.2 Evaluation Criteria

In machine learning model training and inference, slight parameter change can subtly impact the final result. To make a practical reference for pretrained model selection, we compare models' end-to-end performance concerning the pretraining time and cost, fine-tuning time and cost, inference time and cost following the setting of (Coleman et al., 2017).

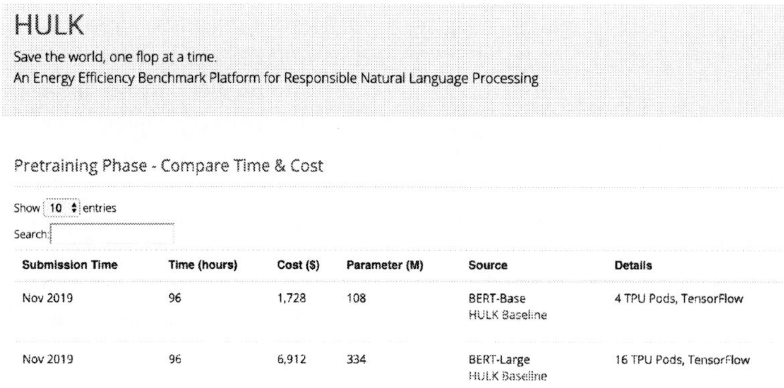

Figure 1: Screenshot of the leaderboard of website.

Datasets	CoNLL 2003		SST-2		MNLI		
Model	Time	Score	Time	Score	Time	Score	Overall Score
$\text{BERT}_{\text{BASE}}$	43.43	2.08	207.15	0.45	N/A	0.00	2.53
$\text{BERT}_{\text{LARGE}}$	90.26	1.00	92.45	1.00	9,106.72	1.00	3.00
$\text{XLNet}_{\text{BASE}}$	67.14	1.34	102.45	0.90	7,704.71	1.18	3.42
$\text{XLNet}_{\text{LARGE}}$	243.00	0.37	367.11	0.25	939.62	9.69	10.31
$\text{RoBERTa}_{\text{BASE}}$	70.57	1.28	38.45	2.40	274.87	7.14	10.82
$\text{RoBERTa}_{\text{LARGE}}$	155.43	0.58	57.65	1.60	397.12	22.93	25.11
$\text{ALBERT}_{\text{BASE}}$	340.64	0.26	2,767.90	0.03	N/A	0.00	0.29
$\text{ALBERT}_{\text{LARGE}}$	844.85	0.11	3,708.49	0.02	N/A	0.00	0.13

Table 3: Multi-task Baseline Fine-tuning Costs. Time is given in seconds and score is computed by the division of $\text{Time}_{\text{BERT}_{\text{LARGE}}}/\text{Time}_{\text{model}}$.The experiments are conducted on a single RTX 2080 Ti GPU following the evaluation criterion. The overall score is computed by summing up the scores of each task. We also use the cost to compute a new score for each task for cost-based leaderboards and summarize similarly. "N/A" means fail to reach the given performance after five epochs.

For the pretraining phase, we design the protocol to explore how much computing resource is required to reach specific final multi-task performance via fine-tuning after the pretraining. Therefore, during model pretraining, after every thousand pretraining steps, we use the current pretrained model for fine-tuning and see if the fine-tuned model can reach our cut-off performance. When it does, we count the time and cost in the pretraining process for benchmarking and analysis.

For the fine-tuning phase, we want to compare the general efficiency of the pretrained model reaching cut-off performance on the selected dataset.

During fine-tuning, we evaluate the current fine-tuned model on the development set after a certain small number of fine-tuning steps. When the performance reaches our cut-off performance, we count the time and cost in this fine-tuning process for benchmarking and analysis. To be specific, for a single pretrained model, the efficiency score on different tasks is defined as the sum of normalized time and cost. Here we normalize the time and cost because they vary dramatically between tasks. To simplify the process, we compute the ratio of $\text{BERT}_{\text{LARGE}}$'s time and cost to that of each model as the normalized measure, as shown in Table 3 and Table 4.

We follow the fine-tuning principles for the inference phase, and we use the time and cost of inference for benchmarking. The models we used for inference experiments are fine-tuned in the last part. Each of the benchmarking results was calculated using the average of time and cost over one thousand samples.

2.3 Performance Cut-off Selection

The selection of performance cut-off could be critical because we consider certain models to be

Datasets	CoNLL 2003		SST-2		MNLI		
Model	Time	Score	Time	Score	Time	Score	Overall Score
$BERT_{BASE}$	2.68	3.18	2.70	3.13	2.67	3.19	9.5
$BERT_{LARGE}$	8.51	1.00	8.46	1.00	8.53	1.00	3.00
$XLNet_{BASE}$	5.16	1.65	5.01	1.69	5.10	1.67	5.01
$XLNet_{LARGE}$	14.84	0.57	14.69	0.58	15.27	0.56	1.71
$RoBERTa_{BASE}$	2.65	3.21	2.68	3.16	2.70	3.16	9.53
$RoBERTa_{LARGE}$	8.35	1.02	8.36	1.01	8.70	0.98	3.01
$ALBERT_{BASE}$	2.65	3.21	2.68	3.16	2.72	3.14	9.51
$ALBERT_{LARGE}$	8.49	1.00	8.44	1.00	8.78	0.97	2.97

Table 4: Multi-task Baseline Inference Costs. Time is given in milliseconds and score is computed by the division of $Time_{BERT_{LARGE}}/Time_{model}$.The experiments are conducted on a single RTX 2080 Ti GPU following the evaluation criterion similar to the fine-tuning part. The inference time between tasks is more consistent compared to the fine-tuning phase.

"qualified" after reaching specific performance on the development set. Meanwhile, particular tasks can reach a "sweet point" where after a relatively smaller amount of training time, the model reaches performance close to the final converged performance with a negligible difference. The cut-off must be high enough to make sure any model that surpasses the threshold can be competent for the task. On the other hand, if the cut-off is too high, we will not have enough data points to evaluate the model's multi-task performance.

Here, our cut-offs were selected by observing the recent state-of-the-art model's performance on the selected dataset for the task[4]. A wise choice would be choosing the performance of some classic methods like LSTM-CRF or Bi-LSTM models as the cut-off. In this way, we can easily compare the efficiency of most models with a solid performance bar.

2.4 Submission to Benchmark

Submissions can be made to our benchmark through sending code and result to our HULK benchmark CodaLab competition[5] following the guidelines in both our FAQ part of website and competition introduction. We require the submissions to include detailed end-to-end model training information, including model run time, cost (cloud-based machine only), parameter number, and part of the development set output for result validation. A training / fine-tuning log, including time consumption and dev set performance after certain steps, is also required. For inference, development set output, time consumption, and hardware/software details should be provided. For model reproducibility, source code is also required.

3 Baseline Settings and Analysis

We adopt the reported resource requirements in the original papers as the pretraining phase baselines for computation-intensive tasks.

For fine-tuning and inference phase, we conduct extensive experiments on given hardware (RTX 2080Ti GPU) with different model settings as shown in Table 3 and Table 4. We also collect the development set performance with time in fine-tuning to investigate how the model is fine-tuned for different tasks.

In our fine-tuning setting, we are given a specific hardware and software configuration. We adjust the hyper-parameter using grid search to minimize the time fine-tuning towards cut-off performance. For example, we choose the proper batch size and learning rate for $BERT_{BASE}$ to make sure the model converges and can reach expected performance as soon as possible with parameter searching.

As shown in Figure 2, the fine-tuning performance curve differs a lot among pretrained models. The x-axis denoting time consumed is shown in log-scale for a better comparison of different models. None of the models take the lead in all tasks. However, if two pretrained models are in the same family, such as $BERT_{BASE}$ and $BERT_{LARGE}$, the model with a smaller number of parameters tend to converge a bit faster than the other in the NER and SST-2 task. In the MNLI task, such a trend does

[4]For example, we referred to the performance data points on Papers With Code for candidates.

[5]The CodaLab competition is available on the website.

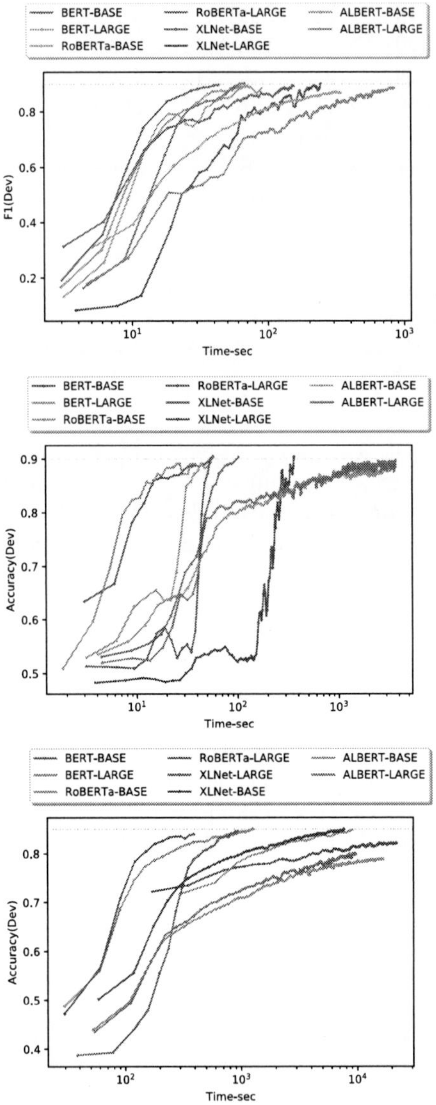

Figure 2: The comparison between different pretrained models for CoNLL 2003, SST-2, and MNLI datasets trained on a single RTX 2080Ti GPU. The curves are smoothed by computing the average with two adjacent data points. The experiments are conducted by selecting hyper-parameters to minimize the time consumption, yet making sure the model can converge after a certain amount of time. Results are demonstrated using performance on the development set after being fine-tuned for specific steps on the training dataset.

not apply because of the increased difficulty level and the number of training instances, which favors a larger model capacity.

Even though ALBERT model has a lot fewer parameters than BERT, according to Table 1, the ALBERT model's fine-tuning time is significantly more than BERT models because ALBERT uses large hidden size and more expensive matrix computation. The parameter sharing technique makes it harder to fine-tune the model. $\text{RoBERTa}_{\text{LARGE}}$ model is relatively stable in all tasks.

4 Related Work

GLUE benchmark (Wang et al., 2018) is a popular multi-task benchmarking and diagnosis platform providing score evaluating multi-task NLP models considering multiple single-task performances. SuperGLUE (Wang et al., 2019) further develops the task and enriches the evaluation dataset, making tasks more challenging. These multi-task benchmarks do not consider computation efficiency but innovates the development of pretrained models.

MLPerf (Mattson et al., 2019) compares training and inference efficiency from a hardware perspective, providing helpful resources on hardware selection and model training. The benchmark focused on several typical applications, including image classification and machine translation. However, it does not separate different training phases, thus making it hard to find the reference for fine-tuning only applications.

Previous work (Schwartz et al., 2019; Dodge et al., 2019) on related topic working towards "Green AI" proposes new metrics like FPO and new principle in efficiency evaluation. We further make more detailed and practical contributions to model energy efficiency benchmarking.

Other work like DAWNBenchmark (Coleman et al., 2017) looks into the area of end-to-end model efficiency comparison for both computer vision and NLP task SQuAD. The benchmark is very detailed and intuitive. However, it does not compare multi-task efficiency performance and covered only one NLP task. Similar to MLPerf, it does not separate fine-tuning efficiency from training efficiency.

The *Efficient NMT* shared task of The 2nd Workshop on Neural Machine Translation and Generation proposed an efficiency track to compare the inference time of neural machine translation models. Our platform covers more phases and supports multi-task comparison.

5 Conclusion

We developed the HULK platform focusing on the energy efficiency benchmarking of NLP models based on their end-to-end performance on selected NLP tasks. The HULK platform compares models in the pretraining, fine-tuning, and inference phase, making it clear to follow and propose more training-efficient and inference-efficient models. We have compared the fine-tuning efficiency of given models during baseline testing and demonstrated more parameters lead to slower fine-tuning when using the same model design but do not hold when the model architecture changes.We expect more submissions in the future to flourish and enrich our benchmark.

Acknowledgments

This work is supported by the Institute of Energy Efficiency (IEE) at UCSB's seed grant in Summer 2019 to improve AI and machine learning's energy efficiency.[6].

[6]https://iee.ucsb.edu/news/making-ai-more-energy-efficient

References

Kevin Clark, Minh-Thang Luong, Quoc V Le, and Christopher D Manning. 2020. Electra: Pre-training text encoders as discriminators rather than generators. *arXiv preprint arXiv:2003.10555*.

Cody Coleman, Deepak Narayanan, Daniel Kang, Tian Zhao, Jian Zhang, Luigi Nardi, Peter Bailis, Kunle Olukotun, Chris Ré, and Matei Zaharia. 2017. Dawnbench: An end-to-end deep learning benchmark and competition. *Training*, 100(101):102.

Jacob Devlin, Ming-Wei Chang, Kenton Lee, and Kristina Toutanova. 2018. Bert: Pre-training of deep bidirectional transformers for language understanding. *arXiv preprint arXiv:1810.04805*.

Jesse Dodge, Suchin Gururangan, Dallas Card, Roy Schwartz, and Noah A Smith. 2019. Show your work: Improved reporting of experimental results. *arXiv preprint arXiv:1909.03004*.

Zhenzhong Lan, Mingda Chen, Sebastian Goodman, Kevin Gimpel, Piyush Sharma, and Radu Soricut. 2019. Albert: A lite bert for self-supervised learning of language representations. *arXiv preprint arXiv:1909.11942*.

Yinhan Liu, Myle Ott, Naman Goyal, Jingfei Du, Mandar Joshi, Danqi Chen, Omer Levy, Mike Lewis, Luke Zettlemoyer, and Veselin Stoyanov. 2019. Roberta: A robustly optimized bert pretraining approach. *arXiv preprint arXiv:1907.11692*.

Peter Mattson, Christine Cheng, Cody Coleman, Greg Diamos, Paulius Micikevicius, David Patterson, Hanlin Tang, Gu-Yeon Wei, Peter Bailis, Victor Bittorf, et al. 2019. Mlperf training benchmark. *arXiv preprint arXiv:1910.01500*.

Pranav Rajpurkar, Jian Zhang, Konstantin Lopyrev, and Percy Liang. 2016. Squad: 100,000+ questions for machine comprehension of text. *arXiv preprint arXiv:1606.05250*.

Erik F Sang and Fien De Meulder. 2003. Introduction to the conll-2003 shared task: Language-independent named entity recognition. *arXiv preprint cs/0306050*.

Victor Sanh, Lysandre Debut, Julien Chaumond, and Thomas Wolf. 2019. Distilbert, a distilled version of bert: smaller, faster, cheaper and lighter. *arXiv preprint arXiv:1910.01108*.

Roy Schwartz, Jesse Dodge, Noah A Smith, and Oren Etzioni. 2019. Green ai. *arXiv preprint arXiv:1907.10597*.

Richard Socher, Alex Perelygin, Jean Wu, Jason Chuang, Christopher D Manning, Andrew Ng, and Christopher Potts. 2013. Recursive deep models for semantic compositionality over a sentiment treebank. In *Proceedings of the 2013 conference on empirical methods in natural language processing*, pages 1631–1642.

Emma Strubell, Ananya Ganesh, and Andrew McCallum. 2019. Energy and policy considerations for deep learning in nlp. *arXiv preprint arXiv:1906.02243*.

Alex Wang, Yada Pruksachatkun, Nikita Nangia, Amanpreet Singh, Julian Michael, Felix Hill, Omer Levy, and Samuel R Bowman. 2019. Superglue: A stickier benchmark for general-purpose language understanding systems. *arXiv preprint arXiv:1905.00537*.

Alex Wang, Amanpreet Singh, Julian Michael, Felix Hill, Omer Levy, and Samuel R Bowman. 2018. Glue: A multi-task benchmark and analysis platform for natural language understanding. *arXiv preprint arXiv:1804.07461*.

Adina Williams, Nikita Nangia, and Samuel R Bowman. 2017. A broad-coverage challenge corpus for sentence understanding through inference. *arXiv preprint arXiv:1704.05426*.

Thomas Wolf, Lysandre Debut, Victor Sanh, Julien Chaumond, Clement Delangue, Anthony Moi, Pierric Cistac, Tim Rault, R'emi Louf, Morgan Funtowicz, and Jamie Brew. 2019. Huggingface's transformers: State-of-the-art natural language processing. *ArXiv*, abs/1910.03771.

Zhilin Yang, Zihang Dai, Yiming Yang, Jaime Carbonell, Ruslan Salakhutdinov, and Quoc V Le. 2019. Xlnet: Generalized autoregressive pretraining for language understanding. *arXiv preprint arXiv:1906.08237*.

Association for Computational Linguistics
209 N. Eighth Street
Stroudsburg, Pennsylvania 18360

ISBN 978-1-7138-2916-4

9 781713 829164

CURRAN ASSOCIATES INC.
proceedings.com